DO IT YOURSELF

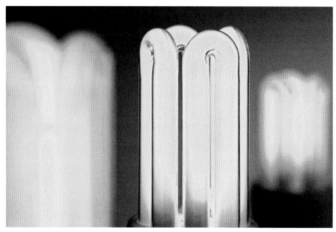

A step-by-step guide

DO IT YOURSELF

A step-by-step guide

JULIAN CASSELL • PETER PARHAM
Adapted for Canada by JON EAKES

REVISED CANADIAN EDITION
Project Editor Bob Bridle
Senior Art Editor Sharon Spencer
Canadian Editor Barbara Campbell

Production Editor Tony Phipps
Production Controller Rita Sinha

Managing Editor Stephanie Farrow
Managing Art Editor Lee Griffiths

ORIGINAL CANADIAN EDITION
Editor Julia Roles
Project Editor Carolyn Jackson
Canadian Photography Ed Homonylo
DTP Designer Pushpak Tyagi
Production Controller Rita Sinha

Second Canadian edition 2010

Dorling Kindersley is represented in Canada by
Tourmaline Editions Inc.,
662 King Street West, Suite 304,
Toronto, Ontario M5V 1M7

Library and Archives Canada Cataloguing in Publication

Cassell, Julian
        Do it yourself : a step-by-step guide / Julian Cassell, Peter Parham;
adapted for Canada by Jon Eakes. -- 2nd Canadian ed.
Includes index.
ISBN 978-1-55363-119-4
        1. Dwellings--Maintenance and repair--Amateurs' manuals.
2. Do-it-yourself work. I. Parham, Peter II. Eakes, Jon III. Title.
TH4817.3.C38 2010   643'.7   C2009-902655-4

Colour reproduction by Colourscan, Singapore
Printed and bound by Toppan Printing Co Ltd, China
10 11 12 13   5 4 3 2 1

Discover more at
www.dk.com

IMPORTANT
All do-it-yourself activities involve a degree of risk. Skills, materials, tools
and site conditions vary widely. Although the publisher and authors have
made every effort to ensure accuracy, the reader remains responsible for the
selection and use of tools, materials and methods, and for compliance with
local codes and laws, the manufacturer's operating instructions, and proper
safety precautions. If you feel uncomfortable or uncertain about undertaking
a particular project, consult or hire a professional. Neither the authors nor the
publisher shall be responsible for any damages, injuries or losses suffered or
incurred as a result of following any information published in this book.

CONTENTS

TOOLS, EQUIPMENT, AND MATERIALS   22

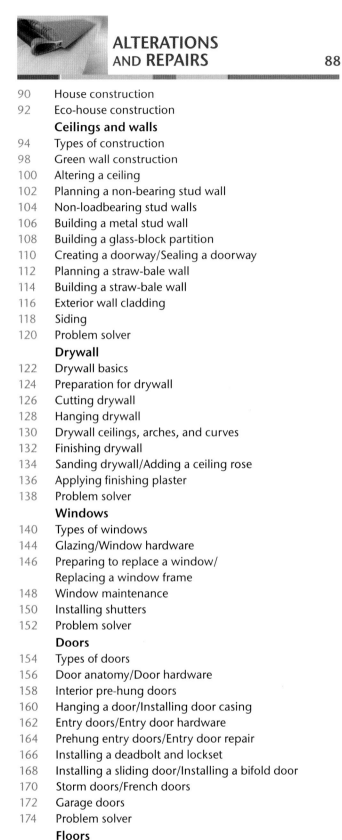

ALTERATIONS
AND REPAIRS 88

KITCHENS
AND BATHROOMS 236

DECORATING AND FINISHING 272

IMPROVING HOME PERFORMANCE 352

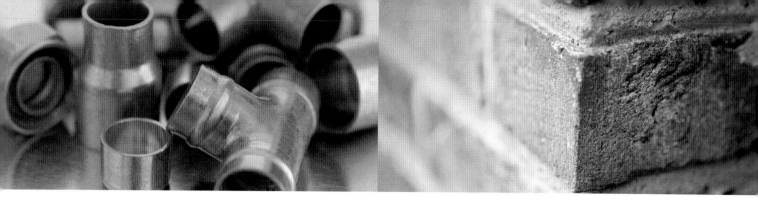

HOW TO USE THIS BOOK

The unique photographic approach of *Do It Yourself* shows you every step of every task, while a wealth of backup information shows you how to prepare and plan for the best results. Nine major sections cover every aspect of DIY within the home. These are broken down into smaller subsections. Before trying any of the tasks shown in the step-by-step sequences ensure that you have read the relevant preparation spread and that you have all the tools and materials listed in the brown tools and materials checklist box. These checklists are in addition to the basic toolkit shown on pp.24–25.

Introduces whole subsection

Each section is color-coded

SUBSECTION OPENER

Each section is divided into several subsections that cover distinct areas of the home or of DIY. The opener introduces the spreads that follow.

Practical technique denoted by colored square with stripe

Information box

Identified by a colored panel across the top of the box, these provide additional information or advice on other techniques.

PREPARATION SPREAD

The spreads give advice on techniques, planning, and the tools and materials that you will need to complete the tasks that follow.

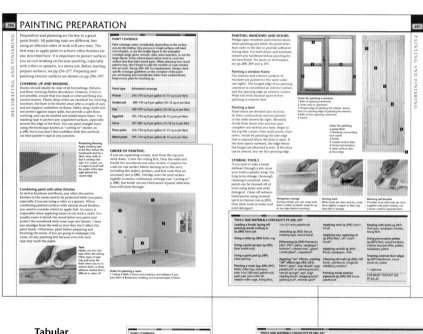

SAFETY BOX

Highlighted in red, these boxes cover important information about safety- or health-related matters. Ensure that you read this information before completing any task shown on the spread. Some of these boxes also contain information on planning and building regulations that you need to consider before commissioning or carrying out certain types of building and electrical work.

WORKING SAFETY

Always follow all manufacturer's guidelines and local building codes when attempting any new DIY project, especially when the project involves electricity and heating elements. Check if you are allowed to install a new radiant flooring system in your jurisdiction. Even if you are, you may need to file paperwork and plans with your local planning office for approval before you begin a project involving the heating system in your home. If you are not confident about completing any projects yourself, contact a professional organization for qualified leads.

Tabular information box

Systematic layout gives an at-a-glance view of quantities, materials, and methods used.

Tools and materials checklist

Gives the tools needed for the tasks on the following pages. These are in addition to the basic toolkit (pp.24–25).

Each step-by-step
sequence is numbered

Solid green options symbol

GREEN OPTIONS

Eco-friendly options are featured
throughout the book. To find these
green options, look out for the
following symbols and boxes:

Green options symbol

A solid green house indicates that
all of the content on the page
is eco-friendly

An outlined green house indicates
that there is some eco-friendly
content on the page

Green options box

Highlighted in green,
these boxes contain
environmentally-
friendly information.

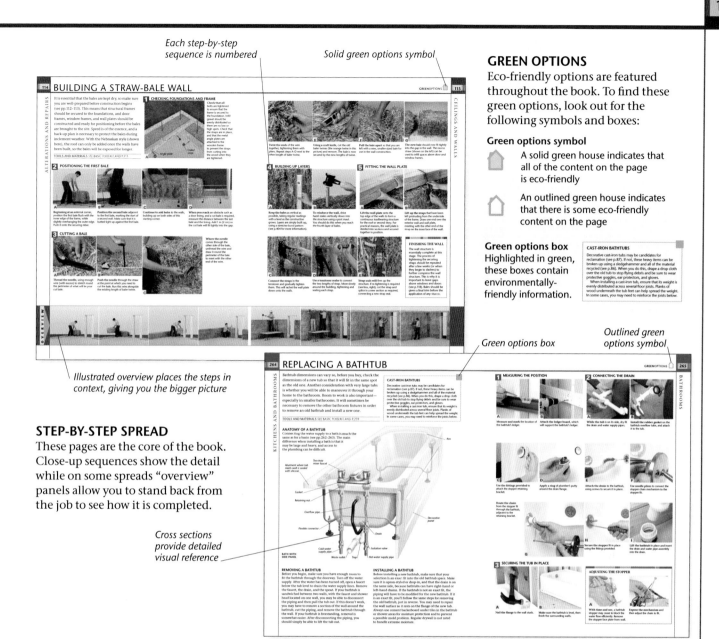

Illustrated overview places the steps in
context, giving you the bigger picture

Outlined green
options symbol

Green options box

STEP-BY-STEP SPREAD

These pages are the core of the book.
Close-up sequences show the detail
while on some spreads "overview"
panels allow you to stand back from
the job to see how it is completed.

Cross sections
provide detailed
visual reference

A short
introduction
outlines the
solution to
the problem

Succinct
sequence
shows
you the
quickest fix

Tools and
materials
checklist
details
everything
you need for
the task

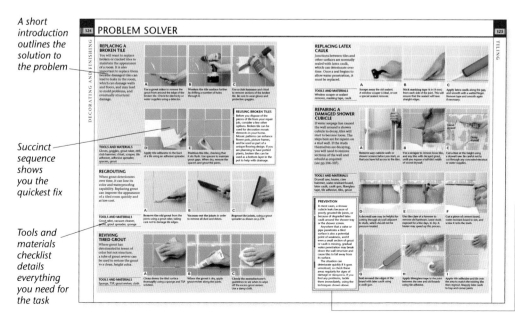

PROBLEM SOLVER
SPREAD

These stand-alone spreads
contain one-stop, quick-fix
solutions to problems,
which you can carry out
around the home.
They fall at the end
of each subsection.

Hints and tips

Provide additional
hints and tips related
to the main subject
or task. Identified by
a colored bar down
the left-hand side
of the box.

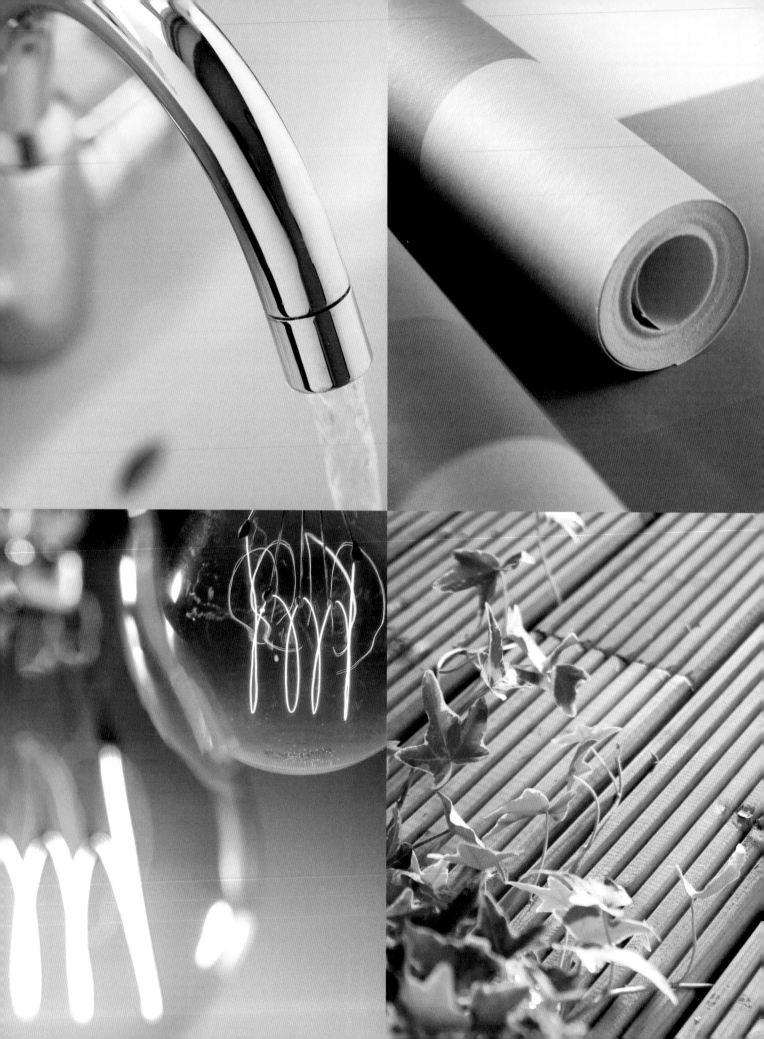

INTRODUCTION

This book is aimed at showing you both how your home is constructed and functions, and how you can make repairs or changes. Once you have browsed the magazines and watched the makeover programs, the book will both tell you, and show you, how the job is done.

In this edition, we have also included practical advice on eco-friendly Do-It-Yourself options, such as renewable energy sources and the use of sustainable materials. As well as combining new and old technologies, we look at the characteristics of raw and recycled building materials, examine their ability to insulate and store energy, and recommend how they may best be used.

Although "eco", "green", and "sustainability" are undeniably the buzz words of the moment, this is not simply an issue of environmentalism—shifting the focus of your home toward sustainability makes good financial sense as well. Achieving this change is easier than ever before, whether you are refitting an old house or starting anew. A sustainable house should be cheaper to run than a more conventional one, and there is a Do-It-Yourself solution for every circumstance that will almost certainly save you money.

One of the most rewarding aspects of writing this book was combining the benefits of traditional methods and materials with the advantages of cutting-edge technology. After all, a home constructed from straw bales and powered by alternative energy from solar panels is both an environmentally friendly and economically sound alternative to a more orthodox building.

The ideas outlined in this book present some rigorous but enjoyable challenges for Do-It-Yourself enthusiasts. We wish you luck with them, and hope you find satisfaction in the worthwhile and exciting projects ahead.

NOT DOING IT YOURSELF

For all of us, there are tasks for which we need professional help to complete a home improvement project. Whatever help you require, these pages provide some guidelines for hiring professionals. Finding good tradespeople can be difficult. Seek out help through personal recommendations or through professional organizations, and preferably view their previous work before hiring them. Always insist on a "price." This should be the amount you pay for the job specified—no less and no more. The only reason a price should change is if you alter the specifications of your particular job or if the professional discovers "unforeseen problems." Both should be clearly defined in the contract.

Architects

An architect will draw plans required for construction, if you are seeking a building permit, for example. Architects generally charge a flat fee for drawings, and then extra to oversee work being carried out (normally a percentage of the final building bill, ranging from 5 to 25 percent). If the architect is going to oversee work, check what this entails and get it in writing.

Masons and bricklayers

Bricklayers tend to solely lay bricks and blocks, whereas masons will also build natural stone walls and construct special stone features. Charges for stone and masonry work are normally based on every 1,000 bricks laid, or a lump-sum price for a specific job, such as building a chimney. If you hire a bricklayer, specify the brick type and insist on seeing samples.

Builders

Large building companies manage trade contractors to do the work on your behalf. Smaller building companies or general contractors will normally have trade skill sets themselves, such as carpentry or bricklaying, but may also become the project manager for part or all of the work being carried out. The builder may include this cost in the submitted price, or charge a further percentage on top of the final cost. Get this in writing before work starts.

Carpenters and joiners

Finish carpenters assemble custom-made, wood-based items such as doors and windows, whereas rough carpenters or framers will fit these items into your home, and tackle structural tasks. There are overlaps between the two. A good carpenter can be invaluable in complex tasks, such as calculating complex roof layouts. With a finish carpenter, be clear on specifications for any items

that you have commissioned him to make. If he is making custom cabinets, for example, make sure that he specifiesthe type of wood and the finish detail. The difference in quality and price can vary greatly.

Electricians

An electrician will carry out all types of electrical work, usually for the wiring of outlets, light switches, phones, and televisions. All provinces require electricians to be certified. Some jurisdictions allow owner-occupied DIY electrical power wiring on condition of obtaining permits and inspections. Low voltage wiring (some lights and all communication wires) is not generally controlled. Check with the city building department about local requirements and permissions.

Flooring installers

General flooring companies can tackle any floor requests, ranging from initial leveling to waxing a hardwood floor, for example. However, make sure they have the relevant experience in all areas. You can also employ carpet installers, wooden floor specialists, or floor tilers.

Excavators

Before a building starts to go up, excavators generally do all the preparatory work, including digging for foundations and routes for drainage and utilities. Many are employed by a builder, but some work independently. It can save time and money to employ an excavator and his equipment for the day to carry out all of the heavy earth-moving requirements on a project.

Laborers

Skill and experience in this trade vary greatly. Good laborers are skilled at helping another trade to finish a job. General laborers will price themselves based on knowledge and experience,

and hourly rates will vary widely. Personal recommendation is essential.

Painters and decorators

A good decorator will carry out all aspects of decorative coatings, including painting, papering, and, in some cases, tiling. Specialist tilers may do both walls and floors. Good decorators can provide very-high-quality finishes—a preferable option when hanging expensive wallpaper, for example. Make sure that the number of coats, type of paint, and general quality of materials is specified in any painting job. Decorators can be a source of ideas for new effects and finishes.

Drywall repair

Minimal drywall repair is easily done by the "do-it-yourselfer" but large scale jobs require skill. Pricing for repair work is usually set according to square footage or estimated time. Check that the price includes all coats required and whether painting is included. They may also offer "tacking" services—cutting and fixing drywall before repair.

Plumbers and heating contractors

There is often an overlap in expertise between plumbers and heating contractors. When installing, servicing, or maintaining a gas- or oil-fired furnace, they must have the relevant certification/licensing. Few jurisdictions alow DIY work on gas or propane piping because of the dangers. For general plumbing work such as installing tubs or toilets, the law is less exacting but most often also requires provincial licensing or renovation permits. Check local requirements before hiring or doing it yourself.

Project managers

A general contractor may be the best choice for project management. He can schedule the job, coordinate the various trades, and communicate on your behalf with everyone involved in the project. If you are employing an architect on new building work, it may be best for them to project-manage. If the size of job warrants a professional project manager, be certain of their credentials based on proven experience.

Roofers

Usually, roofers only deal with roof coverings, such as tiles, shingles, felt, and finishing and any mortar work on the roof. A carpenter will deal with any structural elements. Large companies have carpenters working with the roofers. Smaller firms subcontract out structural carpentry. Roofing bids or prices can be complicated. If weather delays work, this can have effects such as increasing the price of scaffolding rental. On large jobs, a roofer may actually scaffold over the top of the house and provide a waterproof "tent" so that work can continue in most weather. This increases cost and is only worthwhile on larger jobs. Check samples of materials, such as tiles and felts, before they are bought and make sure your choices are specified in writing.

Other installers

This category includes all those trades and services that offer a product with their own installation service. This can be anything from new windows, to garage doors, blinds, or custom kitchens. Make sure the product you receive is the same as the specification you were sold to avoid problems with your installers. As the number of different installers a project involves increases, more vigilance is required to ensure that the job runs smoothly. Make sure that you specify each installer's individual responsibilities. For example, a company that installs blinds only has to supply what you ordered and use relatively basic skills to install them. A company that offers a custom kitchen installation service needs to supply carpenters, plumbers, electricians, and possibly heating engineers, decorators, and tilers.

Structural engineers

As their name suggests, structural engineers assess the structural and load-bearing issues of a building and provide specifications. For example, they can calculate requirements for headers and for foundations. They are often consulted by architects when plans are being made, and generally charge a flat fee. Many municipalities require a stamp from structural engineers for new or remodeling jobs and ignorance of this requirement could cost you serious money in fines or replacing work in place.

Payment and extras

On small jobs, never pay the entire fee up front. It's not uncommon to pay a deposit but be clear on what your recourse is. Pay the full amount only when you are satisfied that work has been completed to specification. On larger projects, it is common to stagger payments through the course of the project. Link these to clear stages, such as the completion of excavation, for example. On large projects, a builder may require some money up front. This acts as a deposit and allows the builder to order and buy materials. The builder usually has a clear "progress schedule" for payments and you should feel comfortable with the requirements. It is standard practice to retain a portion at the end until all work is complete to satisfaction. Any payment in addition to that originally estimated, or quoted, should be backed up by reasoning agreed between both parties, in writing.

Building permits

As building materials, environmental protection policies, and health and safety standards change, so do planning and building regulations. Local authorities deal with most planning issues under an umbrella of provincial policy. Further rules apply to listed buildings and conservation areas. If you are considering structural work, always contact the local building department first. They are there to help, not hinder. A quick phone call can often put your mind at rest about what does or does not need a permit. Construction is supervised by an inspector. Again, a quick phone call can often solve many problems. If you are carrying out work, the inspector will often need to check various stages to ensure that regulations are being adhered to. Insulation, ventilation, electrical wiring, water supply, and drainage systems have all recently become more stringently regulated. Use these highly trained professionals as allies. They offer excellent advice and help.

ASSESSING YOUR HOUSE: EXTERIOR

The exterior of your house has to withstand the elements through all seasons. An annual inspection is important to ensure that all aspects of exterior structure are maintained. It pays to be vigilant in checking for any potential problems, because this may prevent them from escalating into something more serious. Some problems worth checking for are shown here and in the photographs below, though not all will apply to your home. You should also inspect the interior of your home for evidence of exterior problems (see pp.18–19).

WHAT TO DO NEXT?

Whenever you find evidence of a problem, consider these key issues before taking any action. First, assess the physical extent of the problem, and check whether it is symptomatic of a larger issue. For example, a loose tile may simply need to be secured, or may be symptomatic of an underlying problem. Consider whether it is something you can fix yourself, or if you need to call in a professional for advice or to complete the work. Once you know what you are dealing with, assess whether the problem needs to be tackled immediately, or whether it can wait until you have the funds and the time to deal with it more easily. Problems such as leaking pipes or constantly running overflows are damaging and wasteful, and if you have a water meter they will be costing you a considerable amount of money. If the problem is a seasonal one, such as leaves blocking an eavestrough, it is worth planning for annual maintenance work. Remember that if you are hoping to sell your home, any problems with the exterior can seriously affect first impressions, and therefore the price you can expect to receive for your property.

DRAINAGE

Many exterior maintenance tasks involve ensuring smooth and efficient drainage from your home and into underground drainage systems in order to keep your home free from flood problems. Waste water is directed into the sewer system or septic tank through a network of underground pipes. Inspection chambers, situated below manhole covers, allow access to the pipes should problems occur. Rainwater is channeled into a separate system, or may run into the sewer. In older homes, both rainwater and waste water may drain into the sewer through the same network of pipes. Older systems should be regularly maintained, and updated when possible.

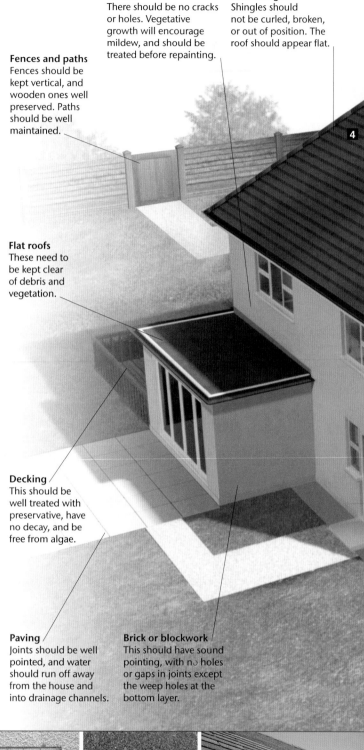

Stucco
There should be no cracks or holes. Vegetative growth will encourage mildew, and should be treated before repainting.

Roof shingles
Shingles should not be curled, broken, or out of position. The roof should appear flat.

Fences and paths
Fences should be kept vertical, and wooden ones well preserved. Paths should be well maintained.

Flat roofs
These need to be kept clear of debris and vegetation.

Decking
This should be well treated with preservative, have no decay, and be free from algae.

Paving
Joints should be well pointed, and water should run off away from the house and into drainage channels.

Brick or blockwork
This should have sound pointing, with no holes or gaps in joints except the weep holes at the bottom layer.

1 Eavestroughs and downspouts should be free of corrosion and leaks, and water should run easily. Remove blockages immediately.

2 Eavestrough downspouts must be clear of vegetation and leaves to ensure that water drains away efficiently.

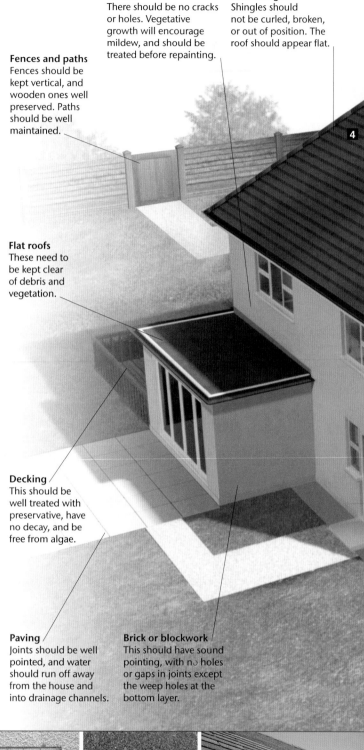

3 Vents must be clear of obstruction. This should be included as part of your boiler service schedule.

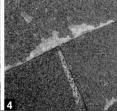

4 Shingles in need of repair or replacing are loose, have curled corners, or large spaces between tabs.

5 Flashing on roofs must be properly installed to ensure that water cannot penetrate the roof.

Chimney
Pointing and flashing should be sound.

Siding
Boards should be sound, with no flaking paint or varnish.

Downspout
Pipes should have no leaks at joints, and water should flow easily to the bottom.

Drains
Drains should direct water as far away as possible from the foundation. Keep free of debris.

Doors
These should have a protective or preservative finish. Vinyl should be kept clean.

Windows must have a protective coat of paint or finish; vinyl should be kept clean.

Trees should be away from the house, as they can cause subsidence, and leaves may block gutters.

Fascia board should be in sound condition and show no sign of decay.

Driveways should be free of holes, craters, and standing water. Vegetation should be cleared from the surface.

ASSESSING YOUR HOUSE: INTERIOR

Many parts of your home's interior can be affected by the exterior problems described on pp.16–17. For example, a damp area on the inside can be a result of exterior issues that need addressing. When carrying out an interior inspection, always bear this in mind. Many other interior problems relate to aesthetics and safety. The photographs below highlight some of the issues. Poor paintwork won't affect the structure of your house, but it will certainly detract from its look. Other issues, such as leaking faucets, require more urgent attention.

WHAT TO DO NEXT?

Since you cannot physically do everything at once, prioritize the most important tasks. Tackle problems related to safety first. For example, ensure that all smoke detectors function correctly. Be certain that you have regular servicing schedules for items such as boilers and any other gas- or oil-fired appliances. Aside from these more obvious items, appliances such as water softeners also require regular checking and in many cases periodic servicing. Also, if you have air-conditioning systems, be sure to check the manufacturer's recommendations on servicing. Remember that many problems will require professional help, particularly those involving gas. With all such items, servicing may not only ensure safe operation, they may also avoid costly breakdowns and repairs or replacement. Make schedules and budgets for improvements to decoration and/or permanent appliances and make sure you follow through on them. Also consider whether the improvements you make would be appreciated by anyone buying your property.

HOUSE FILE

It is a good idea to keep a record of checks, important phone numbers, service schedules, and general information about your home and its appliances, but organization is key. One good way to keep track is to have a house file where all such information is kept. People often buy notebooks with a plan to transfer all the important details into them, but a ring binder is an easier alternative since scraps of paper, schedules, and instructions can simply be clipped into place. At the very least, keep a drawer in your home that is the sole place for accumulating household maintenance, repair, and improvement information.

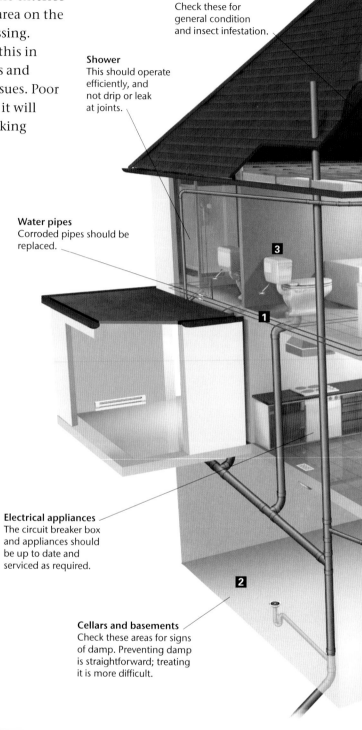

Rafters
Check these for general condition and insect infestation.

Shower
This should operate efficiently, and not drip or leak at joints.

Water pipes
Corroded pipes should be replaced.

Electrical appliances
The circuit breaker box and appliances should be up to date and serviced as required.

Cellars and basements
Check these areas for signs of damp. Preventing damp is straightforward; treating it is more difficult.

1 Radiators should heat up correctly and have no cool spots, leaking valves, or broken thermostats.

2 Concrete floors should be dry. If wet, you may need to waterproof.

3 Toilets should flush easily. If not, replace the relevant valves (see pp.490–491).

4 Faucets should operate efficiently and not leak at joints or drip.

5 Roof space insulation should be checked for general condition and depth.

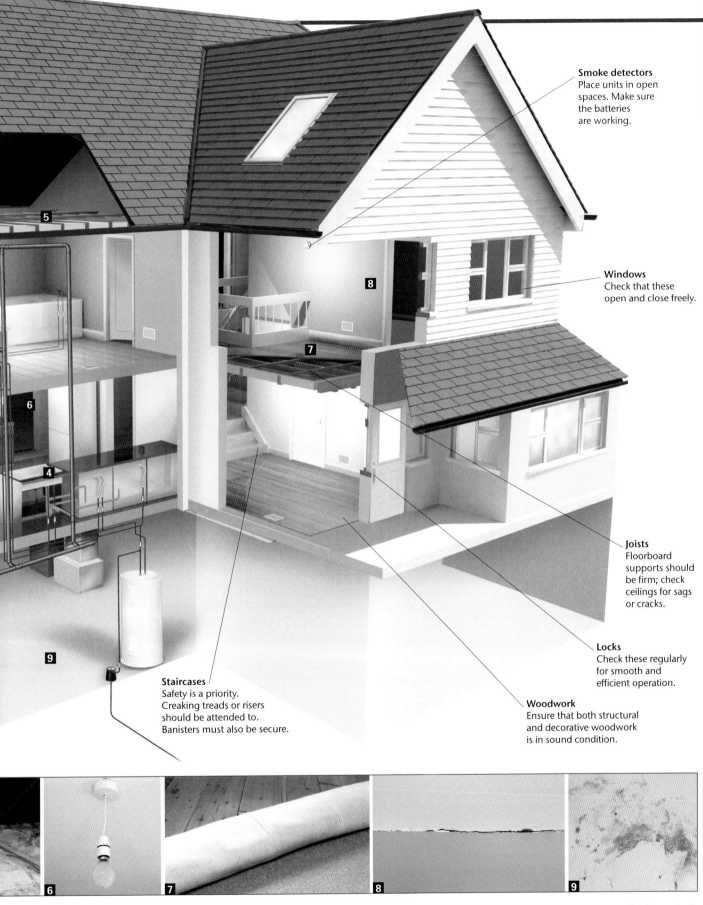

Smoke detectors
Place units in open spaces. Make sure the batteries are working.

Windows
Check that these open and close freely.

Joists
Floorboard supports should be firm; check ceilings for sags or cracks.

Locks
Check these regularly for smooth and efficient operation.

Woodwork
Ensure that both structural and decorative woodwork is in sound condition.

Staircases
Safety is a priority. Creaking treads or risers should be attended to. Banisters must also be secure.

Cables and cords should be in good condition, with no signs of fraying or damaged sheathing.

Floorboards should be checked for signs of rot or infestation.

Walls and ceilings must be sound, with no cracks or holes. Drywall should be smooth for decorative purposes.

Moisture can be the result of a flood or lack of ventilation, and can lead to mold. Treat it immediately (see pp.234–235).

When assessing the green credentials of your house, or investigating where green improvements could be introduced, there are a number of areas to explore. Many green solutions are relatively straightforward, while some will involve major upheaval and may be more suited to a new-build project than a retrospective fit. Use the information given here as a link to more detailed analysis later in the book. You will see that there are greener options for nearly all aspects of DIY.

GREEN RESEARCH

There are advantages and disadvantages with any building technique or material, and eco-friendly options are no different. If possible, it is always important to substantiate a manufacturer's claims with hard evidence. As in any aspect of life, manufacturers are concerned primarily with selling goods, so it is necessary to compare products, research different ideas, and make sure they meet your own needs. The areas covered here deal with most aspects of what is currently available in terms of making your home a greener place to live. Using the relevant page references, you can refer to various parts of the book for more in-depth information—and to learn how to carry out green projects yourself.

1. **Wind power** Wind turbines can produce electricity to supplement the electricity supply (see pp.386–387).
2. **Green living roof** Generates oxygen, provides good insulation, and offers a habitat for wildlife (see p.93).
3. **Heat pumps** Various different designs offer a green alternative for space and water heating (see pp.504–505).
4. **Biomass boilers** A carbon-neutral option that offers a viable alternative to conventional boilers (see p.504–505).
5. **Insulation** This is key for energy efficiency. Try using natural or recycled materials (see pp.356–365).
6. **Passive solar power** Sunlight can be used with good house design to provide heat and light (see pp.382–383).
7. **Active solar power** Solar energy collectors can generate hot water and electricity (see pp.384–385).
8. **Paint** Natural, eco-friendly paints are readily available or can be produced at home (see pp.282–283).
9. **Rainwater** The rainwater that falls on our homes can be harvested on a small or large scale (see pp.390–391).

THE PAY-OFF WITH GREEN LIVING

If all houses featured many of these ideas, the energy usage of the population as a whole would be significantly reduced. However, the initial financial outlay must always be considered. With low-energy lightbulbs, for example, the initial cost is low, so the pay-off is fast—in terms of saving both energy and money. But with larger, more expensive projects, such as installing solar panels, the energy-saving pay-off may be quick, but it will take far longer to recoup the initial costs. The best advice is to address the key options first (insulate well, use low-energy electrical goods, and recycle), leaving the more complex projects to form part of the decision-making process of any future home improvements.

Compost
Making compost is the ultimate expression of green living (see pp.404–405)

Wooden patio doors
Double-glazed windows need not be UPVC or aluminum—wood is a greener option and will last just as long if well looked after (see pp.144–45)

Recycling storage
A good system of sorting materials for recycling is essential for every home (see pp.250–51)

Roof shingles
Consider installing light-colored shingles, which reflect the sun's heat rather than absorbing it

Low-energy lighting
A small investment can have a large impact on saving electricity (see p.435)

Proper venting
Ridge vents are required for cathedral ceilings (see p.205)

Rafter insulation
In a lived-in roof space, ensure the ceiling is insulated sufficiently (see pp.358–59)

Mortar
Lime mortars are far greener than those that are cement-based (see p.99)

Appliances
Be sure to choose energy-efficient models (see pp.380–381)

Natural flooring
Flooring from sustainable sources is an eco-friendly option (see p.330)

Windows
Choose Energy Star-rated energy efficient windows (see p.144)

Gray water
As well as using collected rainwater in the home, you can also recycle water from sinks, baths, and showers (see p.391)

Insulation
Use recycled or sheep's wool insulation (see p.357)

Sustainable wood
Make sure that any wood you use in your home comes from a sustainable source (see p.75)

Reclaimed slabs
It is not always necessary to buy new—consider using reclaimed materials (see pp.86–87)

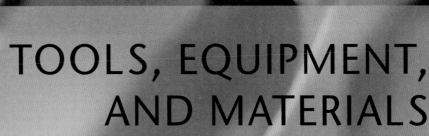

TOOLS, EQUIPMENT, AND MATERIALS

HAND TOOLS
POWER TOOLS
MATERIALS

BASIC TOOLKIT

A good toolkit is something every home should have, but you do not need to buy a lavish kit all at once. Most people will need a screwdriver, flashlight, or wrench from time to time, and it is worth accumulating individual items as and when you need them, and adding to these when you are able to afford it. Tools can be expensive, and as a general rule it is best to invest in quality, since a well-made item will last a lifetime for most household needs. Invariably, cheaper tools will break or fail to do the job, so buy the best you can afford.

THE TOOLBOX

Sturdiness and an adequate capacity are the most important factors to consider when choosing a toolbox. Most toolboxes come with many compartments that help to keep tools organized.

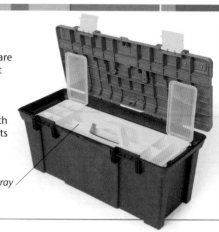

Compartmentalized tray may be lifted out

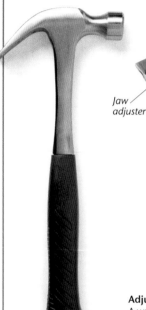

Jaw adjuster

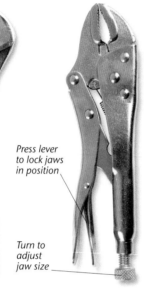

Press lever to lock jaws in position

Turn to adjust jaw size

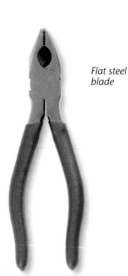

Flat steel blade

Claw hammer
This most versatile of hammers can be used for driving in nails and levering them out.

Adjustable wrench
A wrench suited to many tasks, since its jaws may be adjusted to fit nuts and bolts of different sizes.

Locking pliers
A multipurpose gripping tool, with size-adjustable jaws, ideal for gripping nuts, pipes, and fixtures.

Combination pliers
A gripping tool that you may use to hold, turn, or pull out different types of nails.

Scraper
Useful for removing old decorative coverings or scraping down loose, flaky surfaces.

Flashlight
A vital tool when the power is off, and for viewing in dark, secluded areas.

Robertson screwdrivers
A set of Robertson or "square" socket screwdrivers will handle most Canadian home improvement screws.

Pencil
A sharp pencil is essential for marking accurate measurements.

Phillips screwdrivers
A set of Phillips or "cross" socket screwdrivers will allow you to deal with drywall screws and US imports.

Nail set
Used for pounding in nail heads below surface level.

Slottted screwdrivers
Slotted screws are still used widely in the US. Slotted screwdrivers are necessary for imported products.

Utility knife
A sharp knife used for many precision and general cutting purposes.

Awl
Useful for marking and starting off nail or screw holes. Also used for detecting studs or blocking in studwork, or joists in ceilings.

Electrical detection screwdriver
This combines a small slot-headed screwdriver with a power detector, and has an indicator light located in its handle.

Chisels
Bevel-edged chisels are the most multi-purpose.

Handsaw
A handsaw is the most versatile member of the saw family since it can be used for cutting a wide variety of different materials.

Junior hacksaw
A small, fine-toothed saw that is designed to cut through metal and other materials such as vinyl.

ADDITIONAL ITEMS TO COMPLEMENT YOUR TOOLKIT

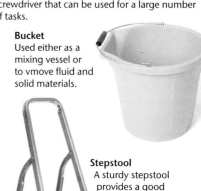

Electrical tape
This insulating tape is used in many electrical tasks.

A selection of hardware
Keep a good selection and number of general-purpose nails and screws so you always have a range of choices available.

Compartments help to separate nail types and sizes

Cordless drill/driver
A multipurpose, battery-powered drill and screwdriver that can be used for a large number of tasks.

Bucket
Used either as a mixing vessel or to vmove fluid and solid materials.

Teflon tape
This lightweight, thin tape is part of every plumber's toolkit. Teflon tape is used on threaded connections to prevent leaks.

Small size means it will fit in a toolbox

Mini level
Provides horizontal and vertical guide lines when positioning fixtures and hardware.

Stepstool
A sturdy stepstool provides a good access platform for a variety of tasks.

Tape measure
Essential for providing accurate measurements. Retractable, lockable tape measures are easy to use and space-saving.

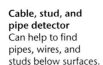

Made of lightweight aluminum

Retractable metal tape

Cable, stud, and pipe detector
Can help to find pipes, wires, and studs below surfaces.

Dust masks
Essential when sanding or sawing to prevent you from inhaling harmful substances.

Calculator
Always useful for quantity and measurement calculations and estimates.

Extension cord
Allows you to take a power supply to any area inside or outside your home.

Safety glasses or goggles
Essential for any toolbox since eye protection is vital for many DIY tasks.

Work gloves
Invest in a good-quality pair of work gloves to protect your hands when handling building materials and using heavy tools.

Portable workbench
This makes an ideal workstation for many DIY tasks. It can be easily moved from area to area in the home, and may be folded away for easy storage.

LADDERS AND ACCESS EQUIPMENT

When gaining access to an area that is otherwise out of reach, ladders, in their various forms, are still the most versatile type of access equipment. However, your primary concern must always be to ensure that your equipment is set up safely, and used in the correct way. When purchasing a ladder, check that your choice meets current safety standards. Find out the maximum load that it can support. Store ladders horizontally and out of reach of children and potential burglars. Other types of access equipment, including platforms and scaffolding, are discussed opposite.

WORKING SAFELY

■ Never use a ladder near overhead electrical wires or equipment.
■ Never use a ladder in front of a doorway unless someone else guards it.
■ When positioning a ladder against a wall, make sure that the height of the top of the ladder is four times (4:1) the distance between the wall and the ladder's base. Many ladders have an angle guide printed on the side to help with this.

■ Inspect a ladder thoroughly before use, to ensure that there are no cracks or breaks. Check a wooden ladder for rot, and a metal ladder for corrosion. Never paint a ladder: paint may hide any damage to the structure.
■ Check ladder feet. A metal ladder should have rubber, slip-resistant feet.
■ Check that the ladder is sturdy enough to support your weight.

LADDERS

Most modern ladders are made from lightweight metals such as aluminum, although it is still possible to buy more traditional wooden designs. Shown here are the modern ladder types, but there are many variations on all these designs. Unlike other ladders, stepladders can stand alone and do not need to be rested on a vertical surface. There are also many types of accessories for use with ladders, such as ladder stays that hold the top of a ladder away from a wall surface, or tool trays that clip onto ladder rungs.

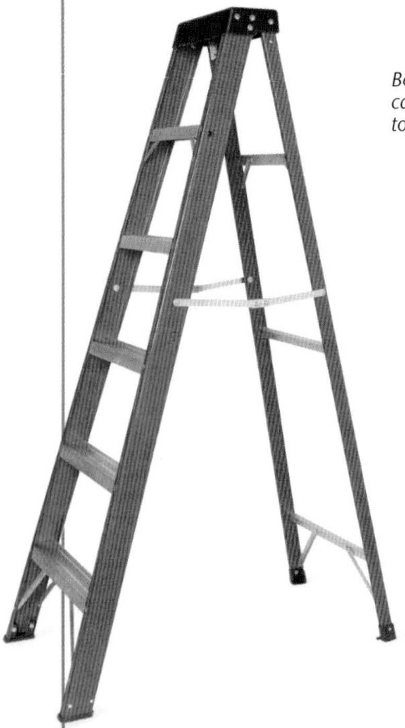

Bottom section can clip onto top section

EXTENDED POSITION

Unused rungs

Strengthening ribs

Cleat

COLLAPSED FOLDING LADDER

Stepladder
A sturdy stepladder is an essential piece of household equipment because of its versatility and portability. Open it to its full extent for safe use, and never stand on the top two steps.

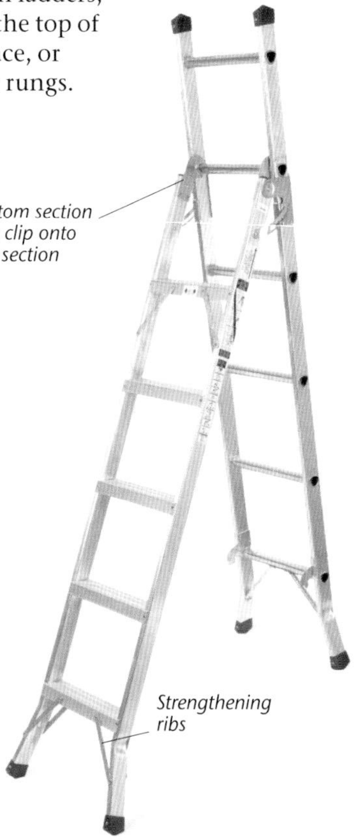

Combination ladder
This can be used as a stepladder or as a conventional ladder, depending on how it is set up. Designs vary considerably: follow the manufacturer's guidelines carefully when setting up a ladder.

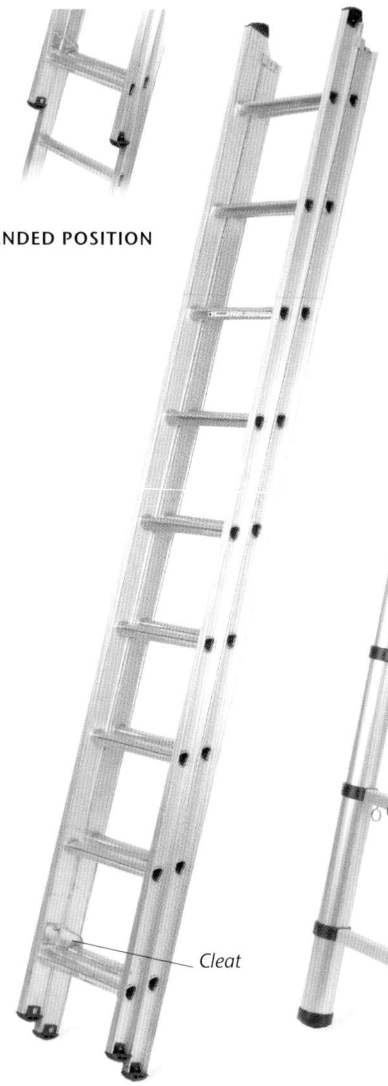

Extension ladder
These have two or three sections. For storage and moving, the sections are retracted. Brackets attached to each ladder section allow sections to slide over each other up into an extended position. Cleats at the lower level of the upper section secure the ladder in an extended position.

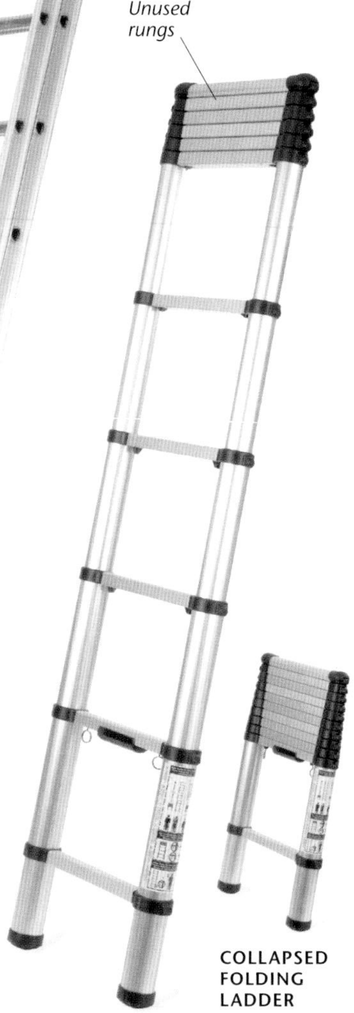

Folding ladder
The stiles of the "telescopic" ladder shown here collapse into the ones below. Other folding ladders fold down into a very small, compact area. Whatever the particular design, the aim is to produce a ladder that is space-saving when stored.

PLATFORM LADDERS AND TRESTLES

The advantage a work platform has over a ladder is that it leaves your arms free to work. Various designs are available, and each provides a stable and level raised surface.

Platform

Hinge with locking mechanism

Combination ladder with platform
Some combination ladders are multi-functional. For example, they may support a raised working platform that clips onto its rails and/or rungs.

Trestles
These can be used as the base for a working platform, by laying planks across the top of them. Most trestles are height-adjustable.

Platform support

Height-adjustable legs

RENTED PLATFORMS AND SCAFFOLDING

Power lift

A number of designs are available for rent, and these differ according to the surface on which they can be used and the height they can reach. Some you can operate yourself; for others, you will need to hire an operator. The rental company should be able to advise you as to the power lift that best suits your requirements. Lifts are expensive to rent, and therefore might be used only when there is no other option or if the amount of work and time saved by using a lift is of clear benefit.

Pipe-staging tower

This provides a safe platform for one or more people, depending on its specifications, and is useful for work that would be too arduous on a ladder. Most towers have several sections that slot and clip together in stages, building up to the required height. They are best used on solid ground; where a tower is built on soft ground, place sections of board under its feet to spread the weight, and ensure that it is level. Add stabilizers at the bottom to secure the tower in position, and tie it in to the building on the upper level. Some towers have wheels, and can be moved to different working positions, if resting on solid, level ground. Never move a tower when people, tools, or materials are on any part of it.

Fixed scaffolding

The access provided by fixed scaffolding is essential for some jobs, such as roofing. It can also offer an opportunity to carry out exterior maintenance. For example, if the scaffolding is erected for roofing work, use the access to check the gutters, and reattach any loose downspouts. Erecting fixed scaffolding is a job for professionals, but check that the firm you employ has the correct certification or license, and suitable insurance.

USING LADDERS

Many of the safety issues involving ladder use have been identified opposite. However, aside from these standard guidelines, there are many other factors to consider.

Whether using an extension ladder (below, left) or constructing a working platform in a stairwell (below, right) safety must always be the most important concern.

Securing a ladder before climbing
The top of the ladder must rest against a solid surface. If possible, tie the top part of the ladder onto a solid structure on the wall, securing rope around the stiles rather than the rungs. It may also be possible to tie it to a strong furring strip braced across the inside of a window, with padding to protect the inside walls.

Aim to work on dry, solid, and level ground. On a soft surface, use a strong board underneath the feet to prevent them from sinking, and hammer stakes into the ground and tie the stiles to the stakes with rope.

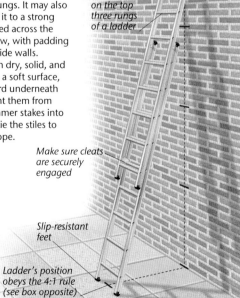

Both stiles must touch the wall surface

Never stand on the top three rungs of a ladder

Make sure cleats are securely engaged

Slip-resistant feet

Ladder's position obeys the 4:1 rule (see box opposite)

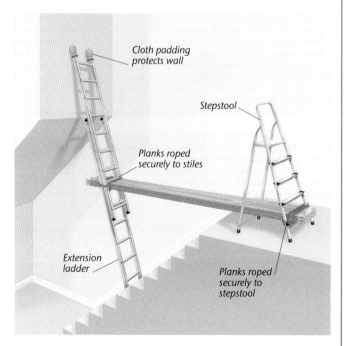

Cloth padding protects wall

Stepstool

Planks roped securely to stiles

Extension ladder

Planks roped securely to stepstool

Using two ladders and a scaffold board
Shown here is an example of how to gain safe access to a stairwell. You should use two scaffold planks tied together and secured at each end. The stepstool position shown here is very secure, but you may also reverse its orientation. Make sure the ladder obeys the 4:1 rule (see box opposite).

There is a large range of tools and equipment that you may rent for home improvement tasks, and many rental companies have a good variety of both hand tools and power tools. The degree to which you will rely on renting tools will depend on the equipment you own, but however extensive your tool collection, there are some items that are so expensive that it would be uneconomical to own them unless you used them very regularly.

DRILLS AND BREAKERS

A power drill is essential for many tasks (see pp.54–57) but you may need to rent a heavy-duty drill for large projects. It is possible to burn out a drill's motor if it is not sufficiently powerful for the task. Some large drill bits, such as a core drill bit, require a large drill to house them. Breakers are designed for breaking up thick beds of concrete, general masonry, or asphalt.

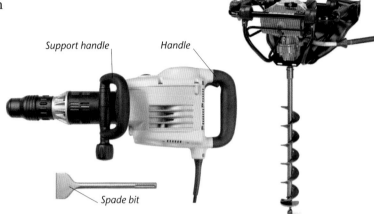

Support handle   *Handle*

Diamond-encrusted cutting edge

Spade bit

Removable handle

Heavy-duty drill
A household hammerdrill (see pp.54–57) will be sufficient for most domestic tasks, but a heavy-duty drill will cope with greater demands, such as drilling a large number of holes in concrete and masonry.

Core drill bit
Use this to cut holes for ducting or plumbing. The best core drill bits are diamond-encrusted for effective and efficient cuts. Rental companies may charge extra for each $\frac{1}{32}$ in (1 mm) of diamond coating used.

Demolition hammer
Choose from electirc pneumatic (operated by compressed air) and hydraulic (operated by pressurized fluid) demolition hammers. Smaller versions called chipping hammers are also available.

Auger
Mechanical augers make excavating deep holes much easier than if working by hand. Their sizes and designs vary, and some will require two people to operate them.

SAWS

Circular saws, miter saws, and handsaws can tackle most DIY tasks, but when you plan to tackle a large repetitive job, a specialty saw designed for the task at hand will give you greater ease and efficiency in the work.

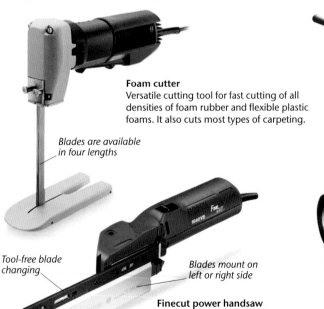

Foam cutter
Versatile cutting tool for fast cutting of all densities of foam rubber and flexible plastic foams. It also cuts most types of carpeting.

Blades are available in four lengths

Tool-free blade changing

Blades mount on left or right side

Finecut power handsaw
Handsaw is designed for flush cutting applications like door jamb flush-trim cuts. The tool provides precision sawing in wood, wood composites, and plastics.

PLUMBING AND DRAINING

If you are working on major plumbing repairs, you may need the help of specialty plumbing tools that include drain cleaners, toilet augers, pipe cutters, and snakes.

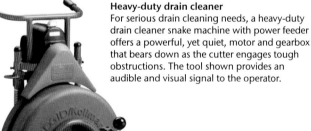

Heavy-duty drain cleaner
For serious drain cleaning needs, a heavy-duty drain cleaner snake machine with power feeder offers a powerful, yet quiet, motor and gearbox that bears down as the cutter engages tough obstructions. The tool shown provides an audible and visual signal to the operator.

Viewing screen

Plumbing SeeSnake
This small, lightweight system allows you to view inside drain lines and other types of piping in order to determine the exact cause and location of problems with a camera head that easily maneuvers through right angles and P-traps.

ROLLERS, SCREED MACHINES, AND COMPACTORS

These are used for flattening and compacting areas of soil, hardcore, asphalt, and concrete. Rollers, screed machines, and compactors remove air pockets in material to reduce the risk of future settlement and provide a solid base for construction. Machines with vibrating mechanisms are the most effective, but you must follow advice about taking breaks during use.

Pedestrian roller
Self-propelled with vibration mode for improved compaction.

Diesel-powered motor

Weighted rollers

Gasoline-powered motor

Hand grips

Fold-down handle

Ride-on roller
Heavy-duty "ride-on" rollers are only really needed for work on drives or where large areas of compaction are required.

Power screed
This gasoline-driven screed machine vibrates to remove air from concrete to increase its strength. Vibrating pokers are also available. Finish with a power float for a strong, dust-free surface.

Gasoline-powered motor

Plate compactor
A more common option than a roller for domestic situations, a plate compactor is ideal for compacting gravel and sand.

EARTH MOVERS

You will need special training before attempting to use an excavator. Models vary, so ask for training at the rental company. Check whether fuel is supplied as part of the deal, or if it is your responsibility, and always be sure of the particular type of fuel required. Check also if delivery is included in the rental price, and consider insurance.

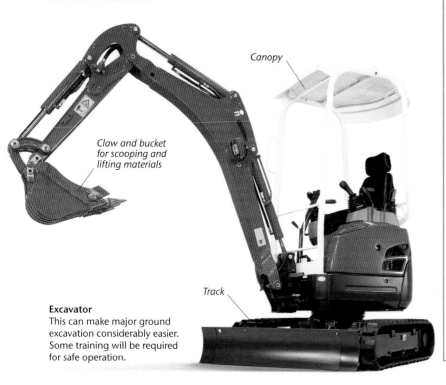

Canopy

Claw and bucket for scooping and lifting materials

Track

Excavator
This can make major ground excavation considerably easier. Some training will be required for safe operation.

OTHER RENTAL EQUIPMENT

It is possible to rent tools and equipment to help you with most DIY tasks. Remember that all rental equipment should come with safety guidelines and documentation proving that the equipment has been regularly checked or serviced. Be sure to look for any damage before signing rental contracts.

Generators
Where an electricity supply is switched off or not yet installed, generators offer a portable option for a continuous supply. You will need to establish capacity and size requirements.

Compressor
Air compressors power pneumatic tools. They are available with power up to more than 5 hp and they can have tank sizes up to 80 gallons (300 liters). The frequency and duration of use will determine the horsepower and tank size that you'll need for your DIY project. A 2 hp compressor will be adequate for typical tasks around the house.

WORK CLOTHING

Work clothing falls into a number of categories. These include those items that are essential for a specific type of protection, those items that aid a particular task, and those items that can be considered to be sensible options for a working environment.

BODY PROTECTION

Look for hardwearing materials that allow you to move freely. Coveralls and gloves can be taped together at the sleeve when complete cover is required (see pp.360–363).

WORKING SAFELY

Make time before you start a job to consider your clothing, footwear, and headgear. Most building materials and tools are now supplied with specific manufacturer's guidelines on what kind of safety equipment should be worn when handling or using that product. These guidelines should always be followed carefully. All protective equipment will have a certain working life. Filters on face masks will specify this life, but on other equipment, such as helmets and goggles, it will be up to you to make sure they are in good condition. This applies not only to clothing, but also to tools and equipment as a whole.

Toolbelt
Useful to keep a number of tools at hand. Do not use to carry sharp tools that could pierce the toolbelt. Leather toolbelts are more hardwearing.

Coveralls
Choose long-sleeved coveralls made from tough fabric to protect your clothing while working. Many include pockets and loops for carrying tools, such as hammers and screwdrivers.

Knee pads
Protect knees when kneeling down for work. They usually attach to the knee using Velcro straps.

Nail pouch
Designed to carry small items such as nails and screws. May also have side loops for tools.

GLOVES AND FOOTWEAR

When choosing hand protection, consider whether you need gloves for avoiding bumps or scrapes, or to protect skin against contact with harmful substances. Good-quality footwear that covers the feet entirely will protect against falling objects or sharp or abrasive materials. Choose boots with a firm sole rather than athletic shoes.

Leather gloves
Heavy-duty gloves offer some protection against bumps and scrapes, and also provide some padding support.

PVC gloves
Protect against some chemicals and substances that cause skin irritation. Wearing PVC gloves reduces the need for harsh hand-cleansers.

Latex gloves
Tighter-fitting and thinner than PVC, these are useful for precise tasks. They protect against some chemicals, but are normally used to keep hands clean.

Boots
Good work boots are important to offer protection from falling objects, and when using tools close to your feet. Those with steel toes provide best protection.

HEADGEAR

Protective headgear must be worn when working high up or in an area where items may fall on you. You also need to apply a certain amount of common sense. Wearing protective goggles or glasses is essential when you may be exposed to flying debris, but they also may be useful when painting or sanding a ceiling, for example.

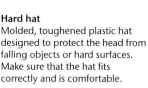

Ear plugs
A disposable, inexpensive alternative to ear protectors. Take care not to push the plugs too far into the ear.

Safety goggles
Offer all-around eye protection, creating a tight seal completely around the eye area.

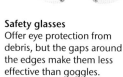

Choose wraparound for maximum protection

Safety glasses
Offer eye protection from debris, but the gaps around the edges make them less effective than goggles.

Hard hat
Molded, toughened plastic hat designed to protect the head from falling objects or hard surfaces. Make sure that the hat fits correctly and is comfortable.

Ear protectors
These provide effective hearing protection when using noisy power tools.

Visor

Ear protectors

Machinery helmet
Combines eye, ear, and head protection. Visor and ear protectors clip onto a hard hat. Helmets may be supplied ready-assembled, but if assembling it yourself, follow the instructions carefully so that the helmet functions correctly.

HARNESSES

When working in raised areas, you may need a harness to safeguard you from falling. Harnesses vary in design, so check for fit before buying one. A harness must be checked and serviced regularly to be sure it is in sound and safe working order. Designs will vary between different manufacturers, and even subtle differences may change the way in which one type of harness is worn compared to another. Harnesses may be attached to fixed scaffolding via a connecting lanyard with a specially designed hook.

MASKS

Protective masks are designed for use with different products. Some are designed to stop large particles such as sawdust, whereas others can protect against the inhalation of fumes and small particles. Check the type of mask recommended for use—failure to heed guidelines can compromise health and safety. Many masks have a limited effective life span and need to be replaced often. Others are designed for use with disposable cartridge filters. When working with paint, chemicals, and/or dust, make sure the area is well-ventilated with open windows. Ensure that you take regular breaks in fresh air.

Metallic strip

Dust mask
Offers some protection against inhaling large particles. Choose a design that fits tightly. A metallic strip over the bridge of the nose keeps the mask in position and makes it as airtight as possible.

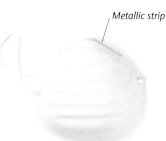

Valved mask
This is more comfortable than a dust mask as the exhalation valve helps to reduce humidity inside the mask. It may also offer a slightly higher level of protection.

Cartridge filter

Respirator mask
Equipped with cartridge filters and exhalation valves. Filters can be changed to protect against the particular substance you are working with.

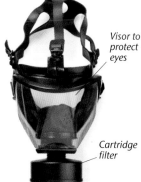

Visor to protect eyes

Cartridge filter

Face mask
Required when working with toxic substances, where a manufacturer specifies use. Regular correct cleaning and inspection of parts are essential.

Hand tools

ALTHOUGH POWER TOOLS HAVE TRANSFORMED DIY, HAND TOOLS REMAIN ESSENTIAL TO A HOUSEHOLD TOOLKIT. DESPITE THE ADVANCEMENT OF POWER TOOLS, THERE ARE SOME CIRCUMSTANCES IN WHICH HAND TOOLS ARE MOST SUITABLE. DESIGNS ARE ALWAYS IMPROVING, SO AS WELL AS LOOKING FOR QUALITY, LOOK FOR FEATURES SUCH AS ERGONOMIC DESIGNS THAT MAKE A TOOL EASY TO USE.

SCREWDRIVERS

Screwdrivers vary according to the type of screw that they are designed to drive. Different sizes correspond with screw sizes, so always use a screwdriver of the correct size to avoid damaging the tool or the screw head. Subtle variations in screwdriver design reflect the many different jobs for which they are used. For information about screws, see pp.76–77.

TYPES OF SCREWDRIVERS

The most common fastener in Canada is the Robertson square socket screw because of the no-slip fit between the screw and the screwdriver. The Phillips cross socket type is particularly useful when you need to drive slightly off angle from the screw, but it does not give the ease of use of the Robertson. Slotted screws are occasionally found on imported products. With all screwdrivers, take care to match the correct type and size of driver to the screw.

TIP OF ROBERTSON SCREWDRIVER

Robertson screwdriver
These square socket screwdrivers are the easiest to use because of the good grip between driver and screw.

TIP OF PHILLIPS SCREWDRIVER

Phillips screwdriver
These cross socket screwdrivers are common in the US. Useful for bad angles and always used for drywall.

TIP OF SLOTTED SCREWDRIVER

Slotted screwdriver
These match the very first screws. Still common in the US, but rare in Canada. It is difficult to drive slotted screws.

USING A SCREWDRIVER

Be sure to select an appropriate screwdriver to match the size and type of screw. Hold the screwdriver at right angles to the screw head, then ensure that the tip of the screwdriver is fully inserted into the head of the screw before turning it. Turn the screw clockwise to tighten it and counterclockwise to loosen it. Depending on the length of the screw, it may be necessary to adjust your grip several times.

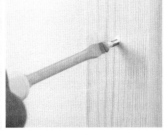

To insert a wood screw without damaging the wood, first you may need to drill a pilot hole.

SPECIALTY SCREWDRIVERS

Some screwdrivers are designed to enable you to fix screws in inaccessible areas, while others have been developed to make the task of driving screws easier.

Stubby screwdriver
As the name suggests, this screwdriver is very short and is designed for use in areas that a regular screwdriver will not fit into.

Short shaft

Jeweler's screwdriver
This type of very fine screwdriver is designed for particularly intricate tasks. To use it, apply pressure to the revolving head with your index finger, and use your other fingers and thumb on the middle section of the handle to turn the shaft.

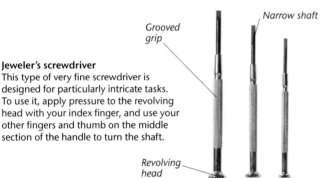

Grooved grip

Narrow shaft

Revolving head

Electric screwdriver
An electric screwdriver can make working with screws much quicker. It is usually powered by a rechargeable battery and comes with a selection of interchangeable bits that fit into the neck of the shaft. In this model, a central switch sets clockwise or counter-clockwise rotation, and a button next to the handle activates the shaft's turning mechanism. In many ways, cordless drill-drivers have taken over from the simple electric screwdriver shown here. However, these still have a function for lightweight work.

Turning shaft holds bits

Direction switch

On/off button

UNDERSTANDING A SCREWDRIVER

The tip
Good screwdrivers will have hardened tips to withstand the work we demand from them. Many multiple-head screwdrivers allow for using the driving bit by hand or chucking it into a drill for power driving. Good Robertson tips will be slightly tapered to fit more snugly into the square socket of the screw. Small Phillips bits will be pointed, while larger ones will be flattened off to ensure that they fit all the way into the screw. Using a flat-headed screwdriver requires a good fit between the driver and the screw or you will damage the screwdriver itself.

FLAT   PHILLIPS   ROBERTSON

The shaft
Screwdriver shafts can be either round or square in cross-section. Square sections in shafts allow a wrench or pliers to clamp on, which can make it easier to apply greater torque to drive in or remove a screw. High-quality shafts are usually made of a hardened steel and chrome vanadium alloy.

Square section

The handle
Traditionally, screwdriver handles have a bulbous section designed to fit comfortably in the palm of the hand. Modern designs place emphasis on a soft grip with a bulbous but less exaggerated section. Fluted handles are much thinner, and the fluted section along the handle shaft provides finger control of the screwdriver.

BULBOUS HANDLE   **SOFT HANDLE**   **FLUTED HANDLE**

ASSORTED SCREWDRIVER BITS

Ratchet screwdriver
You can use a ratchet screwdriver to drive in or take out a screw without having to readjust your grip. A three-position switch selects different functions. With the switch in the central position, the screwdriver operates like any other. With the switch to one side, the handle will rotate in one direction but lock when turned the opposite way. This enables you to simply rotate the handle one way and then the other to screw in or unscrew a fastener. Some ratchet screwdrivers have a spiral action in the shaft that turns the bit as you apply downward pressure.

Although traditionally associated with cutting wood, many different types of handsaws are now available for cutting through a great variety of building materials, including metal and even stone. Shown here are the most common types of handsaws, but you will also find other design variations. Owning one of each kind will equip you to tackle most cutting tasks.

CUTTING WOOD WITH A SAW

Draw a guide line across each face of the wood, marking where you will cut. Use a carpenter's square to ensure that the line is accurate.

A

B

Use a utility knife to score along the guide line. This will enable you to get a clean cut through each side without splintering the wood.

C

Hold the saw as shown. Place the blade just to the offcut side of the guide line and make a few backward strokes across the corner of the wood.

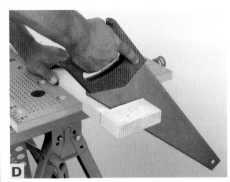

D

Once you have cut a shallow groove, begin to saw through the wood, back and forth, using long, deliberate strokes.

PREPARING TO USE A SAW

Using any saw—handsaw or power saw—requires careful setup in order to make sure your cut is clean and to avoid injury. Always secure a board with clamps to the cutting work surface before attempting to cut through a board with any saw.

If using a miter box, the box provides a snug place for the board. Still, fasten the miter box in place so the work and box do not move while cutting.

Do not hold the cut-off piece—the part of the board you are attempting to cut from the longer length—while using the saw. Always let the cut-off piece fall.

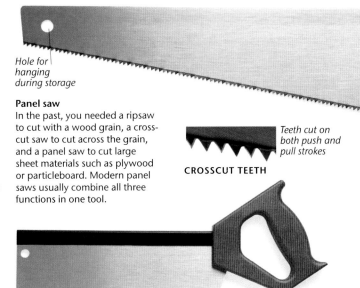

Hole for hanging during storage

Panel saw

In the past, you needed a ripsaw to cut with a wood grain, a cross-cut saw to cut across the grain, and a panel saw to cut large sheet materials such as plywood or particleboard. Modern panel saws usually combine all three functions in one tool.

Teeth cut on both push and pull strokes

CROSSCUT TEETH

Tenon saw

Used for detailed woodworking, or when cuts need to be extremely accurate, a tenon saw makes fine cuts in wood. It has a relatively short but deep blade, and the fine teeth provide a clean cut and edges that require little sanding or smoothing. For this reason, a tenon saw is excellent for making mitered cuts, which need an accurate joint.

FINE TEETH

Regular, fine teeth make accurate cuts in wood

Use point to break through material and start cut

Drywall saw

This saw can cut irregular shapes, and is used to make holes in drywall, for example, when installing electrical outlets. The blade is narrow, and tapers away from the handle to a point.

UNDERSTANDING SAW TEETH

The size, shape, and frequency of teeth on a saw's blade dictate the kinds of materials that the saw is able to cut. Teeth along a blade are measured in teeth per inch (TPI). The larger the TPI figure, the finer the cut, but the longer it will take. A saw with a high TPI is designed for precise cuts. Conversely, a low TPI saw is designed to cut quickly but less accurately.

A saw's teeth are slightly offset, so the groove cut by a saw is slightly wider than the blade. This groove is called the kerf, and it enables sawdust to leave the cutting area, helping the saw blade to move easily through a cut.

Body of blade

Tooth offset from body of blade

EDGE OF SAW TEETH

The angle and design of teeth vary according to the uses for which a saw is designed. Saws that cut metal have very fine teeth, whereas a rough, general-purpose saw has larger teeth. Some manufacturers have patented tooth designs aimed at greater efficiency and ease of cutting, and some make "hardened" teeth, designed to stay sharp for longer than traditional stainless- or tempered-steel blades.

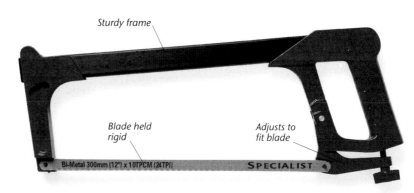

Sturdy frame

Blade held rigid

Adjusts to fit blade

Bi-Metal 300mm (12") x 10TPCM (24TPI)   SPECIALIST

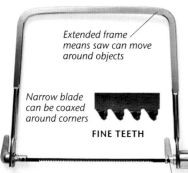

Extended frame means saw can move around objects

Narrow blade can be coaxed around corners

FINE TEETH

Swiveling pins fix blade in different directions

Coping saw
The easiest way to cut irregular shapes or curves in a piece of wood is to use a frame saw, which has a thin blade held on a bow-shaped frame. A coping saw is a common example. Maneuver the blade to cut curves. It is easy to break blades doing this, so buy extra blades when purchasing the saw.

Hacksaw
Use a hacksaw to cut metal. Like the coping saw and fret saw, its blade is housed in a frame. However, it has a deeper blade that is not designed for cutting curves. A hacksaw's teeth are very fine, and cutting through metal is always a slow process. Renew blades at regular intervals, and always fit the blade so that its teeth are facing forward.

Hardened steel blade

Bow-shaped frame keeps fine blade under tension

Fret saw
This is another common type of frame saw, and is used for very fine work. It has a very thin blade held in position on a bow-shaped frame, and should be used in exactly the same way as a coping saw.

Junior hacksaw
This smaller version of a hacksaw fits easily into a toolbox. It is often used for general fine-cutting jobs.

FINE TEETH

Forward-facing teeth create a fine cut

Thumb screw and plate

Miter saw
A combination of a saw and a miter box, the miter saw is a tool that can make accurate cuts at any angle. The saw is housed in a frame that enables you to shift the blade to the angle required.

Saw frame

Clamp for holding wood

Lever lifts to change saw angle

CARE AND MAINTENANCE
It is now comparatively inexpensive to replace a saw, so sharpening handsaw blades is becoming a thing of the past. However, rather than throwing away a panel saw that is becoming blunted, use it to cut softer materials such as drywall or insulation sheets. When a coping saw, fret saw, or hacksaw is blunted, the removable blades are easy to replace.

Miter box
A miter box has channels to guide a saw (usually a tenon saw) through a material at precisely the correct angle for a mitered joint—45 degrees.

Channels at 45 degrees to the block

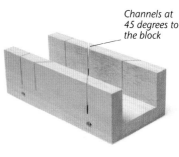

HAMMERS AND FASTENER REMOVERS

TOOLS, EQUIPMENT, AND MATERIALS

A hammer is a particularly versatile DIY tool. As well as positioning and removing nails, it can be used as a driving tool to pound in posts, or as a wrecking tool for demo work. The descriptions here will help you to decide which type of hammer you need for different types of jobs. A selection of robust fastener removers, including pliers, pincers, and pry bars, is an essential part of any toolkit.

NAIL SET

This tool enables you to set a nail just below the surface. Nail sets are available in several sizes and weights to suit varying nail sizes. See p.79 for how to use a nail set.

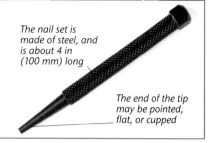

The nail set is made of steel, and is about 4 in (100 mm) long

The end of the tip may be pointed, flat, or cupped

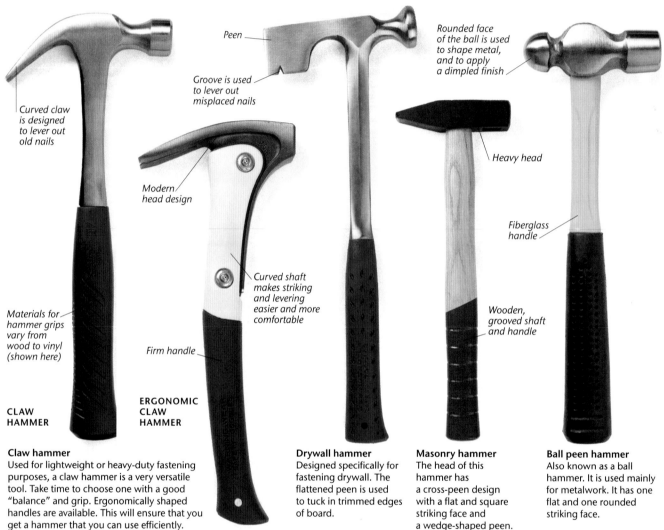

Peen

Groove is used to lever out misplaced nails

Rounded face of the ball is used to shape metal, and to apply a dimpled finish

Curved claw is designed to lever out old nails

Modern head design

Heavy head

Curved shaft makes striking and levering easier and more comfortable

Fiberglass handle

Materials for hammer grips vary from wood to vinyl (shown here)

Firm handle

Wooden, grooved shaft and handle

CLAW HAMMER

ERGONOMIC CLAW HAMMER

Claw hammer
Used for lightweight or heavy-duty fastening purposes, a claw hammer is a very versatile tool. Take time to choose one with a good "balance" and grip. Ergonomically shaped handles are available. This will ensure that you get a hammer that you can use efficiently.

Drywall hammer
Designed specifically for fastening drywall. The flattened peen is used to tuck in trimmed edges of board.

Masonry hammer
The head of this hammer has a cross-peen design with a flat and square striking face and a wedge-shaped peen.

Ball peen hammer
Also known as a ball hammer. It is used mainly for metalwork. It has one flat and one rounded striking face.

USING A HAMMER

A

Grip the hammer so that the end of the handle farthest from the head is only just visible.

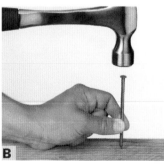

B

Hold a nail in place and set its position with a few gentle taps.

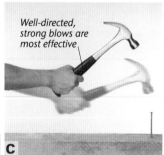

Well-directed, strong blows are most effective

C

Strike the nail firmly with the center of the hammer's face. The face should be at a right angle to the nail to ensure a straight strike.

SOFT HAMMERS

Some jobs require the use of a hammer, but without the hard impact of a metal striking face. Soft hammers include wooden and rubber mallets. Wooden mallets are designed for use with chisels (see opposite) or for tapping wood joints into position. Rubber mallets are commonly used on blockwork, pavers, and slabs (see p.49).

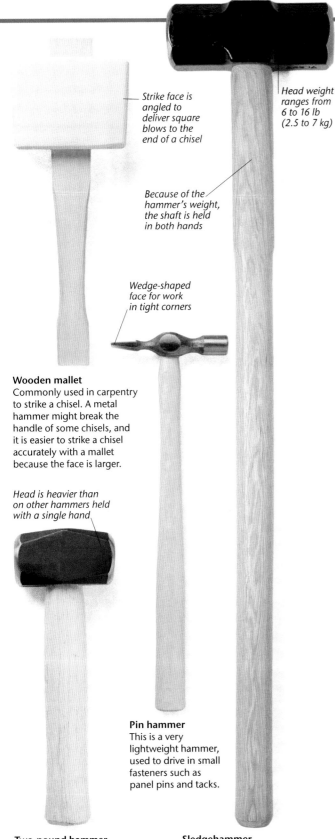

Wooden mallet
Commonly used in carpentry to strike a chisel. A metal hammer might break the handle of some chisels, and it is easier to strike a chisel accurately with a mallet because the face is larger.

Strike face is angled to deliver square blows to the end of a chisel

Head weight ranges from 6 to 16 lb (2.5 to 7 kg)

Because of the hammer's weight, the shaft is held in both hands

Wedge-shaped face for work in tight corners

Head is heavier than on other hammers held with a single hand

Pin hammer
This is a very lightweight hammer, used to drive in small fasteners such as panel pins and tacks.

Two-pound hammer
Also called a lump hammer. It is the heaviest hammer that can be used with one hand. It has a large striking face, and is used commonly with a chisel to split bricks (see p.39). In addition, it is useful for driving large nails into landscape timbers.

Sledgehammer
A large hammer that can be used to break up masonry surfaces such as old hardcore or paving. It is also a driving tool, and may be used to pound in posts, for example. Wear a hard hat, steel toe boots, gloves, and goggles when working with a sledgehammer.

HAMMER CARE AND MAINTENANCE
It is important that you keep a hammer's striking face clean, to prevent it from slipping during use and therefore striking inaccurately. The easiest way to keep your hammer in good condition is to rub its face from time to time with a piece of sandpaper.

FASTENER REMOVERS
These tools are related to hammers. Some can be used as an alternative to the claw hammer, for removing nails from a surface, while others are used for more heavy-duty jobs such as breaking up masonry.

Pliers
These are very useful for small-scale work, since they enable you to get a good grip on the fastener. The toothed jaws have a curved section for gripping, and side cutters for cropping wire.

Scissorlike arms help to grip the fastener

Curved jaws assist rocking lever motion

Pincers
Use these to remove lightweight fasteners and large nails. Grip the shaft of the fastener with the pincer jaws, and rock the pincers to lever the fastener free.

Hooked end allows large items to be levered out

Flattened, chiseled end can be positioned in narrow gaps

Pry bar
You can use a pry bar to remove heavy-duty fasteners. Use the same technique as with a claw hammer. A pry bar is also suitable as a wrecking tool, to lever out or to break down masonry or woodwork.

REMOVING A NAIL

Offcut of wood protects surface

Lay an offcut of wood next to the nail. Resting on the offcut, slide the claws of a hammer around the nail.

Keeping contact with the surface, pull the handle toward you. The rising claws should pull out the nail.

CHISELS

Chisels are cutting and shaping tools that are essential to many carpentry jobs. Heavy-duty chisels are also available for use on masonry. Blade shape and size and handle design all contribute to the function of a chisel and how easy it is to use. A vast range of chisels is available for the serious woodworker, but a small selection should enable you to tackle most DIY tasks. All the chisels shown here have straight blades, but it is also possible to buy chisels, known as gouges, that have curved blades. These are used to cut out curved sections of wood and rounded corners—jobs that are more associated with woodcarving.

WOOD CHISELS

Most wood chisels are based on one of two designs—the firmer chisel and the bevel-edged chisel. Of these, the bevel-edged chisel is by far the most multipurpose and widely used. You can strike wood chisels with a hammer or mallet, or simply use hand pressure and your body weight. For example, you may use a paring chisel by hand to remove small amounts of wood at a gradual pace. Use only a wooden mallet when striking a chisel with a wooden handle. Hammers should be used solely on chisels with synthetic, impact-resistant or shatterproof handles.

◾ USING A WOOD CHISEL

Clamp the wood securely in place, so that you can use both hands to control the chisel. To remove a depth of wood, first use a paring chisel to make vertical cuts along the marked guide lines. Make any cuts running across the grain first to protect the wood from splitting.

A

B

Place the chisel with its bevel-edged side facing downward. Hold it at an angle, and strike the handle squarely with a hammer or mallet.

C

Neaten the edges of the cut using the chisel laid flat. Control the movement of the chisel by hand, gradually finishing the joint.

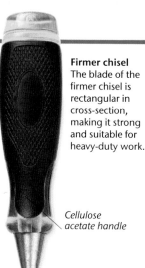

Firmer chisel
The blade of the firmer chisel is rectangular in cross-section, making it strong and suitable for heavy-duty work.

Mortise chisel
Designed for cutting deep mortise joints, the mortise chisel is a stronger version of the firmer chisel. The deeper blade is often more square than rectangular in profile.

Cellulose acetate handle

Bevel-edged chisel
One side is completely flat, but the other face has tapered edges. This chisel is designed for multiple uses, and provides the most accurate cuts. As well as general use, this design lends itself to removing wood in the construction of many different joint types.

Paring chisel
The blade tends to be much longer than the bevel-edged chisel, but otherwise they are very similar. Paring is the gradual removal of small shavings of wood, which can be done with most chisels, but the longer blade on a paring chisel makes this tool easier to control when used by hand.

UNDERSTANDING CHISEL HANDLES

Chisel handles are struck repeatedly and so need to be exceptionally hardwearing. Traditional handles are wooden, but modern handles are often made of shatterproof and impact-resistant materials, such as cellulose acetate. These handles are so strong that most manufacturers provide a lifetime guarantee. Further protection is sometimes provided by a metal cap on the end of the handle. As well as withstanding hammer or mallet blows, a chisel also needs to sit comfortably in the hand, so some manufacturers give them a soft handle, made of rubber or plastic rather than wood, which also helps with shock absorption.

MASONRY CHISELS

The nature of their work means that masonry chisels are much heavier and wider than wood chisels. They are used in conjunction with a two-pound hammer (see p.37) to remove sections of masonry or other "hard" materials, such as wall tiles.

Guard protects hand from missed blows

Wide blade cuts bricks or blocks without shattering them

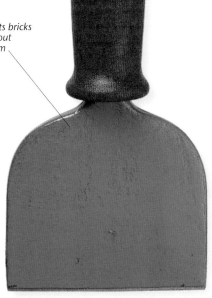

Brick chisel
This chisel has a short, broad, and flat blade, with a handle that may have a guard to protect the user's hand. You can use it to remove masonry or to cut bricks and blocks (see below).

Narrow blade fits between bricks

Cold chisel
This is a narrower version of a brick chisel (above). The blade shape is ideal for removing mortar from brick or block joints in a masonry wall.

CUTTING A BRICK

Use a light tap of a two-pound hammer on a brick chisel to mark a cutting line across each side of the brick.

Lay the brick flat, place the chisel on the guide line, and strike it with the hammer. This should split the brick along the guide line.

SHARPENING A BLADE

For chisels to work easily and effectively, they should be kept razor-sharp. The best tool for this maintenance is a sharpening stone (see box, below). Chisels that are in a very poor condition, and need a lot of sharpening, may benefit from initial sharpening using a bench grinder (see p.65). It is also possible to buy a special guide that can hold a chisel at specific angles when you move it across a sharpening stone.

Moisten the surface of the stone with a few drops of oil or water. You may wish to secure the stone in a clamp or vise while sharpening the chisel. Use the chisel's bevel angle to guide you in getting the correct angle alignment between chisel and stone face.

Move the chisel, briskly but rhythmically, backward and forward across the stone to hone the blade edge to a sharp finish.

To finish off, turn the chisel over, laying it flat on the stone. Ride the blade flat on the stone to remove burrs from the cutting edge.

CARE AND MAINTENANCE

Sharpening stones
Oil stones composed of silicone carbide are the most common sharpening stones. There are other types available, such as more expensive diamond stones. Different grades of stone are available. It is best to buy more than one so that you have a coarse stone to remove large amounts of metal from a chipped blade and a smoother one for final honing. In fact, some stones are made with one coarse side and one fine side. Depending on the stone's composition, apply water or oil to the stone's face to lubricate it for sharpening.

Silicone carbide stone

Storage
Because chisels must be kept sharp, they need to be stored carefully. Chisels are often supplied with plastic covers that clip over the end of the chisel's blade to protect it. These covers should always be replaced when the chisel is not in use. The alternative is to store the chisels in a specially designed tool roll or case, as shown here.

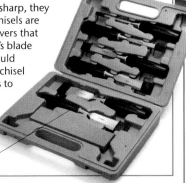

Chisels held securely in individual compartments

PLANES, RASPS, AND FILES

Like chisels, planes are used to shave off fairly small sections of wood, but the broad iron (blade) of a plane is designed for use on long wooden edges. Many designs are available, but most DIY jobs can be completed with just a few. Many tasks are now carried out with a power planer (see p.62), but hand planes still have a role to play. Planes have a number of components, but are straightforward to use. Rasps and files have functions similar to planes, but remove material in a different way.

BENCH PLANES

These are generally categorized according to length. The largest version is a jointer plane, which can be around 2 ft (600 mm) long. It is ideal for jointing or getting one edge square on particularly long boards, but its size makes it relatively unwieldy for more detailed work. Shown here are smaller bench planes: a jack plane and a smoothing plane.

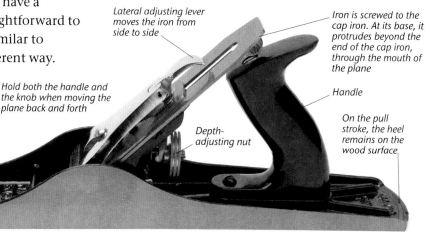

Lateral adjusting lever moves the iron from side to side

Iron is screwed to the cap iron. At its base, it protrudes beyond the end of the cap iron, through the mouth of the plane

Hold both the handle and the knob when moving the plane back and forth

Handle

Depth-adjusting nut

On the pull stroke, the heel remains on the wood surface

Jack plane
The most versatile of the bench plane family, you can use a jack plane for most planing tasks. It is fairly heavy-duty, and removes wood quickly and efficiently.

On the push stroke, place greater pressure here on the toe

The iron end emerges through the mouth in the base. The smaller the amount of iron showing, the finer the planing work will be

CLOSE-UP OF THE PLANE'S UNDERSIDE

Smoothing plane
A smoothing plane is a smaller version of the jack plane that is used for final finishing. It might be used after a jack plane, or it may simply be used for less rigorous planing on smaller pieces of wood.

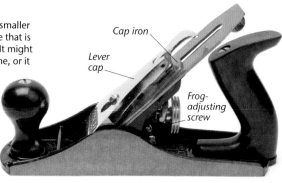

Cap iron

Lever cap

Frog-adjusting screw

SETTING AND ADJUSTING A PLANE

Lift the lever on the lever cap, and slide it out of the plane. Next, lift out the cap iron and the iron. Undo the cap iron screw.

A

B **Lift out the cap iron** and iron, and slide the cap iron back until a small area of the iron is visible—up to ½ in (2 mm).

C **Retighten the cap iron** screw. Do not yet replace in the plane—the mouth settings need to be adjusted, as shown in the next steps.

D **Use a screwdriver** to turn the frog-adjusting screw. Move the frog forward to reduce its mouth size, and backward to increase it.

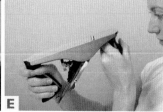
E **Reassemble the plane.** Turn it upside down, hold it at eye level, and look directly along the base from the toe to the heel.

F **Turn the depth-adjusting** nut until the iron protrudes from the mouth. This is used for removing small, not large, layers of material.

G **Finish setting the** plane by moving the lateral adjusting lever to provide a uniform gap at the plane mouth, with the iron parallel to the foot.

BLOCK PLANES

Smaller than a smoothing plane, a block plane is capable of finer shaving because its iron is set at a shallow angle. The iron is positioned bevel-up in a block plane, but bevel-down in a bench plane. A block plane is normally used one-handed, but pressure can be applied with the other hand if necessary. It is particularly useful for planing the end grain.

Compact plane
The compact size of a block plane makes it very easy to handle, as well as being easy to store in the toolbox. It does not have a cap iron, but the iron is adjusted in the same way as other planes.

Twist knob to move iron from side-to-side

Cutting-depth adjustor

Finger rest with mouth-adjustment lever

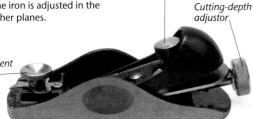

USING A PLANE

Planes are best used for removing wood from relatively thin edges, such as doors or sections of prepared lumber. A sound technique for using a plane is important for achieving good results. Here is the basic technique for plane use.

A **Position the plane** on the edge of the lumber. Move it forward steadily, keeping the pressure on the toe of the plane.

B **As you reach** the end, transfer the pressure to the heel of the plane. Repeat until you have removed the desired amount of wood.

SHARPENING THE IRON

Hone the iron before its first use. The iron should be curved for general work, with corners slightly rounded for finer planing, and it should have a 30-degree bevel. Some planes are supplied with a 25-degree bevel, to avoid damage before purchase. Use an appropriate stone for honing.

A **Hone the bevel side** of the iron up and down the sharpening stone to produce a bevel of about 30 degrees. Lubricate as shown on p.39.

B **Hone the flat side** of the iron to remove burs. Work the iron across the entire surface of the stone, so that it wears evenly.

RASPS

Use a rasp for rounding edges and curves. Traditional rasps have a series of abrasive blades, varying in coarseness. Modern rasps, like those below, have holes punched across the entire surface of the blade. Each hole has a sharpened edge that shaves off layers of wood.

Two-handed surform rasp
As the surform passes across the wood, the shavings come up through the holes and clear of the blade.

Large handle leads the pulling and pushing action

UNDERSIDE OF RASP IN CLOSE-UP

One-handed surform rasp
This has a cutting area similar to its two-handed counterpart.

FILES

Like rasps, files have an abrasive blade and are used for rounding edges and curves on wood, metal, and stone. They are often supplied just as blades, so fit a handle before use.

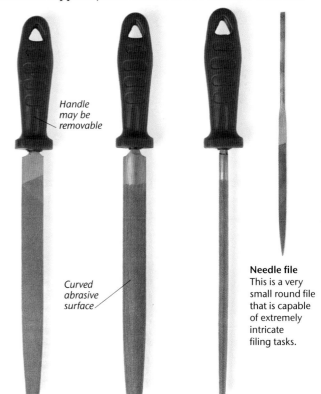

Handle may be removable

Curved abrasive surface

Needle file
This is a very small round file that is capable of extremely intricate filing tasks.

Flat file
Some files are also used for metalwork. The flat file is a commonly used design.

Half-round file
The cross-section of this file is partly rounded, making access to curved areas easier.

Round file
This file has a completely rounded blade for accessing curved areas.

Levels are essential to many DIY jobs, since they ensure that guide lines or marks are precisely horizontal (level) or vertical (plumb). You can also use them to set accurate angled guides, although this is a less common function. Layout tools include the plumb bob and chalk box, which use the tension in taught strings to determine perfectly straight lines.

LEVELS

The most commonly used basic levels come in various sizes. They usually consist of a plastic or metal straight bar containing two or more vials of liquid. Each vial contains a bubble. Hold a level against the item or surface to be checked. When the bubble in the appropriate vial rests between the two center guide lines marked on the vial, the surface is shown to be either exactly vertical or exactly horizontal. Some levels have rotating vials that can be set at precise angles, for when you require guide lines at specific angles.

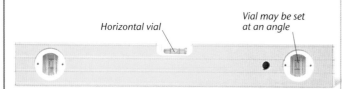

Horizontal vial — *Vial may be set at an angle*

Carpenter's level
This contains three vials and is the most versatile level. The vial in the middle is used to determine the horizontal level, while some carpenter's levels have an end vial that can determine plumb. Carpenter's levels are available in several sizes, ranging from 24 in (610 mm) to 6 ft (1.8 m) in length.

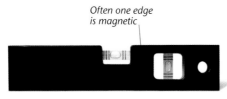

Often one edge is magnetic

Pocket level (torpedo level)
This small level is designed to be used where a carpenter's level is too long. One face of a pocket level is often magnetic, so that it can be stuck to a metal surface, such as a refrigerator door or a range hood, to determine whether it is level.

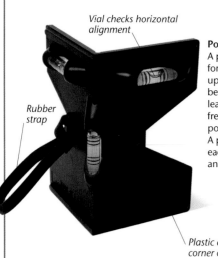

Vial checks horizontal alignment

Rubber strap

Post level
A post level is a level used for accurately positioning upright posts. The level can be strapped onto a post, leaving you with both hands free to adjust the post's position until it is plumb. A post level has three vials, each positioned at right angles to the others.

Plastic casing fits around corner of post or upright

LASER LEVELS

These combine the principles of the basic level with laser technology. They project a beam that can be set to provide an accurate guide line on any surface. A laser level can also work in the same way as a string line, helping to position fence posts.

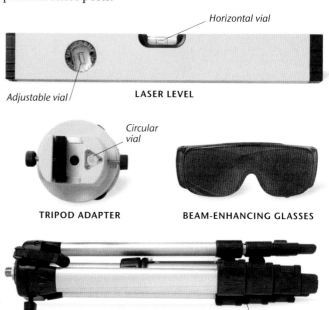

Horizontal vial

Adjustable vial — **LASER LEVEL**

Circular vial

TRIPOD ADAPTER   **BEAM-ENHANCING GLASSES**

TRIPOD — *Retractable legs*

Laser level equipment
The laser level projects a beam from the end of the level. It is used on a tripod, and the adapter has its own leveling vial and an angle-adjusting mechanism so that its level can be adjusted without moving the tripod.

USING A LASER LEVEL

A Set up the tripod and attach the adapter.

B Use the adapter's built-in level adjuster to center the bubble in the vial and make sure it is perfectly horizontal.

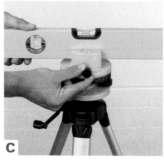

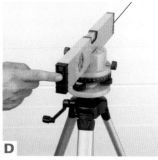

C Clamp the laser level into position on the tripod adapter, and check that it is level.

D Turn on the beam to project either a dot or a line, as required. The beam can be projected horizontally or vertically.

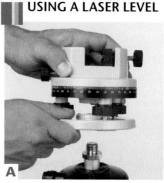

Laser projector

Different vials to denote level and plumb

Laser gradient level

There are several vials along the length of a laser gradient level. One will be set to give a horizontal guide; the others are set to four different gradients. The laser projects a line showing your chosen gradient over several yards. This can be useful when installing gutters (see pp.208–209), for example, or laying out a patio (see pp.412–413). In both cases a slight gradient is required, and this level can provide that measurement with great accuracy.

WATER LEVEL

Although rarely used now, you can use a water level to calculate levels and gradients over long distances or around obstacles. Run water into a tube until it is nearly full. Fasten one end in place so that the water level is at the required height, and take the other end to where you need to mark a guide line at the same level. The water levels at each end of the tube will always be at exactly the same height.

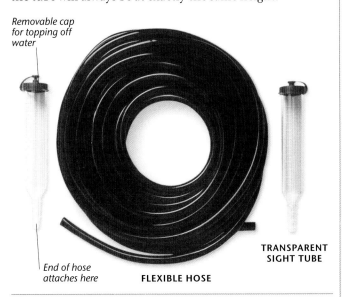

Removable cap for topping off water

End of hose attaches here

FLEXIBLE HOSE

TRANSPARENT SIGHT TUBE

LAYOUT TOOLS

These are among the simplest and most useful elements in a toolkit. A plumb line uses gravity to ensure that vertical lines are accurate. A chalk line will enable you to mark a straight guide line on any surface. It is straightforward to make your own plumb line and chalk line.

Plumb line

A plumb line consists of a symmetrically shaped weight, or bob, suspended from a piece of string. Gravity ensures that the string will always fall in a direct, vertical line, and therefore provide a completely accurate guide.

BOB   **STRING**

Chalk line

This is used to mark guide lines, often created by levels. A manufactured chalk line has a chalk reservoir in its body, so that the line is chalked whenever it is extended or wound back in.

Hook

USING A CHALK LINE

A chalk line is a quick and accurate way to mark a guide line without using a pencil and straight edge. When you no longer need the chalk line, you can simply rub it away. Make sure that the line is taut and that when you lift the chalk line before snapping it, you lift it at right angles to the surface. If you lift the string inaccurately, it may snap down and mark a line in the wrong position. You can use a length of string and some chalk to make your own chalk line.

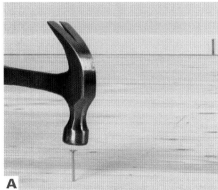

A

Make the required measurements to work out where you need your guide line, and mark both ends. Drive in a temporary fastener—you can use nails or screws—at each end of the planned guide line.

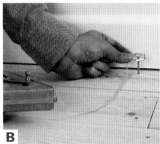

B

Hook the chalk line over the fastener at one end.

C

Unroll the line, and wrap it around the other fastener, ensuring that the line is held taut.

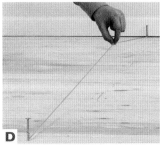

D

Grip the line at its midpoint, and pull it vertically a small distance away from the surface.

E

Let go of the line, allowing it to snap onto the surface. It will leave a chalk guide line where it has hit the surface. Remove line and fasteners.

CARE AND MAINTENANCE

Checking accuracy

It is wise to check the accuracy of a level from time to time. Hold the level against a wall and draw a line that it indicates is horizontal. Turn the level around 180° and draw a second horizontal line parallel to the first. Measure the gap between the two lines at several points. If the gap is uneven, the level is no longer accurate and should be discarded. Use the same principle to test the vertical accuracy of the level, by measuring the gap between two lines that the level considers vertical.

MEASURES AND SQUARES

Accurate measurements are often the key to successful home improvement tasks. Whether you are measuring a length many yards long or creating millimeter-tolerance guide lines for precise cuts, there are many different measuring tools available to you. Tools such as squares and gauges are often used in conjunction with these, especially when working with wood. They convert your measurements into accurate guide lines.

MEASURES

Devices for measuring distances range from traditional metal rules and tape measures to high-tech machines using ultrasonic sound waves. Their varied forms and functions reflect the great variety of DIY tasks.

Ultrasonic sound waves are projected to calculate distance or volume

Easy-to-read digital display

Digital estimator
This measures distances using ultrasonic sound waves. Some may also be used to calculate areas and volumes.

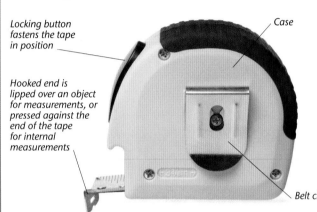

Locking button fastens the tape in position

Case

Hooked end is lipped over an object for measurements, or pressed against the end of the tape for internal measurements

Belt clip

Retractable tape measure
This is the most commonly used measuring tool. Sizes vary, as do the calibrations along the sides of the tape, but 25-ft (7.6-m) tape measures are the most popular. The first inch of the tape is fractionally short to accommodate the width of the metal hooked end.

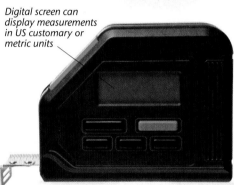

Digital screen can display measurements in US customary or metric units

Button illuminates counter

Digital tape measure
Technology has taken the traditional retractable tape measure to another level. A digital display provides a measurement once the tape is locked in place. Laser measures are also available, although they are a more expensive option.

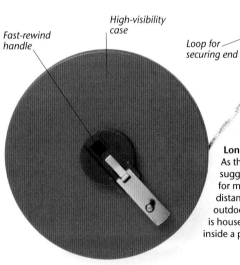

Fast-rewind handle

High-visibility case

Loop for securing end

Long tape
As the name suggests, this tape is for measuring long distances, often outdoors. Flexible tape is housed on a reel inside a protective casing.

MEASURING WHEEL FOLDED DOWN

Gear-driven counter, in a weather-resistant case

Telescopic handle

 INSIDE MEASURING

Place the tape measure inside the space. Note the reading at the point where the tape enters the tape measure case. Measure the length of the case, then add the two measurements.

Measuring wheel
This tool is used for measuring very long distances. The user walks along holding the handles, with the wheel out in front. The machine calculates distances by counting wheel rotations. Allow for a small degree of user error when guiding the wheel, especially when measuring over uneven surfaces.

SQUARES

The main function of a square is to provide an accurate right-angled guide that can be used in any variety of applications. This simple design has been adapted into a number of tools for different types of guide lines. Some, such as measuring rules and levels, have additional features.

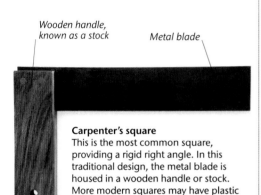

Wooden handle, known as a stock

Metal blade

Carpenter's square
This is the most common square, providing a rigid right angle. In this traditional design, the metal blade is housed in a wooden handle or stock. More modern squares may have plastic or metal handles. The carpenter's square is a simple and reliable tool that is straightforward to use (see box below).

Framing square

Generally a larger square that sits flat on a surface and combines the right-angle guide line function with calibrations along the square's edges, for calculating stairs and rafters. Framing squares are ideal for square-checking corners.

Combination square

Features include a steel rule that slides within the stock of the square. As well as determining a right angle, and a 45-degree angle, other functions of the combination square include scribing (marking a material to fit exactly against a wall or ceiling) and finding levels. It is also ideal for measuring a small rabbet or grooved cut.

Combination set

This takes the combination square one stage further, adding increased functions such as a 180-degree protractor for producing angled guide lines, and a try square for producing accurate 90-degree guide lines.

▌▌ USING A SQUARE

Position the stock against the edge of a section of wood. The blade will form a right angle. Using a carpenter's pencil, draw along the edge of the blade to create your right-angled guide line.

BEVELS AND PENCILS

Two useful items for making guide lines are a bevel and a carpenter's pencil. A bevel provides a guide line for angled cuts; the carpenter's pencil is designed for marking rough surfaces.

Adjustable bevel
The metal blade is first set at an angle using a protractor or other guide, then locked in position by a screw or wing nut. The handle may be moved along the blade to find the required position. Draw the guide line along the edge of the blade.

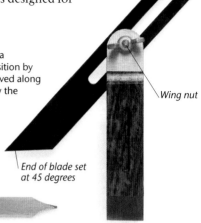

Wing nut

End of blade set at 45 degrees

Carpenter's pencil
This is a thicker and flatter version of a regular pencil. The lead is usually wide and flat to enable it to mark rough wooden surfaces.

GAUGES

These are used to score guide lines on pieces of wood. They are comprised of two main sections of wood—the stem and the stock. One or more marking pins is positioned on the stem. These pins score guide lines (see below).

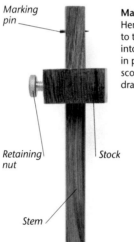

Marking pin

Retaining nut

Stock

Stem

Marking gauge
Here, the marking pin is positioned close to the end of the stem. The stock is moved into the appropriate position, and locked in place with a retaining nut. The pin scores a guide line when the gauge is drawn along the edge of a piece of wood.

Marking pins

Stock

Mortise gauge
This version can score two parallel lines, and may be used to mark off the edge of a door for a mortise lock, for instance. It has two pins—the top one is fixed in place, and the lower is adjustable—and is used in the same way as the marking gauge. On some models, one fixed pin is provided on the reverse, so that the tool can also serve as a marking gauge.

▌▌ USING A MARKING GAUGE

A

Move the stock into the desired position, corresponding with the area to be marked off. Turn the nut to lock the gauge in place.

B

Draw the gauge along the wood, holding the stock against the edge. The marking pin will score a guide line to the set measure.

METRIC OR IMPERIAL?

Two measurement systems
All new Canadian building codes are written in metric measurements and more and more products are produced in metric sizes, but most exisiting houses are built on 16- or 24-inch centers. We are stuck with both systems for some time to come.

WORKBENCHES, VISES, AND CLAMPS

When working on any material, if it is not already fixed in position, you will need to hold it firmly in place. This will enable you to work accurately and safely. You will need to use a workbench and additional vises or clamps, depending on the material involved and the task at hand. Clamps are very versatile tools that come in a great variety of designs.

Broad top

Sawhorses
A pair of sawhorses can support large items, such as sheets of board or lengths of lumber, that a workbench might not accommodate. Traditionally, this type of bench was only made of wood, but now you can buy metal or plastic versions that are height- and width-adjustable. The manufacturer will indicate the maximum weight that a particular sawhorse can support.

Plastic legs fold down for storage

WORKBENCHES

A workbench provides a stable surface for marking, cutting, and general construction tasks. Several types of benches are available. Fixed or freestanding, they vary in size, weight, and accessories, each designed for different purposes. When selecting a workbench, it is essential to consider its suitability for your DIY needs.

Toggles

Handles turn to adjust the gap between the slats that hold materials in place

Folding legs

Portable workbench
These popular benches are good for securing materials, easy to use, and most fold away for easy storage. On some models, measurement calibrations or angle guides are marked on the adjustable slats to help with marking guide lines.

Integral vise

Tightening handle

Storage drawer

Handy shelf also improves stability

Fixed workbench
If you have the room for one, a fixed workbench provides an excellent working platform. It gives greater stability than a portable bench can, and large ones can support bulky materials. It is easy to attach vises and clamps to a fixed workbench.

USING A WORKBENCH

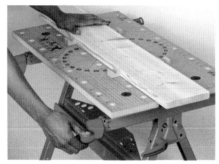

Clamping wood
Turning the handles on the side of the bench adjusts the positions of the wooden slats, allowing you to clamp material securely in place. Do not overtighten the slats.

Using toggles
Another way to hold a material in place is to insert toggles into the holes in the slats and hold the material between them. Use an additional clamp if necessary.

Stabilizing the bench
If your bench has a footrest, use it not just for comfort, but also to apply downward pressure, which will hold the bench in a more stable position.

VISES

A vise is a simple and solid set of adjustable jaws that holds materials in position. Unlike a clamp, a vise must be attached to a stable surface such as a workbench before use.

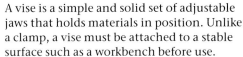

Plate fits to underside of workbench

Turning the threaded central bar adjusts jaws

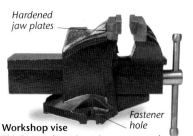

Hardened jaw plates

Fastener hole

Jaws have large surface area

Workshop vise
This heavy-duty vise grips square and cylindrical materials, such as pipes, and should be secured to the top of a fixed workbench.

Woodworker's vise
This should be attached to the underside of a fixed workbench, so that its jaws sit flush with the top of the workbench. Place offcuts of wood against the jaws to protect the material you are working with.

C-clamp fixes vise to surface

Portable vise
This can be attached to any surface, though the maximum thickness of that surface will depend on the dimensions of the vise.

CLAMPS

Clamps are similar to vises in that they are gripping tools, but they are more portable and vary considerably in design, depending on their intended use. They hold materials in position for cutting, and are also useful for holding together glued joints while adhesive dries.

Corner clamp
This type of clamp is designed for use on corner sections of material. It applies pressure to each side of the right angle.

Screw tightener

Inside jaw

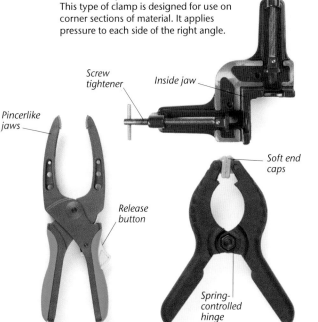

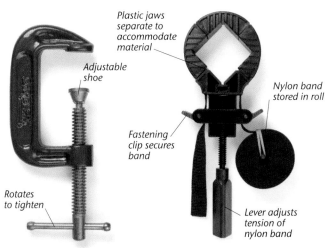

Plastic jaws separate to accommodate material

Adjustable shoe

Nylon band stored in roll

Pincerlike jaws

Soft end caps

Fastening clip secures band

Release button

Rotates to tighten

Lever adjusts tension of nylon band

Spring-controlled hinge

C-clamp
Available in many sizes, a C-clamp is a very versatile tool. Adjust the threaded bar to the required jaw size, placing offcuts of wood between the material being clamped and the jaws to protect it from being damaged.

Band clamp
Use a band clamp on awkward pieces of material. Its jaws are threaded together by a length of nylon, which is released to make the jaws separate. Once placed around the material, pulling the band tightens the jaws.

Ratchet clamp
The ratchet mechanism in this clamp offers you greater control over the pressure it applies. Once you have gripped the material, apply a little further pressure and you will feel the ratchet tighten up until it has an adequate grip.

Spring clamp
Thanks to its very simple design, this clamp can be used with just one hand. Open the jaws by gripping both handles, and release the handles to apply clamping pressure by allowing the jaws to close around the material.

Fixed jaw

Threaded bar

Serrated bar

Movable jaw

Jaw controlled by screw mechanism

Securing pin slotted through hole

Bar clamp
A bar clamp is a type of elongated C-clamp, with one fixed jaw and one adjustable jaw. The adjustable jaw slides along the serrated central bar, as required, and is secured in position using a threaded section with an easy-grip handle. For fine adjustments when securing the clamp, the movable jaw is equipped with a threaded bar that may be tightened.

Large bar clamp
This bigger bar clamp is designed to hold larger materials in place. Fix one end of the clamp in position and adjust the other as required. On some models the central bar is serrated to grip the movable jaw. On others, the bar has a series of holes through which a pin is inserted to hold the movable section in position.

BRICKLAYING TOOLS

Many of the tools used in bricklaying are actually used for other aspects of masonry work. The wide range of tools on the market can be grouped into a few basic categories: trowels, string lines, joint tools, and hammers. Each has an important role to play, and mastering a few simple techniques is the key to successful bricklaying projects.

TROWELS

Trowels are the most important bricklaying tools. Bricklayers use trowels for handling and shaping mortar and laying it between courses of bricks. Professionals use trowels of different types and shapes for specific bricklaying tasks, but a brick trowel is probably most essential. Traditional handles are made of hardwood, although modern trowel designs have softer grips designed for greater comfort and ease of use. The blade of a trowel is made from steel—hardened and tempered carbon steel is commonly used.

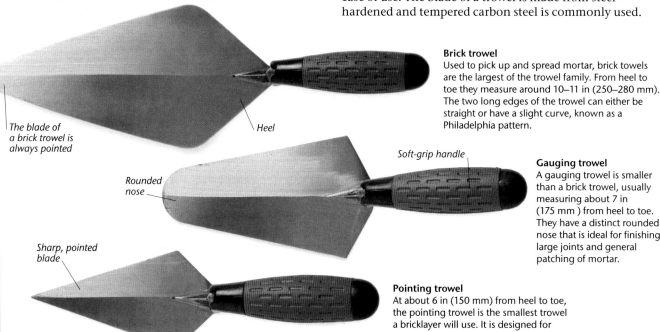

The blade of a brick trowel is always pointed

Heel

Rounded nose

Soft-grip handle

Sharp, pointed blade

Brick trowel
Used to pick up and spread mortar, brick towels are the largest of the trowel family. From heel to toe they measure around 10–11 in (250–280 mm). The two long edges of the trowel can either be straight or have a slight curve, known as a Philadelphia pattern.

Gauging trowel
A gauging trowel is smaller than a brick trowel, usually measuring about 7 in (175 mm) from heel to toe. They have a distinct rounded nose that is ideal for finishing large joints and general patching of mortar.

Pointing trowel
At about 6 in (150 mm) from heel to toe, the pointing trowel is the smallest trowel a bricklayer will use. It is designed for pointing work.

▌ BRICKLAYING TECHNIQUE

The simplest way to set out a straight and level brick wall is to wrap string around a brick at each end of the first course. The bricks should hold the string line taut and provide an initial guide. You may then move the line up each level of bricks as you lay them. Use a level to check that each course is level. Sometimes you may need to use stakes to hold the string line in place.

A

Grip the handle of the trowel toward the blade end. Pick up a good scoop of mortar on the blade, and slide it onto the bricks.

B

Make sure that the mortar sits on the central line of the brick course. Even off the mortar, leaving it slightly longer than brick length.

C

Apply some mortar to the end of a new brick, and smooth the mortar down to each edge. This is known as "buttering."

D

Position the brick, pressing it down into the mortar on the bricks below, and up against the adjacent brick on the same level.

E

Use the handle of the trowel to tap the brick into position.

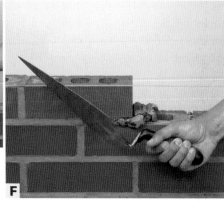

F

Remove excess mortar from the brick face with the edge of the trowel. Continue with this process along the length of the wall, and be sure to check that each brick is level, and aligned with the string line.

MASONRY HAMMERS

A building job may require a certain amount of reshaping of bricks and masonry, and some jobs require masonry to be knocked into position. Since most bricks are fairly brittle, use a trowel to tap them in place. Other types of masonry will require a much heavier mallet.

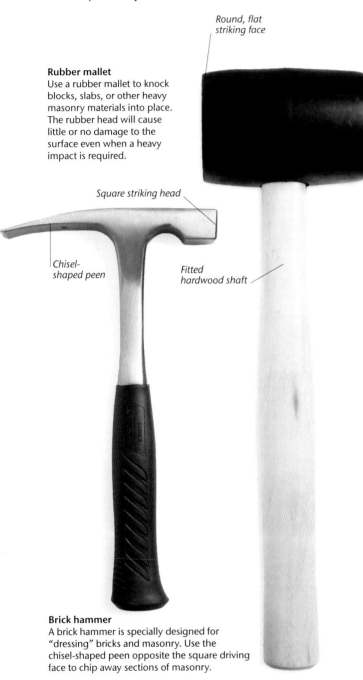

Round, flat striking face

Rubber mallet
Use a rubber mallet to knock blocks, slabs, or other heavy masonry materials into place. The rubber head will cause little or no damage to the surface even when a heavy impact is required.

Square striking head

Chisel-shaped peen

Fitted hardwood shaft

Brick hammer
A brick hammer is specially designed for "dressing" bricks and masonry. Use the chisel-shaped peen opposite the square driving face to chip away sections of masonry.

FURTHER INFORMATION ON BRICKLAYING
During laying, bricks should be moist, but not wet. Too much moisture dilutes the mortar, causing the bricks to slip. Spray the bricks the day before you intend to use them, or about four hours before use if using them the same day. The correct mortar mix is essential for bricklaying (see p.71). Do not use mortar more than two hours after mixing it—its usability will have diminished, making adhesion very poor.

JOINT TOOLS

Joints are key components of masonry work. Not only are they integral to a wall's structure, but they also form part of the design, particularly in the case of brickwork. Usually a jointer is used only for new pointing. A raker is used for removing old mortar or producing patterned joints.

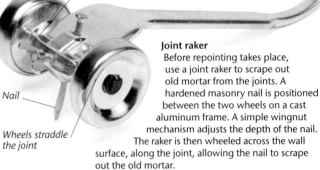

Different thicknesses allow different joint depths

Brick jointer
These are used for finishing brick joints. This example is a double-ended brick jointer, providing options for two different joint depths.

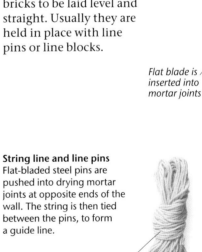

Wingnut

Nail

Wheels straddle the joint

Joint raker
Before repointing takes place, use a joint raker to scrape out old mortar from the joints. A hardened masonry nail is positioned between the two wheels on a cast aluminum frame. A simple wingnut mechanism adjusts the depth of the nail. The raker is then wheeled across the wall surface, along the joint, allowing the nail to scrape out the old mortar.

STRING LINES

A string line is an essential bricklaying tool, enabling bricks to be laid level and straight. Usually they are held in place with line pins or line blocks.

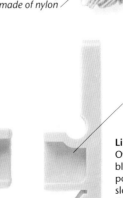

Flat blade is inserted into mortar joints

String line and line pins
Flat-bladed steel pins are pushed into drying mortar joints at opposite ends of the wall. The string is then tied between the pins, to form a guide line.

Mason's string, made of nylon

Front view of the shorter arm of the "L," which lips around the end of the wall

Line blocks
Often bricklayers use these L-shaped blocks, made of wood or plastic, to position guide lines. A continuous slot at one end of the block holds the string line in place.

LANDSCAPING TOOLS

Many of the tools required for landscaping are very versatile, and may be used as general gardening tools. Therefore, it is well worth investing in a few high-quality tools that will last many years. Excavating is very strenuous, so know your limitations.

D-HANDLE **T-HANDLE** **STRAIGHT HANDLE**

SHOVELS AND SPADES

Generally, spades are lighter than shovels and have a straighter, sharper blade, which makes them better suited for digging. The side edges of a shovel's blade are curved, making it more suitable for lifting large loads. A shovel is ideal for lifting loose material, such as aggregate, and perfect for loading cement mixers with sand and cement.

Handles and blades

Although the handles of shovels and spades are traditionally made of wood, it is now possible to buy tools with handles made of nonconductive, synthetic materials such as fiberglass or poly-propylene. These come in a variety of shapes and lengths, and are aimed at providing greater comfort.

Blades are generally made of some form of hardened steel. The best-quality shovel or spade blades should make a ringing sound, rather than a dull thud, when tapped against a hard object.

Rotating handle grip means there is no need to adjust your grip when shoveling

Long, rigid blade

Pointed end for cutting into surfaces

Modern synthetic shaft and handle

Sharp, flat blade

SIDE VIEW OF SPADE

Curved edges increase capacity

SIDE VIEW OF SHOVEL

Square-mouth shovel
This has a wide, square blade with curved edges, ideal for lifting material.

Trench shovel
Ideal for digging channels, as it has a long, narrow blade.

Round-mouth shovel
A wide, pointed blade suits both digging and lifting.

Spade
A spade's straight, sharp blade is made for digging.

DEALING WITH HARD GROUND

On hard ground, grip a D-handle at the sides so that when the blade strikes, your hands can slip slightly down the sides of the D and reduce the effect of the impact. Make sure that your grip is strong enough to control the tool, but not so tight that you risk injury. Keep your wrists and forearms straight, and wear gloves or fix padding to the handle to reduce jarring.

USING A SPADE

Keep back straight

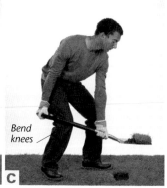

Bend knees

A **Keep the spade** vertical, with both hands on the handle, and push the blade into the ground with your foot.

B **Steadily lever** the blade backward, pushing on the handle with both hands.

C **Slide one hand** down the handle shaft and lift the load on the blade, while keeping a straight back.

HEALTH AND SAFETY

Always wear the appropriate protective clothing when performing excavation work or when using these types of heavyweight hand tools.

Digging into the ground outside your home can pose a potential safety hazard due to underground cables and pipes. Call your local utility notification phone number at least 48 hours before you dig in any area where electric, phone, gas, or cable TV lines may be located.

OTHER LANDSCAPING TOOLS

As well as shovels and spades, there is a large variety of other landscaping tools available for digging, carrying, shaping, and smoothing soil and other materials. Some of these, such as rakes and brushes, are essential garden tools, while others, such as pickaxes or post-hole diggers, may be rented for occasional use.

USING A WHEELBARROW

A wheelbarrow presents the most efficient way of moving heavy materials and large volumes. However, it is important to follow a few simple guidelines to reduce the risk of injury, especially to your back. Before use, check that the wheelbarrow's wheel is sufficiently inflated, so that your passage over uneven surfaces is smooth. Keep your back straight throughout and use your legs to lift the weight of the wheelbarrow, as shown below. Most importantly, know your limitations and do not overload the wheelbarrow.

Top of wheelbarrow is angled so that it is horizontal when lifted

Tubular steel frame

Inflatable tire

Bend your knees, keep your back and arms straight, and position your body between the handles, rather than behind them. Grip the handles.

Straighten your knees and ensure that the weight is centralized over the wheel and that the wheelbarrow is comfortably loaded.

Wheelbarrows
A lightweight garden wheelbarrow may be too flimsy to deal with some heavy-duty tasks. Wheelbarrows used for landscaping should be sturdy enough to deal with relatively heavy building materials and rubble.

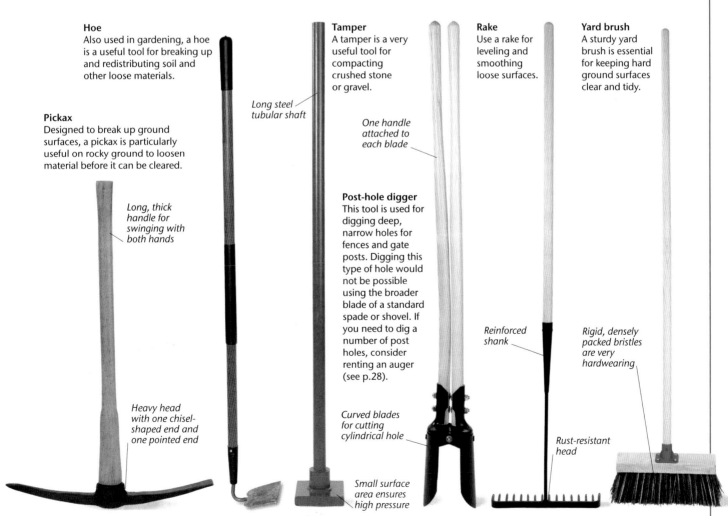
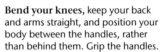

Hoe
Also used in gardening, a hoe is a useful tool for breaking up and redistributing soil and other loose materials.

Pickax
Designed to break up ground surfaces, a pickax is particularly useful on rocky ground to loosen material before it can be cleared.

Long, thick handle for swinging with both hands

Heavy head with one chisel-shaped end and one pointed end

Tamper
A tamper is a very useful tool for compacting crushed stone or gravel.

Long steel tubular shaft

Post-hole digger
This tool is used for digging deep, narrow holes for fences and gate posts. Digging this type of hole would not be possible using the broader blade of a standard spade or shovel. If you need to dig a number of post holes, consider renting an auger (see p.28).

Curved blades for cutting cylindrical hole

Small surface area ensures high pressure

Rake
Use a rake for leveling and smoothing loose surfaces.

One handle attached to each blade

Reinforced shank

Rust-resistant head

Yard brush
A sturdy yard brush is essential for keeping hard ground surfaces clear and tidy.

Rigid, densely packed bristles are very hardwearing

Power tools

POWER VERSIONS OF MANY TOOLS, IF USED CORRECTLY, CAN MAKE DIY WORK QUICKER AND EASIER. THEY MUST BE TREATED WITH RESPECT, TO AVOID SERIOUS INJURY, AND THEY NEED TO BE CARED FOR. AS WITH ALL TOOLS, QUALITY VARIES, AND COST REFLECTS THIS. MANY ARE DESIGNED FOR PROFESSIONAL USE, SO CONSIDER WHETHER IT IS WORTH PAYING FOR A TOP-QUALITY TOOL, OR WHETHER RENTING MAY BE BETTER.

POWER NAILERS AND STAPLERS

Nailers can dramatically speed up a DIY job. Some can drive nails into concrete and/or steel; others are suitable only for wood. Larger nailers are more suitable for heavy-duty carpentry tasks such as erecting a stud partition wall; smaller nailers are good for decorative carpentry work such as crown molding. Some models can use a greater range of nail sizes than others. Staplers can be used for many tasks, such as securing sheets of hardboard for a subfloor, or installing lightweight building boards in general.

CHOOSING AN AIR COMPRESSOR

A compressor may be used to operate several tools, so if you decide to buy an air nailer, choose a compressor that will work with any other pneumatic tools that you are considering purchasing. The most versatile compressors have tanks that store up a quantity of compressed air, producing a ready supply to keep your tools running.

The rate at which compressed-air tanks fill is usually measured in cubic feet or liters per minute (cfm/clm). This affects the frequency at which nails can be fired, but very few DIY tasks will need a high cfm. Air pressure is measured in pounds per square inch (psi); make sure to match your compressor to your tools.

When selecting a compressor, don't choose one that greatly exceeds your DIY tool needs. Weight and portability can be key factors in finding the right compressor, especially if you are working alone. Light compressors that are easy to navigate don't necessary mean they cannot do the job of a larger, heavier machine. But as weight does determine the size of the air tank, you will not be able to run as many tools off a lightweight compressor.

PNEUMATIC TOOLS

These tools use compressed air to drive the nail or staple home. Some compressors are designed for use with one tool at a time, whereas larger ones can run two or three tools (see box at left for details).

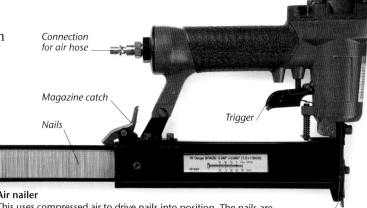

Connection for air hose

Magazine catch

Nails

Trigger

Tip

Air nailer
This uses compressed air to drive nails into position. The nails are more expensive than traditional nails because they come in strips that feed into the nailer's rail assembly. To operate, position the nailer tip at the required point before pulling the trigger to fire the nail.

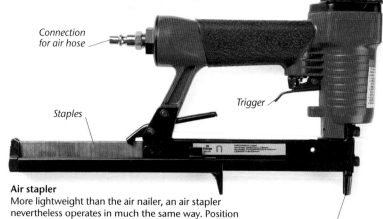

Connection for air hose

Trigger

Staples

Tip

Air stapler
More lightweight than the air nailer, an air stapler nevertheless operates in much the same way. Position the tip and then pull the trigger to fire the staple.

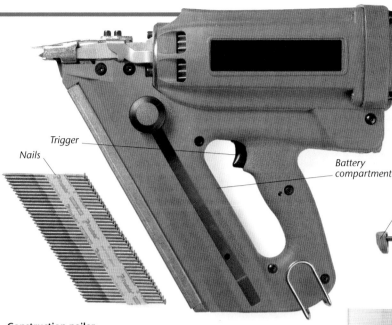

Trigger

Nails

Battery compartment

Construction nailer
This requires both a battery and a gas cell. It is the most portable nailer, because there are no cords. Despite its power, it is relatively lightweight. A metering valve, attached to the top of the gas cell, controls the amount of gas that is released for combustion.

GAS NAILERS
Gas nailers are more portable than air nailers, since they require no connection to a compressor. There is also no power cord, since they operate using a rechargeable battery and a gas canister.

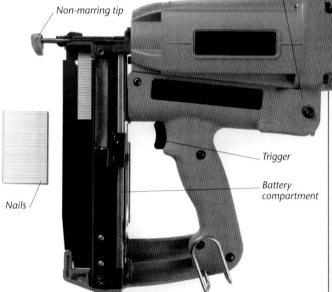

Gas cylinder compartment

Non-marring tip

Trigger

Battery compartment

Nails

Finish nailer
This smaller version of the gas nailer works in the same way as the construction nailer but is more suited to decorative carpentry work.

▌▌ USING A GAS NAILER

A

Load the battery into the nailer's battery compartment, and press firmly until the battery locking clip engages and the battery is secure.

B

Insert the gas cell into its compartment, aligning the valve with the adapter. Close the lid firmly.

C

Load a strip of nails into the nailer's rail assembly, sliding the follower button for access.

D

Press the nailer's tip onto the surface where you want the nail.

E

Pull the trigger. The battery ignites the gas/air mixture and powers the motor to drive a nail into the surface.

F

Release the trigger. This causes the internal fan to cool the motor assembly, and to release any exhaust gases.

CONSTRUCTION NAILER GAS **FINISH NAILER GAS** **BATTERY** **BATTERY CHARGER**

WORKING SAFELY
Always follow the manufacturer's guidelines carefully when using any power tools, and take particular care when loading batteries or gas cells. Wear eye protection and work in a well-ventilated area. Keep all power tools locked away from children. Some tools will require regular servicing to work efficiently, but contact your supplier to do this rather than attempting it yourself.

POWER DRILLS

Drills are very versatile tools and are necessary for many construction tasks. Competition has forced down their cost, making it possible to buy an exceptionally good piece of equipment for a very reasonable price. There are several different types of drills available; some have a screwdriving facility. The main types of drill bits and screwdriving bits, which slot into a drill's chuck, are shown here.

WORKING SAFELY

Wear goggles or safety glasses to protect against flying debris when drilling any hole in any material. It is also a good idea if using a drill-driver as a screwdriver. Ear protection is also recommended when using a drill, especially with larger, more powerful drills, and during prolonged drill use. Wear a dust mask if you are drilling into masonry or concrete. Make sure cords are not split or damaged in any way. Follow the manufacturer's recommendations on servicing any drill.

CORDLESS DRILL-DRIVER

The most versatile drill, this is both a power drill and an electric screwdriver. It is battery-operated, which makes it highly portable, and easy to use. The battery detaches so that it can be recharged. The differences between types of drill-drivers are usually indicated by their level of power. The higher the battery's voltage, the more powerful the drill—most are in the range of 9.6 volts to 24 volts. Some drill-drivers also have a hammer action.

Selector for drill torque, drill action, and hammer action

Bit

Keyless chuck holds bit

Gear selector switch

Forward/reverse switch allows drill to operate in reverse, e.g., to undo screws

Trigger allows control of the drill's speed

Grip

Loop for optional strap

Clip holds driver bit when not in use

Base plate

Battery release button

Battery

MAINTAINING A DRILL

Drills need periodic maintenance to ensure that they remain in good working order. Taking drills apart is not recommended, but some attention to the casing and drill chuck can ensure that the drill works efficiently and will not become damaged. Check the cord regularly for signs of wear.

Greased SDS bit will lubricate chuck when inserted

Cleaning the drill body
Unclog vents with a paintbrush to stop dust from damaging the motor or causing overheating.

Lubricating the chuck
Check your drill's manual for instructions to lubricate rotary hammer bits with grease.

RECHARGING A CORDLESS DRILL

Drills often come with two batteries, so that one can be recharging while the other is in use. Press the battery release button to take a battery off a drill. Invert the battery to put it in the charger. Plug in the charger. Recharging may take a few hours, depending on the drill's quality and size.

CORDED DRILLS

Cordless drills have developed from corded drill designs. These traditional designs still have an important role to play, and some are more powerful than cordless drills, so they are useful for the jobs cordless drills cannot manage. Corded drills do not need recharging, so running out of power is never a problem.

Speed switch
Mode selector
Forward/reverse switch

Chuck

Variable speed trigger

Standard power drill
A corded power drill usually has more power than a cordless drill, and often has two speeds, forward and reverse action, as well as the option of a hammer action for drilling into concrete or brick. This one has a traditional chuck, meaning that a key is needed to operate the chuck when drill bits are changed (see next page).

Switch lock allows continuous drilling without holding trigger

Keyless chuck

Switch lock

Forward/reverse switch

Holder for chuck key when not in use

Lightweight corded drill
Fairly powerful drills are now incorporated in a very lightweight body, making them easier to use than older drills. Keyless chucks make changing bits quicker. A small drill such as this can therefore be a good toolkit companion for a cordless drill-driver.

SDS chuck
Mode selector

Switch lock

Variable speed trigger

Rotary hammer
Heavy-duty power drills are usually SDS ("special drive system") drills with a chuck that requires a special bit. SDS chuck technology grips the drill bit to support the most efficient hammer action for drilling into very hard masonry. Rotary hammers can be corded or cordless.

Side handle for extra control when drilling into very hard surfaces

THINGS TO CONSIDER WHEN BUYING A DRILL
The basic homeowner drill should have a 3/8-inch chuck, be variable speed and reversible. Choose a light weight 9- or 14-volt model for general maintenance, a heavier 18-volt model for more serious renovations.

USING A DRILL

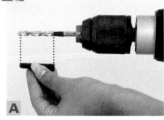

A

Position some insulating tape around the drill bit to indicate the depth to which you need to drill. Here, it is the depth of a wall plug.

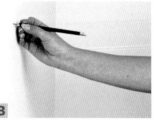

B

Mark on the wall where you need to drill a hole.

C

Use a hammer and a nail set to make a small indent at the marked place. This will prevent the drill from slipping across the wall.

D

Begin drilling with a fairly low bit speed. This enables you to get the hole started easily and to keep the drill at a right angle to the wall.

Keep the drill at a right angle to the wall

E

Once the hole is established, increase the bit speed. Drill to the depth required, as marked by the tape on the bit. When the hole is finished, use the reverse function to get it out of the hole. Release the switch once the bit is out of the wall.

USING BOTH HANDS TO OPERATE A DRILL

Many drills have an extra, detachable handle. This allows one hand to support the drill's weight and keep it at the right angle while the other holds the main grip and operates the trigger.

A

First, position the handle so that it is vertical. If this is comfortable, use the drill in this posture. If it feels awkward, move on to step B.

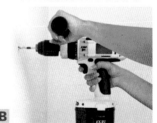

B

Rotate the handle so that it is horizontal. This should give you a more comfortable working posture.

INSERTING A DRILL BIT

Tightening a keyless chuck
Insert a drill or driver bit. Rotate the chuck by hand to tighten it and hold the bit in place.

Using a chuck key
The key's serrated edge engages with the chuck's shaft to tighten it around the bit and hold it in place.

Using an SDS chuck
Push the bit into the chuck. The chuck will engage the bit shank. Pull back the chuck to release the bit.

WORKING SAFELY

Take care when changing a bit after operating a drill: the bit may be hot. Wear gloves to avoid a burn.

WOOD DRILL BITS

These are suitable for all types of wood, and come in a huge range of sizes and lengths. There are three main types of wood drill bits, which are shown here.

Spur

Brad point (dowel) bits
These are characterized by the small point at the tip of the bit. Spurs on either side of this point cut clean, straight holes.

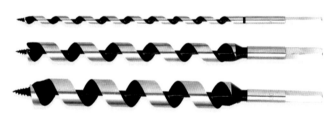

Auger drill bits
These cut large, deep, accurate holes. The spiraling shaft comes to a fine, threaded point. Carbon-steel bits are best, and can be resharpened.

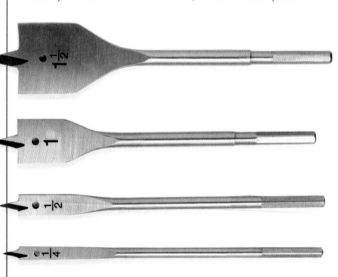

Spade or paddle bits
The pointed tip begins the hole, and the paddle-shaped blade bores a large, wide hole. The size is clearly marked on the paddle's face.

METAL DRILL BITS

These are known as HSS (high-speed steel) bits. They can also be used on wood or plastic, but they last better if reserved for metalwork.

Coatings vary

Standard HSS bits
These are characterized by their black color. More expensive, durable ones may contain cobalt or be titanium-coated.

MASONRY DRILL BITS

These can cut into many masonry surfaces. The shaft spirals up to a tip that is often composed of an extra-hardened material. For instance, a chrome-vanadium shaft may be finished with a tungsten-carbide tip.

Tip often hardened

Standard twist bits
Bit colors vary, because of the different materials used. The tip may be a different color from the shaft as well, due to the hardened coating.

STORING DRILL BITS

Most types of drill bits are available in a wide range of sizes and qualities, and often in sets, which can be economical if you do a lot of drilling. For the best results, always use the bit that is recommended for a specific job. Some sets contain many bits of the same type (those shown here are HSS bits); others contain the most common sizes of masonry, wood, and HSS bits.

SET OF BITS

OTHER DRILL BITS

In addition to the standard drill bits shown opposite, a wide range of specialty bits is available. These are made for a specific task, or to fit a particular type of chuck. The most common of these bits are shown here.

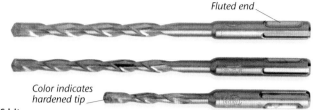

Fluted end

Chuck

Flexible shaft maneuvers bit into tight spaces

Color indicates hardened tip

SDS bits
Some bits are made specifically to fit an SDS chuck mechanism, and won't work with any other. The end that fits into the chuck has a fluted appearance; the drilling part of the shaft is normal.

Spear-shaped tip

Tile and glass bits
The spear-shaped tungsten-carbide tip penetrates a tile or piece of glass, then enlarges the hole to the diameter of the tip's base.

Flexible drill shaft
This attaches to the chuck and allows a drill to be used in an otherwise inaccessible area—just insert the bit into the chuck on the end of the flexible shaft. These attachments cannot be used with the drill in reverse action.

Bit with integral countersink function
As well as drilling a hole, these bits also cut a space for screw heads. They are ideal for preventing splits.

Tip drills pilot hole to prevent cutter from slipping

Remove plug through the side opening

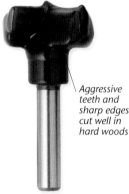

Carbon-steel tip

Cutter: comes in various sizes. Some are for cutting wood, some for metal

Arbor connects the round cutter to the drill bit

Aggressive teeth and sharp edges cut well in hard woods

Countersink bit
This enlarges a hole's opening so that a screw can sit flush.

Plug cutter
Cuts wooden plugs to cover screw heads and disguise them.

Hinge cutter
A tungsten-carbide tip cuts holes for kitchen cabinet door hinges.

Hole cutter
The drill bit cuts first, then the round cutter makes a larger hole.

This end goes into the drill chuck

DRIVER BIT HOLDERS AND NUT DRIVER

To work as a screwdriver, a drill-driver needs an attachment to hold bits in place. It is also possible to insert specialty bits into the chuck, such as a nut driver, for example.

SCREWDRIVER BITS

Some bits insert directly into the chuck, but most (such as those below) need to be put in a bit holder, which is then inserted into the chuck. Specialty bits are also available.

Drywall dimpler
A dimpler has a clutch that stops the screw at the right depth for drywall installation.

Quick-release bit holder
Bit changes are easy due to quick-release action.

Nut driver
Tighten nuts or bolts with this driver.

Flat-head bits
Slotted screws are very difficult to drive with a power tool.

Phillips bits
Screws with a Phillips head must be driven by a corresponding bit.

Posidriv bits
As for Phillips bits, these are made to drive a particular type of screw.

Square drive bits
These bits are the standard driver for most renovation work.

Used correctly and carefully, power saws are great labor-saving devices that speed up progress on a host of jobs. As with any power tools, safety is a concern. Always switch off and unplug a power saw before changing its blade, and wear protective goggles if there is a danger of flying debris. The saws shown on these pages are the ones most likely to be used for DIY jobs. Bandsaws and bench saws are covered, along with other bench tools, on pp.64–65.

HEALTH AND SAFETY

- Always employ standard safety precautions when operating a power saw. Never change a blade, or carry out any maintenance work, with the power supply switched on.
- All power saws generate a lot of heat when in use, so give a machine time to cool before you change a blade.
- Always keep hands clear of the cutting blade, and keep children away from saws.
- Wear goggles to protect your eyes from flying debris.
- Never force a saw. Ensure that the material being cut is correctly supported and clamped firmly in position.
- Sweep up dust.

RECIPROCATING SAWS

These are very flexible and versatile tools. The jigsaw can be used with many materials, especially wood; the heavy-duty version shown opposite is for more arduous tasks. As well as an up-and-down (reciprocating) motion, some saws have a back-and-forth (orbital, or pendulum) action that cuts more easily and quickly, minimizes blade wear, and aids sawdust removal from the cutting point. Blade and orbit setting changes vary by saw.

METAL-CUTTING BLADE

WOOD/PLASTIC-CUTTING BLADE

GENERAL WOOD-CUTTING BLADE

UNIVERSAL BLADE

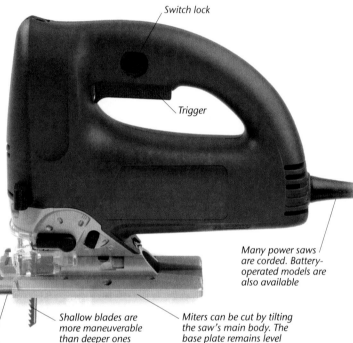

Switch lock

Trigger

Many power saws are corded. Battery-operated models are also available

Guides can be clamped onto base plate, for making parallel or circular cuts

Shallow blades are more maneuverable than deeper ones

Miters can be cut by tilting the saw's main body. The base plate remains level

USING A JIGSAW

Guide line to cut along

A

B

Adjust the orbital action on the saw to match the type of material you are working with.

Position a new blade against the guide roller. Release the blade change lever to secure it, or tighten according to the tool's mechanism.

Jigsaw
This cuts an accurate curved line. Blades are available in mixed packs for materials such as wood, PVC, and metal sheeting. Precision depends on a blade's qualities. Use on a high speed for wood, and a slower speed for metal or ceramic tiles. Some have a dust extraction facility.

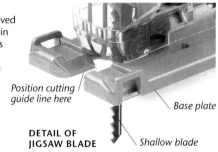

Position cutting guide line here

Base plate

DETAIL OF JIGSAW BLADE

Shallow blade

C

D

Rest the front edge of the base plate on the material to be cut, with the blade at a right angle to the marked guide line.

Adjust the speed and rotary action settings, if necessary, before starting up the saw. Progress along the guide line to make the cut.

CUTTING OUT A CENTRAL SECTION

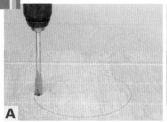

A

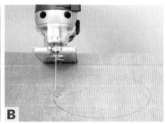

B

Drill a hole at one edge of the cut, using a wood bit with a diameter large enough to accommodate the jigsaw blade.

Insert the jigsaw blade through the hole, and make your cut. Take care to support the wood, and follow the guide line carefully.

Blade

Keyless blade-change lever

Heavy-duty reciprocating saw
Used for more arduous tasks like demolition work. As for a jigsaw, blades can be chosen for different materials, but the blades may be considerably longer than those for a jigsaw, and therefore give greater flexibility in terms of the depth of cut possible. The technique for installing blades is similar to that for a jigsaw but, again, details may vary from brand to brand. Plunge cuts, going directly into soft materials instead of starting at an edge, can be made with a short blade.

Battery

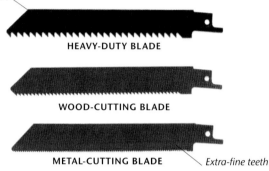

Tungsten-carbide-tipped blade

HEAVY-DUTY BLADE

WOOD-CUTTING BLADE

METAL-CUTTING BLADE *Extra-fine teeth*

USING A RECIPROCATING SAW

A **Insert a blade** as described by the manual. In this instance, an Allen key is needed.

B **Press the base plate** onto the material to be cut, and apply even pressure as you progress through the cut along a guide line.

CIRCULAR SAWS
These use circular blades that rotate to cut through materials. The type of material that can be cut depends on the blade; some are for specific tasks. The saw shown here, for instance, is designed for cutting wood, but will cut metal if a suitable blade is inserted.

Handle requires two-handed use

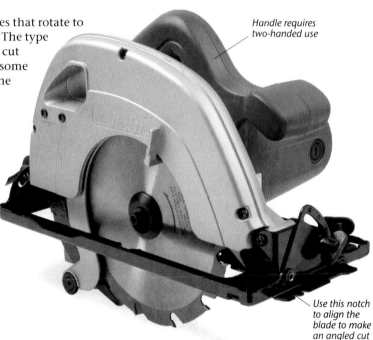

Circular wood saw
Cuts accurate, straight lines through wood; with the right blade, can cut sheet goods, framing, concrete, and masonry. The blade's radius dictates the depth of cut possible. Blades are not changed often—a multipurpose blade usually copes with most cutting requirements.

Use this notch to align the blade to make an angled cut

Teeth can cut wood with nails in it

NAIL-CUTTING BLADE

Hard steel body with a tungsten-carbide tip

STANDARD BLADE

Teeth treated for smooth operation

LONG-LIFE BLADE

USING A CIRCULAR SAW

A **Adjust the depth setting** to ensure that you do not sever underfloor pipes when cutting through floorboards, for instance.

B **Hold the saw** in two hands, to enable you to control it, and switch it on. Allow the blade to reach full speed before beginning a cut.

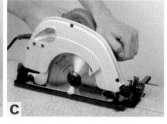

C **Align the relevant** notch in the front of the base plate with the marked guide line, and apply even pressure as the cut progresses.

CHANGING A BLADE
A specially designed wrench is usually needed to remove or insert a blade; the specifics vary according to brand. Always pay close attention to your instruction manual, and follow the recommended sequence of steps to ensure that you work safely and attach a new blade securely.

Miter saw

This housed circular saw is used for any accurate straight or angled cuts in wood—not just for mitering. Whereas a circular saw is ideal for use with large sheets, a miter saw is more use for cutting across the grain of a length of securely clamped lumber. Depth of cut is determined by blade size, and whether the saw is "compound." Some compound saws slide on a rail, increasing the width of material that can be cut.

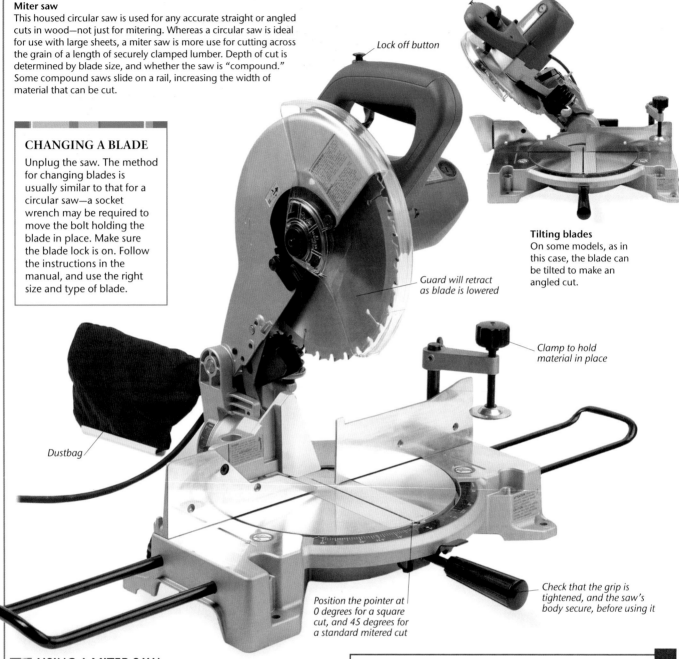

Lock off button

CHANGING A BLADE

Unplug the saw. The method for changing blades is usually similar to that for a circular saw—a socket wrench may be required to move the bolt holding the blade in place. Make sure the blade lock is on. Follow the instructions in the manual, and use the right size and type of blade.

Guard will retract as blade is lowered

Tilting blades
On some models, as in this case, the blade can be tilted to make an angled cut.

Clamp to hold material in place

Dustbag

Check that the grip is tightened, and the saw's body secure, before using it

Position the pointer at 0 degrees for a square cut, and 45 degrees for a standard mitered cut

USING A MITER SAW

A

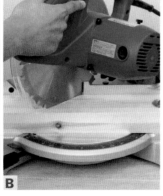

B

Adjust the saw by moving the grip until the pointer is directed at the correct angle. In this example, a 45-degree cut is being made.

With the material held securely, and the blade aligned with a guide line, press the safety button, then the trigger, and make the cut.

HEALTH AND SAFETY

A miter saw has a safety cover over the blade, which rises when the blade is lowered to cut. Never remove or tamper with this cover. To operate the saw, both the safety button and the power trigger must be pressed. Some saws have other levers or switches that must be operated to allow the saw to work. Some of these switches or levers may even be removed when the saw is not in use, so that it cannot be accidentally started. As with all safety issues, proceed according to the manual.

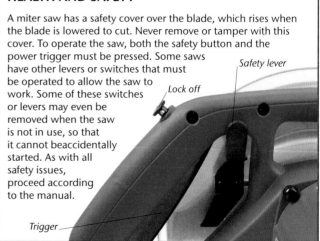

Safety lever

Lock off

Trigger

Angle grinder

This is designed for cutting metal and stone. The blades, or "cutting discs," vary according to the material they are designed to cut. A thinner disc should be used on marble rather than on a paving slab, for example. Angle grinders can be used for cutting and also for grinding (smoothing rough edges or areas on a heavyweight surface, such as masonry). Some discs are designed to cut, others to grind. Use the correct disc for the task. Some discs have diamond-impregnated surfaces for greater resilience. This coating is often visible around the rim. With standard discs, the surface wears away in cutting, so the disc gradually becomes smaller in diameter. Diamond blades last much longer, and so are more expensive.

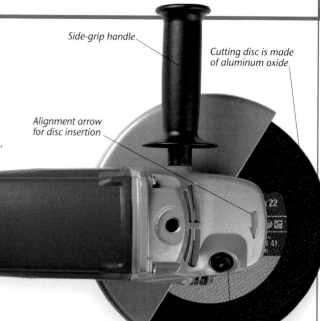

Side-grip handle

Cutting disc is made of aluminum oxide

Alignment arrow for disc insertion

Locking button for disc insertion

Power cord

Engages with clamping nut

TWO-PIN WRENCH

USING AN ANGLE GRINDER

An angle grinder is designed to operate in only one direction—upward. Pushing the angle grinder in the other direction is dangerous, and reduces control. Avoid any sideways pressure on a disc.

Some discs have segmented rims. The diamond versions of these have a diamond coating along the rim of each segment

Abrasive surface

STANDARD DIAMOND BLADE

GRINDING DISC

A

Start the grinder and position yourself so that it can be guided away from you along a marked guide line.

B

Score an initial line in a thick material such as a slab, then make two or three further passes across it to make the cut.

CHANGING AN ANGLE GRINDER DISC

Check the manufacturer's specifications before choosing a disc for an angle grinder, and buy discs of the right size and capable of withstanding the model's operating speed. The mechanism for locking on a disc will vary according to manufacturer, so check your specification. There may be a locking button (see top) to press, which helps tighten a disc onto the angle grinder.

A

Before mounting the disc, check that it is the right way up, and that the rotation arrow on the disc matches the one on the tool.

HEALTH AND SAFETY

Protective clothing is necessary when working with an angle grinder: goggles, ear protection, dust mask, gloves, and work boots should all be worn. Remove all combustible materials from the area before cutting metal, because showers of sparks will be produced. A large amount of dust is produced when stone is cut or ground, so use any dust extraction equipment that is supplied with your angle grinder. If possible, use the angle grinder outside, to reduce mess. If the material being cut is not heavy enough to remain in position under its own weight, clamp it securely before starting.

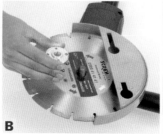

B

Mount the disc on the grinder's central spindle. Position the clamping nut on the disc, threading it over the spindle.

C

Fasten it in position (often by turning a clamping nut with a special two-pin wrench). Press the locking button if there is one.

PLANERS AND SANDERS

Power planers and sanders are smoothing tools. Planers are designed for use only with wood, but some sanders can also be used on metal or masonry surfaces. Use the dustbag if your model comes with one, and make sure the machine has stopped moving before putting it down after use, to avoid accidental damage to surfaces. Unplug the machine before adjusting any settings or changing sandpaper on a sander, or adjusting or changing blades on a planer.

PLANER

Planers remove sections of wood that are too small to be cut easily and accurately with a saw, but are also too thick to be smoothed down simply by using a power sander. They come in a number of sizes, and the larger, heavy-duty types are best suited to professional use. Smaller ones are fine for DIY.

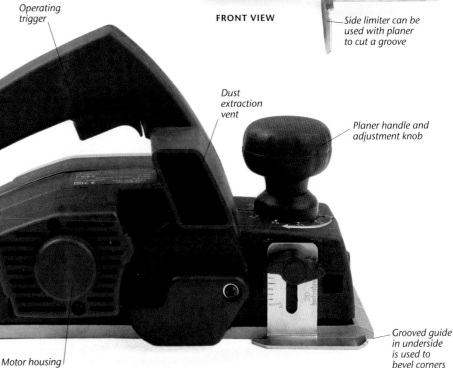

Trigger lock

Main planer

Side limiter securing nut

FRONT VIEW

Side limiter can be used with planer to cut a groove

Operating trigger

Dust extraction vent

Planer handle and adjustment knob

Motor housing

Grooved guide in underside is used to bevel corners

Power planer
This type of planer does the same thing as a hand planer (see p.40) but with much less effort. Blades have a reasonably long life span, depending on usage, and replacing them is straightforward for most models. The most common reason for blade failure, or reduction in the tool's lifespan, is accidentally planing a nail or screw embedded in a wooden surface. Inspect wood carefully before planing it.

■ USING A POWER PLANER

Use the depth gauge to determine the amount of wood to remove, remembering that if a large amount of wood needs to be shaved off, the depth gauge should initially be set high, then reduced as you reach the full extent of the cut. Refer to your model's instruction manual for details on using the depth gauge. Most planers have a dust collection facility; use it if you have one.

When the planer reaches full speed, sweep it evenly across the surface to remove the wood gradually.

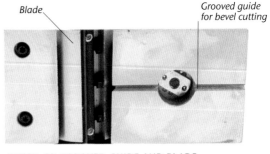

Blade

Grooved guide for bevel cutting

DETAIL OF GROOVED GUIDE AND BLADE

SANDERS

Power sanders smooth a wooden surface quickly and easily. Different designs are suited for sanding large areas, smaller sections, and difficult spaces. Always wear a mask when sanding. Sandpaper is supplied in the shape needed to fit a particular type of sander. Several grades are available for all sanders, ranging from papers that sand coarsely to remove material quickly, to those that give a very fine finish. Use the grade most suitable for your task. Move to increasingly fine paper to achieve a smooth finish.

CARE AND MAINTENANCE

Maintaining a belt sander
You may occasionally need to adjust the belt tracking; see the instruction manual for your model's adjustment requirements. To change a sanding belt, first switch off the sander and unplug it. Pull the belt release lever to enable you to remove the old paper, then insert a new belt of sandpaper and push the release lever back into position.

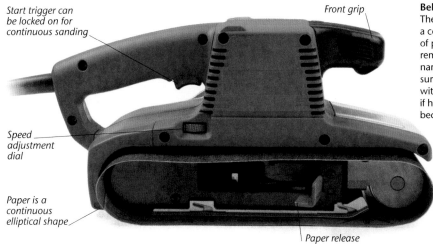

Start trigger can be locked on for continuous sanding

Front grip

Speed adjustment dial

Paper is a continuous elliptical shape

Paper release

Belt sander
The most abrasive of hand-held power sanders: takes off a considerable depth, so it is good for removing layers of paint. Similar in function to a power planer, but removes wood more gradually. It is ideal for smoothing narrow lengths of wood, but can also be used on larger surfaces that a planer cannot tackle. Keep the belt flush with the wood's surface—it will cut grooves into the wood if held at an angle. Do not apply too much pressure, because it can damage the operating mechanism.

DETAIL OF SANDPAPER PARTIALLY LOADED

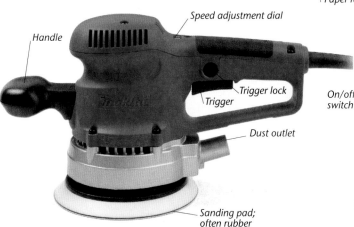

Handle

Speed adjustment dial

Trigger lock

Trigger

Dust outlet

Sanding pad; often rubber

Power cord

Dust bag

On/off switch

Sandpaper securing levers

Orbital sander
Useful for working large wooden surfaces. A large circular sanding pad vibrates with a near-circular motion, which means it can be used for a wood grain in any direction. However, a coarse paper will leave circular abrasions; use increasingly fine sandpaper as you progress for a smooth finish. The sander has a simple hook-and-loop mechanism to make changing sandpaper easy. A soft pad can also be attached to an orbital sander to turn it into a polishing tool for buffing waxed wooden surfaces. The trigger-lock mechanism keeps it switched on for continuous sanding, and speed settings control how vigorously and abrasively it sands.

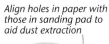

Align holes in paper with those in sanding pad to aid dust extraction

SANDING DISC

Palm sander
Small tool, often with an orbital action. For use on small areas or in awkward corners, often being drawn across a surface in a circular motion. Palm sanders have limited speed settings. The paper is held in place with a lever clamp and is easy to change.

USING A PALM SANDER

A

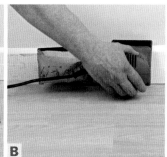

B

Position and attach the dustbag, following the instructions given in the manufacturer's manual. Switch it on and let it reach full speed.

Sweep the sander across the surface to be treated. In this instance, the flat face of a length of baseboard is being sanded.

BENCH TOOLS

If you have ambitious projects in mind, and a home workshop is an option, consider buying some bench tools. These are heavy-duty, specialty machines that can save a lot of time and effort when tackling certain tasks. Although such tools were once left to professionals, they are becoming much cheaper, and therefore more accessible.

JOINERS

As their name suggests, joiners are used to make various joint types between sections of wood, and for shaping and preparing wood for joining. Portable biscuit joiners are particularly useful for making joints in kitchen countertops.

Hand grip

Level adjustment lever

On/off switch

Cutting blade retracts into main body

Biscuit joiner
Though most often used for furniture, biscuit joints have many other applications. The joiner makes precise plunge cuts into each side of the joint, then a "biscuit" (a wafer of compressed wood chips) smeared with glue is inserted, with one side in each slot (see right). Biscuits are commonly manufactured in three sizes, for different thicknesses of board. Biscuit joiners do not have to be bolted to a bench before use.

Biscuits
Common biscuit sizes and shapes.

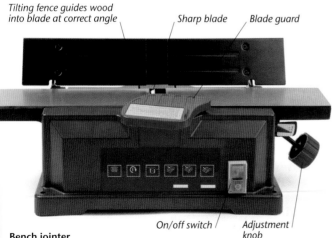

Tilting fence guides wood into blade at correct angle

Sharp blade   Blade guard

On/off switch   Adjustment knob

Bench jointer
Often used for making cabinets or other items of furniture, bench jointers shape and prepare wood for joining. However, they are also useful for tasks such as restoring and replacing damaged sections of woodwork from all around the home. Bolt the jointer down securely and be aware of the maximum depth of material it is capable of working with before you start.

MAKING BISCUIT JOINTS

Biscuits are a quick and simple way to join wood. They can be used in many situations where a strong, inconspicuous joint is required—a butt joint in a wooden countertop is shown here. Whatever you are making, you need to judge how many biscuit joints you need for a good connection. Thickness of the biscuit should be judged on wood depth.

A

Butt the sheets together, aligned as they will be joined, and draw a pencil line across the two sheets to mark the biscuit joint's position.

B

Set the level adjustment lever according to the depth of the material, so the joiner will cut into the middle of the sheet.

C

Use the cutting depth adjuster to set how deep the biscuit joiner will cut. It should be marked with the depths needed for standard biscuits.

D

Cut a slot in each piece of board by lining up the guide on the joiner with your guidelines, and pushing the cutter into the edge.

E

Apply white wood glue inside the slot. Special applicator bottles wipe glue on both sides of the slot. The biscuit expands to fit tightly in its slot.

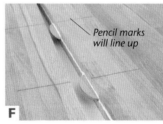

Pencil marks will line up

F

Push one side of the biscuit into the slots in one section of material. Apply a thin bead of glue between the biscuits, down the length of the seam.

G

Push the other end of the biscuit into the corresponding slot to join the two sections, and clamp. Use a damp cloth to wipe away any excess glue.

HEALTH AND SAFETY

With these large tools, the set-up and operating procedures can be complex: make sure you know how to use a machine before attempting a project. Read the manual carefully and pay attention to the guidelines. Use any dust-extraction devices that are available to you, and make sure you wear suitable protective clothing. On some occasions, help from another person may be needed so you can work safely, such as when feeding a large sheet material through a band saw.

BENCH GRINDERS

The high-speed, rotating wheels on bench grinders are used for sharpening and maintaining tools, and other metalwork tasks such as grinding off rough edges. Tools or metalwork are held ("trailed") against the wheels, which can either sharpen or abrade, according to which function is selected. Some grinders have a single wheel that can be changed as required; others have two wheels.

Dual-wheel grinder

One wheel of this grinder is suitable for rough grinding, while the second is for finishing or fine grinding. Dual-wheel grinders have varying designs: some may have wet and dry grinding wheels, while in others the second wheel may be replaced by a finisher—basically a belt sander mounted in a fixed position on the grinder body. Always bolt the grinder securely to a fixed workbench.

Grinding wheel housing

Hinged plastic guard

Grinding wheel

Dust-protected power switch

WORKSHOP SAWS

There are many different designs and types of workshop saws, some designed for specific purposes, so decide what you need before purchasing one. The two saws shown here are arguably the most multipurpose, and so the most commonly used. As with all bench tools, be sure to follow all operating instructions and safety guidelines.

PUSH STICK

Right-angle shaped end

Transparent plastic guard

Parallel fence

Saw blade

Miter guide

On/off switch

Blade tension adjuster

Adjustment to blade angle

Adjustment to blade height

Flexible dust blower

Miter fence

Saw table

Table saw

Essentially a table-mounted circular saw, a table saw is designed to make straight cuts in wood that you feed toward the blade. Most manufacturers supply a push stick with the saw. This is used to push materials across the saw table, and is most useful with smaller items rather than larger sheet materials.

Band saw

This is perhaps the most versatile of all workshop saws, and can be used to make many different types of cuts—much like a fixed version of the jigsaw. Using a band saw is straightforward, but take the time to familiarize yourself with the adjustment and setting guides before you start. Some resetting is required each time you change blades. To avoid mistakes, check that everything is adjusted correctly each time you cut. Mount a band saw on either a workbench or the stand supplied by the manufacturer.

ROUTERS

Routers use bits that cut, mold, and rabbet (cut a groove or step into) wood. Bits are available for numerous cutting and shaping tasks. The detail of operation will vary from model to model, and there is usually a correct direction for a router to face when in use, so read your model's instruction book carefully. Routers can seem very complicated, but they provide professional finishes and increased options in many areas of DIY. It is a good idea to practice using a router on a spare piece of wood before beginning your project.

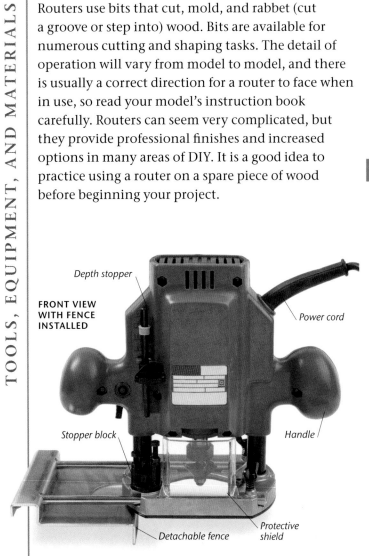

FRONT VIEW WITH FENCE INSTALLED

Depth stopper

Power cord

Stopper block

Handle

Detachable fence

Protective shield

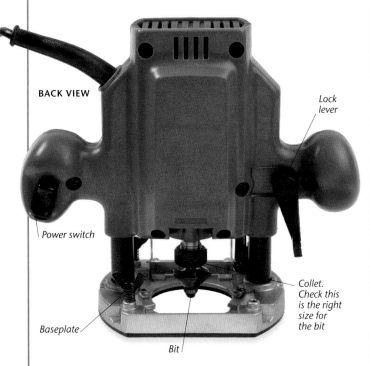

BACK VIEW

Lock lever

Power switch

Collet. Check this is the right size for the bit

Baseplate

Bit

HEALTH AND SAFETY

Always take care when working with a power tool. Some routers have a protective guard to shield the user from flying debris, but you should always wear safety goggles and a dust mask while using a router. Also, remember that the bit will become very hot during routing, so be careful when touching it or putting it down after use. Routing is a particularly dusty job, so attach a vacuum hose to the dust port, if one is recommended by your model's manufacturer, to clear away the dust.

USING A ROUTER

Check the manual for details of your model. On the plunge-style router the stopper block can store three settings at once, to save time when a job involves routing at different depths. Use an even speed when pushing the router across wood: go too fast and the cut will be rough, but go too slowly and burn marks may appear. Do not reduce the bit speed until it is clear of the surface.

A

With the router unplugged, and resting on a steady workbench, insert a bit into the collet.

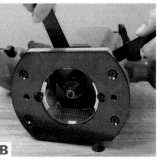

B

Tighten the collet nut with the two wrenches that come with the router, securing the bit in place.

C

Place the router on a flat surface and loosen the lock lever. Press on the router until the bit touches the surface, and tighten the lock lever.

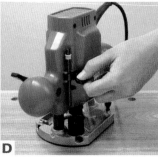

D

Set the depth stopper to the depth of the cut you want to make. Then loosen the lock lever again and allow the router to lift.

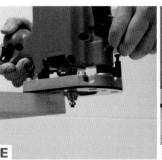

E

Start the router and let it reach full speed. Then press on the two handles to lower the bit and bring it into contact with the wood.

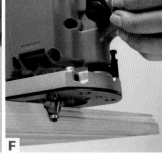

F

Move the router across the wood with its base flat on the surface. Judge the speed according to the cut's depth and the wood's hardness.

CUTTING A STRAIGHT LINE

You may need a fence (guide) to direct the bit for an accurate straight line. Attach the fence to the base plate, then butt it against the wood's straight edge. Make sure it remains in contact with the edge as the router moves across the wood, so that the cut is precisely straight. You will be unable to use the fence if the straight cut is not near the wood's edge. Instead, use a straight edge as a guide. Clamp the straight edge to the wood and pass the router along it, ensuring that it stays in contact with the straight edge. To cut out an area wider than the bit can make in one pass, use two straight edges to provide straight guide lines.

USING THE FENCE TO GET A STRAIGHT LINE

CARE AND MAINTENANCE

See your router's instruction book for information on servicing and maintenance. Make sure that you oil the machine as recommended.

Storage

Most routers are sold in sturdy boxes, which are ideal for long-term storage, if you have the space. Use a specially designed case to protect cutting bits when they are not in use.

ROUTER BIT CASE

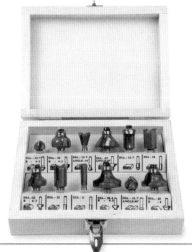

CUTTING BITS

Many different bits are available, each one producing a particular effect. A number of common bit types are shown below, subdivided into groove bits and edge bits. Tungsten-carbide-tipped bits offer high quality, and some may be titanium-impregnated. HSS (high-speed steel) is another common material. Bits are often purchased in boxed sets, but can be bought separately.

Groove bits

To create a channel through a section of wood, a groove bit is needed. This type of bit is useful for creating joints. For example, a straight bit can create a recess for jointing to another piece of wood (see p.393).

Straight bit
This is used to cut straight, precise lines through a section of wood.

This end fits into collet

V-groove bit
Use this bit to cut a groove with a sharp apex.

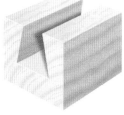

Dovetail bit
This is designed to make the cuts necessary for dovetail joints in woodworking.

Edge bits

When creating decorative profiles or grooves for joints along the side of a wooden section, use an edge bit. These bits often have a ball bearing in their tips that acts as a guide along the edge of the wood. This eliminates the need for a fence or other guide, while still producing a perfect, uniform cut.

Cove bit
This bit produces a curved channel along the edge of the wood.

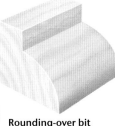

Rounding-over bit
This produces a uniform rounded edge with a slight rabbet—a finish commonly found in kitchen countertops.

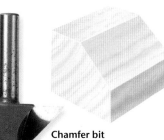

Chamfer bit
This bit creates an angular chamfered edge. Commonly, the chamfer angle produced is 45 degrees, as shown above.

MIXING TOOLS

Mixing is a crucial part of DIY—achieving the correct consistency of compound or concrete, for instance, can make the difference between success and failure. The tools used for mixing are therefore very important. Some are designed to blend large quantities, others for relatively small amounts. Concrete mixers used to be prohibitively expensive, but if you have a lot of concrete work to do, it can be worth buying one. Otherwise, rent one when needed. Power stirrers have become a very popular and cheap option for mixing all kinds of materials.

Power stirrer
A shaped mixing paddle designed for use with a power drill that has a standard chuck. Some materials need less powerful drills than others: paint requires less power than plaster, for example. So an average-sized cordless drill-driver may be used to mix paint, provided it is not overworked. For mixing heavier materials, a high-power cordless drill or, preferably, a corded power drill is advisable. In either case, take care not to burn out the drill's motor through prolonged use.

Clip for hanging up

Shaft

Mixing spiral

POWER STIRRER

USING A POWER STIRRER

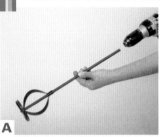

A

Insert the stirrer bit into the drill's chuck. Tighten the chuck.

B

Do not start the drill until the mixing spiral is totally submerged. In this example, paint is being mixed.

C

Slowly start the drill, and mix the paint. A slow speed is sufficient. Stop the drill before removing the mixing spiral from the paint.

Heavy duty concrete mixer
These mixers are the largest jobsite mixers and are ideal for high production. The model shown here can mix large volumes. It is important to clean the drum immediately after use. Removing hardened concrete from a drum causes dents.

Steel drum

Electric and gasoline engine options with punched ventilation

Multi-position dump latch

Dump wheel

Heavy duty retractable tow tongue

Axle spring for reduced bounce

MIXING RECEPTACLES

For small-scale concrete mixing tasks, hand-mixing trays, buckets, and wheelbarrows are ideal. You should always wear work gloves when mixing concrete and one of the best tools to use is a hoe.

If you are using a wheelbarrow, make sure you are on level ground before you start mixing concrete. You will need to use a stiff brush and plenty of water to clean the tray or wheelbarrow after use.

MIXING TRAY

SAFETY CHECKLIST

■ Never place any part of your body inside a mixer drum unless the power is off. In the case of an electrically operated machine, unplug the mixer first.
■ Do not operate a gasoline or diesel mixer in a confined space. Ventilation is vital: exhaust fumes can be lethal.
■ With a gasoline or diesel model, follow the manufacturer's guidelines with particular care when handling the fuel.
■ Remember that a mixer has many moving parts, and pieces that become very hot. Take care around these parts, and never operate a machine with any guards removed.
■ Be careful to keep your tools well clear of the moving parts inside the mixer.

Concrete mixer
Concrete mixers are heavy but still fairly portable. "Tip-up" versions normally come apart, so that they may be easily moved and stored when not in use. Some models are designed to fit inside a car trunk. Some are electric, while others run on gasoline or diesel.

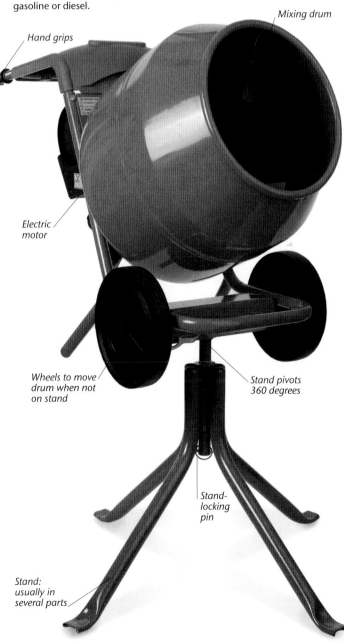

Mixing drum

Hand grips

Electric motor

Wheels to move drum when not on stand

Stand pivots 360 degrees

Stand-locking pin

Stand: usually in several parts

USING A CONCRETE MIXER

When assembling a new mixer, follow the manufacturer's guidelines carefully to ensure that the setup is correct. When renting a mixer, you will still need to assemble its main components. Mixers are heavy items, so it is advisable to have somebody help you. The mixer's maximum capacity will be specified in the instructions; never overload it. After using the mixer, or when finishing for the day, clean it immediately. Add clean water and some coarse gravel to the drum. Turn it on and allow this mixture to clean the inside of the mixer. After a few minutes, pour these contents away and check that the drum is clean. Wash the outside of the drum with water and a stiff brush.

A

Position the main body of the mixer on a flat, level surface, with the drum face-down.

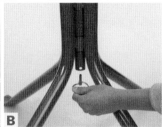

B

Assemble the stand and engage the stand-locking pin.

C

Insert the support stand into the base of the body. On some models, you will also need to engage a stand-locking clip.

D

Stand in front of the mixer and, after making sure that the ground is not slippery, tilt it into an upright position.

E

Make absolutely certain that the mixer is on solid, level ground. Tilt the drum back. It is now ready to use. Switch on the mixer.

Do not allow the shovel to enter the drum

F

Use a shovel or spade to load half of the ingredients, in the correct ratios (see p.71), into the mixer. Be sparing with water to start with.

The drum is still spinning, so do not allow it to touch the wheelbarrow

G

Allow it to mix for a minute or two, and then add the rest of the ingredients to the drum. Let mixing continue for several minutes. When the mix is of the required consistency, pour it into a wheelbarrow. Keep other objects clear of the drum while it is still moving.

Materials

CONSTRUCTION MATERIALS CAN BE DIVIDED INTO THOSE FOR GENERAL USE, AND THOSE THAT ARE SPECIFIC TO CERTAIN TASKS. THE MATERIALS DETAILED OVER THE NEXT FEW PAGES ARE THE MORE GENERAL ONES. THEY INCLUDE LUMBER AND BOARDS, NAILS AND SCREWS, ADHESIVES, AND BRICKS AND BLOCKS. YOU WILL NEED TO REFER TO THESE PAGES TO SELECT MATERIALS FOR MOST DIY TASKS EXPLAINED IN THIS BOOK.

CONCRETE AND MORTAR

Aggregates and cement are mixed together to make mortar or concrete. Mortar is used as an adhesive that can hold bricks and blocks together, or hold paving slabs in place. It can also be used as an exterior finish. Concrete, which contains coarse aggregates, is used for foundations and hard landscaping. By Canadian code, all exterior concrete must be "air-entrained" so frost doesn' t damage it. Special air-entrained mixes can be bought in a bag. Aggregates and sands can be bought in bags, in bulk, or in ready-mixed bags.

CEMENT
The adhesive in a mortar mix, cement binds together the components and dries to a stable, hard finish. It must be stored in a dry atmosphere and is unusable if it gets damp.

Portland Gray in color; the most commonly used cement.

White Portland A lighter version of Portland cement.

Fast-set Sets very quickly, so is ideal for small DIY tasks.

Sulfate-resistant (Type II Portland cement) For cement in contact with a clay-rich soil, or soil that is high in sulfates.

Expansive Hydraulic cement that expands during the hardening process.

READY-MIXED
These are quicker to use, but are more expensive.

Mortar mix A general-purpose mortar.

Slab mix For laying paving.

Concrete mix A general-purpose concrete.

HOW MUCH DO YOU NEED?
Seek advice from your supplier on how much of each constituent you need for your project. To give you a rough idea, to lay 100 bricks with general-purpose mortar you would need: 55 lb (25 kg) of cement, 220 lb (100 kg) of sand, and 22 lb (10 kg) of lime. In practice, this is one bag of cement, four bags of sand, and half a bag of lime. The table opposite gives the proportions needed for a variety of mixes.

USING A MORTAR TUB

A

Pour the appropriate portion of a premixed bag of ready-to-mix concrete into a tub.

B

Add the minimum amount of water recommended. The less water used, the stronger the dried, finished product will be.

C

Use a garden hoe to mix the concrete. This way, you will reduce the strain on our back.

D

Mix the concrete, adding water if needed, until the mixture is the consistency of soft peanut butter.

AGGREGATES

Particles smaller than ⅜ in (5 mm) in diameter are considered a fine aggregate; anything larger is a coarse aggregate. Both materials are used to make a mortar or concrete mix. Fine aggregate varies in color depending on where it comes from. Washed aggregate contains fewer of the impurities that can weaken the adhesion of a parging mix to the surface and stain the finish.

Coarse aggregate

Crushed stone
Large stones and gravel—the coarsest aggregate. Used as a base for concrete and other hard-landscape surfacing.

Ballast
An "all-in-one" combination of fine aggregate and larger stones or gravel. Ideal for use in general concrete work where exact proportions of individual aggregates are not required.

Coarse aggregate
Graded stone, also known as gravel. It may be used in concrete, or as a drainage aid, or as a finished surface for a drive or path.

Fine aggregate

Sharp sand
Coarse sand with fairly large particles. Often used in concrete mixes, but may also be used to produce a very hard, durable mortar.

Builder's sand
Builder's sand is fine-textured and is used in mixes for laying blocks or bricks. An even finer grade of sharp sand is used for parging.

Kiln-dried silver sand
Very fine, dry sand, light in color. Mainly used dry to grout exterior paved areas.

OPTIONS

These can be used in all mixes, according to your requirements.

Lime Cement already contains lime, but adding more makes mortar easier to work with and less likely to crack when set. Traditional mortar mixes (without cement) are based on lime. Lime retains water well, and is less likely to shrink as it dries out. Nonhydraulic lime is sold as powder or as a putty containing water. Use powder for cement-based mortar, and putty for a traditional building mortar. Hydraulic lime sets more quickly, is harder, and is less widely used.

Plasticizer Makes mortar more workable, and is used as a modern equivalent of lime. It normally comes in liquid form.

Cement pigment Powdered pigment that colors cement.

Waterproofer May be mixed with mortar, especially when parging is to be applied in an area prone to damp. Some parging waterproofers slow down the parging's drying, keeping it workable for a longer period.

Accelerator Speeds up curing time, and can be used to protect the mixture while it dries if frost may be a danger.

GETTING THE PROPORTIONS RIGHT

The proportions given indicate ratios by volume, not weight. For most uses, proportions can be "measured" by the shovel-load, but if accuracy is required to maintain a particular strength or color, measure quantities by the bucket-load. The ratios given are best suited to moderate weather conditions; if the mix will be exposed to punishing weather, use more cement for strength.

Mix	Uses	Cement	Lime	Fine aggregate	Coarse aggregate	Ballast	Consistency
General-purpose mortar	Laying blocks or bricks, pointing	1	1	5 (builder's)			Should stick to an upside-down trowel
Slab mix	Laying slabs	1		4 (sharp)			Stiffer than above
Foundation concrete	Laying foundations for house or extension	1		2.5 (sharp)	3.5		Should pour easily
Alternative foundation mix	Less exacting mix for garden walls, etc.	1				5	Should pour easily
General-purpose concrete	Base for slabs, shed, oil tank, etc.	1		2 (sharp)	3		Should pour easily
Alternative concrete	As above	1				4	Should pour easily
Parging	Undercoat for plaster or exterior coating	1	1	6 (builder's)			Should stick to an upside-down trowel

SHEET MATERIAL

Sheet stock is used to create and/or cover large, flat surfaces. Sheet materials are usually supplied in standard sizes, 4 x 8 ft (1,200 x 2,400 mm) being the most common size. The main types are drywall and wood-based sheet material. These are described here to help you choose the most suitable type for your particular requirements. Some need special screws or nails to secure them in place (see pp.76–79). Eco-friendly sheet materials are also available (see p.85).

DRYWALL

This is the most common wall and ceiling material. It is made by compressing gypsum plaster to create rigid sheets, which are covered on each side with thick paper. Treated varieties are available (see below). These are often color-coded for easy identification. Some sheets have more than one quality, e.g., moisture-resistance and fire-resistance. All types are available with square or tapered edges.

Choosing a sheet size

Drywall comes in sheets. While the most common size is 4 x 8 ft (1,200 x 2,400 mm), you can purchase much larger lengths. Use a sheet size that minimizes the number of seams that will appear in the finished product.

Choosing a thickness

Drywall comes in various thicknesses, ⅜ in (9.5 mm) and ½ in (12.5-mm) being the most common. Thicker sheets are needed if nails or screws will be far apart—for example, if there is a large gap between studs (see pp.104–105) or joists.

SCRIBING DRYWALL

This is a way of marking where to cut a sheet to fit against an undulating surface, such as an uneven wall. The method shown here is the basic technique for the first sheet. Examples of when it may be needed include altering a ceiling (see pp.100–101) and drywalling (see pp.122–135). Use the same method, if you need to, against an uneven ceiling. Place the sheet so that it is just touching the uneven surface. Cut some wood to the length of the largest gap between sheet and wall (it is exaggerated for clarity in the picture, right). Then cut one end into a point. Place the pointed end against the uneven surface and, holding a pencil at the other end, run it along the surface to draw a guide line.

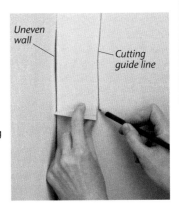

Uneven wall

Cutting guide line

Which side is which?

Standard drywall is pale gray or ivory on one side, and a darker gray or brown color on the other. The lighter surface should face into the room. The other side may have manufacturers' logos on it, and visible seams down its edge.

Square-edged vs. taper-edged sheets

The choice depends on how the drywall is to be covered. Square-edged sheets are best for plastering, and taper-edged sheets for drywalling.

DRYWALL

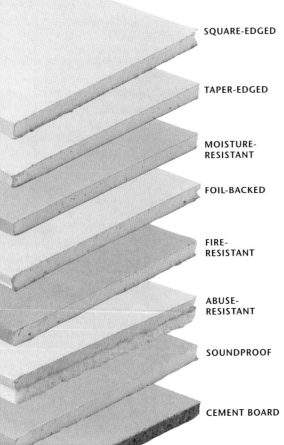

SQUARE-EDGED

TAPER-EDGED

MOISTURE-RESISTANT

FOIL-BACKED

FIRE-RESISTANT

ABUSE-RESISTANT

SOUNDPROOF

CEMENT BOARD

DRYWALL	Uses include
Square-edged Standard drywall. Sheets butt against each other and should be plastered over.	Walls and ceilings to be plastered
Taper-edged Regular drywall with a tapered end that allows for easier filling between gaps with joint compounds.	Finishing walls
Moisture-resistant Core is impregnated with waterproofing materials, but is breathable so the surface beneath the board can "breathe" through the wall's surface. Can be used in areas of high water usage—as a base for tiles in a shower stall, for example.	Bathrooms and kitchens
Foil-backed Has vapor-resistant paper on one side, so is less protected than moisture-resistant sheets. Has a silver foil-like layer on nondecorative side.	Used in cold climates; not for moisture-resistant materials or humid climates
Fire-resistant Has greater fireproofing qualities than standard drywall.	Integral garage ceilings, some corridors, stairwells
Abuse-resistant A polystyrene layer bonded to the nondecorative side provides greater heat insulation than normal. Thicker than other drywalls.	Garages
Soundproof Has greater soundproofing qualities than other drywalls.	Walls and ceilings in apartments or condos
Cement board Not a drywall, but has similar properties and uses. Is a strong, moisture-resistant base board, often used as a subfloor, beneath ceramic tiles, or as a backing for wall tiles. Board thicknesses and sizes vary.	Can be used as a subfloor beneath ceramic tiles, or as a backing for wall tiles

WOOD-BASED SHEETS

Wood is the main constituent of many sheet goods. Some of these may be used in the main structural components of a house; others for decorative finishings.

Plywood

Thin layers of wood, with the grain of each layer at a right angle to that of the previous layer, form plywood. Each layer is bonded tightly to the next, creating a very strong structure, and thickness adds further strength. Some plywoods are available as marine plies, which are impregnated with water-repelling chemicals.

Other boards

Sheet materials such as MDF and particleboard are made from pieces of wood compressed together at high pressure. Water-resistant versions of these sheets are also available for use in areas where humidity may be high.

CUTTING A SHEET

Using a handsaw
If the sheet is coated (with melamine, for example), mark the guide line on the side that will be visible and cut with this side facing upward. This is because the edge of the coating on the lower face will chip during cutting; this way, the chipped edges will be invisible. Score along the guide line on all sides of the sheet with a utility knife, and use a fine-toothed panel saw to reduce the chances of chipped edges.

Using a power saw
The blade cuts as it rises, so to avoid chipped edges on the visible side of a coated sheet, mark the guide line on the rear of the sheet and cut with the rear side facing upward.

Cutting drywall
To cut a straight line in a sheet of drywall, place a straight edge along the guide line, and score along it with a utility knife. Fold the sheet to snap it along the line, and cut through the paper backing.

PLYWOODS	Uses include
3-ply and 5-ply These common types of plywood get their name from their number of layers: e.g, 3-ply has three layers.	Boxing in or decorative internal uses
Multi-ply This is composed of many layers.	Heavyweight construction, e.g., house framing

OTHER BOARDS	Uses include
Blockboard Not technically a ply, but shares its characteristics. Has two thinner outer layers that enclose thicker, square-cut lengths of wood. It is therefore stiff and durable. May have a decorative veneer or a finish of a lesser grade of wood.	Ideal for shelves and cabinets, and can be finished with paint
Medium-density fiberboard (MDF) Very versatile. Made up of highly compressed wooden fibers glued together. This method of manufacturing means that cut edges are neater than those on other materials. It can provide a rigid structural component, or can be intricately shaped to form a decorative surface ready for paint. Available in various thicknesses. Main drawback is that it gives off a very fine dust when cut, which must not be inhaled. Wear a mask when MDF is being cut.	Cabinets, cabinet doors, boxing in, shelving
Moisture-resistant MDF A version of MDF that can resist moisture attack. It is often green.	Areas prone to moisture: e.g., kitchen or bathroom
Fiberboard A lightweight version of MDF. Joints between sheets can be taped, and the boards painted.	Underlay for flooring, or as an alternative to drywall on a ceiling
Oriented Strand Board Central core is composed of small wooden fibers. Has no decorative quality, so is usually covered. Some sheets fit together using a tongue-and-groove mechanism. Available in various thicknesses.	Often used as floor sheathing
Moisture-resistant particleboard is more water-resistant than normal particleboard. It is often colored green.	Flooring
Veneered particleboard Has a melamine (plastic) or decorative wooden veneer.	Commonly used for shelves
Hardboard Thin, compressed fiberboard. Standard hardboard has one smooth side, and one rougher side. Different grades and a variety of finishes are available.	Often used for parts of kitchen cabinets with a melamine (plastic) surface or veneer

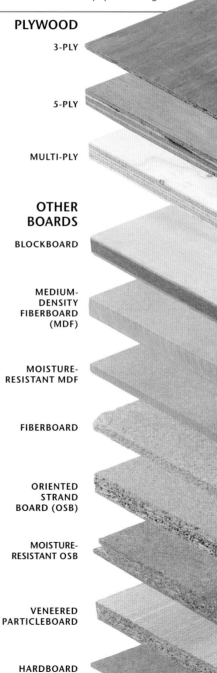

PLYWOOD

3-PLY

5-PLY

MULTI-PLY

OTHER BOARDS

BLOCKBOARD

MEDIUM-DENSITY FIBERBOARD (MDF)

MOISTURE-RESISTANT MDF

FIBERBOARD

ORIENTED STRAND BOARD (OSB)

MOISTURE-RESISTANT OSB

VENEERED PARTICLEBOARD

HARDBOARD

LUMBER

Lumber is essential in Canadian homebuilding and remodeling. Even a solid masonry house may have a large proportion of wood elements, including rafters and joists, and the studs in a stud wall (see p.104). In addition to these, there are decorative aspects: doors, moldings, and stairways. These pages deal with the different types of lumber used in homes, the properties of different woods, and sourcing sustainable lumber. For details of woodworking joints and how to use them, see pp.396–397.

HARDWOOD AND SOFTWOOD

Hardwood is usually harvested from deciduous trees (ones that shed their leaves), and softwood from coniferous trees (which bear cones). Hardwoods take longer to grow, and are more resilient than softwoods, so they are considered to be higher-quality woods. Because of this, they are more expensive. This does not mean that softwood is a less effective building material—indeed, it makes up the bulk of all lumber used in the home. It is used planed on all four sides in structural components such as wall studs, and planed for moldings such as baseboards. Some of the more common hardwoods and softwoods used in house construction and decoration are detailed below.

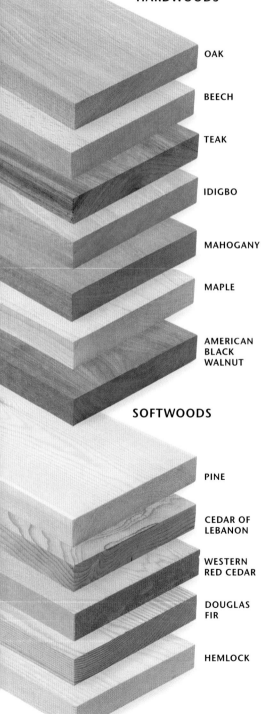

HARDWOODS

- OAK
- BEECH
- TEAK
- IDIGBO
- MAHOGANY
- MAPLE
- AMERICAN BLACK WALNUT

SOFTWOODS

- PINE
- CEDAR OF LEBANON
- WESTERN RED CEDAR
- DOUGLAS FIR
- HEMLOCK

HARDWOODS	Uses include
Oak A traditional building material, oak is common in many homes. "Green" (newly harvested) oak is still sometimes used to make timber frames for houses; when green, it is still soft, so is more easily cut and shaped. As it dries, oak acquires a hardness more like concrete than like wood, making it a very strong construction material. In addition to structural elements, oak can also be used for decorative elements to provide a high-quality finish.	Structure of many houses in Europe, decorative beams, kitchens, veneer on kitchen units, flooring, decorative carpentry such as baseboard and architrave
Beech A straight-grained hardwood with a fine, even texture. American beech is light or reddish brown in color, while European beech is a lighter, yellowish brown color.	Kitchen counters, floors (veneer), decorative moldings such as quadrant, scotia, etc.
Teak Teak is a dark hardwood, sometimes used in finish carpentry to provide a high-quality finish.	Staircases, garden and indoor furniture
Idigbo Resilient and easily worked, Idigbo is also very reasonably priced for a hardwood.	Woodworking
Mahogany More commonly associated with furniture than with house construction.	Furniture, door veneers, paneling in period properties
Maple A highly decorative hardwood with a light, attractive appearance and hardwearing characteristics.	Flooring, cabinets, stair parts, veneers
American black walnut A coarse, dark hardwood used in some aspects of interior carpentry.	Kitchens, veneers

SOFTWOODS	Uses include
Pine One of the most commonly used woods. Some species of pine can contain more orange or red streaks.	Rough carpentry, finish carpentry
Cedar of Lebanon Another light-colored softwood. Often used in interior carpentry.	Rough carpentry, finish carpentry
Western red cedar Has a red-tinged appearance. Used mainly for exterior applications.	Paneling, shingles, decking
Douglas fir Has a definite reddish brown tinge, and is commonly used in plywood.	Construction, decking, flooring
Hemlock A light, nonresinous wood.	Doors, windows, framing

CHARACTERISTICS OF WOOD

In addition to choosing a type of lumber, think about other qualities it needs. These are not mutually exclusive; a piece of lumber can be both seasoned and treated, for example.

Seasoned wood

Wood has a high moisture content when it is first cut, and needs to dry out ("season") before being used. When you buy wood, it will often still have a relatively high moisture content. Wood can distort during the drying process. To overcome this, store it horizontally, above ground level, and supported evenly along its length. Before using lumber, leave it to acclimate for a few days in the environment where it will be used. Most suppliers produce kiln-dried lumber, on which seasoning has been accelerated and the wood artificially dried. Using kiln-dried wood can prevent problems later.

Treated wood

Lumber that is protected from moisture inside the house shell does not need to be treated. Any lumber exposed to the weather or in contact with concrete (like bottom plates in a basement wall) must be treated. Pressure-treated wood (PTW) is usually impregnated with a preservative and has a green or brown tint. It can be used where there is a risk of damp attack or insect infestation. All wood, however well treated, will break down eventually, but the degree to which it has been treated will influence its working life span.

PTW PLANK

BUYING LUMBER

Regardless of the type of wood, and whether it has been seasoned or treated, make sure you know whether your supplier is selling it by its rough-sawn or its planed size.

Rough-sawn wood vs. planed wood

Wood may be supplied either rough-sawn or planed (smoothed on all sides). This can make buying it confusing because lumber is usually priced and sold according to its dimensions when it is first cut into rough-sawn lengths. Rough-sawn lumber is therefore close to the size stated when you buy it, although it may be slightly smaller due to shrinkage during the drying process. But planed lumber is smaller than its labeled size, because it has been smoothed with a plane on all sides. All consumer renovation stores sell planed structural lumber, so your 2 x 4 will probably be 1½ x 3½ in (38 x 89 mm).

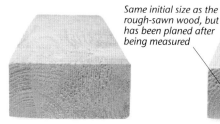

Same initial size as the rough-sawn wood, but has been planed after being measured

Rough-sawn wood
Used where it will not be visible—in a stud wall, for example. It will be close to the size quoted, because lumber is measured when it is rough-sawn.

Planed lumber
Used where it will be visible, such as for a baseboard. It may not be the stated size, because wood has been removed from every face to give the smooth finish.

GREEN SOURCES OF LUMBER

Sustainable wood
The most important issue when buying new wood is to know whether it has come from a sustainable source. Lumber from recognized sources usually bears a stamp, such as that of the internationally-recognized Forest Stewardship Council—a not-for-profit organization that promotes the responsible management of forests.

FOREST STEWARDSHIP COUNCIL'S STAMP

Reclaimed lumber
Reclaimed wood has the advantage of being thoroughly seasoned, and may look more appealing than new lumber. However, some of it may be unusable, so check for damage when buying. For more on reclaimed materials, see pp.86–87.

RECOGNIZING PROBLEMS

When buying wood, look out for splits, knots, and uneven grain. Splits can occur naturally in wood due to shrinkage or growth defects, but it is more likely that the wood has been dried too rapidly or the planks stored incorrectly. Softwoods damage and warp more easily when being stored. You will pay more for defect-free wood, but it is worth examining lumber thoroughly before purchasing.

Look along the lumber for signs of bowing or warping

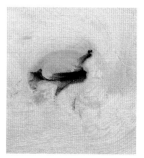

Warped lumber
Bent or twisted wood is difficult to saw accurately. Bending is usually caused by stacking or otherwise storing wood badly. Bowed or warped lumber may have unseen stresses due to the twisting.

Knots
In rough carpentry, knots are hidden and don't matter. They may spoil finish carpentry by bleeding (especially on softwood) or showing through paint. Treat them with knotting solution first.

CHECKLIST WHEN BUYING LUMBER

- Make sure that the wood you are buying comes from a sustainable resource.
- Find out how it has been treated and seasoned, and how it has been stored.
- Check lengths to see if they are bowed or warped, are split, are damp, or contain excessive or dead knots.
- Find out whether the quoted sizes are nominal or actual, so that you get the correct quantity of lumber.
- Ask if the supplier will deliver to your home. This can be useful if you require a large quantity and/or particularly long lengths. Check lumber carefully when it is delivered.

Screws vary considerably in terms of size, purpose, and quality. Some are purely functional, and their appearance is of no importance; others have an aesthetic role as well as a practical one. Once you have chosen the most appropriate screws for your project, check that you have the correct screwdriver to drive them (see pp.32–33, 56–57). Screw heads are quickly damaged by the wrong screwdriver, so always use the correct size—it also makes the job easier.

HEAD DESIGN

Screws are designed to be turned by particular types of screwdrivers. You can tell which type to use by looking at the pattern of slots in the top of the screw head.

Some modern screws have unusual head designs that require special bits rather than traditional screwdriver designs.

Flat head
Traditional design with a single slot crossing the diameter of the screw's head.

Robertson
Square-headed, the most common screw because of good fit with the screwdriver.

Security
Similar to a standard screw except that once inserted, it cannot be removed.

Phillips
Cross-headed, with two slots bisecting one another. The slots are deeper in the center.

Security
A second type of security screw.

Hexagonal-headed
Hexagonal (hex) screws need to be tightened with a hex screwdriver or bit.

Pozidriv
A cross-head screw similar to the Phillips, but with smaller divisions between the cross's slots.

HEAD PROFILES

There are three main types of screw-head profiles, each with a different function, illustrated below. The main difference is how proud the head sits in relation to the surrounding surface.

COUNTERSUNK HEAD   PAN HEAD   ROUND HEAD

SCREW-HEAD COVERINGS

These provide decorative finishes for exposed screw heads. Some fit to the top of a fixed head; others are positioned as the screw is inserted, because it feeds through the cup.

Screw sits in cup

Top folds down

Top

SCREW CUP

Screw sits in cup

Back

INSET CUP

SNAP-ON CAP

COVER CAP

SIZE AND MATERIAL

Screws are sized in terms of length and gauge. The length measurement refers to the part of a screw that goes into the material, so it includes the head of a countersinking screw, but does not for a round-headed one. Choose a screw that is three times longer than the thickness of the smaller of the pieces being joined. The gauge refers to the shank's diameter, and is a label not an exact size. The smaller the figure, the narrower the screw. Most screws are available in gauges 2 (⅛ in/2 mm) to 14 (⁹⁄₁₆ in/6.5 mm), but other sizes are available for some types, especially the most commonly used ones.

Higher-quality screws usually have stronger heads, which reduces the risk of rounding off (damaging) the head with a screwdriver. Where screws will suffer exposed conditions or possible corrosion, use resistant fixings, such as stainless-steel, coated, or galvanized ones.

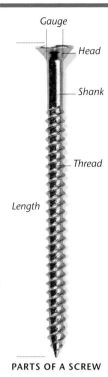

Gauge

Head

Shank

Thread

Length

PARTS OF A SCREW

PILOT HOLES AND COUNTERSINKING

Before driving a screw into wood, drill a pilot hole to guide the screw into the correct position and to prevent the wood from splitting as the screw is tightened. Use a drill bit that is slightly narrower than the screw's gauge. To drill a pilot hole for a wall plug, use a bit with the same diameter as the plug's gauge. See p.54 for the drilling technique.

Before inserting a screw with a countersunk head, use a countersink drill bit to enlarge the pilot hole's opening. The bit widens toward its top, so drill a shallow hole for a small screw head, and a deeper hole for a larger one.

COUNTERSINKING A SCREW

Pilot hole has already been drilled

A

B

Drill a pilot hole of the correct size to take the screw, and use this as a guide for the center of the countersink drill bit.

Using a countersink bit, drill a hole of sufficient depth to accommodate the screw head.

C

D

Insert the screw through the countersunk hole and into the pilot hole, and tighten it as usual.

The screw's head will sit just below the surface. Fill the hole, covering the screw.

TYPES OF SCREWS

Screw designs vary widely to suit particular tasks or materials. Some of the more specialized screws are available only in a limited range of sizes.

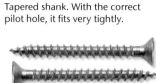

Traditional wood
Tapered shank. With the correct pilot hole, it fits very tightly.

Drywall
Black-phosphate-coated; used to fix drywall to studwork.

Modern wood
Untapered, less likely to split wood. Pilot hole not always needed.

Masonry
For use in masonry with no need for a wall plug, though a pilot hole is still needed. Some have a blue coating.

Decking
Long screws designed for screwing down deck boards.

Single thread   *Twin threads*

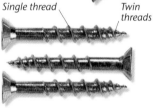

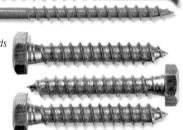

MDF
Sharp point and twin-thread perform initial penetration. Farther up the shank, a single, coarser thread holds the screw tightly in position.

Lag
A lag screw or bolt is a heavy-duty fastener that is inserted by rotating the head with an adjustable wrench.

Chipboard
For fixing down chipboard flooring. Often wax-coated.

Sheet metal
Cuts its own thread. Commonly used with sheet metal. Some general-purpose screws have a self-tapping action.

Decorative dome

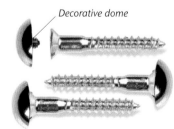

Mirror
Can also hold fittings where access may be required (such as a bath panel). Decorative dome fits over screw head.

Dowel
Threaded at both ends, to join two lengths of wood (curtain poles, for example).

WALL PLUGS AND COMBINATION FASTENERS

Unless you are using masonry screws, a wall plug is required to secure a fastener that is inserted into masonry. Wall plugs are also needed to make strong connections on hollow walls such as stud walls; these are of a different design from masonry ones. You can buy combination fasteners for masonry and hollow walls, which combine a screw and a plug in one product; designs vary according to function and manufacturer. Common examples are illustrated below.

MASONRY-WALL PLUGS

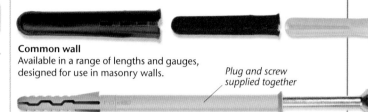

Common wall
Available in a range of lengths and gauges, designed for use in masonry walls.

Plug and screw supplied together

Frame
Screw supplied with correct size of plug. Commonly used to attach a window and door frames in masonry walls.

Hammer
Similar to frame screw except it is hammered all the way into position.

Expanding sleeve   *Turning bolt causes sleeve to expand*

Expansion/masonry bolt
Screw with bolt head and metal sleeve that expands into the masonry material as the bolt is screwed in place.

HOLLOW-WALL PLUGS

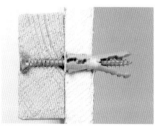

Cavity wall plug
A plug specifically designed for cavity walls. The tapering increases the plug's grip in the pilot hole.

Self-drilling cavity wall plug
The tapered, threaded plug screws into the wall and the screw is then inserted into the plug.

Hollow-wall anchor
Combination fastener for a hollow wall, with a screw inserted with a metal sleeve.

Spring toggle
As the fastener is screwed into place, the toggle section grips the wall tightly. A gravity toggle is similar, but supports greater weights.

NAILS

The most basic of fasteners, nails are essential for construction jobs where the extra strength and expense of a screw is unnecessary. Common nails are for general use and are available in many sizes—if thickness of material allows it choose one that is at least three times longer than the depth of the thinner material being nailed. Specialty nails, traditional nails, and brads are designed for specific tasks or finishes and are made in sizes suitable for their purpose. Most nails are simply hammered in, although where wood is likely to split, or very close to an edge, you may sometimes need to drill a pilot hole slightly smaller than the diameter of the nail (as for screws, see p.76). For details on hammering and removing nails, see pp.36–37.

Head

Shank

ROUND HEAD NAIL

NAIL COMPOSITION AND QUANTITIES

Nails have a head to receive a hammer blow, and a longer shank to provide the attachment. Most nails are made of steel or iron, although masonry nails are made of hardened zinc for strength. Many nails are galvanized (have an outer layer mixed with zinc to protect them from rust), which gives them a pale gray, mottled effect.

Nails are normally sold by weight rather than quantity, so a rough calculation is sufficient for purchasing. Overbuy, since nails are always useful. Nail weights vary between manufacturers, and according to design and composition. As a rough guide, nails are sold by the pound.

COMMON NAILS

The most widely used nail types are shown here. They may vary slightly between manufacturers. Design differences can improve some aspect of each kind. Some nails are lightweight, so, where strength is not an issue, you get more for your money. Others have grooves and twists that give them a greater gripping action to create a very solid attachment.

Round head
A general-purpose nail for joining wood. Widely used where "rough" finishing is acceptable—in studwork, for example. The round head provides a good point of contact for a hammer but may split wood if driven down too far.

Finish
Similar to round-head nails, but the head is much smaller, and sits flush with the wood's surface to give a neater finish with reduced risk of splitting. It can be recessed using a nail set (see opposite) to hide it completely.

FINISH NAILS

Finish nails are designed for fine carpentry work. Their thinness makes them less likely to split wood. The small heads are designed to make them inconspicuous. Brass finish nails provide a decorative detail.

Casing
General-purpose nail for use on small moldings or thin plywood.

Oval head
Similar to the round finish nail, but oval in cross-section to minimize splitting of the wood. Most of the head sits below the wood's surface without the need for setting (see opposite).

Roofing
Commonly used to attach asphalt and for other roofing purposes. Smaller roofing nails are used to attach roofing felt. Because they are exposed to the weather, they are often galvanized to prevent rust.

Masonry
This hard, thicker nail has a small head and is usually made of hardened zinc to enable it to penetrate masonry surfaces. It is generally used to secure wood to stone or brick.

Brads
These very narrow nails give a neat finish to detailed work.

Drywall nail
Used for hanging drywall, the nail head is designed so that it does not cut the paper face and sinks 1 in (2.5 cm) into the frame.

Annular ring shank
Similar to round-head nail, but has rings all along the shank, providing greater grip in wood that results in a more secure attachment.

Siding nail
Siding nails are galvanized. There are four types of galvanization and a variety of sizes are available.

Brass brads
Decorative brads for visible nails, especially on brass door hardware.

Glazing sprig
Wedge-shaped nail used with putty to secure glazing.

SPECIALTY NAILS

Each of these is designed with features suitable for one particular purpose.

Cap nail
This nail has a plastic cap, and is used for nailing down building fabric, such as house wrap.

Upholstery
Small, decorative, dome-headed nails used for securing upholstery to furnishings. Available in a variety of finishes to suit the style of furnishings.

Plastic-headed
Used to hold vinyl siding materials. The shatterproof heads are available in a range of popular colors to help disguise them.

Carpet
Used to hold down carpet before the introduction of gripper rods, and still used in awkward corners, especially on stairs. Also known as carpet tacks.

FASTENERS

Although these do not look like nails, they perform the same function and, like nails, are driven into position with a hammer. The most commonly used are shown here, but a variety of fasteners is available.

Corrugated
Has a corrugated cross-section, and is usually used as an invisible connector for a mitered frame joint (see below).

Staple
The arched shape is designed to hold wire firmly in position—for example, on fence posts.

USING A CORRUGATED FASTENER

A **Position a fastener** so that it bisects the joint at a right angle, then hammer it into place.

B **Drive in another fastener** across the joint, so that the wood is securely held in place by two parallel fasteners.

TRADITIONAL NAILS

These simple designs predate modern nails, and are still used to provide period detail in modern homes. Their rigid, broad design makes them ideal for securing large wooden sections.

Cut clasp
An all-purpose nail, often used today for traditional-look, ledge-and-brace door construction (see p.157).

Cut floor
Similar to the cut clasp, but the head's flat design is suited to nailing down floorboards (see pp.180–181).

SETTING A NAIL BENEATH THE SURFACE

You may wish to drive in a nail to sit just beneath the surface of the material it is securing. This is normally for aesthetic reasons and, in areas where people could brush past, may be needed to prevent injury or damage to clothing and other materials. The only tools needed are a hammer and a nail set (see p.36). In many cases the hole is filled so the nail becomes completely invisible.

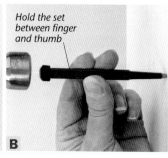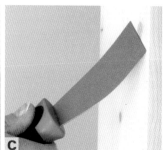

A **Use a nail set** of the right size for the nail. Place its tip onto the nail head, holding the set straight so that the nail will be driven true.

Hold the set between finger and thumb

B **Lightly tap the head** of the set with a hammer, striking it squarely. It will not take much force to drive the nail head below the surface.

C **Use a filling knife** to press wood filler into the hole, covering the nail completely. Then sand and decorate the surface.

ADHESIVES, FILLERS, AND SEALANTS

Many projects require some kind of adhesive or sealant, and it is important to use the one most appropriate for each task. A vast array is available, some of which can act as an adhesive and/or a sealant. Sealants for joints between surfaces are detailed here. For details of surface sealants and primers see pp.276–281.

ADHESIVES
The most widely used adhesives are described here. Other types are designed for use with particular products, such as vinyl. Mirror adhesives, for example, do not affect mirror backings that might be stained by all-purpose adhesive.

Wood glue Yellow in color, this is designed specifically for bonding sections of wood. Working time is about 15 minutes. It has a shelf life of about one year.

Contact adhesive (contact cement) A very strong solvent-based adhesive, this can be used to bond a large range of materials including wood, metal, many plastics, and decorative laminates. It is not suitable for use with some materials, such as polystyrene and bitumen, or as a mirror adhesive, so check the manufacturer's instructions before using it.

Construction adhesive Used to bond surfaces that cannot easily be joined with screws or nails, or combined with mechanical fasteners to form very strong bonds. Available in tubes and sealant-like cartridges. Most (especially water-based and solvent-free types) need at least one of the surfaces being bonded to be porous.

Resin Made up of two elements that mix once they are dispensed from the cartridge, resin creates very strong bonds. Where a secure anchoring point for a wall fixture is required (on shelves, for instance), resin is injected into the hole before the fixture is inserted.

Expanding foam Supplied in an aerosol can, this foam is used to fill large gaps, bonding to their edges.

USING A RESIN ADHESIVE

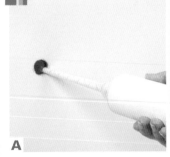

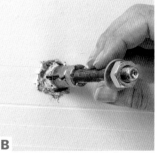

A Aim the nozzle into the hole in the masonry wall, and discharge the resin adhesive into the hole.

B Immediately press a heavy-duty fastener into the resin, and allow the adhesive to set before hanging any heavy item from the fastener.

USING EXPANDING FOAM

Polyurethane-based expanding foam can fill large gaps or holes, and bonds the surfaces in the process. It should never be left exposed to the sunlight as the ultraviolet rays will destroy the integrity of the foam. In this example, foam is being used to fill the gap around a drainage pipe.

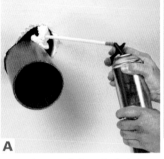

A Point the nozzle into the hole in the wall, and discharge the foam into the hole.

B After about five or 10 minutes, the foam will begin to bubble and expand. It will then set.

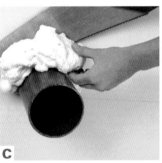

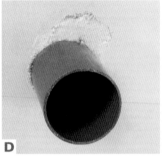

C Once it has set, the foam can be cut away using a saw to neaten the overall finish. Finer trimming can be carried out with a utility knife.

D Holes in the trimmed area can then be filled with an all-purpose filler compound, sanded, and decorated as required.

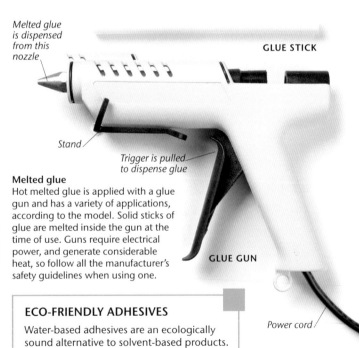

Melted glue is dispensed from this nozzle

GLUE STICK

Stand

Trigger is pulled to dispense glue

Melted glue
Hot melted glue is applied with a glue gun and has a variety of applications, according to the model. Solid sticks of glue are melted inside the gun at the time of use. Guns require electrical power, and generate considerable heat, so follow all the manufacturer's safety guidelines when using one.

GLUE GUN

Power cord

ECO-FRIENDLY ADHESIVES
Water-based adhesives are an ecologically sound alternative to solvent-based products. They are non-toxic and low in VOCs (volatile organic compounds). For more information about VOCs, see p.282.

JOINT SEALANTS

Some sealants prime or seal a surface (see opposite and pp.276–297), while others create a decorative, waterproof, or durable joint. Most joint sealants have a waterproofing element. Many sealants are made for specific uses, such as in kitchens, bathrooms, or on windows.

Joint sealants usually come in cartridges and need a separate dispenser to apply them. Dispensers vary in size and design, so check for compatibility. Most sealants come in an extensive range of colors. Latex sealants can be painted but those made with silicone can not. Sealant remover is available, but can damage some surfaces.

The sealant must cope with movement, such as that caused by temperature changes, in the materials they join. Some sealants are not very flexible, but dry to a relatively hard finish, and are recommended for use in bathrooms—however, check for resistance to mold. Other types are more flexible, and are used in glazing.

Curing and longevity

Most sealants form a skin fairly quickly, but take several hours, or even days, to dry or cure completely. High-modulus sealants give off strong acidic fumes while curing. A few brands are "fast-cure." A sealant should never get completely hard, because of the need for flexibility. Be sure to check the cartridge for the length of guarantee. High-quality sealants may be expensive, but they are easier to work with and last the longest.

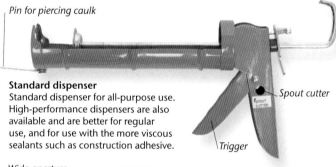

Pin for piercing caulk

Standard dispenser
Standard dispenser for all-purpose use. High-performance dispensers are also available and are better for regular use, and for use with the more viscous sealants such as construction adhesive.

Spout cutter

Trigger

USING A SEALANT DISPENSER

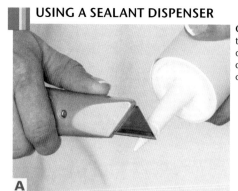

Cut off the tip of the cartridge. The opening at the tip determines the size of the caulk bead.

A

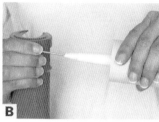

B

Insert a metal pin into the tip of the cartridge and remove.

C

Pull back the dispenser's plunger or rod and load the cartridge into the dispenser.

D

To dispense the sealant, apply even pressure to the trigger. When you release the trigger, sealant will continue to dispense due to a buildup of pressure.

E

Push the catch plate to make it stop. To store a half-used tube, insert a nail into its nozzle to prevent clogging, or replace the nozzle next time you use the tube.

Wide-aperture nozzle

Plunger

Barrel or refillable cartridge

Specialty dispenser
Several variations are available, designed for specific tasks. An example is a repointing gun with a refillable cartridge for applying pointing mortar.

Trigger allows for variable speed control

Battery-operated dispenser
Easy to use and control, this is the top-of-the-line sealant gun. Batteries are recharged much the same way as those of a cordless drill (see p.54).

Rechargeable battery

HEALTH AND SAFETY

Follow all manufacturer's instructions when using an adhesive or sealant, because the chemicals involved can be dangerous. Ventilate your working area and wear all recommended protective equipment and clothing.

BRICKS, BLOCKS, AND WALL TIES

Bricks, blocks, and stone are the main components of masonry construction, whether inside the home or outside it. A wall (a cavity wall, for instance) may contain several of these materials, or just one (as in a brick garden wall). There are several materials to choose from, including eco-friendly options (see pp.94–95). See p.48–49 for bricklaying tools and techniques. Garden brick-wall construction is shown on pp.408–411.

DETERMINE HOW MANY TO BUY

When estimating quantities, remember that the measurement of a brick or block does not usually take into account mortar joints, which will influence the eventual dimensions of your wall. However, some suppliers do quote block sizes in nominal figures including mortar joints. For brickwork, an average joint is ⅜ in (10 mm); it is sometimes a little larger for blockwork—½ in (12 mm). To get a rough idea of how many bricks or blocks to buy, calculate the surface area of your planned structure and divide this by the nominal size of your chosen brick or block.

TYPES OF BRICKS

Many kinds of bricks are available, in terms of composition, color, and texture. The main types are shown here. Bricks are also categorized in terms of quality, referring to their resistance to such things as frost attack. This is not instantly apparent in the brick's appearance, so seek advice from your supplier.

Common
Common bricks are clay-based and must not be used in gardening as they will decompose in contact with the soil.

Facing/Faced
Facing bricks have good faces on all sides. Faced bricks have one good face and one or both good ends.

Engineering
Engineering bricks are very dense and are made of clay. They are used for extra strength and resistance to weather conditions.

Calcium silicate
Made from lime and sand, these bricks come in a vast range of colors. They are also relatively smooth to the touch, and provide a very uniform finish.

Fire
Made from a special form of clay that can withstand particularly high temperatures, these bricks are commonly used in fireplaces.

Concrete
These bricks are composed of concrete and made in a large range of colors and textures.

BRICK DESIGN

Bricks are made in different sizes, although 8½ x 4 x 2⅝ in (215 x 102.5 x 65 mm) is a common size. There are also other aspects of brick design that vary, such as whether they are solid, cored, or indented. These are the three most common brick designs, although many others exist, often designed for specific purposes.

Solid
Solid throughout the structure, with flat surfaces on all sides. Both fire bricks and concrete bricks are commonly solid in structure.

Cored
Have holes that extend from their upper to their lower faces, and so are not suitable for capping on top of a wall. They are laid in exactly the same way as other bricks.

Faced/Indented
Indented bricks have a wedge-shaped indentation (a "frog") in the upper face (some also have this in the bottom face). Bricks can be laid frog up or frog down. Laying them frog up is stronger, but requires more mortar.

Specialty bricks
Less angular bricks are available for certain tasks such as capping a garden wall, creating a curved wall, turning a corner (as shown), or creating specific sill designs. Most manufacturers and suppliers will have catalogs to display their full range of specialty bricks.

BLOCKS

Blocks are a modern development, and are generally larger than bricks. Unless they are faced, blocks are normally covered over for decorative purposes—usually with stucco on an exterior wall, or drywall on an internal wall. Sizes vary, but blocks are often 18 x 9 in (450 x 225 mm). Depths also vary.

Glass
Decorative glass blocks are usually square and may be used inside or outside, often for small features.

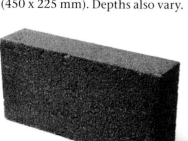

Rectangular concrete
Heavy, solid concrete-based block that is used for general construction work.

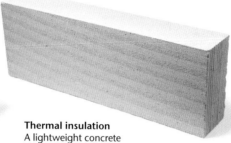

Thermal insulation
A lightweight concrete block that is thermally efficient and easy to handle. Used in loadbearing and non-loadbearing walls, depending on specification.

Concrete with cavity
Continuous cavities allow for strengthening rods through retaining walls. Cellular blocks have discontinuous cavities.

Faced building block
Concrete blocks are sometimes available with a decorative face and in various colors.

STONE

Natural stone varies widely in appearance and properties depending on its origin. Different stones are therefore suitable for different projects. When buying natural stone, quality is important. A load of unfinished stone may produce a lot of waste, while finished stone is more expensive.

Natural stone
Unfinished natural stone generally requires finishing before use. Bear in mind that finished stone needs to have a usable face, as well as the correct dimensions.

Cut stone
Natural stone that has been cut into a block, usually with all faces finished. Cut stone is therefore very expensive and seldom used extensively.

Pitched faced
Stone cut to provide smooth sides for neat mortar joints, but with a rough face.

Reconstituted stone
Made from crushed stone, sand, and cement, these are molded to mimic natural stone.

CUTTING CONCRETE BLOCKS

Angle grinder
To cut a block diagonally from corner to corner, for a gable end, use an angle grinder along a guide line. For square cuts, see p.59.

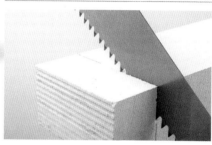

Stone saw
Use a stone saw to cut lightweight blocks by hand, following a clearly marked guide line.

WALL TIES

Wall ties are used in cavity walls to connect the outer and inner walls, or to connect a new masonry wall to an existing one. Designs vary according to whether a tie is for use with masonry or timber. Some common examples are shown below.

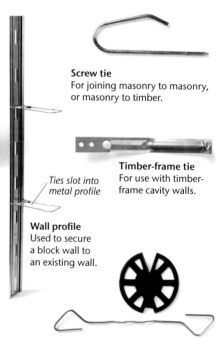

Screw tie
For joining masonry to masonry, or masonry to timber.

Timber-frame tie
For use with timber-frame cavity walls.

Ties slot into metal profile

Wall profile
Used to secure a block wall to an existing wall.

Lightweight wall tie
Stainless steel with a plastic retaining clip designed to hold insulation sheets in place.

GREEN MATERIALS

The materials used in the construction of an eco-house are key to its green credentials. There are various green options available, but it is important to consider loadbearing issues when making your decision. Ask your supplier to identify which type of block is suitable for exterior and interior loadbearing walls, as some may be loadbearing, but still unsuitable in an exterior wall. One of the best ways to help the environment is to source materials locally; transport costs are reduced and you may be able to check production methods and the sustainability of sources.

Since most of the options listed below are not widely used in Canada, you would be well advised to find a knowledgeable contractor that specializes in your chosen material. You will also probably need to get your building plans certified by an engineer prior to obtaining a building permit. Not all alternative building materials are suitable to all locations and climates in Canada, so do your research before making a final decision.

STRENGTHENING THE STRUCTURE

Laying a block flat, rather than on its edge, can make a significant difference to a wall's strength. Some compressed earth blocks, for example, have a minimum compressive strength of 435psi (3 N/sq mm) on their edge, rising to 2,465psi (17 N/sq mm) when they are laid flat. On their edge, most loadbearing concrete blocks have a minimum compressive strength of 1,015psi (7 N/sq mm).

Combining conventional bricks and blocks with green bricks and blocks in the same structure is not recommended. While conventional bricks and concrete blocks are often combined, green blocks should be used consistently. In addition, as green blocks can vary in size dramatically, complete walls should be built with cut blocks rather than alternating sizes.

STORING GREEN MATERIALS

Care must be taken when storing green materials. Most do not store well outside so should be kept inside. If they must be stored in the open air, they should be covered accordingly. Although some blocks can form part of a stucco exterior wall, they will be susceptible to rain damage prior to stucco. It is important to note that most green blocks and bricks cannot be used below the damp-proof course level.

Clay brick
This is an unfired clay brick, commonly used in cobwork. They can be used for non-loadbearing walls or infills in lumber-frame constructions.

Cob block
This sun-dried block is made from mud held together by straw, and is normally used to repair existing cob buildings.

Hemp block
The base material of these blocks consists of fibers from the hemp plant mixed with sand and lime. Hemp is still a developing industry in Canada. Declared an illegal crop in 1938, industrial hemp was legalized in Canada in 1998 for research and commercial purposes. Hemp plants mature in 3–4 months, making them environmentally preferable to wood and well adapted to growing conditions in many parts of Canada.

Compressed earth block
To make this block, clay, aggregates, and water are pressed into a mold and dried. Traditional blocks of this nature, such as adobe blocks, were sun-dried, but modern versions are mechanically compressed.

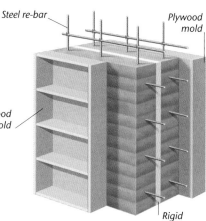

Steel re-bar
Plywood mold
Plywood mold
Rigid insulation

Straw bale
Made from the dry stalks of cereal plants, such as wheat, oats, barley, rye, and rice, straw is an excellent insulator and consequently a good material for blocks. Since straw bales are made up of what is usually waste material, it is a viable green option. However, the quality of the straw used and the consistency of the bales are important issues, so make sure that you're working with an experienced contractor when ordering and accepting bales.

Rammed earth wall
Rammed earth walls are made by compressing gravel, sand, and clay into a mold. A small amount of cement can be added to the mixture if desired, along with rigid insulation inside the wall and steel re-bar for reinforcement. A rammed earth structure requires little lumber and has excellent fire resistance and insulating properties.

FINISHES
The most common finishes for green materials are lime-based. Lime mortars and stuccos are considered greener than modern cement and gypsum-based stuccos because, although their manufacture gives off carbon dioxide, it is reabsorbed as the lime sets, making it a carbon-neutral product. Lime is also recyclable and biodegradable.

It is important to ascertain the type of mortar needed for green masonry blocks, mortars, or stuccos. Each application has its own strength requirements.

Non-hydraulic lime
This mortar is so called because it does not harden underwater. It is produced by heating a pure form of limestone to a very high temperature, burning off carbon dioxide and leaving quicklime. This is then mixed with rainwater to form lime putty—a process known as "slaking".

Lime putty
Left to mature for a number of months, lime putty is the raw material in stuccos and mortars that are completely lime-based. It is mixed with sand to create mortar.

Non-hydraulic hydrated lime
Sold in bagged powder form, this has had less water added to it during production than lime putty (see above). It is considered inferior to mature lime putty.

Hydraulic lime
This mortar is produced by heating up a less pure form of limestone than that used for non-hydraulic hydrated lime. The impurities found in the mix include materials such as clay.

Hydraulic lime
The manufacturing process for hydraulic lime means that it dries to a more hardened finish than non-hydraulic lime. It is breathable, but is much less flexible than non-hydraulic lime.

Additives
Sometimes small amounts of portland cement are added to lime, to hasten the setting processs. Purists do not do this, due to the possibility of segregation occuring as the mixture dries. Animal hair—typically horse or goat—can be added, as can modern, synthetic products. Minerals called pozzolans, which allow the mortar to harden quicker, are also used.

Horse hair
For stuccos, horse or goat hair may be introduced to the mix. This lessens the chances of cracking in mortar that is still drying, or mortar that is prone to flexing.

WORKING SAFELY
When mixing lime and water, be sure to add the lime to the water, and not the other way around. This is particularly important when making lime putty from quicklime, as there can be a risk of explosion. Lime is a skin, eye, and respiratory irritant, so wear protective clothing.

BUILDING BOARDS
The following examples are greener alternatives to the more conventional types of building board shown on pp.72–73. They are made from natural products, so they are eco-friendly and suited for use in conjunction with the other materials shown on these pages. All these products are 100-percent biodegradable, avoiding the disposal problems of drywall, which is often left in landfill.

Drywall alternatives

Clay board
The primary component of this board is clay, often bound together with reed and hessian. It offers a direct alternative to gypsum-based drywall. Clay board is heavier and thicker than drywall, and is best cut using a saw or jigsaw.

CLAY BOARD

Straw board
Manufactured from straw, and free of formaldehyde, straw board can be used for flooring, or wall applications.

STRAW BOARD

Reed board
This is a drywall alternative made from natural reeds laid side-by-side and bound together to form a rigid board structure.

Reed on a roll
A more flexible version of reed board, this is ideal for ceiling applications and walls on which the studwork may be undulating. This makes it ideal for use in restoration work on walls that have bowed over time.

REED BOARD

FLEXIBLE REED BOARD

WOODEN LATH
The forerunner to drywall, wooden laths are nailed to studwork and used as a base for the application of lime plaster. They are extremely eco-friendly as they are produced from a sustainable resource. Sweet chestnut and oak laths are typically handmade using traditional methods.

Production methods
Both sweet chestnut and oak laths have a rough key because they are made by hand. This makes them ideal for use on ceilings. In contrast, larch laths are machine-made and square-edged, which makes them better suited for use on walls.

SWEET CHESTNUT LATH

OAK LATH

LARCH LATH

REUSE AND RECLAMATION

When working on any project, consider where old materials may be reused. Lumber, and particularly structural lumber—the sort found in an old stud wall, for example—is usually suitable for reuse as long as it is sound. Sheet materials can be hard to reuse, however some regions require you to recycle drywall. Wooden sheet materials may also be cut to shapes that make them unsuitable for a future project.

VISITING RECLAMATION YARDS

Increasingly, many old and discarded items are becoming stylish centerpieces in modern renovations. As a result, reclamation yards are now big business and, while this means bargains are harder to come by, the increased competition has led to some stabilization of prices. Positive consequences of this expansion are greater choice and the potential to compare products in different yards. When visiting a reclamation yard, it often pays to go with an open mind as they are places where inspiration can strike. However, it is also important to be as certain as you can that the products you buy fulfill their specifications.

RECYCLING MATERIALS

Recycling building materials is not only very green, in some cases, it can be financially beneficial. The most notable example of this is the current enthusiasm for old metal fittings and fixtures, such as copper pipes, brass plumbing fittings, lead pipes, and flashings. All materials of this kind can be taken to scrap yards, where they are weighed and, from this measurement, a price is calculated. Although the price obviously varies, in the current market all these materials seem to be increasing in value. It is always best to take a sizeable pile of goods to the yard, as they may only pay for items over certain weights. Try to arrange the goods by type, as the more sorted the metal, the higher the price received—the price paid for a mixed load of metal will be far less than for metal that has already been sorted into different categories. Other goods that can be recycled, but are unlikely to fetch a price, are plastics such as PVC, rainwater goods, and wood. These can be taken to a recycling center. Remember that if you are carrying out major works, any rubble or building spoil could potentially be recycled directly as hardcore.

Copper pipe
Metal fittings and fixtures are prime recycling candidates.

▌▌ DE-NAILING LUMBER

Structural lumber that you take down—such as joists—may be used in a future project, as long as it has retained its structural integrity. In many cases, the only work required is the removal of a few nails.

A Use a pry bar for large nails, or a claw hammer for smaller nails, to prize them out of the surface of the wood.

B Older, rusted nails may snap off on removal. Use a hammer and punch to knock the broken shaft of the nail below the wood's surface.

▌▌ DE-ROTTING AN OLD BEAM WITH AN AXE

Old lumber often has areas of woodworm or rot. However, once the worst areas are removed, the remaining lumber is normally structurally very sound. The shapes produced can add great character to a project if beams are left exposed.

A An ax or hatchet is the ideal tool for cutting along the edge of old beams to remove woodworm or rot.

B Once the worst is removed, brush down and treat the wood to protect it and kill any woodworm. For green treatments, see p.294.

▌▌ REFURBISHING FLOORBOARDS

Old floorboards can break when lifted and, like other wood, are susceptible to infestation. Edges are especially prone to damage, so to make a board reusable you need to trim the edge back a little. Accuracy is required, so a circular saw or router is ideal.

A Use a straight cutter and guide, or clamp a furring strip to the plank to act as a guide for the router (for more on router use, see pp.66–67).

B Simply run the router along the edge, trimming a few fractions of an inch. Sanding will be required for a smooth finish.

▌▌ CLEANING BRICKS

After demolition, bricks may be reused, but in most cases they will need cleaning, as old mortar tends to stick to their surface. Soft mortar (lime-based) may scrape off with a trowel, but for persistent lumps, and cement-based mortars, a sledge hammer and bolster chisel will be required.

A Position the brick on a flat surface and gradually knock off the mortar. Be sure to wear protective gloves and goggles for this procedure.

B Wipe off any residue with a sponge and warm water, and you will be left with bricks that are now ready for reuse.

THE RECLAMATION INDUSTRY

Reclamation is big business and, with the increased interest in environmentalism, the industry has expanded significantly. You should bear in mind that approaching a reclamation yard from a buyer's perspective is very different to approaching it as a seller. It is certainly possible to sell goods to these yards, but you are unlikely to receive as high a price as you would selling to a private buyer.

Consequently, you should not be surprised to find similar items to yours being sold for much higher prices than you are being offered. Condition of goods is also very important for both a buyer and a seller; buyers should be aware that slightly damaged items tend to be competitively priced, and may be reasonably straightforward to repair. Keep an open mind, as you are unlikely to find exactly what you're looking for.

COMMON RECLAMATION-YARD ITEMS

Reclamation yards may have a specialty, or be more general in their stock, but it is always sensible to expect the unexpected. Most of the larger reclamation companies now have websites, but you would be well advised to inspect the goods before purchase wherever possible. The following categories of materials frequently appear in reclamation yards.

Category of materials	Example items	Comments
FLOORING	Tiles, flagstones, floorboards	All these items are subject to a reasonable amount of waste, such as split or damaged boards and chipped tiles. Adjust your quantity calculation requirements accordingly to compensate for this
FIREPLACES	Mantelpieces, complete fireplaces, hearths	When buying a complete fireplace, make sure all items are present. For period fireplaces, check that tiles are original and that they fit the surround. Look out for cracks or chips in stone components
STRUCTURAL MATERIALS	Bricks, natural stone, beams, joists	Condition and grade of stone or bricks is important—are there enough and are they suitable for your needs? Wooden items must be checked for condition, such as rot or insect infestation.
DECORATIVE MOULDINGS	Wooden paneling, handrails, balusters, decorative drywall	Condition must be thoroughly checked. Be certain of your size requirements. Reclaimed drywall is often very delicate and prone to damage
BATHROOM FURNITURE AND FITTINGS	Roll-top baths, basins, shower trays, faucets	These items may need lots of restoration, so think carefully before purchase. Faucets will almost certainly need new washers and a general overhaul to restore to good working order
COUNTERTOPS	Plastic laminate, Corian, granite	Check for damage and chipping. Buy larger than you need and cut down to a perfect fit.
DOORS AND WINDOWS	Internal doors, external doors, windows, door and window fittings	Check doors and windows are "square"—old doors are often warped. Stripped doors may also be loose at the joints. Check for rot. Make sure fittings already work or are repairable
PLUMBING ACCESSORIES	Radiators, towel rails	Bear in mind that valves may require changing. There will often be size-compatibility issues with new fittings. Radiators will require thorough flushing out and possibly sand-blasting
RAINWATER GOODS	Cast-iron guttering, downpipes, hoppers, outlets	Check general condition, as old cast-iron guttering cracks and rusts—both of which can put it beyond repair. Check for correct size of fittings and brackets for installation
GARDEN ARCHITECTURE	Capping and coping stones, ornamental stonework, paving slabs	Carry out general damage inspection, and check size variations. Different slab depths will make laying them much more difficult

ALTERATIONS AND REPAIRS

The illustrations shown here demonstrate the most common types of house structure. Variations often arise from architectural innovation, using new materials or using established materials in different ways. While wood frame walls are most common across Canada, masonry was historically used in the East. Today insulated concrete and even steel-stud construction are gaining popularity. Details for identification, construction, or repair of individual elements can be found in the relevant subsections.

LOADBEARING AND NON-LOADBEARING WALLS

The walls in any house can be divided into loadbearing or non-loadbearing. Loadbearing walls, as well as supporting their own weight, carry some of the load of other parts of the building, such as the roof and floors. Non-loadbearing walls support only their own weight, and are not structural components of the house. Always assume that all exterior walls are loadbearing (even though, in the majority of cases, it is only the internal leaf of a cavity wall that is loadbearing). It can be difficult to identify the other loadbearing walls in a house, but establishing whether a particular wall is loadbearing or not is vital when planning renovation work. The subject is discussed in more detail on pp.102–103.

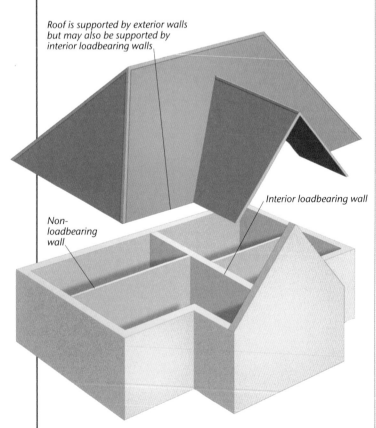

Roof is supported by exterior walls but may also be supported by interior loadbearing walls

Interior loadbearing wall

Non-loadbearing wall

Basic features of a house
Loadbearing walls transmit the weight of the roof and floors to the ground, while non-loadbearing walls act only as partitions. Foundations spread weight. Within these basic areas of construction there are many variations according to architectural preference and need.

TYPES OF CONSTRUCTION

Three main types of roof, four types of wall, and four types of foundation are shown here. They may be used in any combination so different foundations, walls, and roofs can appear together.

Types of foundation

Foundations are the supportive structures on which all houses are built. The type used depends on a property's age, local codes, and the type of ground on which it stands.

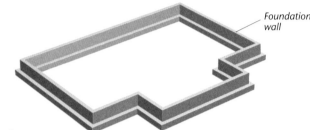

Foundation wall

Crawlspace
A crawlspace uses a footing below loacl frost depth with a foundatin wall that lifts the house high enough for easy access to ductwork and pipes and to keep siding free of snow accumulation. It is useful in damp areas and less expensive than a full basement.

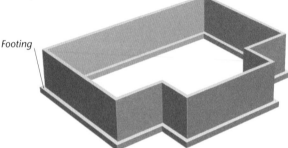

Footing

Basement
Basements are built the same way as crawlspaces but with taller foundation walls; the soil is excavated to the level of the footings. A concrete slab is poured over footings after the foundation is complete.

Ground level

Slab-on-grade
A concrete pad, reinforced with steel, covers the area on which the house sits. In some cases the edges of the slab, directly below the exterior walls, will be thicker than the rest of the slab. Modern slab foundations are well insulated.

Girder

Ground level

Pile

Pile and Girder
The walls are supported by a column of reinforced concrete, or steel, drilled into the ground. The depth and frequency of beams depend very much on the type of ground below the building, and the building size. Piles may also be required for internal loadbearing walls.

Types of wall

The four main types of house construction are generally defined by the way in which the exterior walls have been built. Much more detail about the many variations on these basic categories can be found over the next few pages.

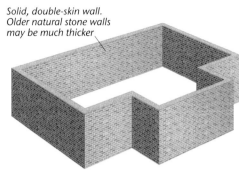

Solid, double-skin wall. Older natural stone walls may be much thicker

Traditional solid masonry

In Eastern Canada, older houses tend to have solid exterior walls. Internal loadbearing walls are usually also masonry, but may be wood. Ground floors may be concrete or suspended wood, and very old properties may have traditional floor coverings such as flagstones laid directly on a soil base. Upper floors are usually constructed of wood.

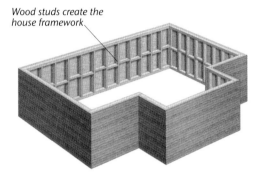

Wood studs create the house framework

Wood

Exterior walls are constructed of wood, and clad in vinyl, masonry, or wood. If the cladding is masonry, metal ties attach it to the internal wall face. Interior walls, whether loadbearing or not, are wood. Upper floors are wood, but the ground floor may be wood or concrete. For more on wooden-frame constructions, see pp.102–103.

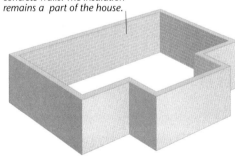

Insulated concrete form (ICF) houses use insulating foam structures as moulds for concrete walls. The insulation remains a part of the house.

Modern solid masonry

Some newer houses have solid exterior walls, often built with different materials to their traditional counterparts. Internal walls may be wood or masonry, or there may be some of each. Floors, on all levels, may be concrete or wood.

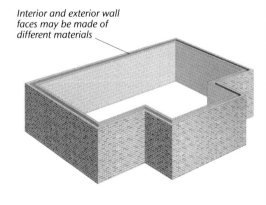

Interior and exterior wall faces may be made of different materials

Masonry with cavity

Exterior walls have an inner and an outer face, held together by metal ties with a cavity between them. They may be made of the same or different materials. Interior walls and floors may be masonry or wood.

Types of roof

Most roofs are angled to divert rainwater away from a house. The internal supporting frame is usually constructed of wood studs. The intersection between separate pitched roofs is achieved by forming valleys between each structure. Pitched roofs are commonly covered with asphalt shingles, although other materials are gaining popularity. Valleys require some form of flashing to create a waterproof seam. Flat roofs either slope to one side or to a central drain for rain run-off. They are always covered with continuous membranes, not shingles. See pp.198–207 for more information on roofs.

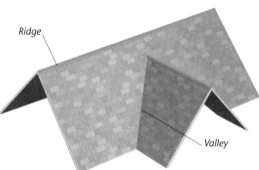

Ridge

Valley

Gable

The gable roof is characterized by the triangular wall shape formed where the pitched roof surfaces meet along an apex known as a ridge. This design creates a greater attic area than a comparable hipped roof design.

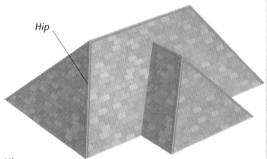

Hip

Hip

On a hipped roof, the gable is effectively cut back at ridge level to provide a triangular sloping roof. The angled ridge that joins this section with the main roof is called a hip.

Flat

A flat roof looks level, but has a slight pitch to allow water to run off the surface. This design is often used on ground-floor extensions, but may form the main roof structure for some houses.

ECO-HOUSE CONSTRUCTION

There are many different ways to build an eco-house, just as there are many different structures for most modern conventional houses. Determining which is the best (and greenest) option is a matter for debate, but architectural and personal preference, geographic location, current trends and, of course, cost all play an important part. Some of the most traditional materials and methods are outlined here, along with more recent developments.

AN UNGREEN MEANS TO A GREEN END

There is often a conflict of interest when it comes to determining what is and what isn't "green". While the structural elements of an eco-house may ultimately perform in an energy-efficient way, their initial production may involve the use of materials or techniques that are far from ecologically sound. A house constructed entirely from poured concrete, for example, with thick, well-insulated walls, is a green option in the long term. However, the initial outlay of energy to produce the concrete in the first place is high—and consequently very ungreen.

MIXING GREEN AND CONVENTIONAL MATERIALS

Building an entirely green house or renovating an existing structure to completely green specifications is rarely a practical option. Instead, it is more likely that a green solution is reached by combining green and conventional methods. When considering a green new-build, such as a straw-bale house for example (see pp.112–115), using a solid concrete foundation could be the best option because the risk of subsidence and egress of moisture is greatly reduced. Equally, with a renovation project, using thermally efficient walls for an extension will improve the green credentials of a house, even though much of the existing structure may be made from less green alternatives.

TYPES OF FOUNDATION

Many green homes are built on conventional foundations (see p.90), however it is possible to use less conventional methods. In Canada, protecting your foundation from frost damage is necessary and required by building codes. In order to use the two examples of green foundations shown below, you would either have to build on soil with high drainage capacity (sand, not clay), or insulate the perimeter of your foundation according to the Frost Protected Shallow Foundations specifications (FPSF).

Rammed earth
Rammed-earth foundations consist of compacted subsoil. For the rammed earth to form a solid base for the structure's walls, it needs to be contained within an effective mold. A modern example of a type of mold is shown here—the compacted earth is being contained within old car tires.

OVERVIEW OF A RAMMED-EARTH TIRE FOUNDATION

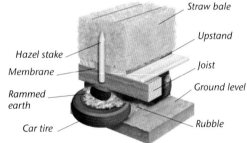

CROSS SECTION OF A RAMMED-EARTH TIRE FOUNDATION

Rubble foundations
In this example, a trench is filled with compacted rubble or stone. Some blockwork or natural stone is required above ground level to provide a solid base for the structure. Rubble foundations form an ideal base for a straw-bale home, as reinforced steel bars can be buried into the rubble for extra strength and support.

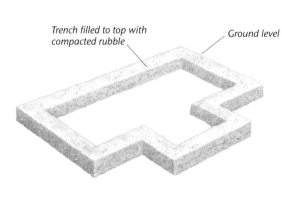

OVERVIEW OF A RUBBLE FOUNDATION

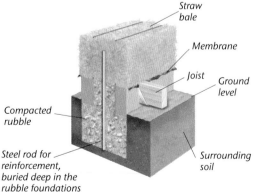

CROSS SECTION OF A RUBBLE FOUNDATION

TYPES OF ROOF

Most green roofs follow the same structural design as conventional roofs (see p.91), with the main difference being that any materials must be obtained from sustainable sources. Wood is the most common component and should be sourced from responsibly managed forests (see p.75). Equally, roof coverings must be green—wooden shingles are a green alternative to concrete tiles, and thatch is a material with excellent green credentials but potential fire code restrictions.

Green living roof

A green living roof is a truly "green" option as the covered surface consists of plant matter. A living roof offers good insulation, retains a high percentage of rainwater (reducing stormwater run-off), and provides a habitat for wildlife. However, the main roof structure must be strong enough to support its weight—a key concern, especially if considering a retrospective fit.

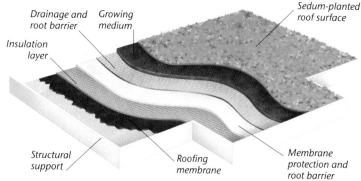

Drainage and root barrier · Growing medium · Sedum-planted roof surface · Insulation layer · Structural support · Roofing membrane · Membrane protection and root barrier

Extensive green living roof
A green living roof may be described as "extensive" (see diagram above) or "intensive". An extensive roof is typically planted with sedum, which requires a low-level of maintenance for use on often inaccessible roofs. An intensive roof is similar in nature to a roof garden: it has good access and a greater variety of plants. Higher maintenance, however, is usually required. All green roofs must be weeded to eliminate plant varieties that can penetrate the roof membrane.

TYPES OF WALLS

A green structure must score highly in terms of sustainability and performance—the materials should come from a sustainable source and the building should be well-insulated. Some conventional structures (see p.91), such as modern timber-framed houses, can be considered green as long as they conform to these principles. The alternative methods described below, however, arguably come closest to the ideal of a truly green construction.

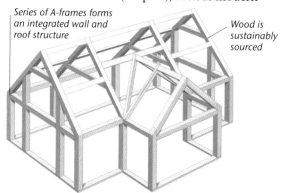

Series of A-frames forms an integrated wall and roof structure · Wood is sustainably sourced

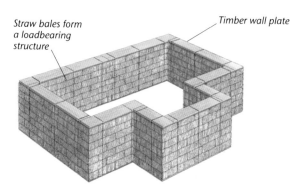

Straw bales form a loadbearing structure · Timber wall plate

Wood—post and beam
Large wooden timbers are used to create the loadbearing structure of the house. Wooden post and beam differs from a conventional timber-framed house in that the size of the timbers often means they form an integral part of the aesthetic finish of the house, and may be visible from the inside, outside, or both. Straw bales may be used as infill (see right).

Straw bale
Bales can be used as either loadbearing blocks or infill for a timber-framed house (see left). Although straw-bale constructions have been built around the globe, climate is an important consideration as it is vital that water is kept out of the structure. Straw bales are a perfect example of what is essentially a waste product being used in major construction.

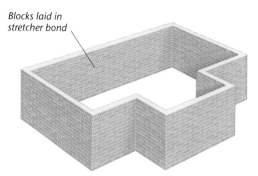

Blocks laid in stretcher bond

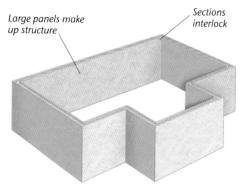

Large panels make up structure · Sections interlock

Earth block
After wood, earth- or soil-based structures make up the next biggest category of green structures. Compressed soil, usually in the form of blocks, is used to build the structural walls of the home. Although modern building standards question the integrity of such structures, history has shown that they can easily withstand a variety of climates.

Structural insulated panel
This type of eco-house construction is an example of green building at its most developed. Highly efficient insulation is integrated into building boards to form large panels. These panels can then be clipped together in a custom-made design. Structural insulated panels may be used to form the roof structure as well as the walls of a house.

Ceilings and walls

THE WALLS AND CEILINGS OF A HOUSE ARE SOME OF ITS MOST IMPORTANT STRUCTURAL ELEMENTS, BUT ALSO OFFER CONSIDERABLE SCOPE FOR CREATIVITY. THE PAGES IN THIS SECTION WILL HELP YOU UNDERSTAND THE STRUCTURE OF CEILINGS AND WALLS, SO THAT YOU CAN WORK OUT WHICH OPTIONS ARE MOST SUITABLE WHEN UNDERTAKING REPAIR OR RENOVATION WORK.

TYPES OF CONSTRUCTION

A knowledge of how ceilings and walls are put together is important to fully understand the structure of your home. In the most general terms, ceilings usually have a wood-frame structure. Walls are either cavity or single-skin, and may be loadbearing or non-loadbearing. In addition, there is a variety of ways that ceilings and walls may be finished, and there are different combinations of materials that can be used to achieve these finishes.

CEILING COMPONENTS
The illustrations opposite demonstrate the basic structures of frame and concrete ceilings. Beneath these are shown the typical finishes used on their lower surfaces. Frame ceilings are traditional but still widely used. A framework of frame joists provides support for the floor above, and a surface for attachment of the ceiling finish below. Concrete ceilings can take a variety of forms. They are more often found in modern buildings, and their popularity has grown with the general use of concrete in the building industry.

Insulation and finishes
A wide range of materials can be used in finishing either a ceiling or wall—drywall can vary in thickness and density, and can also be purchased with useful retardant properties to make the surface more resilient, or to adhere to building and safety regulations. Different types of drywall are explained on p.72. Insulation is not shown in the illustrations here or overleaf, for reasons of clarity. However, in reality, many ceilings and walls will incorporate insulation. Choices and types of insulation are covered in detail on pp.356–365.

UNDERSTANDING BEAMS AND JOISTS
Beams and joists are not the same—beams support joists. Traditionally, they are made of wood, but modern types are often made of steel, and are known as "I-beams". Rolled steel joists are also available. Wooden beams are often left uncovered to form part of a room's decorative aspect, although they can be clad with drywall. Old beams may even be found beneath lath and plaster.

I-beams are usually boxed in with drywall and then finished. To provide securing points for drywall, blocking (small vertical lengths of wood) is installed inside an I-beam. Lintels and headers look similar to beams, but perform a different function: they support the weight of a wall above an opening such as a window or door. They come in many materials and strengths, designed for a variety of uses.

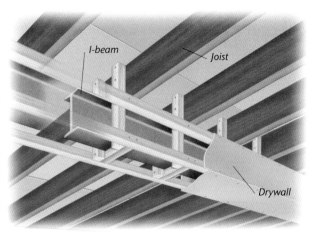

Boxing in a beam
Beams are frequently enclosed and hidden behind a finish, but a little knowledge of basic house construction should allow you to locate them. A traditional method of boxing in is shown here, but it is also possible to use acoustical panels and clips. Ceilings are usually installed flush with the lower surface of the beams.

FRAME CEILING

Frame ceiling and finishes
The type of wood and dimensions of joists will depend on the size of the ceiling and its function—ceilings with a floor above must be more substantial. Blocking at right angles to the joists can connect them to increase rigidity.

Drywall and plaster
Sheets of drywall are screwed directly to the joists, the joints are taped, and the whole surface is covered with finishing plaster (see pp.136–137).

Tape *Fastener hole*

Drywall
The most common system used in the US is drywall. The joints between sheets are taped; fastener holes and joints are then filled with joint compound and sanded smooth (see pp.132–134).

Wooden cladding
Boards are attached directly to the joists, at right angles to them, to give this wooden ceiling finish.

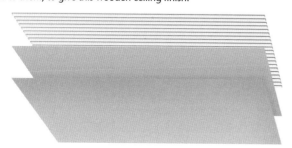

Lath and plaster
This is an old-fashioned construction. Thin, wooden laths sit closely together beneath the joists, and at right angles to them, and are covered with traditional lime plaster.

CONCRETE CEILING

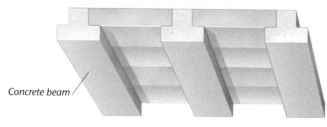

Concrete beam

Concrete ceiling and finishes
There are several ways of using concrete to create a ceiling, but this beam-and-block structure is a common system.

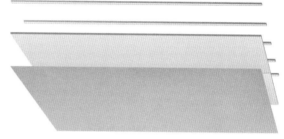

Furring strips, drywall, and plaster
Furring strips are attached to the concrete; boards are attached to the furring strips. Joints are taped, and the whole surface plastered.

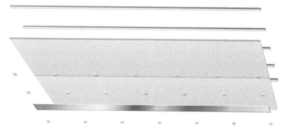

Furring strips and drywall
Board is attached to a furring strip framework, and then treated like drywall (see left).   *Channel*

Metal channels, drywall, and plaster
In this case, metal channels perform the same function as the furring strips in the previous example, plus sound attenuation.

Metal channels and drywall
Again, the channels perform the role of furring strips. The drywall is then finished for decoration.

Most homes in Canada are constructed from wood frames. Even if a house has masonry on the outside, its structure may be wood, as illustrated below.

Exterior walls

Exterior walls all have an internal layer made of wood, and an external cladding layer of siding material. There is a cavity between the two layers. The external face of the wood frame is covered with plywood sheathing for extra strength and rigidity. Building paper or house wrap is required over the sheathing.

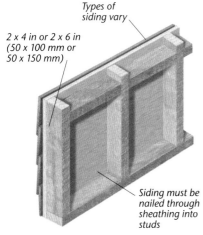

Types of siding vary

2 x 4 in or 2 x 6 in (50 x 100 mm or 50 x 150 mm)

Siding must be nailed through sheathing into studs

Wooden siding
The wooden shakes or shingles are nailed to the external face. Some are made with interlocking edges.

Wall ties connect inner and outer leaf

Typically, studs are placed at 16-in (405-mm) intervals

Framework is normally insulated

Vinyl or aluminum siding
Sheathing is first covered in strips of building paper. Then vinyl or aluminum siding is nailed to the studs starting from the bottom up.

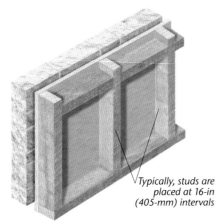

Stone
An exterior layer of natural stone is laid over the foundation and attached to the wall using metal ties.

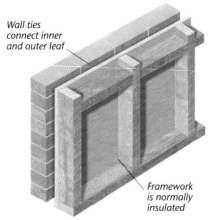

Brick
The inside wood frame is covered on one or more external faces with a layer of brick and installed with a similar method as stone veneer.

Interior walls

These are the walls that create rooms. They may be filled with insulation to dampen sound, and may be loadbearing or non-loadbearing. Stud walls are a good choice in a renovation project because they are straightforward to construct. For more information, see pp.102–107.

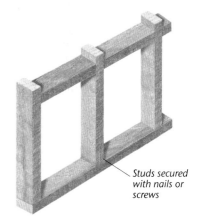

Studs secured with nails or screws

Stud wall
This is an easy-to-make partition consisting of a wood framework that can take any of the finishes listed below.

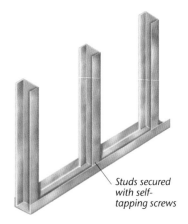

Studs secured with self-tapping screws

Metal stud wall
This modern variation of the stud wall uses metal channels instead of lumber studs to form the framework.

WOODEN WALL FINISHES

All of these finishes can be used on the interior face of an exterior wall, or on either side of an internal wall. They all need a decorative layer such as paint or wallpaper, or in the case of wood siding, perhaps a natural wood finish.

Drywall
Taper-edged drywall is used to cover the frame. The joints are then taped and filled with joint compound to create a smooth surface for decoration (see pp.132–133).

Lath and plaster
In this traditional wall covering, wooden laths (narrow strips of wood) are attached to the wooden wall frame. They are then covered with several coats of lime plaster.

Plastered drywall
Straight-edged drywall is attached to the wooden frame. Joints are taped and filled with joint compound, and the surface is plastered (see pp.132–133 and 136–137).

Wooden paneling
Panels, often in board form, are attached directly to the frame. Stone is tongue-and-groove. Depending on the material used, it may or may not need decoration after installing.

Dry partition drywall
Drywall panels are secured between studs. The finish depends on whether the panels have tapered or non-tapered edges. Dry partition walls are non-loadbearing.

MASONRY WALLS

Masonry houses have block, stone, or brick as the structure for the house. While living spaces with block walls have finished interiors, garages and outbuildings may have unfinished walls.

Exterior masonry walls

These are usually made up of two layers of masonry. The two layers of a cavity wall are held together by metal wall ties. The cavity may contain insulation and a vapor barrier.

Solid brick
The internal and external layers are made of brick, with no cavity between the layers of masonry.

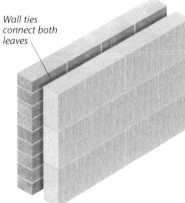

Wall ties connect both leaves

Brick and block with cavity
The external brick layer provides the finished exterior look. The internal layer is of blocks, and requires a finish (see right).

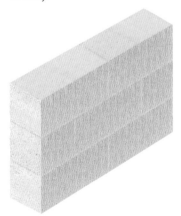

Solid block
A modern construction that uses thick, thermally efficient blocks to create a solid wall.

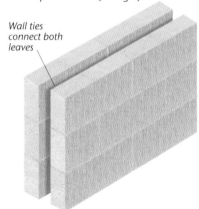

Wall ties connect both leaves

Block and block with cavity
Both layers are made of modern blocks, so both the interior and exterior faces need finishing (see right for finishes).

Solid stone
This may use one or two layers of stone – the space between layers is often filled with broken stone and mortar. Sometimes the external face is stone and the internal brick.

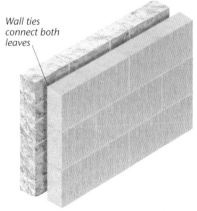

Wall ties connect both leaves

Stone and block with cavity
An external layer of natural stone provides the finished look, while the internal layer is of blocks that need finishing (see right).

Interior masonry walls

These are the walls inside a building, dividing it into rooms. They may be loadbearing or non-loadbearing.

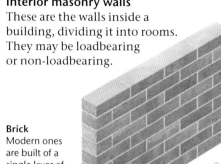

Brick
Modern ones are built of a single layer of bricks, though older ones may have two layers.

Block
A modern wall will be one layer, but an older one may be made of several layers of stone blocks.

MASONRY FINISHES

Any of these finishes can go on any masonry wall, whether it is the internal layer of an exterior wall or either side of an interior wall.

Render and plaster
A coat of render or undercoat is covered with a layer of finishing plaster to give a smooth wall surface (see pp.136–137) – getting this right requires considerable skill.

Drywall
Taper-edged drywall can be attached to a wall. The seam between the boards is taped, and filled with a filling compound (joint compound) (see pp.132–133). The compound is applied in three layers before being sanded smooth with the surrounding drywall surface. The whole wall surface is then ready for further decoration. The drywall may be attached to the wall with screws (see p.128).

Plastered drywall
Straight-edged drywall can be attached to a wall, with the joints between boards taped with joint compound, and then plastered over. The drywall may be attached to the masonry using dabs of adhesive, with a wood furring-strip frame, or using metal channels (see p.128). This avoids the need for render or undercoat, but still demands great skill in plastering to achieve the top layer.

Wooden siding
A frame of wooden battens can be attached to the masonry, forming a base for the attachment of wooden panels.

GREEN WALL CONSTRUCTION

The following pages deal with wall structure in its greenest form, although it is worth bearing in mind that, with proper insulation, the more conventional wall structures shown on pp.96–97 are generally thermally efficient. Consequently, these pages focus on environmentally friendly methods of manufacture, sustainability, and biodegradability, all of which increase a wall's green credentials. The principal types of green wall construction are shown below.

BENEFITS OF STRAW BALES

Straw bales, a waste product of the food production process, can be used to build a green and cost-effective wall. An 18-in (450 mm) thick bale has an R-value that can vary from R-18 (RSI-3.2) to R-43 (RSI-7.5) depending on density and moisture content. In comparison, uninsulated masonry walls have an R-value of about R-1 (RSI-0.2). The simplicity with which bales can be cut and molded into shapes makes them a usefully flexible material. Rendering will leave them as fireproof as most wooden structures, while their compactness, and the lack of any viable food supply, make it difficult for vermin to flourish in the structure.

TRADITIONAL GREEN WALL STRUCTURE

These structures return to the basics of material use; despite their simplicity, however, there is plenty of evidence to suggest that these building techniques are successful. The materials used in these constructions tend to occur naturally, dispensing with energy-hungry manufacturing processes.

STRAW-BALE WALL STRUCTURE

Straw-bale wall structures are a development of traditional techniques (see left). They do, however, still use natural materials as the main part of the wall, with very few man-made components. There are different techniques of construction, with the two main types shown here, although hybrids of these examples do exist.

Compressed earth
Also known as adobe, blocks are laid in rows, and bonded together in a stretcher bond (running bond) with mortar constructed of a slurry mix made from the basic block material.

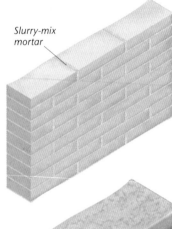

Slurry-mix mortar

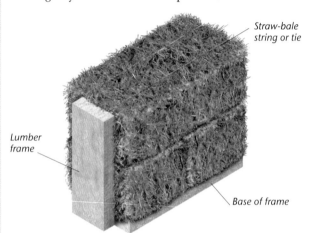

Straw-bale string or tie

Lumber frame

Base of frame

Rammed earth
Rammed earth differs from the compressed block (above) in that formwork is used to create a mold for the wall. Therefore, the wall is effectively a continuous mud form.

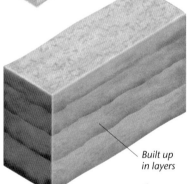

Built up in layers

Straw bale—post-and-beam structure
In this structure, straw is used to fill a loadbearing wooden frame. The frame is traditionally a post-and-beam structure, although modern alternatives include engineered-wood and planed-timber.

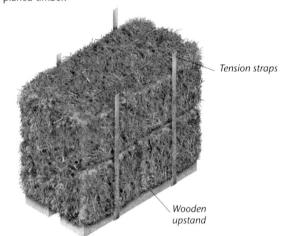

Tension straps

Wooden upstand

Cob
With a cob wall, earth is mixed with a binding product, such as straw, and is piled and molded into a wall structure. These walls are typically much wider at the base than the top.

Wider base

Straw bale—Nebraskan
In this method, the straw itself is used as the loadbearing material and supports the roof. Metal or wooden bars are used to lend the wall solidity.

INTERIOR WALLS

The interior walls of an eco-friendly home may be constructed using similar materials to the exterior walls or—as with conventional building—alternatives can be used. For example, a solid masonry house construction may have interior metal-framed stud walls, while a straw-bale house may have internal walls constructed from wooden studwork. The choice often rests on the creation of as much interior space as possible. Some straw-bale houses do have interior straw-bale walls, but greater space can be achieved with much thinner stud walling. For interior walls, straw bales can also be positioned on their edges to provide more space.

MODERN GREEN WALL STRUCTURE

The theory behind traditional green walls has been technologically modernized, meaning that these ancient techniques are now in commercial production. In most examples, the source material is exactly the same, but there are some examples of recycled materials being used to create green blocks that are then built up in much the same way as their more ancient equivalents.

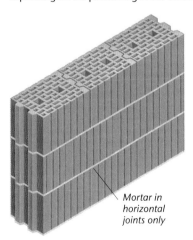

Recycled block
Most closely related to a compressed earth or adobe block (see opposite), these are laid in much the same way, using a running bond, and may be loadbearing or not depending on the positioning of the block.

Lime mortar

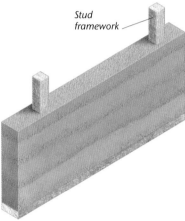

Stud framework

Green infill
Materials such as hemp are used to fill a wooden frame. Similar to a post-and-beam straw-bale structure (see opposite), the hemp may be in block form or cast in a similar way to rammed earth (see opposite).

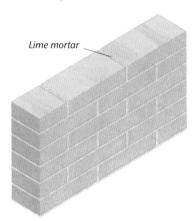

Mortar in horizontal joints only

Aerated clay block
A thin-bed mortar system is used, but only horizontally. The vertical joints interlock, which makes construction very straightforward.

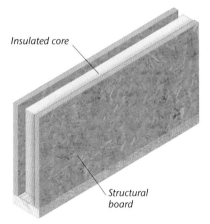

Insulated core

Structural board

Structural Insulated Panel (SIP)
This is a modern construction that uses large manufactured panels to create the wall. Insulating material is compressed between two building boards to create a thermally efficient structure. Some panel systems are made of very green components, such as compressed straw.

WALL FINISHES

The organic nature of green wall construction means it is important that any interior or exterior finish allows moisture to dry out through the wall surface. Exterior coverings are most important, as they protect the structure from the elements. Lime products usually make up the main constituent of these stuccos or plasters (see p.85).

Applying lime finish
A three-coat system of lime stucco or plaster is normally sufficient, and should be applied in the following manner:

■ Apply an initial coat (the "scratch coat") roughly ⅜in (10mm) in depth. For the technique for scratching the surface, see p.133. Leave the scratch coat to dry for 2–3 days, then wet it in preparation for applying the next coat (the "float coat"). If hair is added to the mix, a longer drying time is required—especially on internal walls, which may need 4–5 days.

■ The float coat (made from the same mix as the scratch coat but with no hair added) should be slightly thinner than the scratch coat, and should provide a more even surface. Do not scratch the float coat. Leave exterior walls to dry for another 2–3 days, or interior walls for 4–5 days, before applying the top coat.

■ Always dampen the float coat before applying the top coat. Top-coat stucco should consist of lime putty mixed with very fine sand, rather than the coarser sand commonly used for stucco and interior scratch coats.

■ When applying the putty, ascertain the suction properties of the background wall—very dry block surfaces should be wetted before stucco is applied. In the case of some rough surfaces, such as straw, it may be best to press the scratch-coat stucco on by hand (wearing gloves), as traditional plastering floats can be difficult to use on such surfaces.

Scratch coat

Float coat

Top coat

Lime layers
For most finishes, three layers are standard, but on interior walls, the top coat may in fact be two thin coats. Some manufacturers may also have their own ready-mixed systems, which involve ready-mixed base coats and finishing coats.

ALTERATIONS AND REPAIRS

ALTERING A CEILING

You may wish to create space to run HVAC, reposition an attic hatch, or replace an old ceiling that has become distorted and unsightly. Three ways of replacing a ceiling are shown here. The method chosen depends on your particular needs and preferences. Do not plan any change without considering its structural consequences—a structural engineer can advise on whether a bowed ceiling should be completely replaced, joists and all, for instance. You may take the opportunity, while redoing a ceiling, to add insulation or soundproofing (see pp.356–367). Also plan for later decoration (see pp.372–311).

THINGS TO CONSIDER
■ Remember to use a detector to check whether there are any pipes or wires beneath a surface before inserting any nails or screws.
■ For wood-frame homes, you need to find the joists so that you can screw into them. Do not attach directly to drywall.
■ If you are lowering a ceiling that features a light fixture or fan, simply remove the fixture, extend the wire, and reattach the fixture as shown on pp.448–451.

CUTTING AN ATTIC HATCH

Attic access is important for inspection purposes as well as storage. If you need to make a new hatch, perhaps because your property does not have one, or because alterations mean it needs to be relocated, consider how you wish to use it, as well as the safety aspects.

Positioning the access hole

Consider the angle at which a ladder will extend through the opening, if relevant, and if it will have room to fold or slide into the attic space. Make sure there will be headroom in the attic, and do not position the hatch too close to a staircase. If possible, cut into only one joist to make the opening, because the cuts weaken the structure.

Installing a hatch and ladder

The design of the hatch itself will depend on whether you wish to use a disappearing stair. If you will access the attic via a stepladder, use a simple hatch resting on a section of doorstop. If a disappearing stair is to be installed, you may need a hinged door; check the specifications for the hatch and ladder. Install according to the manufacturer's instructions.

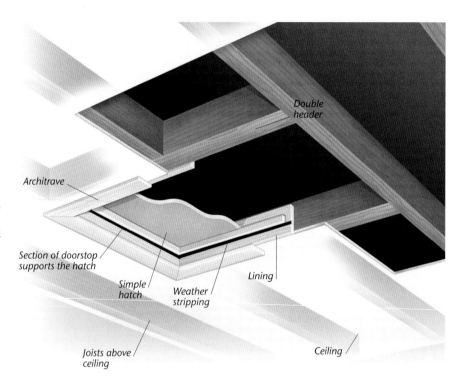

A simple attic hatch
This method cuts only one joist, to minimize structural weakening. The attic is accessed with a stepladder, and the hatch rests on a ledge.

REPLACING A LATH-AND-PLASTER CEILING

If you live in a home that is more than 60 years old, you may have a plaster ceiling. You can either replace it, as described here, or choose one of the options opposite (see pp.122–139 for drywall options, and pp.272–311 on decorating). Removing a ceiling creates a lot of dust and debris, so wear protective clothing, including a respiratory mask (a simple dust mask is not sufficient).

Removing the ceiling

Use a hammer to break away some of the plaster, and then pull away chunks by hand or with a pry bar, working your way across the ceiling. Once all the plaster is cleared, pry out any remaining nails or screws from joists with a claw hammer or pry bar. Then inspect the joists to see if they are in sound condition before applying drywall.

REROUTING WIRES AND PIPES

Any services that run through a ceiling need to be protected from damage and supported while the ceiling is removed. They may need to be rerouted to suit your new ceiling, but you may be unable to plan this very far in advance.

Locating services for re-routing

Switch off the electricity supply at the panel and water supply. Use a detector to locate pipes and wires, or cut a small inspection hatch and look inside the ceiling to see where services run. When removing a ceiling, proceed carefully—removal may expose some services that you hadn't previously found. Support all pipes and wires. Once the ceiling is gone and all services are clearly visible, work out the best way of dealing with them in accordance with your plans for the new ceiling and its fixtures.

LOWERING A CEILING

One way of replacing an unsightly ceiling is to create a new one below the old ceiling. This avoids the mess involved in removing an old ceiling.

Technique

Using a level, draw guide lines on the walls for the new ceiling. Attach 2 x 4s along these lines, and attach joist hangers to two of these wall ledgers. Screw joists into the hangers. Attach blocking (strengthening the wood) between joists, to provide attachment points for drywall. A large span will need more blocking than a narrower span. Then attach drywall to the joists (see pp.126–127).

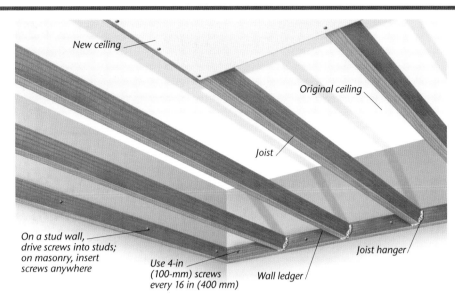

New ceiling

Original ceiling

Joist

On a stud wall, drive screws into studs; on masonry, insert screws anywhere

Use 4-in (100-mm) screws every 16 in (400 mm)

Wall ledger

Joist hanger

A LOWERED CEILING

LEVELLING A CEILING WITH METAL CHANNELS

If joists sag slightly, but not enough to be replaced, achieve a level ceiling by removing the old one, and attaching a metal frame to the exposed joists. Then cover it with drywall.

Technique

Mark guide lines on the wall at the height that you want the ceiling, as described above (Lowering a Ceiling). Attach wall channels along the guide lines, then attach brackets to the joists, at intervals of 16 in (400 mm) for 8-x-4-ft (2.4-x-1.2-m) boards. Attach channels to the brackets, and then apply drywall to the channels as shown on pp.126–127.

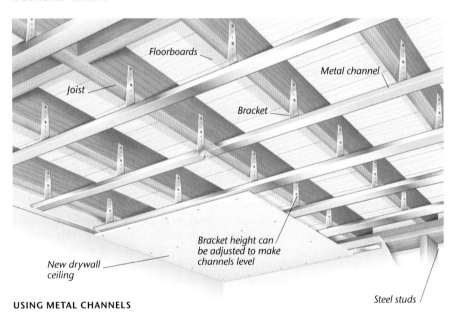

Floorboards

Metal channel

Joist

Bracket

Bracket height can be adjusted to make channels level

New drywall ceiling

Steel studs

USING METAL CHANNELS

ADDING A SUSPENDED CEILING

This gives a different look from other ceilings, and offers other options for lighting, as well as acoustic and thermal insulation. It involves hanging a wooden or metal grid from the ceiling, and filling it with panels.

Planning and technique

The grid may not fit exactly, so you may have to cut panels to fit around the edges. Work out the best position for the ceiling to keep even cuts on all sides. Mark a guide line on the walls (see Lowering a Ceiling, above). Attach wall angles, and insert tees (the main channels) and cross tees. Suspend tees from the ceiling above using wires that can be adjusted to keep the framework level. Then insert panels.

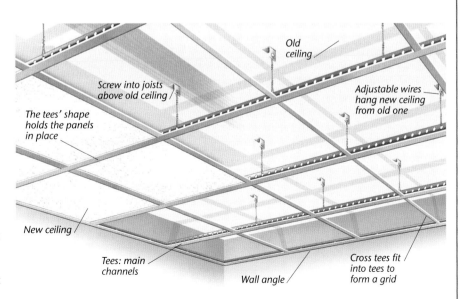

Old ceiling

Screw into joists above old ceiling

Adjustable wires hang new ceiling from old one

The tees' shape holds the panels in place

New ceiling

Tees: main channels

Wall angle

Cross tees fit into tees to form a grid

A SUSPENDED CEILING

PLANNING A NON-BEARING STUD WALL

A stud wall is the most common way to divide a room. Its framework is constructed of wood or metal studs strengthened by horizontal lengths (blocking) attached between them. Wires, pipes, and blanket insulation can sit within the cavity between the drywall sheets, which cover both sides of the frame. The wall can be plastered or drywalled (see pp.122–139) and decorated as normal.

FIRST THINGS TO CONSIDER

Even a minor internal alteration may need planning permission. When planning a stud wall, check the regulations governing lighting, ventilation, and electrical circuits, and get any necessary permits before starting work.

If you need water or electricity in your new room, locate existing pipes and circuits. Work out where appliances such as radiators or sinks should go, so that pipes or wiring are sited where you need them (see pp.466–467 and 432–433).

CHOOSING DRYWALL AND LUMBER

Choosing drywall
Decide how the wall is to be finished, and choose board that is suitable for your plans (see pp.72–73). Standard drywall is available in sheets of 4 x 8 ft (122 x 244 cm) in size. Seams should not be centered on the wall, and should be staggered. The point is to have as few seams as possible. So, lay a panel to the left of the door with a seam off-centered above the door, and then two horizontal pieces to the right of the door. Then, there are just two seams to finish. Place the boards against the ceiling and leave a small gap at the floor, to be hidden by the baseboard.

Drywall sheets
Larger sheets cover a wall quickly but are harder to carry and position.

How much drywall to buy
1. Calculate the wall's area: multiply its height by its width.
2. Divide this by the area of one sheet of your chosen drywall to find out how many sheets to buy. The result will not be exact and, depending on how many cuts you need to make, you may need to buy a little extra to cover the wall, because board edges need to run down the centers of studs, so that hardware can be inserted into the studs.

Choosing lumber
Choose framing lumber (2 x 4 ft or 2 x 6 ft/61 x 122 cm or 61 x 183 cm). Check that the wood you buy is not misshapen: straight lengths are easier to work with, and drywall is easier to attach to straight pieces. See pp.74–75 for more on wood.

How much lumber to buy
Measure the length of each stud, plate, and blocking, and add these together for a total length. Remember that wood lengths will not divide exactly into the lengths that you need.

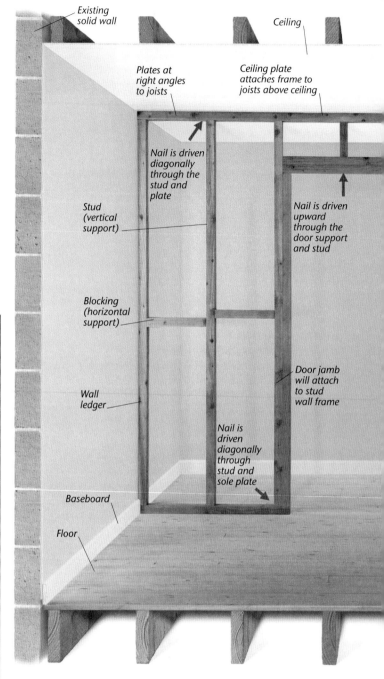

Existing solid wall

Ceiling

Plates at right angles to joists

Ceiling plate attaches frame to joists above ceiling

Nail is driven diagonally through the stud and plate

Nail is driven upward through the door support and stud

Stud (vertical support)

Blocking (horizontal support)

Door jamb will attach to stud wall frame

Wall ledger

Nail is driven diagonally through stud and sole plate

Baseboard

Floor

SECURING THE FRAME TO AN EXISTING WALL

A stud wall must be stable. Securing it to a masonry wall is possible at any point, but with a wooden wall, it is best if it can be secured directly to a stud. Use a stud detector to find the stud nearest to your ideal location. However, if you need to put a wall between studs, place screws at top and bottom, into the ceiling and sole plates, and into the central blocking as well.

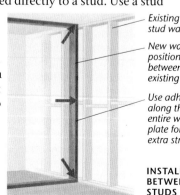

Existing stud wall

New wall position between two existing studs

Use adhesive along the entire wall plate for extra strength

INSTALLING BETWEEN STUDS

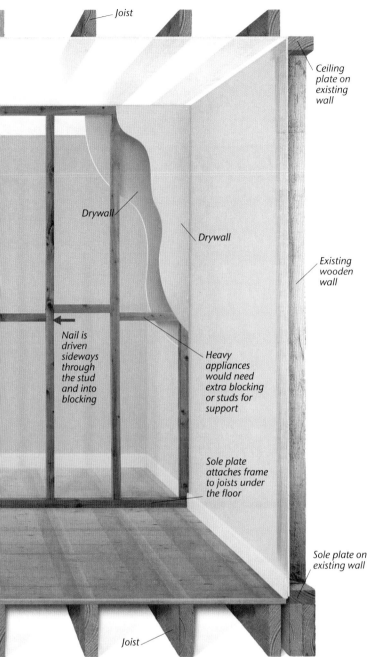

Joist

Ceiling plate on existing wall

Drywall

Drywall

Existing wooden wall

Nail is driven sideways through the stud and into blocking

Heavy appliances would need extra blocking or studs for support

Sole plate attaches frame to joists under the floor

Sole plate on existing wall

Joist

TURNING A CORNER

A corner is two walls butt-joined. However, on one wall, an extra stud is added close to the corner. This provides strength, and is the securing point for drywall on the inside of the corner, because the main stud is inaccessible from that side. Ensure that the corner forms a precise right angle. Site all sole plates on, or at a right angle to, joists.

SECURING THE FRAME TO THE FLOOR AND CEILING

Ideally, plates should cross joists (as shown above). If they run in the same direction, try to build the wall on a floor joist. There may not be a ceiling joist aligned with this, but the ceiling plate must attach to a solid fixture, not just to drywall. If you can't secure it to a joist, add blocking every 2 ft (600 mm) between two joists. Secure the ceiling plate to these. If the wall is not sitting on a joist, this blocking method can be used for support and nailing under the floor.

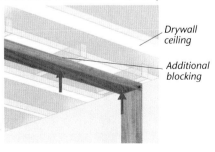

Drywall ceiling

Additional blocking

ATTACHING CEILING PLATE TO SUPPORT BLOCKING

PLANNING A METAL STUD WALL

Metal is a modern alternative to wooden studs. Systems differ between manufacturers, but the basics are the same: metal channels and sectional pieces slot together to form a frame. Metal studs may be thinner than wooden ones, but they are just as strong. Preparation and layout for a metal stud wall is the same as for a wooden one. Drywall is screwed onto the metal channels, in the same way as it attaches to wood. See pp.106–107 for the steps needed to build a metal stud wall.

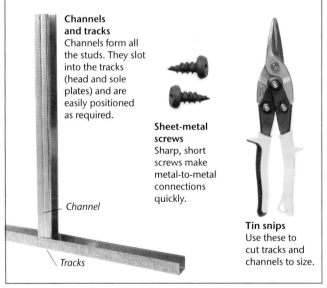

Channels and tracks
Channels form all the studs. They slot into the tracks (head and sole plates) and are easily positioned as required.

Sheet-metal screws
Sharp, short screws make metal-to-metal connections quickly.

Channel

Tracks

Tin snips
Use these to cut tracks and channels to size.

TOOLS AND MATERIALS CHECKLIST PP.94–97

Building a stud wall
(pp.104–105) Plumb line or level and chalk, try square, pry bar*

Building a metal stud wall
(p.106–107) Tin snips, lengths of lumber, level

* = optional

FOR BASIC TOOLKIT
SEE PP.24–25

NON-LOADBEARING STUD WALLS

Before you start, you need to decide where you will position your partition wall (see pp.102–103). The technique shown here uses guide lines to mark where the centers of studs will sit. If you want them to mark the edges, draw them to one side of the joists or studs into which you will drive nails or screws. If your stud wall is to have a doorway, lay a full sole plate as shown, and later cut away a section of it to make the doorway (see step 5A). You may need somebody to hold the ceiling plate in position while you fasten it in place.

TOOLS AND MATERIALS SEE BASIC TOOLKIT AND P.103

1 LAYOUT

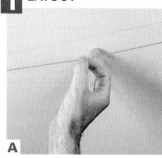

A

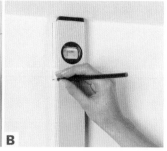

B

Snap a chalk line across the ceiling (see p.41 for technique) to mark either the center or one edge of the ceiling plate's position. Remove the chalk line.

At one end of the ceiling line, use a long level and a pencil to draw a line on the wall, all the way up from the floor. Repeat on the other wall.

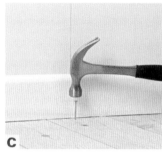

C

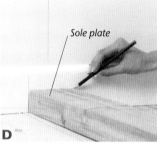

D

Sole plate

Drive a nail into the floor at the base of each wall guide line. Attach and snap a chalk line across the floor to draw a guide line.

Where the wall guide lines meet the floor, mark a section of baseboard on each wall equal to the width of the sole plate.

2 INSTALLING THE FLOOR PLATE

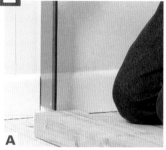

A

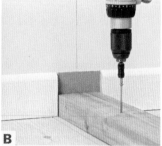

B

Cut away the marked sections of baseboard on both walls, taking care to saw accurate vertical lines. Pry the waste sections away from the wall with a pry bar if they stick.

Cut the sole plate to fit across the room where the baseboard has been removed. Position it along its guide line, and secure it to the floor.

AN ALTERNATIVE TO CUTTING BASEBOARD

Baseboard stays in place — *Notch*

A

B

Notch to lap over the baseboard

C

D

Mark a notch (area to be cut away) on the wall plate so that it will sit over the baseboard and lie flush on the wall.

With the wall-facing side upward, saw along the guide line to the depth marked by the pencil lines on the edges.

Use a bevel-edged chisel and a hammer to remove chunks of wood, working down to the depth required.

Position the plate against the wall and secure as normal.

NAILING A STUD WALL TO A CONCRETE FLOOR

A

B

Use a masonry drill bit to drill through the sole plate and into the concrete floor. This will guide your fasteners into place.

Use hammer-in fasteners (see p.77) through the drilled holes to fasten the sole plate securely into place.

3 INSTALLING OTHER PLATES AND TRIMMER STUDS

Cut the ceiling plate to length. Position it along the guide line, centered along it if necessary, and secure it to the ceiling. This will be easier if two people work together. Cut the wall plates to length and secure them to the walls.

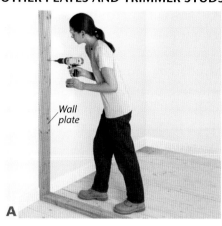

Wall plate

A

Mark the door position on the sole plate, allowing for the door plus its jamb. Mark positions for other studs, usually 16 or 24 in (405 or 610 mm) on center.

B

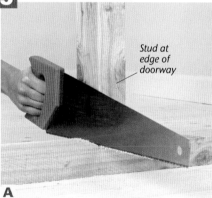

C

Cut and position a stud on one side of the doorway, using a level to keep it vertical and securing it as shown in the next step.

D

Keeping the stud vertical, secure it to the ceiling and sole plates with 3-in (70-mm) nails inserted diagonally. Nail two or three nails this way at the top and bottom of every stud.

4 INSTALLING THE DOOR HEAD

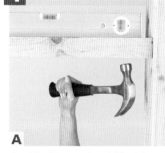

A

B

Cut blocking to the width of the doorway plus ½ in (12 mm). Secure to the door studs at height required for top of door jamb, using a level to make sure it is precisely horizontal.

Cut a stud to fit between the top of the doorway and the ceiling plate. Secure it at the center of the doorway's width.

5 FINISHING THE FRAME

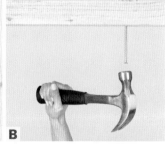

Stud at edge of doorway

A

Saw through the sole plate just inside the doorway studs and remove the offcut, so that the doorway is clear. Be careful not to saw into the finished floor. The frame is now ready to be covered.

BUILDING A METAL STUD WALL

Metal stud walls are a good interior wall option. They are not susceptible to rotting and warping or termite damage. Studs are typically pre-drilled to accommodate plumbing and electric. It is important to order the correct amount of material. Wall track is available in 10-ft (3-m) lengths. Measure the length of the wall in feet, multiply this number by two and divide by 10 for the number of lengths you'll need for the top and bottom tracks. To determine the number of studs necessary, divide the wall's length by the length of the stud intervals, then add one extra.

TOOLS AND MATERIALS SEE BASIC TOOLKIT AND P.103

1 LAYING OUT

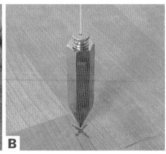

A

B

The first step to building a stud wall is layout. Lay out the location of wall on the floor using a measuring tape and pencil.

Use a plumb bob to mark three corresponding ceiling locations for the metal track.

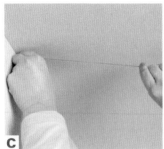

C

D

Lay out the top track of the metal wall using a chalk line. Pull the string line across the marks made in step B.

Measure, mark, and cut the top and bottom tracks. Cut out any sections from the bottom track for door openings.

2 INSTALLING THE OUTER FRAME

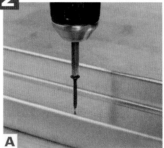

A

B

Attach the bottom track to the floor. Mark the stud locations at 16-in (400-mm) intervals on center on both the bottom and top track.

To help increase accuracy, place the bottom and top track parallel with each other while marking the stud locations with a felt marker.

Align the top track with the chalk lines made on the ceiling. Attach the top track to the ceiling using fasteners. Use a plumb bob to mark the top track for the metal stud positions.

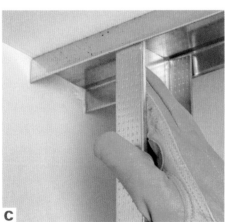

C

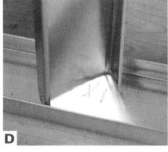

D

Insert the studs into the metal tracks. It is easier to insert them perpendicular to their final position.

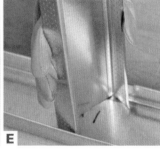

E

Using a twisting motion, move the metal studs in to position. Make sure all of the flanges are facing the same direction.

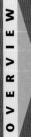

3 INSTALLING THE STUDS

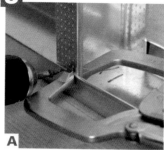

A Clamp the metal studs to the tracks, making sure the stud is plumb, then using screws, attach each stud to the top and bottom tracks.

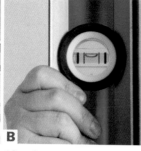

B After the screw is in place, use a level to check for plumb before installing the next stud.

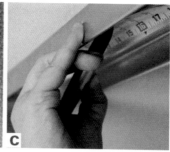

C Use a tape measure to check measurements for the metal studs along the top and bottom track, making sure they are 16 in (400 mm) apart on center.

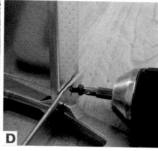

D Hold the last stud in place with a clamp, aligning the stud with the end of the bottom and top tracks, and secure in place.

For doorways and windows, you will need to bridge the header. To make the piece fit with the studs, cut along the creases of the material and bend it back.

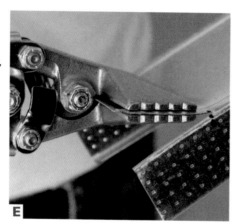

E

F Install the header piece with the flat side on top. The piece will be secured using metal screws.

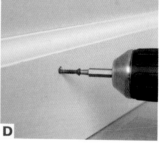

G The end of the flange has a slight lip. You will need to flatten the ends of the horizontal pieces to make a secure connection.

4 INSTALLING METAL STUDS TO A WOOD FRAME

A If you have a wood-framed house, you can still use metal studs to construct new walls in your house.

B Metal stud to wood frame connections, can be made with drywall screws, as with wood-to-wood connections.

C When connecting metal framing members to wood, use the same techniques as above to wrap the end of the horizontal metal member around the stud.

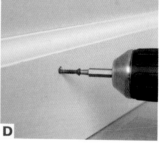

D After you have covered the metal frame with drywall and finished it in paper or paint, use screws to attach any trim. Nails will not make a connection into metal framing.

BUILDING A GLASS-BLOCK PARTITION

A glass-block wall divides a room without shutting out light. It cannot be loadbearing, but it will be a sturdy structure, thanks to metal reinforcing rods that are positioned in the mortar. Blocks sit with the mortar joints aligned and, because the blocks form the wall's decorative finish, white mortar is normally used to give a neat result. Glass blocks can also be used to build a screen across part of a room, as shown here, or (with no lumber frame) as a shower cubicle. Do not build any higher than six courses without stopping to let mortar dry overnight, otherwise the wall may collapse.

PLANNING AND PREPARATION

Most glass blocks measure 7½ x 7½ x 3⅛ in (190 x 190 x 80 mm). They cannot be cut to size, so base your calculations on how they best fit into the space. Half-blocks and corner blocks are available. Use wooden plates to fill any gaps left between blocks and a wall or ceiling. These will be inconspicuous when painted.

Designing a partition
■ Lay out a single row of blocks to judge a screen's extent into the room.
■ A full wall may need a doorway. Its position will depend on how blocks fit across your room. The opening will need suitable ties inserted through the door lining into the mortar.
■ Building within a wooden frame gives clean edges, but the mortar method can be used without a frame, provided you consider your floor surface (see below).

The floor surface
■ Mortar can be laid directly onto a concrete floor.
■ With a wooden floor, lay the first row of blocks on a wooden sole plate, even if you are not building in a frame.

Calculating quantities
■ Multiply the length of the wall by its height to find its surface area. Divide this by the area of one block for a rough

idea of the number of blocks needed, not allowing for mortar joints. Buy 10 percent extra, in case any get broken.
■ White mortar (ready-mixed) is available in 27½-lb (12.5-kg) bags—enough to construct a small shower enclosure.
■ Spacers give even joints. Allow 1½ per glass block, and buy 10 percent extra. The spacer shape can be modified from X-shaped to T- or L-shaped as required.
■ Allow two reinforcing rods per row of blocks. Buy more if you wish to push rods into the vertical joints for extra rigidity.

Sealing the partition
■ Use white mortar and white grout. Use waterproof grout and silicone sealant in a humid room, such as a bathroom, and use silicone sealant on the joint between the glass-block wall and the existing wall.
■ Some manufacturers supply expansion strips for the wall's perimeter in a humid area or one with temperature change.

TOOLS AND MATERIALS CHECKLIST

Lumber, expansion foam, spacers, white mortar, bricklaying trowel, spot board, plasterer's hawk, metal reinforcing rods, wall ties, white grout, grout shaper, silicone sealant*, paint*, paintbrush*

* = optional

FOR BASIC TOOLKIT
SEE PP.24–25

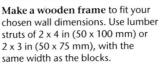

1 CONSTRUCTING THE FRAME

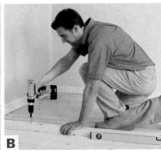

A

B

Make a wooden frame to fit your chosen wall dimensions. Use lumber struts of 2 x 4 in (50 x 100 mm) or 2 x 3 in (50 x 75 mm), with the same width as the blocks.

Fix the frame in place at your chosen location for the wall (see pp.102–103). Remember to use a cable detector to check that it is safe to screw into the floor.

2 LAYING THE FIRST BLOCKS

Nail white expansion foam to the inside of the wooden frame. This foam is a spongy material that allows the wall a small amount of movement without any danger of damage—for instance, if materials expand slightly when the temperature changes. Make sure the foam sits centrally on each length of wood.

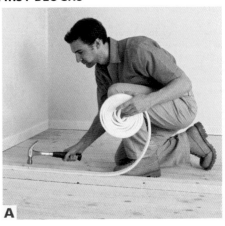

A

B

C

Position spacers inside the floor of the wooden frame, ready to hold the glass blocks. Check that they are level and accurately spaced to fit the dimensions of the blocks.

Trowel white mortar onto the frame's floor, between the spacers. Spread mortar onto one side of a glass block. Try not to get any on the block's face.

D

Place the first block onto the spacers, pressing the mortared side firmly into position against the frame and bedding the block into the mortar along the floor.

E

Lay more blocks and spacers to finish the row, checking that they are level. Wipe off any excess mortar with a damp sponge; dried mortar is hard to remove from glass.

3 BUILDING UP ROWS

A

Apply mortar along the top of the first row. Drill holes in the wall plate and fit the reinforcing rods. Press them down into the mortar. Continue laying blocks on top.

After every two rows, cut through the foam on the wall plate, just above the top edge of the course. Apply mortar to the end block, ready to bed in a wall tie.

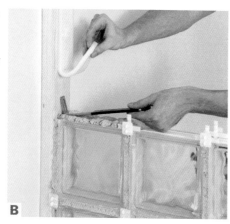

B

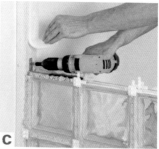

C

Screw the wall tie to the wall plate, behind the foam, and bed the tie into the mortar. Then lay mortar and reinforcing rods, and continue laying blocks.

D

Keep checking as you build up the height that blocks are level and plumb (vertically aligned). If you are going higher than six courses, let mortar dry overnight before finishing.

4 FINISHING THE PARTITION

A

Once all the glass blocks are in place, twist the spacers' faceplates to remove them.

B

Allow the mortar to dry, and then grout the joints (see p.319). Wipe off excess grout from the glass-block faces as you go, because grout is difficult to remove once it has dried.

C

Smooth the grout using a grout shaper, or brick jointer as shown here. Apply silicone sealant around its perimeter if required to make the seams waterproof, and wipe down the wall to give it a polished look. Paint the wooden frame if you wish.

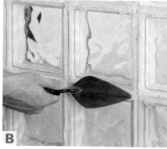

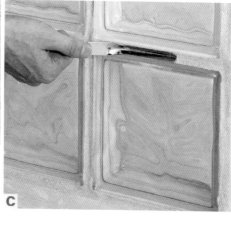

CREATING A DOORWAY

When planning to cut an opening in a wall, whether masonry or wood, establish whether it is loadbearing or non-loadbearing. For advice on this, and on supporting the upper levels of a wall or structure while cutting openings, see box below. The techniques needed for cutting smaller openings such as a doorway or serving hatch are those shown below. If a door is to be placed in the opening, you do not need to be exacting in making good the cut edges, because the door jamb will cover them. In calculating how large to make the opening, allow for a door jamb, and get header specifications calculated by a structural engineer.

BEFORE YOU START
■ Internal alterations may not always need a permit, but check with your local building inspector, because regulations vary. Exterior changes such as adding a new window often have to be authorized.
■ If the wall has a baseboard, remove it before starting work, and reinstall it after making good the walls around the new doorway.
■ Seek professional advice if you have any doubts about carrying out structural improvements to your home.

MAKING AN OPENING IN A STUD WALL

If you are cutting into a loadbearing wall, you should use temporary props, a header, and cripple studs, even for a small opening.

Cutting an opening in a non-loadbearing wall

Use an existing stud as the hinging edge of the doorway. After cutting the opening, add blocking between the trimmer studs above it, and insert a new stud in the open edge of the doorway. Then either attach a door jamb and door (see pp.154–161) or, if the gap is to be an opening with no door, apply drywall and an angle bead, then finish (see pp.136–137). For a serving hatch, cut an opening in the same way. Insert blocking across the bottom edge before drywalling and installing casing (see p.222).

Creating an opening in a loadbearing exterior wall

This is a job for a structural engineer. Specifications for the header and supports will be given. Supporting the frame is possible only on the inside. If the wall is brick- or block-clad, masonry is removed slowly, and angled steel posts placed, until it is possible to insert the header.

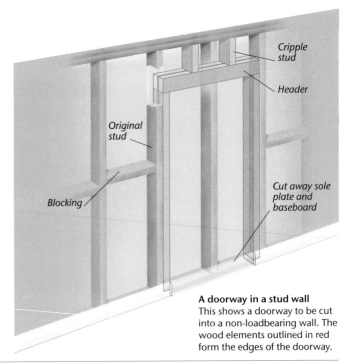

A doorway in a stud wall
This shows a doorway to be cut into a non-loadbearing wall. The wood elements outlined in red form the edges of the doorway.

Cripple stud

Header

Original stud

Cut away sole plate and baseboard

Blocking

MAKING AN OPENING IN A MASONRY WALL

A header is needed for any opening in masonry, no matter how small the span. It will probably need to be concrete or a metal box header; take advice from a structural engineer on the type and strength you need. Some tips specific to small openings are given here, but the techniques for supporting the wall and cutting the opening are those shown above.

Cutting into a non-loadbearing wall

For small openings in brickwork—no wider than 3 ft (1 m), for example—it may be possible to cut the opening without temporary support. If any bricks fall out of their positions, they can be replaced after the header is set in place. With blockwork, however, it is almost always necessary to use a temporary support.

Cutting into an exterior cavity wall

If you need to cut into an exterior cavity wall for a new window or a doorway, use a cavity wall header. This will provide support while retaining the cavity wall's damp-proofing function. It directs any moisture in the cavity out though weep holes in the wall. Your structural engineer will specify the strength to use. Close off the cavity at the sides of the new opening, either using cavity closers or by laying blocks.

SUPPORT NEEDED WHEN CUTTING AN OPENING

This table gives general guidance on the support needed when cutting into a wall. Consult a structural engineer for advice on the size, material, and strength of header needed. Also get advice on temporary support if you wish to cut into a cavity wall.

Wall type	Temporary support	Header required?
Non-loadbearing lumber	Not needed	No
Non-loadbearing masonry	If masonry above opening exceeds two rows of bricks or blocks, use a special support; if it is one or two rows, no support is needed (if blocks fall out, reinsert above the header)	Yes
Loadbearing lumber	Posts on ceiling	Yes, with cripple studs
Loadbearing masonry	Post or special support centrally, or every 3 ft (1 m)	Yes

SEALING A DOORWAY

Filling in an unwanted doorway can be done either with a 2- x 4-in (50- x 100-mm) stud frame or with blocks. It is best to fill in a stud wall with studs and a block wall with blocks, because these materials have different reactions to environmental changes, such as fluctuating temperatures or humidity levels. Using wood is easier, and can be done on a block wall if using blocks seems too difficult. But because the materials used do not match, cracks may later appear at or near the position of the old doorway. These can be filled and painted, but may reappear. By using matching materials, you reduce the risk of having these settlement or movement cracks appear.

PREPARING THE AREA

■ Remove the old door, casing, and door jamb before starting work on the wall. Lift a door off its hinges or unscrew them from the doorjamb. Remove the casing and door jamb with a claw hammer or pry bar.
■ When removing old woodwork, try to keep damage to the surrounding wall to a minimum. It will greatly reduce the amount of finishing work at the end of the project.

USING STUDS

This method for filling in a doorway uses the techniques shown on pp.104–105 (Building a Stud Wall). Use lengths of 2- x 4-in (50- x 100-mm) lumber to line the doorway. In a block wall, use wall plugs and masonry screws to attach the studs to the blocks. In a stud wall, simply attach the new studwork to existing studs with wood screws. Insert more studs and blocking, to strengthen the frame: depending on the dimensions, a central stud and two blockings may be sufficient. Cut some square-edged drywall to fit the gap, and attach it to the wooden frame. Tape the joint between the new drywall and the surrounding wall with self-adhesive tape, and apply joint compound (see pp.136–137), feathering in the seam between the new and the old wall surfaces.

Finishing off

When the joint compound has dried, sand it to a smooth finish. Fill any holes with an all-purpose filler, and sand again, if you wish to for the smoothest possible finish. Attach new baseboard (see pp.224–225) that is the same profile as the rest of the room. You can either use a short section to fill in the gap and match the adjoining boards, or replace the baseboard along the whole wall.

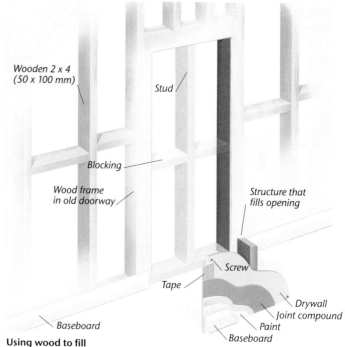

Wooden 2 x 4 (50 x 100 mm)

Stud

Blocking

Wood frame in old doorway

Structure that fills opening

Screw

Tape

Drywall

Joint compound

Paint

Baseboard

Baseboard

Using wood to fill
This method is easier than using blocks. It is normally used in a stud wall, but can also be used in a block wall. Both wall types are shown here.

USING BLOCKS

Blocks can be laid in the opening, using screw-in ties to secure them to the existing blocks, or you can remove blocks at alternate levels from either side of the opening, in which case the new blocks will automatically be securely attached to the existing wall. Both methods are shown to the right.

Once the wall has dried, remove any loose material before attaching drywall panels and feathering in the edges with the existing wall edge. When the joint compound has dried, sand it, paying particular attention to the seam between the old compound and the new. Decorate, and attach a piece of baseboard across the old doorway, or replace the full length (see pp.224–225).

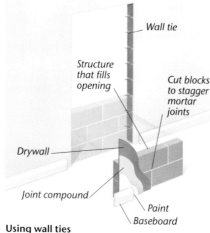

Wall tie

Structure that fills opening

Cut blocks to stagger mortar joints

Drywall

Joint compound

Paint

Baseboard

Using wall ties
Build a small block wall. Match the depths of mortar beds to those on the existing wall, so that wall ties inserted in the old wall's mortar align with the new mortar courses. The blocks will not be an exact fit across the doorway: work out where cuts will be needed.

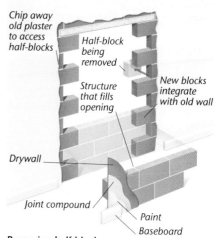

Chip away old plaster to access half-blocks

Half-block being removed

Structure that fills opening

New blocks integrate with old wall

Drywall

Joint compound

Paint

Baseboard

Removing half-blocks
This method takes longer than the wall-tie one. Use a club hammer and bolster chisel to take out half-blocks from the edge of the doorway. Chip away any hardened mortar. Then insert new blocks. If they are not an exact fit, make cuts, or add slightly more mortar, to fill the space appropriately.

PLANNING A STRAW-BALE WALL

There are several ways to build a straw-bale wall (see p.98). The main consideration is whether the straw bales will be loadbearing or whether they will act as infill for another loadbearing structure, such as post and beam (see p.93). The method shown here is for a type of loadbearing wall known as the "Nebraskan style". While there are alternative techniques within this style, all of the key steps are shown, with alternative materials suggested where relevant.

CONSTRUCTION CONSIDERATIONS

These techniques apply to an exterior wall, so you will first need to choose a suitable foundation. There are a variety of options available (see p.92), but here the walls are being built on concrete. While concrete is not the greenest or most sustainable option, it is one of the best for reducing the risk of moisture egress. In fact, the most successful straw-bale structures incorporate many features to guard against moisture. Wrapping the first course of bales in a damp-proof membrane, for example, protects the structure at this crucial level. Designing a roof with a large overhang to deflect rainwater away from the wall surfaces is also important. While the exterior wall will be clad in a protective skin—usually lime stucco (see p.99)—it is still best practice to keep as much water as possible away from the walls.

Frames

It is essential that the bales are raised off the immediate surface of the floor. This is achieved by laying a wooden frame on the foundation wall and bolting it to the floor. The frame must be slightly narrower than the width of the bales. Treated timber measuring 2 x 4 in (50 x 100 mm) is ideal for use in constructing a frame. Here, reinforcement bars are set in the foundations and extend upwards through the center of the frames to secure the first layer of bales in place. Frames also allow you to accurately position doorways in the wall.

Wall plates

Similar in design to a frame, a wall plate is a wooden framework that sits on top of the bale wall to ensure that the structure is loadbearing. The upper and lower surfaces of a wall plate are strengthened by attaching structural ply or orientated strand board (OSB). This board should be ¾ in (18 mm) thick and, like the frame, made from 2 x 4 in (50 x 100 mm) lengths of treated lumber.

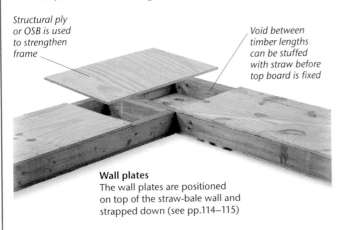

Structural ply or OSB is used to strengthen frame

Void between timber lengths can be stuffed with straw before top board is fixed

Wall plates
The wall plates are positioned on top of the straw-bale wall and strapped down (see pp.114–115)

Cross section of the wall plate

Layers of lime plaster to finish wall surface (see p.99)

Wire mesh acts as key for plaster

Wall plate provides support for roof timbers or floor joists

Wooden frame

Bales laid stretcher bond

Reinforced bar

Concrete raft foundation

Damp-proof membrane

Doorways and windows

When planning doorways and windows, keep in mind that the height of these openings may decrease during the build. This is because the bales will compress as the walls are built upward and the roof is added. Consequently, the area above a door or window head should be left open until the wall plate (see left) has been tied down. A box frame for the opening (within which the door or window frame itself will sit) can be made from a framework of structural ply and treated lumber lengths. Once any compression of the bales has occurred, any gaps can be stuffed with straw.

There is usually no need for an extra header above the door or window in a single-story building as the wall plate should be able to support the roof. Equally, if a second story is planned, the wall plate should be able to bear any joists for the next floor. However, always make careful structural calculations regarding loadings, especially with two-story structures.

Fixing points

The bale structure alone does not offer suitable fixing points for screws or nails, so you will need to use wooden dowels. If, for example, fixing points are required for clipping a cable to a wall, drive wooden dowels into the straw-bale structure and

Tensioning Strap

Door lining-box frame construction

Infill above doors and windows after compression of walls

Half bales rebound with baling wire

Gravel infill

Temporary bracing and framing

Due to the lack of framework associated with the Nebraskan style, it is advisable to construct some temporary bracing as the wall develops. This is especially important at corners, where a temporary framework makes it easier to maintain a vertical structure prior to the wall plates being attached. It is also best practice to secure door and window frames in place during the build rather than after the walls have been completed.

Tools

Although many tools required for straw-bale construction can be found in a standard toolbox, certain items are specific to this building technique.

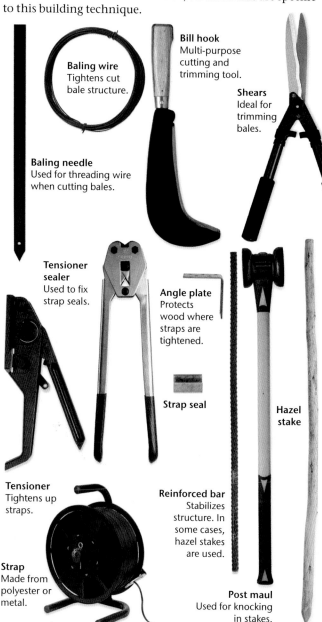

Baling wire Tightens cut bale structure.

Bill hook Multi-purpose cutting and trimming tool.

Shears Ideal for trimming bales.

Baling needle Used for threading wire when cutting bales.

Tensioner sealer Used to fix strap seals.

Angle plate Protects wood where straps are tightened.

Strap seal

Hazel stake

Tensioner Tightens up straps.

Reinforced bar Stabilizes structure. In some cases, hazel stakes are used.

Strap Made from polyester or metal.

Post maul Used for knocking in stakes.

fix the cable to the end of the dowel. This procedure is relatively straightforward during construction, before any finish is applied to the walls. However, when hanging heavy objects, such as kitchen units, more planning is necessary. Sturdier wooden fixing points need to be introduced into the bale surface. One way of doing this is to drive threaded bolts through the wall, bolting them to blocks of wood on the outside surface of the wall, and to lengths of wood on the inside surface, to provide a secure fixing rail.

CABLES AND SERVICES

Electrical cables can be run through the structure of a straw-bale wall, or surface-mounted to the bales and covered with lime stucco and plaster. In either case, it is important to enclose the wires in plastic conduit. Avoid burying water pipes in the walls as any leak could have a devastating effect on the integrity of the structure. If you have no option but to pass water pipes through a wall, keep the pipework continuous (i.e. don't bury a joint in the wall) and aim to position them in internal walls wherever possible.

TOOLS AND MATERIALS CHECKLIST PP.114–115

Building a straw-bale wall
Angle plates, baling needle, baling wire, bill hook, reinforced bars, hazel stakes, post maul, strap, tensioner, strap seals, tensioner sealer, shears

FOR BASIC TOOLKIT SEE PP.24–25

BUILDING A STRAW-BALE WALL

It is essential that the bales are kept dry, so make sure you are well-prepared before construction begins (see pp.112–113). This means that structural frames should be secured to the foundations, and door frames, window frames, and wall plates should be constructed and ready for positioning before the bales are brought to the site. Speed is of the essence, and a back-up plan is necessary to protect the bales during inclement weather. With the Nebraskan style (shown here), the roof can only be added once the walls have been built, so the bales will be exposed for longer.

TOOLS AND MATERIALS SEE BASIC TOOLKIT AND P.113

1 CHECKING FOUNDATIONS AND FRAME

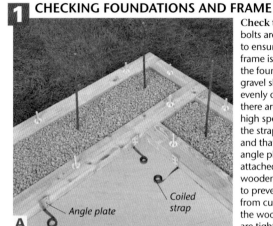

Check that all bolts are tightened to ensure that the frame is secured to the foundation. Infill gravel should be evenly distributed so there are no low or high spots. Check that the straps are in place, and that the metal angle plates are attached to the wooden frame to prevent the straps from cutting into the wood when they are tightened.

Angle plate | Coiled strap

2 POSITIONING THE FIRST BALE

Beginning at an external corner, position the first bale flush with the inner edge of the frame, while slightly overhanging the outer edge. Push it onto the securing rebar.

Position the second bale adjacent to the first bale, marking the start of a second wall. Make sure that it is butted tight up against the first bale.

Continue to add bales to the walls, building up on both sides of this starting corner.

When you reach an obstacle such as a door lining, and a cut bale is required, measure the distance between the last bale and the lining. Add 1 in (2 cm) so the cut bale will fit tightly into the gap.

3 CUTTING A BALE

Where the needle comes through the other side of the bale, unthread the wire and draw it round the perimeter of the bale to meet with the other end of the wire.

Thread the needle, using enough wire (with excess) to stretch round the perimeter of what will be your cut bale.

Push the needle through the straw at the point at which you need to cut the bale. Run this wire alongside the existing length of baler twine.

D

Twist the ends of the wire together, tightening them with pliers. Repeat steps A–D next to the other length of baler twine.

E

Using a craft knife, cut the old baler twines (the orange twine in this picture) and remove. The bale is now secured by the new lengths of twine.

F

Pull the bale apart so that you are left with a new, smaller-sized bale for use in the wall construction.

G

The new bale should now fit tightly into the gap in the wall. The excess straw (shown on the left) can be used to infill spaces above door and window frames.

4 BUILDING UP LAYERS

A

Keep the bales as vertical as possible, taking regular readings with a level as the construction grows. Layers are simply built up, using a stretcher-bond pattern (see p.408 for more information).

B

To reinforce the wall, drive hazel stakes vertically down into the structure using a post maul. You should do this when you reach the fourth layer of bales.

5 FITTING THE WALL PLATE

A

Lift the wall plate onto the top edge of the walls to form a continuous loadbearing structure for the roof or second story. For practical reasons, the wall plate is divided into sections and secured together in position.

B

Lift up the straps that have been left protruding from the underside of the frame. Draw one end over the exterior wall and wall plate, meeting with the other end of the strap on the inner face of the wall.

C

Connect the straps in the tensioner and gradually tighten them. This will rachet the wall plate down onto the walls.

D

Use a tensioner sealer to connect the two lengths of strap. Move slowly around the building, tightening and sealing each strap.

E

Strap seals will firm up the structure. If re-tightening is required (see box, right), cut the strap and splice in a new section as required, connecting a new strap seal.

FINISHING THE WALL

The wall structure is essentially complete at this stage. The process of tightening the securing straps should be repeated after a few weeks (or when they begin to slacken) to further compress the wall structure. This is why it is important to leave gaps above windows and doors (see p.112). Bales should be given a final trim before the application of any stucco.

EXTERIOR WALL CLADDING

Sometimes an exterior wall's structure provides the decorative finish, but most require extra material for decorative or weatherproofing purposes. For example, a brick or stone wall provides structure and finish, but a wood frame or block wall needs to be stuccoed or covered in siding. For most homeowners, the systems and techniques for these coverings become relevant only when they are faced with repairs (the most common repair jobs are shown on pp.120–121). You will need to understand how these coverings are created if you want to match them on an extension, or if you wish to refurbish an entire section of wall.

STUCCO

This can be applied directly to blocks or bricks, or onto metal laths (sheets of wire mesh that help adhesion) to provide a decorative, weatherproofing coat that protects a wall's structure. There are several finishing options, the most common of which are shown to the right. Some topcoats have extra features, such as enhanced water-proofing properties, or suitability for finishing with outside-quality paint. Investigate your options with your builder or supplier, who will also be able to advise you on the quantities needed, and any waterproofing measures that may be necessary.

Planning to stucco

Stuccoing large walls is not a job for an amateur—advanced plastering skills are required, as is experience in achieving the chosen finish. Unless you are very experienced, hire somebody to do the work for you. It may need several coats—usually an initial scratch coat followed by one or more further layers of stucco. Avoid application at times of extreme weather conditions, which can seriously affect the way stucco adheres, and may therefore reduce its life span. For those less experienced at DIY or the novice who wants the look of stucco, EIFS is an option. Made in panels, EIFS is similar to finished stucco and easier to install but requires careful flashing, so you will need professional help even for this option.

Smooth stucco
The smoothest of stucco finishes will still have some slight texture.

Patterned stucco
Smooth stucco can be tooled to produce various patterns if needed.

Rough
A uniform rough finish that is applied over smooth stucco.

Pebbledash
Achieved by throwing pebbles onto damp stucco.

REGULATIONS AND PERMISSIONS

The rules covering exterior alterations vary from area to area, and according to whether the building is historic or in a historic district. Before your plans advance too far, check with your local authorities and home owner's association as to whether you need permission. It may also be necessary to get permission to use certain paint colors. In all cases, a quick phone call can normally confirm any local guidelines or requirements.

SIDING

Siding is often found on most newer houses, forming the outer layer of a wood cavity wall. Some homes are partially covered in siding for decorative effect—boards can be placed horizontally or vertically—but siding also performs a vital weatherproofing function. Boards may be wooden, but synthetic options such as fiber cement board, vinyl, and aluminum are also available. These need less maintenance than wood, and some can be painted. Metal-based boards are usually attached to the house with special clips and channels, bought with the boards.

Siding should be applied on top of either building paper (a moisture barrier) or a breather membrane (which stops water from entering a wall, but allows vapor within the wall to escape). If you have a block house you may need a series of furring strips over the paper or membrane, to provide anchor points for the nails or screws to attach the siding.

Using furring strips

Horizontal siding goes onto vertical furring strips (see right), which provide a cavity for drainage channels between boards and wall. To maintain channels behind vertical siding, which attaches to horizontal furring strips, fit vertical furring strips first. Chamfering the top edges of the horizontal furring strips directs water away from the wall. If untreated, furring strips must end 6 in (150 mm) above the ground, so that siding does not touch damp soil. Use treated softwood measuring 1 x 2 in (25 x 50 mm). Some manufacturers will produce siding systems that incorporate an insulation layer between siding and the wall. Ask for professional advice, because it is important to use the correct insulation and vapor barrier to avoid problems with condensation.

FURTHER INFORMATION

Choosing the right exterior cladding material depends on your climate, personal preference, and budget. Follow all manufacturer's guidelines and local codes to ensure the material you choose performs well over time. One part of this is choosing the correct fasteners for the material and your weather conditions. Most often, you will need to use rust-resistant nails for exterior work.

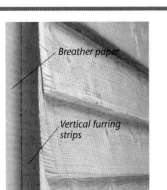

Breather paper

Vertical furring strips

FEATHER-EDGE BOARDS

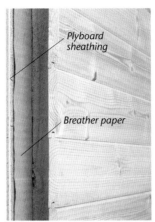

Plyboard sheathing

Breather paper

TONGUE-AND-GROOVE BOARDS

VINYL SIDING

BRICK

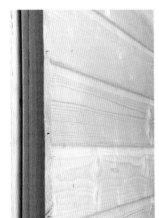

SHIPLAP BOARDS

Vertical furring strips beneath horizontal

SHINGLES

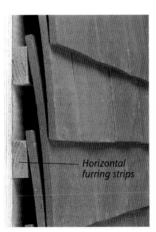

Plyboard sheathing behind breather paper

Vertical furring strips

FIBER-CEMENT SIDING

Horizontal furring strips

TILES

Siding products

Most types of exterior cladding materials are illustrated here. Typically furring strips are nailed over building paper and into studs. Siding is usually installed from bottom to top and must be nailed into either furring or framing, never just into sheathing through building paper. Each product has its benefits and special installation instructions.

▮▮ APPLYING FIBER-CEMENT SIDING

Having attached building paper and furring strips at 16-in (400-mm) intervals, you can start building up rows of siding. You will need the following: nail gun and nails, corner strips, boards, kicker strip, sealant, and dispenser.

A **Apply corner strips** with a nail gun, taking care to use the tool safely (see pp.52–53).

B **Attach a kicker strip** to the bases of the furring strips to push out the boards at a slight angle, helping with positioning and water runoff.

C **Apply boards, nailing** into every furring strip. Build up rows, overlapping the previous layer each time by at least 1 in (25 mm).

D **Use sealant** at corners and where boards meet another surface. A common option for a corner is to use a corner trim piece.

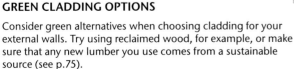

GREEN CLADDING OPTIONS

Consider green alternatives when choosing cladding for your external walls. Try using reclaimed wood, for example, or make sure that any new lumber you use comes from a sustainable source (see p.75).

Aluminum cladding produced from recycled aluminum—rather than a virgin source—is another viable option. For clay tiles, visit a reclamation yard, as reuse is the most eco-friendly option and may save you money (see pp.86–87). While cement board is not the greenest option, if you are determined to use it, find manufacturers that use high quantities of recycled material.

SIDING

The most common types of siding material are attached horizontally, starting at the bottom of the house. Each type of siding has nuances as to how it is attached to the exterior of your house. There are also tools and blades designed specially to cut and install some siding materials. Make sure you use the proper tool for the type of exterior material you choose to cover the outside of your home. Shown on the following pages are the most common ways to install vinyl siding and cedar siding, along with a few tips on working with fiber cement siding.

TOOLS AND MATERIALS SEE BASIC TOOLKIT, P.24–25

CUTTING VINYL SIDING

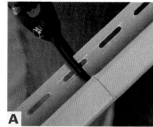

A Measure and mark the piece of vinyl siding to fit. Use snips to cut through the flanges.

B Continue to cut through the material, cutting the rest of the J-flange.

INSTALLING VINYL SIDING

Measure and cut a corner post, so that there will be a ½-in (13-mm) gap between the top of the post and the eave of the house.

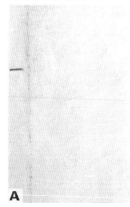

A

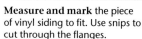

B Measure the length of siding needed. Mark and cut the piece to length.

C Nail the corner post at the top of the post. Check for plumb. Fasten the posts every 12 in (305 mm).

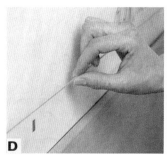

D Determine the lowest part of the wall that will be sided. Make a chalk line across the house for the first horizontal piece.

E Lay out the top of the strip along the chalk line. Check for level.

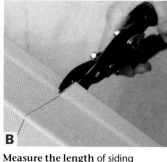

F Nail the starter strip to the house every 10 in (255 mm).

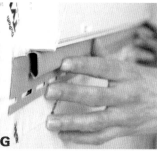

G Miter the ends of a J-channel trim piece to fit two channel widths wider than opening of window. Attach the trim piece under window.

H Cut the side trim pieces to length, and install them on either side of the window.

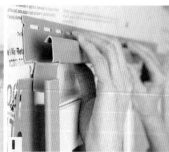

I Nail the trim piece in place on top of the window.

Cut the first piece of siding to length. Install over the starter strip from step F.

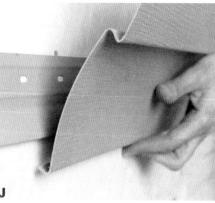

J

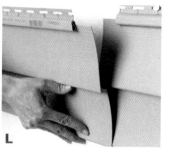

K. **Nail each siding piece** so that it is not driven all of the way into the house. There should be a gap of about ⅛ in (3 mm).

L. **Overlay each successive** piece of siding to cover the house.

OVERLAPPING SIDING

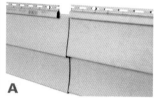

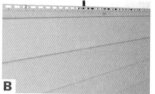

A. **When planning** to overlap siding, you may want to overlap the material so that the top piece is closest to the house's front door.

B. **By overlapping away** from the house, the siding appears seamless when looking at the exterior from the front door.

INSTALLING CEDAR SIDING

Cedar siding offers a few options for treating corners. Mitering is a popular option to create a neat finish. The technique here uses corner boards. They are sized according to the siding's thickness, but are often ¾-in (19-mm) or 1¼-in (32-mm) material. Check that each piece is flush with the house before nailing it in place.

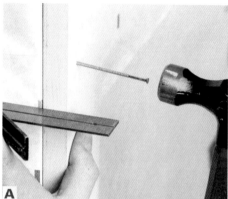

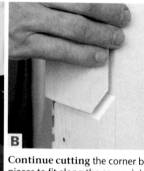

B. **Continue cutting** the corner bead pieces to fit along the corner joint.

C. **Nail the corner bead** in place. Fill any joints with caulk to seal.

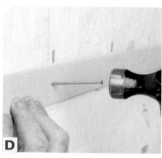

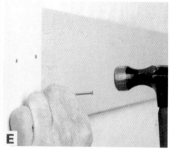

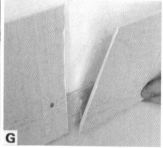

D. **Cut and attach** a furring strip to support the lower edge of the first board.

E. **Face nail to studs** penetrating 1¼ in (32 mm) into solid wood. Use one ring shank nail per bearing spaced at maximum 24 in (610 mm) on center.

F. **Cut and install** each row to length. Use a foam brush to apply sealant.

G. **Make sure that** each course overlaps the previous by about 1 in (25 mm) to allow for shrinkage. Do not overlap more than 2 in (50 mm).

INSTALLING FIBER CEMENT SIDING

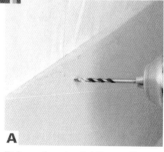

A. **Drive galvanized siding nails** or screws through the top of each length of siding into the studs. You may want to make pilot holes.

B. **Each row overlaps** the row below, (as with cedar siding, above). Create an overlap of at least a 1½ in (38 mm) to cover up the fasteners.

FIBER CEMENT TOOLS

Fiber cement siding can be tougher to cut than wood or vinyl siding. Manufacturers have created special tools and blades to help you cut through the material, making it almost as easy as cutting through wood. You can use a special scoring tool, or a carbide-tipped blade in a circular saw (shown here).

FIBER CEMENT BLADE

REPOINTING MORTAR

If old mortar has cracked or deteriorated, get advice from a structural engineer about whether it is a sign of serious structural problems or simply due to age. If age-related deterioration is the cause, mortar can be repointed (shown here) or "stitched" (a technique involving special "stitching rods" and an epoxy resin). If the problem is more serious, follow your engineer's advice before attempting to tackle it.

TOOLS AND MATERIALS
Gloves, joint raker, two-pound hammer, chisel, brush, misting spray, pointing trowel, brick jointer, small paintbrush

A Use a joint raker to remove any loose, crumbly bits of old mortar until you reach sound material.

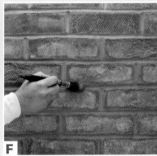

B Use a two-pound hammer and chisel to "peck" out the more obstinate, solid chunks of mortar from between the bricks.

C Dust out the old mortar joints to remove all debris.

D Use a spray to wet the bricks and mortar joints. This stops bricks from soaking up the new mortar and ensures that it will adhere.

E Use a pointing trowel and a brick jointer to press new mortar into place. Use the jointer to mimic the profile of existing mortar joints.

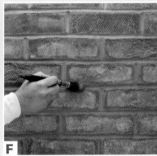

F Use a dry brush to remove any excess mortar from the joints.

REPAIRING VERTICAL TILES ON AN EXTERIOR WALL

Because layers of tiles overlap each other, a new tile cannot be nailed into the furring strip below. Instead, use adhesive to secure a new tile. If you need to replace several tiles, you will be able to nail all but the last one, which will need to be attached using the method shown here. A slate ripper can be used as an alternative to a hacksaw blade. This technique can also be used to repair tiles on roofs.

TOOLS AND MATERIALS
Gloves, masking tape, hacksaw blade or slate ripper, grab adhesive, new tile, heavy-duty tape, caulk gun

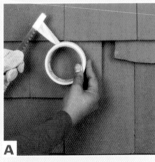

A Wrap some masking tape or similar tape around one end of a hacksaw blade to enable you to hold the blade without injury.

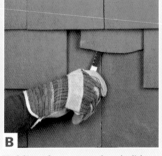

B Holding the wrapped end, slide the saw blade under the broken tile and cut through the fasteners that hold the tile in place.

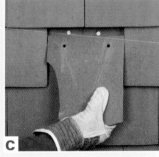

C Slide out the broken tile.

D Apply all-purpose grab adhesive to the back of a new tile, at the top and bottom, where it will sit on the furring strip and the tile below.

E Slide the new tile into position, ensuring that its top edge lies on the strip and its lower edge rests on top of the tile in the row below.

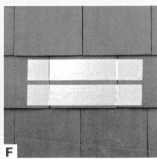

F Tape the new tile so the surrounding tiles hold it securely in position while the adhesive dries. When it is dry, remove the tape.

REPAIRING SPLIT CLAPBOARDS

Boards are difficult to remove, so aim to repair, not replace, them. If you do have to remove boards, cut through joints, or pry boards out and cut through nails with a hacksaw.

TOOLS AND MATERIALS
Chisel, adhesive, hammer, nails, nail set, patching plaster, paint

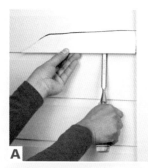

Pry away the split section of board and remove it.

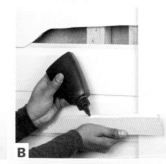

Apply a water-resistant wood adhesive along the edges of the removed piece of board.

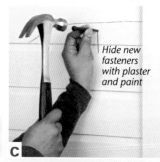

Hide new fasteners with plaster and paint

Reapply the broken piece to the board it came from, and use nail or screw the repair securely together.

REPAIRING VINYL SIDING

Vinyl siding can chip or dent. The good news is that it is fairly easy to remove and replace. When removing the siding and the nails, remember to use care as you do not want to damage any house wrap underneath.

TOOLS AND MATERIALS
Zipper (siding removal tool), pry bar, vinyl siding, hammer

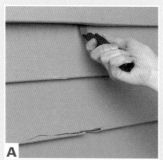

Insert a zipper into the seam between the top damaged panel and the one above it. Pull out slightly so that it is clear of the damaged area.

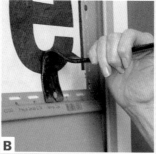

Remove the nails from the damaged boards. Then, remove the damaged panels.

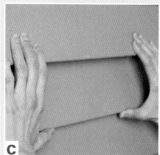

Starting at the bottom, fasten new boards in place.

REPLACING SIDEWALL CEDAR SHINGLE

Cedar shingles can crack or split due to weathering or a direct impact. They can curl or bow over time, too. It is best to replace damaged or bowed shingles instead of attempting to repair the shingle in place. For more information about cedar shingles and shakes visit the Cedar Shake & Shingle Bureau at www.cedarbureau.org.

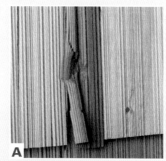

Identify the damaged section of shingle you want to replace.

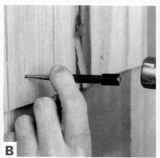

Remove the shingle by using a nail set to drive the finish nail through the shingle.

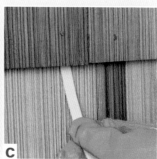

Another option to remove the shingle is to use a hacksaw to cut the nail underneath the shingle.

Carefully remove the damaged shingle from the wall.

Cut the new shingle to size and plane any excess material.

Install the new shingle and nail in place.

TOOLS AND MATERIALS
Nail set, hammer, hacksaw blade, cedar shingle, block plane

Drywall

DRYWALL IS THE STANDARD WALL COVERING IN CANADA, COVERING THREE OUT OF FOUR INTERIOR WALLS IN OUR HOMES. WHILE IT TAKES PRACTICE TO PROPERLY FINISH DRYWALL, IT DOES NOT REQUIRE MANY TOOLS AND IS FAIRLY STRAIGHTFORWARD. IF YOU ARE PLANNING TO ALTER OR BUILD ANY WALLS IN YOUR HOME, YOU WILL NEED TO KNOW THE BASICS OF DRYWALL.

DRYWALL BASICS

Drywall is a specific type of sheeting material made of gypsum sandwiched between paper. Also referred to as gypsum board, wallboard, or plasterboard, drywall started to replace plaster as the typical interior wall finish in Canada more than 60 years ago. Drywall is less expensive than plaster, and it is very easy to attach to stud walls. The panels are typically screwed to wall studs and the joints between them are filled with joint compound, which is then finished to a flat surface. For information on greener finishes for internal walls, see p.109.

PLASTERING
- If you have a home built before 1950, you may have plaster walls.
- Plaster is heavy, and it needs a solid, well-anchored base made of strips of wood or metal wire, called a lath, to support its weight.
- Over time plaster can dry out and lose its holding strength, or the lath beneath can pull away from the framing. If you see your plaster walls sag, you may need to repair them.

PLASTERING AND DRYWALLING OPTIONS

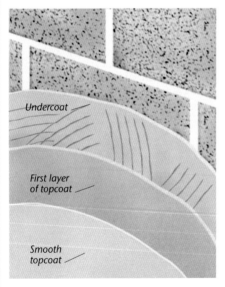

Undercoat

First layer of topcoat

Smooth topcoat

Plastering a masonry wall
A traditional method for preparing a large area of wall, ready for decorating.

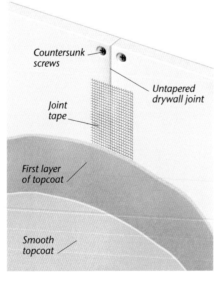

Countersunk screws

Untapered drywall joint

Joint tape

First layer of topcoat

Smooth topcoat

Plastering a stud wall
A smooth finish over untapered board, achieved by plastering across the entire surface.

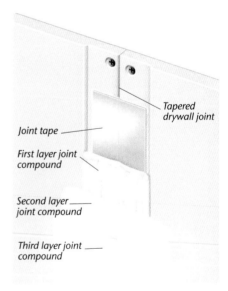

Tapered drywall joint

Joint tape

First layer joint compound

Second layer joint compound

Third layer joint compound

Drywalling
Layers of compound fill the joint, which is then sanded to provide a smooth finish.

PREPARING TO USE DRYWALL

Drywall developed as an alternative to plastering walls. Some say the name drywall is characteristic description of the material. Unlike the plaster-and-lath wall surface that is completely moist and must be left to dry, drywall only has its joints that are moist from joint compound and they dry much more quickly than plaster.

Even with the benefits of drywall installation and repair over plastering, you still may decide to take on plaster repairs if you live in an older home or if you are restoring a home to its original materials. For finishing plastering techniques, see pp.136–137.

Before you even begin to drywall or plaster your walls, make sure you have a flat working surface. When taking on the task of drywalling your home, the most important objective is to achieve a smooth finish. Each step in the multi-step drywalling process is designed to help you achieve this. The first part is making sure your stud walls are framed correctly. If the walls are not flat, the drywall panels will show the imperfections. It will be very difficult to overcome this type of imperfection through finishing techniques. It must be fixed prior to drywalling.

DRYWALL MATERIALS

Drywall is available in 4-ft (1.2-m) and 4½-ft (1.4-m) widths, and ranges in length from 8 ft (2.4 m) to 16 ft (4.8 m). Due to the rectangular shape of the pieces, it is recommended that you hang the sheets parallel to the floor to reduce the amount of finishing work required. You will save time and money on the tape and joint compound needed to finish a larger number of vertical seams. If you are able to transport the larger-sized sheets, buy sheets that are the width of the wall, if possible. This will further reduce the amount of taping required.

MEASURING FOR DRYWALL

When planning to use drywall materials, first determine the total square footage of the walls and ceiling that you are aiming to cover. Include the window and door openings, and always estimate high. Never buy exactly what you think you may need to just finish the project. This will save you time spent traveling back and forth to the home center during the project.

If you are using the standard 4 x 8 ft (1.2 x 2.4 m) sheets of drywall, divide the square footage number by 32 (4 x 8 = 32). This will provide an estimate of the number of sheets you will require. You will also need about 400 ft (120 m) of tape for every 1,000 sq ft (90 sq m) of drywall. And you will need about 150 lb (70 kg) of joint compound. Make sure you estimate for the fasteners you plan to use, and rent any equipment and scaffolding that is needed to finish ceilings.

For ceilings and walls with 16-in (405-mm) on-center framing use standard ½-in (13-mm) drywall. For 24-in (610-mm) on-center framing, use ⅝-in (16-mm) drywall.

TYPES OF DRYWALL

There are many types of drywall available at your local home center. From thicknesses that range from ¼ in (6 mm) to ⅝ in (16 mm) to wall sizes that start at 4 x 8 ft (1.2 x 2.4 m), there is a drywall product that is designed to suit your interior wall needs. If you are finishing a garage or another area where a fire rating is required, look for fire-resistant drywall. If you need to finish a wet wall, make sure you use a product that is able to handle more than average moisture content.

Regular
The most typical drywall used in standard interior applications is ½-in (13-mm) drywall in 4- x 8-ft (1.2- x 2.4-m) panels. It is also available in ¼-, ⅜-, and ⅝-in (7-, 9.5-, and 16-mm) thicknesses.

Moisture-resistant
Sometimes called greenboard, due to its color, this has the same gypsum core as drywall, but with a water-resistant facing. It is typically used in wet areas such as around a bathtub. Not waterproof.

Fire-resistant
This type of drywall has a core with additives that contain fires well. Fire rating for panels is measured in time. Due to its tougher core, it can be more difficult to cut.

Flexible
When you have an arch or a curved wall, ¼-in (6-mm) flexible drywall is the best type to choose. It has a stronger paper face than regular ¼-in (6-mm) drywall and is more resistant to cracking.

Cement board
Sometimes called concrete backerboard or the brand names of Durock and Wonder Board, it is used as a surface for ceramic tiles. It is not a gypsum-based product, as it has a solid concrete core.

GP's Denshield
This is a mold-resistant board used for tiling. It has a glass face and an acrylic coating that prevents moisture from entering the wall cavity.

PREPARATION FOR DRYWALL

Preparing for drywall work involves more than just choosing the right type of drywall and the number of sheets you require. You will need to make sure that you have tools that will suit your situation and the room will need to be prepared for the work. Temperature and humidity can also affect your work and determine how quickly the joint compound dries. To make the process even easier, the delivery of drywall panels should be planned to fit within the installation schedule, so you do not have to worry about storing the panels.

BUILDING REGULATIONS

Before starting to apply drywall to your wall frames, it is important to schedule an inspection for any interior wall systems: electrical, plumbing, mechanical. If you do not fulfill the requirements of your local inspections, you may need to open walls later. You must comply with all building codes.

ROOM PREPARATIONS

As with any DIY work, the room must be prepared for the task at hand. Safety precautions must be made and space must be created for the tools and materials required. At the end of each stage of the process, properly store and stack all materials and tools.

Temperature

Drywall is best completed in rooms that are ventilated and are no warmer than 55°F (13°C) for at least two days prior to beginning work.

Dust

Gypsum dust from cutting drywall can cause eye and respiratory irritation. Protect your eyes and lungs by wearing safety glasses and particle masks, when appropriate, and provide proper ventilation for the work site.

DRYWALL TOOLS AND FASTENERS

Successful drywalling depends upon you having the appropriate tools, and there are tools designed specifically for drywall installation (see right). However, most of the basic tools that you will need are not unique to drywalling. A tape measure, T-square, framing square, chalkline, and pencil will be needed no matter the size of the space and the height of the ceiling. You will also need drywall screws or nails, mixing tools, taping knives, and sanding tools.

Screws and nails

Drywall screws are the preferred method of installing drywall, as they provide a more secure and longer-lasting connection. If you have a large drywall job to tackle, try using a self-feeding screw gun (see right) to speed up the task. The depth of the screw gun can be modified to work with different thicknesses of board. Screw guns are available in both corded and cordless models. If you use nails, use a drywall hammer (see right).

Mixing tools

When working with joint compound to fill nail holes, secure tape, and fill gaps, you will need mixing tools. You can either mix the compound by hand or use an attachment to your drill–a powered paddle (see p.68).

Taping knives

Depending on the stage of the drywall process, you may select a knife that is 1–6 in (25–150 mm) wide. Knives are used to embed the tape along a seam and to spread and smooth joint compound.

Sanding tools

After you complete the taping and joint compound application process, you will most likely still need to smooth any imperfections. Sand paper is ideal for small areas and corners. Sanding sponge is another option. For ceilings, a pole sander is a good option.

Peen

Notch

Use point to break through material and start cut

Utility knife
Used to make cuts through the face of the paper to score the panel before snapping it to length. Make sure the blade is sharp.

Drywall hammer
Has a gently tapered head that creates a natural recess for joint compound. When it strikes the paper surface, it creates a waffle contour that helps lock the compound.

Drywall saw
These are designed to rip through the paper face and gypsum core of drywall. The one shown here is a drywall utility saw.

Turning shaft

Drywall screw gun
Used to drive screws into drywall. It has a clutch so that the drywall screw will go just below the surface of the drywall sheet and dimple the sheet.

TAPE AND JOINT COMPOUND

After you have cut and installed in place each drywall sheet, you will need to smooth the joints. Creating a smooth finish between drywall panels requires both tape and joint compound.

Tape

Joint tape is used to reinforce the seams between drywall panels. You can also use it to repair any cracks in your walls. Paper tape used to be the only option available for drywalling, and it is still in use. Paper tape is 2 in (50 mm) wide with a light crease along the center for folding to create straight inside corners. Fiberglass mesh tape is more popular than paper tape because it is easier to work with. Available in widths of 1½ and 2 in (40 and 50 mm), mesh tape can be found in non-adhesive and self-adhesive rolls. It is used along gaps and around holes in walls. It is more difficult to create a straight seam in corners with mesh tape and it is more easily torn than paper tape. If you are drywalling a large space, mechanical taping tools are available.

Joint compound

Premixed and powdered joint compounds are available, and are rated by drying time.

You may hear about taping and topping compounds. Taping compounds are used for the first coat, where you embed the tape along the drywall seam. Coarser, fast-drying compounds are usually used during this first pass. Thinner, topping compounds are used on the top coats. All-purpose joint compounds are somewhere in between. These are a good choice for small areas, and for DIYers wanting to tackle drywalling for the first time.

Powdered joint compounds need to be mixed with water, and come in a variety of textures. Usually available in bags, the powder can be stored at any temperature.

Premixed joint compound is available, ready-to-use, in buckets. Keep out of sunlight, and do not allow it to freeze. It lasts about a month after opening.

Fast-setting joint compound is called "setting type." Products are available that can set in as little as 20 minutes. The benefit of working with fast-setting joint compound is that you can apply a second coat sooner. If you choose to work with fast-setting, be aware that you have limited time to apply the mixture, so be careful to mix only an amount that you can use in the time you have available.

Fiberglass non-adhesive tape
This has to be stapled over seams to be secured in place. It is harder to work with than self-adhesive tape (below). It can be cut using a utility knife.

Fiberglass self-adhesive tape
Self-adhesive tape can be simply pressed over seams to adhere in place. With the ease of use comes a higher price tag—it is more expensive than non-adhesive tape (above).

CORNER BEADS

While inside corners are finished with drywall tape and joint compound, outside corners are covered with corner beads to create a sharp 90-degree angle. Since walls take the brunt of wear and tear in a home, corner beads also protect the corner surface of a wall. Available in a variety of types, most can be either nailed or screwed in place. If you choose metal over plastic, you will need to use a crimper to set the metal and hit it firmly with a rubber mallet. No matter what type of corner bead you choose, try to install it in one piece to create a seamless finish. Standard length of corner bead is 6 ft 10 in (2 m), but it ranges up to 10 ft (3 m).

Types of bead

Metal bead used to be the only type available, but vinyl and plastic covered in paper are also common. Metal corner beads are available in varieties with a paper cover. Bullnose corner beads give a rounded corner.

Flexible wire bead
This has plastic beaded edges, and is nailed in place.

Bullnose bead
If you want a rounded corner, these are a good option.

Vinyl bead
Has a pre-snipped edge that is glued and stapled in place.

Composite bead
Composite bead usually has a PVC core and a paper surface.

J-trim bead
Used to cover the edges of drywall panel at shower stalls or windows.

L-channel bead
Finishes drywall that butts up against other types of material.

Metal corner bead
Can be nailed or screwed in place. Some have a paper face.

CUTTING DRYWALL

Unless your room is a perfect 4 x 8 ft (1.2 x 2.4 m) square, with no openings, you will need to cut drywall to complete your project. Take time before you begin to accurately measure and purchase drywall panels to reduce the amount of cutting you will have to do. Use full sheets wherever possible during the project, and always cut the drywall panel to length so that the end falls in the center of a joist or stud. You will then be able to attach the next panel to the other half of the joist or stud.

TOOLS AND MATERIALS SEE BASIC TOOLKIT AND P.126

CUTTING TIPS

Making cuts along the length of a sheet can be tough. One method is to snap a chalkline along the sheet and then score the line by hand (see below). You may also use a tape measure to mark out accurate guide lines (see below).

When you need to cut inside corners, cut one side with a drywall saw. Then score the other side of the drywall with a utility knife and snap it back as you would any other cut.

Bend the back panel away from the score line to break it along the score. It is usually easier to snap the panel away from you. Be careful to not rip the paper face when using a drywall saw. Make cuts away from the hand holding the straight edge.

CUTTING THE DRYWALL VERTICALLY

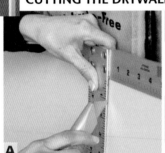

A Mark the panel and score it using a straight edge and a utility knife. Pass the knife just through the top layer of paper and into the core.

B Snap the drywall panel along the score line, and away from cut side.

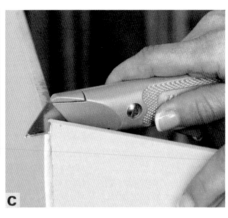

Score the back of the panel with a utility knife to break the paper, and snap forward to break.

C

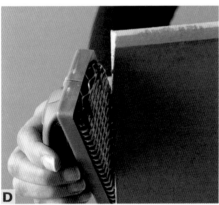

Rasp and sand the edges of the drywall panel to remove any bumps or imperfections.

D

MARKING HORIZONTAL GUIDE LINES

A Mark the panel according to your measurements. Snap a line across the panel to provide a straight line for scoring.

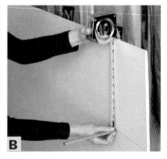

B Alternatively, use a tape measure as a straight edge to mark the cutting line.

MEASURING TIPS

Circular light fixtures
Measure from the center of the fitting to the sides of where the drywall sheet will be attached, then transfer the measurements to a sheet of drywall. Take this mark as the center point of the hole. Use a circular hole cutter to score the hole's outline several times, so that you may then tap it out with a hammer.

Lights switches and outlets
Cutting square holes takes careful measuring and marking (see opposite). Measure from the side edge of where the sheet will go to the right and left sides of the box. Then measure from the top and bottom edges to the top and bottom of the box. Transfer these marks to the sheet of drywall and cut it with a saw.

TOOLS AND MATERIALS CHECKLIST PP.112–114

Cutting drywall vertically (p.126) Carpenter's square or metal ruler, rasp

Marking horizontal guide lines (p.126) Chalk line

Cutting window openings (p.127) Drywall saw, rasp

Cutting small openings (p.127) Drywall saw, rasp

Using adhesive to hang drywall (p.128) Sealant dispenser, caulk

Applying tape (p.128) Drywall knife

FOR BASIC TOOLKIT
SEE PP.24–25

PREPARING TO CUT DRYWALL

While many DIYers find that cutting the drywall is the most straightforward part of the job, it can easily turn difficult if you do not use the right tools or if your tools are not in good condition.

It is important that you always use a sharp blade when cutting drywall. A blunt blade can tear the paper face, leaving a more difficult seam to finish later.

Always score the panels before attempting to cut through them. The best way to cut a piece of drywall is to use the "score-and-snap" method shown opposite. Score along one face of the sheet and then snap it back. If there is damage done to the back of the drywall, it will not be noticed on your finished wall. Always snap the panel away from the score cut.

CUTTING OPENINGS

If you need to cut window openings, it is easier to hang the drywall over the opening before cutting out the hole for the window. If your windows are already installed, but the jambs are not, you may still find it easier to install the drywall panel before cutting out the hole. But, if the entire window unit is installed in the opening, you may want to measure and cut the hole in the drywall before you install the panels.

CUTTING TOOLS

Cutting drywall openings can be straightforward with the right cutting tools. In addition to your basic utility knife and tape measure, you will need some of the following special tools for cutting sheets of drywall.

T-square

To make square cuts, use a T-square or framing square. Set the sheet upright with the smooth side out. Set the T-square on the top edge and line it up with your measurement. Run a utility knife along the side of the "T" to score the cut.

Drywall saw

When making cuts around obstacles you should use a drywall saw. Be careful to not damage the paper face with an aggressive motion.

Rasp

When cutting drywall to size, it is best to aim to cut larger rather than smaller. Use a rasp to shave off excess material. Never force into place a piece of drywall that is too big.

Keyhole saw

Keyhole saws are perfect for cutting around electrical boxes. Insert the tip through the drywall and cut along each side of the box.

Circle cutter

For round cuts, use a circle cutter to get a perfect cut. A compass can also help make a good score line, if you do not have a circle cutter.

Rotozip

These power tools are used to cut holes for boxes and fixtures much faster and easier than cutting out by hand. However, they can create more dust than other methods.

▌▌ CUTTING WINDOW OPENINGS

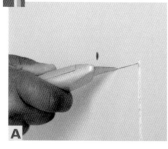  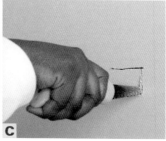 

A Install the drywall in place over the opening. Mark the hole by scoring along the top of the window opening.

B Using the tip of a drywall saw, make an incision through the drywall.

C Cut along the sides of the window opening using the drywall saw.

D Snap the drywall forward. Trim any debris with a utility knife, then smooth the edges.

▌▌ CUTTING SMALL OPENINGS

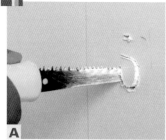   

A Cut a small circular opening through the outlet box with a drywall saw.

B Cut around the inside of the outlet box to create the opening.

C Trim the drywall away from the outside of the box to make room for the box to sit inside the wall.

D Smooth the hole and finish. Insert the box into the hole, then wire as required.

HANGING DRYWALL

After you have cut pieces of drywall to length, the next step is to hang them in the right positions. If you have a small area to cover, it can be a fairly uneventful job. But, if you are covering a large expanse of room with slanted cathedral ceilings, for example, you may need help to lift and secure the panels in place. When installing drywall, make the sheets bridge as many joists or studs as possible to create a stronger connection.

TOOLS AND MATERIALS SEE BASIC TOOLKIT AND PP.125–126

HANGING TIPS

■ Measure the wall and plan the layout, making sure to minimize the number of drywall seams in the wall.
■ Always trim pieces to size. If you force a panel to fit in place, problems could develop later.
■ When hanging drywall, always work from the top to the bottom.
■ Always run the drywall sheets perpendicular to the framing.
■ Hang drywall on ceilings before walls, so the sheets on the walls can help support the ceiling sheets.
■ Start nails across the top of a sheet before lifting it in place, so your hands are free to lift the sheet and nail it in place.
■ Stagger the seams across the wall, so that there is not a continuous seam.
■ As you may be planning to install baseboard later, make sure any small gaps in the drywall are at the bottom of the wall.

HANGING THE FIRST SHEET OF DRYWALL

Lay out and mark the wall for the first sheet. If you are working alone, install a level support to carry the weight of the panel while you secure it in place.

A

B

Place the first sheet in a corner. The sheet should fall in the middle of a stud.

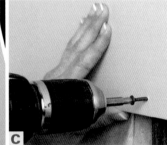
C

Using 1¼ in (32 mm) drywall screws and a screw gun, secure the panel to the wall, starting in the middle.

D

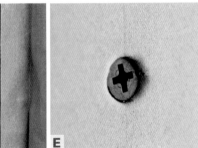
E

Fasten the panel into each stud, with a screw every 8 in (200 mm). Screws should be at least ⅜ in (10 mm) away from the outside edge of the drywall.

Screws should be set just inside the drywall, but should not break the paper covering when you drive the screw into the surface.

DOUBLE-NAILING DRYWALL

If you decide to nail the drywall in place, double-nail. Place nails in rows that are parallel at 2 in (50 mm) apart. Set each nail at the same time. Do not completely drive one nail before setting the second nail.

USING ADHESIVE TO HANG DRYWALL

A

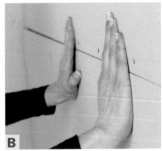
B

Apply a bead of caulk along each stud, leaving a 6-in (150-mm) gap along the edges of where the drywall piece will end.

Press the drywall in place. Nail or screw in place around the perimeter of the drywall sheet.

APPLYING TAPE

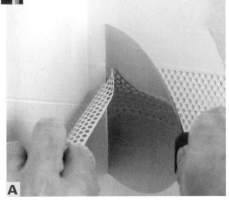
A

After the drywall panels are installed, you will need to cover the joints with tape and joint compound— the first of three layers of compound that you will apply. Cut tape to length, and embed the tape in joint compound along the seam.

INSTALLING CORNER BEAD

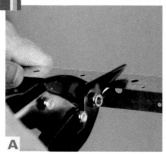

A Measure the height of the wall. Cut the metal corner bead to the required length.

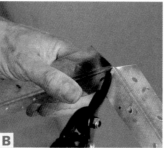

B Bend and cut the metal bead to shear it.

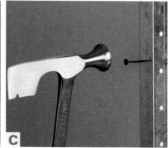

C Nail the corner bead in place at least every 12 in (300 mm).

D Apply joint compound to the corner, covering the corner bead and feathering out.

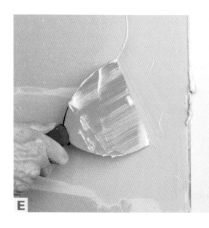

E

After the compound is dry, apply a second coat of compound.

TAPING AN INSIDE CORNER

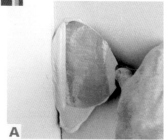

A Apply joint compound to the inside corner using a 4-in (100-mm) knife.

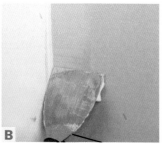

B Smooth the compound out, feathering it in place.

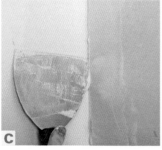

C Apply the joint compound to the other wall.

D Cut drywall tape to length, and crease the tape along the seam. Firmly adhere the tape to the length of the corner.

E Smooth the tape in place, and apply joint compound to the paper, feathering out.

F When the joint compound is dry, sand any ridges from the face of the drywall.

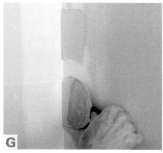

G Apply the second coat of joint compound to the corner.

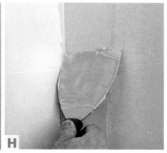

H Feather the compound out to provide a smooth finish.

FILLING SCREW HOLES

A Apply compound to every screw or nail hole in your drywall panels to fill the holes.

B When dry, apply a second coat of compound to smooth out the finish.

Hanging drywall over ceilings, arches, and curves takes more patience and requires more hands then drywalling walls. If you are simply repairing a small area, you may not need the aid of a helper. If you are tackling a larger job without any help, there are special tools that are designed to carry, lift, and position drywall, as weight can be a large factor. Whether you have help or not, drywall carriers and lifts are still worth trying, to make the job move more quickly. Before purchasing panels for the ceiling, keep in mind your resources for positioning them in place.

SEEKING ASSISTANCE

Hanging drywall is often a job that requires more than one DIYer. Never attempt any work that you are not confident that you can complete. Drywall panels can be cumbersome and heavy to lift, carry, and install. Investigate using tools to help with carrying and installing panels. If you need help, it might be a good idea to hire a professional.

DRYWALL CEILINGS

Drywalling ceilings is a job that requires at least two people. Drywall panels are cumbersome and heavy, and lifting them overhead can be tricky. Once they are in position, screwing or nailing the panels in place takes an extra set of hands. There are special tools and simple supports that you can construct to help keep the panels in place, including a T-support constructed of pieces of 2 x 4 in (60 x 120 mm) wood. T-supports and drywall lifts also are available from manufacturers (see opposite).

DRYWALL CARRIERS

Drywall panels are difficult to carry without help. Drywall carriers are designed to help make a very cumbersome job much easier. There are carriers available for two people to use together to lift and move material, and others intended for just one person to carry a panel. Shown below is a carrier for one person.

If your material supply is on the same floor of your home as the room you are finishing with drywall, a drywall cart is also an option to move material around your project. Drywall carts make it is easier to store and move multiple sheets. When you carry drywall with another person, make sure you are on the same side of the panel. Lean the panel toward your body.

Carry drywall
Shown here is a one-person drywall carrier. Its wheels make it easy to transport drywall panels across a room.

ONE-PERSON CARRIER

SUPPORT EQUIPMENT

You may need to access your ceiling and high parts of walls in your house for many types of DIY tasks. If you are planning to drywall a large section of your house, and finish the walls with paint or wallpaper, you may want to investigate renting or purchasing basic equipment that helps you readily access and safely perform elevated work. Scaffolding is a traditional method of increasing your reach. Unlike a ladder, it provides a longer platform so you can tackle more of the wall without having to keep re-positioning yourself. If you want to be completely free from setting up a work station to reach tall tasks, try using stilts.

Scaffolding

Before you begin to consider scaffolding, keep in mind that it is critical to follow all safety guidelines. Each year, one of the top four construction fatalities involves jobsite falls. A few basic safety precautions include making sure that scaffolding has crossbars every 15 in (380 mm). The floor beneath the structure should be sound, rigid, and capable of carrying the load. If the scaffold is higher than 4 ft (1.2 m), you will need guardrails on all open sides. If it is higher than 10 ft (3 m), you will also need toerails. Scaffolding provides a platform for performing work. Available in many different types that are appropriate for a range of construction work, scaffolding can be purchased and rented.

Baker's scaffold

A popular type of scaffold, baker's scaffold is appropriate for most residential remodeling work, as it is narrow enough to fit through door openings. Available in 6-, 8-, and 10-ft (1.8-, 2.4-, and 3-m) lengths, the scaffold can be adjusted to up to 6 ft (1.8 m) in 4-in (100-mm) increments. It is recommend for working on ceilings up to 12 ft (3.7 m) high. It is made of two ladder ends, one platform, and two guardrails. If you use an outrigger, you can stack them two high.

Stilts

If you want to be able to reach the higher parts of walls and ceilings without having to set up scaffolding or benches, try stilts. There are models that are adjustable for different heights and some kinds even flex with your ankle movement. If you are comfortable on stilts, you will save time as you do not need to set up and move benches or scaffolding for each area. Make sure the floor surface is clear and safe for movement on stilts.

DRYWALL LIFTS AND BENCHES

For ceilings that are higher than standard, it becomes even more difficult to position drywall panels and secure them in place. Drywall lifts provide a mechanical advantage to raising drywall to the ceiling. Drywall benches and tall scaffolding are alternatives to get you closer to the ceiling.

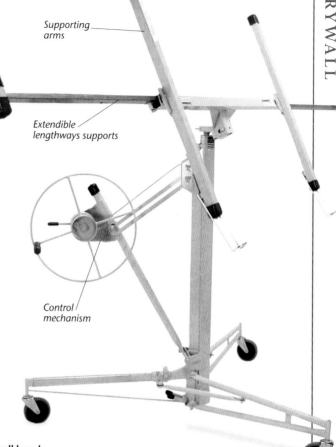

Supporting arms

Extendible lengthways supports

Control mechanism

Wheels lock in place

Drywall lift in use
These allow you to overcome the awkwardness and difficulty of placing drywall on a ceiling. You load the drywall sheet on it, then crank it up to the ceiling. It holds the sheet in place while you nail or screw it to the joists. Lifts are available for rent.

Drywall bench
A drywall bench provides a stable surface for working on the higher parts of walls and ceilings. Some, such as the one shown here, are height adjustable.

LIFTING DRYWALL WITH A PANEL LIFTER

Lifting panels in place is another job where you will need an extra pair of hands. Some DIYers opt to use a prybar to lift panels in place on a wall. There is also a special tool available called a drywall panel lifter. This allows you to adjust the height of the panel on the wall with your foot, freeing your hands to tackle the job of screwing the panel in place. Simply insert the panel lifter under the drywall and step onto it to tilt the panel upward. The small gap created at the bottom of the wall will be covered by baseboard.

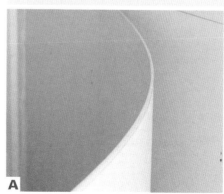

Insert the lifter under the drywall and step on it to tilt the panel upward. When it is positioned correctly, fasten the drywall in place.

A

BENDING DRYWALL

Although drywall panels are flat, it is possible to cover archways and other curves with the material by bending it into shape. Manufacturers make a specific type of drywall to accommodate this need. It is called flexible drywall, and is available in ¼-in (6-mm) thicknesses. It has a heavy paper face and strong liner that makes it easier to bend without being susceptible to cracking. To cover tighter curves, you may need to wet the drywall before attempting to attach it to the wall. To blend into surrounding wall surfaces that have a thicker drywall, you may need to apply two or more sheets.

Either use flexible drywall or bend it to cover archways and curves. To bend drywall, damp one side of the panel with a sponge.

A

FINISHING DRYWALL

Finishing drywall involves typically three to four days of work and a great deal of joint compound. The type of joint compound you use to smooth seams and cover nail holes will depend on the size of your room and your level of experience. The entire process from taping to finishing the final coat can take four days, because of the drying times of the joint compound. Make sure you have allowed enough time to finish each step completely before starting the next.

TOOLS AND MATERIALS SEE BASIC TOOLKIT AND P.125

FURTHER INFORMATION

If you have never completed a drywall project on your own before, and you still do not feel comfortable about tackling a drywalling job after reading the steps in this section, it may be a good idea to hire a professional. In order to find a reputable contractor, scan the Yellow Pages of your phone book or search the Internet for those in your area. When you contact them, ask for references to jobs similar to yours and check those references. Ask the previous client whether the job was done satisfactorily, as well as on time and on budget. Drywall contractors also usually offer painting and other finishing services.

FINISHING STEPS

After reading the previous pages, it may seem like drywalling is a time-consuming, labor-intensive process. In spite of this, the reason drywall has become a standard wall covering is that it takes fewer finishing skills, and less money and time than the traditional alternative of plastering walls. If you have an older home, and want to have a plaster finish to keep consistent with the construction of your home, it is possible to use drywall instead of lath and finish with plaster (see pp.136–137). It will take longer to accomplish, but you will be able to use the plaster to create any texture patterns in the wall or ceiling surfaces that you may want.

At every seam where two pieces of drywall meet, and where there will not be any beadboard or other trimwork covering the panels, you will need to fill the seam and create a seamless transition between the panels. The objective to finishing drywall or finishing with plaster is to create the illusion that the wall consists of one flat piece.

The advantage of installing flat panels of drywall is that there is less finish work after the panels are installed and planning the panel layout to reduce the number of seams will further minimize the time you will need to invest in taping and finishing it. Every seam and every screw hole will need to be covered with joint compound, and each seam requires further steps.

Finishing drywall joints involves three basic steps that can take as many as four days to properly complete. The first step is called the taping step. The second step is called the filler step, and the third step is the finishing coat. Each step involves applying a layer of joint compound that is wider than the one before.

Before starting the taping process, make sure corner bead is installed on all outside corners around the room. Inspect the walls and ceiling to make sure that all of the screw or nails are firmly embedded into the drywall sheets. You can do this by running a taping knife over the surface of the wall. If you hear a tap when going over a surface, it means that a screw or nail will need to be tapped further in.

APPLYING FIRST COAT OF COMPOUND

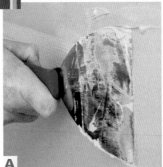 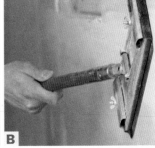

A **Apply a thin layer** of joint compound to the seam. Press tape into the joint compound along the seam. Then apply joint compound over the tape with a drywall knife.

B **Smooth the compound** into place. Let it dry completely and then sand it with a pole sander to remove large imperfections. You do not need to smooth down the finished surface.

FIRST COAT (TAPING COAT)

The first step in the finishing process is called the taping step. During this step you are embedding drywall tape over the joints in the walls and ceiling. Some DIYers will choose to use a fast-setting compound for this first step. While fast-setting compounds will speed up the long process of finishing drywall, the time available to you to work with the material is greatly reduced. This in turn will affect the quantity of compound you will have time to apply, so you will need to judge carefully how much compound you mix with water to begin with.

If you're working with premixed compound, do not stir the compound too vigorously in the bucket. If you stir it too much you can work air into the mixture, which will create little bubbles and craters on the surfaces.

Use a 6-in (152-mm) taping knife to apply the joint compound along the seam. Be generous with the joint compound at this point. Spread out more than you need to fill the seam. Try to work as neatly as possible, but keep in mind that it is not as important to have a perfectly smooth surface when you finish this step. The objective is to make sure that the tape is completely embedded and rests flat over the drywall seams.

Lay a piece of joint tape over the center of the joint, pressing it lightly with your hand to make it stick. Place more joint compound on your knife, and pass it back over the tape. This will embed the tape. Make sure the tape lays smoothly across the joint.

APPLYING A SECOND COAT (FILLER COAT)

After the first coat has completely dried, and you have removed any really noticeable imperfections with a pole sander, it is time to apply the second coat of joint compound. For this step, you may find it easier to use a wider drywall knife, because you will be covering the first strip of compound and blending it further across the wall surface. Select a 6- to 12-in (152- to 305-mm) knife.

You will be building up the drywall joints a little more and then feathering them out smoothly. This step requires a more refined technique than that used to apply the first coat. The joint compound is applied with a little less pressure and a lot more patience. Of the three compound application steps, you will be using the greatest quantity of joint compound. Make sure you have more on hand than during the taping step. In order to achieve a natural-looking feather along the joint, apply more pressure on the outside of the knife and let it ride a little high in the center as you slide it along the seam. If you have applied enough compound correctly, you will not be able to see the joint tape any longer. Be sure to fill and cover all nail and screw holes with joint compound.

The finish coat requires real artistry because you don't want to leave any grooves or streaks after you have finished. The aim is to achieve a base that is as smooth as possible for this final coat. So, before you begin, scrape a wide knife over all the joints to smooth them out a little, which will remove the ridges and tool marks.

▌▌ APPLYING A SECOND COAT

Using a 10-in (255-mm) drywall knife, apply a second coat of joint compound to each seam. Feather the edges of the joint, and make sure there are no air bubbles in the compound.

A

APPLICATION TECHNIQUE

Applying the second coat of compound takes more finesse than the first. Using a wider knife and smoothing any imperfections are ways of creating a successful finish.

Start at the center of the seam, pull the joint compound across the seam. Apply pressure to the outside edges of the knife as you pass over the joint. Pass over the joint to feather the compound out. Continue to pass over the joint until the air bubbles are removed.

APPLYING THE THIRD COAT (FINISH COAT)

If you were able to spread smooth, blended layers of joint compound during the previous two steps, your work during the third coat will be easier. After the second coat is dry, smooth a pole sander across any bumps or humps. You may want to shine a light across the surface to identify the joints that may need extra attention during this third coat.

While some DIYers prefer to use premixed joint compound right out of the bucket, it is possible to add a little water to the premixed bucket during this step. In fact, if you plan to use the paint-roller technique below, you may want to add water to thin the mixture, which will make it easier to smooth the compound onto the wall. Using a paint roller with an extension will also make it easier to apply the third coat to any ceiling joints. You will need a trowel to finish the seam, however, after you apply the compound with the roller.

If you choose to use a drywall knife for this finishing coat, choose a knife that is wider than the one you used during the previous step. A 10- or 12-in (255- or 305-mm) knife will work perfectly well. The objective of this step is to achieve a smooth feather. The aim is to end up with as few imperfections as possible, because each imperfection will require more work during the sanding step.

▌▌ FINISHING DRYWALL

Prepare the drywall joint compound to begin with, adding water to the joint compound mix if needed or lightly stirring a premixed tub. You can add a little water to a premixed tub to make it easier to spread. Only prepare as much of the compound as you plan to use immediately, because it can dry out.

A

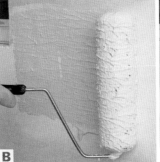

B

C

Using a paint roller and paint tray, spread the joint compound across—and wider than—the previous coat of compound.

Use a trowel to smooth the compound for a seamless finish.

SANDING DRYWALL

Sanding drywall is the final step in the drywalling process. Unlike the muscular work of lifting and installing drywall panels, sanding can be slow work. Make sure you invest in the appropriate equipment and protect yourself and your belongings from dust before you get started. Cleaning up can become a significant part of drywall sanding. You will need to vacuum several times as dust gets into the smallest cracks. Remember that you will be preparing your walls for paint or wallpaper, so make sure you achieve a smooth finish. A good primer or sealer will help hide any imperfections on your walls.

AVOID OVERSANDING

Making sure your walls are smooth is the objective of sanding, but you have to be careful not to oversand. Oversanding joints can damage the paper face of your drywall panels and leave scuff marks or tear marks. Always start out with light sanding and make sure your sandpaper is not too coarse. If you oversand, you may need to fill the scratches in with joint compound (see p.125).

PREPARING FOR SANDING

Sanding drywall creates a lot of dust. Before you begin to sand, you will need to prepare the room and protect yourself from dust inhalation. Even though you will want to completely seal off the room to protect your house from the buildup of a layer of dust, you will also need to properly ventilate the room. Open a window and place a fan in the window to blow the air outside, or use an air cleaner. As you prepare to sand you should keep in mind the following advice:

■ Seal off the room with plastic in the doorway so that dust does not escape into the rest of your house.
■ Properly ventilate the room, but do not open all windows, as this will cause the dust to circulate.
■ Lay a drop cloth on the floor to catch the dust.
■ Cover any furniture in the room with plastic.
■ Wear goggles and a dust mask to protect yourself from dust inhalation.
■ You might also want to wear a hat to keep dust out of your hair.

Reducing dust

If you are sensitive to dust or just want to try to avoid the dust from sanding, try wet sanding. Use a small-celled polyurethane sponge to wet the walls–the smaller cells help hold the water and prevent it from dripping. However, wet sanding does not create the same fine finish as dry-sanding. Another option for dust-free sanding is using a commercial sanding machine or dust-free tool designed to be attached to a vacuum.

Sanding tools

While you may opt for traditional sandpaper to finish your drywall job, there are special sanding tools to help make the work move faster and help minimize dust. Unless you are an experienced drywaller, you will find bumps and ridges along your walls that will take a lot of care to sand smooth. As with all DIY tasks, choosing the right tool for the job is essential. Personal protective equipment, including dust masks, is important to use while sanding drywall, especially if you are sensitive to dust.

STARTING TO SAND

After you have prepared the room for sanding, take a first pass at the walls with a pole sander with 120-grit sandpaper. Make sure that you use even pressure across the wall and ceiling surfaces. Glide the pole sander across all of the taped seams, blending the joints into the surface of the

drywall. You may find it difficult to smooth the inside corners and smaller areas with a pole sander.

The next step involves hand sanding. Before you begin to hand sand, inspect the walls. Pass the palm of your hand over the joints. Use a light to shine on the wall surface you plan to sand, so that it will illuminate the seams, casting light across imperfections and making them evident. Use sandpaper or a hand sander with 150-grit sandpaper. If you use sandpaper, fold it to create an edge.

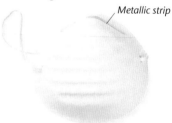

Metallic strip

Dust mask
A mask offers some protection against large particle inhalation. Choose a design that fits tightly. A metallic strip over the bridge of the nose keeps the mask in position and makes it as airtight as possible.

SANDING TECHNIQUES

Hand sanding
For details and finishing work, hand sand your walls. Use even pressure in a circular motion to buff out scratches and imperfections.

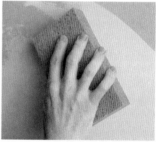

Wet sanding
It may take practice to get the same type of finish as hand sanding. Use a sponge to wet the walls and clean the sponge frequently.

Pole sanding
Pole sanders are used for a first pass at walls and ceilings. You can twist the handle to control the ball joint on the sanding head to allow the sander to switch directions and turn around the inside corners.

ADDING A CEILING ROSE

Accessories can enhance the look of your room. If you have a plaster wall finish or if you've just completed drywalling, adding the touch of a plaster, wood, or polyurethane ceiling rose, also called ceiling medallion, can make a dramatic impression, especially in a dining room or living room. The method for installing a ceiling rose is fairly similar for each type of material–shown below is the installation of a plaster ceiling rose. Follow all manufacturers' instructions for the material you choose.

TOOLS AND MATERIALS SEE BASIC TOOLKIT AND P.125

INSTALLING YOUR CEILING ROSE

■ Consider your electrical wiring. Consult with an electrician if you need to move your electrical work before installing the ceiling rose.

■ If your ceiling is already painted, you will need to rough up the surface area by scoring back and forth where the rose will be attached.

■ Large plaster ceiling roses are heavy and need to be attached very firmly to the ceiling.

■ Polyurethane ceiling roses are lightweight and can be installed with double-stick tape and finish nails.

INSTALLING A PLASTER CEILING ROSE

A

Use a detector to find the joists nearest your chosen point for the rose. Mark their position and the direction in which they run.

B

Hold the rose in position, and mark where the joists cross it. Also draw a pencil guide line on the ceiling around the rose's circumference.

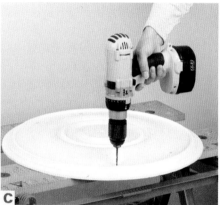

C

Drill holes for attachments in the areas that will align with the joists. Use a slow drill speed to avoid cracking the rose.

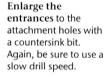

Enlarge the entrances to the attachment holes with a countersink bit. Again, be sure to use a slow drill speed.

D

E

Withdraw the countersink bit when a hole is large enough to accommodate the heads of your chosen attachments.

F

Prepare the adhesive and use a filling knife to apply a good covering of adhesive across the back of the rose.

G

Position the rose on the ceiling, inside the edge guide line and with holes in line with the joists. Apply light, even pressure.

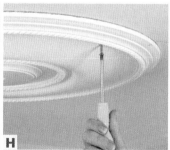

H

Attach wood screws through the holes in the rose and into the joists. Do not over-tighten them, or the rose may crack.

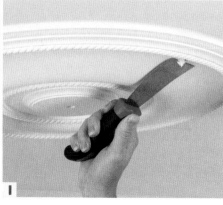

I

Use adhesive or filler to fill the attachment holes. Fill around the edge of the rose, and smooth with a damp sponge. Once filler is dried, sand the filling holes and around the edge of the rose if necessary to achieve a smooth, even finish.

Finishing (skimming) with topcoat plaster is an art that takes practice to get a smooth finish. No guides can be used. The technique is the same whether you skim over drywall sheets (as here), render, or undercoat plaster, though the surface preparation varies (see p.129). An undercoat should be slightly damp when plaster is applied; use a mister to dampen it, if necessary. Practice using plastering techniques on a small area before tackling a whole wall.

TOOLS AND MATERIALS SEE BASIC TOOLKIT AND P.125

COVERING BOARD

Drywall can be skimmed with plaster to make the surface suitable for painting or papering. Use tape to cover the joints between boards. Apply a layer of plaster across the entire surface. Then follow the steps below to achieve a smooth surface. The same type of plaster should be used for each layer.

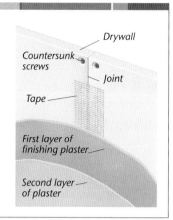

Drywall

Countersunk screws

Joint

Tape

First layer of finishing plaster

Second layer of plaster

1 SMOOTHING DRYWALL JOINTS

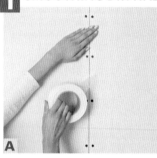

A

Use drywall tape to cover joints between drywall sheets, attaching it with a little prepared plaster.

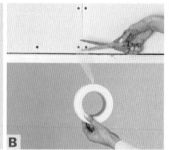

B

Trim tape with scissors to get a neat edge. Fill any gaps greater than ⅛ in (3 mm) with pre-mixed plaster.

2 PREPARING PLASTER

A

Half-fill a bucket with clean tap water, and slowly add the plaster, carefully following the manufacturer's instructions. Mix more as you need it.

B

Use a power stirrer to mix the plaster. Submerge the stirrer before starting the drill and use at a low speed. You can also mix manually.

C

Keep adding plaster and mix until it has a creamy consistency. Run a trowel around the edge of the bucket to incorporate all the dry plaster.

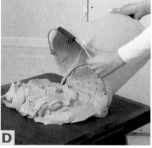

D

Pour the plaster onto a board. It should be thick enough to spread evenly over the board without running over the edge.

3 APPLYING THE PLASTER

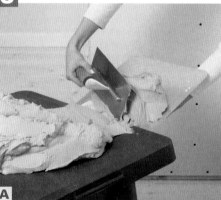

A

Use a trowel to cut away a section of the mixed plaster, and transfer it to a hawk. Use a small amount at first to get used to handling the hawk.

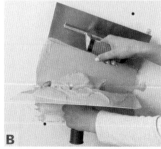

B

Holding the hawk in front of the wall, cut away a section of plaster, using the plastering trowel. Push the plaster up and onto the wall surface.

C

Spread the plaster across the wall surface, pressing firmly and distributing it as evenly as possible. Work from the top of the wall to the bottom, in broad, vertical and horizontal strokes. Aim to work quickly to cover the surface before the plaster starts to dry.

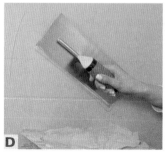

D

Continue to add more plaster, building up a rhythm of loading the hawk and transferring the plaster to the wall surface.

4 SMOOTHING THE PLASTER

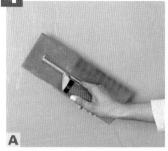

A

Once the surface is covered, go back over it, smoothing the plaster to an even thickness. Do not try to achieve perfect smoothness yet.

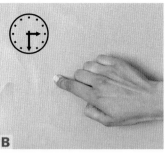

B

Leave the plaster to dry for at least half an hour, until the surface is firm enough to touch without moving the plaster, but is still damp.

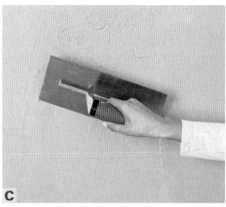

C

Sweep a clean, dampened trowel blade across the entire surface, smoothing the plaster and redistributing any excess to fill small indents. Hold the blade at a slight angle with only one edge on the plaster to achieve a smooth finish.

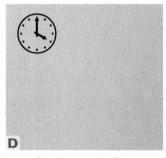

D

Leave the plaster to dry for another half hour, until it is harder, but still slightly damp.

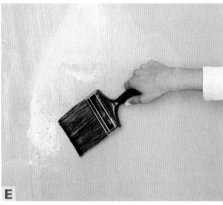

E

Repeat the smoothing process, again using any excess surface plaster to fill small depressions. If necessary, use a wet brush or garden spray gun to dampen the plaster as you work. Aim for a smooth finish at this final stage; it is more effective than trying to sand rough plaster when dry.

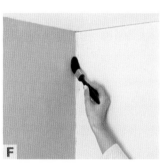

F

Use a small, damp brush to finish edges and corners neatly.

5 FINISHING AN OUTSIDE CORNER

To produce a sharp, straight edge when plastering an outside corner on drywall, use a corner bead. This acts as a guide for the finishing plaster, but is covered by the plaster to give a clean finish. Saw the corner bead to the length you need using a junior hacksaw or tin snips (see p.103).

A

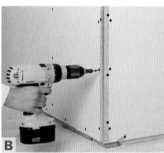

B

Attach the bead to both walls at the corner ensuring that the bead is tight against the corner.

C

Apply plaster over the top of the corner bead, allowing the plastering trowel to rest on the apex of the bead to give you a good finish.

APPLYING A SECOND LAYER

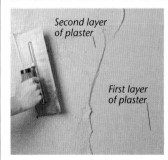

Second layer of plaster

First layer of plaster

An alternative to smoothing off the first layer of plaster is to apply a second, thinner layer, giving two topcoats. If you want to follow this option, do it between steps 4A and B. Most professional plasterers do this to achieve the flattest, highest-quality finish. Once the second layer has been added, follow steps 4B onward to smooth the plaster.

FINISHING AN EXTERNAL CORNER

An alternative to using a corner bead on an external corner is to smooth the plaster with a corner trowel. This gives a more rustic finish, rather than a clean, straight line. A corner trowel is not suitable for achieving a high-quality finish; corner beads give better results. A similar finish is achieved on an internal corner by using an internal corner trowel.

REPAIRING OVERSANDED DRYWALL

A common DIY mistake is trying too hard to smooth a drywall joint. If you sand too vigorously, you can actually remove part of the paper face, and this will need to be repaired.

TOOLS AND MATERIALS

Sandpaper, drywall knife, joint compound

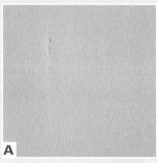

A

If you have sanded through the joint compound and the paper face of the drywall, you will need to repair it.

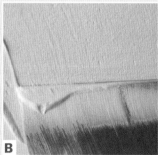

B

Apply new joint compound if damage is extensive. Use the same methods as shown on p.122.

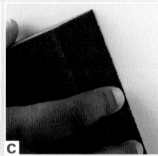

C

After the compound is dry, sand the area with fine-grit sandpaper.

REPAIRING DRYWALL WALL POPS

Common in newer homes, drywall pops are nails that have moved from under the surface of the drywall and popped through the finish. Screws are less likely to create pops.

TOOLS AND MATERIALS

Drywall knife, joint compound, screwdriver

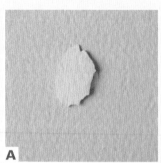

A

Over time, nails may pop through wall surfaces, as shown above.

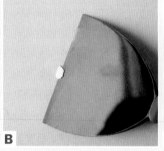

B

Carefully chip away any material that is not flush with the wall or ceiling surface.

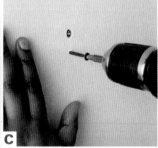

C

Drive screws into the surface of the drywall to securely attach it. Finish the surface with joint compound, and sand when dry.

REPAIRING OVERCUTS

Cutting out electrical boxes may seem fairly straightforward, but overcuts can occur. If you are replacing an electrical box, and the drywall hole is too large for the new box, you can follow these same directions.

DRYWALL REPAIR KITS

Available at most home improvement centers, drywall repair kits make repair jobs much easier. These kits offer you pieces that are cut to fit around standard electrical openings and to fill in small holes.

TOOLS AND MATERIALS

Sandpaper, drywall knife, joint compound, mesh tape

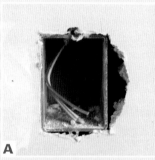

A

If you have overcut a drywall hole, as shown here, you will need to fill in the hole before finishing.

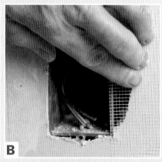

B

The first step is to measure a piece of mesh tape to fit over the hole.

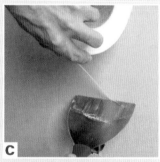

C

Using a knife, trim the mesh tape to the appropriate length.

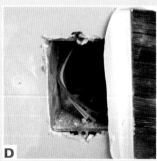

D

Apply joint compound to the mesh tape. The joint compound should fill all of the holes in the tape.

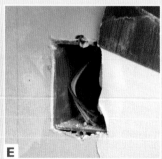

E

Cover the area completely with the joint compound. Let dry.

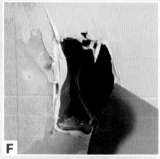

F

Apply a second coat to the area and feather into the wall. Let dry and sand smooth.

REPAIRING BUBBLED TAPE

Bubbled tape appears when the tape has not been completely embedded into the joint compound or the bond has been unsuccessful. The tape becomes loose and a bubble appears on the wall.

TOOLS AND MATERIALS
Utility knife, sandpaper, drywall knife, joint compound

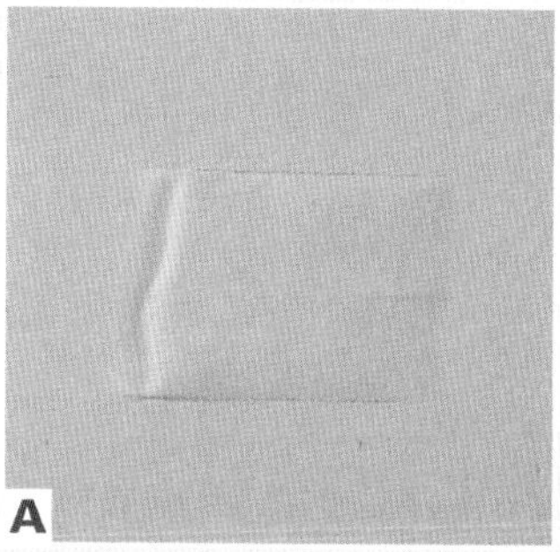

A

Drywall tape can pull away from the wall, creating a bubble along the surface of the wall.

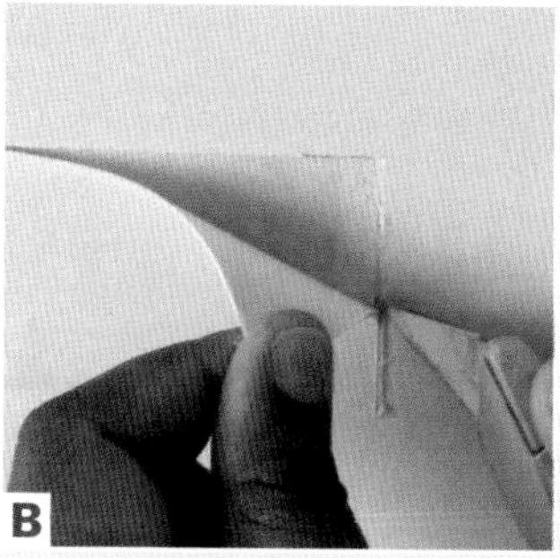

B

To repair a bubble, carefully cut out the affected area with a utility knife.

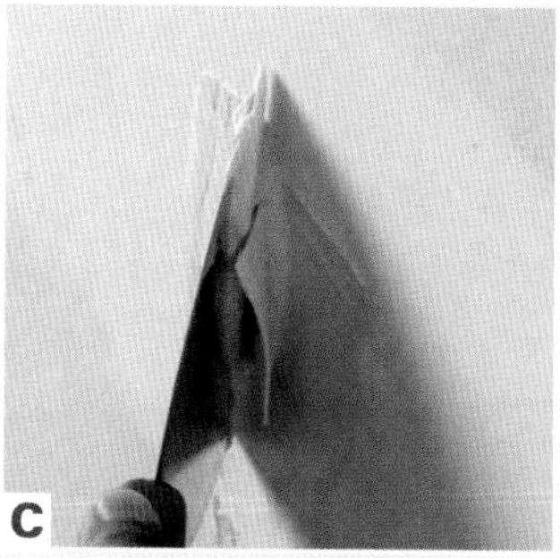

C

Retape and apply joint compound to the surface. Allow it to dry and then apply a second coat. Sand smooth.

REPAIRING A HOLE IN DRYWALL

Holes in walls happen. Whether it's from moving in large furniture or something else, the method to repair it is the same. You will need more supplies to fill a larger hole than the one shown on the opposite page, and it requires a few more steps, too. Cut the damaged area out to calculate how large a patch you will need to have on hand to repair the hole.

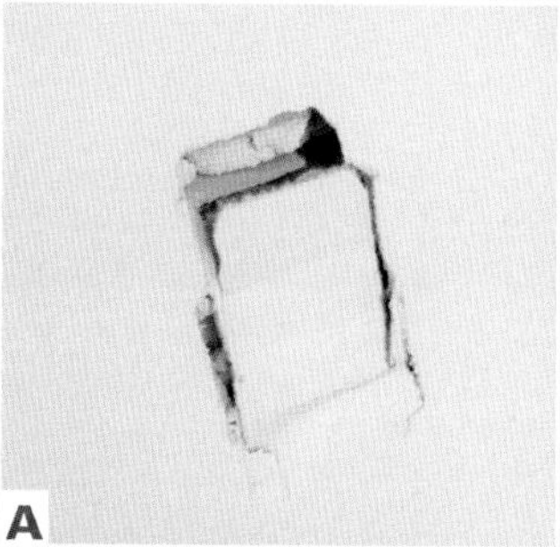

A

If you have a large hole or damaged area in your wall or ceiling, you will need to patch the hole.

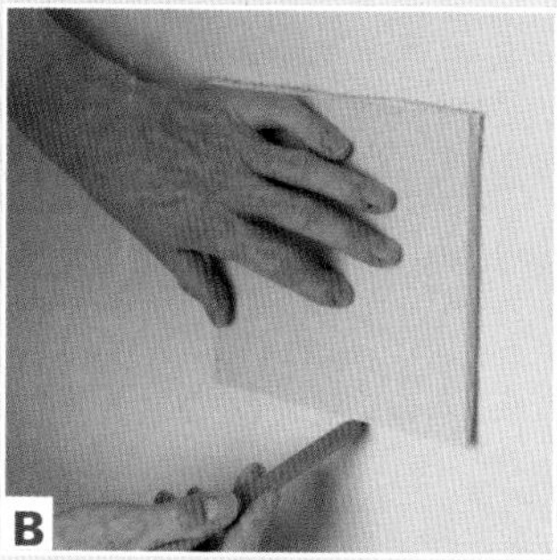

B

Cut a piece of drywall to a size just larger than the damaged area. Use this as a template to trace on the wall.

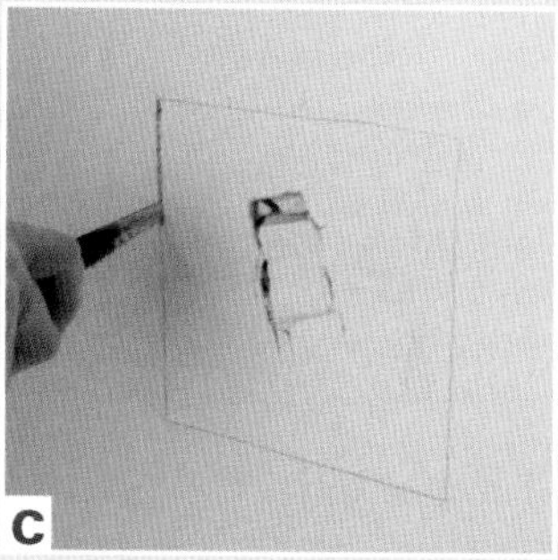

C

Following the pencil mark from step B, cut out the wall section with a drywall knife.

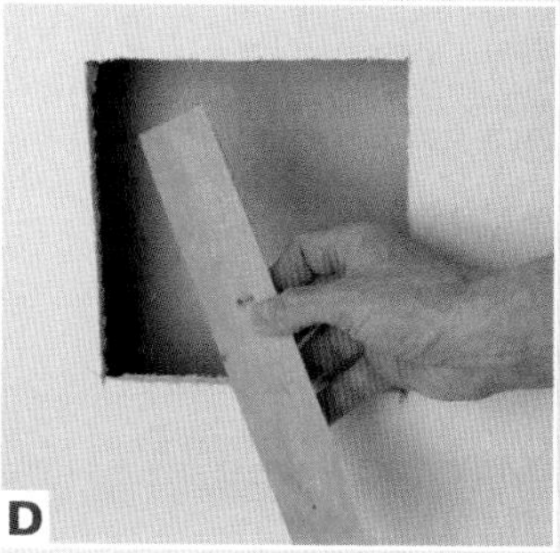

D

Cut two furring strips about 6 in (152 mm) wider than the hole. Insert the strips into the hole.

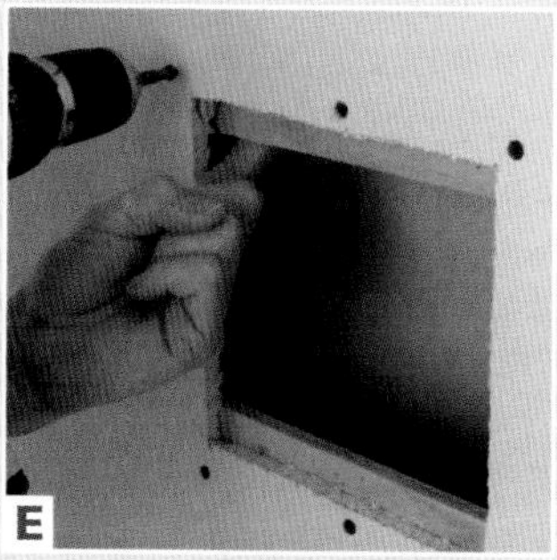

E

Secure each furring strip to the outside edges of the hole with screws.

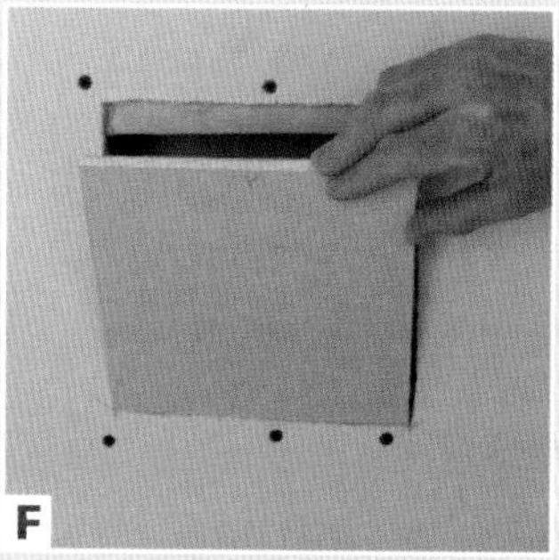

F

The furring strip is used to attach the drywall patch in place. Insert the drywall patch from step B into the hole.

HOLES IN DRYWALL

The repair method for a hole in a wall depends on the amount of damage. To repair a fairly large hole, such as the one shown here, you will need furring strips and a piece of drywall to cover the area before you can apply joint compound and finish the wall. For smaller holes, a piece of mesh tape is enough to hold the joint compound in place.

TOOLS AND MATERIALS
Drywall knife, sandpaper, joint compound, drywall patch, pencil, furring strip

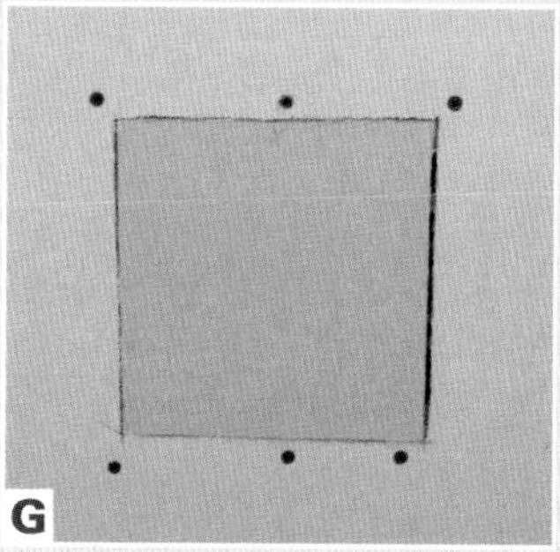

G

Make sure the drywall patch fits, without large gaps around the edges.

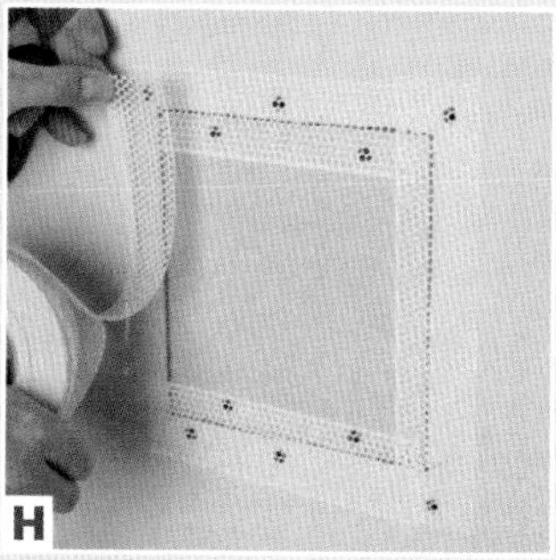

H

Apply tape along the seams between the drywall patch and the wall.

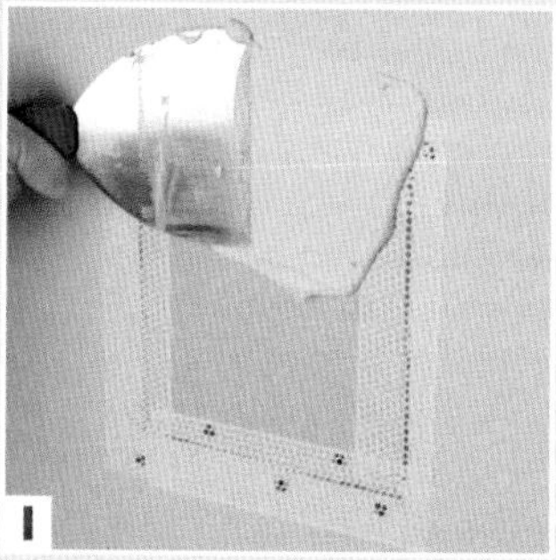

I

Cover the tape with joint compound. Follow the steps for finishing drywall to finish the repair (see pp.132–133).

Windows

WINDOWS ARE AVAILABLE IN A VARIETY OF DESIGNS AND SIZES. THERE ARE DIFFERENCES IN OPENING MECHANISMS AND STRUCTURE, AS WELL AS THE TYPE OF GLASS THEY CONTAIN. THE FOLLOWING PAGES CONTAIN INFORMATION ON REPLACING AND RENOVATING WINDOWS, AS WELL AS INSTALLING CATCHES, SHUTTERS, AND GLAZING. COMMON MINOR REPAIRS FOR WINDOWS ARE SHOWN ON PP.152–153.

TYPES OF WINDOWS

There are several different types of windows. Traditionally, most windows were side-hinged windows, referred to as casements, and sliding sash windows. New opening mechanisms such as friction and pivot hinges (opposite) are increasingly popular. Window materials, shapes, and sizes vary considerably (see p.144), as does terminology, so you should read your manufacturer's literature carefully. Replacement windows for older homes often need to be custom-built to your requirements.

CHOOSING WINDOWS

Commonly, the material and mechanism of a replacement window is chosen to match the originals. There are some exceptions—new sash windows, for example, will often be equipped with modern spiral balances, although they look the same as original lead counterweight versions (see opposite and p.147). If you are replacing all the windows in your property, or building a new home, then take time to consider energy-efficient products such as double and even triple glazing. Frames may have a sill attached, an optional sill, or none at all. If your old frame has a sill attached, make sure your replacement has one.

Parts of a casement window

Casement windows are widely used. Many of the terms used to describe the parts that make up a casement window also apply to other windows.

The window is made up of one or more opening casements, hinged along one side. Top-hung and side-hung casements are available. The metal casement shown here combines opening, non-opening, and side- and top-hung casements.

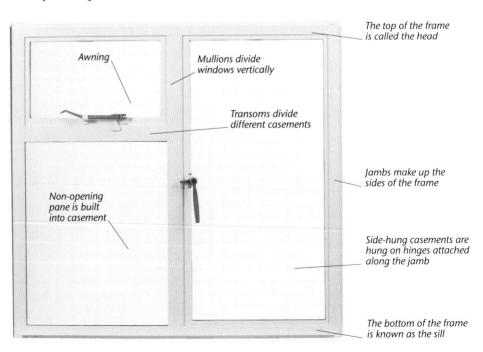

Awning

Mullions divide windows vertically

Transoms divide different casements

Non-opening pane is built into casement

The top of the frame is called the head

Jambs make up the sides of the frame

Side-hung casements are hung on hinges attached along the jamb

The bottom of the frame is known as the sill

Common types of windows

Side-hinged casement and sliding sash windows are still very popular, although pivot and awning windows are becoming common. There are variations on these themes, with each type of window made in many different sizes, shapes, and styles.

Casement windows

As well as the metal casement shown opposite, vinyl and wood casements are also common. See p.144 for information on the properties of different materials.

VINYL CASEMENT WINDOW

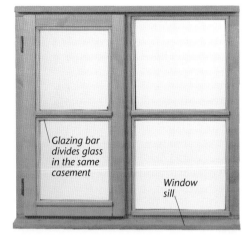

Glazing bar divides glass in the same casement

Window sill

WOODEN CASEMENT WINDOW

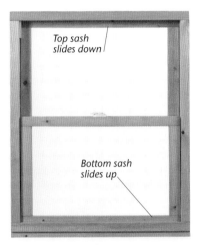

Top sash slides down

Bottom sash slides up

Double-hung window

A distinctive, traditional design with two vertically sliding sashes. Modern sashes are made of wood or vinyl, and some versions allow tilting of sashes for easy cleaning.

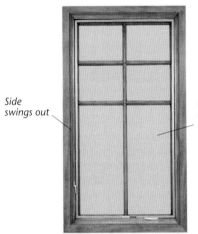

Side swings out

Screen fabric rolls down

Custom casement screened window

Custom windows offer you a selection of sizes and styles that can meet any needs. When you order custom windows, you have options to include special glass, lites, or other features like this window screen.

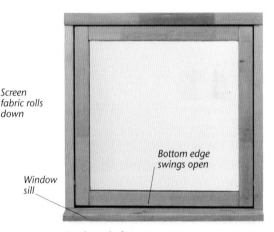

Window sill

Bottom edge swings open

Awning window

Butt hinges are used along the top edge of older designs; newer awning windows use friction hinges at either end of the top edge (see below). Both arrangements allow the bottom edge of the window to swing open.

TYPES OF MECHANISMS

There are several different mechanisms used to open windows. How a window opens can have implications on how space in a room is used—clearance may be needed to enable you to open some windows. Some types, known as "tilt-and-turn windows," have combination hinges and can open vertically or horizontally, depending on how the handle is operated. The opening mechanism of an existing window cannot normally be changed.

Butt hinge

This is the simplest opening mechanism. Hinges are attached down one side, or along the top edge on a "top-hung" casement.

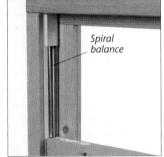

Spiral balance

Weights and balances

Vertically sliding sashes use lead weights or modern spiral balances to hold them in position. Horizontally-sliding windows run on tracks, similar to those for patio doors (see pp.156–157).

Pivots

Tilting casements pivot halfway down each side, or midway along the top and bottom of the frame. The pivots are designed to hold the window in any position.

Friction hinge

These are used on awning and casement windows. The hinges are at either end of the hinged edge, rather than along the edge itself. The "friction" holds the window in any open position.

WINDOW MATERIALS

Most styles of windows are available in a number of different materials. Each material has advantages and disadvantages in terms of maintenance and appearance.

Wood

Windows were traditionally made of wood, and it is still popular because it is so versatile. If old windows are drafty, you can install weather stripping (see p.343). Hardwood is expensive, but is durable and only needs the protection of oil (see pp.294–295). You can also paint hardwood windows or give them a natural finish. Softwood windows need to be protected by paint or a natural wood finish, and regularly maintained, see pp.294–297.

Vinyl

Double-glazed, vinyl windows offer excellent heat and sound insulation. Old windows are often replaced throughout a house by new vinyl windows. In addition to white, other finishes are available, such as wood-grain. Vinyl requires little maintenance.

Aluminum

Where maximum light is required, aluminum windows can be an excellent option—the strength of aluminum means a thin frame can support a large expanse of glass. However,

BUILDING REGULATIONS

■ Check with the local building code department before replacing any windows. New windows may be subject to energy regulations or emergency escape and rescue requirements.

■ If you are working on a historic building, you must check with the local building department and/or the historical preservation board before replacing any windows.

aluminum conducts heat out of the home and is prone to condensation. Double-glazing may be required by building regulations to reduce heat loss. Old aluminum windows were prone to rust, but modern versions are coated during manufacturing and are durable and low-maintenance.

Other materials

Windows can be made from a combination of materials. Aluminum windows, for example, often have a wooden core, and steel casements can be housed in wooden frames to reduce heat loss. Frames with decorative real wood on the inside, and maintenance-free fiberglass or vinyl exteriors are also available. Traditional lead lights are made up of small pieces of glass held between strips of lead within a wood frame. Other types of windows are available with lead-light-effect double-glazing.

SHAPE DIFFERENCES

Although most windows are square or rectangular, many shapes and architectural variations exist. Round windows and arched windows are often used above doors, for example. Windows that project out together with, or proud of, the walls of a house are referred to as bay windows, or bow windows if their profile is rounded. These are generally composed of a number of casements that are joined by a larger and more substantial frame. Large windows with a single, non-opening pane of glass are often referred to as picture windows because of the way they frame the view.

When replacing a window with an uncommon shape, you will usually need to go to a specialty supplier, who will often measure up and install the window for you, as well as manufacture it. If you want a wooden window, then consider hiring a master carpenter.

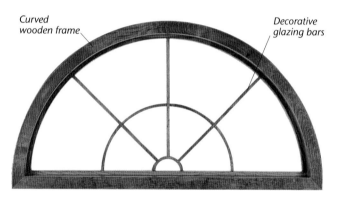

Curved wooden frame
Decorative glazing bars

Curved windows
Decorative, curved fixed windows are often used above square or rectangular windows, or sometimes doors. Their frames are fixed in place using the same method as for other types of window.

Bay windows
This period design is made up of a combination of fixed and opening sashes or casements. Large windows may help support the walls above, so seek professional advice before replacing them.

Bow windows
Despite their curved profile, a bow window is usually made up of flat casements. Always seek professional advice before replacing very wide windows—they may have reinforced mullions with a structural role.

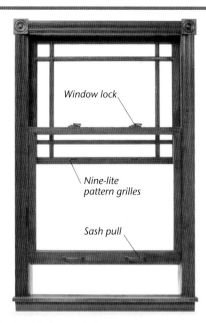

Window lock

Nine-lite pattern grilles

Sash pull

Custom designer window
Windows are available to match the style of the home you are renovating. This double-hung window is shown in a Prairie-style with a unique nine lite pattern.

Custom combination
Window shapes can be combined in custom patterns. In spaces with tall ceilings and views that are desirable to highlight, custom combinations are ideal.

Custom circle window
For a special feature like over a two-story entryway, a dynamic shaped window not only allows light into the home but it also adds a decorative touch to the space.

FURTHER INFORMATION

Choosing the type of window for your home may seem like the most important part in the process of replacing your windows, but making sure you understand all of the operating and maintenance directions is even more important. For example, awning windows are designed to open to only about 45 degrees. And, wood windows that are installed unfinished should be painted or stained as soon as possible to protect them from wear and weather. Finishing windows seals wood from UV rays, preventing them from turning a gray color.

Finish your wood windows with the appropriate outdoor wood sealer that your manufacturer recommends. Always use a water-repellent preservative and do not use caustic or abrasive cleaners. Make sure to caulk between the window and the wall opening after installation. Learn how to properly open every type of window installed, and the recommended ways to clean the glass of the exterior parts of the window to protect your investment in your home. If there are any accessories with your windows, make sure you know how to care for each of them.

GRILLES AND DIVIDED LITES

Windows divided with smaller panes were historically easier and much more affordable to produce than large sheets of clear glass. Today, even though technology allows us to create larger panes of glass that are much less expensive, the traditional look has become very popular. The smaller panes of glass in a window are called divided lites. They are separated by strips of wood called grilles. True divided lite windows are manufactured in the traditional method with a solid wood frame broken into shapes with wood strips.

Grille

Historic style
Grilles are a popular choice on newer homes' windows. Adding a touch of historic style, grilles are offered in the same material as your window frame. Some manufacturers offer removable grilles.

REMOVING OR ADDING GRILLES

If you would like the look of a divided lite window, but are not concerned about having true divided lites, manufacturers offer detachable grilles. These provide the same look as the true divided windows, but are available at a lower cost. With detachable grilles you also have the option of removing them and cleaning behind the grilles when necessary.

INSTALLING A RETRACTABLE INSECT SCREEN

Window screens are a great way to keep the bugs out of your home, while the fresh air flows in. While some DIYers like to remove the screens when the temperature changes, manufacturers offer another option to get the screens out of view. Installing a retractable insect screen on your windows enables you to roll down the screen for use.

There are many types of glass and several installation techniques to consider. Modern manufacturing techniques have produced glass to meet a number of specific needs. Some types of glass are required by law in certain situations, so check the building code. For example, wired or fireproof glass needs to be used in fire doors, and laminated or tempered glass in floor-to-ceiling windows. To install glass in wooden frames, you can choose between putty or glazing beads. Metal and vinyl frames often have special systems built into them.

SHATTERPROOF GLASS

Impact-resistant glass is designed to reduce hurricane damage. This glass has a rigid laminate layer heat-sealed between two layers of glass, one of which provides greatly increased rigidity and "tear" resistance.

LAYERED PANEL

TYPES OF GLASS

Standard glass

Float glass
Clear, "normal" glass. The perfectly flat finish is created by floating the hot, liquid glass on top of molten tin.

HEAT-EFFICIENT GLASS

Double-glazed unit
Two sheets of glass have a layer of inert gas sealed between them to provide heat and sound insulation. For information about triple-glazing, see pp.382–383.

Low-emissivity glass
A special coating lets heat from the sun in, but prevents warmth from escaping back through the glass. A common component of double-glazed units.

Solar control glass
Excessive heat from the sun is blocked from passing through the glass. This reduces heat build-up in buildings with large expanses of glass.

Strong glass

Laminated glass
Clear plastic bonded between layers of glass produces a very strong product. If it does break, the plastic prevents shards from flying.

Tempered glass
This glass is strengthened against impact, and shatters into granules rather than shards. It is commonly used in glazed doors.

Wired glass
The wire stops glass from shattering in high temperatures, so it is used in fire doors.

Fire-resistant glass
New fire-resistant glass is not strengthened by wire but is just as strong, although expensive.

Speciality glass

Mirror glass
To make household mirrors, normal float glass is "silvered." A reflective layer is applied to the back of the glass.

Self-cleaning glass
This glass has a special coating on its exterior surface that makes sunlight break down dirt. Rainwater washes any debris away.

Reduced visibility glass

Privacy glass
Allows light in but distorts the view through the glass. Commonly used in bathroom windows and front doors.

Etched glass
Also known as "frosted" glass, this is similar to privacy glass, but does not distort outlines. Patterns can be etched, instead of the whole surface.

BUYING GLASS

Selecting the type of glass in your windows is an important decision. Depending on which part of the country you live in, your windows may need to protect you from hurricane-force winds, excessive heat, or extreme cold. Often you can select windows with lower U-values for north-facing windows and low e-coatings for the other sides of the house, or choose windows that let passive solar heat in through your winter southern exposures, while blocking excessive heat from east- and west-facing windows. Ratings on windows can be quite confusing. Some are rated by U-factor (the lower the U-value the greater the window's resistance to heat flow and the better its insulating value), or by R-factor (the higher the R-value the better it insulates). Different windows perform differently, through glass gaining and losing heat, losing heat through spaces between the glass, through the frame and through the weatherstripping. To facilitate comparative shopping for consumers, the Canadian Energy Rating (ER) System combines all these factors into one single number,

which takes into account both solar gains and thermal losses. Simply put, the higher the number the better the window. Increasingly you will see the US Energy Star labels in Canada as well. These labels provide ratings for specific climate zones. For extensive up-to-date information, visit the Office of Energy Efficiency, Natural Resources Web site (www.oee.nrcan.gc.ca/publications) and search for "windows."

TOOLS AND MATERIALS CHECKLIST FOR P.148

Using putty Putty, powder filler, glass, putty knife, pin hammer, glazing sprigs or pins, cloth, mineral spirit

Replacing wooden beads Glazing silicone sealant,

dispenser, glazing bead, pins

Installing double-glazed units Packers, vinyl glazing beads

FOR BASIC TOOLKIT SEE PP.24–25

WINDOW HARDWARE

Window hardware typically comes with any new window that you purchase, but you can also replace hardware to match renovations or decorations in your home. Polished brass, chrome, antique brass, satin nickel, and oil rubbed bronze are just some of the many types of finishes you can choose from when selecting new window hardware. It is important to read the manufacturer's instructions on caring for your hardware so that it remains in good condition.

FURTHER INFORMATION

If you are renovating an older home and want to match your older hardware on newer windows, there are antique reproduction hardware options available for many types of windows: sash and pulley windows, casement or crank operated, screen and storm windows, as well as shutters and other related hardware. It is possible to make good discoveries at local specialty shops and flea markets, but if you are seeking something in particular, start by looking on the internet.

CASEMENT FURNITURE

Choose casement window furniture that will work with your window type and style. There are three main types of casement fastener used to hold windows shut. Stays can either keep a window closed, or can fasten it in an open position to stop it slamming. Both a fastener and stay may be fitted to the same window.

Casement fasteners

A wedge or mortise type fastener is used when a casement closes against the frame, a hook fastener when the closed casement and frame sit flush. Some fastener sets include both mortise and hook options.

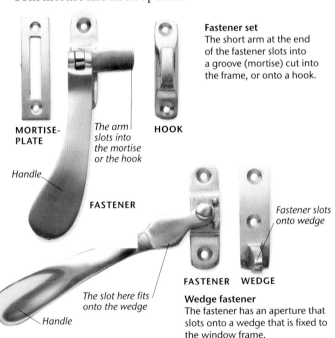

MORTISE-PLATE

The arm slots into the mortise or the hook

HOOK

Handle

FASTENER

Fastener set
The short arm at the end of the fastener slots into a groove (mortise) cut into the frame, or onto a hook.

The slot here fits onto the wedge

FASTENER   **WEDGE**

Handle

Fastener slots onto wedge

Wedge fastener
The fastener has an aperture that slots onto a wedge that is fixed to the window frame.

Casement stays

Stays are long bars with holes in them that are fitted to the opening casement of a window. Separate "pins" are positioned on the window frame. The holes on the stay can be slotted onto both pins to hold the window tightly closed. Alternatively any hole can be slotted onto either pin to keep the window open the desired amount.

Sliding stays are a different design that move within a bracket. A screw mechanism is tightened to hold the casement in the required position.

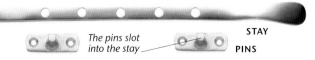

The pins slot into the stay

STAY

PINS

SASH FURNITURE

Sash window hardware is designed to allow you to easily lift and lock the window in place. Sash hardware typically includes sash pulls, sash lifts, and locks. Not as common, sash stops can be used on both sides of the window for extra security. Available in a variety of finishes to match your décor, sash hardware typically has fewer moving parts than casement hardware. Shown below are some specialty sash window hardware.

Sash fasteners

These hold the two sliding sections of a sash window together. They all work as two-part mechanisms, with one part fixed to each sash.

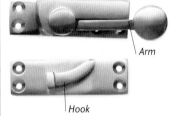

Quadrant arm
The arm swings under the hook on the opposite sash.

Arm

Hook

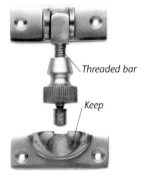

Unsprung fastener
A threaded bar is swung into a keep on the other sash. The bar has a nut on it that is tightened to secure the bar in place.

Threaded bar

Keep

CRANK WINDOW HARDWARE

A very popular casement hardware choice is the hand crank hardware. Crank hardware is available in a variety of finishes and even integrated styles that fold away into the window sill, so that they do not stick out while not in use.

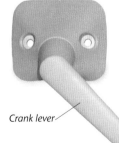

Crank lever

Hand crank
Cranks are levers that are attached to a rotating shaft. Using a rotating motion, the hand crank opens the casement window to the outside.

PREPARING TO REPLACE A WINDOW

If you are replacing an older window, it may need to be custom made, and you will need to measure carefully before ordering. When your window arrives, check that it is the right size. Then remove the old window before fitting the new frame (see opposite). Get professional advice before removing large windows—there may be structural elements in their design. Consider your wall structure before removing the old window (see box, right).

MEASURING FOR A REPLACEMENT WINDOW

Take vertical and horizontal measurements of the window opening (not the existing frame) in at least three places. If there is any variation use the shortest. Then, deduct ½ in (10 mm) from each to give you the frame size for the new window. Take these measurements to your supplier. If you have wood-framed walls, in addition to the window opening, you should also measure the thickness of the walls. If the house is masonry-clad, the height and width of the opening in the masonry must be noted in addition to the dimensions of the window opening itself.

Measuring
Mistakes made while measuring can be costly, so take time to measure accurately.

Edge of aperture

Take three measurements in both directions

Jambs of frame

Only include the sill in your measurements if it is also being replaced

REMOVING THE OLD WINDOW

Don't remove an old window until you have received the new one and checked it for damage. Otherwise you could be left with a hole in your wall. In some circumstances, before removing an old frame you may need to take out any sashes. If all the casements or sashes are removable, simply unscrew or lever them away with the glass intact. Carefully remove glass from fixed panes as shown on p.139. You can then begin to remove the frame. Expect to find most, if not all of the fasteners through the jambs of the frame. While you are removing the frame, take care not to damage any flashing around the edges of the opening.

Removing a wooden-framed window

Use a panel saw to cut through the top and the bottom of one side. Angle your cuts toward the center of the side to create a wedge-shaped section that you can lever out easily. Lever away the side using a pry bar, taking care not to damage the wall (although some damage is often inevitable). Once you have removed the first section, it should be easier to remove the other sides. Remove any fasteners. Finally, clear away loose debris with a dusting brush.

Removing a metal-framed window

Use the same technique as for a wooden frame, but use a hacksaw or an angle grinder with a metal cutting blade (disk). When using an angle grinder, watch out for flying sparks, which can be a fire hazard (see p.61 for technique and safety information).

Checking the window opening

If you have damaged any flashing around the window opening, it should be replaced. Double-check for any rotten wood (see also wall structure, top). If you suspect rot or mold (see pp.230–235), seek professional advice.

This is a much easier job when tackled by two people. You should preorder the replacement window and check its size on arrival. Having removed the old window and prepared the opening using the techniques described opposite, you will usually be able to fix a window directly through the frame into the wall. Always install the new frame at the same depth in the wall as the one you have removed. Seal the frame after installation.

INSTALLING A WINDOW

How you install a window depends on your wall type and window design. Always follow any specific instructions that come with the window you purchased. However, the general technique is always similar. If you need to put in a new window sill, attach this into the bottom of the frame before you install the window.

Positioning the new window

Place the window in the rough opening in the same position that the old window occupied. Place wood shims beneath the sill or frame to get it level. Make sure all windows on the same wall are at the same height. Do not accidentally distort the frame with the shims. Shims should not be placed between the window and the header where roof snow loads could bind the window. Measure the distance diagonally between opposite corners, and make sure both measurements are the same. Adjust the shims if necessary.

Fixing the frame

Open the casements to provide access to the side of the frame. Drill pilot holes for 4-in (100-mm) screws through the frame and into the wall studs at the location of the shims. Screws should not be installed where there are no shims as this can easily distort the frame. Drive the screws deep enough to clear all trim and any moving parts of the window but avoid over-tightening, as this can distort the frame. Do not fix through the top of the frame into the header as this space will allow for minor movement of the house structure due to snow loads. Very wide windows over 78 in (200 cm) may need a screw, but no shims on top, allowing for vertical movement.

Finishing the job

Saw off or chisel away any protruding shims. Fill any large gaps around the frame with expanding foam specifically made for windows and doors, never filling too much at a time to avoid distorting the frame when the foam expands. You will need to protect vinyl window frames with low-tack masking tape (blue painter's tape) if they have no protective film because the foam may damage the finish. Once the foam is dry, trim it neatly using a utility knife. Apply a thin, neat bead of sealant (caulking) around the joint with the wall to hide the foam. On wood-framed homes, use wooden moldings, or for vinyl windows use the cover strips supplied. Create a final seal with a continuous bead of caulk around the edge of the window frame. Glaze windows where necessary (see p.148).

FURTHER INFORMATION

■ A hard hat is advisable, and necessary for work above head height. Goggles, gloves, and work boots are essential.
■ To fit a window, you need interior and exterior access. To work on upper-level windows, fixed scaffolding or pipe staging is essential.

You may also require a raised platform to replace ground-level windows, especially taller designs.
■ Use drop cloths inside the house to protect surfaces from debris and dust.

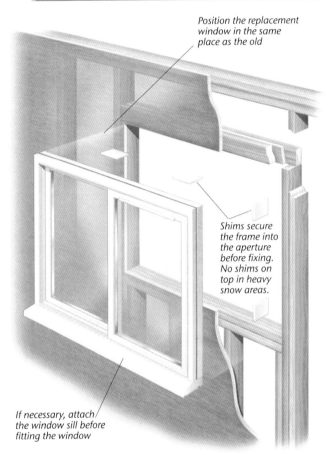

Position the replacement window in the same place as the old

Shims secure the frame into the aperture before fixing. No shims on top in heavy snow areas.

If necessary, attach the window sill before fitting the window

Installing a window frame
Inserting a frame into all types of walls is similar—position the new frame in the same place as the one you removed and fix it in position. Use suitable fixings for the window, and the point to which you are fixing it.

SEALING A WINDOW FRAME

Windows are an historically typical cause of air and water infiltration in a home. Not only can heat loss or heat gain to a conditioned home increase your energy bills, it can also be the source of slow water leaks that cause serious mold problems. After you secure your new window in place, seal around the perimeter of your window frame with a bead of caulking, inside and out. Use thermal plastic or polyurethane sealant on the outside and latex caulking on the inside. Remember that most silicones are not paintable.

Window maintenance is an often overlooked part of home improvement. Replacing older windows with energy efficient windows is a popular DIY project. But not all older windows need to be replaced when you encounter problems, and some historic districts have very strict guidelines. Some windows may need glass replaced, paint removed, caulk to seal the air leaks, or ropes replaced. Older windows are hung on ropes and need to be properly balanced to open and close properly. If you have older windows, you may want to invest time and money in restoring them. Newer windows may be more difficult to update and repair, as they often available only as units.

USING PUTTY

Clean the rabbet before you start, as shown on p.153. Cut some putty from its container with a putty knife. Work it in the palms of your hands so that you achieve a malleable, smooth consistency before you begin. You can also purchase window putty in a caulking tube. Simply gun it to the window, then push it in and tool it as below.

Rabbet

A

B

Work from the outside. Roll the putty into strips about ⅜ in (10 mm) in diameter. Press the strips into the rabbet.

Maneuver the glass into the rabbet. Press gently around the edges of the pane.

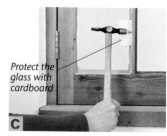

Protect the glass with cardboard

C

D

Hammer glazing pins into the rabbet, not quite touching the glass. Their heads will be hidden by the finished putty.

Press more strips of putty into the junction created by the glass and the rabbet using your thumb.

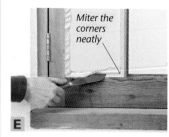

Miter the corners neatly

E

F

Use a putty knife to trim excess putty from behind the glass, then draw the knife along the external putty to create a smooth seal.

Remove smears from the glass with mineral spirit. Before painting, let the putty dry until a hard skin has formed on its surface.

REPLACING WOODEN BEADS

Wooden glazing beads (see pp.216–217) are attached to the exterior of the frame to secure panes of glass. They can be used to glaze a window that was previously puttied. A snug fit is essential to ensure that the glass is secure and weatherproof. Glazing silicone is used to seal the joint.

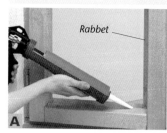

Rabbet

A

Use at least two glazing pins for each bead

B

Apply window caulk around the rabbet to one-third of its depth. Press the pane gently into position to create a seal.

Nail each bead in place on the silicone. The inner edge of each bead should sit flush against the glass. Wipe off any excess silicone.

INSTALLING DOUBLE-GLAZED UNITS

Double-glazed windows have two layers of glass separated by air space, which creates nearly twice the insulation as single glazed units. Glass does not provide insulation value. It is the air between the layers of glass that creates the insulation of an air pocket. Some types of double-glazed windows also use a plastic film as an inner glazing layer. While you can achieve a similar result with a storm window, it is not as effective as there is heat loss along the frame of the storm window.

If you add a third or fourth layer of glass, the insulation value of your window will increase. Each layer of glass traps some of the heat that passes through, increasing the window's resistance to heat loss. When double glazing windows are manufactured, the air between the glass is dried and then the space is sealed airtight. This eliminates possible condensation problems later. Some double-glazed windows are made with a reflective coating, which helps the insulation value.

A

Place two packers along the bottom of the glazing rabbet. Vinyl glazing systems vary, so follow guidelines specific to your system. Further packers may be required around the edge of the unit to ensure that it is positioned centrally and securely within the frame.

B

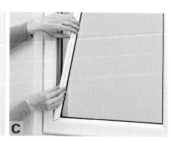

C

Position the unit on the packers and push it into the rabbet. Take care not to crease the waterproof seal or gasket as you push.

Clip the glazing beads and gaskets into position to hold the unit securely.

REPLACING A BROKEN SASH CORD

Work from the interior. Use a chisel to pry away the beading holding the inner sash in the frame. Cut any unbroken cords attached to the sash so that you can lift it out. Remove the central staff beads and repeat the process to remove the outer sash. Undo the knots or remove the nails holding the old cords to the sashes. With the sashes removed, you should be able to pry the four weight covers out of the frame to expose the weights.

Threading in the replacement cords

The easiest way to thread the new sash cord over the pulley mechanism is to use a piece of string with a small weight tied to one end—a small screw or nail is fine. Tie a length of sash cord to the other end of the string. Then, push the nail over the pulley, so it drops down next to the weight. Use the string to pull the new cord over the pulley, being careful not to pull the whole length over. Tie the cord to the weight—you may need to remove the weight from the frame to do this. Repeat for the other three cords.

Replacing the sashes

Hold the outer sash up to the frame in the fully open position. If your sash cords are knotted in place, pull the cord taut, and mark the cord where it reaches the hole. Lower the sash, then thread the cord through the retaining hole, and knot it at the marked point. If your cords are attached with nails, the technique is similar but you should mark the position of the top of the sash on the taut cord. Lower the sash, realign your mark, then nail the cords in place along the sash edge. Check that the sliding mechanism still fits. Fasten the staff beads in position and refit the inner sash. Finally, replace the weight covers and beading.

REMOVING BROKEN GLASS

Wear thick gloves, work boots, and goggles when working with glass. Put masking tape over the glass to prevent falling shards, then remove the putty or beading and tap out the pane in one piece. If this is not possible, break the glass and dispose of it carefully. Clean the rabbet before you reglaze. For information on how to remove glass, see p.139.

Glass is traditionally held in place by putty or glazing beads. However, aluminum and vinyl windows often use gaskets and cover strips to form a watertight seal. If you purchase windows with a special system, use it as instructed.

BROKEN WINDOWS

It is unlikely that you will be able to replace a broken pane immediately, so do one of the following in the meantime:
- Patch small cracks with clear glazing tape.
- Stick masking tape across badly cracked glass, then stretch polythene sheeting over the window, using furring strips to stop it from tearing. This will keep the weather out until you can reglaze.
- If security is an issue, cut a sheet of plywood or hardboard to size and screw it to the frame.

TOOLS AND MATERIALS CHECKLIST FOR P.135

Installing a mortise casement fastener Wood filler, sandpaper

FOR BASIC TOOLKIT
SEE PP.24–25

▌▌INSTALLING A MORTISE CASEMENT FASTENER

Most side-opening casements require one fastener, although larger ones may need two, as will large awning windows. Installing fasteners is a straightforward procedure that simply requires accuracy in positioning. For hook or wedge fasteners follow steps A-C, then pilot and screw the hook or wedge in position on the window frame.

A

Remove the old fastener. Fill the holes with wood filler. Sand the filler smooth when it is dry. You can buy colored fillers that are almost invisible in wood with a natural finish. If your window is painted, you will need to prime over the filler before touching up the paint.

B

Hold the fastener in position and mark the screw holes.

C

Drill pilot holes in the casement frame at the points you have marked. Screw on the fastener.

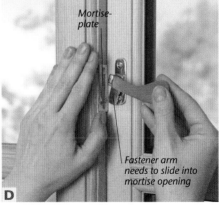

Mortise-plate

Fastener arm needs to slide into mortise opening

D

Close the casement. Swing the fastener toward the window frame. Position the mortise-plate so the arm touches the frame in the middle of the opening. When you are happy with the position, use a pencil to draw around the edge of the mortise-plate and its central opening. This will provide a guide for chiseling out the mortise (slot).

Rabbet for the plate

E

Chisel out the mortise and a rabbet for the plate. The mortise depth should be slightly greater than the length of the arm.

F

Mark and drill pilot holes at the attachment positions. Reposition the mortise-plate and screw it in place.

INSTALLING SHUTTERS

Window shutters can be installed internally or externally and are available in a variety of traditional and modern styles. Most shutters are decorative, but some provide increased security and privacy. Protect windows from weathering with external shutters. Internal shutters can be used instead of curtains—they take up less room and don't become damp in steamy bathrooms and kitchens. Shutters are easily cleaned, and allergy sufferers often find them preferable to curtains.

SECURITY SHUTTERS

Exterior roll-down security shutters are available in some parts of Canada. These are often motorized and can be easily operated from inside. The modern, unobtrusive designs also offer excellent heat and sound insulation. They are not common everywhere because freezing rain can freeze them shut or partially open. Verify references to ensure a specific shuttter will function well in your location.

CHOOSING SHUTTERS

Once you have decided whether you want internal or external shutters, choose what style you prefer. Solid or louver panels are most common—some louver designs are adjustable so you can control the amount of light that you let in. Manufacturers may offer a range of other options such as tongue-and-groove, solid panels with designs cut out of them, or shutters that only cover the lower half of the window. Shutters can be made of traditional wood, as well as aluminum, vinyl, and a range of other materials. Wooden shutters require more regular maintenance than other materials such as aluminum and vinyl. Whatever material you choose, it is worth buying prefinished shutters— louvered shutters are very time-consuming to paint. Shutters are usually supplied with catches to hold them closed and tie-backs to secure them in an open position.

CLOSED   OPEN

Adjustable louver shutters
These are an excellent choice if shutters are being used instead of curtains. You can vary the amount of light (and air) you let into the room by swiveling the louvers, and angle them to increase privacy.

MEASURING

Shutters are usually custom-built for your windows or recesses. Before placing an order for shutters, take note of any mechanisms and installation procedures and make sure they are compatible with your window. If you are installing the shutters into a window recess, make sure there is enough room to fit them without blocking out light. You will need to measure carefully. Most companies will provide specific guidelines on how and where to take the crucial measurements. When you are measuring a window recess, make sure that you take at least three measurements for the width and height of the opening. Use the smallest of the three, because walls are rarely dead straight. This is a technique similar to that used for measuring for a new window frame (see p.146).

MOUNTING OPTIONS

When you have decided on the style of your shutters, there are two main options for installing them. Frame-mounting is the most straightforward technique. The shutters are built into a two-, three-, or four-sided frame, which is then attached around or into the window recess. Alternatively, the shutter hinges can be attached directly to the existing window frame or jamb. This is known as hinge-mounting. With either option, you need to decide whether the shutters are going to be mounted within the window recess or around the opening. Internal shutters are often installed in the recess. External shutters are usually mounted so they are flush with, or just proud of the wall when they are closed.

Interior shutters
You can maximize the feeling of space and light that shutters give an interior by installing them inside the window recess. The frame of the window will need an adequate depth to accommodate the shutters and their fastenings without cutting out light. Large shutters are available that fold like an accordion to rest neatly against the wall surface.

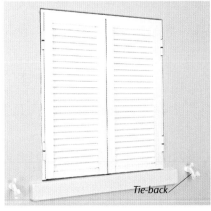

Tie-back

Exterior shutters
These can be mounted to open out flat against the wall on either side of the window. This requires free wall space, and room for them to swing into position. You can use offset hinges to allow the shutters to shut into the mouth of the window recess when closed (shown here). Alternatively, you can mount the shutters on the wall around the window.

TOOLS AND MATERIALS CHECKLIST FOR P.151

Installing interior shutters
Level, wooden offcuts, molding strip*, filler*

Installing exterior shutters
Level, wooden offcuts

FOR BASIC TOOLKIT
SEE PP.24–25

* = optional

INSTALLING INTERIOR SHUTTERS

Here, shutters are being frame-mounted into a window recess. The shutter frame is fixed to the window frame so the shutters take up as little space as possible when they are open or closed. Most types of shutters are installed in a similar way, but you should precisely follow the assembly and installation guidelines specific to those you purchase.

INSTALLING EXTERIOR SHUTTERS

Exterior shutters are often mounted on a three-sided frame so that there is no frame member along the window sill. This type of design is neater, and allows rainwater to run off the sill easily to prevent problems with rot or mildew. Because exterior shutters are exposed to the elements, make sure you choose hardwearing or factory-coated materials.

Tap dowels into position with a hammer

A

B

A

B

Construct the frame using the fasteners provided. Here, dowels are used at each corner to hold the frame together.

Position the shutter frame in the recess and make sure it slides neatly into place against the window frame.

Construct the frame as specified, unless it is supplied ready-made. Position the frame at the front of the recess. Check the fit.

Use a level to check that the frame is square. If packing is required, get help holding the frame while you make any adjustments.

C

Use a drill-driver

D

C

You might distort the frame if you overtighten fixings

D

Use a level to check that the frame is precisely square. Wedge wooden offcuts between the frame and recess if any packing is required.

Drill pilot holes, then screw through the shutter frame and into the window frame at the top, bottom, and center of each member.

Mark the predrilled hole positions on the wall. If holes are not predrilled, then attach each member at the top, bottom, and center.

Remove the frame and drill the pilot holes using a suitable bit. Plug the holes if necessary, then reposition the frame and attach it in place.

E

F

E

Lower the hinge sections on the shutter onto the hinge sections secured to the frame. The shutter should easily slide into place when the hinges are correctly aligned. Check that the shutters open and close smoothly.

Position the shutters. Align the two sections of the loose-pin hinges. Follow specific instructions if your shutters use different hinges.

Insert the pins into the hinges. Check that the shutters open and close smoothly—try adjusting the frame packing if they don't.

G

Clip or stick lengths of molding over the frame to cover the fasteners. If there are gaps between the frame and the wall, you can fit more lengths of molding to hide them. Alternatively, mask the shutter frame with low-tack tape while you fill the gaps, then paint the filled areas to match the wall.

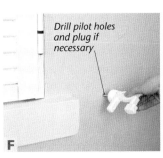

Drill pilot holes and plug if necessary

F

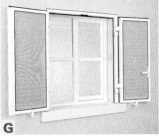

G

Position the tie-backs. Open the shutters to get the right level, then make sure you will be able to reach them from inside. Screw into place.

Check that the tie-backs operate smoothly and make any adjustments as required.

FREEING STUCK WOODEN WINDOWS

Wooden windows can swell in wet weather. Try rubbing candle wax along the sticking edge of the window. If that does not work, plane away some wood as shown here. For protecting exterior wood, see pp.296–297.

TOOLS AND MATERIALS
Plane, hammer, screwdriver

Tap a screwdriver with a hammer to free painted-in screws

Sticking opening edge
You can plane the opening edge of a casement. Take off enough extra wood to allow for painting.

Sticking top or bottom edge
Unscrew the casement from its hinges so that you can plane the sticking edge.

REPOSITIONING FASTENERS

Movement of wood due to damp weather can also make fasteners difficult to close, or lead to loose, rattling windows. Fix the problem by adjusting the positions, as if you were installing from scratch (see p.146). If adjustment only requires minimal movement, you may have to move the fastener so you can attach into solid wood.

MAINTAINING VINYL WINDOWS

Vinyl windows need little maintenance, apart from washing to keep them clean (see box, right). Hinges may sometimes need lubricating, and occasionally you might need to replace a catch.

TOOLS AND MATERIALS
Screwdriver, oil

The screw is often covered

Broken catch
Pry off the fixing cover with a screwdriver then remove and replace the catch.

Stiff friction hinges
Lubricate metal hinges with low-viscosity oil. Spray plastic hinges with polish containing silicone.

CLEANING VINYL

With warm water, remove as much dirt as possible. Use a mild detergent on stubborn marks, then rinse well, especially the seals. Some cream cleaners can be used on vinyl, but keep them off the seals and rinse very thoroughly. Some cleaners are only suitable for smooth, white vinyl, not wood-grain effect types. Never use an abrasive cleaner on vinyl.

ADJUSTING A MORTISE-PLATE

If the mortise-plate for a mortise-type catch (see p.145) is poorly fitted, it makes the catch difficult to use and can prevent it from holding the window closed securely. Remove the mortise-plate and refit it properly.

TOOLS AND MATERIALS
Screwdriver, pencil, chisel

A

B

Mortise

C

Unscrew the mortise-plate from the window frame.

Reposition the mortise-plate. Draw around the outside and the inside of the mortise-plate with a pencil.

Use a chisel to adjust the size of the mortise if necessary. Reattach the mortise-plate and check that it fits snugly.

REPAIRING A ROTTEN SILL

If a small area of a wooden sill is rotten, but the rest of the window is sound, you can just replace this part of the sill. For protecting exterior wood, see pp.296–297.

TOOLS AND MATERIALS
Pencil, saw, router, wood, screws, drill-driver, plane

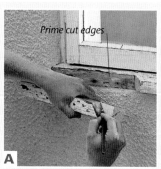

Prime cut edges

A

Countersink screws to allow plane clearance

B

Cut back the sill to sound wood. Use it as a template for the patch. Mark the position of the groove under the sill (the drip groove).

Cut the patch slightly larger than the rotten section you removed. Rout out the drip groove. Screw the patch in place, and plane it smooth.

OTHER WOODEN FRAME REPAIRS

■ Another option for fixing loose joints is to strengthen them with dowel.
■ If a whole section of your window is rotten, then pry the piece out and make a replacement, using the old section as a template. For woodworking joints, see pp.396–397. If rot is more widespread, you should replace the entire window.

REMOVING GLASS SAFELY

Broken glass can cause serious injuries. Always wear protective gloves, work boots, and goggles when you are removing glass from a window. Remove the glass safely and clean old putty and fixings from the rabbet, as shown here, before reglazing (see p.148).

The technique for glass fixed with glazing beads is similar. Tape the glass before prying off the beads (you can reuse them). You should be able to free the pane from any glazing silicone fairly easily by cutting around the silicone with a craft knife. With the glass removed, scrape out the old caulk, prime any bare wood, and reglaze.

TOOLS AND MATERIALS
Goggles, gloves, masking tape, hammer, hacking knife/old chisel, pliers, paintbrush, exterior primer

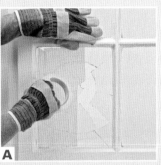

A

Apply strips of masking tape over the surface of the window pane to prevent shards from falling when you remove the remaining glass.

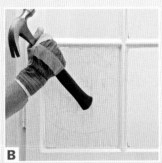

B

Protect surfaces below the window with drop cloths to catch broken glass. Tap the glass with the butt of a hammer to loosen it.

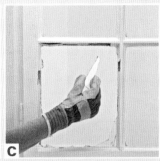

C

Carefully remove the loose, large sections of glass first, then pick out the smaller shards. Dispose of broken glass safely.

D

Use a hacking knife or old chisel to remove the old putty and stubborn pieces of glass from around the glazing rabbet.

E

Remove any old pins or glazing sprigs using pincers or pliers.

F

Dust off surfaces. Use an exterior wood primer on any bare wood before installing a new pane of glass.

REPLACING GLASS IN LEAD LIGHTS

You can repair single-glazed lead lights using caulk sealant. Take a cardboard template to a specialty supplier to buy replacement glass. Caulk can also be used to repair old putty.

TOOLS AND MATERIALS
Putty knife, caulk glazing sealant, sealant dispenser, replacement glass, cloth

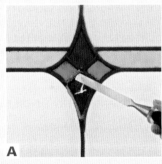

A

Carefully fold up the lead around the broken pane using the end of a chisel. You may find this easier if you run a craft knife under the lead first.

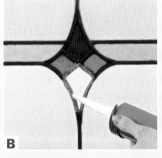

B

Apply a continuous bead of caulk sealant, using a dispenser (see p.81), around the folded lead.

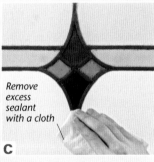

Remove excess sealant with a cloth

C

Position the new pane. Fold the lead back in place and smooth its edge flush with the glass surface.

REMOVING VINYL BEAD TRIM

With beaded and double-glazed units try to remove the trim carefully so they can be reused. Only carry out DIY work on old double-glazed units—if they are still under guarantee, get the manufacturer to repair them.

TOOLS AND MATERIALS
Scraper, packers

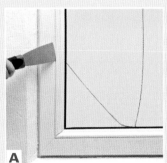

A

Work a scraper blade under the edge of the first bead.

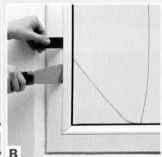

B

Pry up the bead so you can position a packer underneath, beside the scraper. Insert another packer on the other side of the scraper.

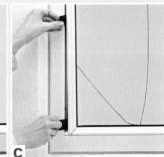

C

Move the packers outward to unclip the bead from the frame. Repeat for all beads. Remove the double-glazing unit carefully.

Doors

BOTH EXTERIOR AND INTERIOR DOOR SYSTEMS SHOULD KEEP WITH THE ARCHITECTURAL STYLE OF YOUR HOME. EXTERIOR DOORS ARE OFTEN THICKER AND MORE DURABLE TO WITHSTAND THE ELEMENTS. WHEN BUYING A NEW DOOR, REMEMBER THAT ALL DOOR HARDWARE, SUCH AS LOCKS AND LATCHES, IS NORMALLY BOUGHT AND FITTED SEPARATELY. A RECLAIMED DOOR IS A CHEAPER, ECO-FRIENDLY OPTION (SEE PP.94–95).

TYPES OF DOORS

The simplest way to categorize the wide range of doors is to consider if they are for exterior use, such as a front door or a garage door, or for interior use within the home.

| WOOD | VINYL | FIBERGLASS | SLIDING PATIO | STEEL |

ENTRY DOORS

A wide range of entry doors is available, the most common of which are shown here. The material of the door is an important indicator of its durability, and will also determine if a finish is required. The age of the building will affect your choice—a paneled design is more appropriate for an older building, for example. The manufacturer should supply details of recommended locks. Many exterior doors are supplied as part of a doorset (i.e., with, or already installed in, a frame). If you are replacing a door that also needs a new frame, see opposite.

COMMON ENTRY DOOR TYPES

Type	Information	Finish
Wood	Hardwood is most durable. Softwood is cheaper, but higher-maintenance.	Use a varnish or paint suitable for exterior work
Vinyl	Thermally efficient, and low-maintenance. Always supplied as part of a doorset.	Factory-finished. No need to paint after installation
Fiberglass	Made of a wooden framework with large areas of insulation. Often pressed or molded for a wood-grain effect.	May be supplied prefinished. If not, finish with varnish or paint
Sliding patio	Supplied in sections, with a frame. Some have both doors on runners; others have only one door sliding and opening.	Door shown left is vinyl in a vinyl frame
Steel	May comprise a wooden core, covered with steel; or may have a steel internal frame with wooden covering.	May be factory-finished. Handles and locks may be factory-fitted

INTERIOR DOORS

As with entry doors, there is a wide range of interior doors on the market—the most common are shown here. Interior doors are lighter, and tend to cost less than exterior doors. Flush doors are generally cheaper than paneled ones. Again, choose a design appropriate to the age of your home. The manufacturer should supply details such as whether the door is fireproof or has soundproofing capabilities.

| PANEL | GLAZED | LOUVER | FRAMED LEDGE-AND-BRACE | FLUSH |

DOOR SECURITY

Choosing a door based upon curb appeal is usually the top consideration on most homeowners' list. But don't overlook security when selecting entry doors. If you must decide first the style and color of door that best fits with your home's design, weigh the security and strength issues for the doors in that category. Doors with steel cores and solid wood doors are the best options for resisting break-ins. Door locks are the most obvious step to securing doors, but if the door is not installed correctly, the lock won't matter. Check the entry doors periodically to make sure they close tightly and they hang plumb in their frames.

Entry doors that feature glass panes will let in light and allow you to see who is at your door, but glass in parts of the door or as sidelights can make your home more vulnerable to break-ins. By breaking the glass, a burglar can simply reach inside your home to undo the locks. If you are concerned about burglars, you may want to choose a door that has glass panels on the top or small panes that don't allow easy access to the locks.

COMMON INTERIOR DOOR TYPES

Type	Information	Finish
Panel	Two types: solid and pressed. Solid is of hardwood or softwood; sometimes made of knot-free wood. Pressed version mimics the grain and panels of solid, with molded hardboard, making it cheaper and lighter.	Solid may be painted, or finished using a natural wood system. Pressed is only suitable for painting
Glazed	Glass is often supplied. Ideal door for a room requiring light.	Tape glass before priming and painting
Louver	Angled slats for ventilation/decoration. Ideal door type for closets. Hung with hinges, or used as a bifold or as a sliding door.	May be painted, or finished using a natural wood paint or finish
Bifold	Fixed to the door jamb with butt hinges. Butt hinges also connect the sections. May have a sliding rail mechanism at the top.	May be painted, or finished using a natural wood paint or finish
Ledge-and-brace	Made up of tongue-and-groove sections, braced with horizontal and diagonal lumber. Softwood or hardwood. Ideal for rustic-style home.	May be painted, or finished using a natural wood paint or finish
Framed ledge-and-brace	Ledge-and-brace construction, in a frame for extra strength. Sometimes used as an exterior door. Stable doors are based on this design, cut horizontally in two.	May be painted, or finished using a natural wood paint or finish
Flush	Cheaper than panel doors. Two types: solid and hollow. Better-quality versions have solid timber core, with a softwood frame for hinging and latch fitting. Hollow flush doors are cheaper.	Solid may be prefinished with a wooden veneer. Hollow versions are mostly designed for a paint finish

DOOR ANATOMY

The way pre-hung doors are installed is similar in both entry door and interior door applications. Entry doors are generally heavier and wider than interior doors. Most interior doors are 2 ft 6 in (750 mm) and entry doors are typically 3 ft (900 mm). When a standard-sized door is being replaced, the new door will fit in the same place as the old one. When putting in a new entry door, the frame should be aligned with the external skin of the wall and then recessed inside the exterior wall surface.

CHOOSING SIZE AND NUMBER OF HINGES

Once quality and finish have been decided, the number and size of the hinges required relates directly to the weight and function of the door. Interior doors may have two or three hinges. A third hinge, positioned centrally, may be necessary for heavy interior doors. A minimum of three or four hinges are used on entry doors. Large hinges with four or more fastener holes are normally used on entry rather than interior doors. Also, remember that hinges should be oiled after installing (they rarely come ready-oiled). Finally, if a hinge is used on a fire door, make sure that it has the required resistance rating (for fire doors see p.379).

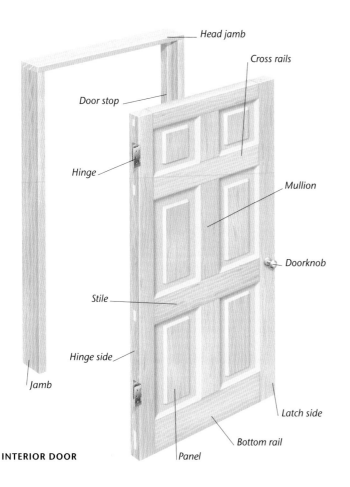

INTERIOR DOOR

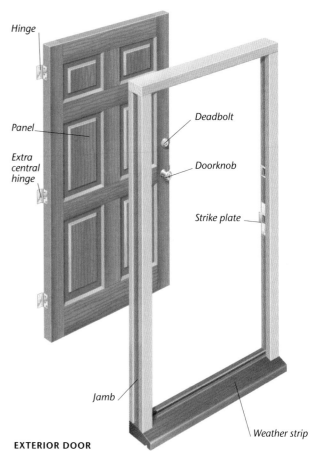

EXTERIOR DOOR

LOCKS AND LATCHES

Doors normally require a latch mechanism so that they can be securely closed. Interior doors tend to have a simple mortise catch. The main body of the latch is attached to the closing edge of the door. The catch then engages with a plate that is attached to the door jamb or door frame.

Entry doors and many interior doors may also have door locks for security reasons or just privacy within a home. Common types of door locks include mortise lock sets, cylinder and tubular locks, and unit locks. Cylinder locks are most common in residential use. Deadbolts are used in addition to a standard doorknob lock on entry doors. When selecting door hardware, it is important to know which way the doors swing.

Passage latch
Used on interior doors where security is not an issue. The latch is opened as the handle is turned.

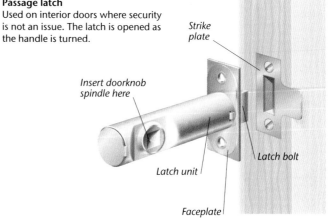

DOOR HARDWARE

When choosing door hardware, ensure that it is in scale with the door itself. Two hinges are usually sufficient for interior doors, but use three or four on entry doors. Entry doors are generally heavier, and call for more durable hardware. Choose locks according to the level of security you require.

HANDLES
Latches require a handle that turns, moving the internal mechanism, whereas with catches (see below right), a simple pull knob or handle is sufficient.

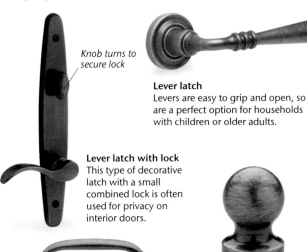

Knob turns to secure lock

Lever latch
Levers are easy to grip and open, so are a perfect option for households with children or older adults.

Lever latch with lock
This type of decorative latch with a small combined lock is often used for privacy on interior doors.

Pull handle
Used on accordion doors, bi-fold doors, and cabinet door fronts, pull handles are easier to grip than knobs.

Knob
Simple doorknobs are used on interior doors, cabinetry, and furniture. Available in a variety of styles and finishes.

DOOR STOPS
In addition to the door stop on the door frame, other door stops can be installed at the bottom of the door to limit the movement of the door or keep the door open.

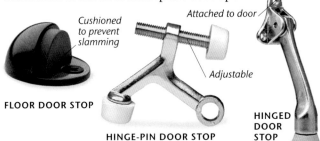

Cushioned to prevent slamming

Attached to door

Adjustable

FLOOR DOOR STOP

HINGE-PIN DOOR STOP

HINGED DOOR STOP

HINGES
Butt hinges are the most common form of hinge. Good-quality hinges come in brass and stainless steel. Some have extra features such as washers and ball bearings. Oil hinges once they have been installed.

Standard butt
Has three or four holes on each leaf, and a fixed pin in the hinge barrel.

Rising butt
Lifts the door upward as it is opened, to allow for a sloping floor.

Parliament
Extended leaf allows a door to open fully, where the frame might otherwise prevent it.

Doorset
Specific hinge for a doorset.

Strap/Tee
Used on a ledge-and-brace door, or a door needing extra support.

Ball bearing
Installed like a butt hinge. Ball bearings give smooth action.

Loose pin
The pin allows you to detach the door without removing the hinge.

Flush
Surface-mounted so no need to cut into the door edge to install it.

Vinyl
Specific hinge for a vinyl door.

CATCHES
Catches are either screwed directly to the door and door lining, or they may need recessing—as is the case with ball catches, for example. Catches are commonly used on closets (see pp.398–399).

Magnetic
Often used on glass doors. Made of high-impact plastic.

Ball
Used on closets. The ball pushes into the strike plate.

Roller
A quiet alternative to the clicking sound of a magnetic catch.

TOOLS AND MATERIALS CHECKLIST PP.158–168

Hanging an interior pre-hung door (pp.158–159) Drywall saw, shims, nail set, spackle

Installing door hardware (p.159) Combination square, auger or flat bit, chisel

Hanging a door (p.160) Hinges, combination square, plane

Installing door casing (p.161) Combination square, mitre saw, wood glue, spackle

Securing exterior prehung doors (p.164) Level, shims, pry bar, caulk

Installing a sliding door (p.168) Level, shims, circular saw, plane

FOR BASIC TOOLKIT SEE PP.24–25

INTERIOR PRE-HUNG DOORS

Installing pre-hung doors is the most popular method of hanging new doors or replacing old ones. All you have to do is install the unit into a rough opening. When ordering a pre-hung door, you will have the choice of a right- or left-hand swing, as well as having the manufacturer drill the holes in the door for the locksets. If the unit arrives with a brace to keep the door and frame aligned, leave the brace on until the door unit is plumbed, shimmed, and secured into place.

TOOLS AND MATERIALS SEE BASIC TOOLKIT AND P.157

HANGING AN INTERIOR PRE-HUNG DOOR

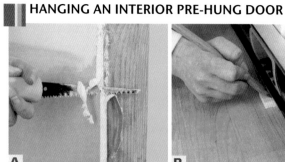

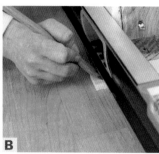

A
Trim any excess drywall around the doorway to make sure the new door will hang plumb.

B
Check that the floor is level, marking for any shims that are needed under the level.

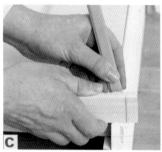

C
Measure and mark against the jamb where any shims are needed.

D
Cut the door to the appropriate length.

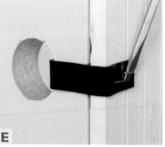

E
Remove the plug that comes on the pre-hung door, as well as the temporary trim on the bottom of the door.

F
Tack one nail on a shim in the doorway to get started.

G
Place the door inside the opening. Position the door so it is plumb, and the door is able to swing open.

H
Secure the jamb with nails along its length.

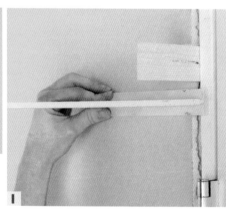

Use a straight edge to check the door opening, ensuring that it has room to open and close.

I

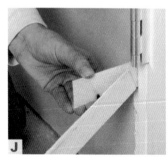

J
With the door closed, place a shim by the bottom hinge to accommodate any adjustments from the previous step.

K
Check the top gap above the door, and check the door again to make sure it is level.

L
Check the center shim and the gap to make sure the door is plumb. Nail the door in place, from the jambs through the shims.

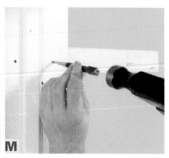

M
Use a nail set to set the nails beneath the wood, creating a smooth finish. Fill the holes with spackle.

Check the door to make sure it opens and shuts properly.

N

MAKING ADJUSTMENTS

Place a level on the vertical surface to check that the door is plumb.

A

If you need to adjust the door, try using a sledgehammer with a very gentle tap.

B

FITTING A MORTISE LOCK

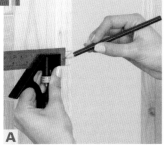

A

Mark the top, bottom and end of the latch case. Draw a vertical guide line through the horizontal guide lines at the mid-point.

B

Measure the distance from the center of the spindle's position on the latch to the latch plate.

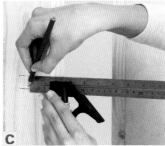

C

Mark, on the appropriate line, the distance from the front of the plate to the center of the spindle position on the door.

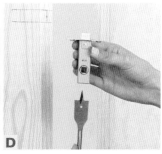

D

Select an auger bit or flat bit that is slightly larger than the latch casing (in this case a flat bit is used). Mark off the latch depth with tape.

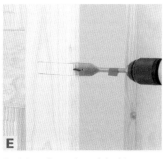

E

Position the point of the bit on the vertical guide line between the horizontal guide lines showing width.

F

Start drilling slowly. It is essential that the drill bit enters the door at a precise right angle to the door edge. If it does not, the latch will not sit flush in position. You may also split the door face if the bit is misaligned.

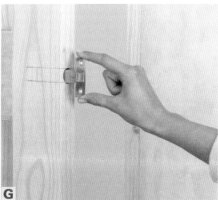

G

Drill to the depth of the latch. Push the latch into the hole, positioned precisely vertical. Draw a guide line around the latch plate.

Remove the latch and chisel out the wood from inside the guide line, to a depth equal to that of the latch plate.

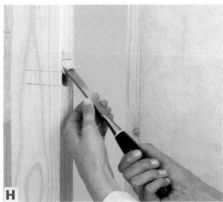

H

I

For the marked-off spindle position, gently drill into each face of the door, taking care not to split the wood surface.

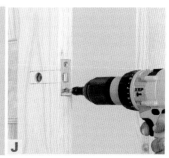

J

Push the latch into position. Drill pilot holes for the screw positions on the latch plate. Secure it with retaining screws.

HANGING A DOOR

It is usual for the door to require some height and width adjustment for a perfect fit. This is achieved by temporarily holding the door in place and measuring for fit. Get someone to help you lift the door, or else use a board lifter. Once you are satisfied with the fit of the door, the next task is to attach the hinges. For information about hinge choices, and deciding on the number required, see p.157. In the example shown here, standard butt hinges are being installed.

TOOLS AND MATERIALS SEE BASIC TOOLKIT AND P.157

1 ADJUSTING THE DOOR TO FIT

A

Use a butt hinge to gauge the gap

B

Drive two temporary nails into the jamb head and two in the sides, to the exact door depth. Position the door against the nails in the jamb.

There needs to be a gap of ⅛ in (3 mm) between the hinging edge of the door and the jamb. (This is the thickness of most butt hinges.)

C

D

E

Always plane from the outer edge inward, to prevent wood from splitting

F

Move to the closing edge. Measure a gap of ⅛ in (3 mm) between the door and the jamb. With a level, draw a line down the door.

Remove the door from the jamb. Place it on the floor, with its closing edge facing upward. With a plane, take the wood down to the line.

Reposition the door to check that the sides fit with the clearances of ⅛ in (3 mm). Repeat the measuring process for the base of the door.

With a level floor, 1 in (25 mm) is needed, but any undulations may require more. Plane off the required amount and check for clearance.

2 FITTING THE HINGES AND HANGING THE DOOR

Place the door on the floor, hinge-side up. Make a pencil mark 6 in (150 mm) down from the top of the door. Place the hinge below the mark, and trace around it. Repeat for the lower hinge, but this time position it above the mark.

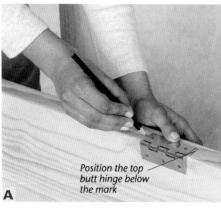

Position the top butt hinge below the mark

A

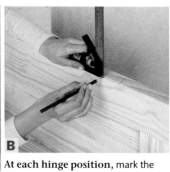

B

C

At each hinge position, mark the thickness of the hinge onto the door's front edge. Use a chisel to remove the marked-off depth of wood.

Cut across the grain first, so that you do not split the wood at the next stage. Make cuts every ⅛ in (3 mm).

D

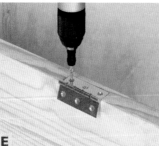

E

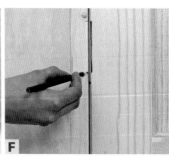

F

G

Now use the chisel blade along the guide line on the door's front edge. Gently remove the cut wood from inside the hinge guide lines.

Holding a hinge in each hinge area, mark off the screw holes. Pilot drill and test a hole with one screw to make sure it fits.

Repeat the layout process on the door jamb. Repeat steps A–E on the jamb and screw the hinges to the door.

Wedge the door open and screw the hinges to the jamb. The latch and handle can now be installed.

INSTALLING DOOR CASING

Door casing, or trim, finishes the look of a newly installed door and updates the style of an older doorway. Care must be taken when installing casing, as the main purpose is not decorative, it is functional. Casing conceals gaps between the door jamb and the rough opening. If you are installing a new door, the casing may come mounted on one side of a pre-hung door. If you choose to replace existing trim, you will need to remove it with a pry bar and a hammer.

TOOLS AND MATERIALS SEE BASIC TOOLKIT AND P.157

1 MEASURING

Mark ¼ in (6 mm) from the inside of the door frame. This will be your guideline for installing the trim.

A

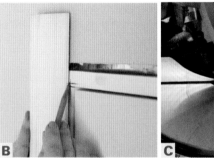

B **Place a piece** of trim on each side of the side of the door, aligned with the ¼ in (6 mm) mark. Transfer the mark onto the trim.

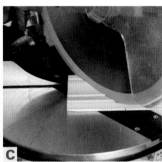

C **Cut each piece** to length, mitering each end at 45 degrees.

2 ATTACHING THE TRIM

A **Nail each side** casing in place, starting at the top.

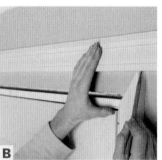

B **Mark and cut** the top piece to length, mitering each end.

Apply a line of wood glue to the end of each miter to help secure the pieces of trim to each other.

C

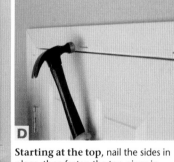

D **Starting at the top,** nail the sides in place, then fasten the top piece in position.

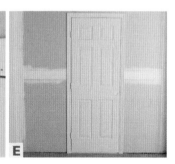

E **Fill the nail holes** with spackle. Let dry and sand smooth.

ADJUSTING THE MITER

The most important part of installing door casing is making sure that you cut the miters so that they fit together at the corners. Some DIYers choose to install the top piece first, making sure it is level and on the mark, before installing each side piece. With the top in place, you can use the top miters to mark the side pieces.

If you need to make adjustments, use a sanding sponge to gently remove material and shape the miter.

FURTHER INFORMATION

Design options
Casing is available in a variety of design styles and profile options, from square-edged designs to colonial-style molding. Rosette blocks, decorative squares that butt the casing pieces at the top corners of the door, are a great Victorian-style option that eliminates the need to miter the ends of the trim.

Painting before installation
If you are using paint-grade door casing, you may want to paint the pieces before you cut to length and install. Use semi-gloss paint for door casing. Flat paint is harder to clean, and flat painted casing will show any dirty fingerprints.

ENTRY DOORS

Curb appeal starts with selecting the perfect front door for your home. The idea behind curb appeal is to present your home so that it makes a positive first impression and appeals to passersby and potential buyers—if you are planning to flip your house for a resale—from the street. Consider the overall architectural style of your house, the type of materials that will fit within your budget, the color of your house, the range of door hardware available, and safety features. Most importantly, to make sure that replacing your front door is an easy, straightforward DIY project, select a door that fits within your current opening.

DOOR LITES

Most doors are available with different options involving lites and decorative glass. Among the many options are energy-efficient insulated glass and stained glass with genuine brass caming. A door may comprise one large lite or have a grille that separates the glass into several lites. Sidelites are available on one or both sides of a door.

DOOR STYLES

When it comes to front doors, there is a very wide range of options available in prehung easy-to-install styles. Color, material, and lite options are the major characteristics you'll sift through at your local home improvement store. Lites are offered in many combinations, shapes, and styles, and can be placed centrally, at the top, or on either side of the door opening. Keep in mind that you also will need to make sure the door you select fits inside your current door opening, swings the desired way, and is prepared with the hardware on the correct side.

15-lite entry door
If you want maximum exposure in your entryway, the 15-lite entry door provides your home with the most natural light that can be achieved without using a glass door.

4-paneled with a half-circle lite
Providing more privacy than the 15-lite door, the 4-paneled with a half-circle light offers some natural light exposure in your entryway.

6-paneled door
The popular 6-paneled door is the standard entry door on offer at most home improvement centers. This door provides maximum privacy for the homeowner.

2-paneled with a window
The 2-paneled door with a window allows you the view and the natural light, but with some privacy. The example shown here features a stylish window.

Custom door
This is an example of a custom-made door with a patterned center lite. It is a left-hand door, because the hinges are on the left and the door swings into the house.

Custom door with oval lite
A popular option, the oval lite is a stylish way to make an impression. The door shown here is a right-hand door; the hinges are on the right and the door swings inward.

Entry door hardware is more than just doorknobs and locksets. Most door hardware manufacturers offer entire coordinated product lines of hardware for the doorbell, letterbox, door knocker, and even exterior lights. Finishes range from polished brass to oil-rubbed bronze and styles range from Victorian to Arts and Crafts, to sleek modern examples. Select the style of doorknob and lockset that enhances the look of your chosen door, and the rest of your house façade. If you are replacing entry hardware on an existing door, make sure you take careful measurements before you order the new set.

DEADBOLTS

Single-cylinder deadbolts are operated with a key from the outside of a home and a thumb turn from the inside. A double-cylinder deadbolt is operated with a key from both outside and inside the door. This offers a more foolproof security option against the burglar who relies on gaining access to a home by breaking through the door glass and turning the thumb turn to open the door. Always keep a key near a double-cylinder deadbolt, in case of fire or other emergency.

DOOR KNOCKERS

While you may have a doorbell and not have a practical need for a door knocker, you may still want to select a door knocker as an accessory to enhance the style of your entry door. Door knockers lend a traditional appearance to any style of door and are available in a wide selection of finishes. Some of the most common types of door knockers available are featured below.

Traditional door knocker
This door knocker is the most commonly seen in the US. It is usually paired with a traditionally styled door.

S Door Knocker
The S door knocker gets its name from the shape. Unlike the traditional knocker it has a vertical handle.

Imperial-styled knocker
The knocker shown here is a variation on the traditional knocker. It has a more stately appearance. Shown with a nickel finish.

Ring door knocker
The ring door knocker is another popular style, and gets its name from its shape. It is shown here in satin brass.

DOORBELLS AND CATCHES

Doorbell hardware surrounds the face of the doorbell button. Often screwed in place.

LETTERBOX PLATES

Letterbox slots used to be standard on most homes, fell out of favor and now are back in vogue with concerns about the security of mail sitting in an outside box. Modern, weathertight slots with spring-loaded sealed covers on both sides are now available.

MORTISE LOCKS

Mortise locks are locking latch mechanisms that require a rectangular hole in the door edge. Some have a second round hole above for key operation.

Oval doorbell
Features a brass lifetime finish that warrants against defects in material.

Door catch
Compensates for swelling, shrinking, drafts, and weights.

Letterbox
This letterbox is a sleek, streamlined modern version of the traditional letterbox. It is shown here in satin nickel.

Arts and Crafts
The Arts and Crafts style is popular in many parts of the country. This mortise lock features a pattern reminiscent of the style. It is shown with an oil-rubbed bronze finish.

Traditional
Many homeowners opt for a more traditional look with hardware, as it typically has great appeal. This traditional-looking lock features elegant styling.

PREHUNG ENTRY DOORS

Entry doors are available as both slabs and in standard prehung sizes that fit most newer houses. If you have an opening with an unusual size or would like a custom-made door, you may need to buy a slab. Slabs require a few additional steps to those shown below for a prehung door, which arrive with the jambs and hinges already in place. Replacing an older entry door with a new insulated door can save energy, as well. The most important part of hanging a door is to make sure it is plumb and level.

TOOLS AND MATERIALS SEE BASIC TOOLKIT AND P.157

1 PREPARING TO HANG THE DOOR

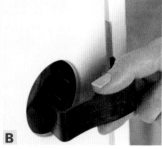
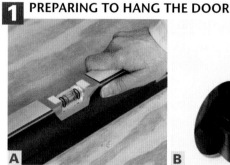

A Check the floor to make sure it is level. If it is level, you will be able to align the door with the floor.

B Remove all of the packaging from the door, except any braces that keep the door square.

2 POSITIONING THE DOOR

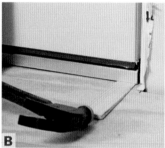

A Center the door inside of the opening to make sure that the door will fit.

B Use shims, if necessary, to make sure the door is plumb in the opening.

C After the door is centered, trace the molding on the exterior of the house. Drive nails at the top of the door unit to keep it in place as you make adjustments.

D Once centered, trace the molding onto the exterior of the house. Drive nails at the top of the unit to keep it in place as you make adjustments.

E Check for plumb. Use a pry bar to adjust the hang. The gap between door and wall must be small enough to be covered by the door casing.

3 INSTALLING THE HINGE AND LOCK

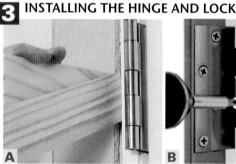
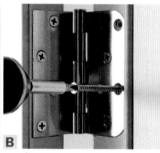

A Insert shims behind each hinge. The shims help distribute pressure.

B Screw the hinges in place. Check to make sure the door opens properly.

4 INSTALLING THE DRIP EDGE

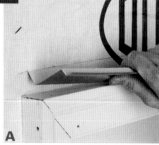

C Drive nails every 12 in (305 mm) along the molding into the house.

A Measure the width of the opening. Cut and install a drip edge at the top of the opening. This provides a moisture barrier.

B Making sure to firmly press the molding in place, center the door inside the opening. Run a bead of caulk around the molding. Adjust the threshold. From the inside, insulate the gap around the door with fiberglass insulation or window and door foam. Work in two or three passes rather than all at once to avoid warping the frame with the expanding foam.

Entry doors have to withstand outdoor elements of rain, wind, and changing temperatures, as well as the wear and tear of everyday life. They are stronger than interior doors, with impact-resistant materials and are finished to withstand the elements. Eventually a door dents or weatherstripping needs to be replaced. Below are some of the more common adjustments that you may need to make on your entry door. Keep in mind the material; you may need to take precautions for exotic woods versus manufactured products.

TOOLS AND MATERIALS SEE BASIC TOOLKIT PP.24–25

MAINTAINING AND REPAIRING DOORS

Over time you may notice that your entry door sticks, creaks, or does not close as easily as it did when it was first installed. Because a house is usually constructed from organic material, it is susceptible to wear and tear. In addition, wood expands and contracts through changing weather. Therefore, after your house has "settled" you may need to make simple adjustments to make sure your entry door is still plumb in the doorway and can easily open and shut. In addition to the natural changes that occur with an aging house, there are other factors that may make it necessary to spend time repairing your entry door. If your house sees a lot of foot traffic, your door is more likely to suffer from damage due to use.

Repairing a sticking entry door

If your door is sticking, you may need to adjust the size of the door to fit the entryway. It may be as easy as cleaning all of the hinges and removing any buildup of dirt along the door edges. The next step is to see if adjusting the hinges will alleviate the problem. Try tightening them. If the door continues to stick, try sanding the edges of the door.

Repairing dents

Dents in entry doors can be repaired. If you have a steel door, you may be able to repair it using an auto filler. You will need to sand down the damaged area until you see the metal. The auto filler is then applied in layers until the door is smooth. This requires some sanding. When you have achieved a smooth surface, you can prime the area and paint it.

Squeaky hinges

If your door makes a squeak every time you open and shut it, you may need to lubricate your hinges with silicone. Remove the pin and lightly scrub the pin, barrel, and hinge leaves with steel wool. Then coat with a thin layer of silicone spray or a light penetrating oil.

Stopping air leaks

If you notice a cold draft around your entry door during the winter months, your door may need to be sealed. A few simple DIY tasks can help reduce your energy bills and keep your home a steady temperature. Check the caulk around the door, and replace it if it shows any damage or gaps. Weatherstripping is another option for stopping air leaks. Shown here is a weatherboard. Available in a variety of finishes, a weatherboard seals the bottom of the door. The angle of the weatherboard directs rain away from the bottom of the door.

Loose hinges

Remove one hinge screw and drive a 3-in (76-mm) screw into the framing to hold the door in place. Do not overdrive the screw, because you will move the door frame.

REPLACING A THRESHOLD

■ If you have an older home, it may be necessary to cut out a new threshold by sawing through the joint between the doorframe stiles and the top surface of the threshold. It should then be possible to ease it out of position.

■ Apply wood preservative to all surfaces before installing them. Apply several coats to the underside because this can't be accessed again once it has been installed.

■ The new threshold may need to be cut to fit if you are installing a custom door of new side lites.

■ If necessary, replace any rotten wood below the threshold.

▌▌ INSTALLING A WEATHERBOARD

A weatherboard can be installed into the doorframe or cut to fit against the frame's profile. This decision often depends on the design of the door. If you choose to cut the weatherboard into the frame of the door, use an offcut section to draw a profile on the edge of the frame. The unwanted wood may then be removed, using a chisel.

A

At the base of the door, measure the distance between the stiles of the frame. Cut the weatherboard to this length.

B

Draw a line along the top of the weatherboard. Predrill some holes in the front of the board and countersink them.

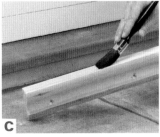

C

Apply wood preservative to the underside of the board. Once dry, apply wood adhesive along the back edge of the board.

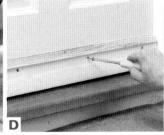

D

Screw the board in place. Test by closing the door; plane off any parts that catch the frame. Fill any holes, then sand and decorate as required.

INSTALLING A DEADBOLT AND LOCKSET

If you plan to purchase a door slab, instead of a pre-hung door, or if you are adding a lock to a door, you will need the following steps on installing deadbolts and locksets. As shown on page 163, there are many types, styles, and finishes available for door hardware. Some are easier to install than others, and when selecting your new locksets, consider your level of expertise with this type of DIY work. If you require a lockset or special hardware that requires more skill to install, contact a professional for help.

TOOLS AND MATERIALS SEE BASIC TOOLKIT PP.24—25

1 LAYOUT THE POSITION

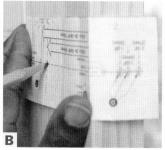

A Measure and mark the location for the new lockset on the door slab with a pencil and tape measure.

B Most manufacturers supply a template to aid with lay out. Some are meant to be taped to the door, others are used to make marks.

2 DRILLING HOLES FOR LOCKSET AND DEADBOLT

A Using a hole saw and a drill, make a hole for the lock and deadbolt through the door slab. Do not go all of the way through.

B Turn the door over and drill the hole from this side to complete the hole for the lockset. Repeat for the deadbolt.

The next step is creating a hole for the latch bolt. Drill holes with a spade bit through the side of the door, following the manufacturer's template.

3 INSTALLING THE DEADBOLT AND LOCKSET

Insert the latch bolt inside the hole made above in step 2c. Trace around the strike plate on the door.

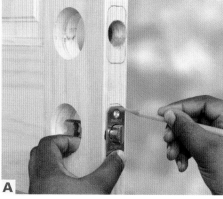

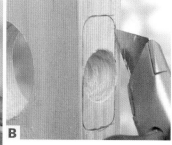

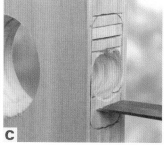

B Using a utility knife, score the door along the outline.

C Strike a chisel at intervals within the score lines to create cuts. This will make it easier to remove the material.

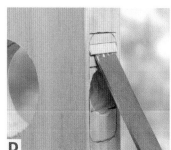

D Using a chisel at less than 45 degrees, remove the material inside the score mark, so that the strike plate can fit flush with the door.

E Insert the latch bolt in the hole, making sure the strike plate is flush. Attach the latch bolt assemblies with fasteners.

Connect the deadbolt face and the lockset handle to the latch assembly according to the manufacturer's instructions.

4 FINISHING THE LOCKSET

A

B

Finish assembling the lockset and deadbolt, using fasteners provided or recommended.

Line up the door with the door frame. Make a mark where the top of the latch bolt hits the frame.

5 LAYING OUT THE STRIKE PLATE

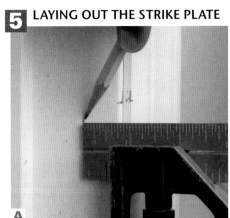

A

Lay out the strike plates on the door jamb, making sure that the marks are level and plumb, and that the lay-out marks will allow the door to close within the frame. Refer to the manufacturer's directions.

B

C

D

E

Drill the holes into the door frame for the latch bolts to fit.

Follow the directions on the previous page to cut a mortise for the strike plate.

Use the template provided by the manufacturer to mark the holes for the fasteners.

Place the strike plate in the mortise cut.

Using the screws provided, attach the strike plate to the door jamb.

F

G

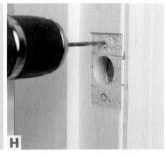

H

Using the lockset strike plate as a guide, mark the location for the fasteners.

Drill pilot holes at the marked locations for the fasteners.

I

J

Place the strike plate inside the mortise cut on the door jamb. Attach the strike plate.

Test the locking mechanisms to make sure the strike plates align.

FURTHER INFORMATION

If your door does not latch well, slowly open and close the door, to see where the latch bolt lands on the door jamb. If the door latches well, the latch bolt will enter the strike plate. If not, check for the following:

■ Hinge screws may be loose. Ensure all fasteners are tightened.
■ The gap between the door and the jamb may be too wide for the latch bolt. You may be able to adjust this with shims. Off-center latching can be fixed by shimming the door in the appropriate direction. If you are unable to fix misalignment with shims, you may need to reset the latch plates.
■ The doors may be warped and causing misalignment. It is possible you will need to purchase and hang a new door.

INSTALLING A SLIDING DOOR

Sliding doors are popular on bedroom closets, and are available both finished and unfinished, and in solid and hollow core options. It will make installation much easier if unfinished doors are finished before you install them. Replacing closet doors is fairly straightforward. You need to lift the doors off of the track, and then attach the hardware to the new doors. If you have built a new closet and are hanging sliding doors for the first time in a room, you will need to follow all of the steps below.

TOOLS AND MATERIALS SEE BASIC TOOLKIT AND P.157

1 BUILDING THE FRAME

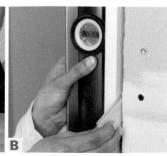

A Measure the door opening. Cut the door frame to length. Lay out the pieces, making sure they are square. Nail the frame.

B Set the frame inside the opening. Use a level to ensure the legs of the frame are plumb. Insert shims to adjust and provide a nailing surface.

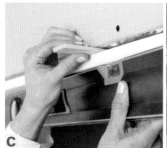
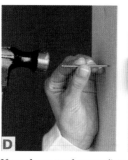

C Use the level to check the top member of the frame. Insert shims to adjust and provide a nailing surface.

D If you have made any adjustments, check to make sure the frame is level and plumb. Nail or screw through the shims to attach the frame in place.

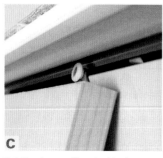

C If the cut end of the door is not perfectly smooth, you may want to plane the surface. Use slow, even pressure on the door, removing material gradually from the surface.

2 TRIMMING THE DOOR

A Measure the door opening; add in the track dimension. Measure and trim the door to fit. Score the door's bottom with a utility knife.

B With the door on a level surface, use a circular saw to trim the door to length using the score mark as your guide.

3 INSTALLING THE TRACK AND GUIDES

A Using the hardware provided by the manufacturer, attach the top track to the door frame according to their instructions.

B Mount the brackets and rollers on the upper end of the door, making sure the hardware will not interfere with the movement of the rollers.

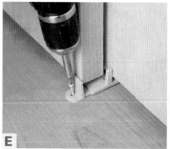  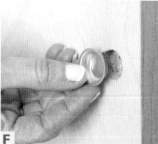

C Set the door rollers inside the top track and hang the door in place. Repeat for the second door.

D Check to make sure the doors are plumb and level. Make any needed adjustments with the roller and bracket hardware.

E Attach the floor brackets according to the manufacturer's directions. Check to make sure the doors can easily move through the opening.

F Install the door hardware. Sliding doors typically have hardware inset inside the door, as shown above, to allow for easy movement.

INSTALLING A BIFOLD DOOR

If you want to be able to view the entire contents of a closet, and don't have enough room for the doors to swing open, bifold doors are a good option. Used on closets and in laundry rooms, bifold doors fold out of the way, leaving room around the door for furnishings and foot traffic. Each door is made of two hinged panels, and the top of the doors slide within a track. The mounting hardware is at the top of the door. There is also hardware at the bottom of the door that allows the door to pivot open.

TOOLS AND MATERIALS SEE BASIC TOOLKIT, PP.24–25

1 INSTALLING THE TRACK

Install the top guide track to the head jamb of the door opening. Use the hardware provided, or recommended, by the manufacturer.

Lay out the location for the pivot hardware on the floor directly below the top track. Secure the hardware to the floor.

Attach the pivot hardware to the doors. Make sure the lower pivot hardware aligns with the hardware on the floor.

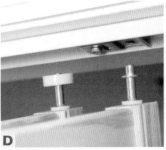

Attach the hardware to the top of the door. Align the top of the door with the track.

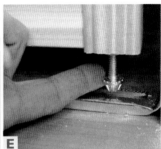

Begin to install the bifold doors by putting one door's bottom pivot point into the lower track socket.

Insert the door's top pivot point into the top pivot socket inside the track. Secure the door in place.

If the top pivot point is spring loaded, retract the pivot point, place it into position, and release it.

Attach the door brackets on the inside edge of each door to allow for the doors to close snug.

2 ATTACHING THE HANDLE

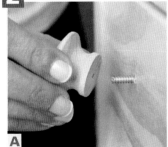

If your doors don't have predrilled holes, measure, mark, and predrill a hole. Insert the hardware through the hole and attach the knob.

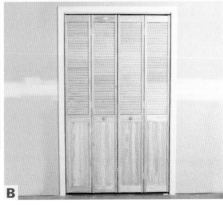

The finished door should open and close smoothly. The doors should be plumb and level. Make any adjustments using the lower pins and track sockets.

ACCORDIAN DOORS

Accordian doors completely fold out of the way. Installed in a similar manner to bifold doors, accordion doors allow even more floor space around the door opening and they also fit smaller door openings.

Entry doors are often installed with extra room inside the opening for a storm door. Storm doors help protect the entry door from weathering and damage, while helping to increase your home's insulation and security. They are made to close automatically, but most have a locking mechanism to keep the door ajar. Never leave the door fixed in the open position, as it can be damaged in heavy winds. Storm doors can have a full pane of glass or have just half of the unit made of glass. Frequently the storm door's glass can be removed for a screen. Screens are commonly used in parts of the country when the season is temperate.

INSTALLATION GUIDELINES
While most storm doors are manufactured so that you can choose whether to install the door with either a right or left swing, some storm doors are available specifically with a right- or left-handed swing. Be sure to check the model you purchase so that it opens compatibly with your current entry door.

STORM DOOR DESIGN
Storm doors are typically full or half-view doors, meaning that the door consists of mainly one piece of glass or the door is solid at the bottom with glass at the top (as shown, right). Glass is available in single-pane and double-pane options from some manufacturers, increasing the opportunity to insulate and seal your house. Weather-stripping is another way to seal the opening around the storm door. The non-glass surface of the door is usually aluminum, and can be available with solid inner cores or foam insulation, with low-maintenance finishes. While the door may be aluminum or a composite, some manufacturers offer wood-grain looks to enhance your house's curb appeal.

When selecting a new storm door for your house, be mindful of how the entry door opens. If you select a storm door that only works with a right-hand opening entry door, it will make entering the house quite difficult. Some entry doors also are installed without an entry door in mind, and there may not be sufficient room in the opening for a storm door. Make sure there is room, before purchasing a storm door.

MAINTAINING A STORM DOOR
Storm doors receive the brunt of activity. If you want to prevent dents and other problems, keep the door's hinges oiled and check that the latches connect properly. At the start of each season, check that the door closers are properly adjusted and working smoothly.

Make sure the tracks are clean and free of any debris to eliminate unnecessary material that makes it harder to open and shut the door, potentially wearing out the mechanism. Sweep out the track with a brush or using a vacuum. It will help the operation if you lubricate tracks with a little silicone or Teflon spray.

REPAIRING A STORM DOOR
If a storm door is wrenched open by a gust of wind, the door-closer's plunger may be damaged and bent. In extreme cases the closer may be torn completely away from the jamb. If the closer is torn off, it will need to be replaced. Lock the door in the open position to replace the closer. Remove the pins that attach the closer and unscrew the bracket from the jamb. Follow the manufacturer's instructions to attach the new closer. If you have a pneumatic closer, you can adjust the speed of closure. Simply turn the adjustment screw in the end cap. If a door track is bent, you may be able to straighten it by tapping it with a block of wood and a hammer.

Classic storm door
This classic design for a storm door features a half window view and a flat panel. This right-hinged door is installed over a left-hinged entry door. However, it is best to have the hinges of the storm door on the same side as those of the entry door.

If your storm door has interchangeable glass and screen panels, make sure you create a snug installation when changing them. The clips must be tight. Replace any clips that become damaged. If your storm door's screen is damaged, you may need to replace it.

FRENCH DOORS

French doors are used as both entry patio doors and as interior doors that separate two spaces. These doors are popular because they allow some privacy, while allowing a visual connection between two spaces. Patio French doors often open on to a deck or a backyard patio, and may be used with a screen door system. Interior French doors are often found in the entryway between a dining room and kitchen or living room, the doors allow light to flow between the spaces. Curtains and blinds are sometimes installed, just as with an exterior window, to provide more privacy. A divided-glass-panes design is the most popular.

INSTALLATION GUIDELINES

French doors are offered in both in-swing, and out-swing fittings. When selecting doors for the interior or exterior opening of your home, be sure to plan for space around the door swing. Unlike pocket doors and sliding doors, French doors command more space for operation. Take the width of the door and layout a radius around the pivot point on both sides of the jamb to see how much space you'll need to allow.

FRENCH DOOR DESIGN

Design options for French doors include window types, glass types, material of door, color, and size. Manufacturers offer standard French door styles that are readily available to fit standard door openings, and custom options that suit unique and older spaces. Usually installed as a pair of doors that swings out from the center of the door opening, there are two standard types of French doors available: In-swing and Out-swing. There are a number of design options available. Your doors can have a flat panel of glass with no grills or grills with simulated divided lites, which are more common. The lites usually extend the entire height of the door, as shown to the right. Lites also are available in half-view and three-quarter view options, allowing some light to filter into the space and affording more privacy.

Standard door sizes start at 1 ft 6 in (460 mm) and are offered at 2-in increases to 3-ft (915-mm) wide. Fitting with standard door openings, stock door heights are 6 ft 8 in (2 m); 7 ft (2.15 m); and 8 ft (2.5 m). If you live in an older house or have an unusual door opening, there are manufacturers who offer custom sizes. Doors are also available in a variety of colors. Blinds and shades are commonly used, just as on windows to filter light and add privacy to a space.

INSTALLING FRENCH DOORS

The most important part of installing a French door is measuring the radius of the swing. Make sure there are no furnishings planned for the area within the door's swing path. The next thing to check is the jamb depth of the opening, and plan to purchase a door that will fit inside that depth. If you have a newer home, you will probably have an easy fit with a standard-sized French door. Older homes have non-standard sized openings, so you may need to install a new jamb inside the opening to fit the French doors of your choice. For standard door frames, French doors also are offered in pre-hung kits, making installation much easier and more straightforward. Pre-hung doors eliminate many of the steps necessary to installing a door (see pp.160–161). Always follow the guidelines supplied by the manufacturer.

If you are planning to install French patio doors to replace sliding doors for deck or patio access, you will need to purchase entry French doors. Some French patio doors can be purchased with inactive doors, meaning there are door panels that match the look of the doors that open, but these inactive door panels do not open and close. Offered typically in wood, steel or aluminum, they should be maintained and painted as often as windows.

Full-view interior French doors
French doors are typically constructed of glass panes surrounded by a frame, similar to the look of a standard window. This set of full-view 10-lite French doors has levered hardware.

For security, always look for French patio doors with a three-point locking system. The three-point system locks the door to the head jamb and the sill, instead of just to each other. Hanging these doors involves a similar process to hanging an entry door (see p.164). Just with any other type of door, make sure the door is hung plumb inside the door frame, so that your doors stay open when desired and close tightly.

GARAGE DOORS

When choosing a garage door, it is important to consider the appearance, material, construction, and method of operation (manual or automatic). Garage doors are usually either tilt-up or sectional roll-up. They are offered with flush, raised panel, or recessed panel designs. Your decision will depend on budget, design, and the structure of the garage itself—you may need more than one door in a double garage.

TYPES OF DOORS

Garage doors, traditionally made of wood, are now available in various materials. Steel and aluminum are commonly used, as is fiberglass. The latter is particularly popular, because it is lightweight, strong, and easy to maintain. Weight is an important consideration; a lightweight door is particularly desirable if it is large, or if an automatic system is being installed. If you plan to install doors yourself, even lightweight ones will be difficult to handle alone, so make sure you have help during installation. Also remember to think about your old doors. They are not small items, and you may have to make special arrangements for their disposal.

MATERIALS

Steel tilt-up
Although not as light as fiberglass doors, steel canopies still provide a relatively lightweight feel, and are easy to open and close by hand.

Fiberglass tilt-up
This type of door is made of lightweight material, and has a pivot mechanism allowing for easy opening and closing by hand.

OPENING AND CLOSING MECHANISMS

Garage doors have a wide variety of opening and closing mechanisms. Some are similar to those used by other entrance doors, and some are used only with garage doors. Sectional (roll-up) garage doors are the most popular type offered. One-piece doors are typically less expensive, but require more headroom in the garage. These doors are often called tilt-up or swing-up doors. Almost any type of door can be automated (see opposite).

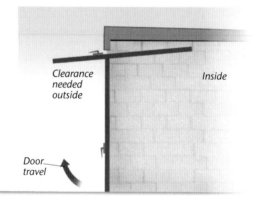

Tilt-up: canopy
Canopy tilt-up doors have a pivoting hinge mechanism that allows the door to be lifted upward and slid back at ceiling level into the garage. A portion of the base of the door protrudes from the garage, providing a small overhang or "canopy." This is the simplest tilt-up mechanism, and the system is secured to the sides of the frame, saving space.

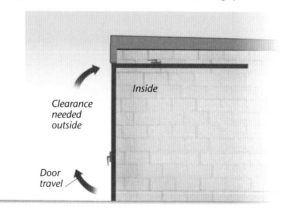

Tilt-up: retractable
A retractable tilt-up door operates in much the same way as a canopy door, except that the door retracts fully into the garage at ceiling level; it is suspended on a framework independent of the doorframe, and therefore occupies a little more space than a canopy mechanism.

Sectional roll-up

Subdividing a door into four or more horizontal sections provides the basic structure of a sectional garage door. The divisions in the door allow it to roll straight up into a retracted position so there is no need for door clearance outside the garage. The sections slide through channels fixed to the doorframe, which keep the door rigid when shut.

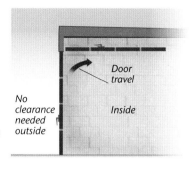

Door travel

Inside

No clearance needed outside

MAINTAINING YOUR GARAGE DOOR

Like anything you use everyday, you grow accustomed to counting on your garage door to function without problem. To keep your garage door running smoothly, tracks should be cleaned, rollers lubricated, and screws checked and tightened. Springs should not be rusty or have bulges. Also test your garage door's reversing feature monthly to make sure it is operating safely. For more information about garage doors and safety, visit the International Doors Association at www.doors.org.

ELECTRIC DOOR OPERATION

There are three basic types of electronic garage doors: screw drive, chain drive, and belt drive. Most electronic systems are based on a ceiling-mounted electric motor, linked to the door through a mechanism that pushes or pulls the door closed or opens it. Another type of system, called torsion, does not need a chain, belt, or screw. And unlike other systems, a torsion-operated garage door does not require the overhead tracks and ceiling-mounted box.

Some systems can be added to existing doors, in which case it may not be necessary to purchase a new door. However, there may still be a need to modify the opening mechanism of the existing door in order to incorporate an electric opener, so if you are adding the electric system retrospectively, take the time to choose a design of opener that best suits your existing door. The systems illustrated here are for use with tilt-up doors, but there are other types available that work equally well with side-opening doors.

Motor

The motor is electrically operated and secured to the ceiling. A belt or chain held in the rail mechanism connects the motor with the door. Most motors are operated by remote control, and have safety devices that prevent the door from trying to close when obstructed. A ½ hp motor should lift most typical garage doors.

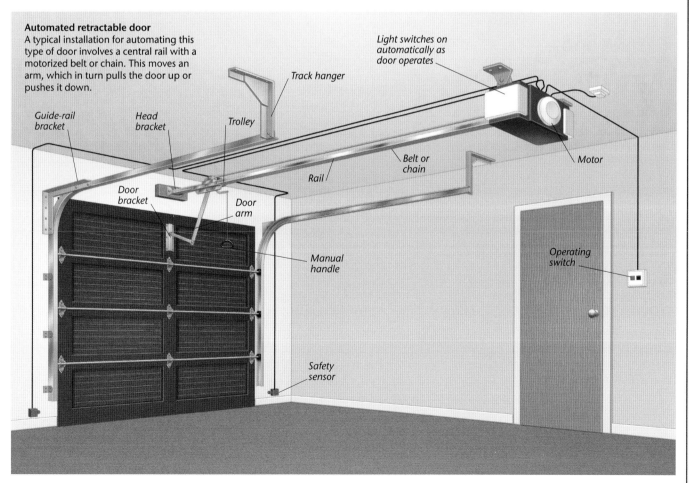

Automated retractable door

A typical installation for automating this type of door involves a central rail with a motorized belt or chain. This moves an arm, which in turn pulls the door up or pushes it down.

Track hanger

Light switches on automatically as door operates

Guide-rail bracket

Head bracket

Trolley

Belt or chain

Motor

Rail

Door bracket

Door arm

Manual handle

Operating switch

Safety sensor

PROBLEM SOLVER

STICKING DOORS: PLANING SIDES

Doors can stick when part of the door edge is binding against the frame or floor. Gently removing wood from these areas will return the door to an easy opening and closing action.

TOOLS AND MATERIALS
Pencil, plane

A

Mark on the door edge, with a pencil, where it touches the frame. For elongated areas, draw a pencil guide line along the door edge.

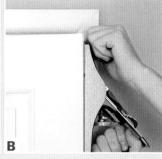

B

Open the door and plane along the edge, down to the guide line. Check that the door fits; replane if necessary.

AWKWARD AREAS

■ **The sticking area is very close to the floor.**
If there is not enough room for a plane, remove the door from its hinges.
■ **The sticking area is very close to the latch.**
The latch may not be able to move back because the handle cannot be moved. Remove the door and plane the hinge side. Reset the hinges deeper.

STICKING DOORS: SCRIBING BOTTOM

Doors can also stick when the entire bottom edge binds against the floor.

TOOLS AND MATERIALS
Measure, panel saw, wood, pencil, block plane

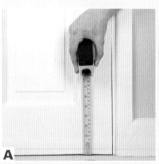

A

Measure the exact height needed to clear floor level. Cut a small offcut of wood to the height that you have just measured.

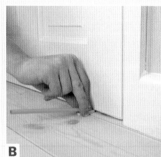

B

With a pencil on top, move the offcut across the floor to trace an exact line on the door.

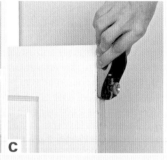

C

Remove the door from the frame and plane down the guide line. If a large amount of wood needs to be removed, use a saw.

RATTLING DOORS: MOVING THE STRIKE PLATE

Doors that fit too loosely in their frame rattle in a draft. This is often due to the strike plate being in the wrong position. Measure the area accurately and move the strike plate.

TOOLS AND MATERIALS
Combination square, pencil, screwdriver, drill-driver, chisel

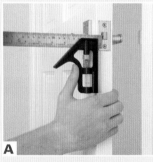

A

Measure the gap between the door latch and the closing edge.

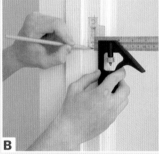

B

Transfer this measurement to the area between the frame edge and the strike-plate opening. Move the strike plate to this position.

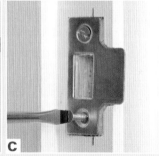

C

Pilot hole the screw points. Chisel out any further wood from the door jamb to accommodate the strike plate's new position.

RATTLING DOORS: MOVING THE DOORSTOP

The other reason a door rattles in a draft is that the doorstop has been wrongly positioned. Moving the doorstop to the correct place should fix the problem.

TOOLS AND MATERIALS
Chisel, hammer, nails

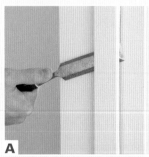

A

Pry off any doorstop sections that do not fit properly against the door when closed.

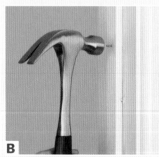

B

Reattach the removed sections, making sure they touch the door edge along their full length when the door is closed.

LATCH PROBLEMS

■ **The latch does not catch when the door closes.**
The strike plate may be too far forward in the frame. Filing the plate's inner edge may be all that is needed.
■ **The latch does not catch in the strike plate.**
The plate may be too far recessed in the frame. Pack out the plate, in the same way as shown for packing out a hinge (opposite).

TIGHTENING HINGE ATTACHMENTS

A door may not close properly because the hinges are loose. You can fix this by drilling out the old holes and plugging them with wooden dowels. New pilot holes are then drilled in the surface created by the dowels. Begin by unscrewing the leaves of the hinges attached to the jamb.

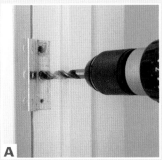

A

Use a large wood drill bit to bore out a hole in the door jamb at each existing screw hole.

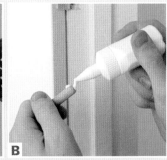

B

Apply wood adhesive to the end of a cut section of dowel.

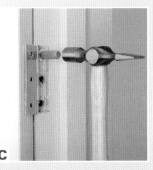

C

Tap the dowel into the hole.

D

Continue adding dowels into the holes as required. Allow the glue to dry.

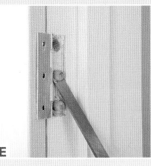

E

Cut off the exposed dowel ends with a chisel.

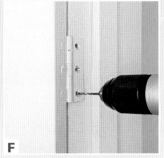

F

Redrill pilot holes for screws into the dowels, and rehang the door.

TOOLS AND MATERIALS
Drill-driver, dowels, hammer, chisel, wood adhesive

FILLING OLD HINGE POSITIONS

If you are moving the door to the other side of the frame, you will need to fill in the old hinge recesses in the frame.

TOOLS AND MATERIALS
Wood, adhesive, block plane

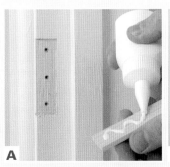

A

Cut a piece of wood with the exact dimensions of the former hinge position.

B

Glue the wood in position, with the patch sitting slightly above the surrounding surface.

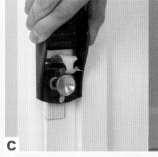

C

Once dry, plane the patch down to the exact level of the surrounding wood, then fill and decorate as required.

PACKING OUT A HINGE

"Packing out" can help a door to open and close if it is binding on its hinges. It is also a good solution if too much wood has been removed from the frame or door to fit a hinge.

TOOLS AND MATERIALS
Scissors, cardboard, drill-driver

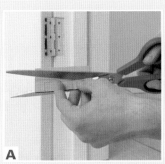

A

Remove the door. Cut out pieces of cardboard to the exact shape of the hinge recess.

B

Position the cardboard in the hinge recess. Rehang the door.

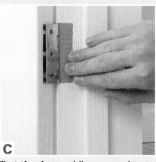

C

Test the door, adding more pieces of cardboard if required. Repeat for other hinges on the frame.

Floors

IF YOU ARE RENOVATING AN OLDER HOME, YOU MAY PEEL BACK CARPET TO REVEAL WOOD PLANKS AND DECIDE TO LEAVE THIS STRUCTURAL FLOOR EXPOSED. CONCRETE AND WOOD ARE THE MOST WIDELY USED FLOOR STRUCTURES. TYPICALLY WOOD JOISTS ARE COVERED IN PLYWOOD. CONCRETE FLOORS, SUCH AS A GARAGE FLOOR, MAY BE PAINTED AND NEW CONCRETE CAN BE DYED.

WOOD FLOORS

A platform-framed wood floor is the most common method of construction above ground-floor level. The floor is constructed using wood joists resting on double plates. The method of securing these in place is dependent on a floor's age and local building codes.

WOODEN FLOOR CONSTRUCTION

Floor joists are supported by exterior walls (the interior section in cavity walls) as well as interior load-bearing walls. Smaller sleeper walls are often used to add support below suspended wooden floors at ground level. The floor surface is constructed by laying wooden boards or Oriented Strand Board panels (OSBs) across the joists.

Joist hanger
Joist hangers attach directly to the wall face.

Brick or block hanger
This hanger's top section is installed into the mortar.

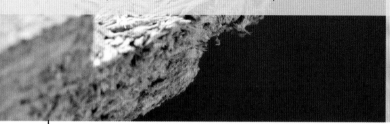

Wood joist
These are made out of solid lumber and vary in size. They are typically 2 x 6 in (50 x 150 mm) or 2 x 8 in (50 x 200 mm) in cross-section.

Joist hanger
This type of hanger is designed for use with joists.

Lateral restraint straps
Used for bracing joists and floor structures.

Engineered joist
Modern versions of sawn lumber, joists are made of laminated layers of wood, and are lighter than sawn lumber.

Wooden boards
Rather than using plywood, these are the traditional covering for joists and are available with flat edges and with tongue-and-groove edges.

Wooden bridging
Used to brace floor joists by adding diagonal support.

Sawn lumber connector
Used to connect two joists together in order to give greater support.

OSB floor sheeting
These sheets are available with tongue-and-groove edges and in moisture-resistant forms.

Metal bridging
Modern version of a wood strut. Used to brace floor joists.

PLATFORM FRAMING

Since the 1930s, the most common type of floor framing in this country has been platform framing, also called "western" framing. Joists, studs, rafters, and plates are the members that are used to construct platform framing. Each floor is constructed as its own unit, helping to prevent fire from spreading between floors. Wall sections for each floor are also constructed as one-story units. Settling does occur after a house is framed, but most shrinkage occurs uniformly over a structure. Typical construction methods for platform framing are shown below.

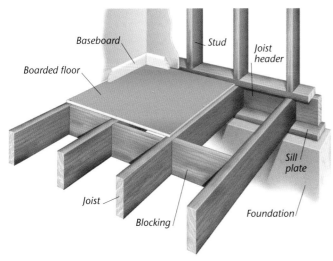

Platform framing and foundation
Platform frames are started with a sill plate attached to the foundation, and joists run perpendicular from the sill plate. A joist header attaches to the end of each joist. The studs are then attached to the joists, running the ceiling height of the floor. The subflooring is installed on top of the joists. A sole plate is then installed on top of the subflooring material.

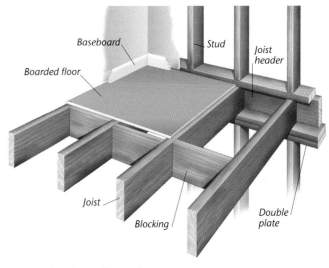

Platform framing and upper floors
The details in upper floor framing are similar to the ground floor (as shown left). No firestopping is required, as the construction method provides a joist hanger, which is a built-in firestopping and structural system. The height of the studs for each floor are determined by the desired ceiling height for that particular floor.

BALLOON FRAMING

Introduced during the mid-1800s, balloon framing is no longer a popular framing system. Balloon framing uses the same type of members as platform framing, but with more substantial sized material for studs. Studs in a balloon frame run continuously from the sill all the way to the rafter. The second floor joists are supported on a ribbon (see below) instead of a joist header. Firestopping is added to the spaces between the studs, which provides a space for mechanical system installation. Typical construction methods for balloon framing are shown below.

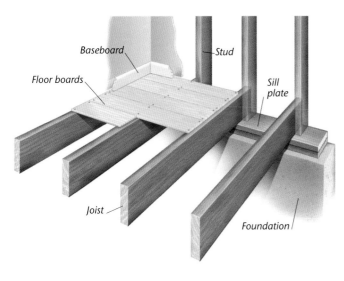

Balloon frame and foundation
The foundation for a balloon frame is constructed the same as in the platform framing method, shown above. There is a sill plate attached to the foundation, and joists run perpendicular from the sill plate. The studs are then attached to the joists, and run the entire height of the house. The subflooring is installed on top of the joists.

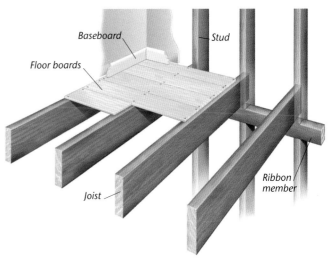

Balloon framing and upper floors
The details of upper floor construction are different in balloon framing. Each floor's joists are run off of the same stud members that continue through the height of the house. In order to hang the joists, ribbon members are installed to the studs. This type of construction provides great stability. Firestopping is included in the stud bays.

OTHER FLOOR STRUCTURES

Not every house is built from wood frame construction, and some houses are built with a combination of materials and techniques. Typically the building practices for residential construction vary according to region, availability of materials, and climate. Block houses, made of stone, concrete, or brick, are found more often in regions with older construction. When gutting an older block house to begin a major renovation, you may find that in addition to building new floors and walls, the shell of the house needs insulation and waterproofing to improve the home's performance. Here are a few alternatives to a standard wood frame building.

FURTHER INFORMATION

Another alternative to wood frame construction is incorporating steel into the design. For example, steel beams are an alternative to wood girders. The wide flange (commonly called I-beam) used most often in residential applications. The appropriate size of the beam is dependent on the calculated load of your house and the length of span.

SAWN TIMBER JOISTS METHOD

In this traditional floor construction, the ends of joists or beams are built into the walls of a block building, and are therefore directly supported by the wall structure. Sometimes joist ends rest on wooden wall plates secured to the wall surface. Old lumber joists secured within a wall may eventually become damp, and might need replacing over time. Joist size can vary according to the floor span, and this is an important consideration when building a new house or creating an addition.

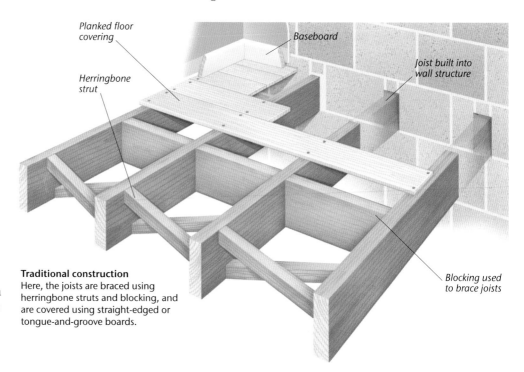

Planked floor covering

Baseboard

Herringbone strut

Joist built into wall structure

Blocking used to brace joists

Traditional construction
Here, the joists are braced using herringbone struts and blocking, and are covered using straight-edged or tongue-and-groove boards.

JOIST HANGING METHOD

In modern buildings, metal joist hangers are often used to support the joists. Joist depths, widths, and designs vary, so there is a wide range of hangers available to match. It is also an option to use joist hangers when renovating an old floor as these do not require large holes in walls, and are straightforward to fix.

Metal lateral joist straps are used to brace joists in position. One end of the strap is attached to the exterior wall, and the other end is attached to joists (either across or in line with them), to secure their position. Lateral joist straps are mainly used in new building projects.

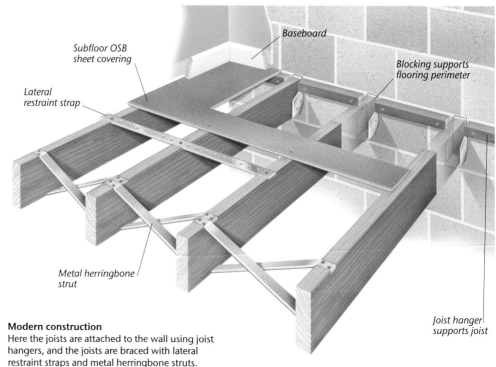

Subfloor OSB sheet covering

Baseboard

Lateral restraint strap

Blocking supports flooring perimeter

Metal herringbone strut

Joist hanger supports joist

Modern construction
Here the joists are attached to the wall using joist hangers, and the joists are braced with lateral restraint straps and metal herringbone struts.

CONCRETE FLOORS

Ground floors made from concrete have been common for many years in residential construction, but as concrete grows in popularity as a building material, upper floors also are being constructed from concrete. If you build an upper floor from concrete, you will most likely use concrete beams and blocks, as opposed to the slab we commonly find in basements and ground floors of homes without basements.

When preparing a bottom floor for concrete, it is essential to insulate and prepare the floor for moisture control. Your floor will need compacted fill, possibly a drain tile, vapor barrier, and perimeter insulation (see below) to effectively combat potential moisture problems. Vapor barriers not only help keep the house sealed from moisture, but they also help speed the curing process of the concrete. A 6-mil polyethylene vapor barrier is laid over any mechanical systems, but the connections need to be accessible and above the finished floor level.

Pouring in the concrete and leveling it off by "eye" is possible, but it is far more accurate to create some shuttering within which a level floor can be laid. To achieve a smooth surface, concrete floors are usually covered with a topcoat of screed. Screed is a 3:1 mix of flooring sand and cement, and ready-mixed screed is available.

Floor alignment

When altering floors—for example, in a renovation project where two rooms are to be made into one—you may need to align the floor level. To level between two concrete floors, adjust the screed using mortar or self-leveling compound, depending on the degree of change. Rather than leveling across a large area, you may need to build a small step. If there is only a small height difference, it may also be possible to simply create a small slope across the floor surface.

Solid concrete floor
The structure shown here is suitable for renovating or replacing an old floor. However, this type of structure is also used in new properties. In this case the damp-proof membrane would be lapped into the main wall structure.

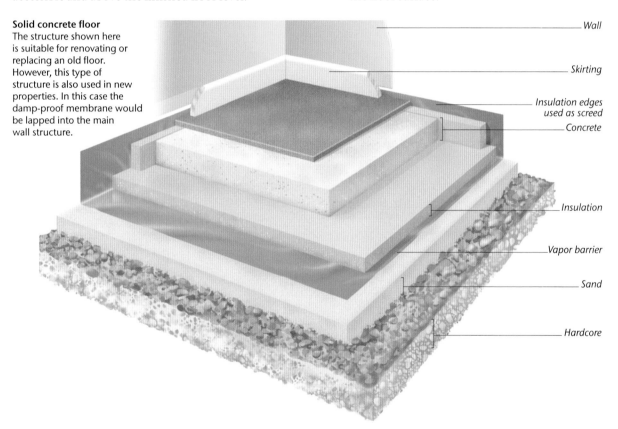

Wall

Skirting

Insulation edges used as screed

Concrete

Insulation

Vapor barrier

Sand

Hardcore

FURTHER INFORMATION

■ The strength of your floor frame depends on the accuracy of your cuts and how well the pieces fit together.
■ When building a floor frame, first set the trimmer joists in place. Joists are usually spaced at 16" on center. Headers are then attached before tail joists are installed.
■ The parts of a floor frame can be assembled using a pneumatic nailer. Joist hangers and framing anchors can also be used.
■ Caulking compound can help seal the joint between the header and the sill in colder climates.
■ Wood is not always perfectly straight. Always lay the crown (hump) side of a board up when nailing it in place.
■ While you are working on the floor frame, lay a piece of plywood across nearby joists to provide a more stable work area.

TOOLS AND MATERIALS CHECKLIST PP.182–183

Laying concrete (p.182)
Concrete, straight-edged plank, float, trowel, battens

heavy-duty drill, spirit level, wood offcuts

Laying a "floating" floor (p.183) Insulation boards, damp-proof membrane, boards, wood glue, cloth, skirting board

Attaching floor furring strips (sleepers) (p.183) Damp-proof membrane, furring strips,

FOR BASIC TOOLKIT SEE PP.24–25

LAYING A PLYWOOD SUBFLOOR

Plywood is the most common type of subfloor in new homes. Plywood is rated for use, based on whether it's for interior or exterior applications, and what type of material you plan to use for the finished floor. Available in standard sheets of 4 x 8 ft (1.2 x 2.5 m), your work will be easier if you minimize the number of cuts you need to make to cover the floor. Lay out your floor carefully before you start attaching sheets to the joists. Also, plan the layout so that the cut edges are against the perimeter of the room. Make sure the sheets are spaced evenly and butt each sheet tightly.

TOOLS AND MATERIALS SEE BASIC TOOLKIT AND P.180

FURTHER INFORMATION

Lay sheets of plywood measuring 4 x 8 ft (1.2 x 2.5 m) across the floor joists, starting at one corner of the room. Make sure the edges parallel to the joists fall on the joists. In addition, make sure that the sheets are spaced evenly, butt each sheet tightly, and run a circular saw set to the depth of the subfloor between the sheets. A floor will have less bounce if both adhesives and screws are used rather than just nails.

▌▌ LAYING A PLYWOOD SUBFLOOR

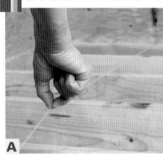

A

Snap a line across the floor joists to mark the position of the first sheet of plywood.

B

Apply a consistent bead of construction adhesive on the floor joists.

C

Keeping a space of about ⅛ in (3 mm) away from the walls to allow the material to expand, lay the first piece of plywood on the chalk line.

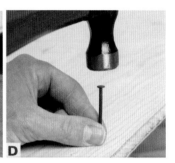

D

Starting at one end of the floor, drive nails in every 6 in (150 mm) along the joists. Screws or staples may also be used.

E

To cut plywood to size, use a pair of sawhorses and 2 x 4s to create a stable cutting station.

F

Using a circular saw with the depth of the blade at ½ in (13 mm) deeper than the plywood sheet, cut the plywood to size.

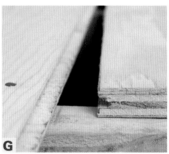

G

Lay additional pieces of plywood, inserting the tongue into the groove joints of each piece of plywood.

H

Use a piece of lumber as a smash block to protect the plywood tongue. Smash the additional pieces of plywood in place.

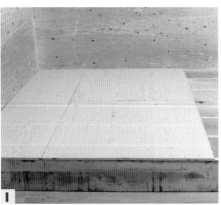

I

Check the butt joints of each piece of plywood to make sure the floor is level. If a sheet is raised, drive extra staples (or nails) to force the sheet into place. Using a flat trowel, cover all of the seams and fasteners with reinforced flooring patch. Sand the floor smooth with a hand sander.

TOOLS AND MATERIALS CHECKLIST PP.180–181

Laying a plywood subfloor (p.180) Chalk line, construction adhesive, sheets of plywood, pair of sawhorses, circular saw, sledge hammer, trowel, flooring patch, hand sander

Laying tongue-and-groove boards (p.181) Tongue-and-groove boards, nail set, jigsaw

Laying tongue-and-groove chipboard (p.181) Tongue-and-groove chipboard, wood glue, offcut block, sponge

FOR BASIC TOOLKIT SEE PP.24–25

Older houses have plank subfloors. If you are remodeling your house and find that some areas of the subfloor are damaged, you may choose to replace them with new tongue-and-groove boards that fit with the character of your house. You may use a hammer, nails, and a nail set, or you may decide to rent a floor nailer. This fires a nail at precisely the correct angle through the tongue of the board and into the joist below, securing it below the floor surface.

TOOLS AND MATERIALS SEE BASIC TOOLKIT AND P.180

▌▌ LAYING TONGUE-AND-GROOVE BOARDS

Position the first board in the way described opposite for laying plywood. Check that the board is the right way up. The tongue should be facing you. The following steps show you how to attach tongue-and-groove boards using blind nailing.

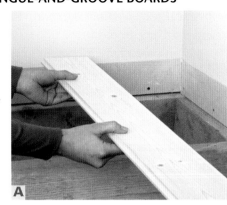

A

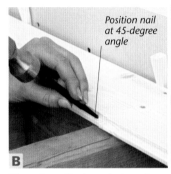

Position nail at 45-degree angle

B

C

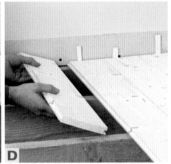

D

E

Place the nail where the board's tongue meets the vertical edge. Using a nail punch, tap it in place, until it sits below the surface.

Place the groove of the next board over the nailed tongue, covering the nails. Make sure that you join boards together over a joist.

Continue to position rows of boards across the floor. Use blind nailing, in the way shown, as you progress.

On reaching the final board, scribe and cut to fit as required. A jigsaw is ideal for this. Fasten with finish nails.

▌▌ LAYING TONGUE-AND-GROOVE ORIENTED STRAND BOARD (OSB)

Flooring-grade OSB is usually made with tongue-and-groove edges, including the board's shorter sides. Supporting blocking should be placed around the room's perimeter. Position the first board across the joists. Insert wedges between the board and the wall, to create an expansion gap of ⅜ in (10 mm).

A

B

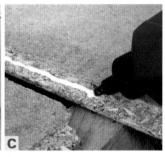

C

Screw the board in place, using flooring screws. These should be inserted at 6-in (150-mm) intervals, positioned along a joist.

Apply wood glue along the tongue of the board. Then slot the next board in place.

D

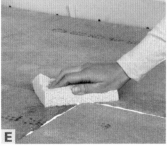

E

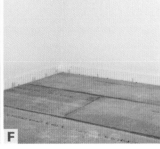

F

To create a tight joint, tap the boards in place, using an offcut of OSB as a knocking block.

As you tighten the boards, you will probably need to wipe away excess glue with a damp sponge.

Continue to lay the OSB. At the edge of the room, mark and cut the boards to fit the remaining space and fix them with screws.

ACCESS PANELS

Gaining access underneath a tongue-and-groove floor is difficult, due to its interlocking structure. Note where access may be required. Remove the tongue from the board, and screw the board down. It can then be unscrewed and lifted easily. Fix extra blocking to support the edges of the access hatch.

LAYING A CONCRETE FLOOR

Laying an interior concrete floor is usually a renovation project that takes place in your basement. Here an old wood floor is removed and a base is prepared on which concrete can be laid. It is possible to pour the concrete and level it off by eye, but it is far more accurate to use a screed board. Here, insulation is used as screed and as a leveling guide. However, you could use wood offcuts to make a temporary frame around the floor edge, which you would remove after use.

TOOLS AND MATERIALS SEE BASIC TOOLKIT AND P.179

PREPARING TO LAY THE FLOOR

A

Remove the baseboards by prying them away from the wall using a pry bar.

B

Use a pry bar to remove the floorboards one by one. Once the floor is out, mark the required height of the floor with a chalk line.

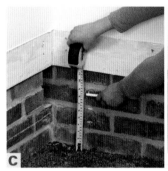

C

Excavate to the required depth. Snap chalk lines to indicate infill layer levels.

D

Fill to the height of the appropriate marked-off level, with crushed stone. Compact with a rammer.

E

Cover the stone with sand, up to the height of the next guide line. Move the back of a shovel in a circular motion, to smooth the sand.

F

Lay the 6 mil sheet plastic on the sand. Take it up the wall above the finished floor level. Tape it to the wall to hold it in place.

LAYING INSULATION BOARD

Place the insulation foam board across the sand and membrane, cutting sections to fit as required. Cut 4-in (100-mm) widths of insulation board and lay them around the edges of the room. The insulation provides a guide for the height of the concrete pad, as well as a rest for a leveling plank as you lay the concrete.

A

LAYING CONCRETE

A

Shovel the concrete over the floor, starting at the wall farthest from the door. See pp.70–71 for mixing concrete.

B

Scrape a straight-edged plank across the concrete to level it, using the top edge of the insulation as a guide.

C

Fill in any gaps or indentations using a trowel as you work backward. You may need to go over the area more than once.

D

Use a plastering trowel to smooth any rough areas, right to the edges of the insulation foam. Leave the concrete to set for two to three days.

E

Place furring strips on the dry concrete. Apply a top layer, leveling it to the top of the furring strips. Remove the furring strips and fill the gaps.

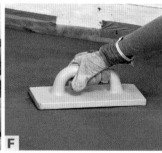

F

Level the surface using a float. Work to the edges and back toward the door. Leave for another two to three days to set completely.

The decision to lay a wood floor on a concrete base is often made when a decorative wood or laminate floor is to be created. Another reason is to create a warmer, insulated floor (see opposite and p.364), on which you can lay various types of flooring. In the first sequence, particleboard panels are laid "floating" on top of insulation board. In the second sequence, furring strips are secured to the floor, on top of which floorboards may then be attached. This method is demonstrated on pp.180–181.

TOOLS AND MATERIALS SEE BASIC TOOLKIT AND P.165

LAYING A "FLOATING" SUBFLOOR

Position insulation board directly onto the concrete base, then lay a damp-proof membrane over the insulation board. Cut the corners to allow it to lap up the walls. Make sure it is higher on the wall than the depth of the floor. Overlap the joints in the membrane sheets by at least 12 in (300 mm), and tape using waterproof tape.

A

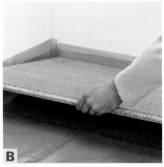
B
Lay a particleboard panel directly on top. Make sure you leave an expansion gap of ⅜ in (10 mm) around the edge of the floor.

C
Glue then interlock the tongue-and-groove joints. There will be no need for screws or nails.

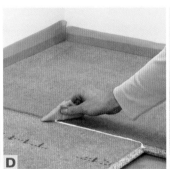
D
Wipe away any excess glue, then lay the remaining boards using the same method.

E
You can then attach the baseboard. For installing baseboard, see pp.224–225. It will hold down the board edges, and cover the gap.

ATTACHING FLOOR FURRING STRIPS (SLEEPERS)

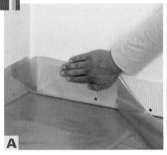
A
Lay down the membrane, as shown for a floating floor, cutting the corners to enable it to lap up the wall about 4 in (100 mm).

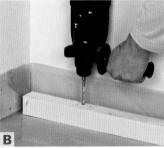
B
Position the first furring strip against the wall, and drill pilot holes through the wood, the membrane, and into the concrete floor.

C
Use 2½-in concrete screws, including plugs, to secure the furring strips. Initially, set the screw and plug in place with a hammer.

D
Once driven in, use a cordless drill-driver to tighten the screw. As an alternative, hammer fasteners for steps C and D (see p.77).

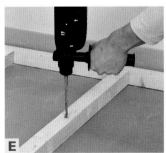
E
Install furring strips around the edge of the room, then across the floor, at intervals of 1 ft 8 in (500 mm), in parallel lines. Drill pilot holes.

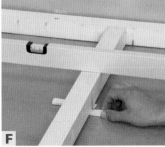
F
Where necessary, insert wedges underneath the furring strips to ensure that they are at the correct floor height. Use a level to check that they are level.

G

Once the correct height has been achieved, screw through the furring strip, down through the wedge, and into the floor. Repeat for all furring strips, making sure you screw down through all wedges where necessary. Lay insulation boards between the furring strips. The strips are ready for floorboards to be laid on top (see pp.180–181).

PROBLEM SOLVER

REPLACING OLD TONGUE-AND-GROOVE BOARDS

The interlocking design of tongue-and-groove boards means that it is necessary to cut through the board joints to release them from their position. A circular saw is ideal for this purpose. Take care to avoid damaging any utilities below floor level.

TOOLS AND MATERIALS

Metal cutting blade, circular saw, pry bar, chisel, replacement board, finish nails, hammer, nail set

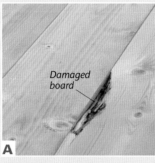

A *Damaged board*

Use a nail cutting blade to cut through any concealed nails. Set the circular saw to the exact depth of the damaged board.

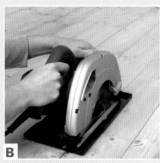

B Run the saw down the entire length of the board on either side of the damaged area where possible.

C Pry out the damaged board using a pry bar. Rest the bar on a wood offcut to prevent the bar from damaging adjacent boards.

REPLACING OSB FLOORBOARDS

Replacing a section of OSB floor is similar to replacing tongue-and-groove boards. A circular saw is the best tool to use. Any superficial damage caused to other boards is not important, since the floor will be covered.

D Remove the tongue from the new board, using a sharp chisel. If the boards are very thick, you may need to use a saw.

E Reposition the board in place. Since blind nailing is not possible, use finish nails and fill the holes.

CUTTING ACROSS THE GRAIN

An alternative way to cut the damaged board is to cut it across the grain, along a joist. In this way a smaller section of board can be removed. However, the adjacent boards would also have small cuts on their edges. For an exposed floor these would have to be disguised with an appropriate filler.

REPLACING OLD SQUARE-EDGED BROKEN BOARDS

It is simpler to replace square-edged boards than tongue-and-groove boards, since they do not have interlocking edges. Take care to avoid damaging cables and pipes below floor level.

TOOLS AND MATERIALS

Pencil, ruler, pry bar, replacement board, nails, hammer, offcuts

A Mark a pencil line on the damaged board over the nearest joist. If the damage is central, mark lines on joists either side of the damage.

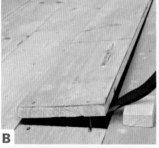

B Lever up the broken board, using a pry bar. Rest the pry bar on a wood offcut to avoid damaging the floor.

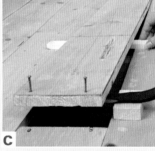

C Once the board has been raised high enough, place wood offcuts underneath to hold it in a secure position.

MATCHING BOARD DIMENSIONS

It may be difficult to buy replacement boards with matching dimensions.
■ If the new boards are too wide, reduce the width with a power plane.
■ If an exact depth match is not possible, buy boards that are slightly less deep than the desired depth. Position pieces of hardboard on the joists below to level the boards.

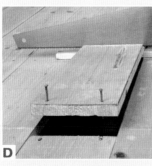

D Saw along the pencil lines to remove the damaged section of board. Protect the floor with a spare piece of board.

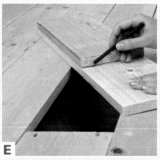

E Using the damaged section of board as a template, mark the new board and cut it to size.

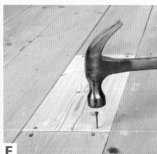

F Position the new section of board in the gap, and nail it in place.

SECURING LOOSE BOARDS

Loose or creaking boards are a common problem, particularly in older buildings, but they are straightforward to fix. Take care to avoid damaging cables and pipes below floor level.

TOOLS AND MATERIALS
Drill, nails, hammer, nail punch

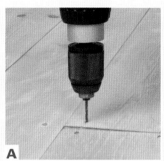

A On one side of the loose floorboard, drill a pilot hole down through the board and into the joist below.

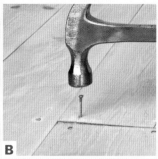

B If the floor is exposed, hammer a nail into the hole. If appearance is not important, use a screw, which will be more secure.

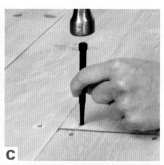

C Use a nail set to drive nail heads (if using nails) just below the surface. If required, repeat on the other edge of the board.

FILLING GAPS BETWEEN BOARDS

Gaps between boards look unsightly and can cause drafts. This is not normally a problem with tongue-and-groove boards. For square-edged boards, large gaps should be filled.

TOOLS AND MATERIALS
Sliver of wood, wood glue, hammer, block plane

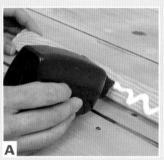

A Cut a strip of wood to fit in the gap. Apply wood glue to both sides of the strip.

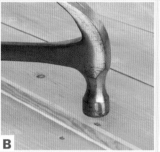

B Insert the wood strip into the gap, driving it in with a hammer for a tight fit. Allow it to sit slightly above the floor surface.

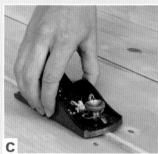

C After the glue has dried, use a block plane to remove the excess wood, and to create a smooth finish flush with the floor.

MENDING HOLES IN CONCRETE FLOORS

If only a small area is damaged, patch the hole only and level it off. For large holes, patch with a strong mortar mix before applying self-leveling compound.

TOOLS AND MATERIALS
Dusting brush, paintbrush, white glue, mortar, gauging trowel

A Dust out any loose material or debris from the hole using a dusting brush.

B Dampen the hole with some glue solution made up of four parts water to one part glue.

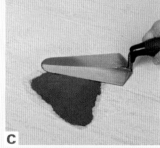

C Once the glue is tacky, press some mortar into the hole and use a gauging trowel to smooth it over.

EXPOSED BOARD SOLUTIONS

If floorboards are exposed, finding a replacement board that matches the existing boards is an issue.
■ Use an original board from a less visible area of the room, such as under a sofa. You can then use a new board in the less conspicuous area.
■ If you are replacing more than one or two boards, try reclaimed or seasoned boards.

Often their dimensions are more likely to work, and a certain degree of wear on replacement boards may better match the existing floor.
■ If you have no alternative but to use a replacement board made of a different type of wood, you may be able to treat the wood with wood dye or stain. There are many different types available.

CONCRETE FLOOR SOLUTIONS

■ It is possible to improve a rough floor surface by adding a self-levelling compound to fill in cracks and gaps.
■ After removing an old floor covering, such as cork tiles, use floor scrapers and commercial solutions to remove adhesive remains and bitumen-based products before laying a new floor covering. Otherwise, most self-

leveling materials laid over a bitumen base will fail to adhere properly and may cause further problems.
■ To protect a new concrete floor, seal it with a concrete sealer.
■ If you suspect water leaks from an existing concrete floor, see pp.230–233.

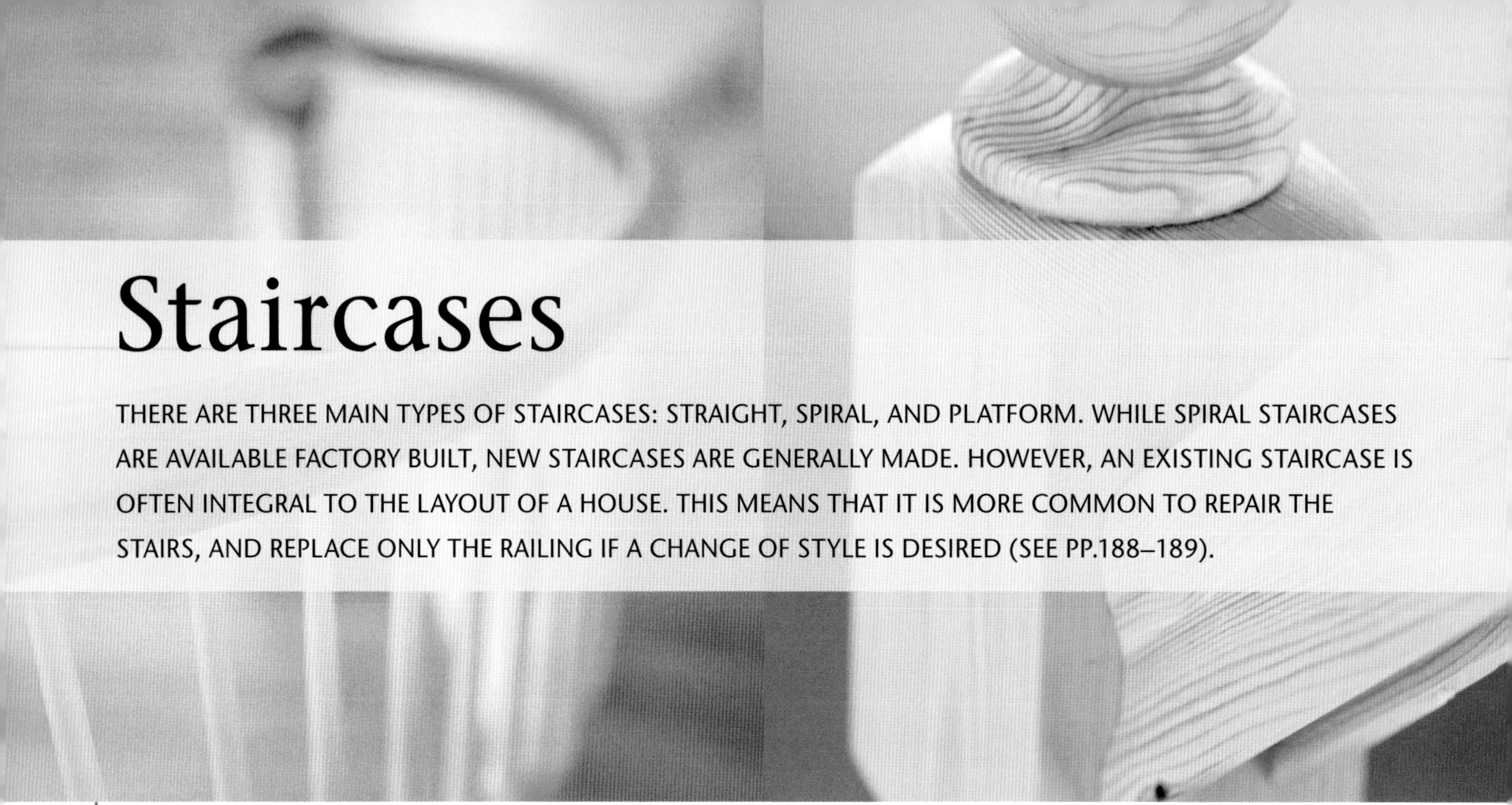

Staircases

THERE ARE THREE MAIN TYPES OF STAIRCASES: STRAIGHT, SPIRAL, AND PLATFORM. WHILE SPIRAL STAIRCASES ARE AVAILABLE FACTORY BUILT, NEW STAIRCASES ARE GENERALLY MADE. HOWEVER, AN EXISTING STAIRCASE IS OFTEN INTEGRAL TO THE LAYOUT OF A HOUSE. THIS MEANS THAT IT IS MORE COMMON TO REPAIR THE STAIRS, AND REPLACE ONLY THE RAILING IF A CHANGE OF STYLE IS DESIRED (SEE PP.188–189).

TYPES OF STAIRCASES

Staircases are complicated constructions. Traditional straight flights are most common, and easiest to attempt. However, in new homes and renovations other designs, such as spiral stairs, are often used. If you want to change the style of your existing staircase, you can purchase new stair parts at your local home improvement center.

STAIRCASE CONSTRUCTION

A staircase may be composed of one material or a combination of several—wood, concrete, and metal are most often used. Boards, such as MDF, are increasingly popular. Methods of construction vary depending on the materials. Standard designs are 3 ft (900 mm) wide, with 2 ft 8 in (800 mm) clearance to the handrail.

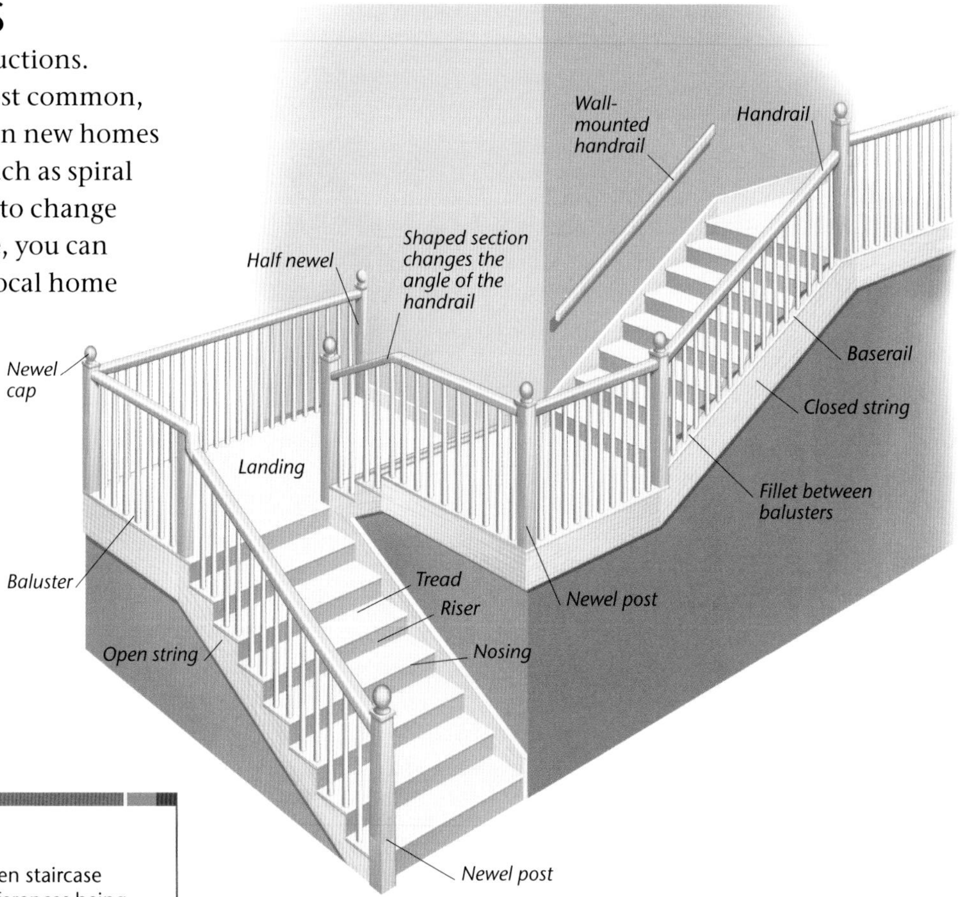

CONCRETE STAIRCASES

Most of the terminology used for a wooden staircase is also relevant for a concrete one, the differences being in construction and installation.

A concrete staircase can be built on site to your requirements and is a professional job. A plywood form is created, steel bars are inserted to strengthen and reinforce the structure, and then concrete is poured in. Once the concrete has cured, the form is removed.

Parts of a staircase
There are many terms associated with a staircase and railing and it is important to understand what they describe, and how the parts relate to each other. The staircase shown here has a traditional design with landings, but an alternative is to use winders—kite-shaped treads that turn a corner in a similar way to a section of spiral staircase. Many of the terms used here also apply to other designs of staircases, such as spiral stairs.

STAIRCASE DESIGNS

Traditional staircases are based around a straight flight or flights of stairs. Spiral stairs have long been used as an alternative, and modern designs are popular in open-plan spaces. Disappearing fold-away stairs, and alternating tread stairs are often used to access attics. The steps are wider at alternate ends so your foot can always rest on a deep tread. Spiral and disappearing stairs are available ready to install.

TRADITIONAL STAIRCASE

Components slot together on site

SPIRAL STAIRCASE

ALTERNATING TREAD STAIRCASE

BALUSTRADE MATERIALS

Staircases are not usually replaced, although a railing can be updated using a kit (see below and pp.188–189). Several styles are available, modern and traditional, and may have solid wood or metal balusters. Newel posts and handrails are usually made of wood. If you want to replace the whole staircase, you will probably need to get one custom-built. Most stair parts are available in standard sizes, and can be installed following the manufacturer's instructions.

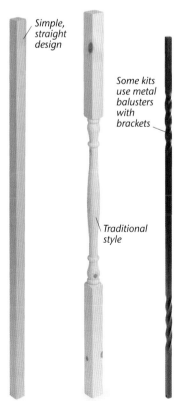

Simple, straight design

Some kits use metal balusters with brackets

Traditional style

STRAIGHT BALUSTER

TURNED BALUSTER

METAL BALUSTER

Cap

Spigot of newel cap

Turning

Spigot of newel turning

Dowel

Base

MODULAR NEWEL

WHOLE NEWEL

Constructed from one section of lumber

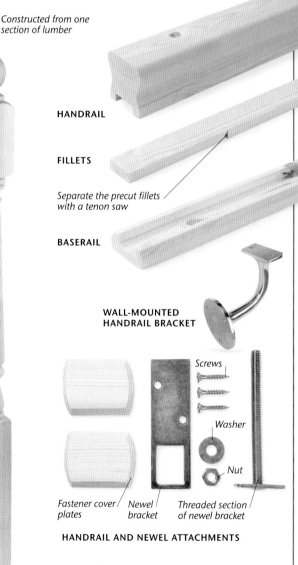

HANDRAIL

FILLETS

Separate the precut fillets with a tenon saw

BASERAIL

WALL-MOUNTED HANDRAIL BRACKET

Screws

Washer

Nut

Fastener cover plates

Newel bracket

Threaded section of newel bracket

HANDRAIL AND NEWEL ATTACHMENTS

Stair railings

All of the components needed for the new railings should be available—handrail, baserail, newel posts, balusters, and special brackets and fasteners. Newel posts may come whole, or be made up of several pieces (modular). Modular newels are better for an existing staircase.

STAIRCASE PREPARATION

The layout of your home is generally designed around the staircase, so it is unusual to replace it unless it is unsafe or if you are doing extensive remodeling. Staircases are custom-built. Installing a staircase is a complex job and may be best left to a professional who will measure and build the stairs. Replacing the balustrade can update a staircase, and with a kit it is fairly straightforward. Staircase design must meet local building codes.

STAIRCASE REGULATIONS

The staircase should comply with these rules:

■ The top of the handrail must be located between 34 and 38 in (860 and 970 mm) above the pitch line.

■ Along any open side of a stairway, the balusters must be located such that a 4⅜-in (110-mm) sphere cannot pass through.

■ The riser height is limited to 7¾ in (200 mm).

■ A minimum tread depth of 10 in (250 mm) is required, measured horizontally between the nosings of adjacent treads.

■ The headroom clearance along any point of the must be at least 80 in (2 m).

REPLACING A STAIRCASE

Most specialty manufacturers will measure and install a new staircase for you, and ensure it complies with building codes (see box, above right). If you are building stairs yourself, always read any manufacturer's instructions—they will explain where and how to take the crucial measurements. Generally, you will need to measure from floor to ceiling to get the "rise"—the height of the staircase. Remember to take the thickness of the finished floor into account. The advance of the staircase across the floor is known as the "run." It is measured as the distance between the face of the first riser and the face of the last riser. If you are building a staircase between two walls, measure the width of the space in several places and work with the smallest figure.

REPLACING A BALUSTRADE

You may wish to replace a balustrade if it is broken, or purely for cosmetic reasons. Traditionally, balustrades are secured into the staircase, and require considerable expertise to replace (see pp.396–397 for woodworking joints). An alternative is to purchase replacement newels, balusters, and rails (see p.187). These can be adapted to fit around most stairs and landings. Make sure you buy the right kind for your stairs—the system needed will vary depending on whether the staircase is closed- or open-string (see parts of a staircase p.186). If your stairs have an open string, then metal balusters are ideal because they can be attached directly to the treads with brackets.

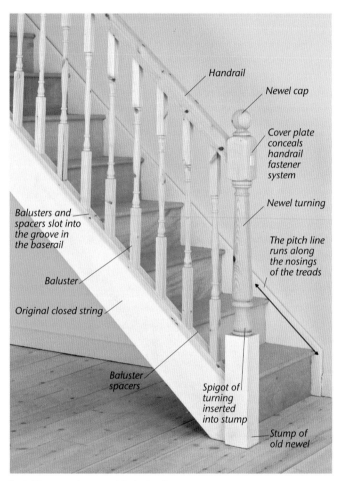

Handrail

Newel cap

Cover plate conceals handrail fastener system

Newel turning

Balusters and spacers slot into the groove in the baserail

Baluster

Original closed string

The pitch line runs along the nosings of the treads

Baluster spacers

Spigot of turning inserted into stump

Stump of old newel

Installing a replacement balustrade
You should comply with building regulations (see above) and you should install it using the instructions supplied. It is particularly important to cut the old newel at the right point to avoid weakening the structure.

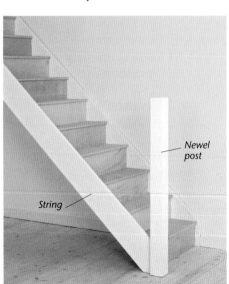

Removing the old balustrade
Before you can install new stair accessories, you need to use a pry bar to remove the old balusters and handrail. Strip back the baserail. You should be left with the bare string and old newel post.

Newel post

String

TOOLS AND MATERIALS CHECKLIST PP.175–177

Repairing creaking stairs from below (p.189) Wood glue, new wedge, block of wood

Repairing creaking stairs from above (p.189) Basic toolkit only

Replacing a broken baluster (p.189) Replacement baluster, pin hammer, panel pins

Installing basement stairs (pp.190–191) Carpenter's square, circular saw, wood glue, pin hammer, panel pins

FOR BASIC TOOLKIT SEE PP.24–25

Staircases are exposed to a lot of wear and tear. Small amounts of damage are not uncommon but can be dangerous, so you shouldn't put off fixing them. Check your staircase regularly for any minor problems. Joints can loosen over time, or wood may crack, but the affected parts can almost always be easily fixed or replaced.

TOOLS AND MATERIALS SEE BASIC TOOLKIT AND P.188

CREAKING OR DAMAGED TREADS OR RISERS

Treads and risers are usually wedged tightly in position. The wedges can loosen so the stair moves and creaks. If this happens, you should carefully check all the stairs (see box, below right), and carry out any repairs necessary, from below the stairs if possible, or from above if not.

If the treads or risers split, they can be replaced in an open-string staircase (see p.186). Remove the balusters and the fasteners from the damaged tread or riser (fasteners are under the stairs). Slide out the broken part and use it as a template to cut a new one. Slip the new part into place and replace the fasteners and balusters. You will need professional help to replace treads or risers into a closed-string staircase.

If the nosing of a tread is damaged, it can often be fixed without removing the whole tread. Cut away the damaged area and use it as a template to cut a new section. Then glue and screw the patch in place. This is a method similar to that used for window sills (see p.152).

LOOSE-FITTING NEWEL POST

Take the loose joint apart, clean it, then install it with glue and screws. Adjust the fit of a modular newel turning into the newel base by using wedges and dowels (see p.190) if required. Resin can also be used to form a strong joint.

REPAIRING CREAKING STAIRS FROM BELOW

A If a wedge is loose under the squeaking stair, remove it. Use it as a template to cut a new wedge, and apply wood glue to its sides.

B Drive the new, glued wedge firmly into place. The wedge needs to fit tightly to prevent any movement in the joint.

C Once the wedges are tight, glue a reinforcing block across the joint between the tread and riser.

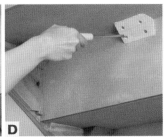

D Drill pilot holes through the block and into the stair, taking care not to penetrate the outer surface. Screw the block tightly into place.

REPAIRING CREAKING STAIRS FROM ABOVE

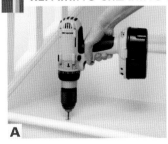

A Drill pilot holes through the squeaking or moving tread and into the edge of the riser below.

B Screw tightly into the riser. The screw head should recess into the tread. Fill the hole when you have finished. Repeat along the riser edge.

CHECKING THE STAIRS

The treads and risers of the staircase are exposed to the most damage. Many problems aren't obvious, so it may be worth checking the condition of old stairs occasionally, and certainly if you detect any movement when using the stairs. If you can get under the stairs, this is the easiest way both to inspect for damage and to fix it—especially if the stairs are carpeted. Ask someone to walk up and down the stairs while you check for any movement in the joints underneath. Mark any that need attention, then strengthen them using the technique above. If you have no access underneath the stairs, you will have to fix them from above (see left).

REPAIRING A BROKEN BALUSTER

If you have a closed-string staircase (see p.186), simply replace the broken baluster as shown here. If the baluster is secured into the tread of a step, it may be necessary to remove beading around the step in order to replace the spindle. If lots of spindles are damaged, you can replace the whole balustrade.

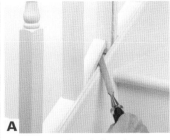

A Lever up the fillet below the broken baluster using a chisel.

Slide the new baluster into place

B Take the damaged baluster out and use it as a template to trim a replacement.

C Replace the fillet and pin it into place using a panel pin. You can then decorate to hide the repair.

INSTALLING BASEMENT STAIRS

Building stairs requires careful planning, the right tools, and some installation know-how. Good rules of thumb are: when you add the height of a stair riser and tread width, the result should be to 17– 18 in (430–460 mm). Risers usually rise 7–7¾ in (180–200 mm) and treads usually run 10 in (255 mm). And once the stringers are installed they should sit at about a 35-degree angle. These measurements are somewhat adjustable, to make the stair assembly fit in an opening, for example.

TOOLS AND MATERIALS SEE BASIC TOOLKIT AND P.188

1 LAYOUT

A

B

Measure the height (called "rise") from the floor to the landing, where the top of the stairs will go.

Divide the measurement by 7 or 7.5 to determine the number of risers the stringer needs. Round this to the closest whole number. Re-divide the total rise by this number.

C

D

E

F

With riser height determined and tread run known (10 in/255 mm) fasten brass stair gauges to your framing square.

Check your stringer stock. Make sure it is straight. If there is a crown, place the crown facing up.

Place the square on the stringer stock. Apply pressure with your thumb to keep it flat and scribe the riser height.

Without moving the square, mark the tread run. Keep gentle, even pressure on the square to keep it stable.

G

H

Step the square down the stringer stock by placing it next to the previous mark. Repeat the process until all stairs are marked.

Remove the stair gauges for the last mark so you can mark all the way across the board.

2 CUTTING OUT

A

A circular saw is the ideal tool for cutting most of the stringer, however, do not over cut the stringer. Instead, use a hand saw to finish cuts. This ensures the stringer stock (usually 2 x 12 in/50 x 300 mm) remains as strong as possible for heavy use.

B

C

D

E

Using a sharp handsaw to finish circular saw cuts ensures accuracy and ensures the stringer will be as sturdy as possible.

Clamp the pattern piece to new stock and trace it. This ensures accuracy between stringers, and speeds up the process.

Cut carefully. Make sure you always keep the saw blade on the same side of the line during every cut.

When cutting the bottom riser, be sure to cut it one-tread-thickness shorter than all the other risers.

3 ATTACHING THE STAIRS

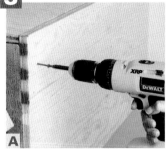

At the location where the stairs will contact the landing, place riser stock (plywood) to create a connection point for the stringers.

Place the stringers in place and on your layout marks. Fasten from behind the riser stock.

Install riser material on the stringers. Cut each one exactly the same so the stair is the same width at all points.

To really fasten the treads, glue and screw them down. This prevents squeaks and makes a permanent bond.

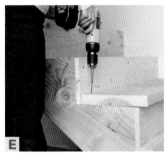

Use screws, rather than nails, to fasten tread stock to the stringers. Screws will form a tighter bond with the glue.

Sink screws from behind the riser stock into the edge of the tread. This binds everything together into a unit.

4 ATTACHING THE RAIL

A sturdy rail is an important safety feature of any stair. It is vital that they are built properly and to local building code, to prevent accidents. The newel post should be set plumb and fastened with screws while the rails should follow the exact rise-angle of the stairs.

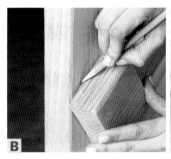

After running the bottom rail along the stair nosings and fastening securely, use a block to transfer the measurement up to the next rail piece.

Once you've marked where the next rail segment goes, fasten it to the newel post with screws.

Run rail segments long and cut them off, once fastened in place, with a handsaw. This saves you from having to calculate angles and lengths.

Above the last rail, install a handrail. Install all handrail hardware the same distance from the last rail section to maintain the proper angle.

Pre-miter and fasten the railing returns. Doing this prior to installation makes installation much easier. Pre-drill each side of the miter and set nails to fasten.

Set the railing on the railing hardware and fasten from the bottom side. It often helps to pre-drill holes to prevent splitting the wood.

Fastening all parts of the stair together with screws and installing a sturdy railing are the key to safe, sturdy stairs.

Fireplaces

FIREPLACES CAN BE PURELY DECORATIVE OR THE MAIN SOURCE OF HEAT OF A HOUSE. FIRES BURN SOLID FUEL OR GAS. ELECTRIC FIRES ARE ALSO AVAILABLE. THE KIND OF FIRE YOU CAN HAVE DEPENDS ON YOUR FLUE TYPE (SEE P.194). INSTALLING A FIREPLACE IS A JOB FOR A PROFESSIONAL, BUT YOU CAN INSTALL A FIRE SURROUND (SEE PP.196–197) OR COVER UP A FIREPLACE (SEE P.195) YOURSELF.

TYPES OF FIREPLACES AND FUELS

Several types and styles of decorative fireplaces are available. A fireplace can simply be a display area, or it may contain a solid fuel, gas, or even electric simulated fire. Each fuel has advantages and disadvantages, and some regions have pollution restrictions on burning wood. The kind of fireplace you choose will be influenced by the existing hearth size, and flue size and type (see p.194).

TYPES OF FIREPLACES

If you have an original fireplace designed to burn solid fuel, understand that the throat and chimney were designed for that fuel. Converting to any other type of fuel requires the advice of a professional and probably a flue liner. All open-hearth fireplaces can be made a bit more energy efficient by simply installing glass doors, restricting the quantity of air that goes up the chimeney.

FIREPLACES AND FUELS

Your options when changing to a different fuel type, or installing or renovating a fireplace, depend on your starting point. If you already have a chimney and fireplace, you can put any type of appliance in the opening as long as the flue conforms to regulations, or you may prefer to close it up and decide on a wall-mounted design. If you don't already have a fireplace, you can install a wood stove, construct a false opening and install a "real-effect" fire, or choose a contemporary style.

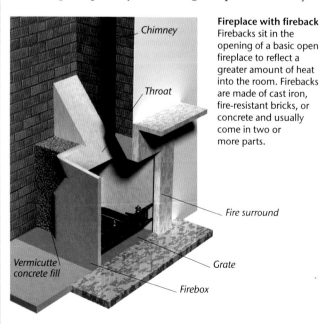

Fireplace with fireback
Firebacks sit in the opening of a basic open fireplace to reflect a greater amount of heat into the room. Firebacks are made of cast iron, fire-resistant bricks, or concrete and usually come in two or more parts.

Chimney

Throat

Fire surround

Vermicutte concrete fill

Grate

Firebox

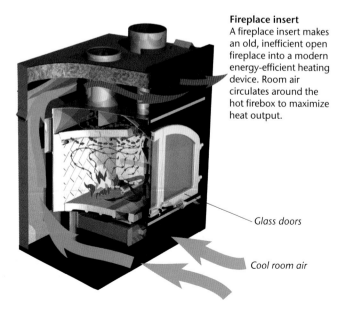

Fireplace insert
A fireplace insert makes an old, inefficient open fireplace into a modern energy-efficient heating device. Room air circulates around the hot firebox to maximize heat output.

Glass doors

Cool room air

TYPES OF APPLIANCES

Your choice of fireplace type will be narrowed down by what fuels are available to you, the construction of your chimney, and whether it has a flue liner. If you have no chimney, you can install an electric fireplace, or a gas fireplace designed for use with a balanced or power flue (see p.194).

Solid-fuel open fireplaces

A real fire burns wood or coal, or some can burn a range of solid fuels. The most efficient fires have a grate so that a good flow of air can get to the fire. Real fires may be in an open fireplace or one with a fireback. Canopies can be used over large fires that do not draw well. The canopy helps to direct combustion gases up into the flue.

Solid-fuel stoves

A woodburner or stove burns solid fuels. They are installed on the inner hearth of an open fireplace, or project onto the outer hearth. The flue may connect directly to a flue liner that either continues all the way up the inside of the chimney, or ends on the other side of a so-called register plate fitted across the bottom of an unlined flue.

Gas fireplaces

These are fuelled by natural gas or liquid propane. Running off the household gas supply, they are very clean and convenient. Manufacturers will specify flue requirements—they commonly use balanced or power flues (see pp.194–195), so a chimney is unnecessary.

Traditional and modern designs are available, including stove and open-fire styles. Contemporary designs that don't mimic real fires, such as fireplaces containing pebbles, are also available. Wall-mounted types are also popular.

Electric fireplaces

Real-effect electric fires can mimic traditional fires with a fireback, woodburner styles, and contemporary and wall-mounted designs. No flue is necessary.

FIRE SURROUNDS

Traditionally, a fire surround is made up of a mantel, a back panel, and an outer hearth. These items are sold separately or as part of a kit. Reclaimed antique and reproduction fire surrounds are popular, especially for older properties (see pp.94–95). Modern styles are also available. Existing surrounds may require refurbishing. For example, an antique cast-iron surround may need to be stripped of old paint layers, and its tiles, or the whole surround may need replacing. Although installing a new fireplace is a job for a professional, you can change a fire surround yourself. See pp.196–197 for more information.

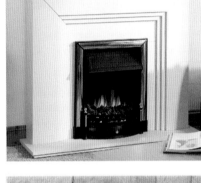

Traditional fireplace
Stone, cast iron, and wood are popular materials for traditional fire surrounds. Traditional styles are available for all fuel (see above) and flue types (see p.194). For use with "real" fires, reproductions of antique designs, as well as old reclaimed fire surrounds, are available.

Stoves in fireplaces
A stove or woodburner positioned in a basic open fireplace (see opposite) provides a traditional look. Doors can be opened on most stoves, except for those with a balanced flue (see p.194). With a real, solid-fuel burning fire, remember that the flue will require periodic sweeping.

High-efficiency insert
Basically a freestanding stove inserted into an old fireplace opening, an insert gives you modern energy efficiency with the look of an old-fashioned fireplace. Glass dors may become hot. A railing guard helps prevent accidents.

Freestanding stoves
With our emphasis on energy conservation and air sealing our houses in Canada, flueless stoves are generally not permitted because of concerns for indoor air quality. The look of a flueless stove can be obtained with an electric stove.

Wall-mounted fireplace
This is a modern, space-saving option. Electric and direct vent gas types can be extremely thin and can be installed almost anywhere in the home. Other types need a chimney and so are more complicated to install. See p.194 for more information on flue types.

FLUES, CHIMNEYS, AND FIREPLACES

There are several things you need to consider when choosing a new fireplace or refurbishing an old one. You may need to install a new flue, or have an existing chimney lined or relined—the main types of flue are shown here. If your current flue does not need renovating or replacing, it will be easier to choose a fireplace suitable for it. Unless you have a direct vent fireplace or balanced flue, you need to consider ventilation; fires require an air supply to burn well. A lack of wall space can make it desirable to cover up a fireplace, either leaving the recess or making it flush with the wall.

GAS SAFETY

Vent-free gas fireplaces are common in Europe, permitted under certain conditions in the US, and not permitted in most Canadian jurisdictions. Great efforts have been made with catalytic converters and the like to assure pollution-free output, but in Canada's modern, very tight houses, any combustion device that does not vent outdoors is considered an indoor air quality hazard. If you do install one in one of the few areas that permit such devices, be sure you have an oxygen detection safety pilot (ODS) and install a CO detector.

FLUES

As fires burn, they give out combustion gases, which are carried out of the home by a flue. The main types of flues are discussed below. As the gases are carried out of the house, they must be replaced by fresh air. In older houses, natural drafts were relied upon to provide this constant airflow. In modern, well-insulated homes, it is unlikely that a natural airflow exists, so ventilation must be provided. Some flues (balanced flues) have a built-in air intake. Ventilation requirements should be specified for particular fires. See pp.368–369 for more on providing ventilation. Fires and flues need to be checked annually by a professional to ensure that they are working safely and efficiently, according to the National Fire Protection Agency.

Fireplaces without chimneys

There are several types of flues that do not need a chimney. Two common designs are shown below and flueless fires (right) are also available. The type of flue you need will normally be specified by the fire manufacturer. Some fires only radiate heat, but the fires shown here also warm air from the room by circulating it inside of the body of the fireplace, separately from the combustion process.

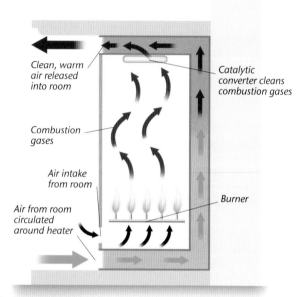

Flueless (vent-free)
The combustion gases are double-burned by a catalytic converter and released into the room, making flueless stoves energy-efficient because no heat is lost via the flue. Only a few Canadian jurisdictions permit them as they are still considerd an indoor air quality hazard.

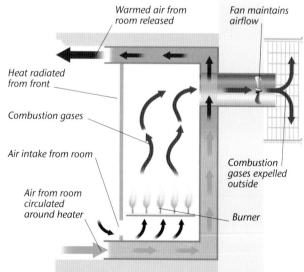

Balanced flue
This kind of flue is built into the fire and runs straight through the wall behind. It takes fresh air in and lets combustion gases out. A balanced flue is used with glass-fronted fires so there is no contact between the fire and the air in the room.

Power direct flue
This type of flue has a fan to suck combustion gases through the flue and expel them outside. Power flues can be extended, so it may be possible to install a fireplace away from an external wall. An electric supply is required for the fan.

Flues in chimneys

Modern chimneys are built fully lined with a corrosion-resistant, rectangular, precast concrete flue suitable for any fire. If you have an older chimney, it may have an unlined flue. If there are cracks in the mortar you should have it lined. Seek advice from a professional—they may recommend installing a concrete or metal flue liner compatible with your fuel type.

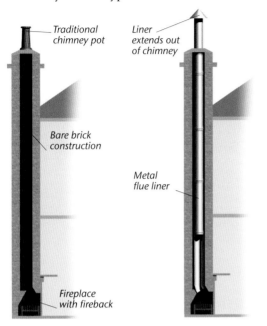

Traditional chimney pot

Liner extends out of chimney

Bare brick construction

Metal flue liner

Fireplace with fireback

Unlined flue
Basic chimney constructed of brick or stone.

Lined flue
A chimney with a concrete or metal liner in it.

OLD FIREPLACES

Closing up a fireplace

If you are blocking up a fireplace, it is important to understand the potentially damaging effects that can come from trapped moisture. You need to cap the top to prevent rain penetration, but usually the top is not sealed air tight. It is the fireplace opening itself, as well as the clean-out opening in the basement that need to be sealed up air tight to prevent moist household air from escaping into the chimney. With the fireplace blocked up, there is no longer heat from the fire to push the moist air out the top nor to dry it out. Condensation can saturate the bricks on the top. With our freeze/thaw climate that eventually leads to the breaking up of the bricks and the chimney begins to fall apart.

Opening up an old fireplace

Exposing an old fireplace is a journey into the unknown—there is no way of knowing what you will discover behind the boarding or blockwork. There might be an intact period fireplace, or little more than debris. If the latter is the case, you will need to get a new or reclaimed surround, and a grate and a fireback installed.

If you plan to use the fireplace, then notify your local building inspector. A previously blocked-off chimney must be tested before reuse to ensure that it is sound, gas-tight, and free from blockages. An old hearth must also be checked to ensure that it complies with current building regulations.

If the fireplace looks like it was blocked off recently, there may be little to do once it is uncovered, other than getting the fire and chimney structure checked and swept. Get professional advice on how to proceed when unblocking very old hearths because you may need to get the integrity of the structure checked before removing any rubble or brickwork. You will then probably need to have some work done on the chimney and fireplace before you can safely use it.

CHIMNEY CAPS

Chimney pots provide a decorative finish and raise the top of the chimney above the roof line, where the airflow draws combustion gases out. A chimney cap is often attached to the top to improve ventilation and keep out rain and animals. If any damp problems are associated with a chimney, check that the flashing and pointing are intact, and that a cap has been installed. Different cap designs are used with different fire types, so make sure you have the right cap. If you are opening up an old fireplace, you should enlist professional help to check that the top of the chimney has not been blocked and is fitted with the right type of cap, and that the chimney is in good repair. They may also install or replace a flue liner (see above).

Uncoated chimney caps are only suitable for some types of fire

Pins secure the chimney cap to the chimney pot

Pamper cap
This type of chimney cap can be adjusted to fit most chimney pots. It is designed to prevent downdrafts from blowing smoke and fumes back into the house, and to prevent entry of rain, hail, animals, and birds.

Coating resists corrosion

Chimney cap is tied to the chimney pot

Standard chimney cap
If your chimney is well-situated and has no significant downdraft problems, a basic chimney cap will prevent entry of rain, hail, animals, and birds.

Fins catch the breeze

Hinged versions are available to make chimney cleaning easier

Draft-assist chimney cap
Revolving chimney caps or wind-vane type caps that keep the opening always down wind are designed to encourage air flow in chimneys that don't draw air well or are prone to wind-driven downdrafts.

INSTALLING A FIRE SURROUND

The technique for installing a fireplace surround is straightforward. If you are replacing a surround for a working fireplace, then you need to make sure that it is compatible with your type of fireplace and fuel, as temperatures and fire hazards vary—check the manufacturer's instructions. If you are working on an old fireplace, you need to follow all the guidelines and make sure that your local building inspector has been informed (see p.195).

BUILDING REGULATIONS

Regulations govern the construction of masonry and factory-built fireplaces and chimneys, so seek professional advice if you are unsure of any installation. The construction or installation of a new fireplace, as well as the reconstruction of an existing fireplace, will need to be inspected by the local building safety department. The installation of a gas-fired appliance must also be inspected for compliance with the applicable codes. For both factory-built and custom fireplaces, it is important to provide an exterior air supply to ensure proper fuel combustion.

INSTALLING A FIRE SURROUND

If replacing an existing surround for a working fireplace, check that the new surround is compatible with the type of fuel and fireplace. Some are designed for ornamental use and may not be heat-resistant. Building regulations state that surrounds for working fires need a superimposed, or outer hearth (see right), which is at least 2 in (48 mm) thick, and extends at least 18 in (450 mm) from the front of the fire. Before purchasing a new fire surround, check the dimensions of your opening and make sure new items will fit. Depending on the fireplace type you have, the inner hearth may also need to be built up to bring it to the same level as the outer hearth that you have installed.

If you want a purely ornamental fireplace, you can fit a surround around a blocked opening, or even on a flat wall. A kit designed for a decorative purpose will usually be cheaper than a fireproof surround.

Installing a wooden surround

This is normally a very straightforward task that simply requires brackets. The order of work for installing the mantel, back panel, and hearth may vary, but a typical procedure is shown here. Wooden surrounds often incorporate a stone (marble, for example) back panel. Or the back panel area can be tiled.

Installing a stone surround

Because of the weight of a stone surround, it needs to be broken down into more sections than a wooden surround, which in turn means that assembly involves joining these sections together. Hearths are likely to come in a number of pieces, as are the mantel and back panel. In this example, a typical stone fireplace surround is shown but the order of work may need modification according to the particular design you have chosen. Some manufacturers will recommend using a stone sealer on the surround to prevent staining when using the fireplace.

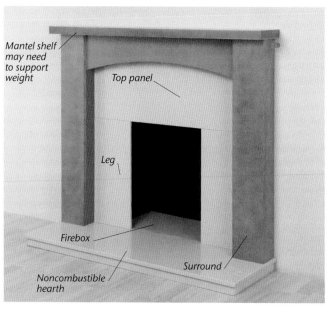

Surround kits
This type of surround is normally sold in kit form. Manufacturers generally offer a range of mantel shelves, back panels, and hearths, so you can choose which combination you prefer.

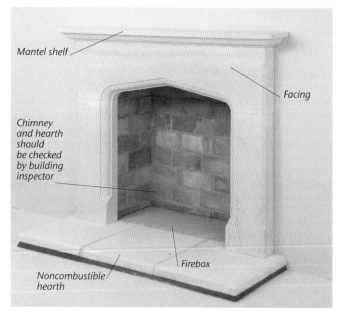

Stone fireplaces
Some manufacturers sell standard sizes and styles of stone surrounds, but more often they are custom-built. The components are very heavy, so you will need help with installation.

TOOLS AND MATERIALS CHECKLIST P.197	
Installing a marble hearth and wooden fire surround Level, drp cloth, adhesive spreader, white mortar*, fire cement*	white mortar*, threaded bolts, resin * See pp.70–71 for cement and mortar mixes
Installing a stone hearth and fire surround Level, slab mortar* trowel, corner braces,	FOR BASIC TOOLKIT SEE PP.24–25

INSTALLING A MARBLE HEARTH AND WOODEN FIRE SURROUND

A Apply a thin bed of thinset mortar to the constructional hearth. Position the marble hearth and check it is central and level.

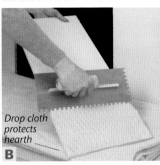

Drop cloth protects hearth

B Apply thinset mortar to the legs. An adhesive spreader is the ideal tool to texture the surface of the mortar to increase grip.

C

Position the upright, using a level to get it plumb. Don't worry about getting mortar on the wall—it will be covered by the surround—but make sure you keep the marble clean. Check that the two legs are level, then allow the mortar to set.

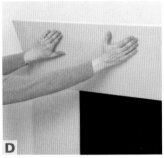

D Spread thinset mortar across the top panel and place it by resting it on the legs to get the bottom edge level before pressing it into the wall.

E Position the mantelpiece and mark the fastener points. An option is to draw around the brackets, then cut notches in the wall surface for them.

F Remove the surround. Drill pilot holes in the wall at the marked off points. Reposition the mantelpiece and screw it in place.

G Carefully fill any gaps between the surround and the fireplace using fire cement.

INSTALLING A STONE HEARTH AND FIRE SURROUND

A Mark out the exact position of the hearth and lay a ¾-in (20-mm) bed of slab mortar (see p.71). Roughen the surface with the trowel.

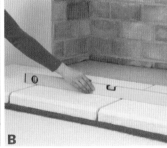

B Position the slabs that make up the hearth. Adjust the mortar until the slabs are precisely level. Grout them with thinset mortar (see pp.70–71).

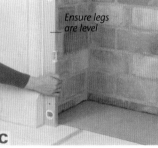

Ensure legs are level

C Position the legs. Mark the layout points of the corner braces on the wall and upright for the fasteners. Remove the legs and drill pilot holes.

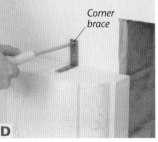

Corner brace

D Spread a thin bed of thinset mortar underneath the legs. Reposition them and screw them into place.

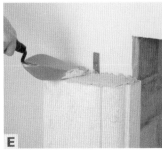

E Apply a thin layer of thinset mortar to the tops of the legs.

F Place the mantle and check that it is level. You will need help to lift it. Screw the corner braces into the wall.

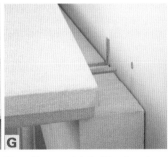

G Place the mantel shelf and mark the position of the bolts. Drill holes at the marked points. Fill them with resin, then reposition the shelf.

H Clean up all the joints in the hearth and surround with a pointing trowel, then clean any excess mortar from the stone faces.

Roofs

ROOFS MAY BE PITCHED (ANGLED), OR "FLAT" (WHICH, IN REALITY, IS VERY SLIGHTLY ANGLED). A NEW ROOF IS ALMOST CERTAINLY A JOB FOR A PROFESSIONAL. BUT YOU CAN TACKLE MINOR REPAIRS YOURSELF, AS LONG AS YOU ARE COMFORTABLE WITH HEIGHTS. THE NEXT FEW PAGES DETAIL TYPICAL REPAIR JOBS—INCLUDING REPAIRING OR REPLACING GUTTERS.

PITCHED ROOFS

Most roofs are pitched. There are many types of pitched roof to suit different situations. As a result, there are many variations on the basic design and numerous combinations of design elements with construction methods.

TYPES OF PITCHED ROOFS

Four main designs of pitched roofs are shown here. There are many variations on these themes. Roofs are usually defined according to their shape. Each type can be built in different ways, and from different materials.

Gabled
The roof slopes around a triangular extension of the end wall. This piece of wall is the gable.

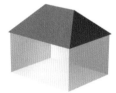

Hipped
A hip is the joint between two adjacent slopes of a roof. Some complex roofs have several hips.

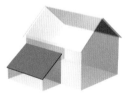

Shed
This simple roof has only one slope. It is commonly used on lean-to structures, such as additions.

Mansard
A modified version of the pitched roof that creates a spacious living area in the roof space.

ROOF DETAILING

Ridges, hips, and valleys are the corners or joints where a roof changes direction; they are the points at which pitched roofs meet. Verges, abutments, and eaves are the "edges" of a roof. The eaves are horizontal joints between a roof and a wall, whereas the verges are angled joints between a roof and a gable wall. Not all roofs feature all of these details, and some of them can be constructed in a number of ways.

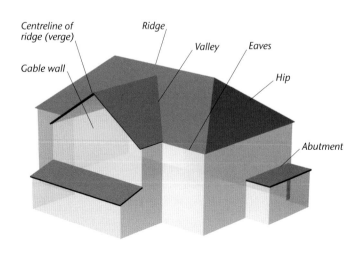

Centreline of ridge (verge)
Gable wall
Ridge
Valley
Eaves
Hip
Abutment

PITCHED ROOF FRAMES

A pitched roof has a network of frames to support the structure and its covering. There are two main types of wooden frames—stick-built and trussed roofs—which are sometimes combined to achieve more complex roofs. Both types of construction will support any common roof coverings (see pp.204–205).

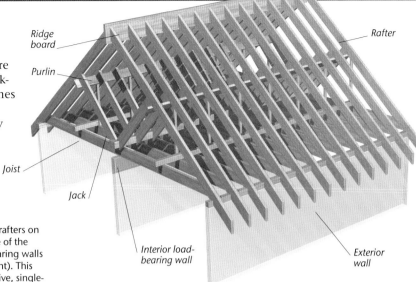

Ridge board *Rafter*

Purlin

Joist

Jack

Interior load-bearing wall *Exterior wall*

Stick-built roof framing

Traditionally, all roofs were stick-built—carpenters cut rafters on site during construction. To cover greater spans, some of the roof's weight may be transferred onto internal loadbearing walls using purlins (beams that brace the rafters; shown right). This forms a "double" roof. Although they are labor-intensive, single- and double-stick-built roofs are still constructed.

Common trussed roof framing

Often referred to as A-frames because of their shape, modern trusses (lumber frames) are manufactured off-site by specialist companies. The A-frame combines rafters, joists, and jacks. A roof is made up of several A-frames. Because of technological advances in calculating the stresses and loading requirements of roof lumber, trusses can be made slimmer than the boards in a cut roof. Trusses are manufactured in a number of different shapes and sizes to suit the needs of various types of roofs. For example, some trusses are designed to leave a lot of open space in a roof, so that it can be used as a room. Lean-to, or shed, trusses are commonly used for additions.

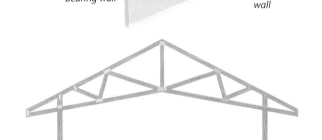

A-frame *Rafter*

Joist

Interior load-bearing wall *Exterior wall*

TRUSSES DESIGNED FOR COLD CLIMATES

With increased insulation levels in modern houses, there became a need for more room between the ceiling of the house and the roof to allow for the increased insulation as well as more ventilation. Icicles and ice dams on the roof are avoided with these special truss designs.

Raised hip truss
A hip is installed between the roof and the wall.

Cold-climate scissor truss
More space is provided over the outer walls than with similar trusses in warm climates.

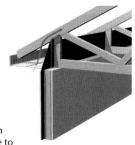

The insulation does not have to taper down at the edge of the attic for air to pass.

There is room for both heavy insulation and roof air flow.

ROOF STRUCTURE

Before you can start any work on a roof, you need to understand how the roof's elements combine to create a waterproof layer. This varies according to design, age, type of covering, and climate. Some roofs have all the elements shown below; others have only some, but the principles tend to remain the same. Roofs are supported by outside walls, ceiling joists, and interior bearing walls. They are sheathed in layers of plywood, waterproofing, and shingles. The roof's job is to shed water away from the structure.

BUILDING REGULATIONS

Check your local regulations regarding roofs. There may be requirements for almost every detail, including materials, ventilation, and fasteners. The regulations are much stricter with regard to historic buildings, for which certain styles have to be maintained, and attic conversions, for which stringent safety rules must be followed.

THE PARTS OF A ROOF COVERING

The features described here are standard on most residential roofs. Further information on roofing felt, vapor barriers, shingles, and other roof coverings is on pp.204–205. In order to shed water properly, make sure you overlap these materials in the correct direction. Typically material is installed from the bottom of the roof toward the ridge, so that the lower layer is overlapped by the next layer of the same material.

Shingles

Most roofs have shingle, tile or membrane coverings (see p.204) to provide the waterproofing. Ways of overlapping roofing materials are shown below and on pp.206–207.

Battens

These provide attachment points for tiles, and hold down felt. They are evenly spaced to give the correct overlap between rows of tiles. The spacing (gauge) depends on roof pitch, tile type and fastening method (see p.204), and climate. Roofs to be covered with asphalt shingles do not need battens (see p.207).

Roofing underlayment

Felt, or another kind of underlayment (see p.205), is laid below shingles to create a waterproof and wear barrier. It is not always required by code, but it is always recommended by the manufacturers. It may not be present on older buildings. It is laid over the sheathing, which may be made of plywood or another material (see below), in overlapping horizontal strips.

Sheathing

Boarding laid on top of the rafters is known as sheathing. It is required by local codes. Sheathing adds rigidity to the roof frame and provides a nailing surface for fasteners. OSB and plywood are common sheathing materials. Center each sheet of sheathing on a rafter below. If you plan to install wood shakes or shingles, you may want to space sheathing to provide more ventilation, as it helps to dry out wood roofing materials after wet weather. When installing roof sheathing, only walk where the rafters run underneath to help prevent any problematic bowing. You may want to make chalk lines along the rafters.

Roof structure
A typical roof is constructed from a roof truss, covered with roof sheathing, underlayment, and a roof covering on top. The layers are carefully overlapped to ensure the roof is fully waterproof.

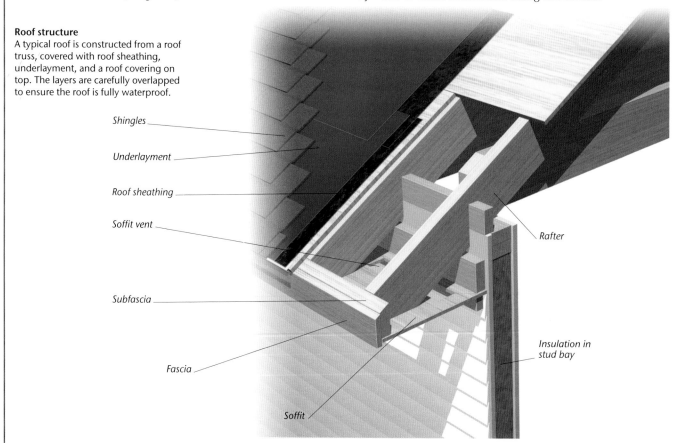

Shingles

Underlayment

Roof sheathing

Soffit vent

Subfascia

Fascia

Soffit

Rafter

Insulation in stud bay

TYPES OF ROOF DESIGN

Roof designs can be complicated. In order to shape a roof, hips and ridges combine with the trusses to create the spaces inside the home. The shape of the roof must also shed water effectively. When detailing a roof hip or ridge, it is important to make the connection secure, and to properly install the sheathing, underlayment, and flashing materials so that water does not enter the structure. Shown below are a few common details used to create most rooflines. See pp.202–203 for more information about detailing roof flashing.

Valley
A valley is used if the external walls of the home turn an internal corner. It is designed to direct water down towards its intersection point, and then the water runs down the valley and off the roof.

Hip
A hip design can sometimes be found at a corner of the external walls of the home. Just like a mountain, a hip allows rainwater and snow to fall off either side of the hip and then slide off of the roof.

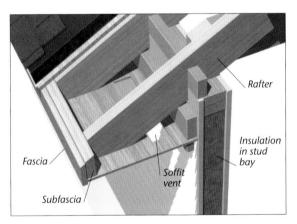

Deep eaves
Typically, deep eaves should have 12 in (300 mm) or more continuously vented to ensure that sufficient air intake is available. This is required to properly vent the attic.

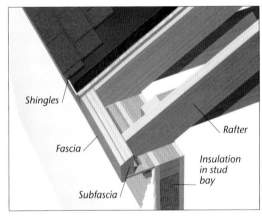

Shallow eaves
Typically, shallow eaves have less than 12 in (300 mm) of continuous venting. This is popular among more contemporary designs. Avoid this design in regions of heavy rainfall as the walls will get wetter.

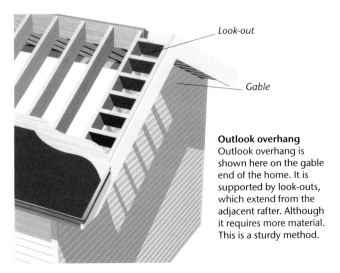

Outlook overhang
Outlook overhang is shown here on the gable end of the home. It is supported by look-outs, which extend from the adjacent rafter. Although it requires more material. This is a sturdy method.

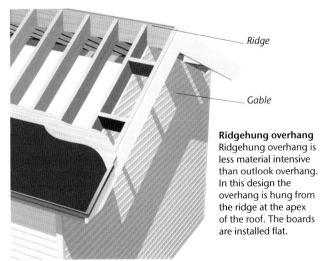

Ridgehung overhang
Ridgehung overhang is less material intensive than outlook overhang. In this design the overhang is hung from the ridge at the apex of the roof. The boards are installed flat.

FLASHING

Flashing helps direct the flow of water around openings. Since water can seep into your home's walls, deteriorating building materials, causing structural damage, and creating moisture and mold problems, it is very important to properly install flashing when constructing a new house or altering the exterior of a house. Flashing is used beneath the first course above ground level in a masonry building, above all wood trim on shelves, doors, and windows, where exterior stairs and decks attach to the house, and around any features in the roof structure. Below are some of the common flashing details on residential roofs.

FURTHER INFORMATION

When working on the roof, make sure you take the necessary precautions. In order to safely work, you will need secure scaffolding and a roofing ladder. If you are installing a skylight, remember to never step on the skylight. Never put tools or materials on the skylight. Screens and platforms are available to protect you from falls. If you are unsure about how to make your DIY jobsite safe, contact your local workman's safety board.

FLASHING MATERIALS

Flashing can be made of sheet metal, plastic, or composite materials. Sheet metal flashing is the most durable, and usually the most expensive choice. Copper or stainless steel can be used as flashing. Plastic flashing, usually PVC-based, is a less expensive alternative to metal, but if parts are exposed, it can wear with direct sun contact.

Flashing overlaps roofing material

Roofing material overlaps flashing

Dormer

Metal flashing is usually chosen for dormer windows. Flashing squares are inserted between each row of roofing material. Flashing can also be used as a strip that runs around the dormer and under the roofing material. Unlike other windows in your home, the flashing is also extended into a front apron, which overlaps the roof material. As dormer size and window style vary from house to house, the details can be different for your house.

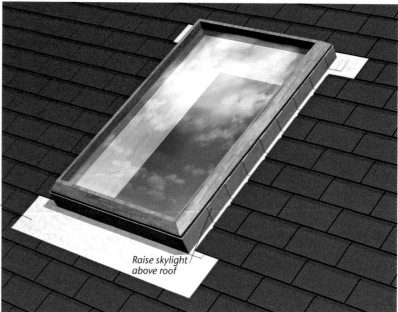

One-piece flashing

Raise skylight above roof

Skylight

Flashings around skylights are usually one continuous piece. Skylights should be raised on a wooden curb at least 8 in (20 cm) high to provide space for flashings, but often much higher to keep the skylight above the snow line if your roof collects snow. If you are reroofing your house you may need to raise or remove your skylight for the installation of proper flashing. Even if your skylight is manufactured with flashing attached, you may need additional flashing.

VENTS

No matter the shape of your roof, vents are a common feature of any roof structure. If you are roofing around an already-installed vent, you may need to alter the height of the flashing detail around the vent. If you are cutting out a hole in your roof to accommodate a new vent, be careful to cut a clean hole, to minimize any extra work that will be needed to complete your project.

Hood vent

Hoods can vent through the wall or through the roof. Low button vents are common, but if you have deep snow on your roof you are better off with a raised vent. If you are installing a new vent, you will be cutting a hole in the roof. After placing the vent in the hole, slip the flashing flange under the shingles above the vent. The flashing will be over the shingles below the vent. Seal the joints. Place the vent cap on top of the vent.

Seal all joints

Flashing extends over shingles below the vent

Pipe vent

When you are roofing around a pipe vent (also called a pipe stack), you will need to cut out the shape of the pipe from the row of shingles. Fit the shingle row around the bottom part of the pipe. Then, slide pipe flashing over the pipe so that it extends 4 in (100 mm) below the pipe, 8 in (200 mm) above the pipe, and 6 in (150 mm) to the right and left. The bottom part of the flashing will overlap the shingle row, as shown.

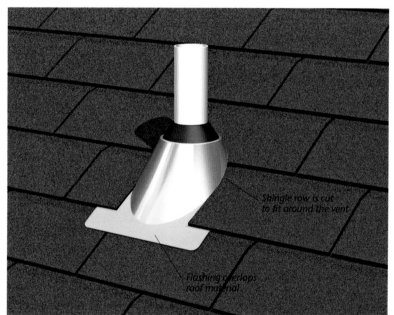

Shingle row is cut to fit around the vent

Flashing overlaps roof material

Chimney flashing

Metal or PVC-based strips cover the joint between the roof and the chimney. They are bent in the corner and overlapped on one side by the edges of the shingles, and on the other by the cap flashing, which is attched into the mortor joints of the chimney's brickwork.

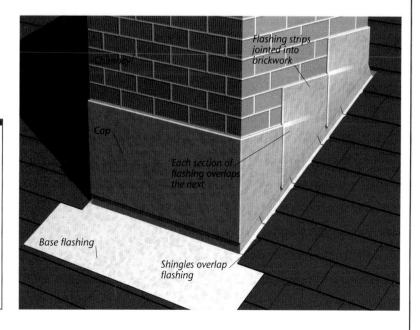

Flashing strips jointed into brickwork

Chimney

Cap

Each section of flashing overlaps the next

Base flashing

Shingles overlap flashing

NEW ROOFS

Hard coverings such as tiles do not easily break down, so they can often be reused. New asphalt tiles can sometimes be laid over old ones, to avoid stripping a roof; ask for your supplier's advice.

If you are considering changing the type of roof covering, find out first whether the new roof can be supported by the existing structure. Get advice from a professional roofer. You may want to consult with more than one.

ROOFING MATERIALS

Roofs are composed of many different materials but, broadly speaking, there are four main components common to the structure of most roof systems: a lumber framework (shown on the previous pages), felt underlay, a roof covering, and flashing (waterproofing at joints). The options in these four areas are shown and explained here, along with some supplementary items used with the materials shown. You may find it helpful to read this alongside pp.200–201.

FASTENERS

The specifications for fasteners such as nails and/or screws used in roof construction can vary according to local building regulations. Coated and galvanized nails are often used. They provide the best protection, because they are anticorrosive. The most commonly used are called roofing nails, such as those shown on p.78.

ROOF COVERINGS

Seek advice from manufacturers when deciding how to install tiles or shingles on a roof. Although it may seem easy to replace like with like, newer regulations may require a different method. If you are planning a new roof, the installation method will be influenced by the pitch of roof, chosen tile type, and prevailing weather conditions. Many older shingles still on roofs in Canada were made in Imperial measurements (inches and feet) while all new shingles are metric. One system fits poorly over the other if you are trying to add shingles over shingles. Although clay shingles and slate tile roofs are relatively uncommon in Canada, modern metal and composite materials imitate their appearance.

Specialty shingles
These new new types of asphalt shingles provide style and are designed to be resistant to fire and high winds.

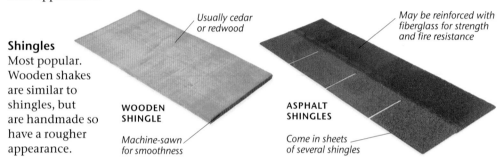

Shingles
Most popular. Wooden shakes are similar to shingles, but are handmade so have a rougher appearance.

Usually cedar or redwood

WOODEN SHINGLE

Machine-sawn for smoothness

May be reinforced with fiberglass for strength and fire resistance

ASPHALT SHINGLES

Come in sheets of several shingles

Cedar
Asphalt shingles can be double-layered to give design relief that looks like cedar shakes.

Concrete tiles
Mimic clay designs and are made to interlock easily.

PLAIN TILE   **PAN TILE**   **ROMAN TILE**

Imitation redwood
An asphalt substitution for redwood shakes. Some shingles are designed to lock corners down for high wind areas.

Other tiles
Give a traditional look.

Interlocking single-lap tile

PAN TILE   **METAL ROOF TILE**

Rustic look
Theses specialty asphalt shingles resemble weathered wood.

Slate tiles
Strong and durable, slate provides long-lasting roofing and is more lightweight than other tiles. Cheaper synthetic slates are another option.

SYNTHETIC SLATE TILE   **NATURAL SLATE TILE**

Scalloped edge
Scalloped edges and a weathered rock finish give a European look.

ROOFING FELT

For a small repair, choose felt to match what is already on the roof. If you need to lay new felt, think about whether you need it to be breathable—for instance, because the roof space is insulated and/or ventilated in a particular way (see pp.360–361).

Often colored

Breathable felt
Allows moisture inside the roof to escape, but prevents moisture that is outside from getting in.

Normally black

Bitumen-reinforced felt
A very effective waterproof barrier.

Sheets should overlap to the dotted line

Plastic "felt"
Alternative to bitumen-reinforced felt. Both types are non-breathable.

STRAPS AND PLATES

Metal straps and plates are used to hold lumber together in roof structures—especially in modern trusses. These types of joints and plates make installation much more straightforward, as there is no need to cut complex wooden joints. Since roof structures have so many joints, they can be a considerable timesaver.

Restraint strap
There are several designs of restraint straps made for various uses and roof types. The example shown here fits across the end rafters next to a gable and attaches to the wall.

Small holes for fasteners

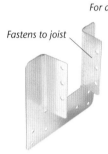

Timber connector
Used at joints in trusses to hold together roof parts.

Fastens to joist

Truss clip
Used to connect trusses to a wall plate.

For deeper joists

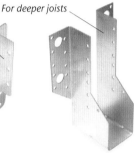

Heavy-duty truss hanger
More robust.

FLASHING TOOLS AND MATERIALS

The waterproofing materials used in valleys, abutments, around chimneys, or at any other joint between different parts of a roof are known as flashing. Galvanized metal flashings are the most common, but flashings can be made of copper, aluminum, and even plastic products.

Ice Shield
A self-adhesive rubberized material about 3 feet (1m) wide is laid on the lower edge of most roofs before shingles to stop problems caused by ice dams.

Self-adhesive flashing repair
Applied over damaged flashing for a repair. Primer may be needed before application.

Glass-reinforced polyester (GRP)
GRP flashing is used in Europe when replacing old lead flashings. Similar products are becoming available in Canada.

Handle
Curved side
Flat side

Lead dresser
This is typical of special tools needed to work with old materials like lead flashings or some new synthetic roofing materials.

VENTILATION MATERIALS

Poor ventilation in a roof is a major cause of mold and wood rot. There are a number of different options for ventilating a roof. Exhaust fans should never be attached to attic vents because of the condensation and frost that would form and drip back into the attic. Exhaust fans that go through the roof require special exhaust vent hoods that attach the exhaust duct to the vent opening in a sealed fashion. Insulating a roof is discussed in detail on pp.356–361.

Button vent
The most common Canadian roof vent slides under the shingles above it and over the ones below it. Two or three to a roof is typical.

Ridge vent
Ridge vents are necessary for cathedral ceilings where every truss space of the roof space needs venting all the way from the soffits through the roof and out the top.

High vent
High vents are becoming the standard in Canada wherever snow accumulates on a roof. The best have baffles to keep blowing snow out.

Reroofing is a major project, and should usually be carried out by a professional contractor with proper safety equipment. DIY work on a roof usually involves carrying out a small-scale repair, perhaps caused by storm damage, rather than total replacement—and that is what these pages deal with. Although the most common roof coverings in Canada by far are three-tab asphalt shingles, these pages will show you how to deal with repairs to such difficult materials as tiles, slates, and wood shingles as well.

REPLACING A DAMAGED TILE OR SHINGLE

The method needed for replacing a roof covering will depend on the type of tile or shingle in use. For instance, the steps below show a simple way of replacing a tile, but you may need to alter them slightly, as described alongside the steps. To remove a slate, you may prefer to use a slate ripper rather than a hacksaw blade (as shown). Slate rippers are specially designed to remove fasteners that are under a row of slates, but they are specialty tools and probably not worth buying unless you are likely to replace a lot of slates. With wooden shingles, the problem may have to do with waterproofing rather than breakages: damp shingles may buckle or rot. Replace split or damaged shingles so that they do not allow moisture to penetrate into or through the roof. Replacing asphalt shingles is easier because they are flexible, so they can simply be lifted up to give access to the fasteners beneath them.

Cutting a tile or shingle

Wooden shingles and shakes can be cut with a saw, and asphalt shingles can be cut with a utility knife. Clay and concrete tiles are best cut using an angle grinder (see p.61, paying attention to the safety issues involved, and wearing all suitable protective clothing). Slates can be scored by running a sharp nail along a guide line, and then snapped along that line, or they can be split apart by tapping the scored line with the edge of a trowel.

▌ REPLACING A TILE

Tiles with nibs may be nailed in place, so those nails may need to be cut free as shown in Replacing a Slate (below). Otherwise, lift the old tile free of the furring strip, and lip the end of a new one over the furring strip. With interlocking or single-lap tiles, wedge up the tiles next to the damaged one, as well as those above it, as shown here, to undo the interlocking joints.

A

Wedge up the tiles above the broken one, so that you can access it. Unhook the tile from the furring strip and lift out the broken tile.

B

Position the new tile, hooking its nibs over the furring strip and ensuring that it is securely attached. Remove the wedges from the adjoining tiles, and check that the new tile is sitting flush with the neighboring tiles.

▌ REPLACING A SLATE

A

Remove any loose pieces of slate, then cut away the nails with a hacksaw blade wound in tape at the "handle" end.

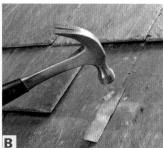

B

Nail a strip of lead over the exposed vertical joint between slates, securing into the furring strip below. You can use clips instead.

C

Position a new slate to replace the old one, ensuring that it fits well.

D

Bend the lead or clip up over the new slate to secure it in position.

REPLACING A WOOD SHINGLE

A Use a hammer and chisel to split and remove the broken shingle.

B Wind tape around one end of a hacksaw blade to form a "handle" by which to hold it. Use the blade to cut through the shingle's nails.

C Slide the new shingle into position and secure it in place with nails as close as possible to the row above. Seal along the edges of the shingle, and across the nail heads, with a sealant (see p.81).

REPLACING AN ASPHALT SHINGLE

A Use a pry bar to lever up the nails in the damaged strip of shingles. Then remove it.

B Loosen the nails at the top and bottom of the strip of shingles above, so that you can slide the new strip of shingles in underneath it.

C Slide the new strip of shingles up and into position.

D Hide nails by placing the end of the pry bar over them, and hitting it farther down the shank of the bar with a hammer to knock them in.

WORKING WITH ASPHALT SHINGLES

Asphalt shingles have the advantage of being flexible, but be careful. You can damage them without realizing it. The older they are, the more brittle they become, and the colder the weather, the more brittle they become, even when they are new. Try to work on a warm, sunny day. Do not use a propane torch to warm shingles up as you will boil the asphalt, causing more problems.

Under the lower edge of each tab there is roofing cement that holds the tab down. On new shingles you can see that cement on the shingle below the tab. After new shingles are laid, it is the sun that activates the cement and locks down the tabs. When trying to loosen a shingle, be careful to use a putty knife to gently wedge up and cut through that dab of cement. Just working away with a crow bar will probably break the shingle right next to the dab of cement.

When repairing loose or damaged shingles, add a dab of roofing cement to the corners of the repair and then push the shingle down into place. Work so as to avoid any cement from being pushed out where it is visible. This is not only for aesthetics, but also to avoid UV sunlight from striking the roofing cement. UV light will break down all such adhesives within just one year. If you must apply roof patching adhesives where they will be exposed, return a week after you have made the repair and paint over the exposed adhesive with aluminum paint, which is an ultraviolet light protector.

Roofing cement

Bend shingle carefully

Glue loose shingles before the wind rips them off.

Apply pressure

Corner must lie flat

Hold or weight down until stuck.

TYPES OF GUTTERS

A correctly installed gutter system will increase the efficiency of water transfer from roof to drainage system. This helps to maintain house structure by eliminating problems often caused by leaking or badly positioned gutters. Gutters do not need to be replaced often. Regularly clear gutters of debris and repair any loose joints as soon as you notice them. Direct water as far away from the foundation as possible.

RECYCLING WATER
Rainwater is usually just sent away from the housse, but it can be recycled. This can be done by collecting it in a rain barrel positioned below a gutter downspout, or with a system of water recycling for use in the household plumbing system (see pp.389–91).

MATERIALS
Gutters are made from a variety of materials, each with different strengths, appearances, and costs. There may be regulations in historic areas about replacing gutters, so check these if they may apply to you before you buy new gutters.

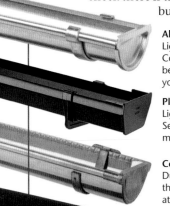

Aluminium
Lightweight. Joining systems vary. Continuous gutters (without joints) can be made on-site by specialists to suit your requirements.

Plastic (vinyl)
Lightweight, and easy to work with. Sections clip together. Requires only minimal maintenance.

Copper
Durable and easy to install. With time, the bright finish weathers to an attractive verdigris (green patina).

Sheet steel
Sturdier than aluminum and copper with a factory-applied finish. Continuous gutters can be made on-site.

PROFILES
Most gutters have a rounded or a squared shape, but several profiles are available (see below). If you are replacing a whole gutter system, your main concerns will be appearance, cost, and ease of installation (if you are planning to do the work yourself).

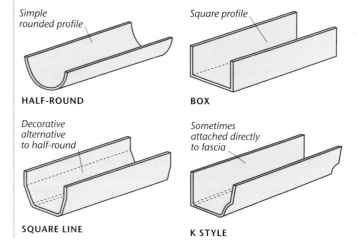

Simple rounded profile

HALF-ROUND

Square profile

BOX

Decorative alternative to half-round

SQUARE LINE

Sometimes attached directly to fascia

K STYLE

GUTTER SYSTEMS
Several different sections fit together to drain rainwater quickly and efficiently. Although the method of joining these elements varies depending on the gutter material used, the components are similar. Shown here is a basic vinyl system. Your system may need some or all of the components shown here.

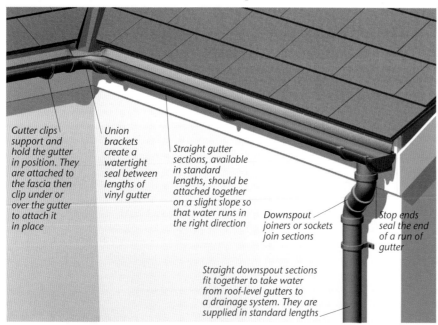

Gutter clips support and hold the gutter in position. They are attached to the fascia then clip under or over the gutter to attach it in place

Union brackets create a watertight seal between lengths of vinyl gutter

Straight gutter sections, available in standard lengths, should be attached together on a slight slope so that water runs in the right direction

Downspout joiners or sockets join sections

Stop ends seal the end of a run of gutter

Straight downspout sections fit together to take water from roof-level gutters to a drainage system. They are supplied in standard lengths

LAYOUT OF A GUTTER SYSTEM

Splash block
Most downspouts empty on to a splash block that directs water away from your foundation.

Installation is a simple, methodical process, but the technique will vary slightly depending on the gutter type. Plan thoroughly the layout and components needed. In most cases it will simply be a case of replacing like with like, so it may be worth making a sketch of how the components of the old system are arranged. Familiarize yourself with how to assemble the joints used with your system, and see pp.26–27 for how to position a ladder and information on scaffolding. Arrange to have somebody to help you do the work.

see pp.26–27

OTHER THINGS TO CONSIDER
■ If fascia boards need to be painted, paint them before attaching new gutters.
■ Trim back any long sections of roofing felt so that they lip into the gutter, but ensure that they do not block the water flow.
■ Use a toolbelt to hold tools safely while you are working on a ladder.
■ After installation, test gutters by pouring in a bottle of water at the highest point to make sure everything is working properly.

REMOVING OLD GUTTERS
Whether or not it is difficult to remove old gutters depends on what material it is made of, and how easy it is to gain access to it. Aim to carry the gutters down the ladder with you, rather than allowing them to drop to the ground. If the gutters are very high, or it is difficult to set up a ladder, get a professional to take down the old gutters and replace them. If you are removing metal gutters, bear in mind that they may be heavy. Make sure the area below where you are working is clear. Another alternative to ladders or fixed scaffolding is to rent either pipe staging or a power lift. For more information on these options, see p.27.

see p.27

MEASURING FOR NEW GUTTERS
Gutters need to slope towards a running outlet to ensure that water drains away efficiently. The gradient needed is very slight – only 1:500, which amounts to 1 in (25mm) in every 50 ft (15 m). In practice, you do not need to work it out precisely, but just make sure that the gutters slope all the way down to the running outlet (as shown opposite) – and that it slopes even while turning any corners. On a particularly long run of gutter, the fascia board may not be deep enough to accommodate the gradient required. In this case, a running outlet may be positioned centrally along the length of a fascia board, with lengths of gutter on either side running downhill toward it. The number and position of downspouts will therefore be very much dependent on the length of a gutter run, and also where the downspout can direct water to drainage. In most cases, these routes will be well established, but on new projects some more detailed planning will be required.

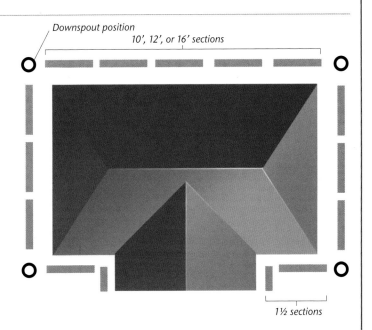

Downspout position
10′, 12′, or 16′ sections

1½ sections

Typical gutter arrangement
A diagram of your property provides the easiest way to work out requirements. It is then possible to calculate how many standard lengths will be required, and how many will need to be cut. It also makes it straightforward to calculate joints (and the requirements for union brackets), corner sections, and the number of running outlets needed.

ESTIMATING QUANTITIES

Basic estimate	If possible, measure lengths of the old gutter and the downspouts. Otherwise, measure around the building at ground level, and measure its height. Feed a rigid tape measure up a wall to find the height for the downspout.
Waste and trim	Buy about 10 percent extra. Gutters tend to come in standard lengths, which you will have to cut to size, so some will be wasted.
Clips	The number of clips needed per length may be specified by the manufacturer. Otherwise, aim for one every 2 yd (2 m) on metal gutters and every 1 yd (1 m) on vinyl gutters.
Union brackets	If you are using vinyl gutters, work out how many joints there will be between lengths: you will need a union bracket for each joint.

TOOLS AND MATERIALS CHECKLIST PP.210–211

Installing vinyl gutters (pp.210–211) Ladder or scaffolding*, string line, file, level or gradient level

hacksaw, sealant dispenser*, sealant*, nuts*, bolts*

* = optional

Installing metal gutters (p.211) Ladder or scaffolding*, string line, file, level or gradient level,

FOR BASIC TOOLKIT SEE PP.24–25

TOOLS AND MATERIALS CHECKLIST PP.210–211; FOR BASIC TOOLKIT SEE PP.24–25

INSTALLING VINYL GUTTERS

Lightweight vinyl can be assembled by one person but, because most work involves handling long lengths up a ladder, it is best to enlist a helper if you can. Move your ladder to the work; do not reach across. See p.209 for details on choosing an appropriate pitch for gutters. The steps show how to fit a straight run of standard lengths of vinyl gutter. If you need to turn corners, simply use the same principles but attach corner sections at the appropriate places.

TOOLS AND MATERIALS SEE BASIC TOOLKIT AND P.209

1 ESTABLISHING THE PITCH

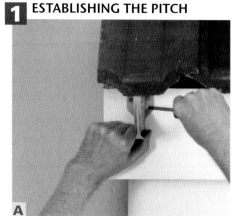

Attach a support clip high up on the fascia board, at the opposite end from where the running outlet will be. You will probably find it easier to tighten screws near the roof covering with a hand-held screwdriver rather than a power drill-driver.

A

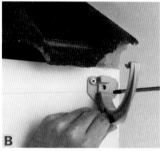

B

Position a clip at the other end of the eaves, lower than the first and at the correct height to give the necessary pitch.

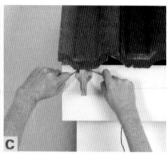

C

Tie a string line between the two clips, to form a guide line.

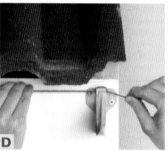

D

Make sure the string line is taut and is not caught anywhere, especially if it has to travel around a corner.

E

Check the pitch with a level. If it is not as you want it, adjust it by slightly repositioning the lower bracket.

2 ATTACHING CLIPS AND THE RUNNING OUTLET

Attach a third clip 3 ft (1 m) away from the first one, with the string line just touching the top edge of the bracket.

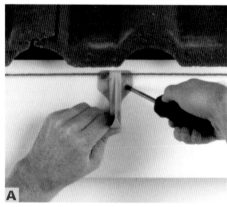

A

B

Attach a union bracket 3 ft (1 m) along from the third clip. Then attach alternate clips and brackets until within 3 ft (1 m) of the end.

C

Remove the string line. Then clip the running outlet into the last, lowest support clip.

3 INSTALLING THE GUTTER

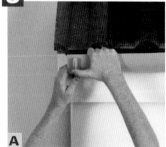

A

Position the first whole length of gutter by snapping one end of it into the highest clip.

B

Snap a stop end onto the gutter before moving the ladder to clip the rest of the length in place.

C

Snap the gutter into the next clip, and then insert its end into the first union bracket.

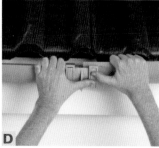

D

Snap the next length into the union bracket. Continue installing whole lengths until near the end.

4 CUTTING TO LENGTH

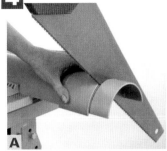
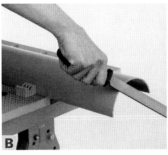

A Mark where you need to cut the last piece of gutter to length. Use an offcut of gutter to guide you for a straight cut with a panel saw.

B File the cut end of the gutter to remove burs.

C Position the last piece of gutter and clip it into the running outlet. Clip a stop end onto the running outlet if it needs one. If the roof overhangs the edge of the house by a long way, you may need to attach a short length of gutter the other side of the outlet, angled down from the eaves into the running outlet.

5 ATTACHING THE DOWNSPOUT

Assemble a bend to connect the gutter with the downspout, using two offset bends with a length of downspout between them. Adjust the middle section of downspout so that the main downspout will lie against the wall.

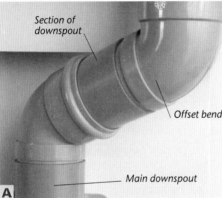
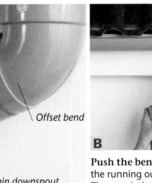

A

Section of downspout

Offset bend

Main downspout

B Push the bend into the bottom of the running outlet to fit it in place. Then push the downspout into the offset bend.

PREPARATION

Before you begin to install gutters, assemble as much of the gutter system as you can while you are on the ground. Working on the ground minimizes the amount of work you will have to do later while you are standing on a ladder or scaffolding.

6 ATTACHING THE DOWNSPOUT BRACKETS

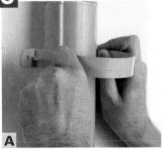
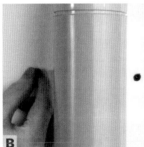
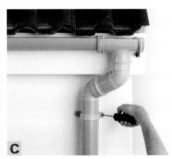
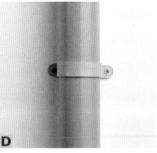

A Hold a bracket in place at the top of the downspout and draw through the fastener holes to mark the wall.

B Use a masonry bit to drill pilot holes at the marked points. Insert wall plugs into them.

C Screw the bracket into position over the downspout.

D Secure more brackets every 3 ft (1 m) along the length of the downspout.

INSTALLING METAL GUTTERS

Set up a string line for metal gutters just as shown left for vinyl. Lightweight aluminum gutters will have union brackets, as shown at right. Some systems have standard running outlets. The system shown here involves using a hole cutter to make holes in gutter lengths, allowing running outlets to be positioned as required.

Joining lengths
The union bracket has a rubber gasket to create a watertight seal.

Attaching a stop end
The stop end has a rubber seal, and clips into place.

Using a running outlet
The running outlet clips over and around the gutter profile, where the hole has been cut.

Some attics are constructed from the outset to be used as additional rooms in a house. Skylights bring natural light into areas that normally wouldn't have windows. They come in a range of designs. Most are made to fit into a pitched roof, although domes and other openings for flat roofs are available. Broadly speaking, there are three standard types of skylights that are used—ventilating, fixed, and tubular.

BUILDING REGULATIONS

Converting an attic into a habitable area needs a permit and building inspections because most attic floors are not designed for the added load living space requires. If the area is to be used as a bedroom, it must have a window or other direct route to the exterior for emergency escape. A complying stairway must be provided to the habitable area.

VENTILATING WINDOWS

Ventilating windows are installed at the same pitch as the roof, so no other roof structure needs to be built in order to accommodate the window. Access for maintenance is also easier with a tilting design and remote controls are available for operation. Because of the ease of installation and upkeep, you can install pivot windows when you renovate other areas. The success of this type of window design has expanded product ranges. In addition to standard tilting windows, it is now possible to buy top- or side-hung variations, as well as specially designed blinds and shutters. These may attach to the inside of the window, or sit between two panes of glass inside the window itself.

Planning and permits

Standard sizes of tilt windows are available, or several windows can be placed alongside each other to make a larger window space—although this may affect the structural integrity of the roof. Before buying the window, seek professional advice. Any required cuts in rafters will weaken the roof structure and will require additional framing. Planning permission is sometimes required for this type of window, and there may be local regulations governing a window's size, its position in the roof, and even its design.

Installing a skylight

Illustrated below are three different designs of windows, all of which are installed using much the same technique. One major advantage of tilt windows is that the installation process can be carried out entirely from inside the roof space. Unless you are adding a very small window that can sit between rafters, at least one rafter will need to be cut to make room. To ensure this does not weaken the roof, support members called false rafters and trimmers will have to be inserted to strengthen the opening. The way in which rafters are cut

Waterproofing
Tilting roof windows are installed in conjunction with flashing kits to make sure the window is waterproof. Flashing kits vary not only with window size and design, but also according to the type of roof shingles.

and trimmers are inserted is very much dependent on window size and positioning. The three examples below are aesthetically quite different, but structurally similar.

Tilt window
This is a variation on a straightforward design. The window opens from an upper hinge instead of tilting around the central window axis.

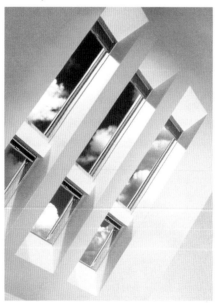

Fixed
Fixed skylights do not provide exterior access, but offer additional light and the opportunity to enjoy views outside.

Escape window
By hinging the window along its side, it can easily be "thrown" open, for use with an emergency ladder (see p.379) if required.

TUBULAR SKYLIGHTS

Skylights are not limited to just the rooms in your attic. When you want to brighten a room that is too small to install a wall window or is simply lacking direct access to the roof to allow traditional skylight installation, there still remains another option to bring natural light in. Tubular skylights are installed using a shaft that starts at the roof and extends down through your home. Capturing sunlight on the rooftop, the tube redirects it down a highly reflective shaft, and diffuses it throughout the interior space. Unlike the direct light of a skylight, tubular skylight uses a type of optics that spread the light out over more floor surface area. The tube can also be angled around attic obstructions.

Tubes are available in a range of sizes. The model shown below is offered in diameters of 10, 14, or 21 inches (25.5, 35.5, or 53.5 cm). The 10- and 14-inch models can easily fit between rafters and ceiling joists so no structural modifications are needed. Such units also offer the Energy Star® rating, designating them as offering optimal energy efficiency. Because of their compact size, tubular skylights are ideal in smaller areas where traditional skylights couldn't be accommodated, such as powder rooms, shower stalls, hallways, and walk-in closets.

These skylights have optional features that are available from manufacturers. Integrated bathroom fans are an optional feature, ideal for use in bathrooms and laundry rooms. Electric light kits can be used to modify the unit, allowing you to use the tube at night as an additional light fixture. There is also a dimmer that allows you to adjust the level of daylight that pours through the tube. The entire unit is sealed to lock out dust, bugs, and moisture.

Tubular skylight installation
When installing a tubular skylight, start by marking the location inside the room. Line up the preferred location with a flat area in the roof before cutting any holes.

FLASHING AND INSULATION

Skylights should be flashed just as chimneys with a separate apron, step, cricket or back and counterflashing. If snow remains on your roof, you should place the skylight on a curb built high enough to keep the skylight above the snow. Some skylights are called "self-flashing," meaning that continuous flashing is prefabricated as part of a low-lying unit, but it is best to avoid these in areas of heavy snow.

If you see condensation form on your skylight's interior, it may be condensation if there is inadequate insulation along a skylight's sides.

Windows can also be added to flat roofs to provide more light. These are often built up on a frame above the main roof deck, and tilted to allow for runoff. Because of the location, installation is straightforward—you can work directly from the roof deck.

FLAT ROOF WINDOW

ATTIC CONVERSIONS

There are a number of factors to consider when converting an attic. One of the most important issues is how much structural work will be needed. If the existing joists are not substantial enough to support a floor, they will require strengthening. If roof-support trusses cross the area you want to use, you may have to alter the roof's structural framework to remove them. Other important considerations include the number and type of windows, and where the stair access will enter the loft from below. You may need to reshingle parts of the roof before or during conversion, and will certainly need to reroute some electrical supplies, and possibly heating, air conditioning, and plumbing as well. One other major thing to consider is stair access and how you will move the building materials into your roof space, and get access to it while you are working.

Tilting windows are a good option for attic conversions

Make sure the roof is properly insulated

Insulated knee wall

CONVERTED ATTIC INTERIOR

PATCHING A FLAT ROOF

Small holes in a flat roof can be patched with a specially made primer and patching system. The technique will vary slightly according to manufacturer; that shown here is typical. This repair requires dry conditions.

TOOLS AND MATERIALS

Primer and patching system, brush, scissors, flat-roof roller

A Cut open the roof membrane at the problem and slide in a patch under the area. Smooth it out, then coat it with roofing cement.

B Apply roofing cement over the area and cover with a second patch.

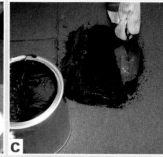

C Coat the entire area with roofing cement. Fibre-reinforced roofing cement is the strongest.

REPAIRING ASPHALT SHINGLES

Asphalt shingles typically last between 15 and 20 years if they are properly maintained. If you have a torn or broken shingle, rain can penetrate around the nails and cause damage to your home.

TOOLS AND MATERIALS

Asphalt shingle, prybar, hammer, roofing nails, roofing adhesive

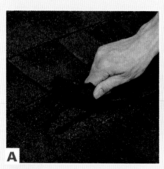

A Lift the damaged shingle from the roof.

B Pull the nails out and completely remove the damaged shingle.

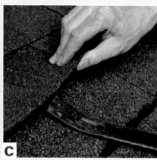

C Use a pry bar to lift the tab above the damaged area.

FIXING OTHER SYSTEMS

■ Laminated roofing shingles are thicker than standard asphalt and may require longer nails or staples to fasten them securely.
■ Wood shake roofing can last about 30 years before it needs to be replaced, but it can become damaged through warping or shrinking and require a similar repair to asphalt.

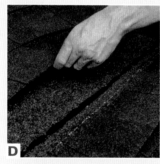

D Cut a shingle to length and slide it into position.

E Using roofing nails to fasten the shingle.

F Coat the head of each nail with adhesive and press the shingle in place.

REPAIRING A LEAK IN FLASHING

Leaks are most likely where flashing is badly installed or old. In masonry and concrete structures, flashing should bend into mortar joints. Lead flashing is seen here but the method is the same for brick chimney flashings.

TOOLS AND MATERIALS

Dusting brush, screwdriver, wedges, sealant and dispenser

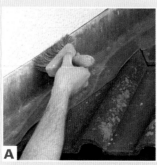

A Dust any debris from the joint, removing any old mortar or sealant as required.

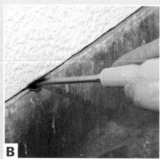

B Use the end of a screwdriver to push wedges into the joint to hold the metal firmly in place.

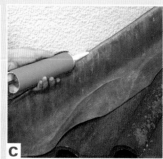

C Run a continuous bead of sealant or mortar along the joint (see pp.80–81 for more information on sealants).

REPAIRING A LEAKING GUTTER

Gutter joints, whether sealed with a rubber gasket or sealant, will deteriorate over time and leak. The repair shown here uses gutter or silicone caulk. For gutters without joints, cut out the damaged section and replace it with a piece that is at least 2 in (5 cm) longer.

TOOLS AND MATERIALS
Cloth, gutter or silicone caulk, caulk gun

OTHER CAUSES OF LEAKS
■ The gutter might be blocked and overflowing. Unblock it to fix the problem.
■ Loose attachments may cause sagging and overflowing. Fix as for a downspout (below).
■ A gutter needs a slope to drain efficiently. Check whether it needs adjusting to the correct angle (see p.209).
■ Cast-iron gutters may rust and leak. Paint often to avoid this (see p.296).

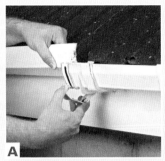

A Disassemble the gutter joint by unclipping the gutter length from the joint clip.

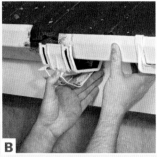

B Remove the adjacent length of gutter to give you clear access to the internal profile of the joint clip.

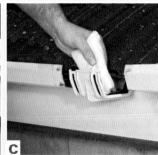

C Dust out the joint, making sure that it is clean and dry.

D Apply gutter or silicone caulk around the edge of the gutter's profile.

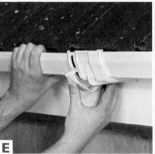

E Reassemble the joint, fixing the clips securely back in place.

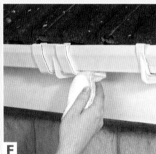

F Wipe away any excess caulk with a cloth.

FIXING A LOOSE DOWNSPOUT

If downspout brackets become loose, joints in the pipe may fracture and cause water to run down the building. This may cause water infiltration problems, so loose pipes should be reattached immediately.

TOOLS AND MATERIALS
Drill, suitable fasteners and wall plugs (see pp.76–79)

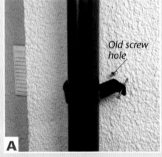

Old screw hole

A Slide the loose downspout bracket to slightly above or below its previous position.

New position

B Hold the bracket in place, and mark where the new fasteners will need to go. Then drill pilot holes.

C Attach the bracket with the appropriate fasteners. Use wall plugs on masonry.

REPOINTING A LEAKING VERGE

The drawback of a pointed verge is that the cement fillet sealing the edge of the tiles may become cracked. This leaves an opening for water penetration, but is easily fixed, as shown here.

TOOLS AND MATERIALS
Chisel, mallet, mortar mix, spot board, pointing trowel, small paintbrush

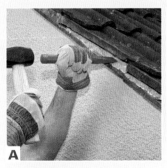

A Rake out loose mortar carefully, using a chisel and mallet, taking care not to dislodge or damage any of the tiles.

B Mix some mortar (see p.69), and use a pointing trowel to press it into the joint below the tile.

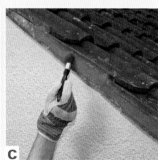

C Use a dry paintbrush to brush lightly along the edge to tidy the joint and provide a smooth finish.

Decorative woodwork

MOLDINGS PROVIDE A DECORATIVE FINISH TO MANY AREAS OF THE HOME. BASEBOARDS, CROWN MOLDING, AND DOOR TRIM ARE THE MOST NOTICEABLE EXAMPLES, ALTHOUGH FINER MOLDINGS ARE OFTEN USED FOR DETAILING ON CLOSETS AND BOOKCASES, AND TO CREATE PANELS ON DOORS OR WALLS. THIS SECTION CONSIDERS THE USES OF THIS TYPE OF TRIMWORK, AND TECHNIQUES FOR APPLYING IT.

TYPES OF MOLDINGS

Moldings usually need either paint or a natural wood finish (e.g., paint or varnish; see pp.286–299) after they are installed. Some types need no finish. Baseboards, for example, may be made in the same color and style as a door. This saves time, but requires careful installation: mistakes are not easily covered with caulk or paint.

BASEBOARD AND CASING

Probably the most common molding, baseboard forms a decorative, protective edge at a wall and floor junction. Casing creates a decorative joint between a door jamb and wall. Casing usually has less depth than matching baseboard. For example, 4-in (100-mm) baseboard is often used with 2-in (50-mm) casing. Provided you measure carefully (see pp.222–225), both are straightforward to fit.

MDF moldings

A common alternative to wood, MDF moldings are normally primed and moisture-resistant. MDF is only prone to splitting at the ends, and has no knots. It also has some flexibility, making it easier to attach when there are slight contours across a surface. A tighter fit to an undulating wall surface will also reduce the need to fill gaps between the molding and wall.

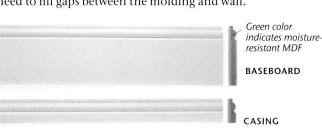

Green color indicates moisture-resistant MDF

BASEBOARD

CASING

Baseboards and casings

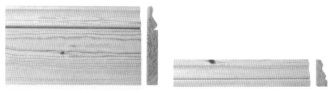

OGEE BASEBOARD AND CASING

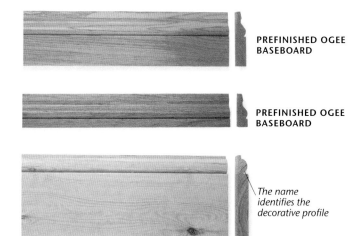

PREFINISHED OGEE BASEBOARD

PREFINISHED OGEE BASEBOARD

The name identifies the decorative profile

TORUS BASEBOARD AND CASING

CHAMFERED BULLNOSE BASEBOARD AND CASING

DECORATIVE MOLDINGS

These moldings provide the finer decorative detailing in a room, such as around a bookcase. Moldings such as quarter-round and scotia are commonly used to fill the expansion gap around the perimeter of wooden flooring (see pp.342–343). A greater range of profiles is available than for larger moldings such as baseboard and casing. It is also more common to find smaller moldings in a range of soft- and hardwoods. Profiles range from the simple to the highly ornamental. The selection shown to the right features the most commonly available moldings, but some manufacturers produce much wider ranges that can accommodate most decorative preferences.

DECORATIVE MOLDING

Molding may be decorative, for example, to break up a wall surface, or practical, for example, to protect a wall from chairs (see pp.218–219). As an alternative to wood, MDF rails and plastic cornices are available (see pp.218–219).

CHAIR RAIL

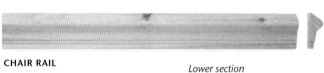

Lower section overlaps here

CROWN MOLDING

USING DECORATIVE TRIM PACKAGES

Lengths of casing are usually mitered at the top of a doorway, and butted to matching baseboard at the bottom of a doorway. Decorative trim, however, creates a more traditional look.

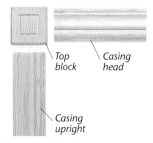

Top block — *Casing head* — *Casing upright*

Casing top block
Available in many designs. This butt-joins with the upright and head lengths of casing to give a traditional appearance.

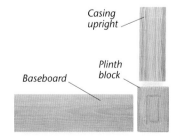

Casing upright — *Plinth block* — *Baseboard*

Casing plinth block
Butt-joins with baseboard and forms the base on which upright lengths of casing are placed, again with butt joints.

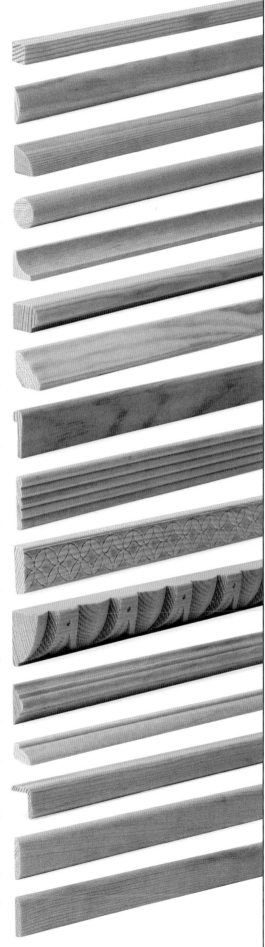

SQUARE

HALF-ROUND

QUARTER-ROUND

DOWEL

COVE

STAFF BEAD

TRIANGULAR

HOCKEY STICK

REEDED

EMBOSSED

CARVED

ORNAMENTAL

GLAZING

ANGLE

DOUBLE D

FLAT D

USING MOLDINGS

Molding selection can transform a room. Traditional ornate, as well as simple plain trim packages, line rooms in homes across the country. The difference between past and present molding options include material choice, which can greatly affect the ease of installation and price. No longer do you have to choose just wood or plaster, as foam and plastic options are also available.

TYPES OF MOLDING

Baseboards
The most popular type of trim in a home is baseboard. Lining the joint where the wall and floor meet, it's available unpainted or primed. Shoe molding is sometimes used at the foot of baseboard to cover a gap of a newly installed floor.

Casing
The trim that covers the gap around the outside of a door in called casing. It also provides extra stability to the door opening.

Crown molding
A popular DIY project is installing new crown molding. It is located at the seam between the ceiling and the wall. Some install crown molding just below the ceiling height in very tall rooms. White crown against a richly colored wall makes a dramatic statement. Crown molding is also a great way to hide paint that has not been cut-in perfectly.

Paneling
You can partially or totally cover a wall with paneling. If it's applied halfway up the wall, to the chair rail, it's commonly referred to as beadboard or wainscoting. If you have a masonry wall, paneling can be attached to battens on the wall.

Chair (dado) rail
Chair rails protect walls from chairs and other items that are pushed against them. The division in a wall's surface can be both practical and decorative. For example, the lower part of a wall often suffers knocks, or is marked by children. If a rail separates this from the upper wall, you need redecorate only the area below the rail to restore the decor.

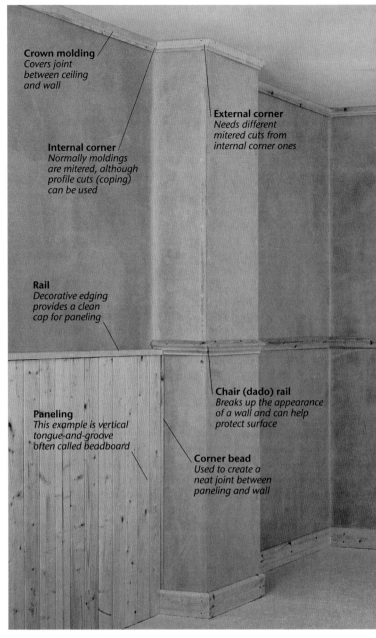

Crown molding
Covers joint between ceiling and wall

Internal corner
Normally moldings are mitered, although profile cuts (coping) can be used

External corner
Needs different mitered cuts from internal corner ones

Rail
Decorative edging provides a clean cap for paneling

Paneling
This example is vertical tongue-and-groove often called beadboard

Chair (dado) rail
Breaks up the appearance of a wall and can help protect surface

Corner bead
Used to create a neat joint between paneling and wall

Examples of moldings in a room
The room above shows a selection of moldings in a typical room. The effect will vary according to whether they are painted or maintain a natural wood finish (see p.294–295).

Self-adhesive panels
Used on flush doors to create the look of a panel door, these can also be used on walls to imitate raised paneling. Most have double-sided tape on the back.

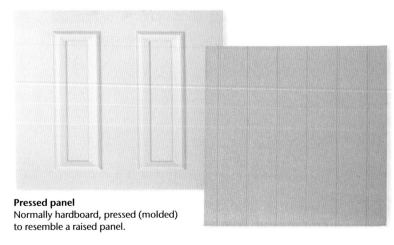

Pressed panel
Normally hardboard, pressed (molded) to resemble a raised panel.

Moisture-resistant MDF paneling
This has been routed (see p.66) to resemble tongue-and-groove paneling. Moisture resistance makes this paneling suitable for use in a kitchen or bathroom. Once painted, it performs well as a backsplash—around bathtubs or sinks in a bathroom, for example.

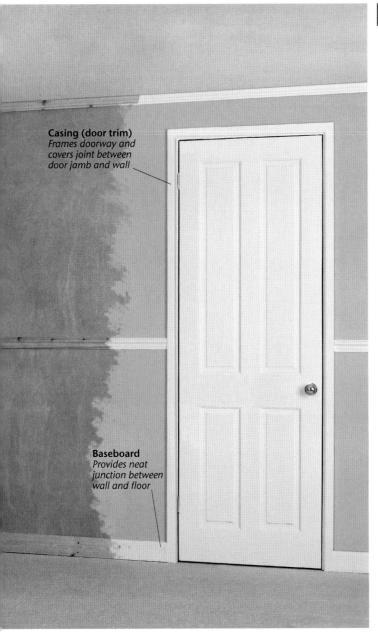

Casing (door trim)
Frames doorway and covers joint between door jamb and wall

Baseboard
Provides neat junction between wall and floor

Radiator cover

This provides a decorative alternative to an exposed radiator. You can make your own, or buy a kit that can usually be adapted to fit most radiators. Covers are usually made of MDF. The grill may be metallic or wood fretwork.

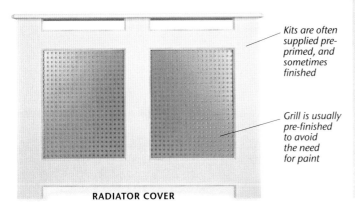

Kits are often supplied pre-primed, and sometimes finished

Grill is usually pre-finished to avoid the need for paint

RADIATOR COVER

DISGUISING NAILS AND SCREWS

When attaching any type of molding, you will probably want to hide screws or nails. If the molding is to be painted, filler can be used to cover these holes. Stainable filler is also available for natural wood finishes. For prefinished moldings, or where expensive hardwoods have been used, the most professional finish is achieved by plugging the holes. This involves filling the hole with a piece of wood that matches the molding in appearance and is thus almost invisible. The technique is shown below; you will need a drill plug bit and the basic toolkit.

A

Use a plug bit to drill into an offcut of molding, to get small pieces of dowel. Drill into the screw holes to the same diameter as these dowels.

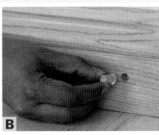

B

Once a screw has been inserted, apply wood glue to a dowel, and insert it into the screw hole.

C

Drive the dowel firmly into place with a hammer. Wipe away any excess adhesive.

D

When the glue has dried, use a chisel to shear off the end of the dowel so that it is flush with the surrounding wooden surface.

E

Use a block plane to smooth the cut end of the dowel.

F

The plugged hole will now be almost invisible. Repeat on all screw holes across the surface.

TOOLS AND MATERIALS CHECKLIST PP.220–227

Installing crown molding (pp.220–221) Miter saw, crown moldings, nail set

Installing casings (p.222) Miter saw, filler, filler knife

Installing a decorative rail (p.223) Nail set, miter box, tenon saw, level, adhesive*

Installing baseboards (pp.224–225) Grab adhesive,

masonry drill*, countersink drill bit*, miter saw, jigsaw*

Paneling a wall (p.226) Wood furring strips, lumber offcuts, rail, block plane, pry bar, quadrant or scotia*

Paneling around obstacles (p.227) Drill, mounting box, tenon saw, lumber offcut

* = optional

INSTALLING CROWN MOLDING

Crown molding adds a dramatic look to almost any room, finishing the wall and providing a stylish transition to the ceiling surface. Traditionally made of plaster, it is available in wood, MDF, foam, plastic and even drywall. The foam and drywall can simply be adhered into place with drywall compound. Crown molding will hide imperfections between the wall and the ceiling. When installing crown molding, always remember to follow safe practices for working on a ladder or scaffold.

TOOLS AND MATERIALS SEE BASIC TOOLKIT AND P.219

1 INSTALLING CROWN MOLDING

Find and mark the wall studs in the room with a stud finder or with nails. Mark studs with just a pencil.

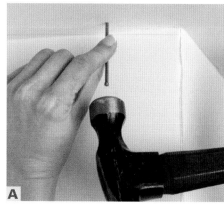
A

B **Measure the height** of the crown molding. Trace the height of a piece of molding on a block.

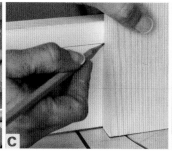

C **Transfer the measurement** to a nailing strip and cut it to length.

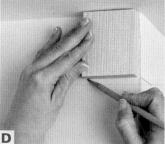

D **Use the nailing strip** to mark layout lines on the walls.

E **Cut a miter** in the nailing strip so it follows the profile of the crown.

Use screws to securely attach the nailing strip along the stud marks.

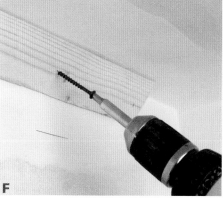
F

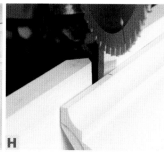

G **Mark the placement** of the crown molding on the wall.

H **Measure and cut** the molding to length.

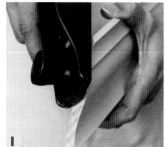

I **Smooth the ends** of mitered pieces to make a clean joint.

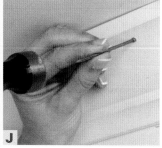

J **Drill pilot holes** in the molding to help prevent splitting. Nail in place.

2 ATTACHING THE MOLDING TO THE WALL

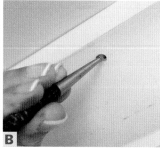

A **Using finish nails,** nail the piece of crown in place.

B **Use a nail set** to make sure the nails are below the surface of the molding.

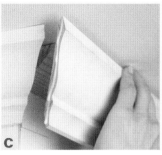

When attaching mitered pieces, line the end of one piece with construction adhesive.

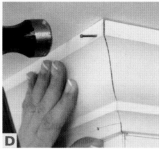

Use a finish nail to secure the two pieces at the joint.

3 MARKING FOR A COPE

When shaped moldings meet at an inside corner, the best way to join them is with a coped joint, which is created by cutting a profile on the end of one piece of molding so it fits over the contours of the face of the second piece of molding.

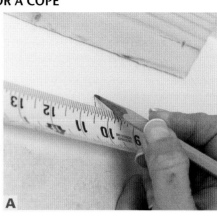

Measure and mark for the length of the molding that will be coped. Then set your miter saw to 45 degrees.

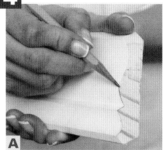

Set your miter saw to 45 degrees. Place the molding on the miter saw with the ceiling edge flat on the bottom. Cut the end of the molding.

4 MARKING FOR BACK CUT

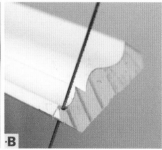

Scribe the profile of the trim to bring out the line.

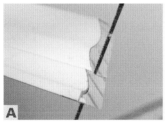

Using a coping saw, cut along the profile of the end, removing material behind the end at about an angle of 45 degrees.

COPING

Coping is not as hard as it may look. And the benefits over mitered joints are worth the extra few steps. Wood tends to contract, and a mitered end will pull away from what seemed like a perfect joint. A coped joint will not open up as much. Use a coping saw to remove the material behind the end of a piece so that it fits snugly with another piece.

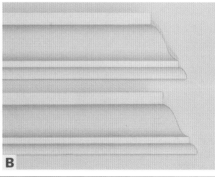

A coping saw has a c-shaped frame, a handle, and a thin flexible blade. The blade can be installed to cut on the push or pull stroke.

Smooth the end of the coped joint for a clean finish. Test the fit of the coped piece by holding it in place against a scrap piece of molding.

MOLDING TIPS

Fit a coped end to the piece of crown. Cut more material or sand to adjust the fit.

Nail the molding in place. Fill any gaps with caulk. Fill nail holes with caulk and wipe the excess with a damp cloth or sponge.

Use a wood block to gently tap crown molding pieces in place or to adjust a fit.

Fence accessories help support tall pieces of molding in the saw.

INSTALLING CASINGS

Before you start, cut three lengths of casing—two for the uprights and one for the horizontal head section—to very roughly the length you need them. Cut them longer than they need to be, because the most accurate way to mark where to cut them is to hold roughly cut lengths in place and mark on them. Transferring measurements from jamb to casing is less accurate. The casing's inner edge should be set back from the edge of the door jamb by ⅛–¼ in (3–6 mm); this is called the margin.

TOOLS AND MATERIALS SEE BASIC TOOLKIT AND P.219

1 ATTACHING THE FIRST UPRIGHT

A

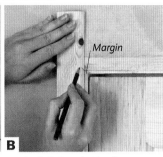
Margin
B

Mark off the margin position around the edge of the door jamb. Join the marks at the corners to provide a right-angled guide line.

On the left-hand side, align some casing precisely with the margin. At the head, mark the piece where it meets the right-angled margin mark.

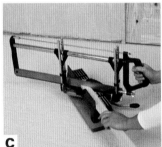
C

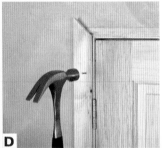
D

Make a mitered cut, using the marked-off point to guide you.

Reposition the casing, with its inner corner at the apex of the margin's right angle. Attach it with two or three nails at the top.

2 CUTTING THE HEAD SECTION

A

B

Make a mitered cut, in the same way, on the head section, to join with the section already fitted on the jamb. Check that it fits.

Hold the head section in position while marking off the cut for the other miter on the right-hand end of the length. Cut the miter.

3 CUTTING THE OTHER UPRIGHT

A

B

Place the right-hand upright section of casing to mark off in relation to the margin requirement, and cut this miter.

Nail the right-hand upright in place, securely at the top.

4 ATTACHING THE CASING

A

B

Check that the head length of casing fits, and nail it into position.

Drive in nails along the entire lengths of casing. Use six nails on the head casing and eight for each jamb.

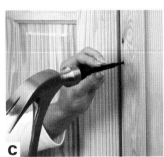
C

D

E

Use a nail set to drive all nails below the surface.

To keep mitered corners tight, you will need nails through both pieces. Prepare for this by drilling pilot holes.

Drive a 1-in (25-mm) finish nail into each pilot hole on the mitered corners. It should run through the outer piece of casing and into the head section, to hold the joint tightly. Then fill nail holes and sand smooth, if necessary.

INSTALLING A DECORATIVE RAIL

The technique demonstrated here on a chair rail may be used to apply other decorative features such as picture rails. You may find it useful if someone else holds the rail steady while you draw guide lines. See pp.76–77 for nails suitable for stud walls and masonry walls, and use a nail set to drive nails in below the rail's surface, giving the best possible finish. Make sure you do not pierce hidden cables or pipes below surface level. Use a detector to help check for their positions.

TOOLS AND MATERIALS SEE BASIC TOOLKIT AND P.219

1 INSTALLING THE RAIL

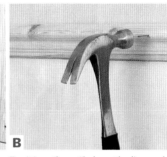

A

B

Draw a level guide line around the room at the height where you want the lower edge of the rail—often 3 ft (1 m) from floor level.

Position the rail along the line and nail through its center (into uprights of a stud wall; plugging as required in masonry). Drive nails in fully.

2 MAKING MITERED CUTS FOR A CORNER

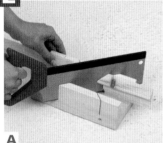

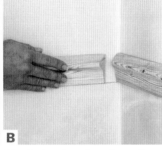

A

B

Use a miter box and tenon saw to cut miters for a corner.

Check that the mitered cuts fit neatly together in the corner before putting the rails in place. The corner shown here is an internal one.

3 MEASURING AND CUTTING FOR A STAIRWELL

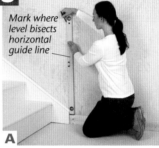

Mark where level bisects horizontal guide line

Original line is at base of chair rail

A

B

To determine where the rail must change direction, hold a level upright where the baseboard meets the stairwell.

Hold a length of rail along the original guide line. Draw a line along the rail's top edge, reaching at least as far as the vertical mark.

Mark distance between rail and baseboard

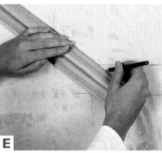

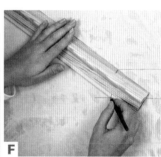

C

D

E

F

Higher up the staircase, make a mark the same height above the stair string as the original guide line is above the baseboard.

Join this mark to the one at the foot of the stairway to provide a guide line in the stairwell for the lower edge of the rail.

Position a length of rail on this guide line. Draw along its top edge, joining and intersecting with the horizontal line drawn in step 3B.

Now that clear guide lines are on the wall, position a length of rail and mark off on either edge to provide the correct angle for mitering the joint.

G

Cut the stairwell rail at the marked angle. Then repeat the process with a horizontal piece of rail to miter that length. Position the lengths, checking that they fit tightly together. Nail them to the wall. Use this technique each time a rail needs to change direction.

USING ADHESIVE

One way to make rails more secure is to use some construction adhesive in addition to the nails.

Rather than using the traditional contact cement that requires precise alignment on the first contact, use modern adhesives that go by the name of Quick Grab. They hold immediately but allow for sliding around for repositioning.

On straightforward runs—between two casings, for example—use butt joints between the end of the rail and the upright casing, installing the rail with adhesive. Mitered joints are best installed with screws or nails, because they sometimes need slight adjustment to get a precise fit.

INSTALLING BASEBOARDS

Installing molding requires accurate measurement and precise joints, and securing it neatly can be difficult. The makeup of a wall defines the method. Molding may be joined with mitered cuts at internal and external corners; internal corners can also be done with profile cuts. Molding may need cutting to keep it level on an uneven floor, and this will involve scribing, a method of accurately marking and cutting a board to fit exactly the profile of the floor on which it is being positioned.

TOOLS AND MATERIALS SEE BASIC TOOLKIT AND P.219

FINDING ATTACHMENT POINTS

Before attaching baseboards, establish whether the wall is lumber, masonry, or drywall. Use the relevant fastening method from those shown below. If you are attaching molding to a stud wall, establish first where the studs are—you will need to secure the molding at these points. If you are building a new stud wall (see pp.104–107) this is not a problem.

Vertical cracks in plaster, or lines of nail heads may indicate edges of drywall—and, therefore, studs. Otherwise, use a stud detector, or simply tap the drywall until you don't hear a hollow sound. Once you have located one stud, look for others at (usually) 16-in (400-mm) intervals. Use a cable/pipe detector to avoid wires and pipes.

ATTACHING TO A MASONRY WALL

Screw the boards to the wall. Fill the countersunk holes with filler, if necessary, and sand.

A **Apply glue** to the back of the molding and place in position. Use a masonry drill to make two pilot holes every 1 ft (300 mm).

B **Enlarge the openings** of the holes with a countersink bit. This will allow the screw heads to sit below the wood's surface.

ATTACHING TO A STUD WALL

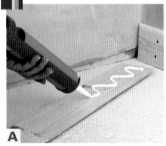

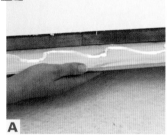

A **Apply some grab adhesive** to the back of the molding, and place it in position.

B **Attach the molding** with two screws or finish nails at each stud. Studs are usually 16 in (400 mm) or 2 ft (600 mm) apart.

FASTENING TO A LATH-AND-PLASTER WALL

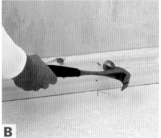

A **If possible, locate** studs and mark their positions. Apply grab adhesive to the back of the molding, and position the board.

B **Attach the molding** to the studs at regular intervals with two screws or finish nails. If you cannot locate studs, attach at regular intervals.

MITERED CUTS

Mitering gives neat joints in a corner or between lengths on a straight run along a wall. A miter box (see p.35) is an alternative to a power miter saw (see right)—but it is difficult to get accurate cuts, and most boxes will not hold the tallest boards.

Make sure you cut in the correct direction; mitering angles differ for internal and external corners.

MITERING FOR AN INTERNAL CORNER

The easiest way to make a mitered cut is with a power miter saw. If the saw has the height, a board can be clamped upright and cut down through its height. In this instance (right), it is laid flat on the stage of a miter saw. Larger boards are best cut this way. Tilt the blade and cut a 45-degree angle in the board.

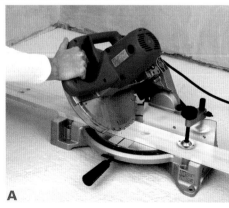

A

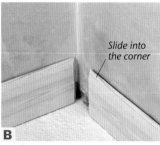

Slide into the corner

B **Repeat for the joining board,** and fit the pieces together in the corner.

MITERING FOR AN EXTERNAL CORNER

A Cut miters as before. Check for fit. Place one board. Apply wood glue to the cut end, position the other board, and wipe away excess glue.

B Drill pilot holes for two brad nails to fit through the mitered joint and hold it together. Pin the corner.

MITER-JOINING LENGTHS

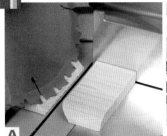

A Mitered joints are neater than butt-jointed boards. Cut the ends at a 45-degree angle, checking that they will fit together when attached.

B Glue the boards into place, and hammer in a brad nail to secure them. Attach the rest of the baseboard as normal (see opposite).

CUTTING ORNATE MOLDING

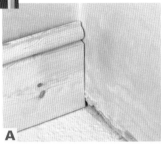

A Butt one piece of molding against the wall and cut the other piece to fit exactly against the first.

B Using an offcut of molding, draw around its profile on the board that needs cutting. This forms a guide line to cut along with a jigsaw.

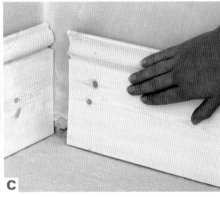

Having cut along the guide line (try a hand-held coping saw or a fret saw if the molding is too ornate to cut with a jigsaw), butt the cut end against the first piece of molding. It will exactly match the profile and give a neat finish. Fix the molding in place and continue fitting the molding around the room.

C

SCRIBING AGAINST AN UNEVEN FLOOR

Undulations in a floor can leave unsightly gaps below molding, which can let in drafts. It is always best to ensure that the top edge of the molding is level, and to trim any necessary adjustments from the bottom edge. In some cases, a slight slope may be acceptable, as long as the joint with the floor is flush. Minor gaps at the bottom may be covered with carpeting, the edge of a wood floor, or a decorative molding.

Cutting off a section from the base of a length of molding may mean that neighboring sections also require trimming, even if they sit flush with the floor, otherwise they may be taller. Therefore, cut all pieces to length and loosely position them all (as shown in step A, right) to find the right height for all boards.

SCRIBING MOLDING

A Position baseboard against the wall, and use a level to check if it is level at the top and flush with the floor. If not, scribing is needed.

B Wedge the molding so that it is completely level—check this with the level. Use a temporary fastener to hold it if required.

Cut a small piece of wood that is slightly taller than the biggest gap between the molding and the floor. You can use this as a scribing block. Place a pencil on top of it, and slide the block and pencil across the floor surface, so that the pencil marks a guide line on the molding matching the profile of the floor.

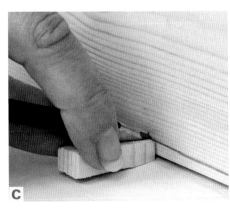

C

D Use a jigsaw to cut away the excess molding, following the pencil line carefully.

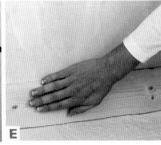

E Fix the length of molding in place. It should be flush with the floor and level along its length.

PANELING A WALL

Tongue-and-groove paneling can be attached to furring strips. Vertical boards need horizontal strips for the panels to attach to, as shown here. This example adds panels to chair rail height.

TOOLS AND MATERIALS
SEE BASIC TOOLKIT AND P.219

1 INSTALLING THE FRAMEWORK

Fix horizontal furring strips around the perimeter of the area to be paneled. They should be at the top and bottom of the area to be paneled, and also at equidistant intervals between these extremes, ideally 16 in (400 mm) apart, taking care not to pierce wires or pipes, and making sure to fasten to studs.

A

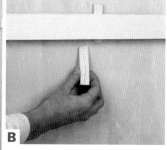

B

If the wall is uneven, shim furring strips as required to get them in plane, using wedges or offcuts of plywood.

2 INSTALLING TONGUE-AND-GROOVE PANELING

A

Using a level, mark a guide for the first board.

B

Position the first length on the level line. Nail it into the furring strip with finish nails, placing nails at the edge nearest a wall.

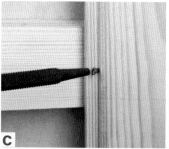

C

At a 45-degree angle, nail through the tongue side of the board into the furring strip below. Use a nail set to drive the nail head in completely.

D

Overlap the groove of the next board onto the tongue of the first.

E

Use an offcut of board as a tapping block. Tap the board once or twice with a hammer to make a tight seam between the boards.

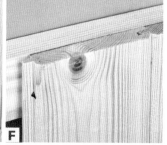

F

Continue across the wall surface. Nails through the boards' tongues at each furring strip are all that is needed to secure the boards in place.

3 DEALING WITH CORNERS

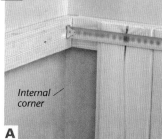

Internal corner

A

Eventually you will need to cut a board to fit the space into a corner. Measure the space and cut a board to slightly smaller than this.

Partial board

B

Position the cut board, placing its groove over the previous board's tongue. With the board a little short, you will have space to maneuver it.

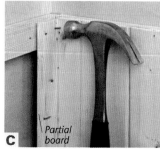

Partial board

C

Finish the inside corner by butting the other piece of the cut board against the paneling. Then continue across the wall as normal.

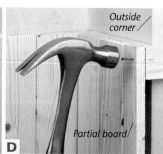

Outside corner

Partial board

D

Deal with an outside corner by cutting a board to fit. Use the other cut piece on the other side of the corner, for a balanced appearance.

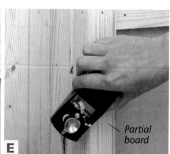

Partial board

E

The corner will seem unsightly because the cut edge is visible. Trim it by using a block plane to finish the edge.

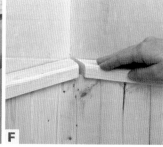

F

When all paneling is in place, add a rail along the top to cover the gap caused by the furring strips between boards and wall. Miter the corners.

PANELING AROUND OBSTACLES

Sometimes you need to cut a panel to fit around an item on the wall or to end a run. A wall may be uneven, so rather than measuring and cutting to fit a board against it, use the method shown below (called scribing) to get a neat fit.

TOOLS AND MATERIALS
SEE BASIC TOOLKIT AND P.219

WORKING SAFETY

Switch off the electricity supply at the consumer unit (see p.436) before removing the face plate from any fixtures such as an outlet or switch plate. Pay attention to all safely advice for working with electricity, and check terminal connections before replacing a switch plate and turning the electricity back on (for details, see pp.432–463).

CUTTING AROUND AN OUTLET OR SWITCH

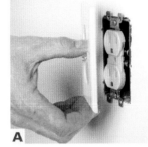

A

Deal with fixtures as you come to them. Remove the switch plate, remembering that wires are still connected to it.

B

Remove the wires from the back of the switch plate and tape the cores separately before taping the wire as a whole to protect it.

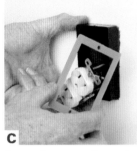

C

Insert a box extension so the outlet sits beyond the paneling.

D

Attach the box extension with the screws provided.

E

Position furring strips around the perimeter of the hole, and nail them in place.

F

Place a vertical board over the opening. Measure and mark the opening.

Cut carefully measured sections of the paneling to sit around the fixture. Position and secure paneling in the normal way.

G

H

Attach the receptacle in place with screws.

I

Reattach the cover plate.

PLACING A PANEL AGAINST A WALL

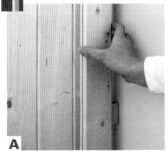

A

Temporarily position a new board exactly on top of the last placed complete board.

B

Cut a small section the width of a board. Hold one end against the wall. Run it down the wall, using a pencil at the other end to draw a cut line.

C

Surface nail along the edge of the board. There is no tongue for blind nailing at an angle, as shown opposite, so you must nail through the face of the board into the furring strip below. Then neaten the seam between the paneling and wall by pinning some quarter-round in place, mitering any seams between lengths if required.

REPAIRING TONGUE-AND-GROOVE PANELING

Boards interlock, making it difficult to repair a small area: releasing one damaged board would mean releasing all the boards. Instead, use this method to replace just the damaged board.

TOOLS AND MATERIALS

Drill, new board, drywall saw, chisel, workbench, claw hammer, nails, filler, sandpaper, paint or finish as required, paintbrush

FURTHER INFORMATION

■ Where the damaged board crosses furring strips on the wall, it may be easier to use a hammer and chisel to cut through the board.
■ If the board is very thick, it may be easier to remove the tongue with a saw.
■ If you want a natural-wood finish, consider using grab adhesive to secure the board in place rather than nails.

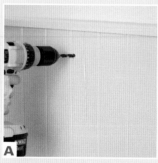

A Drill a hole close to one edge of the damaged board, toward the top, and large enough to take the point of a drywall saw.

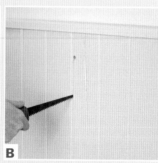

B Insert a drywall saw into the hole and cut all the way down the joint between the boards.

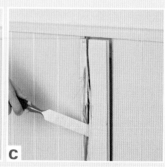

C Use a chisel to pry out the damaged section of board.

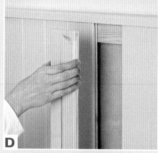

D Cut a new section of board to fit. Secure it in a workbench and use a saw to remove the tongue so that you can position it.

E Secure the new board in place, nailing through its face because there is no available tongue for angled blind nailing.

F Fill the nail holes, and sand when dry. Then decorate the board to match the surrounding surface.

REPLACING A DAMAGED SECTION OF BASEBOARD

If a short run of molding is damaged, replace the entire length, but on a longer run cut out just the damaged section and replace it.

TOOLS AND MATERIALS

Pry bar, wooden blocks, pencil, level, miter box, panel saw, nails, hammer, wood glue, grab adhesive, molding, filler, sealant dispenser, paint, paintbrush

MATCHING OLD BASEBOARD

■ For an entire room, a close match to that in the rest of the house will go unnoticed because the two designs are not sitting side by side.
■ Take a sample of your baseboard to a lumberyard to match.
■ Another option is to pin decorative moldings to the top of lumber (see opposite).

A Pry the damaged section away from the wall. Place wooden blocks between the molding and wall, on either side of the damaged area.

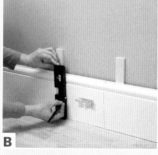

B Draw pencil guide lines vertically down the baseboard on either side of the damaged area, marking the section to be cut away.

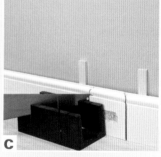

C Using a miter box, carefully cut down each guide line, using short, accurate strokes. Cut at the angles shown here.

D Remove the blocks from behind the baseboard and reattach the existing molding to the wall.

E Measure and cut a new section for the gap. Apply wood glue to its mitered ends and grab adhesive across the back.

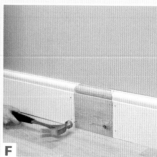

F Position the board, allowing the glue and adhesive to adhere to the baseboard and wall. Drive in nails to strengthen the joints.

REVIVING POORLY DECORATED MOLDINGS

Where moldings have been poorly decorated and/or paint buildup has left them in poor condition, simply sanding the area can help. You don't need to strip back all the previous layers of paint to achieve a marked change in appearance, as this example shows. This technique can be used on all kinds of moldings. Paint buildup in the grooves of the profile often creates an unsightly effect. Filling these areas as shown here improves their appearance. Flexible caulk cannot be sanded when dry, so it must be completely smoothed while still wet.

TOOLS AND MATERIALS
Sanding block, vacuum cleaner, sealant dispenser, decorator's caulk, sponge, paint, paintbrush

A

Sand back the "flats" on the molding as smoothly as possible, and glance across the higher areas of the molding with sandpaper.

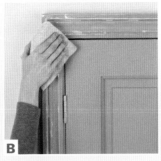

B

Use a vacuum to remove any dust and debris, and then wipe down the area with a damp cloth.

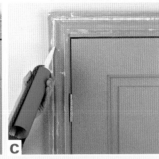

C

Using a sealant gun, apply a bead of decorator's caulk along the molding profile and groove details.

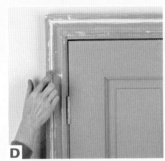

D

Smooth along the caulk with a wetted finger.

E

Carefully remove any excess with a clean, damp sponge. Smooth the caulk again with a wetted finger.

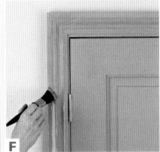

F

Once the caulk is dry, repaint the molding to achieve a much-improved surface.

REPAIRING AN EXTERNAL MITER

External miters can sometimes crack open and become unsightly. In most cases, this is because the joint was not properly glued and secured in place when it was installed.

TOOLS AND MATERIALS
Drill, hammer, wood glue, finish or thin screws, paint or finish as required, paintbrush

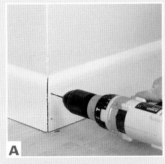

A

Drill pilot holes through the top and bottom of the joint, making sure that you drill into both mitered edges of the corner.

B

Apply some wood glue to the joint, and wipe away any excess.

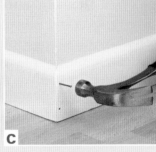

C

Use finish nails through the pilot holes to secure the miter in position or, for larger baseboards or moldings, use thin-gauge screws.

USING DECORATIVE MOLDING TO ENHANCE A PLAIN BASEBOARD

Improve plain molding with wooden moldings. You can use this technique to match a discontinued design.

TOOLS AND MATERIALS
Pin hammer, molding, finish nails, filler, spatula, sandpaper, paint, paintbrush

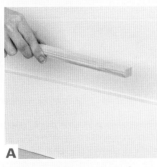

A

Cut the molding to size and position it on the top edge of the molding. Joints may be mitered or butt-joined (as in this sequence).

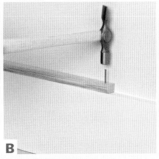

B

Secure the molding in place with finish nails. Continue to install the molding along the baseboard.

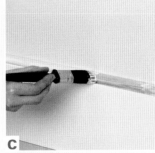

C

Fill nail holes and joints, and sand before painting.

Structural problems

IN THIS SECTION, ALL TYPES OF STRUCTURAL PROBLEMS—THOSE CAUSED BY MOISTURE, ROT, AND INFESTATION OF VARYING KINDS—ARE EXAMINED IN DETAIL. IN MOST CASES, RELATIVELY STRAIGHTFORWARD REMEDIES ARE POSSIBLE. HOWEVER, INITIALLY IT IS A GOOD IDEA TO IDENTIFY WHERE PROBLEMS ARE LIKELY TO OCCUR AND HOW YOU MAY RECOGNIZE THEM.

IDENTIFYING THE PROBLEM

Structural problems can be hard to recognize because they often remain hidden in the fabric of a house. Even if there is an obvious symptom, such as a crack in a wall, initially it can look the same whether it is due to harmless settlement or dangerous subsidence. Similarly, water intrusion caused by blocked gutters—which is easily remedied—may look like damage caused by a leaking roof. With structural problems, if you are not sure of the cause, or if a problem persists after you have attempted to fix it, then seek advice. A professional will be able to make a correct diagnosis, inform you of the right course of action, and, if necessary, complete the required work to prevent future problems.

TYPES OF ROT

There are two types of rot: wet and dry. Wet rot is most common in the wood of window sills and door bases that have been exposed to damp conditions. Dry rot is more common in older properties. It starts in damp wood, usually in poorly ventilated areas, but can cause greater damage by spreading through a property, moving across surfaces.

Early treatment of both types of rot is essential. In both cases, the original cause of dampness must be addressed, and the infected areas removed, but with dry rot you must also cut back into the sound material, to make sure that all traces are removed. Extensive dry rot should be treated by a certified firm that offers a guarantee of their work.

Problems with rot are generally the result of poor maintenance or poor ventilation. Therefore it is best to improve both of these aspects of your home to prevent the presence of rot in the first place.

Damp window reveals
May be caused by condensation, or by penetrating damp due to poor seals at edges or flawed installation.

Damp floor
Generally a result of condensation, a damp covering suggests that ventilation needs improving. If the structure itself is damp, with visible patches on a concrete floor or wooden floorboards, rising damp may be the cause.

Large cracks in walls (interior or exterior) or ceilings
May be due to settlement or subsidence, and therefore require investigation. Cracks are commonly found along wall-ceiling junctions. Central cracks may be due to poorly finished drywall. Cracks in old ceilings may be caused by sagging joists, or the plaster itself beginning to fall away from the ceiling structure.

Damp lower wall
When soil or debris piles up against a wall, water retained by the debris may gradually penetrate the wall surface and create a water problem.

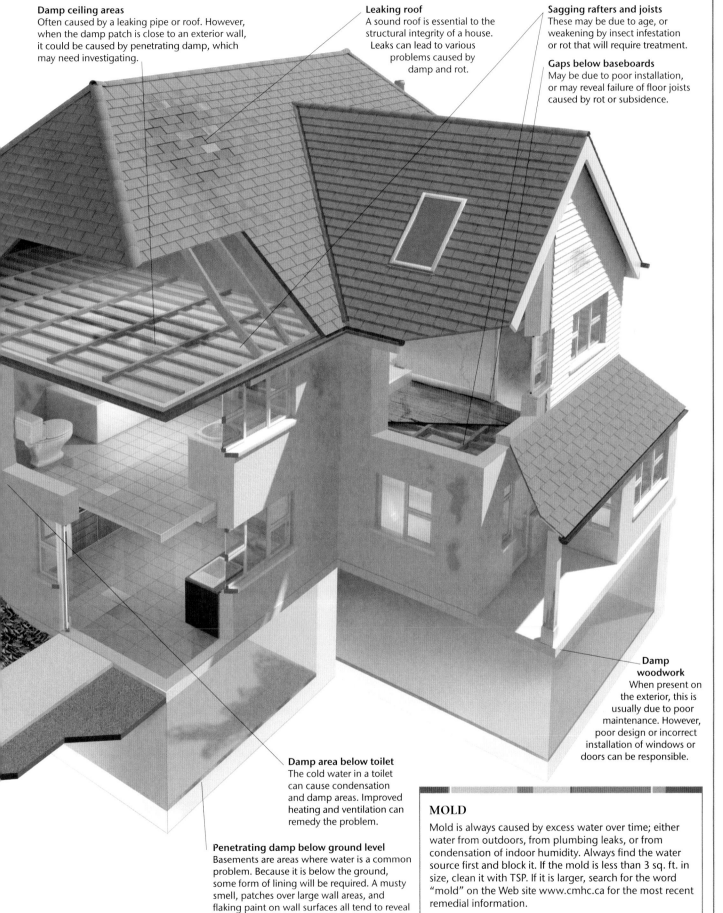

Damp ceiling areas
Often caused by a leaking pipe or roof. However, when the damp patch is close to an exterior wall, it could be caused by penetrating damp, which may need investigating.

Leaking roof
A sound roof is essential to the structural integrity of a house. Leaks can lead to various problems caused by damp and rot.

Sagging rafters and joists
These may be due to age, or weakening by insect infestation or rot that will require treatment.

Gaps below baseboards
May be due to poor installation, or may reveal failure of floor joists caused by rot or subsidence.

Damp woodwork
When present on the exterior, this is usually due to poor maintenance. However, poor design or incorrect installation of windows or doors can be responsible.

Damp area below toilet
The cold water in a toilet can cause condensation and damp areas. Improved heating and ventilation can remedy the problem.

Penetrating damp below ground level
Basements are areas where water is a common problem. Because it is below the ground, some form of lining will be required. A musty smell, patches over large wall areas, and flaking paint on wall surfaces all tend to reveal the problem clearly.

MOLD
Mold is always caused by excess water over time; either water from outdoors, from plumbing leaks, or from condensation of indoor humidity. Always find the water source first and block it. If the mold is less than 3 sq. ft. in size, clean it with TSP. If it is larger, search for the word "mold" on the Web site www.cmhc.ca for the most recent remedial information.

"Wet basement" is a phrase that strikes fear into the hearts of most homeowners. More than half of Canadian homes have this problem to some degree, according to the Canada Mortgage and Housing Corporation. The most typical causes are runoff, condensation, and groundwater swelling. Solutions depend on the cause, and can range from using a dehumidifier to installing a perimeter drain system. If you notice dampness and a musty odor when you enter your basement, you may be experiencing the first signs and should make it a priority to combat the water before more serious damage occurs to your home.

CONSIDERATIONS

- Never ignore a persistent musty smell.
- Find out the cause of a wet basement before beginning any modifications to your home.
- Seek professional advice before attempting to combat a groundwater swelling problem.
- Check with your local municipality for information about changes in the local water table. Health advice on wet basements is readily available at www.cmhc.ca.

CONDENSATION

Condensation occurs when moist, warm air hits cool foundation walls. If you see wet spots on basement floors and walls, you might have a condensation problem. Check it by performing a simple test. Tape plastic wrap onto a damp spot, sealing the edges with tape for a few days. If moisture appears on the wall side of the plastic, it's a leak; if moisture is on the outside, it's a condensation problem.

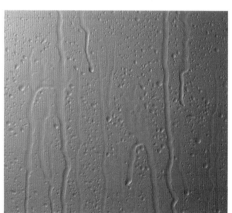

Condensation
Allowing condensation to persist in your home can lead to structural problems. Localized problems, particularly in a basement, can be dealt with by a dehumidifier, but generalized problems indicate a need for better whole-house exhaust ventilation.

RUNOFF

The most typical cause of runoff is melted snow and rainwater that is not directed away from the house. Hydrostatic pressure forces the water through gaps or cracks in walls and footings. You can prevent runoff by making sure the ground outside your home slopes away from your house at least 1 in (25 mm) vertically for every 12 in (300 mm) of horizontal travel and that downspouts are not leaking or pooling near the foundation.

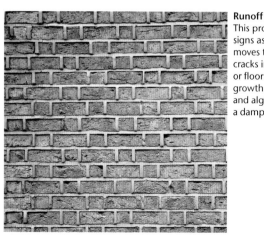

Runoff
This problem shows signs as water moves through cracks in the walls or floors. Here, growths of mold and algae suggest a damp surface.

GROUNDWATER SWELLING

Groundwater swells when the water table has exceeded its high point. Soil surrounding your home is unable to hold the extra water, causing a consistent runoff problem. If you have a wet basement due to groundwater swelling, your basement will be wet for a long period after each storm and there may be water bubbling up from the joints between the wall and floor. Many homes are not constructed with protection from high groundwater, and it is very expensive to install a system to combat the problem.

COMBATING A WET BASEMENT

No matter if your basement is finished or you use it as just a storage room, it is important for the structural integrity of your home to combat a wet basement problem as soon as you discover it. Solutions to tackling a wet basement are plenty. The first step is trying to figure out the type of problem you are encountering. Then, check the grading around your home, downspouts for any leaks or pooling, and cracks in the driveway. Fix all of the problems you encounter as well as patching cracks in the basement walls and floors, as water in the home can cause mold problems as well as a wet basement.

Applying a concrete sealer

Sealers are available for coating basement walls and floors. They offer a quick waterproofing measure and can be decorated. They are easy to apply (see opposite), provided you follow the manufacturer's guidelines. They can be applied to damp surfaces but any standing water should be removed.

Fitting a polyethylene membrane

An alternative to epoxy coatings is to use a polyethylene membrane. Although it holds back water, it may be necessary to install channels and a sump pump to collect and remove water from behind the membrane. Seek professional advice on whether this is required. Measure the surface area you need to cover and make sure you buy enough membrane for your needs.

TOOLS AND MATERIALS CHECKLIST P.233

Filling cracks and holes
Stiff brush, trowel, mixing receptacle, cement, fine sand

Walls under pressure
Masonry chisel, trowel, mixing receptacle, mortar

Parging: Applying waterproofing mix to walls
Brush or sponge, paint brush, latex waterproofing mix

FOR BASIC TOOLKIT SEE
PP.24–25

SUMP PUMPS

Sump pumps channel water away from the house. When groundwater fills the tank to a certain level, a float or some other device activates the pump. They are typically electric powered and some have a battery backup option so they still run during power outages.

While your local municipality dictates where a sump pump drains, they typically drain into a sewer and have an anti-siphon feature to prevent backflow into your home. Sump pumps are usually installed at a low point in the basement and require breaking into the slab to bury the system's sump tank and drain tile.

While a sump pump can effectively move water from your home, if you have a persistent groundwater problem, a perimeter drain system may also be needed to relieve the hydrostatic pressure.

SUBMERSIBLE SUMP PUMP   PEDAL SUMP PUMP

◼ FILLING CRACKS AND HOLES

When cracks and holes appear in basement walls and floors, there is the opportunity for water runoff to enter the basement. It is important to fill small cracks before they have the opportunity to become more serious problems. Small cracks and holes can be filled with a simple concrete paste. For cracks that are ¼ in (4 mm) wide or larger, use a hydraulic cement, which expands as it dries.

A Clean out the crack with a stiff brush.

B Mix one part cement and two parts of fine sand with just enough water to make a paste.

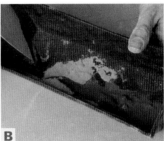

C Use a putty knife to fill the mixture of mortar cement into the crack.

◼ WALLS UNDER PRESSURE

Walls that are already showing signs of leaks through cracks need a more extensive repair solution. You must remove the damp material surrounding the crack so that the mortar has sound material to bind. If filling the crack with mortar does not solve the problem, you may need to install a sump pump or regrade around the exterior of your home.

A Chip a dovetail groove out for the entire length of the cracked area.

B Remove any excess material from the groove.

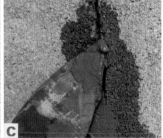

C Fill the hole with a mortar mix and a trowel.

◼ PARGING: APPLYING WATERPROOFING MIX TO WALLS

Parging is a process of applying a waterproofing mix or a concrete sealer to walls. This stops the moisture from entering the basement. If you are experiencing consistent wet basement symptoms, sealing walls may not be the best solution. When you seal walls, the moisture is then trapped inside the walls, which can damage the structure. Parging is best used with a sump pump or a perimeter drain system.

A Dampen the walls using a wet brush or sponge.

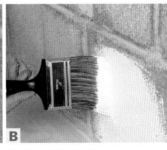

B Starting at the bottom, rub a latex waterproof mix into the wall with a circular motion. Completely cover the area where there was a leak.

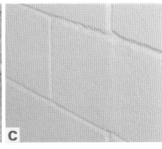

C Soak the wall with water and let the wall set for 12 hours. Reapply the waterproof mix again.

Infestation by insects or animals can be little more than a harmless nuisance, or it can have serious consequences for house structure. It is therefore important to be aware of the telltale signs of infestation, how to recognize the particular animal or its traces, and how effectively to treat and rid yourself of the problem. The table opposite lists some of the pests and the dangers they may pose to a house structure.

HANDLING POISONS

Many of the chemicals used in dealing with infestation are toxic or poisonous. For this reason, adhere strictly to manufacturers' guidelines. Make sure that all such products are stored out of the reach of children (preferably in a locked cabinet). Similarly, make sure that children cannot come in contact with poisons once they have been deployed around the house.

INSECTS AND ANIMALS

With all insect and animal infestations, the general rule is that if you find one (or evidence of one), there are likely to be more. Early identification is key to dealing with the problem before it can escalate into a far less manageable situation. Fortunately, most problems can be brought under control without professional help.

WOODWORM

A group of wood-boring beetles, commonly known as woodworm, can cause serious structural problems. Obvious signs are small flight holes in lumber; dust around the holes confirms that the worm is active. Immediate treatment is essential.

Furniture beetle
This small brown beetle is generally found during the summer months. It is usually about ⅛ in (4 mm) in length.

Deathwatch beetle
This gray-brown beetle prefers old hardwoods. Up to ¼ in (8 mm) long, it lays its larvae in wood; years later the larvae emerge as beetles.

House longhorn beetle
This is less common than the two above, but is equally destructive. It can be up to ⅛ in (4 mm) long.

Weevil
This has an elongated snout which it uses to bore into the wood. Weevils are found in a range of colors and sizes.

IDENTIFICATION

There are various ways of identifying which pests have entered your home. Some distinctive signs of common pests are shown below.

BLUEBOTTLE FLY MAGGOTS

Flies
Apart from the flies themselves, maggots are the most obvious sign of fly infestation. They may be found in decaying food or in any rotting organic matter.

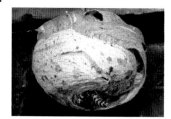

WASP ENTERING NEST

Wasps
A wasp nest is the obvious source of a wasp problem in your home. It may be found in the open (e.g., in an attic), or hidden in a cavity wall.

BEE NEST

Bees
Some bees live in nests (as shown here), while others are solitary and live alone. They tend to nest in enclosed spaces.

ROT IN WOOD

Woodlice
The presence of woodlice suggests a rot problem; they tend to live in damp areas where there is wood decay.

MOUSE

Rodents
Frayed wires, gnawed woodwork, holes in woodwork, nests in attic insulation, and rodent droppings all signify a rat or mouse infestation. Rodents cause minor structural damage, but gnawed electrical wires and cables can cause considerable trouble.

CROW'S NEST IN WALL

Birds
Nests can be found in cracks and crevices in masonry, as well as in attics, or attached to downspouts and soffits. Bear in mind that some birds are protected, so tampering with nests and eggs can be illegal. It is best to discourage nesting before it occurs (see opposite).

Insect and animal pest	Problem	Solution
FLY	Poor hygiene can cause fly infestations. They pose no structural problems, but their body fluids can stain decorated surfaces. They also pose a general health hazard by spreading bacteria.	Keep food covered; promptly dispose of garbage; use insecticides
SILVERFISH	Silverfish can indicate a moisture problem. They are nocturnal and enter the house looking for food and moisture. Among other things, they feed on paper and adhesive, and so can damage wall coverings.	Treat excessive moisture and use insecticide on infested areas
BEE	As well as attics, bees tend to nest in inaccessible areas such as wall cavities. They can enlarge holes in mortar and burrow into wall structures to gain access to a cavity. Some repointing may be necessary.	Insecticide can be injected into nests; large nests should be removed professionally
WASP	Wasps commonly nest in attics. If situated above a ceiling, a nest can drip an unpleasant secretion into the drywall, breaking it down and staining the ceiling. Sections of drywall may need to be removed and replaced.	Inject special insecticide into the nest, or have the nest removed professionally
COCKROACH	Cockroaches appear when hygiene is a problem. This may be due to blocked drains, food debris on surfaces, or lack of cleaning in cabinets.	Poisons are available, but professional help may be necessary
ANTS	Ants are mainly attracted by food debris on work surfaces and on floors. The nest can normally be traced by following the line of an ant column.	Pour boiling water into the nest, then apply insecticide. Insecticide lacquer can be applied to thresholds
WOODLOUSE	Woodlice feed on damp wood, suggesting a damp problem. They also destroy plants, both indoors and out.	Treat damp and use insecticide on plants and thresholds
EARWIG	Earwigs are easily recognizable by the pincers on their abdomen. Though harmless, they are scavengers and eat kitchen waste and plants.	Cut back vegetation from doorways and windows. Use insecticide spray or vapour strips
MOTH	Moths tend to feed on natural fibers, damaging clothing, carpets, and upholstery.	Clean stored clothes, vacuum all cracks and crevices, and use insecticide or mothballs
BAT	Bats are likely to be found in attics or in basements that have exterior access. They pose no structural problems.	Contact a bat professional
RAT	Rodents, especially rats, are disease carriers and should be kept well away from the home. Rats and mice chew all manner of items, including wires, woodwork, plastic, and even metal pipes; damage to all of these can cause serious problems.	Keep food covered; promptly dispose of garbage; use traps and poisons
SQUIRREL	Squirrels tend to live in attics, where they can chew plumbing, wiring, and insulation.	Physical barriers are the best deterrent; various vent meshes and fillers are available
BIRD	Birds can nest in the eaves of a house or in attics. The damage they cause is limited, but in large numbers, droppings can stain painted and masonry surfaces.	Like squirrels, birds are best discouraged with physical barriers

KITCHENS AND BATHROOMS

KITCHENS
BATHROOMS

Kitchens

ONE OF THE MAIN FOCAL POINTS OF A HOUSE, A KITCHEN REQUIRES CAREFUL PLANNING IF IT IS TO BE EASY TO USE AND ATTRACTIVE TO LOOK AT. MOST MODERN KITCHENS FEATURE CUSTOM CABINETS, AND CUSTOM KITCHENS ARE THE MAIN FOCUS OF THIS SECTION. REMEMBER THAT INSTALLING A KITCHEN MAY INVOLVE STRUCTURAL, PLUMBING, AND ELECTRICAL WORK COVERED IN OTHER SECTIONS OF THIS BOOK.

CUSTOM KITCHENS

Custom kitchens are designed to make the best use of space. Attached cabinets combine ample storage and ease of use with a contemporary finish. Standard stock cabinets are made with different styles of doors and drawer fronts, and a wide variety of sinks, countertops, and appliances will match any decor.

FREESTANDING UNITS

As well as custom cabinets, matching freestanding kitchen units are available. The units are made to look more like separate items of furniture than part of a connected run. A few freestanding pieces can be combined with some custom cabinets—a good option if you like their appearance and need extra storage space.

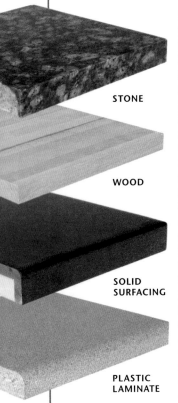

STONE

WOOD

SOLID SURFACING

PLASTIC LAMINATE

COUNTERTOPS

Precut countertops come in 2-ft increments from 4 to 12 ft long, and in thicknesses varying from 1 to 2 in (20 to 40 mm). Choose one wider than you need because you will probably cut some off during installation (see p.244). Countertops may be made of solid wood or stone, veneered chipboard, and stone-effect materials. Solid wood and veneered counters, and some stone-effect types, are sold as standard sizes and can be installed as is. Countertops made of solid stone, such as marble or granite, are generally supplied and installed by manufacturers, who make a template of your requirement, fabricate the countertop at their factory, and then deliver and install it. Countertops are also a frequent object for reclamation (see pp.94–95). A countertop can also be tiled. When tiling a countertop, use moisture-resistant plywood or MDF as a base. On walls behind the countertop it is usual to install backsplashes of tiles, stainless steel, or glass.

KITCHEN CABINETS

Custom kitchens are made up of wall cabinets and base cabinets. Cabinets are either frameless (European) like those shown below or framed (with face frames). Most custom kitchens can be viewed already assembled in a showroom. The price usually depends on the material and the thickness of the carcass members and panels. As a rule, the more substantial a cabinet is, the more expensive it will be.

Base cabinet
Most manufacturers produce these in standard widths and heights. Their depth is usually 1 ft 8 in–2 ft (500–600 mm), although some are shallower to accommodate utilities.

Wall cabinet
These are available in standard widths that match base cabinets, but they are typically only up to 2 ft 4 in (720 mm) high and 1 ft (300 mm) deep.

HARDWARE

Most manufacturers will supply a pack of accessories for each cabinet, some or all of which will be required, depending on how the cabinet is to be used. A selection of the most common hardware is shown here.

Drawer runner
May be preinstalled on drawers and cabinets when supplied.

Cam and cam stud
Two-part fasteners for assembly of some flatpack cabinets.

Connection screw
Two-part screw that joins cabinets.

Wooden dowel
Peg used to strengthen joints.

Hinge
Kitchens use easy-install hinges and usually predrilled holes.

Joining plate
Metal plate used to strengthen joints between cabinets or sections of countertop.

Damper
Small pad that protects surfaces when doors or drawers are closed.

Wall mounting plate
Shaped bracket for hanging cabinets on walls.

Countertop bracket
Attaches a countertop to base cabinets.

Angle brace
Often used to secure cabinets to a wall surface.

Cover cap
Decorative cap for screws and other fasteners.

Toekick vent
Provides airflow to appliances.

SINKS AND APPLIANCES

When planning a kitchen renovation always study both the large and small appliances, as well as the cabinets and cupboards at the same time to be sure that everything is compatible. If your cabinets already exist, you will be limited to appliances that will fit. If you are starting with the appliances, be sure to order counters and cupboards that will accommodate them. Many manufacturers also produce both extra-large appliances for large families, and slimline models for small kitchens. Innovations are always coming onto the market, so take time to select appliances that fit your space and needs best.

Exhaust fan
Housed in cabinets or the more decorative design of a hood and chimney, exhaust fans may either filter then recirculate air, or vent it out through an exterior wall via a duct that you will need to install.

Faucet

Sink
Usually, sinks are cut into a countertop. Most, like the one shown here, have a deep side for a garbage disposal.

Stove
These come in gas (above) and electric versions. Gas stoves are generally sunk into a countertop. Electric ones can have sealed plates or ceramic tops.

Hood

Oven
An oven may be housed in a special cabinet that comes as part of a custom kitchen. Attachment kits will be supplied. Freestanding stoves slide between cabinets.

FINISHING TOUCHES

The carcass structure of a cabinet is ultimately hidden by door fronts, drawer fronts, and a number of other decorative items. If you are happy with your kitchen's current layout but want a new look, changing the finish can be an inexpensive and very effective option. Finishing touches are supplied in styles to suit many different tastes.

Decorative trims
Toekicks are installed between the floor and the underside of base cabinets. They may have a vinyl strip on the bottom edge to stop moisture from penetrating the edge when the floor is cleaned. A molding covers up the bottom edge of wall cabinets and scribe molding runs along the top edge of wall cabinets.

Handles and knobs
For use on door and drawer fronts. Threaded bolts and screws secure them in position.

Door front
These are manufactured to fit all standard cabinet sizes.

Drawer front
Made to fit standard base cabinet drawers. Some act as "dummy" drawer fronts.

TOEKICK

SCRIBE MOLDING

PLANNING KITCHENS

Planning a new kitchen requires considerable time and thought. It can be complicated putting all the components together and, because it is an expensive investment, mistakes can be costly. An existing kitchen layout is a good starting point. If it works, then you can just update the design, often simply by changing cabinet doors and hardware rather than installing a complete new kitchen. However, you will need to modify the layout to update it with new appliances or additional storage, or if you feel the space just does not fit your lifestyle needs.

PLANNING YOUR KITCHEN LAYOUT

Planning a kitchen is a fairly complex task because of the many different factors that need to be considered. It is also an area in which strict budgeting is necessary since much of the cost of a kitchen is not only in the cabinets, but also in the time and cost of installation. This will also depend on how much you wish to tackle yourself.

Appliances

■ Decide what appliances you are going to have in the kitchen. A kitchen should contain a stove and oven, a refrigerator, and a sink. Other options include a microwave, a dishwasher, or a separate freezer. Of course, not all of these have to be in the kitchen—garages and utility rooms can often house appliances.

■ Most food preparation in the kitchen is related to the stove, the sink, and the refrigerator. Generally, a triangular layout of the three essentials is considered ideal—access is straightforward, and there is room for preparation or storage beside each area (see right).

■ It is best not to put your refrigerator next to your stove, since the refrigerator will have to work harder because of the warm air around it when the stove is on.

■ If you want an island in your design, it is best if it does not block your route between sink, refrigerator, and stove. An electrical supply for an island can run under the floor, especially if you are installing a new floor anyway. Many people utilize the additional counter space of an island to contain the stove.

Storage

■ Think about what you would like to store in the kitchen and how you use your kitchen. Pantries and cabinets that extend to the ceiling are great ways to increase the amount of storage in a kitchen. Manufacturers of kitchen cabinets also offer a range of great storage options from lazy susans to integrated garbage cans.

Countertops

■ Countertops are essential for both food preparation and to accommodate electrical appliances such as toasters, blenders, coffeemakers, and freestanding microwaves.

■ Countertops can also provide an eating space, in the form of a breakfast bar, for example. The underside can be left open, or peninsula cabinets can be installed underneath. In the latter, a wide section of countertop provides a large overhang.

USING YOUR SUPPLIER

Once you have formulated some ideas about what design and style you are looking for, the next step is to speak to your supplier. Take accurate measurements of the room. Include existing alcoves, room height and width, and heights and widths of windows and window sills. Your supplier may be able to produce a computer-generated design to give you a good idea of what your kitchen will look like.

Some manufacturers have cabinets in stock, but with others, orders may take weeks or even months to come through. Bear this in mind in your overall planning. Coordinating the delivery of materials is crucial to a smoothly running project, so plan well ahead and confirm delivery dates.

TYPICAL KITCHEN LAYOUTS

In smaller kitchens, the size and shape of the room will often dictate the layout. In larger rooms there are more options to consider. Typical kitchen layouts are galley, L-shaped, or U-shaped, and may include islands, breakfast bars, and dining areas. Most kitchens are a variation on one of these examples. Typical layouts are shown below with "work triangles" indicating the possible positioning of appliances.

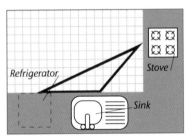

L-shaped layout
This layout has cabinets along all or part of two adjoining walls. In a larger kitchen this may allow room for a dining area in the kitchen. This layout provides ample storage space and floor space and is therefore ideal for a busy family life.

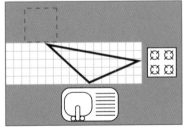

U-shaped layout
Here, cabinets cover three walls, and in a larger room one length of the U may be used as a breakfast bar. In a small kitchen, this layout provides maximum storage and appliance capacity, but standing room is limited. It is best to keep the refrigerator close to the door.

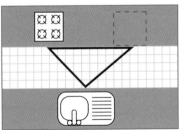

Galley layout
This design uses straight runs of cabinets on opposing walls in a narrow kitchen. As in the U-shaped layout above, floor space may be limited, but wall space is used to its maximum potential.

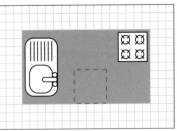

Island layout
This type of layout tends to be used either in large kitchens or as a design feature in smaller ones. When appliances are installed in an island, the "work triangle" theory doesn't apply. Routing utilities may be tricky with this layout design.

Installing a new kitchen
When remodeling a kitchen, consider the order in which you complete each task. Below is an example of a typical work strategy, but there must always be some flexibility built into the work schedule, depending on design elements.

Initially, you will need to remove the old kitchen, but you should take into account such issues as how you will maintain a water supply during renovation work and how you will deal with cooking and bathing needs.

Order of work for refurbishing a kitchen:
1 Reroute electrical wiring, if necessary
2 Reroute plumbing, including gas pipes, if necessary
3 Complete structural work on walls, ceilings, and floors
4 Install base cabinets then wall cabinets
5 Install countertops and backsplash
6 Install sink and plumbing fixtures
7 Install stove (or separate stove and oven)
8 Install exhaust fan

PLANNING UTILITIES

If you are going to keep the layout of a new kitchen similar to that of the old one, this will cut down on a lot of work. However, in most cases some rerouting of utilities will be necessary. The main issues to consider are outlined below.

Natural gas or propane

Consider whether the position of any existing gas pipes needs rerouting or adjusting. When purchasing new gas appliances, check where the connections are. In some situations, the supply pipes may need to be converted. Ask an appliance installer or other qualified professional to hook up new gas appliances.

Electricity

Kitchens are full of electrical appliances, large and small. As well as standard outlets above the countertops for coffeemakers, toasters, and blenders, large appliances may need to be connected to special outlets that run 220 volts.

Lighting should be planned to combine general illumination with directed task lighting above sinks and food preparation areas. As well as ceiling lights, wall cabinets and range hoods can have lighting installed underneath.

Once you have designed your layout, use it to plan how to reroute the electrical wiring. Any rewiring is most easily carried out after an old kitchen has been removed and before the new one is installed. In most places you can do the rewiring yourself, but always check with your local planning department or electrician. For more information on electrical wiring, see pp.400–433.

Plumbing

A kitchen sink needs hot- and cold-water supplies, to be connected to its faucets, and a waste pipe. Dishwashers also need to be plumbed in, and their supply and waste pipes are often extended from the sink plumbing. Therefore, it makes sense to keep them close together, if possible. Waste pipes are particularly difficult to extend, because they must run at a gradient. If you alter waste pipes you may need to notify your local building inspector.

TOOLS AND MATERIALS CHECKLIST PP.244–253

Installing doors (p.244) Hinge plates, hinges

Attaching a handle (p.244) Offcut of wood, C-clamp

Installing a toekick (p.245) Clips, vinyl strips

Installing a scribe molding (p.245) Jointing block, miter saw, wood glue

Cutting a countertop length (p.248) Masking tape, C-clamp, block plane, straight edge

Scribing a countertop to fit (p.248) Block of wood, jigsaw

Joining square-edged countertops (p.249) Wood glue, fixing plate

Joining solid surfaces (p.249) Joining strip, silicone caulk and caulk gun

Securing a countertop (p.249) Clamps, mounting brackets

Fitting a recycling cabinet (p.251) Screwdriver

Fitting a countertop bin for food waste (p.267) Jigsaw, silicone sealer

Cutting a recess hole (p.252) Flat or auger drill bit, jigsaw, preservative primer, paintbrush

Assembling and inserting a sink (p.252) Retaining clips, adhesive, silicone caulk and caulk gun

Installing a garbage disposal (p.253) Garbage disposal, plumber's putty, GFCI receptacle

* = optional

FOR BASIC TOOLKIT
SEE PP.24–25

PREPARATION FOR INSTALLATION

Shopping for kitchen cabinets offers an abundance of choice. Materials, finishes, door profile, configurations, accessories, and door hardware are just the beginning. Before you dream of your perfect kitchen, you'll need to decide on a budget and whether or not you will be installing the cabinets. Most home improvement stores and retailers offer cabinet installation by employees or referrals to independent installers. If you decide to hire someone for the job, always ask for a referral.

TOOLS AND MATERIALS SEE BASIC TOOLKIT, PP.24–25

CABINET SIZES

Stock and semicustom cabinets are built to industry standards. If you buy stock cabinets, use the following as a guide to planning your kitchen. The sizes are developed based on an 8-ft (2.5-m) ceiling height. Always check with the manufacturer for their sizes.

■ Base cabinets are built 34½ in (876 mm) tall and 24 in (610 mm) deep.

■ Wall cabinets are 30 in (760 mm) tall and 12 in (300 mm) deep.
■ Wall cabinets above a sink or stove can be 12–24 in (300–610 mm) tall.
■ Cabinet widths range from 6 to 48 inches (153 mm to 1.2 m), and are available in 3-in (76-mm) increments.

Refrigerator

Wall cabinet

Soffit

Tall end filler

Exhaust fan

Under-cabinet light

Sink

Dishwasher

Oven

Paneled front

Washing machine

Toekick

Base cabinet

ACCESSIBLE KITCHEN DESIGN

If you are planning to design a kitchen to meet your needs for life, you may want to consider including accessible features. The most important considerations are making sure the doorways are wide enough for wheelchairs, that cabinet and counter heights are accessible, and that there is plenty of room to move around the kitchen. Accessories include push-button garbage disposals near the front of the sink, motion-sensor lighting, and lever door handles. Certified Kitchen Designers and the National Kitchen & Bath Association can help you with the design of your kitchen.

Before you start to install your kitchen cabinets, you should have removed the old kitchen, rerouted any utilities, and have the option to replace or finish the floor, if that is your plan. Always check that the entire cabinet order has arrived and is undamaged. Make sure that every item, right down to the screws, is checked off, because waiting for a second delivery can hold up the entire installation process. Installing a kitchen is a job for at least two people, especially when it comes to hanging large wall cabinets.

TOOLS AND MATERIALS SEE BASIC TOOLKIT, PP.24–25

PLANNING AND PREPARATION

Take time to prepare the wall surfaces and assemble the kitchen cabinets before installing them. Drawing the first guide line for positioning cabinets is essential to the success of the whole project. Cabinets and countertops are heavy items, and you will need someone to help you lift them into position.

Laying out cabinets
■ The starting point for installing any kitchen is a level guide line for the top of the base cabinets. A height of about 34½ in (876 mm) above the floor is standard. The countertop is added later.
■ Start in one corner, using a level to guide you. Older floors can be uneven, so check the line's height at intervals to make sure base cabinets and appliances will fit beneath it comfortably along the entire length.
■ Mark a second line to show the thickness of the countertop. Generally, wall cabinets are installed so that they are 19½ in (495 mm) from the top of the countertop, but adjust this height according to the manufacturer's specifications for positioning cabinets around the stove.
■ If you are attaching wall cabinets to a stud wall, you will need to use a stud finder so you attach cabinets to studs, or provide additional support with extra blocking to ensure that fasteners are solid.

Preparing the cabinets
■ Once you have marked up the wall surfaces, you should assemble the cabinets. Follow the manufacturer's instructions for each type of cabinet.
■ Wall cabinets sometimes have installation rails across their backs that you cannot see once the cabinet is held

up to the wall. Note their size and position so you can drill pilot holes directly through the inside of the cabinet once you have positioned it.

Installing cabinets
■ Provided you have measured and marked accurately, installing the kitchen itself should be relatively straightforward. Follow your layout marks and attach cabinets to studs with screws. Predrill pilot holes and countersink screws beneath the surface. It may be easier to install upper cabinets first.
■ If you have a block wall, you can screw the cabinets directly to the wall with brackets. Drill and plug pilot holes in a masonry wall. It may be necessary to cut holes or notch cabinets to accommodate utilities. Wall cabinets will need to be positioned carefully, again, ensuring that they are securely screwed to the wall surface.

LAY OUT

A

Use a tape measure to mark a point 34½ in (876 mm) above the floor level (see left), for the top of the base cabinets.

B

C

Use this mark to draw a horizontal guide line across the wall to indicate the top level of the base cabinets.

Mark a point 19½ in (495 mm) plus countertop height above this line, and draw a line to mark the bottom of the wall cabinets.

D

Measure the width of each of your cabinets and mark their positions across the horizontal guide lines. Mark the location of each stud.

DRILLING PILOT HOLES

A

For all cabinets that have attachment rails, drill a pilot hole through the rail into the cabinet. When you are ready to install the cabinet, you will have the necessary screw holes visible inside the cabinet. Pilot holes also help prevent the wood from splitting.

FINISHING KITCHEN CABINETS

Once cabinets have been screwed in place, they are given their decorative finish. You will need to install doors, any trims such as decorative moldings, and hardware. The final look of the kitchen depends on these finishing touches, so it is important that the correct procedures and techniques are followed, and time and care is taken.

TOOLS AND MATERIALS SEE BASIC TOOLKIT AND P.241

UPDATING AN EXISTING KITCHEN

Replacing doors, drawers, and handles can be a great way of updating a kitchen if changing the layout is unnecessary. If you are on a tight budget, you will be amazed how much the look of your kitchen can change with some paint and new hardware. You can paint almost any finish of kitchen cabinet, as well as tiles, but make sure you use the right paint and other materials—special primers will often be necessary (see p.280). If you decide to change doors or drawers, make sure that the new ones are compatible with your existing cabinets.

INSTALLING DOORS

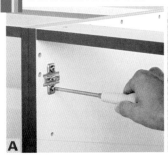

A Screw the hinge plate into its predrilled holes in the carcass. Hinge plates often come with the screws already inserted.

B Insert the hinge into the precut recesses on the doors, and screw it in place. Be sure to use the correct short wood screws.

C Position the door, with the hinges aligning with hinge plates, and use the screw already positioned in the hinge to join them.

D Tighten the central screw in the hinge plate to secure the door. Follow the instructions below to align the doors perfectly.

ALIGNING DOORS

Moving the door left and right Tightening or loosening the screw, as shown, will move the door to the right or left.

Moving the door up and down Loosen the screws in the hinge plate, as shown, and reposition the door before tightening them again.

Moving the door in and out To position the door farther away from the carcass, loosen the central screw in the hinge plate and adjust the door accordingly. Retighten the screw to secure the door.

ATTACHING A HANDLE

A Clamp a scrap of wood firmly against the front face of the door at the position where the drill bit will emerge. Using a drill bit slightly larger in diameter than the threaded screw of the knob or handle, drill through the door until you penetrate the block. This should prevent the front surface from splitting.

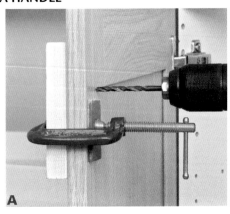

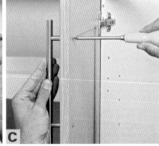

B Remove the block. You should have a perfect pilot hole, with no splintering or other damage around its edge. Insert a screw.

C Because a handle is being installed here, a second hole is required. Position the handle against the door and secure the screw in place.

INSTALLING A TOEKICK

A

Position the toekick, pushing the clips in place onto the legs of the cabinets. Continue to add further sections of toekick until you have covered all areas. A toekick is easy to remove, allowing new floor coverings to lap under cabinets. Toekick height may then be trimmed to accommodate any floor-level change.

PUTTING ON DRAWER FRONTS

A

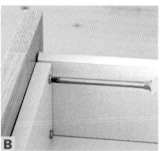

B

First attach the handles to the drawer using the same method for attaching door handles (opposite). Hold the front against the drawer.

Insert screws through the front of the drawer from the inside, so that they are driven into the drawer fronts, and tighten them securely.

INSTALLING A SCRIBE MOLDING

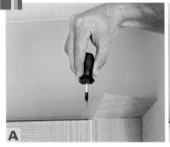

A

B

C

D

Cut the molding to the lengths needed. Cut mitered joints with a miter saw. Screw in place the piece of molding that fits against the wall.

Apply some wood glue to the mitered end to add extra strength.

Butt the next piece of molding against the first and press the mitered joints together firmly.

Secure this length of scribe molding using wood screws.

TYPES OF CABINETS

Kitchen cabinet options may seem endless. While you know that the material, finish, and design style of your kitchen cabinets will determine the overall look of your kitchen, it is also important to keep in mind that how your cabinets are made will determine the timeline of your kitchen remodeling project. There are three main types of cabinets available: stock, semicustom, and custom. The cabinets that you might choose to browse in order to gather design inspiration at a local home improvement center or cabinet discounter are either stock or semicustom kitchen cabinets. If the price tag for new cabinets is more than you expect or if you just want to update the look of your cabinets with new cabinet fronts, kitchen cabinet refacing may be the best option for you.

Stock cabinets

Stock cabinets are preassembled or ready-to-assemble cabinets that are available at most home centers and cabinet discount stores. Manufacturers and dealers keep a selection of stock cabinets in inventory, so they are ready for delivery on ordering. If the cabinets you choose require delivery from the manufacturer or warehouse, it may take a few weeks to receive your order.

Typically constructed of engineered wood and steel-sided drawers in standard sizes, the options are limited. While stock cabinets can be finished, cabinet boxes are usually made of less expensive material than the fronts of the cabinets. Some manufacturers offer a higher-end version of stock that includes standard options of rollout trays and dovetail joints. Stock cabinets are the least expensive option.

Semicustom cabinets

Available at most home centers, cabinet retailers, and design centers, just as the name implies, semicustom cabinets are standard premade cabinet components that allow you to mix and match the pieces to your specification. Oak, maple, and cherry are popular materials, and special finishes are available. They can be framed or European style. Most design centers have assemdled kitchen cabinets, so you can have a look at the possibilities that each offers. Options can include plate racks, sliding shelves, wine racks, and glass doors. Designers employed by the suppliers can help you decide what package might suit your needs the best. While there is a display of the various configurations of cabinet options, you will have to order your

particular cabinet design and wait about six weeks for delivery.

Custom Cabinets

Custom cabinets are the best choice if you are not on a tight budget and if you do not have a fast-approaching time deadline. Unlike stock and semicustom cabinets, custom cabinets are not constructed until you place your order. Material possibilities may seem endless, because you can also choose exotic woods and reclaimed wood. Cabinetmakers can paint or stain to your choice of material, to your specifications. Door profiles and design and storage options are also only limited by your budget and the cabinetmaker you choose. Some cabinetmakers can complete a modest cabinet order in as little as a few months, but be aware that it could take much longer.

APPLIANCES

The right appliance can make an enormous difference to the way you use and enjoy your kitchen. With so many types of appliances available, in unlimited styles and finishes, there is bound to be the perfect refrigerator, oven, dishwasher, or warming drawer to suit your needs. From high-efficiency, climate controls, and quiet operations, there is also a growing number of operational features that distinguish models and brands in the marketplace. While there are standard sizes for most appliances, make sure you measure the appliance you are replacing, or the space you have set aside, before you purchase any new appliance.

MICROWAVE OVENS

New to most homes in the 1980s, the microwave oven has since become a standard kitchen feature. They can be mounted above your gas or electric oven or may be freestanding on the kitchen counter.

REFRIGERATORS, SINKS, AND DISHWASHERS

Refrigerators, sinks, and dishwashers are usually located near each other in a kitchen, as they may all require plumbing. While sinks and dishwashers are commonly integrated into the kitchen counter, refrigerators usually break up the counter surface. Some models even offer paneled fronts that integrate the look of the refrigerator into the kitchen cabinets. All are offered in a variety of finishes, and are usually chosen to match each other.

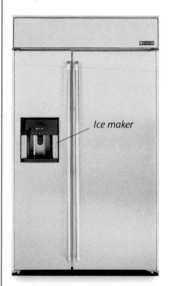

Ice maker

Side-by-side refrigerator
In this type of refrigerator the freezer and refrigerator storage are adjacent horizontally. An ice maker is featured on this model.

Paneled front refrigerator
Integrating the look of the refrigerator into the finish of the kitchen cabinets, paneled fronts are available on some models.

Freezer-on-bottom refrigerator
Traditional refrigerators offer the freezer on top. This model has a freezer drawer on the bottom, making the contents more accessible.

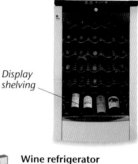

Display shelving

Wine refrigerator
Wire shelves designed for wine are the main difference between a wine and regular refrigerator. Offering ideal humidity, this model also includes display shelving.

WATER FILTRATION SYSTEM

Water filtration systems are designed to remove impurities from your tap water. The most common types available use either carbon or reverse-osmosis filtration. They can be whole-house systems or mounted on the end of a faucet or under the sink.

Dishwasher
Advances in technology have made dishwashers virtually silent features in the kitchen. Rack configurations, energy efficiency ratings, and soil sensors vary.

Directable faucet

Double-basin model

Sink
Available in stainless steel (shown here), solid surfacing, cast iron, and acrylic, sinks can be top mounted or under mounted. The number of mounting holes required corresponds to the type of faucet system.

UNDER-THE-SINK SYSTEM

COOKING AND WARMING APPLIANCES

Cooking appliances are grouped into two general categories based upon their energy source: electric and gas. The other important selection criteria are based upon where and how you plan to install the appliances. There are stoves that integrate into the countertop, ovens that integrate into the wall and cabinets, and then there are freestanding oven ranges.

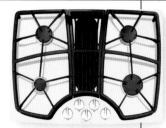

Electric stove
Electric stoves can be smooth, which make them easier to clean. They are offered in a variety of burner configurations.

Gas stove
Offered in various burner configurations and designs, gas stoves offer instant heat. Some offer integrated trivets or special burners for woks.

Temperature controls

Gas stove

Hood chimney

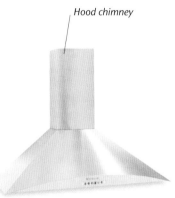

Wall oven
This double wall oven integrates into the surrounding cabinets. Offered in standard widths of 24, 27, and 30 in (610, 685, 760 mm).

Free-standing oven
Usually less expensive than wall ovens, free-standing ovens include a gas or electric range with the oven in one unit.

Hood
Used to circulate air and prevent condensation and cooking odors in the kitchen, hoods can be stylish kitchen features.

Warming drawer
Warming drawers can be installed under a stove or under a wall oven. They are offered with variable temperature controls.

WASTE DISPOSAL

Garbage disposals and trash compactors offer solutions to handling the waste created during food preparation. Always unplug the compactor and turn off the disposal's circuit before attempting any repairs.

WASHERS AND DRYERS

Capacity, size, controls, and style are usually the main features to consider when selecting a washer and dryer. If you are concerned about energy efficiency, look for the Energy Star label when selecting.

Drawer pulls out

Waste enters here

Top-loading washer

Front-loading dryer

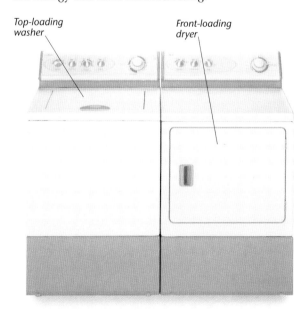

Garbage disposal unit
Once a luxury, now garbage disposals are fairly standard in new home construction. See p.253 for installation instructions.

Trash compactor
Decreasing the load on landfills, trash compactors are available in finishes that match most kitchens.

Side-by-side model
Clothes washers and dryers are offered in front-load and top-load styles, and in side-by-side models (shown here) and space-saving stackable models.

INSTALLING A COUNTERTOP

Installing a countertop is reasonably straightforward. However, joining two lengths of material to take a countertop around a corner requires more care, since the joint needs to be perfect to create a continuous, flat finish. The best joints can be achieved if you use the right techniques, and make good use of factory-cut straight edges. Joining a countertop material with square edges is easier than if the front edge has been finished with a curved profile.

TOOLS AND MATERIALS SEE BASIC TOOLKIT AND P.241

▌▌SCRIBING TO FIT

Any deviations in the wall surface will cause gaps along the back edge of the countertop. In these situations, the best finish is achieved by scribing the countertop to fit the wall. Consider that you will lose some countertop depth, so if the gaps are large, buy a wider countertop and trim it as described below.

Position the countertop with the back edge touching the wall and the front edge overhanging the cabinets by the same distance along the run.

Measure the largest gap between the countertop and the wall and cut a small scribing block of wood the same width.

Hold a pencil at one side of the block as you run the other end along the wall. This will provide a guide line for trimming.

Use a jigsaw to cut along the line. You may need to use a sander or plane where a small amount of material needs to be removed.

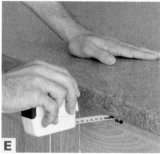

Reposition the countertop and check that you have a good fit between wall and countertop, and a consistent overhang at the front.

▌▌CUTTING A COUNTERTOP LENGTH

For a straight run, the countertop needs to be cut to the right length, including an overhang of about 1 in (25 mm) at each end. Handsaws or power saws can be used. Make sure you use an appropriate blade. For a laminate countertop, place masking tape over the cutting line to help prevent any splintering of the laminate surface. See p.73 for advice on cutting a board or sheet.

Draw a pencil line across the countertop where you want to cut it, and cover the line with masking tape.

Clamp a straight edge to the countertop along the guide line (a metal ruler is ideal). Using a utility knife, score down the line through the masking tape.

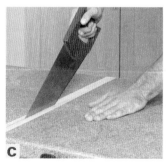

Carefully saw through the scored line using a panel saw. Make sure the countertop is well supported on both sides of the cut.

Remove the remaining masking tape. Use a block plane to smooth the cut end of the countertop.

TRIMMING A COUNTERTOP WIDTH

If you have a wider counter than you need, you can trim it at the same time as scribing it to fit. With the counter positioned on top of the base units, work out the width of material that needs to be removed to leave you with your desired overhang. Subtract the width of the largest gap at the back of the countertop from the trimming amount and cut a scribing block of this length. Use the block in the same way described above.

Deciding on what size of overhang is required at the front of the units is a matter of personal taste. Some people prefer a finish fairly flush with the drawer fronts, other people prefer a larger overhang. The standard overhang is 1½ in (38 mm). Cut through the countertop using the method shown left.

JOINING A COUNTERTOP

If you want your countertop to turn a corner, you will need to join two lengths. Options for joining are limited by the material the countertop is made from, and whether its profile is square or rounded. Once a joint has been cut, it is essential that it is held tightly in position. Mending plates can be installed across the joint on the underside of the counter, or a biscuit joiner will create an exceptionally strong joint. The technique for using a biscuit joiner is demonstrated on p.64.

Round-edged countertops

If your counter is supplied with a curved finished edge, it is not possible to create a simple right-angled butt joint. The best option is to use a joining strip, or a countertop jig. Making a mitered joint is possible, but will be hard to cut accurately unless you use a jig (see above, right).

USING A JIG

Professional kitchen installers use countertop jigs for accuracy. These specially designed tools are relatively expensive, although often they can be rented. The jig provides a template for a router to cut against. With practice, it produces very accurate cuts for each side of the joint required, and guides for notched cuts to fit connector bolts to hold the joint together.

Countertop joint kits

Some manufacturers provide joint kits. Basically, these are colored fillers used to cover a less than adequate miter or butt joint. Some are epoxy-based, so you should remove any excess before it has a chance to dry.

JOINING SQUARE-EDGED COUNTERTOPS

Square edges mean that two sections of countertop can be easily and neatly butt-joined without the need for a countertop jig. Once the countertop is fixed in place, the front edge may then be finished using a router (see p.66).

A Cut the countertop lengths to size and, if necessary, scribe (see opposite). Apply wood glue along one of the joining edges.

B Push the countertop together and secure the joint using a mending plate and screws. You may need to drill pilot holes for the screws, and apply weight to the countertop as you fasten the screws. Wipe away excess glue. For an even stronger joint, use two or even three mending plates.

JOINING SOLID SURFACES

A Cut a joining strip to the width of the countertop, then secure it using selant and screws. Apply sealant along the edge of the other countertop.

B Butt the sections together, and use a cloth to remove any excess sealant.

SECURING A COUNTERTOP

Once a countertop has been cut to size, it should be secured in place using screws inserted through the countertop brackets that are attached to the units and rail. You will need someone to apply weight to the back of the units while you attach them.

A Clamp the countertop to the cabinets along their front edge. Insert screws through the rail into the underside of the countertop.

B Apply weight from above while you secure the back of the countertop using mending brackets.

FINISHING COUNTERTOPS

Laminate countertops

These often have unfinished edges that require covering with laminate strips supplied by the manufacturer. The strips can sometimes be ironed on, but others will need contact adhesive. Once the strip is fastened in place and any adhesive is dry, you can trim the edges flush using a utility knife.

Solid surface countertops

Sawn edges of some types of solid surface can be sanded smooth. Always check manufacturer's guidelines.

Solid wood countertops

These are best sanded smooth, then stain-protected using the oil recommended by the manufacturer. Paint on several coats of oil, removing any excess with a dry cloth. Extra oil may be required at intervals to maintain the finish.

Concrete countertops

After installation, seal the exposed surfaces with a sealing product. The sealer prevents the surface from absorbing food stains and odors, and it makes it easier to clean. When dry, buff out the surface using an abrasive pad. Then apply a coat of acrylic clear finish. To achieve a high-gloss finish, buff the surface.

Stone countertops

You can always seal your stone countertops, but keep in mind that a sealer does not make the stone unstainable. The sealer's main job is to fill the pores in the stone and make the staining process slower, so you have more time to clean a spill before a stain sets in. Marble and granite surfaces should be sealed at least once every year.

GREEN KITCHEN SOLUTIONS

Recycling is a part of daily life in most homes, with food waste and packaging being the most commonly recycled items. Most recycling, therefore, occurs in the kitchen. Food waste can be composted (see pp.404–405), but here we show how a kitchen can be adapted to make recycling a simple process. The precise way in which you recycle will depend on your local services—some materials may be collected from your home while others must be taken to a recycling center—but a good system of sorting and temporarily storing your recycling is needed.

WHAT CAN BE RECYCLED?

Most packaging carries a symbol that states whether it can be recycled—the universal recycling symbol (pictured) means that it can be. Most plastics have a number in the center of the recycling symbol—check with your local municipality to see which plastics they are equipped to recycle. Confusion can occur over whether a product is recyclable, or whether it has been made from recycled materials, so check the packaging carefully.

UNIVERSAL RECYCLING SYMBOL

HOUSEHOLD RECYCLING SYSTEMS

The main way to sort and conveniently store your recycling material in the short term is to make use of a dedicated recycling bin. There are many different styles available, but all are designed to make the process of recycling as simple and convenient as possible. Some manufacturers produce specific designs to fit into their kitchen units, but it is also possible to buy more generic bins that will fit the vast majority of kitchen units.

A selection of different types of bin are shown here—in all cases, the aim of the bin is to make recycling easier, but also to be unobtrusive and make the best use of the available space. It helps if you compact the items for recycling before placing them in the bin, which saves space in your home, and makes it easier to transport them to a recycling center.

CRUSHING PLASTIC BOTTLES

A

Remove the lid and crush the bottle with your hand or foot to compact the bottle (the space taken up by empty plastic bottles consists almost entirely of air).

B

Replace the lid when you have crushed the bottle to create a vacuum that prevents the bottle returning to a larger size. By doing this, a large amount of room is saved in storage and transit.

CRUSHING METAL CANS

A

Place the can in the jaws of the crusher. There are many such gadgets available and a simple design allows most sizes of can to be crushed underfoot.

B

Push down with your foot to flatten the can. As with plastic bottles, this saves space both in storage and transit.

Stacking bins
Some recycling bins are designed to be stacked up, to save on floor space. The stack can be disassembled for transporting to the recycling center, or separate sections can be left for collection by your local crew.

Pedal bins
These are a more stylish solution for recycling. A bin that is internally subdivided makes it easier to sort different types of recycling.

Built-in recycling bins
This is a good option for keeping recycling out of view, as well as utilizing space under a countertop. Most designs are internally divided, meaning recycling can be separated. Styles vary, but the principle remains the same. For more on installation, see opposite.

Countertop bins
Countertop bins conceal the body of the bin, which is set into the countertop. This design is commonly used for recycling food scraps or waste, such as vegetable peelings. These may then be composted domestically, or put out for collection. For more on installation, see opposite.

FITTING A RECYCLING CABINET

Make sure you have chosen a bin that will fit your kitchen units. Depth is very important here, as it tends to vary more across products than the internal height. Remove any shelving from the cabinet to allow for installation of the recycling bin.

Position the bin frame on the floor of the cabinet, so it is central to the door opening. Observe any supplier's guidelines on positioning.

Screw the frame in place—normally into the cabinet floor, but some designs may require securing to the back, or sides, of the cabinet.

Fit the bins into the frame—they tend to be the same size, and usually consist of two or three separate bins.

Fit the lid in place. Sometimes, the lid may be attached to the door to allow it to open automatically when the cabinet is opened.

Replace any shelving if the bin height allows (in this example, the bin is on runners and can be pulled forward to allow the lid to be lifted). If there is not enough space between the shelf and the bin, the shelf brackets can be raised to create space.

FITTING A COUNTERTOP BIN FOR FOOD WASTE

Draw a cutting guideline on the countertop. The bin's manufacturer should provide a template, as well as instructions for fitting, but here the lid ring is being used for this purpose. Positioning is very important with a bin of this type, as it is necessary to cut a hole in the countertop, meaning mistakes are not easily rectified.

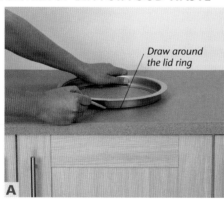

Draw around the lid ring

A jigsaw is needed to cut the guideline. For more on positioning the blade for the initial incision, see p.248.

Position the lid ring in the hole. Some manufacturers recommend fixing the ring with silicone sealant around the underside of the rim.

Position the bin in the ring by simply placing it through the hole.

Create a seal for the lid using an inner rubber ring. These are easily removed for cleaning.

Fit the lid to the rubber seal for a neat finish. Depending on the depth of your bin, it may be necessary to remove shelves below, or at least customize the cabinet design so that the bin sits in its hole.

Most types of sinks and stoves need to be recessed into the countertop, but many kitchen appliances are freestanding and simply slot into gaps beneath the countertop. However, if you have chosen built-in appliances, you may want to choose doors that match your cabinets. For new kitchens, power and water services should be in place, but for renovations some rerouting may be required.
If you are unsure about plumbing or any electrical issues, consult an expert.

INSTALLING A SINK

Depending on design, a kitchen sink may take up the entire top surface of a cabinet, or may be recessed into the countertop. To install a recessed sink, you need to cut a hole in the countertop to accommodate it. Some manufacturers will supply a cutting template with the sink. If not, you can draw your own guidelines. It is advisable to install the faucets and waste to the sink or countertop before the sink is secured in place because access is much easier. The method for connecting faucets is similar to that for a bathroom sink (see pp.262–263). In this example, a stainless steel sink is being installed into a laminate countertop.

TOOLS AND MATERIALS SEE BASIC TOOLKIT AND P.241

1 CUTTING A RECESS HOLE

A

B

Use a drill with a flat bit or auger bit to make a hole in each corner of the sink position, inside the inner guide line. Make sure that the drill is at precise right angles to the countertop, so that you make an accurate hole.

C

Position the sink face-down on the countertop, making sure the space at the front and back is even. Draw a pencil guide line around the sink.

Measure the depth of the lip of the sink, then mark a second pencil line at this distance inside the first, all the way around.

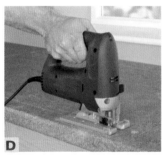

D

E

2 ASSEMBLING AND INSERTING A SINK

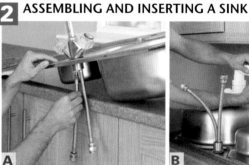

A

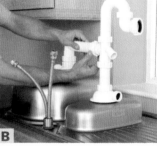

B

Cut around the inside guide line with a jigsaw, using the holes as starting points. Support the countertop underneath as you cut.

Check that the sink fits well in the hole. Seal the cut edges of the countertop with a preservative primer.

Put the faucet into the hole in the sink and secure it on the underside of the sink using the washers and nuts supplied. Install the hoses.

Install the waste assembly and connect the overflow section as guided by any supplied instructions.

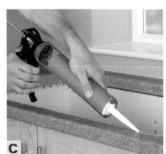

C

D

E

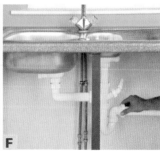

F

Caulk around the hole in the countertop. This may not be necessary if the manufacturer has supplied a gasket or seal.

Install retaining clips around the edge of the sink. Position the sink and check whether you have enough room to connect the faucets.

Tighten the retaining clips to the underside of the countertop. Wipe away any sealant that may squeeze out from around the sink edges.

Connect faucets and waste as for a bathroom sink (see pp.262–263). Flexible connectors are the easiest option for faucets.

INSTALLING A GARBAGE DISPOSAL

Clear the waste lines from the sink. Remove the cover plate from the disposal and wire it according to manufacturer's instructions.

Attach the discharge tube to the disposal body.

Run plumber's putty along the underside of the drain flange into the drain, then the backup ring and fiber gasket. Mount the ring with screws.

Position the disposal into the mounting ring. Adjust the ring until the disposal is set in firmly.

Align and attach the discharge tube with the drain trap.

Tighten the mounting lug for the dishwasher tube.

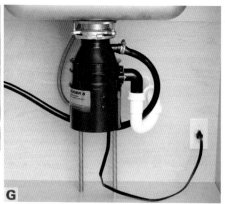

Connect the disposal to a GFCI receptacle.

REFRIGERATORS AND FREEZERS

In some cases, manufacturers offer models with faces that match cabinetry for a built-in look. However, normally the refrigerator or freezer will have to be custom made specifically for built-in use.

BUILT-IN OVENS

Built-in ovens often form part of custom kitchens, and are usually housed in custom-made units. Ovens normally slide into position on brackets, which you will probably have to install. Instructions must be followed carefully according to the precise make and model being installed. There are often differences in procedure and positioning of brackets. As with stoves, you cannot connect a gas oven yourself. You can wire an electric oven—it will need its own radial circuit—but your work must be inspected and permitted.

Some ovens have their own feet, and are simply slid into position between units.

The only adjustment that may be necessary is to use a wrench to adjust the feet to level the oven.

STOVES

Stoves are recessed into countertops using a technique similar to that shown for sinks. Gas stoves are best installed by a qualified appliance installer. However, if you are installing an electric stove you may be able to wire it yourself, although all electrical work must be checked by a professional to comply with building regulations. For more information on electrics, see pp.432–433.

Installing a stove
To install a stove into a countertop, use the method described for installing a sink (opposite). Stoves need to be installed before an oven is positioned so that you can make connections under the countertop.

INSTALLING AN EXHAUST FAN

A kitchen exhaust fan is often housed in a wall unit that matches the rest of the kitchen and is installed in much the same way. There are two extraction methods. If a recirculator is being used, there is no need for any ducting to the outside of the building. However, if conventional extraction is chosen, it may be necessary to cut a hole in an exterior wall to accommodate a ducting channel. Use the method shown on p.364 to make an opening. Decorative chimneys and hoods are often secured on the wall with simple brackets. Great care needs to be taken when handling these items since they can be damaged and dent easily. All fans will require an electrical supply.

PROBLEM SOLVER

REPLACING DOOR HINGES

Hinges themselves tend not to break—if they do, you can simply replace them. What is more likely is that the hinge plate will loosen through wear and tear. If this happens, you can reattach the hinge above or below its existing position.

Note: Step D indicates that you should use a 32-mm hinge-cutting bit. This is neither a mistake, nor an option. All of these European-style hinges are made to go into a 32-mm hole and if it is any other size, it will not hold. Buy the bit where you buy the hinges.

TOOLS AND MATERIALS
Screwdriver, tape measure, pencil, drill, hinge-cutting bit

A Unscrew the loosened hinge plate and remove it.

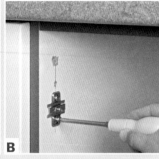

B Mark off a new position where you can get a firmer attachment, slightly lower in this case, and reattach the plate.

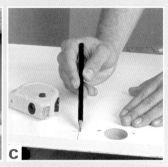

C Measure off the new hinge position on the door using the new plate position as a guide.

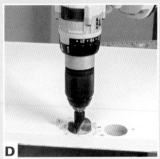

D Use a 32 mm hinge-cutting bit to drill out the recess for the new hinge position. Take care not to drill too deeply.

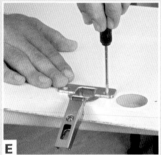

E Screw the hinge in place, making sure that it sits perfectly flush.

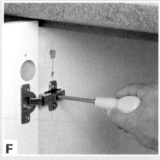

F Re-hang the door. The old hinge plate and hinge holes can be filled and painted if desired.

REPAIRING DRAWER HANDLES

The most common problem with drawers is a loose handle. You may need to strengthen the screws that hold the handle in position or attach the drawer front more securely.

TOOLS AND MATERIALS
Adhesive, washers, clamp, screwdriver, wood glue

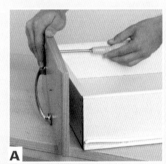

A Unscrew the drawer front and remove the handle from its position.

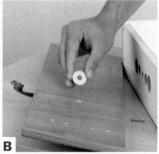

B Apply some strong adhesive to the thread of the handle. Position a washer on the screw before replacing the handle.

C Spread some adhesive on the back face of the drawer front before securing it back in place.

ADJUST DRAWER RUNNERS

Drawer runners may require adjustment because of wear or simply because they were misaligned when the unit was constructed. Adjustment is a straightforward process of reattaching the runner.

TOOLS AND MATERIALS
Screwdriver, mini-level, awl

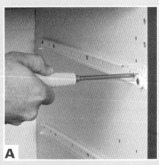

A Unscrew the runner, ideally leaving the rear screw in place.

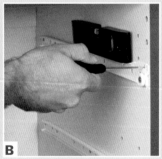

B Position a level on the runner and use an awl to mark new mounting holes.

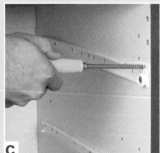

C Screw the runner back in place. Reposition the drawer and check for improved operation. Readjust if necessary.

DRILLING THROUGH TILES WITHOUT CRACKING THEM

Many installations in kitchens involve making attachments on a tiled surface. It is essential to use the correct technique for drilling through tiles so they do not crack. The dust created from drilling ceramic tiles can discolor grout and sealant, so try to vacuum dust from the hole as you drill it.

TOOLS AND MATERIALS

Felt-tip pen, masking tape, drill and bits, vacuum cleaner, wall plug

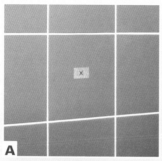

A

Mark the point for the attachment using a felt-tip pen. Apply some masking tape over the mark—it should still be visible.

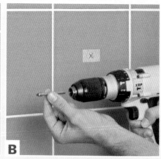

B

Fit a tile drill bit (see pp.56–57) and switch off any hammer action.

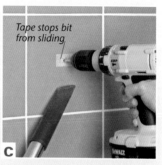

Tape stops bit from sliding

C

Position a vacuum cleaner below the mark and switch it on. Start up the drill on a low speed, and slowly increase the speed.

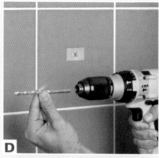

D

Once through the tile, exchange the bit for a masonry bit or wood bit, depending on the surface below. Drill to the required depth.

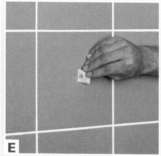

E

Once you have drilled the hole, remove the masking tape from the tile surface.

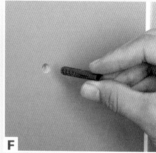

F

Plug the hole with the appropriate anchor and insert the fastener as required.

REPAIRING A LAMINATE COUNTERTOP

A repair is achieved by disguising the damage. Laminate manufacturers' supply fillers that are color-matched for small holes. Reattach broken edging as shown.

TOOLS AND MATERIALS

Contact adhesive, masking tape, pencil or crayon

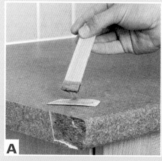

A

Apply contact adhesive to both the countertop edge and the broken section of laminate.

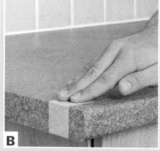

B

Wait for it to become tacky and stick it in place—use masking tape to hold it securely.

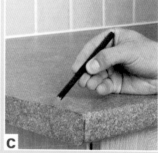

C

Once the adhesive has dried, remove the masking tape and use a pencil or crayon to disguise any white edges along the seam.

REPAIRING A WOODEN COUNTERTOP

Over time, a countertop can be damaged or discolored. In most cases, you can simply sand back the damaged area (though only for solid wood countertops, not veneered ones).

TOOLS AND MATERIALS

Sanding block, latex glove, cloths, wood oil, brush

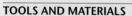

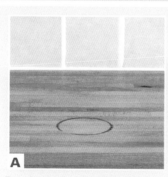

A

Burning and staining can look unsightly, but these problems are easy to repair in two steps, as shown.

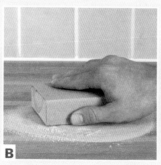

B

Sand the area back to the bare wood, making sure not to create a depression. Then use a cloth to remove all traces of dust and debris.

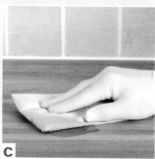

C

Brush on two or three coats of the recommended oil, usually tung oil. Brush on a coat, then remove the excess with a cloth.

Bathrooms

WHEN PLANNING A BATHROOM, YOU SHOULD THINK ABOUT WHAT STYLE YOU PREFER, AND WHAT WILL MAKE BEST USE OF THE SPACE AVAILABLE. HOW TO REPLACE OLD FIXTURES IS DESCRIBED IN THIS SECTION, AND WILL INVOLVE A MINIMUM OF PLUMBING. NEW LAYOUTS OR BATHROOMS WILL CERTAINLY PROVIDE MORE DEMANDING TASKS IN TERMS OF ROUTING SUPPLY AND WASTE PLUMBING.

CHOOSING YOUR SUITE

A huge range of bathroom fixtures and fittings is available. Most manufacturers sell bathroom suites, and bathroom furniture is a popular target for reclamation (see pp.94–95). A basic suite usually includes a toilet, sink, and bathtub with shower. For more information on showers, see pp.266–269. Most bathroom fixtures are available in basic white and then a range of other colors. Modern or traditional styles can be complemented by faucets (see pp.484–489) and tiles (see pp.312–313). For ideas on planning a bathroom layout, see pp.258–259.

PLUMBING

Simply replacing existing fixtures with new ones in the same position usually requires the least amount of plumbing work. However, if you want to move fixtures, or are planning a new bathroom, consider carefully if you are confident with the plumbing involved. The different types of supply and waste pipes and the systems and techniques for routing and joining them are shown in the plumbing section (see pp.464–483). However, you might prefer to choose and design the layout yourself, and then leave the plumbing to a professional.

TOILETS

Most residential toilets have two separate pieces: a tank and a bowl. Some are offered in space-saving one-piece designs. The tank holds the flush mechanism and water. Most toilets are either gravity-flow or pressure-assisted. Gravity-flow toilets have a flapper or ball inside the tank. Pressure-assisted toilets have an air-pressure drum inside the tank. Toilets manufactured before 1992 can use between 3.5 to 8 gallons (13–30 liters) per flush. Now low-volume flush toilets use only 1.6 gallons (6 liters) per flush. There also are dual flush toilets that offer the option of a half flush for liquid waste and a full flush for solid waste. Bowls can be oval or round in shape. Heated seats, lids that automatically open, and automatic flushing are among the options available. Toilets are typically made of ceramic, acrylic, or metal.

Lever flush

Push-button flush

Vitreous enamel coating

Triangular tank

Flush-handle toilet
Most toilets are operated by a side flush handle. Handles usually come standard with the toilet, but can be available in hardware that matches other bathroom hardware.

Push-button toilet
Operated by a button on top of the toilet tank, these toilets are becoming more popular. This toilet shown is offered in a slimmer, space-saving design that suits smaller rooms.

BIDETS

There are two types of bidets available. Over-the-rim bidets are filled in the same way as a sink, and installed in a similar way (see p.263). Rim-supply bidets have heated seats and sprays, but generally require professional installation.

Faucet

Ceramic with a vitreous enamel coating

OVER-THE-RIM BIDET

SINKS

Sinks are traditionally made from ceramic, although contemporary designs made of glass, wood, marble, and other types of natural stone are available. There are several designs—pedestal and wall-mounted. Sinks can be pedestal, wall-mounted, or supported by vanities—countertops with cabinets underneath. Steps for replacing a sink are shown on pp.262–263.

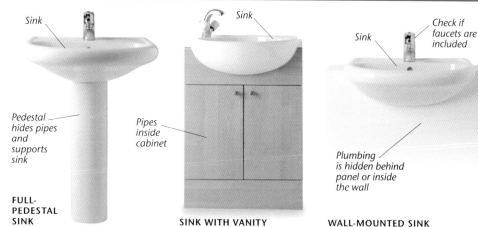

Sink

Pedestal hides pipes and supports sink

FULL-PEDESTAL SINK

Sink

Pipes inside cabinet

SINK WITH VANITY

Sink

Check if faucets are included

Plumbing is hidden behind panel or inside the wall

WALL-MOUNTED SINK

BATHTUBS

Bathtubs can be made from a variety of materials. Enameled steel and iron tubs are cold to the touch. Steel tubs are cheaper but chip easily; iron tubs are expensive and heavy, but long-lasting. Acrylics are light, inexpensive, and warm but can be scratched, and thin acrylic can be deformed by heavy loads of water. Composite resins are sturdy, but lighter than metal and warm to the touch. Other options include tubs with water jets and air bubbles. Walk-in tubs are available with improved access for disabled. Replacing a bathtub is shown on pp.264–265. You can also install a shower-tub (see pp.268–269).

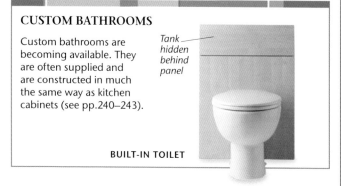

Deep tub

Feet

CUSTOM BATHROOMS

Custom bathrooms are becoming available. They are often supplied and are constructed in much the same way as kitchen cabinets (see pp.240–243).

Tank hidden behind panel

BUILT-IN TOILET

Soaking bathtub
Soaking tubs can either be built into the wall or freestanding, like the traditional footed tub to the left. Soaking tubs typically do not have jets. Soaking tubs oriented vertically, meaning deep instead of long, are called Japanese-style soaking tubs.

HEATING AND VENTILATION

Even if your home has central heating, electric heaters, radiant floor heating, or towel rails are often used in bathrooms to provide extra heating on demand. If there is not one already, build a ventilation system into your bathroom (see pp.368–369) to reduce mildew caused by humid air.

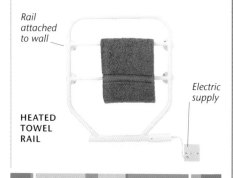

Rail attached to wall

Electric supply

HEATED TOWEL RAIL

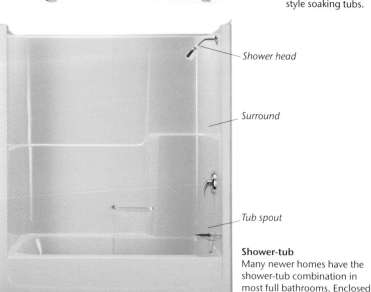

Shower head

Surround

Tub spout

Shower-tub
Many newer homes have the shower-tub combination in most full bathrooms. Enclosed on three sides, with either a curtain or glass sliding doors, the bathtub is typically the most affordable option.

FAUCETS

The final look of the bathroom depends to some extent on the faucets you choose, and your choice is limited by the number of holes in your chosen sink or tub, although you can cut your own faucet holes in some tubs. Choosing faucets is dealt with in more detail on pp.484–485.

Your initial bathroom design should focus on making the best use of the space available. Then consider which utilities would need rerouting for the new design. Decide whether you are going to tile the walls, change the floor surface, or update heating and ventilation. You can then construct an order of work. If you are replacing the whole bathroom, remove all the old fixtures and reroute the plumbing and wiring before installing the new bathroom. If there is little rerouting required, you may prefer to replace each item in turn.

TYPES OF BATHROOM LAYOUTS

Most homes have at least one full bathroom with a toilet, sink, and bathtub. Optional extras to this basic suite include a shower, either in a separate cubicle or above the bathtub, and possibly a bidet. An extra sink is a popular choice in a bathroom used by more than one person.

Custom bathrooms

Like a standard bathroom, custom bathrooms have a full suite of fixtures. The difference is that the final design has matching built-in cabinets and countertops around part of the room. If you are considering this type of bathroom, the manufacturer or professional bath designer can help you plan the layout.

Attached bathrooms

Because of the proximity of the bedroom, noise is an issue. If there is no window in an attached bath, an exhaust fan is essential for removing moisture (see p.369). The noise of a toilet tank refilling can be reduced by installing a quiet, modern inlet valve (see pp.490–491).

Wet rooms

These are bathrooms that include a shower with no enclosure—the water runs away through a drain in the floor. The whole room has to be fully waterproofed.

Powder rooms

Powder rooms are usually located on the first floor of a house near the entryway. Also called half-baths, powder rooms have a sink and a toilet, but they do not have a shower or bathtub.

BATHROOM REGULATIONS

Electrical installations

Water is a good conductor of electricity, so it increases the chance and severity of shocks. There are strict regulations regarding where and how you install electrical equipment in bathrooms. Metal pipes also conduct electricity, so the plumbing system should be grounded with grounding clamps (see pp.436–437).

Waste pipe installations

Changing or installing a new bathroom may involve making a new connection to your home's main soil stack or drain (see pp.482–483). Contact your local building control office should you need to check regulations regarding stack connection.

SPACE CONSIDERATIONS

All bathroom fixtures require space around them so that they can be used comfortably. For example, a bathtub should be at least 2 ft 4 in (700 mm) from a wall or another fixture, to allow you to step in and out and dry yourself easily. You should also make sure there is room for the door to open without scratching or chipping fixtures. Try to provide space for a wastebasket in your plan. Make sure you place items such as mirrors and cabinets to suit the height of all users when possible. Medicine cabinets should be lockable, and be out of the reach of children.

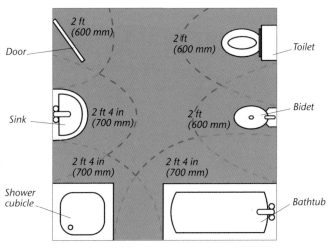

A GUIDE TO FIXTURE CLEARANCE ZONES

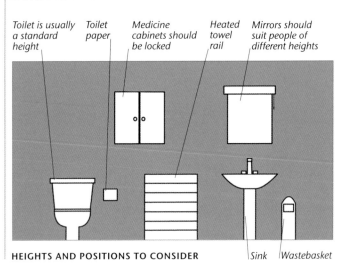

Toilet is usually a standard height · Toilet paper · Medicine cabinets should be locked · Heated towel rail · Mirrors should suit people of different heights · Sink · Wastebasket

HEIGHTS AND POSITIONS TO CONSIDER

NEW BATHROOM CONSIDERATIONS

- Even if replacing fixtures in the same position, check that supply and waste pipes don't need to be extended or otherwise modified.
- A new floor will increase floor height, which can affect the pipe positions. Flexible connector pipes will accommodate changes.
- Check the dimensions of new fixtures; don't assume they are the same as the old. Fixtures can vary in size even if they look similar.
- Consider improving ventilation by installing a bathroom exhaust fan.
- Stud walls need modifying for wall-mounted fixtures.
- Floors may need to be strengthened for a cast-iron bathtub. Get a professional opinion on what is required.

Replacing a bathroom suite
Before installing the new bathroom, you will have to remove the old fixtures. If you are not replacing a tiled floor or moving fixture positions, you may choose to tackle them one at a time. If you are tiling the floor or moving any fixtures, you will probably need to remove all the old fixtures before you start. In tight spaces, you may have to take away the toilet and sink before you are able to remove the bathtub.

Order of work considerations:
1 Reroute or extend plumbing
2 Route wiring, but do not wire in any new equipment. Replace subfloor if necessary
3 Install bathtub and shower tray
4 Install the base of the shower mixer valve into the wall
5 Complete any tiling on floors and walls, and paint if required
6 Install the toilet and sink, and the shower and cubicle
7 Lay soft flooring
8 Install electrical items
9 Seal all joints with bathroom caulk

ATTACHING FIXTURES TO A STUD WALL

As well as modifying the plumbing, if you are attaching fixtures to a stud wall, you need to install extra blocking for added support. Wall-mounted fixtures will need double blocking, one piece on top of the other, or custom-built frameworks inserted into the wall to support their weight.

To put frames into a stud wall, you will need to remove the drywall or cut a hole in the drywall at the attachment point. With the studwork exposed, you can nail any extra blocking in place (see pp.102–107 for more on stud walls and how to install blocking). Alternatively, insert the support frame. While you have access to the studs, you might want to hide supply and waste pipes in the wall. To repair the wall, use a drywall patch and finish the drywall (see p.125).

PLANNING PLUMBING IN BATHROOMS

The simplest option when planning a new bathroom is to position the new fixtures in the same place as the old ones. In this way plumbing work is kept to a minimum. If each item is already plumbed in with isolating valves and flexible connector pipes, you can easily work on each in turn. If there are no isolating valves, then you will have to shut off the water at a nearby gate valve, or drain down the entire system if there is no other option.

When you are repositioning a toilet, rerouting its waste pipe is complex, and in many cases may not be possible. An option is to fit a grinder pump behind the toilet bowl. This can pump waste through small pipes to join the main stack and makes it possible to put a toilet almost anywhere.

Showers may need to take their water supply directly from a pressure tank, rather than from a nearby supply pipe (see p.267). This helps maintain pressure and reduces temperature fluctuations. Repositioning other fixtures requires teeing off the water supply pipes and running waste pipes to the new position. See pp.476–483 for more on routing and connecting supply and waste pipes.

PLANNING ELECTRICAL WORK IN BATHROOMS

Electrical considerations are an important part of bathroom planning. Aside from obvious features such as lighting, it may also be necessary to provide power for an exhaust fan, heated towel rail, or whirlpool bathtub. Water and electricity are a dangerous combination, so bathroom outlets and electricity must be grounded. Use GFCI outlets in bathrooms (see information on electrics, pp.430–463).

TOOLS AND MATERIALS CHECKLISTS PP.261–269

Replacing a toilet (p.261)
Toilet bowl connector, stubby screwdriver*, sealant, caulk gun, level, slip joint pliers, flexible connector

Installing a wall-mounted sink (p.262) Brackets, level, flexible pipe connectors

Replacing a sink (p.263)
Drop cloth, faucet (or faucets, depending on holes in sink), flexible pipe connectors, sink trap, sink wrench, caulk, caulk gun

Replacing a bathtub (p.265)
Drop cloth, faucet (or faucets, depending on holes in tub), flexible pipe connectors, trap, panels*, level, furring strip, wood offcuts, tenon saw, jigsaw, caulk, caulk gun

Installing a solid resin or ceramic shower tray (p.269)
Jigsaw, furring strips, white glue, mortar (see pp.70–71), trowel, level, shower trap, caulk, caulk gun

Installing an acrylic shower tray (p.269) Level, shower trap, caulk, caulk gun

Installing a shower or bath screen (p.269) Level, caulk, caulk gun

* = optional

FOR BASIC TOOLKIT SEE PP.24–25

REPLACING A TOILET

Replacing an existing toilet is a straightforward task because the supply and waste pipes are already in position. Before replacing the toilet, remove the old one, taking care not to damage the outlet to the soil stack. Installing a toilet in a new position requires more complex rerouting that is best completed by a professional plumber.

TOOLS AND MATERIALS SEE BASIC TOOLKIT AND P.259

ANATOMY OF A TOILET

This type of toilet design, where the tank sits on top of the back of the bowl, is popular because it is so compact and simple to install.

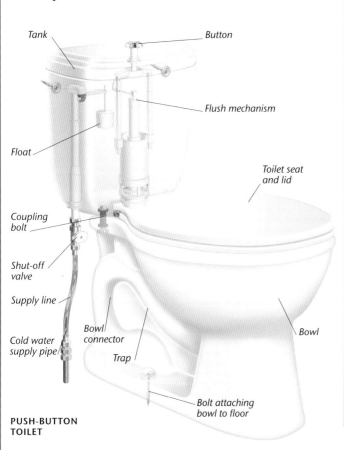

Tank

Button

Flush mechanism

Float

Toilet seat and lid

Coupling bolt

Shut-off valve

Supply line

Cold water supply pipe

Bowl connector

Trap

Bowl

Bolt attaching bowl to floor

PUSH-BUTTON TOILET

MOVING OR ADDING A TOILET

You may need to notify your local building control office if you are planning to modify your main soil stack and/or install a toilet (see building regulations, p.468). Routing toilet waste pipes is complicated, so it is worth seeking professional advice on what the best options are. In some cases it may be necessary to fit a grinder pump, which chops up waste and pumps it through small pipes to provide more options for toilet position.

TOILET FLANGE

The toilet flange helps make a tight connection between the toilet and the waste pipe. The flange sits on top of the floor and connects to a collar that fits through the floor. Historically the flange was secured in place with putty, but today there are several flange gaskets to choose from.

Flange
This is a common plastic insert flange used in houses. The wax gaskets shown below fit on top of this flange, sealing the connection with the toilet on top.

Wax gasket with insert
Other gaskets are available, but wax gaskets are the most popular type. The gasket shown here has a plastic insert used to direct water flow.

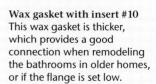

Wax gasket with insert #10
This wax gasket is thicker, which provides a good connection when remodeling the bathrooms in older homes, or if the flange is set low.

Wax gasket without insert
Wax gaskets are available with and without inserts. Even without plastic inserts they can provide a suitable seal against sewer gases.

REMOVING AN OLD TOILET

Before you begin to remove an older toilet, gather the right equipment. You will need newspapers or old towels to set the toilet on when it has been removed from its location. Also, make sure the new toilet fits inside the space occupied by the old toilet. Some newer models are available in longer and larger sizes than traditional designs, and may not fit within a toilet room's design.

Removing the water
The first step is to shut off the water supply to the toilet. After the water supply is disconnected, flush the toilet several times. Flushing repeatedly will remove the water from inside the tank and most of the water from the bowl.

If there is any water left in the bowl, use a container to scoop it all out. If you leave any water in the old toilet it may leak out when you carry it through your home to dispose of it.

Disconnecting the the toilet
To disconnect the old toilet from the pipes and from the floor, first unscrew the nuts that attach the toilet to the water supply line. Then, remove the caps that cover the bolts on the base of the toilet. Unscrew the nuts located under the caps. Lay out your towels or newspapers then lift the toilet from its position, being careful to hold the bowl, not the seat. Place the toilet on the towels or newspapers.

1 REMOVING THE OLD TOILET

Before removing an old toilet, make sure the water is turned off. Disconnect the water shut-off valve.

Lever the caps off of the bolts attaching the toilet to the floor, and use an adjustable wrench to unscrew the nuts beneath them.

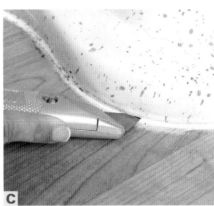

Loosen the seal between the bowl and the floor with a knife, and then free the toilet by rocking it from side to side. Lift the toilet away onto some old towels or newspaper. Block the drainpipe with a rag to prevent sewer gas escaping.

2 POSITIONING THE NEW BOWL

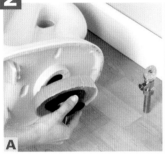

Place a new wax gasket on the outlet of the new bowl. The tapered side faces away from the bowl.

Apply a bead of caulk to the base of the toilet. Remove the rag from the drainpipe. Lower the bowl into place on top of the flange and press down.

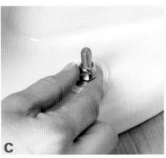

Gently tighten the washers and nuts onto the bolts. Tightening too hard can crack the porcelain.

Use plastic toilet shims if the toilet is not level. Fill the caps with plumber's putty and place the caps over the bolts.

3 SETTING THE NEW TANK

Insert the tank bolts through the base of the tank. Position the tank over the bowl and lower it gently into place.

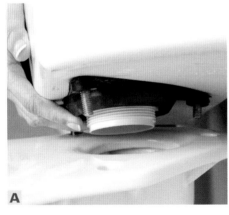

Secure the nuts and washers to attach the bowl to the tank. Make sure the tank is level.

When the tank is level, set the tank lid on top of the tank. Do not seal the join between the lid and the tank.

4 CONNECTING THE TOILET

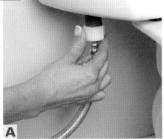

Connect the supply line between the shut-off valve and the fill valve.

To finish connecting the toilet to the water supply, tighten the compression nut and then open the shut-off valve.

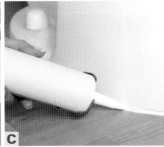

Run a bead of bathroom caulk along the bottom of the toilet. This seals the joint between the toilet and the floor.

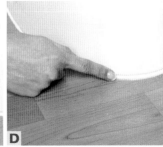

Using a wetted finger, smooth the bead of caulk along the joint for a clean finish.

REPLACING A SINK

Sinks are straightforward to replace. Simply remove the old sink and connect the new one. If a sink is being installed in a new position, you will need to reroute water supply and drainage pipes (see pp.476–483).

TOOLS AND MATERIALS SEE BASIC TOOLKIT AND P.259

ANATOMY OF A SINK AND PEDESTAL
The pedestal helps support the weight of the sink and sits in front of the water supply and waste pipes to partially hide them.

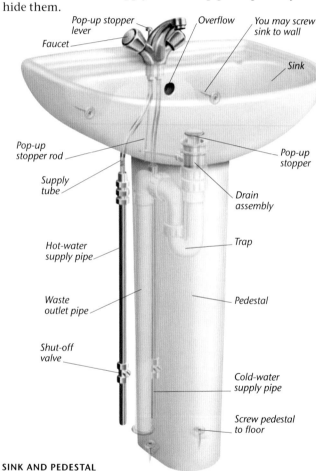

- Pop-up stopper lever
- Faucet
- Overflow
- You may screw sink to wall
- Sink
- Pop-up stopper rod
- Pop-up stopper
- Supply tube
- Drain assembly
- Hot-water supply pipe
- Trap
- Waste outlet pipe
- Pedestal
- Shut-off valve
- Cold-water supply pipe
- Screw pedestal to floor

SINK AND PEDESTAL

REMOVING AN OLD SINK
Before you start, turn off the water at the shut-off valves on the hot- and cold-water supply pipes. If there are no valves, part or all of each system may require draining down. With the water off, open the faucets and allow them to run dry.

Disconnect the supply tubes from the faucets, or on older systems, cut through rigid supply pipes. Unscrew the plastic nut connecting the trap to the waste pipe. When all the plumbing is disconnected, if there are screws holding the sink to the wall then remove them, then lift the sink away. There is no need to remove the faucets from the sink unless you want to reuse them. Undo the screws attaching the pedestal to the floor and remove it.

INSTALLING A SINK AND PEDESTAL
When you have removed the old sink, assess whether you need to reroute the plumbing. You may want to adjust the supply and drainage pipes slightly so that they run up inside the pedestal, rather than simply being hidden behind it. This isn't essential, but you might decide it is worth doing if you have a side view of the sink. The supply pipes should have shut-off valves (see p.467). Then follow the steps shown opposite to install a sink with a pedestal.

Installing other styles of sinks
Assembling the components of the plug, trap, and faucets (shown opposite) is similar for all types, but other aspects of the procedure can differ. For example, you might need to hide supply and drainage pipes in a wall. Units or countertops may need to be cut to house some types of sinks—the manufacturer will generally supply a cutting template. If you are putting a sink into a stone countertop, it may need to be cut at the factory.

Wall-mounted sinks (see below) rely on their brackets to support their full weight. Most manufacturers supply special brackets with wall-mounted sinks. If none are supplied, seek installation advice from your supplier. When attaching a wall-mounted sink to a stud wall, you will need to insert new blocking to provide firm attachment points. You can modify the plumbing to run through the wall at the same time. If you want to hide the supply and drainage pipes of a wall-mounted sink in a solid wall, you will have to chisel out grooves for them to sit in. Run the pipes through protective casings, then finish the wall over the top. This technique is known as "chasing."

INSTALLING A WALL-MOUNTED SINK

Measure the fastener positions on the sink and mark them to the wall. Make sure the two points are level and the supply and waste pipes are centered. Drill pilot holes at the marked off points.

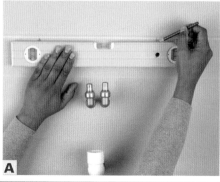

A

B

Screw the brackets provided into the pilot holes. If you are attaching to a masonry wall, insert wall plugs into the pilot holes first.

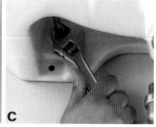

C

Hang the sink on the brackets, then tighten the nuts to hold the sink firmly. Connect the hot and cold water, and the waste pipe.

1 ASSEMBLING THE FAUCET AND STOPPER COMPONENTS

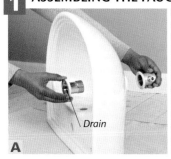

A Balance the sink on its back. Push the top of the drain assembly through the drain hole to meet the bottom section.

Drain

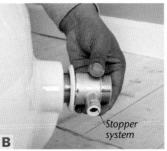

B Hold the top of the drain assembly steady while you screw the bottom on. The pop-up stopper system should point to the back of the sink.

Stopper system

C Insert the washer supplied into the bottom of the faucet (see pp.484–487 for more information on faucets).

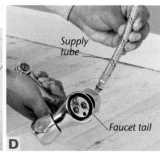

D Screw supply tubes into the faucet tails. You can reuse supply tubes from the old sink.

Supply tube

Faucet tail

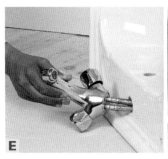

E Insert the faucets, with supply tubes attached, through the hole in the top of the sink.

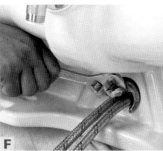

F Slip a washer on before you tighten the retaining nut underneath the sink to hold the faucets in position, but do not over-tighten.

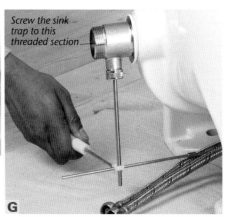

G *Screw the sink trap to this threaded section*

Connect the pop-up stopper system. Insert the rod with the lever attached through the faucet. Screw the other rod into the drain assembly. Connect them using the hardware supplied. See p.485 for more information on pop-up stopper systems. Screw a trap onto the bottom of the drain assembly.

2 POSITIONING THE SINK

A Position the pedestal in front of the supply and waste pipes.

B Place the sink on the pedestal. Adjust the pedestal so that it provides good support and the sink is nestling securely on top of it.

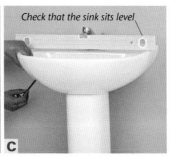

Check that the sink sits level

C Use a level to make the final adjustments, then mark through the sink and pedestal attachment points with a pencil.

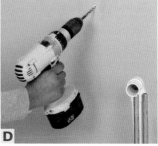

D Drill pilot holes at the points you marked. Make sure you are drilling into studs.

3 SECURING THE SINK IN PLACE

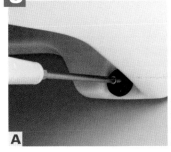

A Reposition the sink. Place rubber washers over the attachment points and then screw the sink into position. Repeat for the pedestal.

B Screw the trap connector nut onto the waste pipe.

C Use slip joint pliers (see p.470) to brace the supply pipes while you tighten the supply tubes onto them with an adjustable wrench.

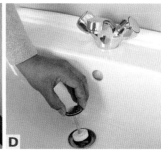

D Position the stopper. Apply bathroom caulk across the back of the sink and around the bottom of the pedestal. Turn the water back on.

REPLACING A BATHTUB

Bathtub dimensions can vary so, before you buy, check the dimensions of a new tub so that it will fit in the same spot as the old one. Another consideration with very large tubs is whether you will be able to maneuver it through your home to the bathroom. Room to work is also important—especially in smaller bathrooms. It will sometimes be necessary to remove the other bathroom fixtures in order to remove an old bathtub and install a new one.

TOOLS AND MATERIALS SEE BASIC TOOLKIT AND P.259

CAST-IRON BATHTUBS

Decorative cast-iron tubs may be candidates for reclamation (see p.87). If not, these heavy items can be broken up using a sledgehammer and all of the material recycled (see p.86). When you do this, drape a drop cloth over the old tub to stop flying debris and be sure to wear protective goggles, ear protectors, and gloves.

When installing a cast-iron tub, ensure that its weight is evenly distributed across several floor joists. Planks of wood underneath the tub feet can help spread the weight. In some cases, you may need to reinforce the joists below.

ANATOMY OF A BATHTUB

Connecting the water supply to a bath is much the same as for a basin (see pp.262–263). The main difference when installing a bath is that it may be large and heavy, and access to the plumbing can be difficult.

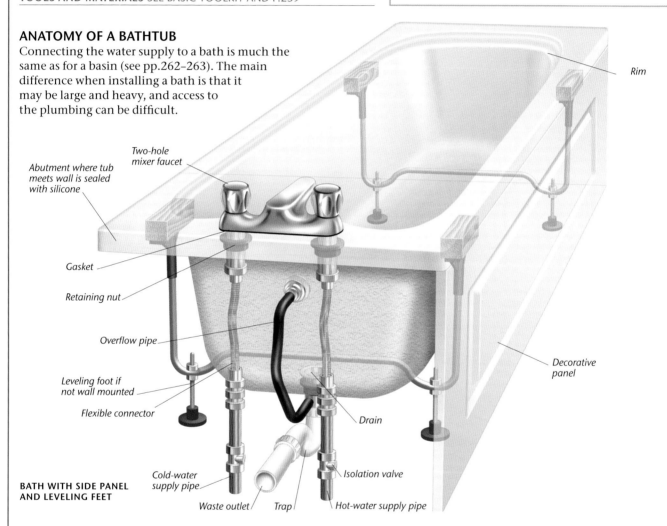

Two-hole mixer faucet

Abutment where tub meets wall is sealed with silicone

Rim

Gasket

Retaining nut

Overflow pipe

Decorative panel

Leveling foot if not wall mounted

Flexible connector

Drain

BATH WITH SIDE PANEL AND LEVELING FEET

Cold-water supply pipe

Isolation valve

Waste outlet   Trap   Hot-water supply pipe

REMOVING A BATHTUB

Before you begin, make sure you have enough room to fit the bathtub through the doorway. Turn off the water supply. After the water has been turned off, open a faucet below the tub level to drain the water supply lines. Remove the faucet, the drain, and the spout. If your bathtub is sandwiched between two walls, with the faucet and shower head located on one wall, you may be able to disconnect the piping and then pull the tub out. If this doesn't work, you may have to remove a section of the wall around the bathtub, cut the piping, and remove the bathtub through the wall. If your bathtub is freestanding, removal is somewhat easier. After disconnecting the piping, you should simply be able to lift the tub out.

INSTALLING A BATHTUB

Before installing a new bathtub, make sure that your selection is an exact fit into the old bathtub space. Make sure it is apron-styled or drop-in, and that the drain is on the same side, because bathtubs can have right-hand or left-hand drains. If the bathtub is not an exact fit, the piping will have to be modified for the new bathtub. If it is an exact fit, you'll follow the same steps for removing the old bathtub, just in reverse. You may need to repair the wall surface so it rests on the flange of the new tub. Always use cement backerboard under tiles in the bathtub or shower areas for moisture protection and to prevent a possible mold problem. Regular drywall is not rated to handle extreme moisture.

1 MEASURING THE POSITION

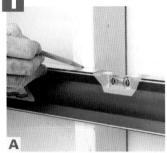

A

Measure and mark the location of the bathtub's ledger.

B

Attach the ledger board, which will support the bathtub's ledger.

2 CONNECTING THE DRAIN

A

While the tub is on its side, dry fit the drain and water supply pipes.

B

Install the rubber gasket on the bathtub overflow tube, and attach it to the tub.

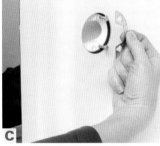

C

Use the fittings provided to attach the stopper retaining bracket.

D

Apply a ring of plumber's putty around the drain flange.

E

Attach the drain to the bathtub, using screws to secure it in place.

F

Use needle pliers to connect the stopper chain mechanism to the stopper fit.

Route the chain from the stopper fit through the bathtub, adjacent to the retaining bracket.

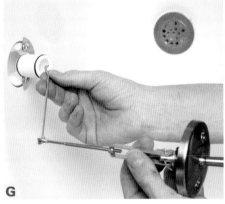

G

H

Secure the stopper fit in place using the fittings provided.

I

Lift the bathtub in place and insert the drain and water pipe assembly into the drain.

3 SECURING THE TUB IN PLACE

A

Nail the flange to the wall studs.

B

Make sure the bathtub is level, then finish the surrounding walls.

ADJUSTING THE STOPPER

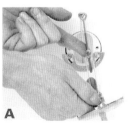

A

With time and use, a bathtub stopper may cease to block the water flow efficiently. Remove the stopper face plate from wall.

B

Expose the mechanism and then adjust the chain to fit.

TYPES OF SHOWERS

There is an enormous selection of shower designs on the market. To add a new shower to your existing suite, one option is to construct a separate stall for one if there is room (see pp.258–259 for bathroom planning). Alternatively, install a shower above the existing bathtub. The type of plumbing system you have will determine the type of shower you can install (see opposite).

CHOOSING SHOWER COMPONENTS

In most cases, a shower stall package comes with most everything you'll need. Separate stalls, trays, and screens are also readily available. Like other bathroom fixtures, white is the most popular color for trays, as well as screen and stall frames.

Shower stalls

These are designed to fit standard sizes and shapes of shower trays. The structure of a shower stall usually relies on tiled areas of the bathroom walls making up one or more of its sides. Use cement board on walls that will be tiled inside a stall. Some manufacturers make all-in-one stalls with a built-in shower. Alternatively, you can create a walk-in shower (see p.268–269).

Shower trays

Acrylic, fiberglass, resin, and ceramic shower trays are available. Solid resin and ceramic trays need to be installed on a bed of mortar. You will need to remove a section of flooring to accommodate the trap under a solid tray. If this is impossible, build the tray up on a base frame or choose an acrylic tray. Acrylic trays usually have legs and side panels (see pp.268–269). They sit higher off the floor than solid trays, which means waste connection is easier, and removing sections of the floor is rarely necessary if it is a simple replacement project. There are many shape variations, and standard sizes start at 32 x 32 in (81 x 81 cm)—make sure you buy one to match the cubicle design you have chosen.

Shower screens and curtains

Screens are used along the edge of a bathtub when a shower is installed above it. Some are single, fixed sheets, whereas others are constructed of a number of folding sections. See pp.268–269 for how to install a shower screen. Alternatively, you can use a shower curtain. These run on straight or curved tracks to fit any shape of bathtub or shower, and styles are available to suit any bathroom.

(see pp.258–259 for bathroom planning)

MAKING A WET WALL

When you are planning your new bathroom, consider saving a wall space of 2 x 6 ft (600 x 1800 mm) for a strategically situated cavity to allow a place for the main drain/vent stack and a cluster of supply and drain-waste-vent lines.

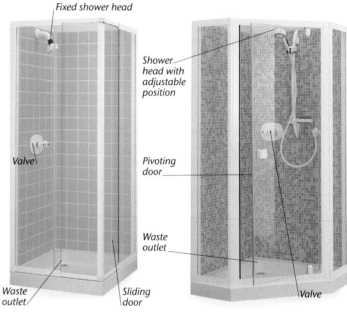

Fixed shower head

Shower head with adjustable position

Valve

Pivoting door

Waste outlet

Waste outlet

Sliding door

Valve

SHOWER STALL—TWO SIDES

SHOWER STALL—THREE SIDES

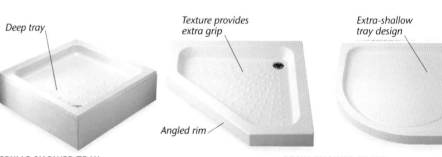

Deep tray

Texture provides extra grip

Extra-shallow tray design

Angled rim

ACRYLIC SHOWER TRAY

RESIN SHOWER TRAYS

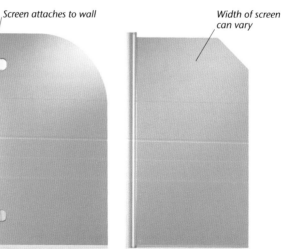

Screen attaches to wall

Width of screen can vary

Folding doors

SHOWER SCREEN WITH CURVED EDGE

SHOWER SCREEN WITH STRAIGHT EDGE

SHOWER SCREEN WITH FOLDING DOORS

CHOOSING THE RIGHT SHOWER

After you've decided between a shower stall and a shower-tub combination, there are still many options to consider.

Shower heads are offered in almost every conceivable shape, size, style, and finish to match all the other bathroom hardware. There are stationary shower head models that attach directly to the wall, as well as hand-held units that can be bought separately.

If the options with off-the-shelf shower heads aren't enough, and you are considering a custom shower, there is a great variety of possibilities. There have also been great advances in the technology behind the shower system, with options ranging from body sprays to steam.

When selecting a new shower system, always compare the plumbing requirements of the systems to the constraints of your home's plumbing. It's important to know the required drain capacity when selecting a new system. Typically, a bigger custom shower requires more hot water. And, while most shower heads are wall-mounted, some are so large and heavy they must be mounted on the ceiling.

Hand-held showers

Fully adjustable hand-held showers are very popular. If your local building code has an anti-siphon ordinance, you may need to have a vacuum breaker on the hand-held shower to prevent backflow and contamination of potable water.

Body Sprays

If you have two or more body sprays in your shower, you'll need a pressure balancing loop. This ensures that each outlet delivers the same spray volume and temperature.

Low-flow shower heads

After you install your new shower head, don't tamper with the flow restrictor. The flow restrictor limits the water flow to 2.5 gallons (9.4 liters) per minute – about half the regular volume. Removing the flow restrictor will increase your water and energy consumption. If you've noticed that your shower's pressure has decreased, clean the shower head.

UNIVERSAL DESIGNS FOR SHOWER ENCLOSURES

After you have selected the type and finish of your new shower and hardware, it is important to layout the shower enclosure so that it fits the rest of your bathroom design, and suits the needs of everyone who might use it.

Shower entrance

Install a shower system that has at least a 3-ft (1-m) wide opening. Make sure there is a very low or curbless entrance into the shower.

Shower tray

Slip resistance material is fairly standard, but extremely important for a universal design shower.

Fold-down seat

If you have the room, seats make a shower easier to use.

Shower valve height

The standard height for a shower valve is 4 ft (1.2 m) off of the tray height. If you are trying to create a more accessible shower, you may want to install the valves lower so they are at a more comfortable reach.

Bracket fixed to wall of shower stall

Shower head

Slide bar

Shower hose

Shower rose

FIXED SHOWER HEAD

Hanging bracket

FULLY ADJUSTABLE SHOWER

MIXER VALVE

Spray direction can be adjusted

DIRECTIONAL SHOWER HEAD   **FIXED SHOWER HEAD**

Shower head height

Depending on the height of the people using the shower, you may want to install the shower head at the standard 6 ft (1.8 m) or opt for a different height. An extendable or hand-held shower head is a good idea for universal design.

Lighting

Motion sensor lighting makes the shower easier to use, and limits the amount of reaching or the need to move light switches from standard heights.

Accessories

If you can, install towel hooks, shelves, lights, and an intercom at an accessible height. Lever doors are usually the easiest to open by everyone.

INSTALLING A SHOWER STALL

Unless a shower is used in a wet-room design, an enclosure is needed to prevent the surrounding area from getting wet. In most cases this takes the form of a shower tray and a stall. Screens or shower curtains are used when a shower is above a bathtub. A third option is to create a large, walk-in shower using screens, or tiled or glass-block walls.

TOOLS AND MATERIALS SEE BASIC TOOLKIT AND P.259

WALK-IN SHOWERS

This type of shower stall is an option in large bathrooms. A "drying area" separates the entrance and the shower, making a door or curtain unnecessary. A walk-in shower can be installed in much the same way as a standard tray and stall. Alternatively, you can build one yourself. Stud walls are the easiest option (see pp.102–107). Use water-resistant wallboard rather than drywall for the interior walls. This provides a good surface for tiling (see pp.312–315) and gives a fully waterproof finish. Alternatively, build a glass-block wall (pp.108–109).

ANATOMY OF A SHOWER

Plumbing requirements vary depending on the type of shower you choose (see pp.266–267). A shower stall with an acrylic tray is shown here.

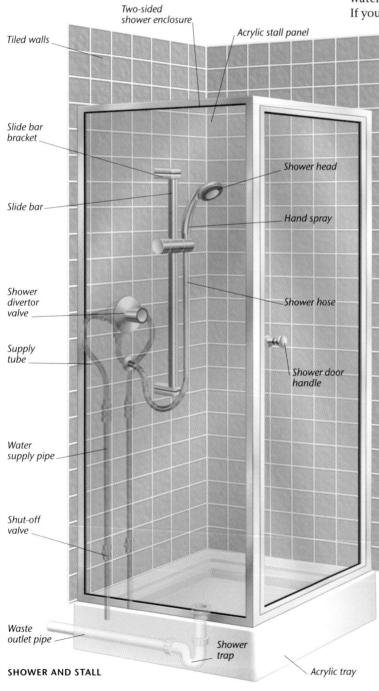

Two-sided shower enclosure

Tiled walls

Acrylic stall panel

Slide bar bracket

Shower head

Slide bar

Hand spray

Shower divertor valve

Shower hose

Supply tube

Shower door handle

Water supply pipe

Shut-off valve

Waste outlet pipe

Shower trap

SHOWER AND STALL

Acrylic tray

INSTALLING A SHOWER

Plumbing requirements differ depending on the shower type—clear instructions should be supplied with your shower. As a general rule, you will want to route ½-in water supply pipes using as few elbows as possible. If you have a masonry wall, the pipes need to be hidden in the wall in protective sheaths. Because walls inside the shower will be tiled and waterproofed, where possible provide emergency access to the shower shut-off valves from the other side of the wall behind the shower. Alternatively, put the valves somewhere more accessible farther down the pipe route, but make sure you label them carefully. Waste pipes will also need to be installed with a P-trap and zinc drain pipes (see pp.476–477 for more on routing pipes). You will need a rubber gasket around the drain to seal the connection.

INSTALLING A SHOWER SCREEN

A screen is required if you are installing a shower over a bathtub. They are attached to the wall at the shower end of the bathtub. It is essential that the rim of the tub is flat to create a watertight seal. If your tub has a curved rim, then shower curtains are a better option.

INSTALLING A SHOWER TRAY AND STALL

Basic instructions for installing a tray and stall are given here, but you should always follow any specific guidelines given by the manufacturer or requirements directed by local code officials. Put the tray in place before you begin to tile the walls or lay any flooring. Choose a position for the shower that will allow you to secure the stall into a wooden stud or a solid wall. There are two main types of trays, each installed by a different technique (see opposite). Once you have installed the tray, the next step is to tile the walls within the shower stall (see pp.312–325). The bottom row of tiles should overlap the top of the tray rim. After tiling, add the stall as you would install a screen (see opposite). Then seal the joints between the stall, tray, walls, and floor with bathroom caulk. Add the shower valve, and connect the supply and waste pipes as required.

INSTALLING A SOLID RESIN OR CERAMIC SHOWER TRAY

A

Place the tray with its drain outlet in a good position to connect to the waste pipes. Mark the position of the drain and the tray on the floor.

B

Remove a section of the floor in the position you marked using a jigsaw. The hole must be big enough to house the trap.

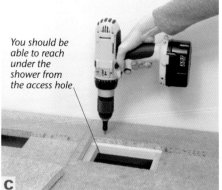

You should be able to reach under the shower from the access hole

C

Remove a second section of flooring next to the first, but outside the tray area. The drainage pipe for this type of tray runs under the floor, so you need to provide access to make the connection with the trap. To create a permanent access hatch, screw furring strips around the edge of the hole to support the section of flooring you have removed.

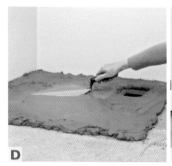

D

Carefully spread a thin bed of mortar over the marked-off area for the tray to sit on.

Clean the edges when tray is level

E

Screw the trap to the drain as for a sink (see p.263). Place the tray on the mortar bed and check if it is level. Adjust the mortar if needed.

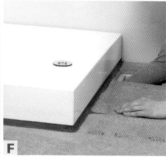

F

Allow the mortar to set for at least 24 hours. Connect the shower trap with the waste pipe, using the access hatch you made in the floor.

G

Use a dispenser to apply a continuous bead of bathroom caulk around the edge of the tray.

INSTALLING AN ACRYLIC SHOWER TRAY AND STALL

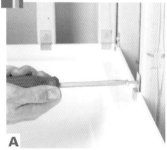

A

Set the shower tray in place and check it is level, then using the fasteners provided, attach the tray to the wall studs.

B

Seal the gaps around the joint between the tray and the wall with a bead of caulk.

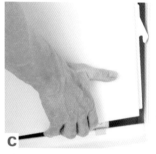

C

Clip together the side panels of the shower according to the manufacturer's instructions.

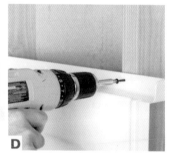

D

Attach the panels to the studs with screws. Be sure to check that the shower is level and all connections are tight.

INSTALLING A SHOWER OR BATH SCREEN

Hold the channel sections vertically

A

Mark the attachment points of the channel. Drill pilot holes though the tiles and insert plugs (see also p.255). Screw the channel in place.

B

Carefully slide the panels into their channels. Make sure they are vertical, and resting on the rim of the shower tray or tub to provide a seal.

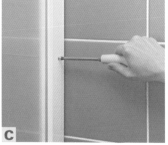

C

Screw the hardware provided into the side of the channel to secure the screens in position.

D

Use a dispenser to apply a bead of bathroom caulk down the outside edge of the channel. Don't apply caulk on the inside edge.

UNBLOCKING TRAPS

One of the most common areas where blockages occur is in traps. A basin trap is shown here. Snakes can unclog many types of traps, but sinks usually need to be dismantled in order for the blockage to be removed.

TOOLS AND MATERIALS
Bowl, bucket, old toothbrush, replacement washers

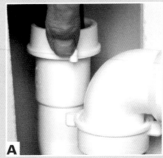

A **Undo the sink trap.** Position a bowl beneath it to catch any water.

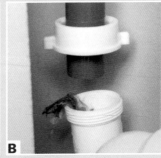

B **Remove debris** and wash the trap in a bucket of clean water. An old toothbrush is an ideal cleaning tool.

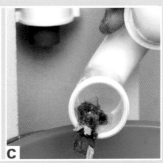

C **Replace the trap.** It is worth replacing worn washers while the trap is disassembled to prevent future leaks.

UNBLOCKING THE SINK DRAIN

Clogs in bathroom sinks are fairly common, and they usually occur near the pop-up assembly of the drain.

TOOLS AND MATERIALS
Drain plug adjustment arm

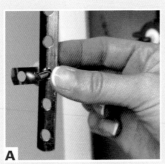

A **Remove the spring tab** from the drain plug adjustment arm.

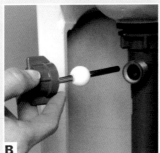

B **Remove the ball valve** from the sink trap.

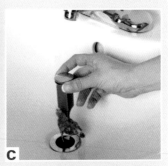

C **Remove the pop-up plug** and then remove the debris clogging the sink.

UNBLOCKING TOILETS

If flush water rises to the rim and then drains slowly, the toilet trap or drain is blocked. To unblock these, use a plunger first, then a snake—the latter burrows into the blockage and loosens it up.

TOOLS AND MATERIALS
Snake

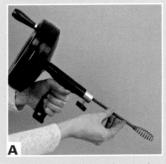

A **Pull a section of the snake** out of the drum.

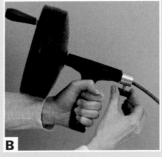

B **Tighten the retaining** nut on top of the snake body.

C **Rotate the drum** of the snake so it burrows into the waste system to dislodge the blockage.

ADJUSTING A LOOSE TOILET SEAT

Toilet lids can be poorly adjusted and may not stay in an upright position. There is usually no need to purchase a new seat and lid; you can simply adjust the lid so that it leans back against the wall or tank.

TOOLS AND MATERIALS
Screwdriver

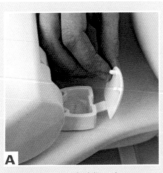

A **Locate the nuts** holding the seat and lid to the pan.

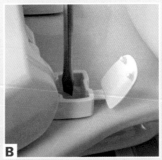

B **Unscrew the nuts** and slide their rubber washers to adjust the opening angle of the lid.

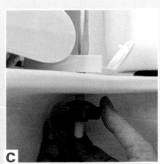

C **Tighten the nuts** and check that the seat and lid now open to the desired angle.

REPLACING A TOILET SEAT

Toilet seats can become worn over time and require a replacement. A new toilet seat is also an inexpensive way to update a toilet.

TOOLS AND MATERIALS
Screwdriver

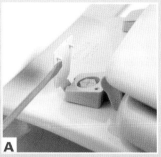

A Lift up the lids that house the nuts holding the seat assembly in place.

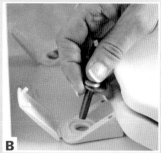

B Remove the bolt from each position and lift the toilet seat.

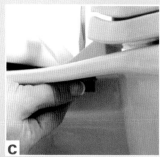

C Secure the new toilet seat in place with bolts, and close the lid.

REPAIRING CHIPPED CERAMIC FIXTURES

Kits are available to repair minor damage to ceramic bathroom fixtures. Instructions for use may vary slightly between different manufacturers, but the example shown here displays the common principles. Some filling compounds can also be used to glue chipped sections back together.

A Dust out the damaged area and ensure that it is completely clean and dry.

B Mix the two-part filler in the ratio specified by the manufacturer.

C Fill the chipped area, leaving it slightly proud of the surrounding area because the filler shrinks as it dries. Repeat if necessary.

D Sand the filled area until it is smooth. Shape it to match the fixture.

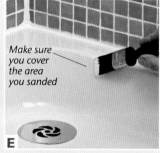

Make sure you cover the area you sanded

E Use the paint supplied to cover the repair. Any excess may normally be removed with acetone.

F The finished patch should be invisible.

TOOLS AND MATERIALS
Ceramic filler, filling knife, mixing spatula, sandpaper, ceramic paint, paintbrush, acetone

WEAK SHOWER

Reduced shower flow is usually due to limescale buildup. This can easily be removed with a descaling product.

TOOLS AND MATERIALS
Screwdriver, bowl, descaling solution

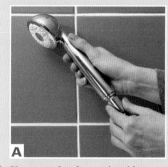

A Unscrew the shower head from the hose.

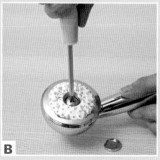

B Unscrew the spray plate and immerse it in descaling solution.

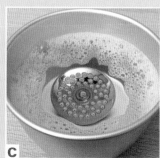

C Leave it in the solution for specified length of time. Flush any remaining scale from the pipes before replacing the shower head.

DECORATING AND FINISHING

HOME DECORATION

Architecture and design provide the framework for the look of your home, but the decoration provides the finish. Options for finishing depend very much on surface type and your personal preferences. The variety of decorative options has expanded greatly in recent years. Many aspects of the home that were once considered purely functional can today offer scope for decoration and expression of personal taste and style. This section considers many of these options, as well as the all-important preparatory steps in any decoration project, which are required in order to achieve the best finish possible.

DECORATION OPTIONS

The opportunity for decoration extends into almost every aspect of the house, including many you might not immediately think of. A huge range of products and techniques are available to enhance the decorative aspects of both interior and exterior walls, floors and ceilings, and fixtures. Lighting can also play an important part in a decorative scheme, and everything from staircases to gutters can be designed or treated to personalize the look of your home. Decorative projects may be large or small, ranging from minor enhancements of an existing scheme to full-scale renovation of a room or even an entire house. Whatever the scale of the job, however, advance planning is key. Work out what you intend to achieve, consider the problems you may encounter, and make sure you have all the equipment you need before beginning work.

DESIGN STYLE

The appearance of your home is, of course, a matter of personal taste, but there are some general issues that are always worth bearing in mind. Consider the age and style of the house's exterior, the shape and size of the rooms, the design of any fixtures such as kitchen cabinets or a bathroom suite and other aspects that you either cannot change, or do not plan to. Bear in mind the amount of natural and artificial light available, and remember that dark colors will tend to make a room seem smaller, while light colors can make it look larger. If you plan to use two or more strong colors in the same room, consider carefully whether they go together. In a historic home, you may want a decorative scheme appropriate for its age, perhaps with brass fixtures and hardware. Or, if appropriate, you may want a bold modern approach with stone and stainless steel.

Carpets
Comfortable and warm underfoot, carpet is ideal for most rooms apart from kitchens and bathrooms. In a bathroom, some people like the feel of carpet, but in practice it can become damp and therefore rot if the appropriate ventilation is not present. Good-quality underlayment increases durability, adds soundproofing, and provides extra comfort.

Vinyl floors
Whether in tiles or sheet form, vinyl is ideal for "wet" areas in the home like bathrooms and kitchens. It is waterproof and easy to clean. Linoleum is a more "natural" alternative to vinyl that achieves a similar finish.

Bathroom and kitchen walls
Wall tiles are commonly used in kitchens and bathrooms to provide durable, easily cleaned decorative surfaces. Wallpaper used in these rooms should be of a vinyl variety. Paints that contain vinyl are also ideal as they provide a good wipe-clean surface. Some manufacturers will also provide paint that is recommended for bathroom and kitchen use.

Tiled floors
Ceramic floor tiles are commonly found in kitchens and bathrooms, and offer a very hard-wearing, easily cleaned flooring option.

Doors (exterior)
The treatment for exterior door surfaces is much the same as for windows. Making sure that the top edge and the underside of the door are painted or treated will increase the life expectancy of the door considerably.

Stucco
Painted stucco will last for up to 10 years before it requires recoating. Only exterior emulsion or masonry paint should be used. Other masonry surfaces, such as brick or stone, can be painted, but these are more often left with their natural finish, since paint will take to some types of brick or stone better than others.

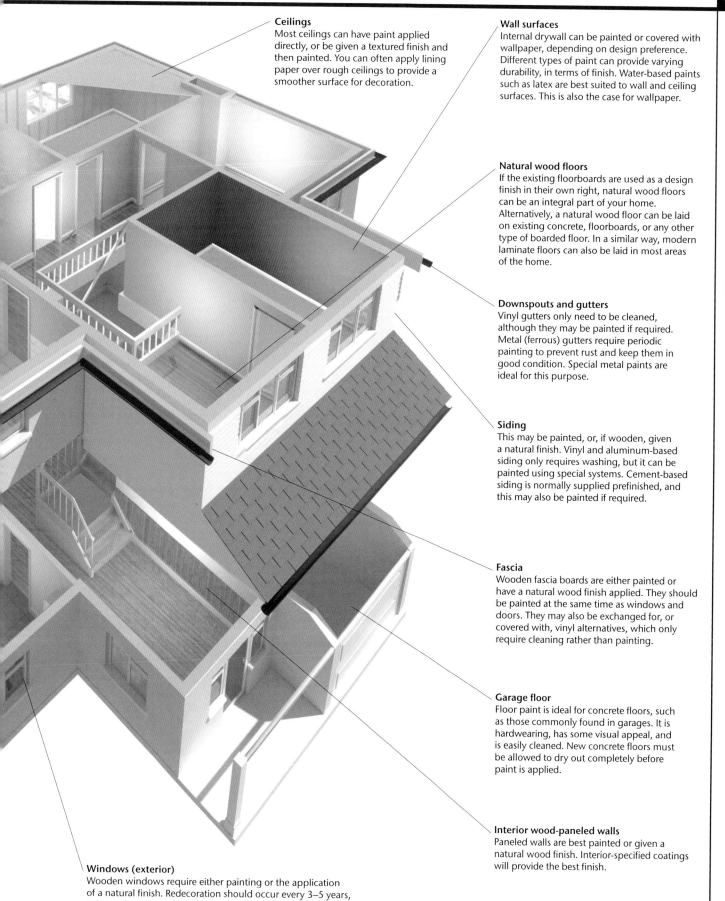

Ceilings
Most ceilings can have paint applied directly, or be given a textured finish and then painted. You can often apply lining paper over rough ceilings to provide a smoother surface for decoration.

Wall surfaces
Internal drywall can be painted or covered with wallpaper, depending on design preference. Different types of paint can provide varying durability, in terms of finish. Water-based paints such as latex are best suited to wall and ceiling surfaces. This is also the case for wallpaper.

Natural wood floors
If the existing floorboards are used as a design finish in their own right, natural wood floors can be an integral part of your home. Alternatively, a natural wood floor can be laid on existing concrete, floorboards, or any other type of boarded floor. In a similar way, modern laminate floors can also be laid in most areas of the home.

Downspouts and gutters
Vinyl gutters only need to be cleaned, although they may be painted if required. Metal (ferrous) gutters require periodic painting to prevent rust and keep them in good condition. Special metal paints are ideal for this purpose.

Siding
This may be painted, or, if wooden, given a natural finish. Vinyl and aluminum-based siding only requires washing, but it can be painted using special systems. Cement-based siding is normally supplied prefinished, and this may also be painted if required.

Fascia
Wooden fascia boards are either painted or have a natural wood finish applied. They should be painted at the same time as windows and doors. They may also be exchanged for, or covered with, vinyl alternatives, which only require cleaning rather than painting.

Garage floor
Floor paint is ideal for concrete floors, such as those commonly found in garages. It is hardwearing, has some visual appeal, and is easily cleaned. New concrete floors must be allowed to dry out completely before paint is applied.

Interior wood-paneled walls
Paneled walls are best painted or given a natural wood finish. Interior-specified coatings will provide the best finish.

Windows (exterior)
Wooden windows require either painting or the application of a natural finish. Redecoration should occur every 3–5 years, using only coatings recommended for exterior woodwork. Vinyl, aluminum, and wood composite windows are best treated by regular washing.

Preparing surfaces

TO ACHIEVE THE BEST POSSIBLE FINISH, ALL SURFACES MUST BE ADEQUATELY PREPARED BEFORE THEY ARE DECORATED. THIS SECTION SHOWS YOU HOW TO GET THE BEST RESULTS ON LARGE AREAS SUCH AS WALLS AND CEILINGS, AS WELL AS TECHNIQUES FOR TREATING WOODEN SURFACES SUCH AS DOORS AND SMALLER AREAS OF EXPOSED DECORATIVE WOODWORK.

CEILINGS, WALLS, AND WOODWORK

Previously painted walls, in good condition, need little preparation—usually only minor filling and sanding—before redecoration. If a wall is papered, remove the paper and make sure the surface is smooth. On a wooden surface, good preparation is the basis for a professional finish. See pp.278–279 for preparing wooden elements or features.

TOOLS AND MATERIALS

Sandpaper
Paper with a rough face that smoothes surfaces. Grades vary from the fine to the very rough.

Shave hook
Strips paint from a wooden surface, whether flat or ornate.

Wire brush
Used to remove debris and clean off flaky surfaces, such as a metal pipe.

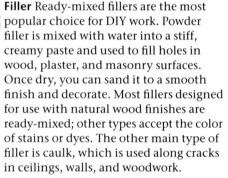

Sanding block
Easy to grip, with a sanding surface on one or more sides. You can make your own by folding sandpaper around a squared-off block of wood.

Heat gun
Blisters paint and makes it easy to remove from a wooden surface. Must be used with caution.

Wallpaper scorer
Perforates paper to let steam or water through. Essential for removing vinyl (waterproof) papers.

Steam wallpaper stripper
Electrically operated. Steam flows from a hot-water reservoir to a stripping pad and bubbles the paper, easing its removal.

Steel wool
Cleans down metal surfaces and is used to apply wax. Comes in various grades of coarseness.

Place pad against wall to steam paper

Filler Ready-mixed fillers are the most popular choice for DIY work. Powder filler is mixed with water into a stiff, creamy paste and used to fill holes in wood, plaster, and masonry surfaces. Once dry, you can sand it to a smooth finish and decorate. Most fillers designed for use with natural wood finishes are ready-mixed; other types accept the color of stains or dyes. The other main type of filler is caulk, which is used along cracks in ceilings, walls, and woodwork.

White-tinted shellac Applied to knots in wood before primer or further coats of paint, to prevent sap from weeping from the knot.

TSP Powdered soap mixed with water and used to clean down surfaces before they are rinsed. Allow surfaces to dry before decoration.

Spray-on stain block Blocks out stains that show through normal coats of paint. Can also be bought as a "paint" in cans. May be water-based or solvent-based; water-based versions dry faster.

Mineral spirits Solvent used for most oil-based paints.

Brush cleaner Restores brushes.

Hand cleaner For easy removal of paint, grime, and grease.

TOOLS AND MATERIALS CHECKLIST

Stripping wallpaper
Drop cloths, steam stripper, warm water, garbage bags

Washing down and filling
TSP, hot water, sponge, oil-based undercoat (optional), brush, spackle, 2-in (50-mm) knife, sandpaper

Filling cracks
Caulk, caulk gun, sponge, brush, oil-based undercoat*

* = optional

FOR BASIC TOOLKIT
SEE PP.24–25

STRIPPING WALLPAPER

Steam strippers work most efficiently when top layers of paper have been removed, exposing the more absorbent backing paper. The impermeable surface layer of vinyl papers often peels dry, relatively easily. Always follow the manufacturer's guidelines. Wear protective gloves, if the tool's manual recommends them, and goggles. Steam and drips may burn, so take all possible precautions to protect yourself. Never use a steam stripper to remove paper from a ceiling. Instead, simply soak the paper with warm water and then scrape the paper off the ceiling surface, an option that can also be used on a wall if you prefer.

A

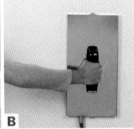

B

Lay drop cloths over the room, and remove as much loose paper from the wall by hand as you can.

Fill the stripper with warm water before plugging it in. When it starts to steam, place it flush on the wall.

C

Hold the pad completely flush on the wall surface. After 15–30 seconds, move it along and scrape paper off the wall in the steamed area. The thicker the layer(s) of paper, the longer you will need to hold the pad in place. But do not hold it still for too long or the wall surface itself may crumble.

D

E

Work your way across the wall, steaming areas and removing paper.

Continue removing paper. Put it in a garbage bag as you remove it, so that it does not stick to the drop cloth or other surfaces.

WASHING DOWN A WALL AND FILLING HOLES

After a wall has been stripped, wash the surface thoroughly to remove all traces of adhesive. Use soapy hot water to sponge the wall. Then rinse with clean water. You can now repaper the wall. If you wish to paint the wall, apply an oil-based undercoat before a water-based latex paint. However well the wall has been cleaned, traces of adhesive may bleed through a water-based paint; oil-based undercoat prevents this. It is needed on a previously painted wall only if the wall is in poor condition.

Deeper holes may need filling twice because spackle contracts as it dries

A

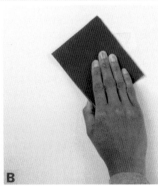

B

Clean out the hole with a dry brush. Apply filler by pressing it in place with a 2-in (50-mm) knife.

Once the spackle has dried, sand it back to create a smooth surface flush with the surrounding area.

FILLING CRACKS

Cracks are best filled using caulk. It is supplied in a tube and is applied along cracks or joints with a caulk gun. It cannot be sanded, and must therefore be smoothed by hand before it dries. Some caulks may be overpainted when dry. Choose a latex caulk if you think you may paint. Others need an oil-based undercoat to prepare them for water-based paints, which may crack if there is no undercoat. A ceiling–wall junction is shown here.

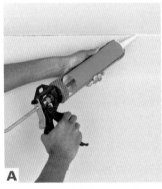

A

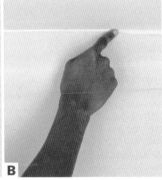

B

Clean out the joint. Prepare the sealant and gun as shown on p.81. Apply even pressure to the trigger, moving the gun along the joint.

Gently smooth the sealant with a wet finger. You may also use a damp sponge to smooth the caulk.

NEW WALL AND CEILING SURFACES

Plaster in a good condition can be directly overpainted with full-strength paint. Alternatively, first apply a mist coat of diluted latex paint (1 part water to 10 parts paint), which provides a base for further coats. Drywall ceilings must be coated with a special sealer before paint is applied, otherwise paint may dry differently on the board than on the jointing compound.

WORKING WITH WOOD

Woodwork provides the finer detailing in a home and its finish is a stamp of quality. To produce good results you must prepare surfaces, including doors, windows, and decorative woodwork for moldings or paneling.

Stripping wood

A good finish is often achievable by recoating the existing surface. However, you may need to strip woodwork before redecorating—the existing coating may be so bad that it cannot be successfully recoated; it may be painted, but you want a natural wood finish; or it could have a natural finish but you want to paint it or apply a different finish. Beware of surfaces with lead-based paint, which is toxic and now found only in older properties. It is a health risk if heated with a heat gun, and fine particles created by sanding are also toxic. Paint-testing kits are available to identify lead-based paintwork.

TOOLS AND MATERIALS CHECKLIST

Using a heat gun
Shave hook

Solution stripping
Old paintbrush, scraper or shave hook, cloth, mineral spirit or water

Paste stripping
Filling knife or small trowel, stripper, covering cloth, cleaning cloth, neutralizing solution/white vinegar, water

Covering old paint
Oil-based eggshell paint, paintbrush, brush-cleaning

solution, mid-oak wood stain, varnish, oil, or shellac, two cloths

Priming and filling before painting
Knotting solution, paintbrush, filling knife, sanding block, filler, primer

Filling for a natural wood finish
Filling knife, filler, sanding block

FOR BASIC TOOLKIT
SEE PP.24–25

USING A HEAT GUN

A

Turn the heat gun on and direct the nozzle at the wood surface, leaving a gap of a few inches between the two.

B

After a few moments, the paint will begin to soften and bubble, at which point use a shave hook or scraper to lift the old paint free.

C

Move the gun along to the next area and repeat the process. Use a shave hook to remove paintwork in recesses, such as on paneling.

WORKING SAFELY

■ Take great care using a heat gun. Wear goggles and a respiratory mask, and perhaps gloves. Take any other precautions that are advised by the tool's manufacturer.
■ Do not hold the gun for too long over the wood, to avoid the risk of scorching it or even setting it on fire.

SOLUTION STRIPPING

Wearing gloves, a mask, and goggles, use an old paintbrush to apply the stripper. Use dabbing strokes to build up a good layer of the stripper on the wood's surface. Allow it to soak in and react with the paint. This may take only a couple of minutes or up to half an hour.

A

B

Once the paint has bubbled up, scrape it off using a scraper and/or a shave hook.

C

Thoroughly clean the surface afterwards. Mineral spirit and cold water are usually best, but check the stripper manufacturer's guidelines.

PASTE STRIPPING

Wear gloves, a mask, and goggles

A

Apply the stripper with a filling knife or small trowel to a depth of about ⅛ in (2.5 mm)—or deeper if there are many coats of paint.

B

If your manufacturer specifies it, cover the entire surface with a special cloth. Leave for 24 hours. Use a scraper to peel away the paste.

C

Thoroughly clean down the area. If the manufacturer suggests it, use a "neutralizing solution"; or use white vinegar and then clean water.

DIPPING DOORS

Removable items such as doors can be "dipped" professionally. The whole item is submerged in a tank of powerful chemicals, which lift all traces of paint from the wood surface. Many companies offer a pickup and delivery service.

▐▌ COVERING OLD PAINT

Sometimes a natural wood finish may not be possible—if the wood is too rough, or the paint too ingrained to strip. Old beams may have stained finishes or may have been painted at some stage. You can have the paint sand-blasted away by a professional company but this is expensive, and extremely messy. An alternative is to apply the paint effect shown here.

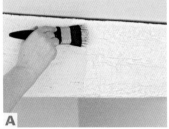

A

Completely paint the beam, using an oil-based white eggshell.

B

Apply a wood stain over the top of the eggshell. A mid-oak color is very effective.

C

Rub varnish, oil, or shellac across the whole surface to provide the effect of an oak beam.

D

After half an hour, buff off the varnish, oil, or shellac with a clean cloth. Some will remain embedded within the wood grain, resulting in the appearance of a natural wood beam.

PREPARING BEAMS

Natural wood beams are often tricky items to prepare for decoration, because of flaky surfaces and often very crumbly edges where the beam meets plaster. Trying to fill the edge is difficult and often ineffective, as the filler too crumbles and falls away.

One way to secure the edge is to apply a clear matt varnish to the beam, overlapping slightly onto wall or ceiling surfaces. The varnish both binds the surface and provides a natural look. The wall or ceiling paint may then be cut in along the edge to create a neat finish.

FILLING AND SANDING WOOD

Wooden surfaces are seldom completely smooth. Filling dents and sanding improves the finish. The type of filler to be used depends on whether the wood is to be painted or a natural finish applied. If it is to be painted, use powder filler (see pp.276–277)—flexible filler can be used in joints or cracks. If a natural wood finish is to be applied, use a "stainable" filler the same color as the finish. See pp.286–289 for choosing a suitable primer.

▐▌ PRIMING AND FILLING BEFORE PAINTING

Prime bare wood before using filler, to make it adhere better. Primer also makes it easier to see areas that require filling. If wood is painted, use primer only if there are large, bare patches—for instance, on external woodwork. Any knots in bare wood must first be coated with knotting solution.

A

B

Allow primer to dry. Mix up filler, and apply to holes, dents, or divots, using the flexibility of a filling knife blade to press in the filler.

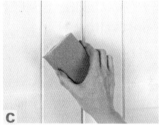

C

Allow filler to dry. Sand to a smooth finish. Deep holes may require refilling and sanding to provide the best finish.

▐▌ FILLING FOR A NATURAL WOOD FINISH

A

B

Apply colored putty to holes in the wood surface with a putty knife. The putty color should match the natural wood finish to be applied.

Once the putty has dried, sand it smooth. Then apply coats of your chosen finish.

FURTHER INFORMATION

Sanding
Sandpaper should be chosen according to the condition of the surface. So, for rough surfaces, begin by using a rough paper. As the surface becomes smoother, reduce the coarseness of the paper

Remember that sanding produces dust. This should always be brushed away before a coating is applied.

A vacuum cleaner nozzle is ideal for removing dust from baseboards or the profiles of moldings.

The best finishes are normally achieved when the wood has been wiped down with a damp cloth before coating, removing the finest residues. This is essential when sanding flat surfaces such as window sills.

Painting and finishing

PAINT AND NATURAL WOOD FINISHES ARE AN EFFECTIVE WAY TO PROTECT AND DECORATE SURFACES. THE FOLLOWING PAGES SHOW YOU HOW TO CHOOSE A PRODUCT, USE THE RIGHT TOOLS, AND PICK THE BEST APPLICATION TECHNIQUE. PLAN IN WHAT ORDER YOU ARE GOING TO TACKLE A PAINTING PROJECT BEFORE YOU BEGIN, AND PREPARE THE SURFACES BEFOREHAND AS SHOWN ON PAGES 276–279.

PAINT TYPES

Most paints fall into one of the general categories of eggshell, semi-gloss, flat, or gloss (see below). You may also need to apply primer or first coat, depending on the surface being painted. These basic paints will answer most of your needs but it is worth looking for formulas that will perform better in specific situations (see box opposite). Always apply paint as recommended by the manufacturer.

BASE COATS

For a decorative finish coat to last and look as good as possible, the right base coats are essential. For interiors, a combined primer-first coat is a good option.

Primer

Used on new, uncoated surfaces, primer protects the material beneath and provides a good base for further coats. Most paints can be sprayed with the right sprayer. Oil-based and water-based primers are available. Traditionalists prefer to use oil-based primer before oil-based paints, especially on exterior woodwork. Plaster and masonry are usually primed with a coat of latex paint diluted with 10 percent water, known as a "mist coat," although a stabilizing primer or solution may be needed if the surface is very flaky or powdery. Special primers for other surfaces such as tiles or melamine are also available, and can be overpainted with normal paints.

First coat

A specially formulated paint used to build up opacity beneath finish coats, one or two coats of first coat paint are usually required before the decorative finish coat is

---

WATER-BASED AND SOLVENT-BASED PAINTS

Paints are made up of pigment and a binder. Water-based (latex or acrylic) paints use water for a binder, solvent-based paints use mineral spirit, and some specialty paints use thinner. Natural wood finishes are also water- or oil-based. If you are using a mineral spirit- or thinner-based product (also sold as solvent-based) plan how you will dispose of excess paint. There are regulations.

More natural or eco-friendly alternatives to oil are available, and include alkyds. They are made of renewable materials such as plant oils, contain fewer preservatives, and their manufacture is less polluting. See pp.300–301 for more on greener paint options.

RECOMMENDED APPLICATION METHODS

Although latex- and oil-based paints can be applied with rollers or pads as well as brushes, cleaning them after using oil paints is difficult and will require lots of white spirit or thinner.

Paint type	Brush	Roller	Pad	Sprayer
Primer	✓	✓	✓	
First coat	✓	✓	✓	
Flat	✓	✓	✓	✓
Eggshell	✓	✓	✓	
Gloss	✓			
Floor paint (on wood)	✓			
Floor paint (on concrete)	✓	✓		
Metal paint	✓			

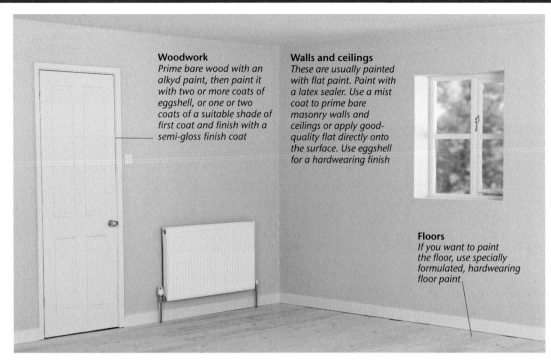

Woodwork
Prime bare wood with an alkyd paint, then paint it with two or more coats of eggshell, or one or two coats of a suitable shade of first coat and finish with a semi-gloss finish coat

Walls and ceilings
These are usually painted with flat paint. Paint with a latex sealer. Use a mist coat to prime bare masonry walls and ceilings or apply good-quality flat directly onto the surface. Use eggshell for a hardwearing finish

Painting a room
New surfaces such as drywall or tongue-and-groove woodwork need an appropriate primer coat before first coats or finish coats are applied. When decorating previously painted surfaces, you will still need to apply first coats as well as finish coats. For information on applying natural wood finishes, see pp.294–295.

Floors
If you want to paint the floor, use specially formulated, hardwearing floor paint

applied. Use pale first coat beneath pale finish coats and a dark first coat beneath dark finish coats. Although most oil-based first coat is suitable for interior or exterior use, exterior first coats are available that will last longer when exposed to the elements. Water-based paints are usually applied in as many coats as are required to provide an even coverage.

FINISH COATS

Once you have applied the base coats, or washed down previously painted surfaces and rinsed them thoroughly (see pp.276–277), you are ready to apply the decorative finish.

Flat

A latex-based, versatile paint type, flat is normally used for walls and ceilings. Many types of finish are available—dead-flat matt, matt, a water-based eggshell (see also below), and silk. Some formulations contain vinyl to make them more hardwearing. Flat is also best used on siding materials. It can help the material cope with moisture. Exterior flat is available with a smooth or rough texture. Apply all flat using as many coats as are necessary for even coverage. For use in a sprayer, dilute flat with 10 percent water.

Eggshell

More durable than flat, eggshell has a slight sheen. Always check the exact finish because the degree of sheen varies between manufacturers. It is most commonly used on interior wood surfaces as an alternative to semi-gloss, although some manufacturers will specify that the paint may be used on exterior surfaces. Eggshell can also be used on wall surfaces where a hardwearing finish is required as it is easier to clean. Two coats will usually give an even color; use primer and first coat as required.

Gloss and satin

A very hardwearing finishing paint, gloss is used mainly on wooden and metal surfaces. Satin is used in the same way as gloss but is slightly less shiny and is increasingly popular, especially for interior woodwork. Both solvent-based and latex-based versions of gloss and satin paints are available. Latex-based paints are easier to apply and less prone to "yellowing" with age, but do not provide as high a shine or hardwearing a finish as solvent-based paints. Almost all gloss and satin paints are suitable for interior or exterior use. Some glosses are formulated especially for exposed exterior surfaces. Gloss is generally applied as a single coat over one or two coats of primer.

SPECIALTY PAINTS

Good-quality paints will perform well in all domestic situations as long as they are used with the right primer and applied on the surface they were designed for. However, sometimes it can be worth using paint formulated for a specific task.

Bathroom or kitchen paints
These flats resist fungal growth and moisture better than standard formulations, although if you have condensation you should consider improving ventilation, see pp.368–369.

Floor paint
Used on concrete and floorboards, floor paints are typically solvent-based and very hardwearing. Gloss or sheen finishes are available. New concrete floors should be left to cure completely before painting; check their progress with a moisture meter.

Metal paint
High-gloss, smooth, and textured (often hammered) metal paints are available. They can be used internally or externally; some types can be applied straight over rust. Thinner is generally required to clean brushes, rather than mineral spirit.

Traditional paints
Products such as distemper and limewash, as well as ranges of traditional colors, can now be purchased relatively easily.

Green paint, sometimes termed eco-paint or natural paint, is becoming a popular option for home decorating. The reason for choosing these paints over conventional ones is directly related to VOCs (see box, right). It has now been established that these compounds—which aid drying times and help with viscosity —can be harmful. Paint manufacturers have therefore been tasked with finding an alternative that still allows the paint to perform to product requirement. Usually, more natural raw materials, such as linseed oil, are used in paint production. In fact, many natural paints have been in existence for hundreds, if not thousands of years.

VOLATILE ORGANIC COMPOUNDS

Characterized by the often pungent fumes produced from drying paint, "volatile organic compounds" or VOCs (found in conventional paints and decorative coatings) are a major area of concern. There are many different types of VOCs, such as benzene and toluene, which can be harmful both to human health and the environment. Many countries are introducing legislation to greatly reduce VOC levels. In Europe, for example, all paints must comply with minimal VOC levels by 2010.

NATURAL PAINTS

All paints contain a binder, pigment, solvent, and sometimes a filler. Binders make up the main film-forming body of the paint, the pigment provides the color, and the solvent essentially creates the paint's liquidity. Sometimes fillers are added to further thicken the mixture and increase its volume. With natural paints, it is straightforward to identify these different components as they are all naturally occurring—there are no synthetic parts. The following table provides information about the ingredients of natural paints—there are many variations on each type shown.

Making your own natural paint

It is possible to produce any of the paints shown in the table below, and there are numerous "recipe books" available, all offering different ideas on how to mix the perfect paint.

When making your own paints, the main concern is to produce the correct quantity for the job ahead—it is impossible to match colors so you won't be able to make a supplementary batch. The second problem can be with sourcing ingredients, as natural paints are not mainstream. You will need to source specialist local suppliers—a process that is far simpler than it once was thanks to the internet.

Paint type	Binder	Solvent	Filler	Comments
Limewash	Lime putty, non-hydraulic bagged lime, or hydraulic lime	Usually water, but some have a small oil content (typically linseed oil), particularly with external applications	Not required in pure limewash	A recommended system would be 3–4 coats for use indoors, and 4–5 coats for outside applications. Must be applied to a porous surface (not on top of other finishes) With casein limewash, casein (derived from milk curd) is also added for greater adhesion
Distemper (including milk paint and cheese paint derivatives)	Soft animal glue, casein (derived from milk curd), or natural oils	Water, linseed oil	Powdered chalk	A small amount of linseed oil is added, but the product is still water based While many milk paints only use the curd, more traditional types would simply mix skimmed milk directly with hydrated lime and pigment Oil-bound distemper may contain borax—an emulsifier that increases durability For interior use only
Flour paint (including clay paint)	Flour (not always used in clay paint)	Water	Clay	Clay often provides the color, although further pigments may also be added
Natural oil paint	Natural oils such as raw linseed oil	Natural oils such as citrus oil	Not required	Natural oil paints have good all round application, both inside and out
Natural silicate paint	Potassium silicate	Water	Colored rocks such as quartz	A more durable version of limewash that is well suited to exterior work
Egg tempera paint	Egg yolk or white	Water	None used	Not normally practical for large-scale work, but is extremely hardwearing and can be effective for the detailing in moldings, for example

Natural pigments (not listed above) come from many different sources. Organic pigments can be derived from flowers and berries (although these tend to fade with light). More stable finishes are provided by natural earth pigments, such as ochre and umber. Most come in powder form, so precautions are required to avoid inhalation of the powder while mixing.

LIMEWASH

A traditional paint, limewash is breathable and has anti-bacterial qualities. Its recent resurgence in popularity is due to its compatibility with eco-friendly building techniques, and to the move away from paints containing VOCs. It can be made from lime putty, powdered lime, and quicklime (although the use of quicklime is not advised as the reactions involved can be explosive).

▌▌ PREPARING COLOR

Natural pigments can be added to limewash, but first check they are compatible, as lime is a strong alkali. Pigments in powder form are best mixed with hot water to aid dispersal (see right). The amount of pigment needed depends on the required intensity of color, with a ratio of 20:1 an average figure. With some earth pigments, it is best to soak them for 24 hours first (check manufacturer's instructions).

Add powdered pigment to a jug of hot water.

Using a hand whisk, mix the liquid to disperse the pigment. Add more of the same, or different-colored pigments, to alter or intensify color.

▌▌ MAKING A LIMEWASH

The sequence shown here describes how to make limewash using lime putty. This method is thought to provide a superior finish to those made using a powdered lime (hydrated or hydraulic lime—see p.85).

While the lime putty will have been pre-mixed, use a trowel to make sure it is sufficiently mixed before use. Aim for a thick, creamy consistency.

Transfer three trowel-fulls of the lime putty to a clean bucket.

Add water slowly to the lime putty. The ratio of water to putty may be 50:50, or even greater, depending on its original consistency.

Mix the lime putty and water with a stirring paddle until the mixture is thin and creamy in consistency.

You may add flaxseed oil, especially if the limewash is for exterior use (the oil aids adhesion and durability). As a guide, use a ratio of 12:1.

Pour the mixture through a sieve and into a second bucket.

Add any colored pigment at this stage, again mixing it together with a stirring paddle.

Mix the limewash again. It should have a thinner consistency (ideally milk-like) because of the dilution with the pigment.

Give the limewash a final sieve and stir. Your homemade limewash is now ready to use.

APPLYING LIMEWASH

Limewash is applied in much the same way as most emulsion or water-based paints. It is important to keep a wet edge as the finish can become patchy where overlaps have occurred. Unlike conventional paints, limewash is always applied to a dampened surface (use a small hand-pumped spray) rather than direct to a dry substrate. It should not be applied in very cold, hot, or wet conditions. It is also essential to wear protective gloves and goggles.

High-quality application tools are essential for an even paint finish. The tools you choose will depend on the size and type of job you are planning. The main options to consider are shown here. It is also necessary to protect surfaces you're not painting. Always wash away grease and dust with a mineral spirit. For some jobs, further preparation is required. See pp.276–279 for more information.

BRUSHES

Paintbrushes are the most versatile and essential of all decorating tools. Ease of application and a successful finish are hugely affected by the quality of a brush. Remember, whether you choose natural or synthetic bristle brushes, a good brush is not cheap, and should have long bristles of equal length. It is normal for a brush to shed a few bristles when it is first used, however, this should not continue through the life of a brush.

Pure bristle brushes
Good-quality pure bristle brushes are expensive but will last for years if they are cleaned well and stored properly after each use.

Pure bristles

Fitches
These are used for detailed work. The angled lining fitch (above left) is useful for straight lines.

Synthetic bristles

Synthetic bristle brushes
Although brushes made from pure natural bristle used to be considered superior quality, vast improvements have been made to synthetic bristle brushes and they are now used by most professionals.

PROTECTION MATERIALS

It is ideal to remove all the furniture and floor coverings from a room before decorating. However, this is often impractical, so drop cloths and tape are used to prevent splashes and spillages damaging surfaces.

Tape
Use low-tack tape to protect surfaces and help you create clean, straight lines where areas with different finishes meet.

Fabric drop cloth
These sheets can be washed and reused, but large spills soak through. Plastic sheets are an alternative, but are easily damaged and slippery underfoot on floors.

PAINTING ACCESSORIES

Besides the more obvious painting tools such as brushes and rollers, there are other items that can be used to make the job easier, restore tools, and provide the best finish.

Steel pins

Paint kettle
Decant paint into kettle so it is easier to carry and to keep debirs such as dried paint on the brush from contaminating hte main tin or tub.

Brush comb
Used to clean and shape brushes.

Dusting brush
Fine bristles remove debris from a surface before painting.

SPRAYING

Paint sprayers can be used to cover large surfaces quickly, or for intricate areas that are very time-consuming to paint with a brush. Small hand-held airless sprayers are most suitable for DIY work, although much larger airless or compressed-air sprayers can be rented. Sprayers can be dangerous, so always read the manufacturer's instructions very carefully. Wear any protective clothing specified and ensure good ventilation while you are spraying. For small jobs, it is better to buy aerosol paints.

PAINT SPRAYER

ROLLERS

There are several different designs of roller and frame. Large rollers can cover flat surfaces such as ceilings and walls quickly and efficiently, although be aware that very large rollers may be tiring to use. Mini-rollers are available for woodwork, although they tend not to provide as pleasing a finish as a brush. Rollers are best used with water-based paints. Cleaning a roller of oil- or solvent-based paints is difficult. It is best to simply throw away the sleeve and buy a new one. The best roller sleeves are pure sheepskin, although synthetic sheepskin also provides a good finish. Smooth, medium, and rough sleeves are available, and should be chosen to match the texture of the surface being painted. Other sleeve materials may produce a rough finish or shed fluff.

Roller cage
The cage holds the roller sleeve and is attached to a handle. Be sure when choosing a replacement sleeve that it fits the cage you are using.

Roller tray
A reservoir for holding paint that also has flatter, ribbed area adjacent to the reservoir, used for distributing paint evenly over the roller surface. The tray needs to be of the same width as your roller.

Cage

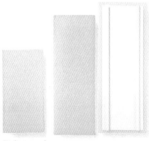

Extension pole
Attaches to the roller-cage handle to extend your reach. Buy a pole that is compatible with your roller.

Radiator roller frame
Used with mini-rollers. The long handle lets you gain access to wall surfaces behind radiators.

Roller sleeves
These fit onto the cage. Rough to smooth textures are available.

Mini-roller kit
A miniature roller cage, tray, and sleeve, designed for painting smaller surfaces and for using with a radiator roller frame.

PAINT PADS

These are designed to cover large, flat surfaces quickly and effortlessly. The flat pads have a painting surface composed of many tiny, tightly-packed bristles.

Pad holder

Paint pad frame
Holds the pad and provides a handle.

Paint pads
Replaceable pads of different sizes are attached to the frame for use.

Mini paint pad
Useful for more detailed work.

Paint pad tray
Similar to a roller tray. Some designs have a wheel that distributes paint evenly onto the pad.

PAINT EFFECTS TOOLS

These tools are used for different paint effects. As well as special tools like these, normal household items such as rags and paper or plastic bags can be used, see pp.292–293.

Stencil brushes
For applying paint over a stencil.

Comb
Several different tooth sizes create straight or curved lines of different widths.

Rocker
Creates a wood-grain pattern in paint or glaze.

Softening brush
Smooth, fine-bristled brush for removing any hard paint lines.

Dragging brush
Extra long and coarse pure bristles create grained effect.

Natural sponge
Used to apply or remove paint to make mottled, cloudlike effects.

Stippling brush
Block-shaped brush with bristles of the same length, used for creating a velvet-like texture on surfaces.

PAINTING PREPARATION

Preparation and planning are the key to a good paint finish. All painting tasks are different, but using an efficient order of work will save time. The best ways to apply paint to achieve other finishes are also described here. It is important to protect surfaces you are not working on because painting, especially with rollers or sprayers, is a messy job. Before starting, prepare surfaces, see pp.276–277. Preparing and painting exterior surfaces are shown on pp.296–297.

COVERING UP AND MASKING

Rooms should ideally be clear of all furnishings, fixtures, and floor coverings before decoration. However, if this is not possible, ensure that you mask or cover anything you cannot remove. Plastic drop cloths are excellent for covering furniture, but have to be thrown away after a couple of uses and are slippery underfoot on floors. Fabric drop cloths will not protect against major spills, but provide a safer floor covering, and can be washed and reused many times. Use masking tape to protect any unpainted surfaces, especially around the edge of the floor. You can paint straight lines using the technique known as "cutting in" shown on p.288, but if you don't feel confident with this method, use blue painter's tape at any junction.

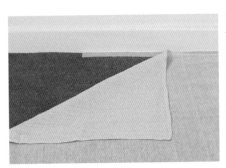

Protecting flooring
Apply masking tape to the floor below the baseboards and lay a fabric drop cloth so that it overlaps the tape. For carpet, use a scraper to push half the width of the tape right behind the carpet edge.

Combining paint with other finishes

As well as furniture and floors, any other decorative finishes in the room need to be protected while you paint, especially if you are using a roller or a sprayer. When combining painted surfaces with natural wood finishes, you need to consider which to apply first. Accuracy is impossible when applying waxes or oils with a cloth. It is usually easier to finish the wood before you paint and protect the woodwork with some tape (see below). Clean any smudges from the wall so that they don't affect the paint finish. Otherwise, paint before preparing and finishing the wood. If you are going to wallpaper the room, do any painting first because even low-tack tape may mark the paper.

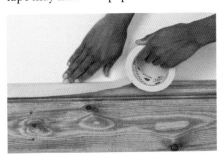

Tape
Ideally, use low-tack tape when decorating. Other types of tape may pull away the finish when you try to remove them, or leave adhesive residue that is difficult to clean off.

PAINT COVERAGE

Paint coverage varies considerably depending on the surface you are decorating. Very porous or rough surfaces will need a lot of paint, so use the smaller figure in the estimated coverage range given; smooth, shiny areas need less, so use the larger figure. Some solvent-based paints tend to cover less surface area than latex-based types. When planning how much paint to buy, don't forget to take the number of coats needed into account. See pp.280–281 for requirements. Always check specific coverage guidelines on the container of the paint you are buying and overestimate rather than underestimate. Keep excess paint for touching up.

Paint type	Estimated coverage
Primer	245–734 sq ft per gallon (5–15 sq m per liter)
Undercoat	489–734 sq ft per gallon (10–15 sq m per liter)
Flat	489–979 sq ft per gallon (10–20 sq m per liter)
Eggshell	391–734 sq ft per gallon (8–15 sq m per liter)
Gloss	587–881 sq ft per gallon (12–18 sq m per liter)
Floor paint	343–734 sq ft per gallon (7–15 sq m per liter)
Metal paint	391–734 sq ft per gallon (8–15 sq m per liter)

ORDER OF PAINTING

If you are repainting a room, start from the top and work down. Cover the ceiling first, then the walls and finally the woodwork and other details. Complete the coats on one surface before moving on to the next, including the sealers, primers, and first coats that are necessary (see p.280). Overlap onto the next surface slightly to ensure continuous coverage (see "cutting in" p.288), but brush out any thick areas of paint otherwise they will show through.

Order for painting a room
1 Ceiling 2 Walls 3 Doors and windows, and radiators if you have them 4 Baseboard, molding, and exposed pipes 5 Floors

PAINTING WINDOWS AND DOORS

Wedge open windows and exterior doors while painting and while the paint dries. Start early in the day to provide sufficient drying time. For both doors and windows, remove any hardware before painting for the best finish. For more on techniques, see pp.288–289 and p.291.

Painting a window frame

The interior and exterior surfaces of windows are painted in the same order (see right). The hinged edge of an opening casement is considered an interior surface, and the opening edge an exterior surface. Wipe sills with mineral spirit before painting to remove dust.

Painting a door

Panel doors are divided into sections by their construction and are painted in the order shown far right. Mentally divide flush doors into sections and complete one section at a time. Begin in the top left corner, then work across, then down. Finish by painting the side edge that is exposed when the door is open. If the door opens outward, the edge where the hinges are attached is seen. If the door opens inward, you see the opening edge.

Order for painting a window:
1 Rails of opening casements
2 Outer rails of casements
3 Hinged edge (if painting the interior, shown here) or opening edge (if painting the exterior)
4 Rails of non-opening casements
5 Frame

Order for painting a panel door:
1 Moldings surrounding each panel
2 Panels
3 Central vertical stiles
4 Horizontal members
5 Outer vertical stiles
6 Door edge

STORING TOOLS

If you need to take a break midway through a job, store your tools in plastic wrap. For long-term storage, thorough cleaning is essential. Latex paints can be cleaned off of tools using water and mild detergent. Clean off solvent-based paints using mineral spirit or thinner (see p.289), then rinse tools in water and mild detergent.

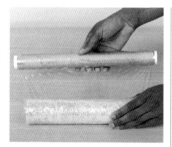

Temporary storage
During a break, you can wrap tools (here a roller) in plastic wrap for up to two days before resuming.

Storing tools
When tools are clean and dry, wrap them tightly in paper so they stay dust-free in storage.

Reviving old brushes
If bristles of an old brush are stuck together with paint residue, use a brush comb to separate them.

TOOLS AND MATERIALS CHECKLISTS PP.288–297

Loading a brush; laying off; painting wood; cutting in (p.288) Paint pail

1-in (25-mm) paintbrush

Using a roller (p.289) Roller tray

Using a paint sprayer (p.289) Basic toolkit only

Using a paint pad (p.289) Paint pad tray

Painting a room (pp.290–291) Roller, roller tray, extension pole, 4-in (100-mm) paintbrush, paint pail, mini-roller kit, radiator roller cage, lining fitch,

Stenciling (p.292) Stencil, masking tape, stencil brush

Distressing (p.292) Petroleum jelly*, PVA*, paints, sandpaper* hammer*, colored wax*, glaze*, crackle glaze*, craquelure*

Applying "on" effects; creating "off" effects (pp.292–293) Paints*, glaze*, clean dowel*, large paintbrush* or softening brush*, natural sponge*, rag*, bag*, stippling brush*, dragging brush*, graining tool*, mineral spirit*

Applying stain (p.295) Stain*, brush

Applying wax; applying oil (p.295) Wax*, oil*, cloth*, brush*

Applying varnish (p.295) Brush, sandpaper, cloth

Cleaning old walls (p.296) Stiff brush, paintbrush, fungicide, stabilizing solution*

Painting metal exterior pipework (p.296) Stiff brush, paintbrush

Dealing with knots (p.297) Heat gun, sandpaper, knotter, lining fitch

Using preservative pellets (p.297) Fitch, wood hardener, exterior two-part filler, pellets, sandpaper, paints

Treating external door edges (p.297) Paintbrush, wood preserver, paints

* = optional

FOR BASIC TOOLKIT SEE PP.24–25

PAINTING TECHNIQUES

Many paints and finishes can be applied using whichever tool you prefer, although some have more specific needs (see pp.280–281 for paint and pp.294–295 for natural wood finishes). Tool choice is also governed by the size and roughness of the surface, and the accuracy needed. Brushes are fairly labor-intensive to use but give fine control over application and can be used on any surface. Rollers, pads, and sprayers cover large areas evenly, quickly, and easily but can be messy and are usually unsuitable for detailed work.

PREPARING PAINT

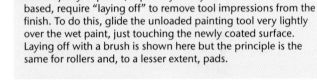

Open the paint can using an old screwdriver or a lid-opening tool. Unless otherwise specified, use a clean wooden dowel or a power stirrer (see p.68) to mix the paint for at least a few minutes before use. Failure to do this can result in poor coverage and noticeable color variation across a surface. If you are using a brush, decant some into a smaller container. This will be easier to carry and prevent the rest of the paint from becoming contaminated.

LOADING A BRUSH

Good brush technique is essential to achieve even coverage. To avoid overloading the brush, only dip it into the paint to one-third of the bristle length for water-based paint, or one-quarter of the bristle length for solvent-based paint. Then scrape off the excess on the rim of the container. With the correct amount of paint on the brush, you can begin covering the surface.

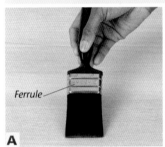

Ferrule

A Hold the brush with your fingers at the top of the ferrule, or lower for a large brush. Small brushes can be held like a pencil.

B Dip the bristles into the paint to one-third of the bristle length. Draw both sides of the brush across the rim to remove excess.

LAYING OFF

The majority of paints, especially if they have a sheen or are oil-based, require "laying off" to remove tool impressions from the finish. To do this, glide the unloaded painting tool very lightly over the wet paint, just touching the newly coated surface. Laying off with a brush is shown here but the principle is the same for rollers and, to a lesser extent, pads.

A Apply the paint roughly to distribute the paint from the loaded brush. Use random strokes in differing directions.

B Lay off the paint, again using random strokes, allowing only the very tips of the bristles to glide across the freshly painted surface.

PAINTING WOOD

Woodwork is usually finished with a finish coat of semigloss or eggshell. These types of paint need to be applied particularly carefully to achieve a good finish. On large, open surfaces such as flush doors, paint should first be applied at right angles to the grain, then brushed out and laid off in line with the grain. On narrow surfaces such as baseboard or panel doors, the paint is easiest applied in line with the grain and brushed out and laid off in the same direction.

Coating a door
Paint each section separately. Take time to lay off the paint carefully, then cut in accurately along the construction joints for a neat finish (see below, and p.287 for orders of work).

CUTTING IN

The technique known as "cutting in" is used to create a precise dividing line. You need a brush to cut in accurately, although small paint pads can sometimes be used (see opposite).

Work in manageable sections along the division line. Load the brush, but take care not to overload it (see top), then position it with its bristles into the junction. Brush it steadily along and allow the bristles of the brush to make a neat "bead"—a tiny, slightly raised line created as the paint leaves the brush. Lay off the other side of the brush stroke to finish.

In a corner
A straight line between two areas of paint, especially a junction between surfaces, enhances the finish of a room.

Decorative woodwork
Carefully cut into the junction between the woodwork and adjoining surface.

USING A ROLLER

Rollers apply paint over flat surfaces very quickly and easily. Several different sizes and sleeves are available (see p.279). You should make sure you have the right kind of roller sleeve for the job. Rough roller sleeves can cope better with texture; smooth rollers are excellent for flat surfaces and applying paints with a sheen. Although you can apply most kinds of paint with a roller (see p.280), solvent-based paint will be difficult to wash out. Rollers are not very accurate tools, so you will still need a brush to cut in to junctions and woodwork.

A

Pour paint carefully into the tray reservoir, keeping the paint below the point where the ribbed section of the tray begins.

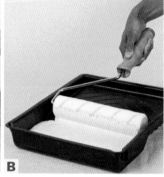

B

Push the roller along the ribbed section of the tray and then glide it over the paint surface—do not submerge it in the paint.

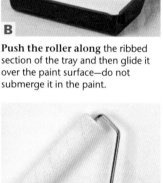

C

Move the roller backward and forward slowly over the ribbed section to distribute the paint evenly over the roller sleeve.

D

Apply the paint onto the surface in sections by rolling up and down, then "lay off" the paint with the roller (see opposite).

USING A PAINT SPRAYER

There are many variations of sprayers, so you should carefully check the manufacturer's safety and operation instructions for the type you intend to use. Whether you are using a powerful compressed-air sprayer on a room or an aerosol can on a radiator, the aim is to build up several thin coats of paint. Spraying is a messy job, so sprayers are most useful in rooms empty of furniture and floor coverings, or for exteriors. When spraying paint you should always wear a mask and goggles, and any other specified safety equipment.

A

Pour paint into the sprayer reservoir. Normal latex paint diluted with 10 percent water, or paint designed for spraying is used.

B

Assemble the sprayer following the manufacturer's instructions.

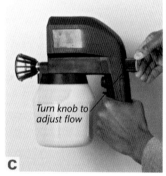

Turn knob to adjust flow

C

Try spraying on a sheet of scrap paper or similar. Adjust the flow until you can achieve a fairly even coat with no drips.

D

Spray back and forth over the surface. Apply a thin coat, allow to dry, then add more coats until you achieve good coverage.

USING A PAINT PAD

The most common design of paint pad is used in a very similar way to a roller. You can use a normal paint tray or a specially designed tray, some of which have a wheel to distribute paint evenly from the reservoir onto the pad.

Small pads are available for more detailed work. They can be used to cut in at a junction. Uneven surfaces are best finished using a brush to follow the slight contours. Cut in with a brush (see opposite), then lay off the brush marks as close as you can to the junction using the pad.

A

Dip the pad into the paint held in the reservoir, then move it across the ribbed section of the tray to remove the excess.

B

Apply paint to the wall surface with an up-and-down motion. The pad should create a very even coat without the need for laying off.

DISPOSING OF PAINT SAFELY

To thoroughly clean tools of water-based paints you need a large amount of water. The waste water must go into the sewer system.

Mineral spirits or thinners used to clean up oil-based paints, and old paint cans, must be disposed of as advised by your municipality, often at a recycling facility. Always try to use up oil-based paints to avoid having to manage disposal issues.

PAINTING A ROOM

All surfaces must be prepared thoroughly before painting—any damage should be filled, sanded, and primed, and surfaces cleaned (see pp.276–279). Choose the right paint type for each surface. See pp.280–281 for your options. The order shown here is for undercoats or topcoats. Finish the ceiling and walls before tackling the trim. Details of the techniques needed to apply an even coat of paint with rollers, brushes, and other tools can be found on pp.288–289.

TOOLS AND MATERIALS SEE BASIC TOOLKIT AND P.287

1 PAINTING THE CEILING

A

Attach an extension pole to the handle of the roller. Decant paint into the paint tray and load the roller, taking care not to overload it (see p.289). Roll the paint onto the ceiling in sections, laying off each area before you reload the roller. When painting a ceiling, it is important to wear goggles to protect your eyes from drips and spatters of paint.

2 PAINTING THE WALLS

A

Once the central area of the ceiling is coated, paint around the edge with a brush. Overlap slightly onto the wall surface.

B

Roll paint on in vertical sections. Use an extension pole to save bending when painting lower sections of the wall, and reaching for the higher areas.

C

Cut in at the junctions between the walls and the ceiling. A roller is not accurate enough, so use a 4-in (100-mm) brush, or a small paint pad if your walls are straight.

D

Slightly overlap the wall color onto the baseboard, or, if your baseboard has a natural finish, protect it with blue painter's tape.

PAINTING AROUND OBSTACLES

After you have rolled paint on the ceiling, and then on the walls, it is time to handle the details and paint around any obstacles. Learning the technique to cut in a straight line saves you time spent lining the obstacles with painter's tape (see p.288).

If you decide to use tape to line your obstacles, make sure to press it firmly down to keep any paint from bleeding underneath.

When it comes to large obstacles like a radiator or even small obstacles like a light switch, there are a few tricks you can try.

Painting behind a radiator
Use a radiator roller to coat the wall behind the radiator. The long handle will reach down easily. An alternative is to remove the radiator while you decorate—see pp.508–509 for more information on how to do this.

Painting around a light switch
It's usually easiest to remove any

wall plates before you start painting to avoid spending time carefully painting around them. But if you live in a house where the previous owners have painted the wall plates to the wall, you may choose to paint around them. Use the cutting-in method described left. Tackle the switches last, after you have perfected your technique. Unlike outlets, the light switches are at eye level in the room, so any mistakes cutting-in are visible.

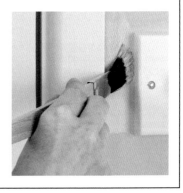

3 PAINTING A WINDOW

Open the window so that you can paint both the opening and the hinged edge, but avoid painting over the hinges themselves. Wedge the window open until the paint is completely dry.

A Remove any window hardware before painting to make the job easier and to provide a neater finish.

B Use a 1-in (25-mm) brush. Follow the order of work shown on p.287, starting with the stiles and the rails of the opening sections.

D Paint the rails of any non-opening casements.

E Create a clean dividing line between the window frame and the wall surface.

4 PAINTING THE BASEBOARD

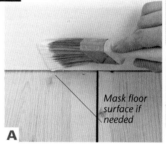

Mask floor surface if needed

A Begin to paint the baseboard, one manageable section at a time. Start by coating the middle of the board, then cut into the floor.

B Cut in neatly at the baseboard and wall junction. Lay off the paint carefully for an even finish, then move on to the next section of baseboard.

5 PAINTING A DOOR

If you stray onto the stiles or rails, brush out the paint to avoid lines

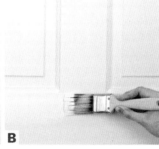

Finish by painting the casing, cutting in precisely along the edge created with the wall surface. Paint the door jamb (see p.160). For inward-opening doors, paint the lining up to but not including the doorstop. For outward-opening doors, continue on to paint the doorstop. Wedge the door open while you paint the opening edge.

A Remove the door hardware before you start painting. Begin by coating the panels and continue to paint the door according to the order of work outlined on p.287.

B Follow the grain of the wood as you paint the stiles and rails. Where they cross, create a line along the joint of the two pieces of wood.

PAINT EFFECTS

Some paint effects are used to add detail, such as stenciling, distressing, and some trompe l'oeil effects. Others are used to decorate whole walls or rooms, using a discontinuous topcoat of color to create depth and texture. The topcoat is chosen to complement the base color of the wall where it shows through. Traditionally a translucent glaze, known as scumble glaze, is used for the finish coat, although other paints are sometimes used. Once you are familiar with the key techniques of the effects shown here, you can experiment with colors, layers, and tools to create effects of your own.

TROMPE L'OEIL

Trompe l'oeil translates as "trick of the eye" and includes all those paint effects that try to mimic a different surface. Examples include marbling, where paint and glaze are carefully applied to create the appearance of marble, and tricks such as recreating the look of old stone on a new plaster surface. To produce convincing trompe l'oeil takes practice, so hone your skills on some scrap paper before tackling a new project.

STENCILING

Stencils are normally made from acetate or cardboard and can be bought ready-to-use, or you can cut your own. Any paint can be used for stenciling, but water-based options dry quickly and are the most user-friendly.

Use a very small amount of paint on a special stenciling or small stippling brush and dab lightly into the stencil. Stencil crayons or aerosol paints can also be used. You can apply a coat of flat color, or create a three-dimensional effect by concentrating color around the edge of a design. This creates a central highlight. You can also apply more paint on one side to suggest directional light.

Using a stencil
Attach the stencil to the surface with low-tack painter's tape. Use a stenciling brush in an up-and-down motion to apply the paint (see also Stippling, opposite). Remove the stencil carefully. Choose the next stencil location randomly, or create a regular pattern.

DISTRESSING

There are several techniques that can provide the illusion of age. Masking areas with petroleum jelly or glue prevents paint from adhering so that once the surface is painted and the area is sanded, the masked areas lose all their paint to provide a patchy, aged finish. Surfaces can also be physically distressed with strokes of a hammer or other objects. Accentuate the texture by rubbing some colored wax into the surface or colorwashing (see opposite).

For a different effect use crackle glaze or craquelure. Used as directed, they create a surface like cracked antique paint or varnish. You can enhance the finish with colored wax.

Creating aging effects
When using these effects, think carefully where you would expect to find natural wear, such as on the edges of a door, or on the area around a handle. The more layers of different colored paint applied to that area, the greater the effect.

APPLYING "ON" EFFECTS

Glaze or latex can be applied over a flat coat of paint to create a textured effect. Translucent glaze, bought ready-to-use or mixed as shown for colorwashing (see opposite), gives a more subtle effect than emulsion. Here, sponging on paint is described, although you can experiment with other "tools"—such as rags or bags. Whatever tool you use, the general technique is similar.

The first step is to paint a base coat of latex or eggshell onto the wall. When this is dry, pour a small amount of your topcoat of paint or glaze into a roller tray. Dip in your chosen tool and make sure it is well coated. Remove the excess paint by dabbing it off on the ridged section of the tray, then on some newspaper, until a light touch produces a mottled mark rather than a solid block of color. Begin to apply it to the wall in a random pattern, varying the side of the tool that you use for each mark. Build up the effect slowly rather than attempting a dense coat the first time. Go over the whole surface with one very light coat first, then check it for even coverage. Apply subsequent layers until the desired result is achieved.

Creating a random yet even pattern is harder than it looks and you may want to practise on some scrap paper first. However, mistakes can be corrected and evened out by applying some of the paint you used for the base coat with the effect tool you are using.

Sponging on
A sponge is one of the easiest tools for a paint-effect novice to get to grips with. Build up the finish in layers until you achieve your desired density of color. If different shades of the same color are used then the final effect will be subtle; if contrasting colors are used then you will get a bolder result.

▌▌ APPLYING COLORWASH

A colorwash provides depth of color and enhances textured and distressed surfaces (see opposite). Create the effect by applying translucent glaze over an opaque base coat.

Water-based glazes are available and can be bought colored, or you can color them yourself using a special dye. For a greater range of colors, tint glaze with acrylic paint. Apply a second coat of glaze if more color is required, or work on the wet glaze to create one of the effects below. The finish is usually glossy.

A

Pour a small amount of dye into the glaze and mix it well with a length of clean dowel. Test the color and adjust if required.

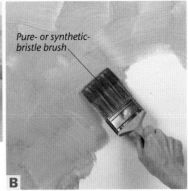

Pure- or synthetic-bristle brush

B

Spread glaze onto the wall, using random strokes. Work quickly because if you let the edges dry they will show on the finished surface.

CREATING "OFF" EFFECTS

The first step for these effects is a translucent colorwash of glaze that is applied over an opaque base coat. Use a vinyl silk or satin latex, eggshell, or even gloss for your base coat because this will prolong the drying time of the glaze while you work with it. You need to work quickly to complete a colorwash and create one of the "off" effects shown below before the glaze dries. If you are inexperienced at creating paint effects, or are tackling a particularly large area, get some help so that one person can apply the glaze while the other follows behind creating the effect. When using these techniques, replace or wash your tool clean often and keep plenty of newspaper and water or mineral spirit on hand. Complete the whole wall surface before taking a break.

Sponging
Press a damp sponge into the glaze, and lift it off to leave a mottled impression. Move the sponge across the surface, pressing and removing the sponge in a random fashion. From time to time, rinse out the sponge to remove excess glaze.

Ragging
Press a dampened, crumpled cloth into the glaze randomly across the wall surface. Rinse the rag regularly or have a few ready for when the one you are using becomes too soaked with glaze. Vary the effect by using different types of cloth or even plastic and paper bags.

Rag-rolling
Crumple a rag and form it into a sausage shape, then roll it down the wall surface to create a subtle effect resembling tumbling material. Rinse or change rags often. You can also rag-roll glaze or latex onto a wall for a similar but more dramatic effect.

Stippling
By pressing the very ends of a specially designed stippling brush into the wet glaze, you can create a very finely textured, almost velvet-like finish. Pat the brush into the wall surface in a random pattern and make sure that you go straight up and down with no drag.

Dragging
This creates a coarse-lined, textured finish running either vertically or horizontally. Hold a long-bristled dragging brush at a low angle, then draw it in a continuous stroke down or across the glazed surface. This effect can be used on wood as well as walls.

Graining
A wood-grain effect often used on MDF or melamine furniture, graining can be applied to any flat surface. Rock the special graining tool gently as you drag it down the wet glaze surface. Vary the pace of rocking to give different effects.

As their name suggests, natural wood finishes enhance rather than cover the grain of the wood. Some also offer protection. Transparent, translucent, and almost opaque finishes are available. There are several things to think about when choosing natural wood finishes—the range available is outlined below. Once you have chosen the finish you require, prepare the surface as shown on pp.278–279, then follow the application tips shown opposite for a perfect result.

TOOLS AND MATERIALS SEE BASIC TOOLKIT AND P.287

GREEN WOOD FINISHES

Natural oils and waxes are the most eco-friendly of wood finishes, although synthetic alternatives do exist. Beeswax and linseed oil are well known green finishes, but look out for safflower oil and carnauba wax as well. Water-based varnishes and stains also have good green credentials. Look at the manufacturer's label, check for any VOC content (see p.282), and determine exactly what ingredients have been used. For the application of eco-friendly products, follow the guide below.

WOOD FINISHES

Natural wood finishes, especially those that soak into the grain, are often difficult to remove, so take time to think about your requirements and choose the right product. Protection offered by natural finishes varies. Dye, for example, may offer no protection by itself. Always buy a suitable interior or exterior formula. Consider if you want an almost invisible coat or would prefer some color or gloss. Also, think about how much time you are prepared to spend on application—there may be one-coat options available. Finally, look out for eco-friendly options, such as water-based varnishes and stains, or products made from 100-percent natural ingredients.

VARNISH

STAIN

DYE

WAX

OIL

WOOD PRESERVER

FINISH AND EFFECT

Finish	Use	Application
Varnish Hardwearing, transparent or colored, decorative, and preservative finish that highlights and protects the wood surface below. Matte and high-gloss versions are available. You can buy water-based and oil-based types	For interior or exterior use as specified. Can be used on bare wood or to protect unsealed finishes, such as dye	Covers 600–900 sq ft per gallon (12–18 sq m per liter). May need several coats. Apply with a brush for the best finish
Stain Soaks into the wood to provide a decorative and sometimes preservative finish. Darkens or colors wood. Matte to gloss, water-based, and oil-based types are available	For interior or exterior use as specified. Use as a finish or coat with varnish for extra durability. Apply to clean, bare wood for a true color	Covers 400–1,000 sq ft per gallon (8–20 sq m per liter). May need several coats. Apply with a brush for the best finish
Dye Subtly enhances natural color or evens out shades on different pieces of wood. Dyes can be mixed to match an existing color. Gives a matte finish. Water-based and oil-based types are available	Only for interior use unless specified, or protected with exterior varnish. Apply as a finish or beneath varnish or wax	Covers 400–750 sq ft per gallon (8–15 sq m per liter). May need several coats. Apply with a brush for the best finish
Wax Transparent or translucent decorative finish; some types can be buffed to a high gloss. Feeds and protects the wood but will not penetrate a sealed surface. Both water-based and oil-based types are available	For interior use only. Apply to bare wood or over unsealed finishes such as dye	Apply with a cloth. Brush-on waxes are also available. Needs several coats and regular maintenance
Oil Transparent finish that nourishes and protects wood. External surfaces lose their finish but stay protected. Buff to achieve mid-sheen finish. Will not penetrate a sealed surface	For interior or exterior use. Must be applied to unsealed wood	Covers 400–750 sq ft per gallon (8–15 sq m per liter). Apply with a brush or cloth yearly. Highly flammable—see "cleaning tools" above
Wood preserver Prevents rot and insect damage. Available clear or colored with a matte or a semigloss finish. Both water-based and oil-based types are available	Exterior use. Used alone, or as base coat for another natural wood finish or paint	Covers 400–1,000 sq ft per gallon (8–20 sq m per liter). Apply in sections as for stain (see opposite) or as specified

APPLYING STAIN OR WOOD PRESERVER

Stain and wood preserver are applied in the same order as you would paint, see pp.286–287. You can apply coats to roughly finished wood quickly, but to get an even coat on smooth wood requires accuracy. Cover each surface without a break—if the stain or preserver dries midway, you will be left with a line.

Apply stain with the grain of the wood. Take care not to overload the brush and to brush out any drips before the stain dries.

Complete one section of wood before beginning the next. Where two sections join, ensure that strokes do not overlap each other.

APPLYING WAX

Wax is normally applied with a cloth, although some types are designed to be brushed on. Repeated application and buffing builds up depth of color and sheen. It is not necessary to follow the grain of the wood, although this is considered to be the best way to efficiently cover the wood surface.

Scoop some wax out of its container with a soft cloth and rub it evenly into the wood until there are no globules of wax left.

Leave the wax to dry, but not harden, for a few minutes. Buff the surface with a clean cloth to provide a smooth finish.

APPLYING OIL

All oils are applied using a similar technique. Pure tung oil is good for countertops and food preparation areas as it is non-toxic. Danish oil and teak oil are good for hardwoods, especially outdoor furniture; teak oil provides a glossier finish. If you choose traditional linseed oil, use boiled or double-boiled types because they are quicker to dry and not as sticky as the raw oil.

Apply liberally, using strokes of a soft brush in line with the wood grain to help ensure full coverage and aid penetration.

Allow the oil to soak in before removing excess with a cloth. Leave for half an hour, or as directed, then buff the surface with a dry cloth.

APPLYING VARNISH

Like stain, varnish must be applied in the direction of the grain, although you don't have to worry so much about accuracy. Because many varnishes are completely transparent, it is easy to miss areas during application. Good lighting and regular inspection of the surface are necessary to ensure good coverage.

Follow the grain of the wood. Finish one section before beginning the next.

Brush out the varnish to give an even coat. Use the technique shown for laying off paint, p.288.

Sand down the surface of the first coat because varnish, especially water-based varieties, tends to lift the grain of the wood.

Wipe the surface with a damp cloth to remove dust and let it dry before applying the next coat. Apply further coats as required.

APPLYING DYE

If you want to mix dyes to a specific shade, make sure they both have the same base—oil or water. Dyed wood needs a protective finish such as wax or varnish over the top.

Working with dye
Apply dye with the grain. Keep a wet edge where you work and take care not to overlap onto areas that have dried. Seal the dye with a protective finish. Check the manufacturer's specifications for compatible finishes.

MAINTAINING EXTERIOR SURFACES

Stained exterior woodwork needs only occasional maintenance. A single coat, applied every year or two, will keep wood protected and looking good.

Once a year, lightly sand and wipe exterior varnish before applying a maintenance coat (see above).

The finish of exterior hardwoods treated with Danish or teak oil can fade quickly. Although the wood will remain protected, manufacturers often recommend that exterior oiled surfaces are recoated at least once a year.

PAINTING EXTERIOR SURFACES

Most of the tools and techniques for painting exterior surfaces are the same as those used for interiors. However, materials are often chosen for their greater durability. Painted masonry can last up to ten years, and wooden windows up to five years before recoating is necessary. Surfaces need to be filled and sanded before you paint (see pp.276–277). Additional preparation is often required. Vegetative growth and rot are more common problems on exterior surfaces, and how to treat them is shown here. If you are working on the outside of your house, remember that ladders and scaffolding will almost certainly be needed for access.

EXTERIOR PAINT

Items painted with light colors reflect the sun's heat. This reduces paint problems due to expansion so they need repainting less often. Exterior latex, also known as masonry paint, is used outside. Apply it in the same way as interior latex. Coverage is often less: 100–1,000 sq ft per gallon (2–20 sq m per liter). Coat woodwork and pipework with gloss. You can use special paint for rusty metal. See pp.280–281 for more on paint types.

PREPARING MASONRY FOR PAINTING

Remove any vegetative growth from masonry walls, and clean them down thoroughly. Small holes in masonry can be filled using all-purpose powder fillers as long as they specify exterior use. New masonry finishes should not need any further treatment.

Old masonry may need some more extensive repair. It will also benefit from an application of fungicide, and stabilizing solution if the surface is flaky (see cleaning old walls, below). Once the surface is clean and dry, fill any remaining holes and sand as normal.

When you come to paint walls, the best choice is exterior latex, often called masonry paint. Apply a mist coat—the paint you are using diluted with 10 percent water—followed by two full-strength coats. Paint from the top down, covering the walls before woodwork and metalwork. Some deviation from this basic plan is often necessary because of access. You may find it easiest to paint roof details such as soffits, fascias, and bargeboards, followed by the top section of wall, before tackling the lower surfaces (see pp.26–27 for information on ladders and platforms).

CLEANING OLD WALLS

A

Use a stiff brush to remove any loose paint, masonry, vegetative matter, or dirt from the wall.

Wear any protective clothing specified

B

Apply fungicidal solution using the manufacturer's guidelines. Leave for 24 hours, then use a pressure washer to clean the surfaces.

C

Check the wall surface. If it is powdery to the touch, you need to use a stabilizing solution.

D

Apply the stabilizing solution with a large paintbrush. When it is dry, the wall is ready to fill, sand, and paint.

PAINTING METAL EXTERIOR PIPEWORK

Exterior pipework is usually made of metal or plastic. Exterior metalwork is treated in the same way as that inside the home, except that special exterior metal paints generally offer greater durability. Plastic items are simply cleaned when any dirt or vegetative growth accumulates. If you do wish to coat plastic pipes, apply two coats of gloss over a primer coat.

A

Brush down the metal. Remove any flakes of paint and rust right down to bare, shiny metal. Some metal paints can be applied directly over rust.

B

Prime patches of exposed metal using a metal primer specified for exterior use.

C

Apply exterior-grade gloss paint, laying off the paint carefully as you work (see p.288). Shield the wall with a piece of cardboard.

PAINTING AND TREATING EXTERIOR WOODWORK

Paint or a natural wood preservative finish (see pp.294–295) are essential for exterior woodwork because it is prone to damage from the elements. Maximize protection by using hardwearing fillers and exterior-grade paints. Problems can still occur. The heat of the sun can cause sap to bubble out of knots, blistering the paintwork. Use a heat gun followed by knotter (shown below) to prevent further damage. This technique can also be used on bare wood, prior to painting. Small cracks in paintwork can lead to minor rot problems.

Pellets of wood preservative or wood filler repair are an excellent way to repair rot damage. Large areas of rotten wood need to be replaced (see p.152).

Wooden siding is treated like any other exterior woodwork, but it must be washed down thoroughly in order to remove all signs of dirt. In some circumstances, fungicide may be required, which can be applied as shown for masonry walls, opposite.

DEALING WITH KNOTS

   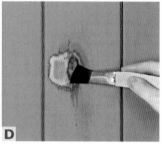

A Scrape all the sap and excess paint away from the affected area.

B Use a heat gun to heat up the sap so that it bubbles out from the knot. Keep using the heat gun until the sap stops flowing.

C Sand the area to remove residue and provide a clean, smooth surface for painting.

D Apply sealer to the knot using a small brush. Once this is dry, you can prime and paint the area using exterior-grade paints.

USING PRESERVATIVE PELLETS

A Scrape the rot back to sound wood. Allow the area to dry out, then apply wood hardener to the exposed wood.

B Use a two-part wood filler specifically for exterior use to repair the damage caused by the rot.

C *Drill bit size will be specified on pellet packaging*

Drill holes around the rotten area. Push pellets into the holes, making sure they sit below the wood surface. You can then fill the holes with more exterior filler. Sand the treated area smooth before priming and painting. Like many preservative products, pellets contain toxins, so be sure to wear gloves when handling them.

TREATING WINDOWS AND DOORS

Wooden windows and external doors rely on paint or a natural wood finish (pp.294–295) for protection. Start work early in the day so you can close the windows and doors before night. The order of work for painting the rest of the window or door is shown on p.287. Apply paint using the technique specified for wood on p.288.

Cracked puttywork can let down the finish of an otherwise well-painted window or glazed door. As long as the putty is sound, fill it with an all-purpose filler, then sand and paint with the wood. Take care not to allow the sandpaper to touch the glass surface, because it will scratch it. Where putty is very loose or missing, remove as much as possible, dust away any debris, and re-putty as shown on pp.148–149.

Vinyl and metal windows

Vinyl doesn't require painting. It can be kept bright and clean with a non-abrasive cleaner. Some cleaners denature and degrade rubber seals or gaskets, so check the manufacturer's guidelines. When painting surrounding wall surfaces, take care to mask up vinyl as removing any paint overspray can be very difficult.

Metal windows or parts of windows are often factory-coated and so don't require painting. Old metal windows can be painted using much the same system as normal wooden windows, except that an appropriate primer must be used to prevent rust damage.

TREATING EXTERNAL DOOR EDGES

 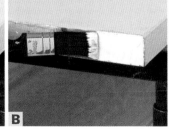

A Take the door off its hinges. Apply preservative primer to the top and bottom edges of the door.

B Prime and paint the edges when the preservative primer has dried using exterior paints.

PROBLEM SOLVER

REMOVING DRIPS

Drips are caused by poor technique—usually overloading the brush during application. See p.288 for the correct technique.

TOOLS AND MATERIALS
Scraper, sandpaper

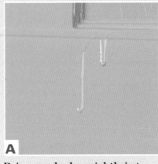

A Drips may look unsightly but can be easily removed.

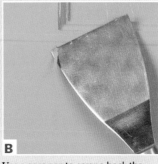

B Use a scraper to scrape back the paint drips.

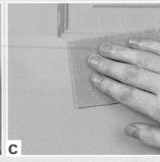

C Sand the area to a smooth finish. Repaint the sanded area.

HIDING A STAIN

Stains are caused by smoke damage or not properly priming before painting. The wall should always be cleaned then primed. You can also treat stains caused by mildew this way, provided the cause of the problem has been fixed.

TOOLS AND MATERIALS
Stain blocker or oil-based undercoat, paintbrushes, topcoat

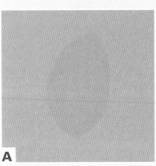

A Clean the area thoroughly with TSP, then allow the surface to dry completely.

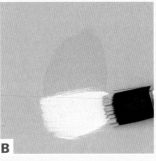

B Apply stain blocker or oil-based undercoat over the stain.

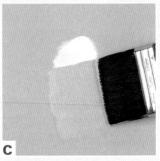

C Allow the stain blocker or undercoat to dry, then recoat with spare topcoat.

SMOOTHING A GRITTY FINISH

Rough or gritty finishes are a result of poor preparation or impurities introduced into the paint during application. Always decant paint into a kettle when using a brush, and stir and sieve old paint before you use it again.

TOOLS AND MATERIALS
Sandpaper, cloth, paint, paintbrush

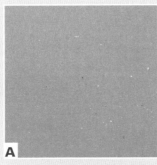

A A gritty paint finish spoils the appearance of a painted surface, as shown, but it is easily remedied.

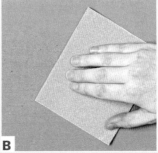

B Use sandpaper to sand the area back. Clean down with a cloth to remove dust.

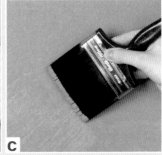

C Repaint the area with topcoat.

REMOVING WRINKLED PAINT

This effect is created by painting coats too quickly, and not allowing adequate drying time. It can also be caused by extremes of temperature while the paint is drying.

TOOLS AND MATERIALS
Chemical stripper or a hot-air gun, scraper, sandpaper

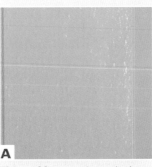

A This problem requires stripping, sanding, and repainting in order to get the desired finish.

B Strip paint completely using chemical stripper or a hot air gun.

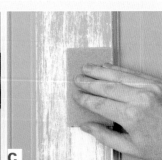

C Sand down the area and repaint.

REMOVING BRUSH MARKS

Prominent brush marks are caused by poor application technique. The problem is also common with natural wood finishes.

TOOLS AND MATERIALS
Sander, cloth, paintbrush, paint

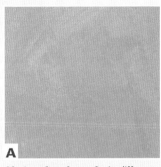

A Obvious brush marks in different directions can make wood finishes look uneven.

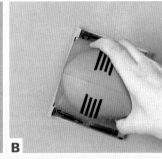

B Machine sand the area. Wipe the area clean of dust with a damp cloth.

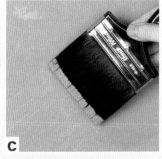

C Repaint the area. If using a natural wood finish, take care to apply stain with the grain, keeping a wet edge at all times.

IMPROVING POOR COVERAGE

Poor coverage is caused by applying the wrong number of coats of paint. Sometimes this problem combines with prominent streaks in the paint caused by paint buildup on roller edges during application.

TOOLS AND MATERIALS
Sandpaper, roller.

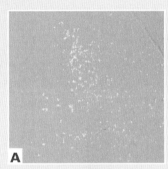

A Poor coverage results in a patchy appearance, as shown above, and needs repainting.

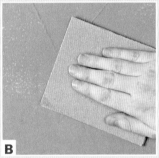

B Sand the area to remove any paint ridges created by roller edge trails.

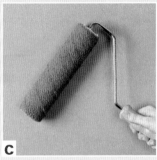

C Recoat the area using as many coats of paint necessary to match the surface.

HIDING FILLER THAT SHOWS THROUGH

This problem sometimes occurs when filled areas are not primed before painting. It is always best to prime filler and/or apply an extra patch of paint to filled areas. This is especially the case for water-based paints.

TOOLS AND MATERIALS
Paintbrush, primer, roller, paint

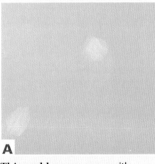

A This problem can occur with some types of filler.

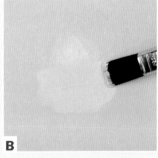

B Recoat the patch of filler with a suitable primer, or if you are painting with latex paint, prime with the full-strength paint.

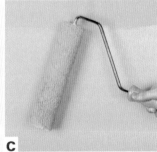

C Recoat the entire wall.

DEALING WITH A BLEEDING KNOT

Where wood has not been knotted and primed, knots can continue to secrete resin that will show through coats of paint. See p.297 for proper preparation of knotted wood.

TOOLS AND MATERIALS
Scraper, sandpaper, paintbrushes, wood sealer, paint

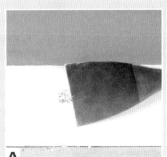

A Scrape back the paint from the knot and sand the area smooth.

B Apply some sealer.

C Apply primer, followed by the required paint finish.

Wallpapering

BEFORE APPLYING WALLPAPER, ALL WALL AND WOOD SURFACES SHOULD BE PREPARED IN THE USUAL WAY (SEE PP.276–279). IF ANY FEATURES NEED TO BE PAINTED, APPLY THE PAINT FIRST; THIS FREES YOU TO OVERLAP ANY PAINT ONTO THE WALLS AND GIVES YOU A NEATER RESULT WHEN THE WALLPAPER IS TRIMMED TO FIT. FOR MORE INFORMATION ON PAINTING, SEE PP.286–287. WALLPAPERING IS ALWAYS THE FINAL JOB.

PAPERING TOOLS AND MATERIALS

This section only covers the application of new wallpaper to stripped and prepared wall surfaces. The tools and techniques required for stripping old wallpaper are shown on pp.276–277.

TOOLS

Aside from the general tools required for wallpapering, such as a tape measure, pencil, and utility knife, several special items are needed. The paperhanging brush, for example, is vital for creasing paper into corners.

Soft brush prevents damage

Bristles apply paste evenly

Paperhanging brush
Broad-handled brush for smoothing wallpaper.

Pasting brush
Large brush to apply paste to wallpaper.

Make sure you can read the scale

Metal rule
Used for drawing accurate guide lines, or for cutting with a utility knife.

Papering sponge
For cleaning paste off equipment and removing excess paste from wallpaper. Ideally, you need more than one, and plenty of clean water.

Keep the roller clean

Measuring cup
Essential for accurately mixing wallpaper paste.

Seam roller
Used to gently press wallpaper seams to ensure good adhesion. Do not use on embossed papers.

Handles have good grips

Paperhanging scissors
Long-bladed scissors for cutting wallpaper.

Long, narrow reservoir

Pasting table
A long, narrow, foldaway table on which wallpaper is cut, pasted, and folded before hanging. Make sure you wipe down the surface with clean water after pasting each length.

Wallpaper trough
Filled with water and used for dipping ready-pasted paper.

TYPES OF WALLPAPER

There are many types of wallpaper available. Your choice will probably be based on design. Textured paper hides uneven surfaces. Vinyl-coated papers can be washed. Always buy rolls with the same batch number to avoid slight variations. Be aware that some papers are prone to fading in direct sunlight. Check the packaging for details on colorfastness.

Standard types of wallpaper

Standard paper and vinyl-coated wallpapers are most commonly chosen. Both can be used in most situations, but vinyl is more hardwearing. Paste-the-paper, paste-the-wall, and prepasted types are available (see below).

Special wallpapers

Unusual wallpapers such as flock or those with hand-printed designs may be subject to very specific handling and hanging procedures. Be sure to follow any guidelines from the manufacturer.

Embossed wall panels

Wall panels are hung in much the same way as standard wallpaper. They are thick and linoleum-based and are commonly used below chair rails in historic properties. Embossed borders can be bought in a roll.

Lining paper
This provides a base for wallpaper or paint. For rough walls use a thicker gauge of lining paper.

Standard paper and vinyl paper
These two kinds of paper vary hugely in quality. Numerous patterns are available.

Woodchip paper
Several grades of texture can hide most rough or pitted walls. Can be painted.

Embossed paper
Disguises uneven surfaces. Hang gently to avoid flattening the relief. Vinyl-coated versions available.

Border paper
Strips used to divide or frame walls and features if required.

TYPES OF ADHESIVES

There are various different types of adhesive associated with wallpapering and some types of wallpaper may require a particular adhesive. Wallpaper paste comes either ready-mixed or powdered, with the latter being mixed with water before use. Size is very diluted wallpaper paste used to prepare walls before lining paper or wallpaper is applied. Diluted with water, PVA is an alternative to size, and can be used to seal walls before wallpapering. Border adhesive is an extra-strong adhesive that ensures a good adhesion between borders and wallpaper. It is also used on overlapping wallpaper seams.

ECO-FRIENDLY WALLPAPER

There are a number of eco-friendly wallpaper options. Check labels for the FSC symbol (see p.75) and ensure that products are made from recycled paper. Look for non-toxic, water-based inks.

The absence of vinyl as a component of "green" wallpaper raises some durability issues, but it is possible to find papers that use a water-based glaze to produce a wipeable finish.

THREE METHODS OF ADHESION

There are three ways in which wallpaper is adhered to a wall surface. Paste-the-paper and paste-the-wall types require wallpaper paste. Prepasted paper is coated in a dry adhesive powder that is "activated" when submerged in water. Both paste-the-paper and ready-pasted types need to be left to soak after pasting or activation. Make sure you keep this soaking time consistent for each length of paper.

 PASTE-THE-WALL

To apply this type of paper, brush wallpaper paste onto the wall, then smooth the wallpaper into place. Make sure you apply an even coat. Unpasted patches will result in bubbles under the paper.

 PASTE-THE-PAPER

The aim is to create a loose "book" of paper, only allowing pasted faces to touch, with no paste on the patterned side. Leave the "book" for the recommended soaking period before hanging.

A

Apply paste down the length, working from the center of the paper out to the edges.

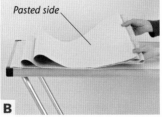

B

Pasted side

Loosely fold up the pasted end of the paper. Paste the remaining length, then fold it up with the rest.

PREPASTED

Once you have wetted the paper (see below) you will need to loosely fold the length, as for paste-the-paper paper, although with the pasted side inward to improve adhesive activation.

A

Keep the roll loose

Roll up a length of the paper, pattern side facing inward, and submerge it in the trough.

B

Take the top of the roll length and draw it up onto the table, patterned-side down, then fold up loosely.

PAPERING PREPARATION

Before applying wallpaper, it is important to consider the right order of work regarding the overall decoration of the room. First finish the wall preparation; then do any painting; finally, apply the wallpaper. When using wallpaper paste, always check the guidelines regarding soaking time. This refers to the length of time the wallpaper has to be soaked after pasting; for heavy-duty papers, this can be 10 or 15 minutes.

ESTIMATING QUANTITIES

To estimate how many rolls of wallpaper you need, add the height of the room to that of the paper's repeat pattern, if it has one (this measurement should be shown on the packaging). Multiply the total by the length of the room's perimeter. This is the total area of wallpaper needed. Divide this number by the area of a single roll of wallpaper (this may be on the packaging, or you should multiply the width by the length). Add an extra 10–15 percent to this figure, depending on how many obstacles there are in the room. Round this up to the next whole figure to give you the number of rolls you need to buy.

CUTTING PAPER TO SIZE

Lengths need to be cut to an approximate size before they are applied to the wall surface. There are various ways of doing this to keep waste to a minimum; the method you use will depend on the paper's pattern.

Free-match papers
Simply measure from the ceiling to the floor (or the top of the baseboard). Add a maximum of 4 in (100 mm) to allow for easy trimming.

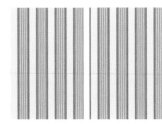

FREE MATCH

Straight-match papers
In addition to the trimming length, add the size of the paper's repeat pattern. If the pattern is very large, this may cause a lot of waste; an alternative is to hold a dry section of paper to the wall surface, cut it to an approximate length, and use this as a template for all the other "standard" lengths in the room.

STRAIGHT MATCH

Offset-match papers
Because of the offset, only every other length will be in the same "position" on the wall surface. You can use the same technique as employed for straight-match papers, but take alternate lengths from two rolls, each with a different starting point.

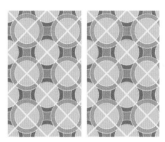

OFFSET MATCH

TEMPORARY WALLPAPER

If you like the look of wallpaper, but are not ready to commit to the seemingly permanent wall treatment or to spending time measuring, cutting, and cleaning up the mess, there are other wallpaper options available for you to try.

Temporary wallpaper, often called removable or peelable wallpaper, is a new wallpaper option that simplifies the process of decorating with traditional wallpaper. If you have never applied wallpaper, aren't sure if wallpaper is right for your home, or if you live in an apartment or college dorm where you cannot alter the walls, temporary wallpaper allows you the ability to experiment with wallpaper borders.

For children's rooms, temporary wallpaper is a perfect decorating accessory. The wallpaper gives you the option of being able to easily update their rooms to match changing ages and interests without having to undergo a complete bedroom remodel each time. With temporary wallpaper, the hours invested to strip old wallpaper with special solutions and tools are no longer always needed.

Available in rolls, borders, murals, and accents, the wallpaper can be applied to most materials. Perfect for any type of wall, temporary paper can be applied to other smooth, flat surfaces, including cabinets, tiles, and lamp shades. Offered in designs that range from contemporary to traditional, you should be able to find a scene or design that suits the look of your home.

Temporary wallpaper is pressed to the wall and adhered using a damp sponge (as shown below). Unlike other wallpapers, you have the opportunity to reposition it without harm until the paper is dry. After the wallpaper is dry, wet the paper again to peel it off the wall. Some manufacturers offer temporary wallpaper that does not even require water to remove it. Since the temporary wallpaper paste is water soluble, you will need to use traditional wallpaper paste to reapply it if you would like to reuse the wallpaper after it has been removed.

CUTTING PAPER CORRECTLY

Unroll the paper on the pasting table. You will probably need to weigh down the end to stop it from rolling up. Measure the length of paper needed. If the table isn't long enough, fold the paper back on itself without creasing. At the required point, mark a pencil guide line, then cut the paper carefully.

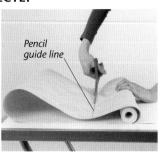

Pencil guide line

APPLYING TEMPORARY WALLPAPER

WHERE TO START PAPERING

Papers with large patterns should generally be centralized relative to any major features in the room (see also tiling, p.315). For small patterns, centralizing is less important. In either case, it is essential to get the first length (drop) perfectly vertical. Ideally, choose a full ceiling-to-floor drop and use a pencil line drawn with a level as your guide. In most cases you can choose an inconspicuous corner for the first drop because the dimensions of the room are unlikely to allow the final papers to match exactly. Draw your line about half a paper width away from the corner, rather than using the wall as your guide.

Ceiling with central light fixture
Start papering across the center of the light fixture. Either trim the paper roughly around the fixture and tuck it under, or loosen the fixture so you can paper under it easily. Be sure to turn off the electricity in this case.

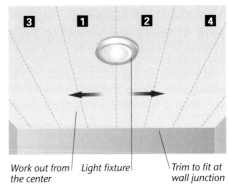

Work out from the center | Light fixture | Trim to fit at wall junction

Starting from a corner
Draw a vertical line away from the corner. Try to position your starting point so that there will be no tiny slivers required when cutting and trimming around doors and other obstacles. Hang the first length of paper against your guide line, then work clockwise around the room.

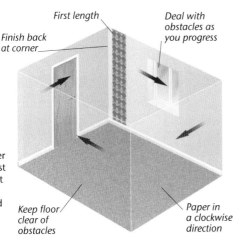

First length

Finish back at corner

Deal with obstacles as you progress

Keep floor clear of obstacles

Paper in a clockwise direction

Starting from the center
If the room has a prominent feature such as a chimney, centralize a large motif in the pattern in the center. Paper out from each side of the first length, then continue to paper clockwise around the room in the usual way.

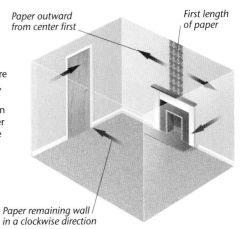

Paper outward from center first

First length of paper

Paper remaining wall in a clockwise direction

Papering around a window
Use the order shown right. Techniques are shown on p.306.
1 Hang the first length so that it overlaps the window.
2 Hang a short length at the top of the first. Then trim neatly to create flaps and fold these into the recess.
3 Hang a short length above the window and fold it into the recess.
4 Hang a whole length so that it overlaps the other end of the window.
5 Create flaps and fold them into the recess as before.
6 Fill in between the window sill and the floor. Trim the first and fourth lengths neatly around the sill.

Work in a clockwise direction

TOOLS AND MATERIALS CHECKLIST (PP.304–309)

Basic papering (pp.304–305) Wallpaper paste, pasting brush, paperhanging brush, sponge, paperhanging scissors, level, seam roller

Papering a room (pp.306–307) Wallpaper paste, pasting brush, paperhanging brush, sponge, level, paperhanging scissors, cutting edge

Papering an external corner (p.308) Wallpaper paste, pasting brush, paperhanging brush, sponge, cutting edge, seam roller

Papering an internal corner (p.308) Wallpaper paste, pasting brush, paperhanging brush, sponge, level

Working around radiators (p.308) Wallpaper paste, pasting brush, paperhanging brush, sponge, paperhanging scissors, radiator roller

Working around outlets and switch plates (p.309) Wallpaper paste, pasting brush, paperhanging brush, sponge, paperhanging scissors

Working around ceiling lights (p.309) Wallpaper paste, pasting brush, paperhanging brush, sponge

Applying borders (p.309) Wallpaper paste, pasting brush, paperhanging brush, sponge

FOR BASIC TOOLKIT SEE PP.22–23

BASIC PAPERING

You may decide to apply lining paper before wallpaper. Lining paper can be hung horizontally as well as vertically, depending on which technique will cover the wall fastest (see p.302). The horizontal technique is shown here; hang vertical lengths as for wallpaper. Use corners as guide lines, and if walls undulate, then allow the paper to overlap, then trim it back. Greater care must be taken with wallpaper; each sheet has to be hung perfectly vertical to achieve satisfactory results.

TOOLS AND MATERIALS SEE BASIC TOOLKIT AND P.303

1 LINING THE CEILING: THE FIRST SHEET

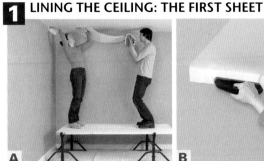

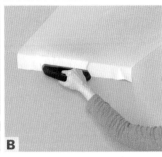

A Take your "book" of pasted lining paper and hold it in position in line with the wall; you will need help with this.

B Use the paperhanging brush to crease the paper into the junction between the ceiling and the wall.

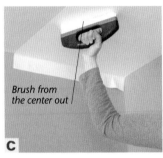

Brush from the center out

C Smooth out the paper with the paperhanging brush; your helper should unravel the paper as you progress.

D Brush out any bubbles trapped under the paper, then draw a pencil line along the junction between the ceiling and the wall.

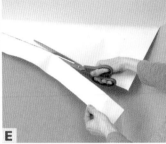

E Pull the paper gently back from the ceiling. Trim the paper along your line using scissors, then brush it back into position.

F Use a damp sponge to remove any excess paste from the walls and the paper surface. Repeat steps D–F at the other end of the paper.

2 ATTACHING THE NEXT LENGTH

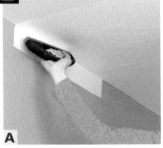

A Take the next "book" of paper and repeat the process. Align the paper with the first sheet, then fold it into the junction as before.

Make sure the seam is tight

B Butt the paper length against the side of the previous sheet. Smooth the entire section before trimming and wiping down.

3 LINING THE WALLS

A Position one end of a length of pasted lining paper into the corner of the wall, tight against the ceiling and overlapping into the corner.

B Smooth the paper across the wall with a paperhanging brush, using the junction between the wall and ceiling as your guide.

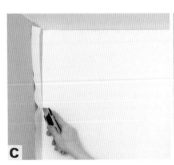

C When the sheet is in place, return to the corner and crease the paper. Slice the sheet with a trimming knife or scissors to remove any excess paper.

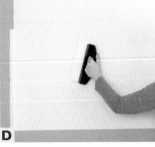

D Take the second sheet of pasted paper and position it below the first. Continue down the wall surface using the same techniques.

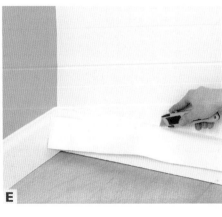

E When you get to the bottom of the wall, trim the paper against the baseboard or floor using a utility knife. Wipe any paste from the baseboard. Before starting on the next wall, cast an eye across each hung length. Check for bubbles and smooth again if necessary.

4 HANGING WALLPAPER

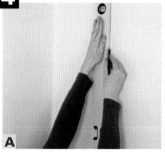

A Draw a vertical pencil line on the wall surface at your chosen starting point (see p.303). Check and recheck this line using a level.

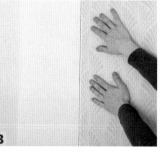

B Pick up the "book" of folded paper and unfold the top section. Position it against the guide line.

C When you are happy that the paper is level, brush it down from the top and crease it into the junction. At the same time, ensure that the vertical edge of the paper is precisely aligned with the pencil guide line.

D Unfold the book and work your way down the wall to the floor or baseboard. Be careful not to crease or tear the paper. Keep checking that the sheet is vertical.

E Use the brush to smooth the paper over the wall and remove any bubbles. Work from the center of the paper to the edges.

Check the paper against the vertical guide

F At floor level, use the brush to crease the paper into the junction between the wall and baseboard.

5 TRIMMING AND JOINING THE NEXT LENGTH

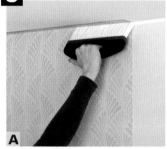

A Brush back up the paper to ensure good adhesion. Pay particular attention to the edges and to removing air bubbles.

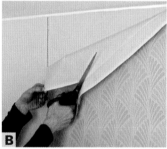

B Trim at the top and bottom of the length using whichever method you prefer. If you use scissors, mark the crease with a pencil line.

C Brush the trimmed edges tight against the ceiling and baseboard.

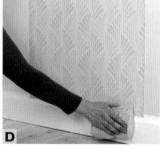

D Use a clean, damp sponge to wipe away any excess paste from wallpaper surface. Do the same for the ceiling and baseboard.

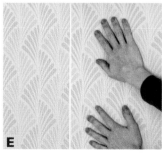

E Make sure that the pattern is matched at eye level; this keeps any pattern drop (or misalignments) at a high or low level.

F Butt the edges together tightly, checking the seam as you work your way down.

G *Apply roller with an up-and-down motion*

Clean the seam with a wet sponge to remove any excess paste; do not apply too much pressure as this creates a shiny seam when the paper is dry. Finish off by gently running a seam roller up and down the seam.

WALLPAPERING A ROOM

Wallpapering a room is a methodical process. Plan the project carefully, making sure you have bought enough paper and are sure of your starting position (see pp.284–285). Clear the room of as much furniture as possible. This example shows how to tackle a typical room layout. Use the basic wallpaper-hanging instructions shown on p.287 in combination with the techniques described here to navigate around the room perimeter. Details of how to negotiate corners and other obstacles you might encounter are shown on pp.308–309.

TOOLS AND MATERIALS SEE BASIC TOOLKIT AND P.303

1 HANGING THE FIRST SHEET

A

Draw a vertical line half a width away from the starting corner and hang your first full length of pasted paper. If you are using patterned paper, try to choose an inconspicuous corner, since the dimensions of the room are unlikely to allow an exact match when negotiating the final joint (see opposite).

2 PAPERING THE SIDE OF A WINDOW RECESS

When you reach a window, hang the next length of paper so that it overlaps the recess. Make horizontal cuts in the paper and bend the resulting flap into the recess. If the paper doesn't reach the window, it will be necessary to insert a further length.

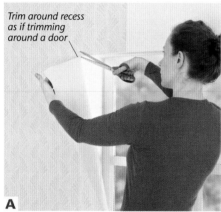

Trim around recess as if trimming around a door

A

B

Using a utility knife, finely trim the paper so that it fits perfectly around the sill.

C

After cutting the ends, brush the flap into place and crease the paper into the corner. Trim the edge so that the paper is flush with the window frame.

3 PAPERING THE TOP OF A WINDOW RECESS

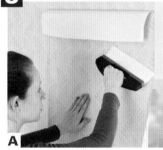

A

Paste a short piece of paper on top of the existing sheet to create a flap to fold into the window recess. Make sure that the patterns on the two sheets match.

Flap to fill recess

B

After cutting the flap, use a cutting edge and a knife to cut a diagonal line through both sheets of paper from the corner of the recess to the edge of the top sheet.

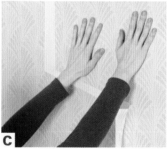

C

Remove both pieces of paper, then peel away the bottom sheet and place the top piece onto the wall. As always, make sure that the pattern fits perfectly with the edge sheet.

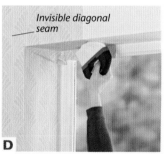

Invisible diagonal seam

D

Fold the remaining flap of the new sheet into the window recess. Brush out any bubbles and trim any ends with the knife. Continue as shown on p.303.

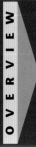

4 PAPERING AROUND A DOOR

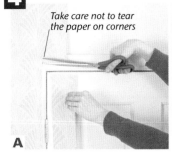

Take care not to tear the paper on corners

A

When you get to a door, apply a sheet as normal. Cut out a rough area of the door with scissors, leaving plenty of excess paper.

B

Cut diagonally through the excess paper over the door to the corner of the casing. Crease the top and side flaps into place, leaving the excess around the casing.

C

Trim the excess paper from the top of the door frame, using a utility or trimming knife.

D

Continue trimming the paper down the side of the door frame. Use the edge of the casing as a guide.

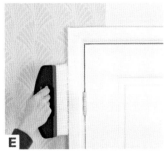

E

Smooth the paper around the casing with the brush.

F

Hang a short length of paper above the door. When perfectly aligned, trim it against the ceiling and casing.

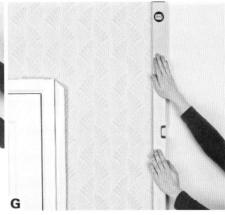

G

On reaching the other side of the door, use the same technique for the opposite edge, except do not trim along the vertical edge of the casing until the next full length of paper is hung. In this way it is easier to maintain the precise vertical position of the lengths and to trim accurately along the casing edge.

5 NEGOTIATING THE FINAL SEAM

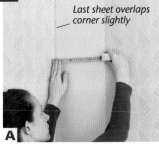

Last sheet overlaps corner slightly

A

Measure from the edge of the first length into the corner and add ¾ in (20 mm). Transfer this measurement to a length of pasted paper and cut along it.

Take care to brush the paper right into the corner

B

Take the measured strip and hang it against the first strip you hung, matching the pattern carefully. Brush the other edge into and around the internal corner.

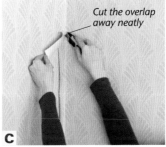

Cut the overlap away neatly

C

Carefully trim into the corner to remove the excess paper, and the top and bottom of the length. Smooth the ends when finished, adding extra paste if necessary.

D

The final edges may not match perfectly, but in the corner this is hardly noticeable. Sponge any remaining paste off the paper to finish.

PAPERING AROUND OBSTACLES

Aside from the obstacles shown on pp.306–307, there are many other areas where precise measuring, cutting, and trimming are required. In most cases, it is simply a further application of the principles demonstrated on those pages. In others, however, some special techniques are needed; the most common of these are illustrated here. As always, remember to turn off the electricity before working around lights and switches, and drain radiators if removing them from the wall (see p.508).

TOOLS AND MATERIALS SEE BASIC TOOLKIT AND P.303

EXTERNAL CORNERS

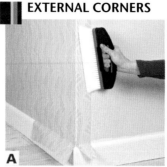

A

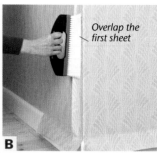

Overlap the first sheet

B

Hang the paper so that it bends around the corner. Slice the bottom to make two separate flaps, then brush the paper flat.

Hang a second sheet around the corner. Make sure it is vertical. Check that the pattern fits, then brush the second sheet flat.

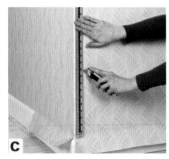

C

D

E

Use a straight edge (a metal ruler is ideal) to cut through both layers of the overlap.

Pull back the overlap and remove the paper below. Then remove the excess from the top sheet. Smooth to reveal a precise butt joint.

Trim the top and bottom of both sheets in the usual way. Remove any excess paste from the paper surface. Use a roller to secure the seam. You are now ready to hang the next sheet.

INTERNAL CORNERS

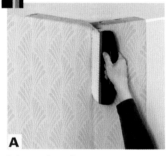

A

B

C

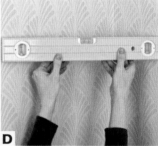

D

It is much easier to paper an internal corner with two vertical strips than with one. Start by folding a sheet into the corner.

Brush the sheet flat, then slice the paper ¾ in (20 mm) to the right of the corner to create two separate sheets.

Move the right-hand sheet to one side, then trim the top and bottom of the left-hand sheet. Move the right-hand sheet back across and trim.

Check that the paper is at the right level by comparing points of the pattern with adjacent lengths.

WORKING AROUND RADIATORS

Radiators can always be removed before papering, but it is also possible to simply work around them. Begin by securing the wallpaper as usual, pasting it to an inch or so above the radiator. Then allow the bottom section of the length to flap over the radiator surface.

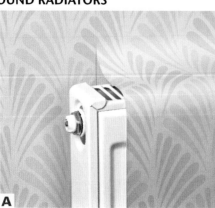

A

B

C

Cut the paper so that it will hang down slightly behind the radiator.

Use a roller to push the paper behind the radiator.

WORKING AROUND OUTLETS AND SWITCH PLATES

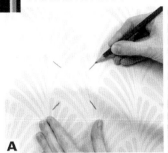

A

Turn off the power. Hang paper over the switch plate (or remove the plate while hanging). Mark the position of the corners of the plate.

B

Cut two diagonal slits from corner to corner, creating four triangular flaps. Fold the flaps out from the wall and cut along the folds.

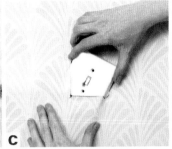

C

Loosen the switch plate by removing its retaining screws. Rotate the plate and feed it diagonally through the hole in the paper.

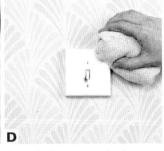

D

Smooth the paper under the switch plate. Reattach the plate and remove any paste with a sponge. Leave the electricity off until dry.

WORKING AROUND CEILING LIGHTS

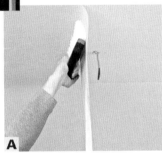

A

Turn off the power, then remove the light fixture and leave the wires hanging. Brush the paper across the ceiling to the wires.

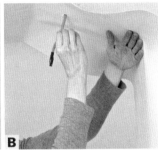

B

Make a hole in the paper where the wires stick out of the ceiling. Draw the wires through the paper. Continue smoothing down the length of paper.

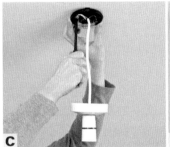

C

Finish hanging the paper, then reattach the fixtures. Screw the base back into the ceiling, making holes in the paper where necessary.

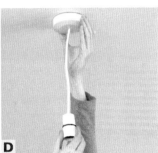

D

Once the wires and base are secure, screw the fixture into place. Leave the electricity off until the paper is completely dry.

APPLYING BORDERS AROUND A ROOM

A

Draw a pencil guide line on the wall at the height you wish the border to hang. Apply the border to the wall with a paperhanging brush.

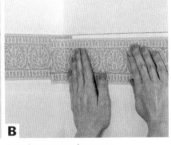

B

Overlap around corners. Move the next length into place, making sure the pattern matches. Trim overlap precisely in corner.

APPLYING BORDERS AROUND A FEATURE

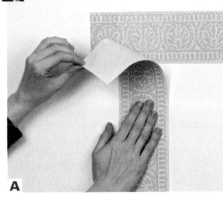

A

Borders are often used to frame mirrors and other features. To make a frame, they need to be joined at right angles. Use a level to make sure the strips are horizontal and vertical. Try to cross the pasted strips through the middle of a motif to get an approximate pattern match.

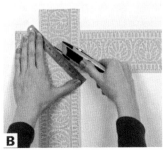

B

After placing the borders, use a straight edge and a trimming knife to cut through the overlap at 45 degrees.

C

Remove the excess paper from the end of each strip. You may need to lift the border to remove the paper from underneath.

D

Having removed the excess paper, flatten the borders against the wall and clean the final surface with a wet sponge.

STAIRWELLS

The most important consideration when papering a stairwell is to build a safe working platform. An example of this is shown on p.27, but the design can be varied, depending on your needs. Pad the tops of the ladders to prevent damaging the wall. You will need someone to help you when hanging long sheets.

PROBLEM SOLVER

FILLING BETWEEN CORNER EDGES ON LINING PAPER OR DRYWALL

A superior finish for lining is achieved by using caulk or flexible filler along all trimmed paper seams. Caulk is applied using a sealant dispenser, and must be smoothed immediately.

TOOLS AND MATERIALS
Caulk, sealant dispenser, sponge

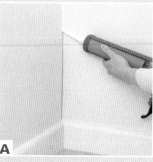

A Apply caulk evenly, creating a uniform bead along junctions.

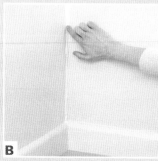

B Smooth with a wet finger to remove ridges and surface imperfections.

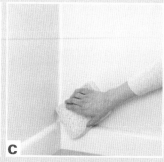

C Use a damp sponge to smooth caulk. Rinse regularly.

FILLING GAPS IN LINING PAPER

Imperfect seams on a lined surface may be improved by using some all-purpose decorating filler. Some manufacturers make ready-mixed "fine-surface filler," which is ideal for use here.

TOOLS AND MATERIALS
Filler, filling knife, sanding block, brush

A Apply filler using a filling knife.

B Let the filler dry, then use a sanding block to smooth any ridges.

C Make sure the filler is "sized" before any wallpaper is hung.

DISGUISING GAPS IN WALLPAPER SEAMS

For a perfect finish, seams can be disguised in a wallpaper finish by painting the background a color similar to the paper "base" color.

TOOLS AND MATERIALS
Paint, paintbrush, pasting brush

A Mark a line on the wall where the papers will meet. Paint over the line with the appropriate paint.

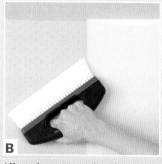

B Allow the paint to dry. Then hang the first sheet of paper and smooth down with a brush.

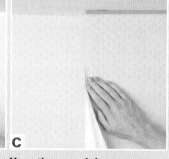

C Hang the second sheet next to the first. If there is space between the two sheets, the paint will disguise the gap.

REPAIRING TORN WALLPAPER

Paper is delicate and can sometimes be torn by a sharp object. You can often repair damage by carefully repositioning the torn section.

TOOLS AND MATERIALS
White glue, small brush, sponge

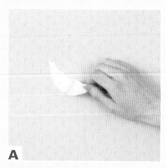

A Carefully pull back the torn section of paper.

B Apply border adhesive or white glue to the wall with a small brush, taking care not to get it on the front of the paper.

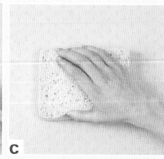

C Smooth the paper back into place with a damp sponge, removing excess adhesive.

REATTACHING PAPER THAT IS LIFTING OFF

Paper commonly lifts at its base, which is normally the junction with the baseboard. Poor initial application or moist air in a bathroom are the main causes.

TOOLS AND MATERIALS
White glue, small brush, sponge, caulk

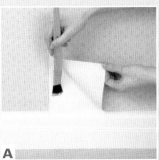

A

Peel back the lifted section of paper, and apply border adhesive or white glue to it.

B

Use a damp sponge to smooth the paper back into place.

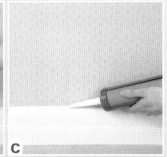

C

When the adhesive is dry, apply caulk along the seam between the paper and the wall.

GETTING A BUBBLE OUT OF WALLPAPER

Bubbles normally occur because of poor initial application. Where there are lots of bubbles, replace the paper. Where there are only a few bubbles, repair as shown.

TOOLS AND MATERIALS
Utility knife, white glue, small brush, sponge

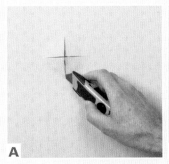

A

Using a utility knife, cut open the bubble with a cross cut.

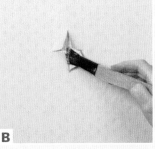

B

Open out the four leaves of the cut and apply a small amount of white glue with a small brush.

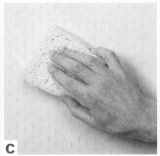

C

Use a sponge to smooth the leaves back into place, and allow to dry thoroughly.

REPAIRING A PEELING SEAM

Seams normally peel because of poor initial application, or because of an overlap. Overlaps are sometimes unavoidable, and (particularly with vinyl papers) they tend to peel easily if white glue was not used on the overlap during initial application.
In either case, overlaps or peeling seams are easily repaired by using the following technique.

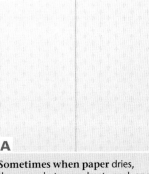

A

Sometimes when paper dries, the seams between sheets peel, and look unsightly.

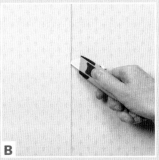

B

Carefully use a utility knife to pry back the overlap just enough to apply adhesive beneath it.

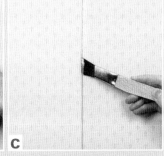

C

Apply a small amount of white glue, taking care not to get it on the front of the wallpaper.

D

Apply gentle pressure with a seam roller to flatten the seam edges together.

E

Wipe the seam clean with a wet sponge.

F

Dry the seam with a cloth, working in one direction to smooth the seam.

TOOLS AND MATERIALS
Utility knife, small brush, white glue, seam roller, sponge, cloth

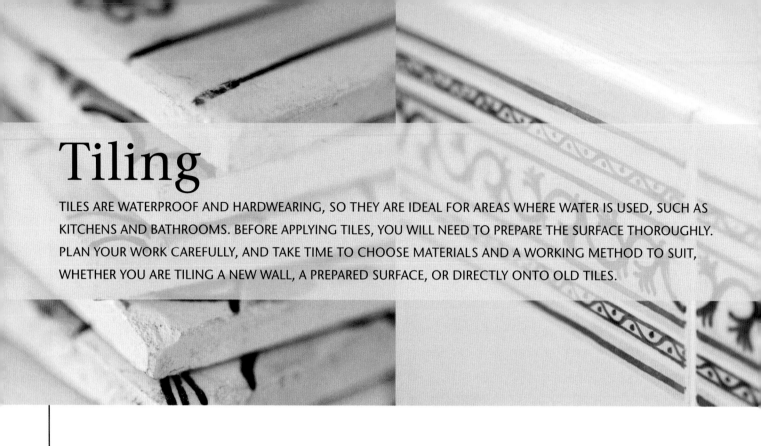

Tiling

TILES ARE WATERPROOF AND HARDWEARING, SO THEY ARE IDEAL FOR AREAS WHERE WATER IS USED, SUCH AS KITCHENS AND BATHROOMS. BEFORE APPLYING TILES, YOU WILL NEED TO PREPARE THE SURFACE THOROUGHLY. PLAN YOUR WORK CAREFULLY, AND TAKE TIME TO CHOOSE MATERIALS AND A WORKING METHOD TO SUIT, WHETHER YOU ARE TILING A NEW WALL, A PREPARED SURFACE, OR DIRECTLY ONTO OLD TILES.

PLANNING TILING PROJECTS

The type and size of tile you choose will affect your overall design and how you work. You can use larger tiles to cover an area more quickly, but you may find it more difficult to lay large tiles on uneven surfaces. In such cases, small tiles may be easier to use and be more forgiving. Consider whether to tile the whole room, just up to a border, or a specific area, like a backsplash. Because of the grid pattern formed by tiles, you need to spend time finding the best starting point in order to achieve a balanced overall effect and avoid thin slivers of tile. Use the next few pages to help you plan the project in its entirety first.

DESIGN OPTIONS

Tiles are usually applied in a regular grid pattern, but you can use other designs—for example, staggered or diamond patterns, or a combination of the two. For complicated designs, drawing a scale diagram will help you to plan your approach. See p.322 for the techniques needed for these effects.

Tiling patterns
The majority of ceramic tiles are square, and the most common design is to apply them in a grid pattern. However, tiles can be laid in a brickbond pattern or in more elaborate designs. Beware of using complicated arrangements in small spaces, since the effect can be overpowering.

REGULAR GRID

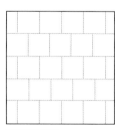

BRICKBOND

DIAMOND PATTERN

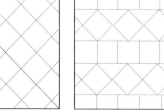

DIAMOND PATTERN IN REGULAR GRID

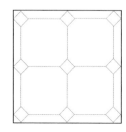

OCTAGONS WITH INSETS

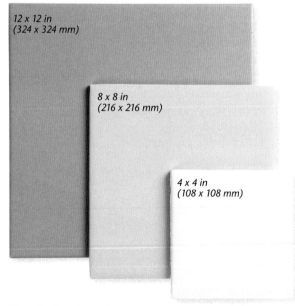

12 x 12 in (324 x 324 mm)

8 x 8 in (216 x 216 mm)

4 x 4 in (108 x 108 mm)

Choosing the right tiles
Size, shape, and color are as important as the material from which the tile is made. The standard square sizes are shown above. When possible, buy tiles of one color with the same batch number. Shuffle tiles of the same color from different boxes, so that any slight color variation will not show once the tiles are applied to the surface.

TYPES OF TILES

Most tiles are ceramic—they are made of clay, have a glazed, smooth surface that is easy to clean, and are very durable. Glazes are generally colored to provide decorative options. Some glazed tiles are prone to surface cracking, which may affect their waterproofing properties, making them unsuitable for constantly wet areas such as showers. Nonceramic tiles are made of materials such as marble or slate, and rather than relying on glaze, their natural texture provides the finish.

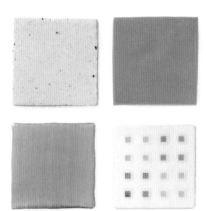

Ceramic tiles
These are usually glazed and are available in many sizes, colors, and thicknesses. Ceramic tiles are also easy to cut to shape. Some manufacturers produce ceramic tiles that look like natural tiles (see top left), but are often cheaper than the real thing.

Inset tiles
These tiles add a decorative detail to the main pattern of a larger design. They are usually small and square, but come in many shapes.

Mosaic tiles
Small ceramic or glass tiles are supplied in sheets on a net backing to control the space between tiles and to make them easier to apply. Some have a protective sheet of paper; it has to be soaked off after the tiling adhesive has dried. Sheets can be cut with scissors to size.

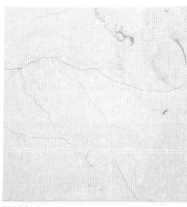

MARBLE

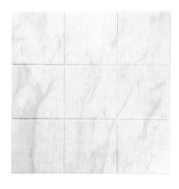

Plastic tiles
These are normally supplied in a sheet, and are applied to the surface with a tile adhesive. Never use plastic tiles in areas that will receive direct heat, such as close to an oven or stovetop.

SLATE   **LIMESTONE**

Natural tiles
Limestone, slate, and marble are common types of natural stone tile. Marble tiles are normally larger than standard-sized ceramic tiles, and are usually applied allowing for small grout joints to give a continuous marble effect. Natural stone is porous, so in areas where water is used, such as a bathroom or kitchen, natural stone tiles have to be treated with a waterproof sealant after application. Suppliers can provide appropriate sealants for the job.

GLASS   **STAINLESS STEEL**

Specialty tiles
Tiles made of glass, stainless steel, and some other materials can be considerably more expensive than ceramic tiles. Check that the material of your choice is suitable for the job. For instance, heat from an oven can crack some types of glass tiles.

BORDER TILES, TILE EDGES, AND CORNER TRIMS

In addition to square tiles, you can buy border tiles to decorate the edges of the tiled area and trims to finish and protect the edges of the tiles. Both are available in a wide variety of finishes and designs. Quadrant tiles are a further option, creating a decorative edge where tiles meet a bathtub, sink, or countertop. They give a more finished look than regular tiles cut to fit a narrow space. Remember to include trims and border or quadrant tiles when estimating quantities (see overleaf).

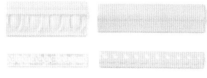

SELECTION OF BORDER TILES

■ **CORNER PIECE FOR PLASTIC TRIM**

PLASTIC TRIM

Border tiles
Narrow border tiles provide a decorative band that runs through a design or along its top edge. Apply adhesive directly to thin border tiles. If the tile widths do not match exactly the width of the main tiles, use spacers cut down into T-shapes or apply cross-shaped spaces perpendicular to the wall, and remove before grouting. Apply full tiles first, leaving cuts until last.

Tile edging and corner trims
Regular, straight-edged tiles are straightforward to apply, whereas you may have to adapt your technique for those with irregular edges. Trims are usually plastic and applied along external corners. Where the design stops in the middle of a wall surface, they can be used to provide a neat finish and cover unsightly cut edges. Tile edges are often unglazed, and trims may be used to protect the edges of tiles.

PREPARING A SURFACE

Surfaces must be prepared before applying new tiles to them. Old painted walls must be sanded and cleaned down. Wallpaper must be removed, and the surface below prepped. Old tiled surfaces can be stripped of tiles, but it is possible to tile over old tiles as long as they are still firmly attached to the wall. The grout joints of the new tiles should not coincide with those of the old tiles, so that if the old joints weaken and crack, the new tiled surface will not be affected.

CALCULATING HOW MANY TILES TO BUY

Follow the steps below to calculate the number of tiles you will need to buy.
1. Measure the height and width of the area you need to tile.
2. Multiply the height by the width to get the surface area.
3. Repeat for each surface. Remember to include small areas such as window reveals.
4. Add together all the areas to get a figure for the total area.
5. Subtract from that total any areas that do not need tiling (e.g., a doorway).
6. Add at least 10 percent to your final figure to allow for waste (broken tiles) and cutting. Then divide the surface area by the area of one of your chosen tiles to find out how many you need.

Using your supplier
If your design uses more than one type of tile, your supplier should be able to calculate for you how many tiles of each type you need. Where a relatively small number of tiles is needed, it should be easier to give your supplier an accurate figure for the number of tiles you require.

▐▐ USING A TILING GAUGE

You can use a tile gauge—a length of marked-off wooden furring strip—to judge accurately the number of tiles you need. By marking the width of the tiles on the wood, you can "gauge" how many tiles are required for a particular area. It is particularly useful for visualizing the tiles in position. When you are calculating how many tiles are needed (see above), use the gauge to see how the different tile sizes will fit in the area you have to tile. If your tiles are rectangular, rather than square, you will need two gauges, one for vertical gauging, one for horizontal gauging.

Spacers mark grout gaps between tiles

A

Cut a furring strip slightly shorter than the smallest width of the area to be tiled. Place the tiles along the furring strip with spacers between them. Mark the tile edges.

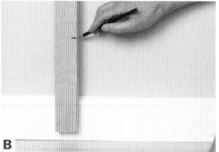

B

Hold the gauge against the surface of the wall and count the exact number of tiles. Use the gauge to plan the position of tiles around obstacles such as windows.

TILING A SMALL AREA

A stand-alone sink or stove may only require a small area of tiling above it. Plan the work so you only need to use whole tiles, with no cutting involved. Use the middle or edge of a tile as a central starting point to see if the tiles will look best centered in the space, or set to either side of the starting point. A slight overlap at the end of a tiled section can look neat if evenly matched on both sides. For sinks that have a slightly curved back edge, lay the first, central tile as before. Then, as you move out from the center, use spacers or card supports to keep the tiles level. Check that the line of tiles is level as you progress.

TILING A SHOWER STALL

You should tile a shower stall after tray installation, but before an enclosure is attached. Standard-sized tiles will often divide exactly into the dimensions of the shower tray, so cuts are often unnecessary, but check with a gauge first. Start at the outside edge of the stall, with the tile extending slightly outside the enclosure.

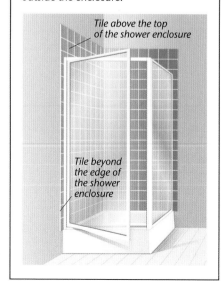

Tile above the top of the shower enclosure

Tile beyond the edge of the shower enclosure

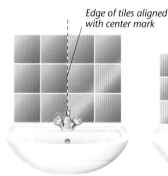

Edge of tiles aligned with center mark

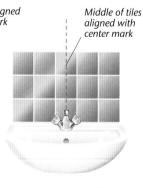

Middle of tiles aligned with center mark

Option 1: Even tiling
If an even number of tiles will fit neatly above the sink, first use a pencil to mark a midpoint on the wall above the back of the sink. Line up the edge of the first tile with the center mark and tile outward.

Option 2: Centered tiling
If an odd number of tiles lines up neatly above the sink, or you cannot put up the tiles without over-lapping the edges of the sink, align the middle of the first tile with the center of the sink and tile outward.

Option 3: Tiling behind a shaped back edge
If possible, loosen the retaining screws that hold the sink or shaped back section against the wall. Apply the first row of tiles behind the edge of the sink and reattach it.

PLANNING A TILE ARRANGEMENT

There is no single starting point that applies to all tiling jobs. In a small room it is a good idea to center your tile layout on a small area, such as a sink or cooktop backsplash, that is the area that you look at most often in the room. Use a tape measure or tile gauge (see opposite) to assess where the tiles would be positioned. Plan to site cut tiles in areas where they would be less noticeable, and avoid awkward,

thin pieces. Although you should plan to start tiling at floor level, you will need to consider how columns and rows of tiles will be positioned in relation to focal points and level surfaces. If tiling from floor level, take into account the temporary furring strip you will use to provide a straight edge and support (see p.318). Eventually you will use cut tiles to cover the space left by the furring strips.

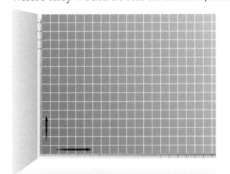

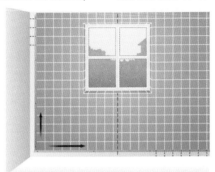

Start at floor level
Some older floors and baseboards are uneven, so you may need to install temporary furring strips to the bottom of the wall to provide a straight edge. Aim to finish with any cut tiles in less conspicuous areas, such as around the floor or ceiling and in corners. You should always aim to start tiling from furring strip level.

Plan around focal points
If your room has a focal point, such as a window, it is vital to consider this in your planning. Use a tile gauge to assess whether you can use whole tiles around it, or cut tiles to match on each side. Although you will start tiling at floor level, accurate planning will mean that the tiles around the window will be well positioned.

Consider level surfaces
A level surface, such as a countertop or bathtub, can sometimes act as a guide and support for the tiles above. Ideally, you should apply a row of whole tiles along the surface. Use a gauge to check how this will affect the positioning of tiles around other features. Even with a level surface, you should aim to start tiling from floor level.

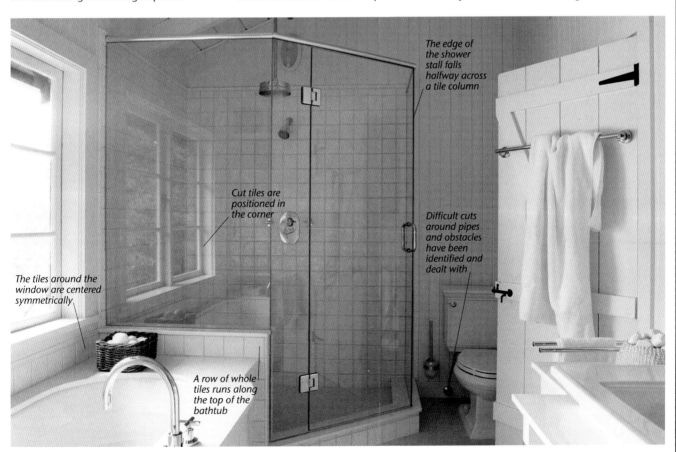

The edge of the shower stall falls halfway across a tile column

Cut tiles are positioned in the corner

Difficult cuts around pipes and obstacles have been identified and dealt with

The tiles around the window are centered symmetrically

A row of whole tiles runs along the top of the bathtub

Visualizing your room
If you are planning to tile a whole room, first you will need to consider some or all of the planning guidelines suggested opposite and above. In this example, the best possible tiling solution for each area of a bathroom has been visualized, and the overall tiling plan has addressed most of the practical and design issues that are covered here. However,

in most cases, your design depends on room proportions and tile size. It is unlikely that you will be able to combine the ideal tile placement for each area of your room. In such instances, you will need to use a tile gauge to measure out possible combinations of tile placement and come up with a solution that offers the most acceptable compromise.

CUTTING TOOLS

For cutting straight tile edges, a score-and-snap cutter is usually the best option, but an electric one is worth considering if you need to do a lot of tiling, or are using floor tiles. To cut curves and irregular shapes you would normally use a tile saw, while special drill attachments are available for making holes in tiles.

Angle grinder
Intricate cuts are made easier when you use an angle grinder with a diamond wheel.

Side handle

Grinding wheel

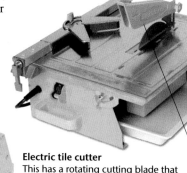

Scoring and snapping handle

Blade

Electric tile cutter
This has a rotating cutting blade that grinds through tiles. It can cut thick tiles more easily than a score-and-snap tile cutter, and it can cut miters. To cut a tile, push it toward the blade using the pushing tool supplied. A cold-water reservoir keeps the blade from overheating. Diamond blades provide the best cuts.

Sandpaper-like surface

Tile file
If a cut tile has a rough edge, use a tile file to get a clean, straight finish.

Score-and-snap tile cutter
This cutter can handle most cutting requirements. Cheaper models will be less accurate than heavy-duty cutters, and cannot be used for floor tiles. To cut a tile, place it inside the central frame. Press the wheel onto the surface of the tile, and push it along to score its surface. Apply pressure on either side of this groove to snap the tile in two.

Spring opens jaws when grip is relaxed

Tile nibblers
Used to remove small portions of tile. Score a guide line first.

Protective cage

Tile-cutting bit

Circular tile cutter
This drill attachment cuts clean circles in tiles for pipework.

Tile saw
Use a tile saw, preferably with a tungsten carbide blade, to cut curves in tiles.

Blade wears quickly but is replaceable

OTHER TILING TOOLS

There is a large range of tools that are designed for measuring tiles, applying them to surfaces, and creating a neat finish. Decide which tools you need for your project using the checklist opposite.

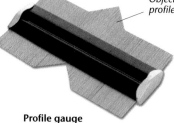

Object's profile

Profile gauge
Press the gauge against any profile or edge to make a guide that can be traced onto a tile.

An indelible pen
Use to mark cut lines on tiles. Used with an electric cutter, so that the water used to cool the blade does not smudge the guide lines.

Sponge float
The rubber blade presses grout into place, and the straight edge limits overspill onto the tiles.

Adhesive spreader for walls
The notched edges distribute adhesive evenly and in a ridged pattern, so that tiles stick firmly.

Notched edge

Grout rake
Scrape the blade along tile joints to remove old grout that you want to replace.

Blade

Adhesive spreader for tiles
Use to apply adhesive to the back of tiles.

Grout shaper
Run along a grout line, after applying the grout, to create a smooth finish.

Sponge
Keep a bucket of water and a sponge on hand to wipe away excess adhesive, and to clean tools as you work.

USING SPACERS

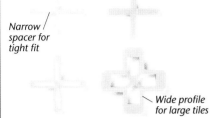

Narrow spacer for tight fit

Wide profile for large tiles

Spacers
These small, plastic crosses are positioned between tiles to provide equal-sized joints. The size of the spacer will determine the thickness of the grout joints. Spacers need to be removed before grouting.

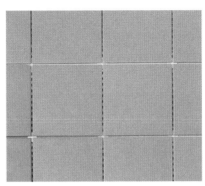

Using spacers flat against a surface
When tiling up from a furring strip with plastic spacers used flush to the wall surface, you can tile from floor to ceiling in a day. The spacers and furring strip stop the tiles from slipping.

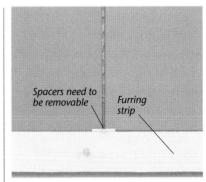

Spacers need to be removable

Furring strip

Using removable spacers or cardboard
When using spacers perpendicular to the wall surface, apply tiles to a maximum height of 5 ft (1.5 m) and let the adhesive dry before continuing with the next rows.

ADHESIVES AND SEALANTS

Good-quality adhesives and sealants are crucial for providing waterproof tiled finishes. Also pay particular attention to the grout you purchase, since some are more waterproof than others. Grout is available in a range of colors. White is the most popular, but you may choose off-white to match natural stone, for example. Natural tiles may also require sealing. Often it is best to apply one coat of sealant to the tiles before application, and one after. As sealants are often tile-specific, you should take advice from your supplier.

Adhesive

Powdered and ready-mixed varieties are available, but the latter are more expensive.

Adhesive and grout

This useful dual-purpose substance acts as both an adhesive and a grout. Close the lid between stages to prevent drying out. Good for small repairs.

Grout

Mix powdered grout with water to form a paste. Only mix as much as you can use in an hour, so that it does not dry out.

Epoxy grout

This is difficult to apply but makes a hygienic seal for joints on tiled kitchen countertops.

Grout protector

This liquid sealant stops grout from discoloring and keeps the finish clean. Leave grout to dry fully before application.

Grout reviver

Apply this paintlike substance to old grout to restore its finish. Available in white and a range of neutral colors.

Sealant

Use this for a waterproof seal between tiles and a countertop, bathtub, wall, or floor.

TOOLS AND MATERIALS CHECKLIST (PP.300–305)

Basic tiling (pp.318–319) Wood battens, level, tile adhesive, adhesive spreader, spacers, measuring jig*, indelible pen, tile cutter, sponge, grout, grout spreader, sponge, grout shaper

Tiling around an outlet or switch (p.320) Pen, tile cutter, tile adhesive and spreader

Tiling an internal corner (p.320) Pen, metal ruler, tile cutter, tile adhesive, adhesive spreader

Tiling a recess (p.320) Furring strips, tile adhesive, adhesive spreader

Tiling a recess (pp.320–321) Pen, tile cutter or saw, tile adhesive, adhesive spreader, corner trim*

Cutting a curve (p.321) Paper, scissors, pen or pencil, tile cutter or saw, profile gauge*

Tiling around a pipe (p.321) Pen, try square, ruler, tile hole cutter, tile adhesive, adhesive spreader

Using inset tiles (p.322) Spacers, tile adhesive, spreader

Creating a diamond pattern (p.322) Tile cutter, level, tile adhesive, adhesive spreader

Laying mosaic tiles (p.322) Paint roller, scissors and/or tile nibblers, tile adhesive, adhesive spreader

Creating a border (p.322) Spacers, tile cutter, tile adhesive, adhesive spreader

Other spacing effects (p.322) Pieces of thin cardboard, spacers

Using sealant (p.323) Masking tape, sealant, sealant dispenser

Sealing and unsealing a bath access panel (p.323) Sealant, sealant dispenser

* = optional

FOR BASIC TOOLKIT SEE PP.24–25

BASIC TILING

Before you start tiling, make sure you have planned your tile arrangement (see p.315). Generally, you can tile from furring strip to ceiling in a day using the method shown here. If you do not use rigid plastic spacers flat against the wall, you should tile to a height of 5 ft (1.5 m), then leave the adhesive to dry for at least 12 hours before continuing. Allow the adhesive to dry fully before grouting. See pp.320–323 for more advanced tiling techniques.

TOOLS AND MATERIALS SEE BASIC TOOLKIT AND P.317

1 ATTACHING THE FURRING STRIPS

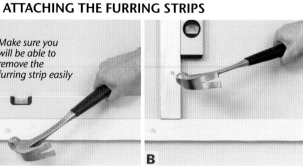

Make sure you will be able to remove the furring strip easily

A **Nail the horizontal furring strip** to the wall at your chosen starting point. Use a level to keep it straight, and use a wire detector to check for wires before hammering the nails.

B **Place the vertical furring strip** at the edge of your design, marking the start of the first vertical row of complete tiles. Nail the second strip at right angles to the first.

2 PLACING THE FIRST TILES

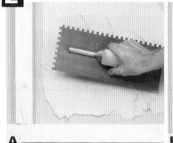

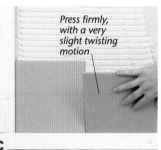

Press firmly, with a very slight twisting motion

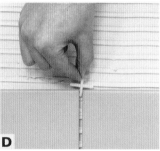

A **Apply the adhesive** with a notched trowel, pushing it into the right angle created by the furring strips. Cover no more than 10 sq ft (1 sq m) at a time.

B **Spread the adhesive** by pulling the notched trowel's serrated edge through it, several times if necessary, to make sure it is even. This improves the adhesion of each tile.

C **Place the first tile** in the right angle of the two furring strips. Place the second tile beside it, remembering to leave a sufficient gap between them for the first spacer.

D **Place the spacer** flat between the inside top corners of the two tiles. Stand a spacer at right angles to the wall at the bottom of the gap between the two tiles.

3 BUILDING UP THE TILE LEVELS

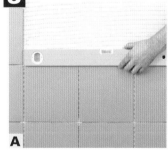

A **Add further tiles,** building up the levels as you progress across the wall, adding spacers between the tiles. Use a level to check regularly that the rows are straight.

B **As tiling progresses,** check that the tile surface is even. Hold a furring strip with a straight edge across the tiles, and see if it lies flat on every tile.

4 MEASURING TO FILL GAPS AND CORNERS

A **Allow the completed area** of tiles to dry fully—for at least 12 hours, but ideally overnight. Then remove the horizontal furring strip by prying out the nails with a claw hammer.

B **Measure the remaining gap** at every point where a tile will be placed, since widths may vary along the wall. Remember to allow space for grout joints.

ALTERNATIVE MEASURING TECHNIQUES

Measuring by hand
For pinpoint accuracy, turn the tile face inward and mark the edges, allowing for grout joints.

Using a measuring jig
Tile cutters often have a measuring jig that quickly calculates widths plus grout space. This is then inserted into the cutter as a guide.

5 APPLYING CUT TILES

Mark the measurements on a tile using a felt-tip pen. If you have planned correctly, you will need approximate half- tiles, rather than slivers.

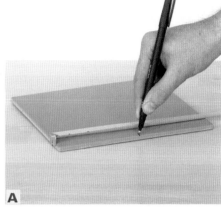

A

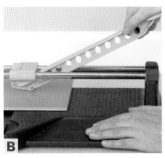

B

To score the tile, grip it in your tile cutter, with the glazed surface facing upward. Push the lever away from you to score along the marked guide line.

Depending on the cutter design, either position the tile in the cutter's jaws or below its mechanism, before applying downward pressure to the lever to split the tile in two.

D

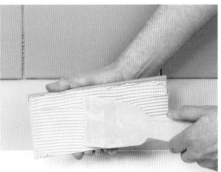

Smooth any rough edges with a tile file. Before placing cut tiles, spread adhesive on the back of the tile. It is easier to add adhesive to a cut tile than to the wall space.

E

Position the tile on the wall. To complete the wall, continue along the row to fill the horizontal gap. Remove the vertical furring strip and repeat the process, working upward. More information on dealing with internal corners is given on p.320.

6 GROUTING TILES

A

Wearing a glove, use a damp sponge to wipe off any excess grout while it is still wet. Avoid rubbing the grout out of the tile joints.

Shape the grout to give a smooth, even finish

B

Use a grout shaper or finger to neaten the grout line, then wipe again with a clean, damp sponge. After the grout has dried, polish the tiles with a dry cloth to remove any residue.

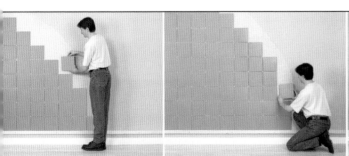

TILING AROUND OBSTACLES

Most surfaces have obstacles that interrupt the run of tiles and make tiling more complicated. Many of the problems that obstacles present can be dealt with by carefully planning your tile layout (see pp.314–315). Remove fixtures if possible, and tile with just the supply pipes in place. Choose those techniques that are most suitable for your own project. Often there is more than one way of tackling some tasks, depending on which tools you have, or the circumstances you face.

TOOLS AND MATERIALS SEE BASIC TOOLKIT AND P.317

CONSIDERING TILE LAYOUT

When dealing with a number of obstacles, you will first need to plan the overall tile layout (see p.317) and work out a solution that addresses most problem areas.

Half-tiles inside the recess

Tiles centered on window frame

Corner trim

Internal corner

Begin at center of outer edge, and work toward window and corners

External corner

TILING AROUND AN OUTLET OR SWITCH PLATE

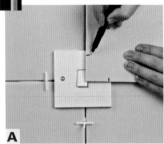

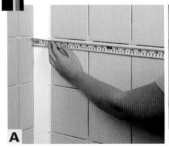

A **Turn off the electricity** supply and loosen the plates. Hold a tile in place and mark it so that the cut edges will fit behind the plate.

B **Use an electric** tile cutter to cut along the guide lines. Another option is to use a tile saw on the first line, then score and snap the second.

TILING AN INTERNAL CORNER

A **Measure the space** between the last full tile and the corner, allowing for grout gaps. The gap may be uneven, so measure at both ends.

B **Mark your measurements** on the tile. For an even gap, mark on one edge. For an uneven gap, or a large tile, draw a guide line right across.

C **Cut the tile,** placing it squarely in the cutter to cut for an even gap, or placing it at an angle in the cutter if the tile needs to fit in an uneven gap.

Apply tile adhesive directly onto the tile, and put it in position, using spacers as required. Repeat until the corner is completely tiled.

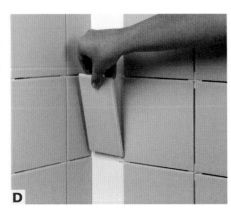

D

TILING A RECESS

A **Start tiling at** the center of the outer edge and work outward toward the corners and up around the inner edge of the recess.

B **Support tiles inside** the top of a recess by wedging a piece of wood beneath them while the adhesive dries, to prevent them from falling off.

ALTERNATIVE TECHNIQUES

There are various ways to finish tiling an external corner. In some cases, such as around a window reveal, a neater finish may be achieved by making mitered corners. For these you will need to use an electric tile cutter with a platform that can be angled (see p.316). Overlapping edges are a simple solution, but may be unattractive if the tile edges are unglazed. Corner profile strips are a neat and protective solution.

Mitered corner tiles
Press the angled edges neatly together at the corner. Leave a gap along the joint for grouting.

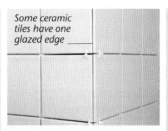

Some ceramic tiles have one glazed edge

Overlapping
Tile to the corner seam so that the tiles on one surface butt up over those on the other.

Using a strip
An L-shaped strip can be used to cover unglazed tile edges. Fix it in place with a sealant.

CUTTING A CURVE

A
Cut some paper to the size of a tile and place it up against the curved surface. Mark the profile of the curve on the paper with a pen.

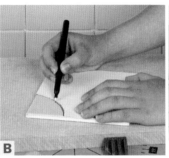

B
Cut along the pen line to create a template of the curve. Place the paper template over a tile and trace a guide line onto the tile.

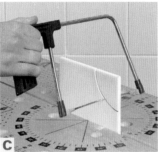

C
Use a tile saw to cut along the guide line. This may take a while. Hold the tile in place to check the fit before placing it in position.

ALTERNATIVE TECHNIQUE

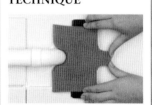

Cutting a curve
Press a profile gauge against the obstacle, and trace the curve onto the tile for a guide.

TILING AROUND A PIPE

Remove the fixture, if possible. Hold a tile to one side of the pipe and mark the top and bottom edges of the pipe's diameter on the tile. Even if the fixture has not been removed, use this technique to measure where the hole will fall.

A

B
Hold the tile below the pipe, in line with its column of full tiles, and mark on it the left and right edges of the pipe's diameter.

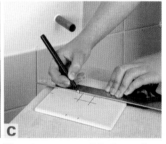

C
Use a try square to join the marks, forming a square where the tile will fit over the pipe. Join opposite corners to find the center.

D
Adjust a tile hole cutter to the size setting you need.

E
Attach the hole cutter to a drill, set its point on the mark in the center of the square guide lines, and remove a circle of tile.

F
Apply tile adhesive directly to the tile, and put the tile in position over the pipe. If it has not been possible to remove the fixture, score and snap the tile along a line through the hole, so that you can fit the tile around the pipe.

USING OTHER TECHNIQUES

There are many different types of tiles and designs available, and, depending on your choice, you may need to adapt the basic application techniques or use alternative methods. Some designs will use regular square tiles in irregular grid arrangements, while other types of tiles, such as inset tiles, border tiles, and mosaic tiles each require a specific approach. Depending on the shape and size of the tiles you select, you may also need to improvise when applying spacers.

TOOLS AND MATERIALS SEE BASIC TOOLKIT AND P.317

USING INSET TILES

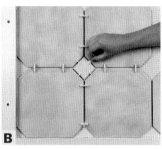

A **Before placing** inset tiles, build up a row of the larger tiles in your pattern, standing spacers on edge, as they will not lie flat.

B **Position inset tiles** as you build up subsequent rows, placing main and inset tiles alternately.

CREATING A DIAMOND PATTERN

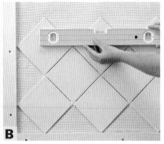

A **Buy extra tiles,** because this design requires cuts, and wastage may be high. Cut some tiles in half diagonally to fill in the design.

B **Keep diamonds even** by checking regularly, with a level, that the corners are horizontally or vertically aligned, as required.

USING MOSAIC TILES

A **Treat each sheet** as a single tile, and use a paint roller to flatten it into place, considering the type of backing you have (see p.313).

B **To fit a sheet** around an obstacle, use scissors to cut through the backing.

CREATING A BORDER

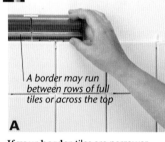

A border may run between rows of full tiles or across the top

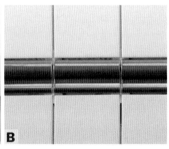

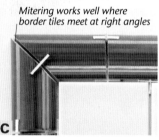

Mitering works well where border tiles meet at right angles

A **If your border** tiles are narrower than the main tiles, spacers may not sit flat. You will need to stand them on edge or cut them into a T-shape.

B **Apply border tiles** adjacent to the last row of main tiles, or at the required height within the main tiles. Leave any cuts until last.

C **Use an electric** cutter to make 45-degree cuts on two tiles. Press them neatly together using spacers on edge to maintain the mitered gap.

ALTERNATIVE TECHNIQUE

Applying adhesive
Where it is difficult to apply adhesive to a wall, you can apply it directly to the back of the tile instead.

OTHER SPACING EFFECTS

Irregular tiles
Judge grout spaces by eye, or use pieces of thin cardboard, rather than trying to force spacers to fit irregular tile edges. Keep rows as level as possible.

Brickwork
Align each row of tiles so that seams between tiles fall at the midpoints of tiles on the row beneath.

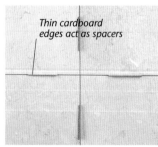

Thin cardboard edges act as spacers

Marble tiles
Create the illusion of a continuous marble surface by keeping grout gaps as narrow as possible.

A seam between a tiled area and another surface is a point of potential weakness, because grout can crack, or water seepage can cause damage to areas under tiling, including floors and ceilings. Silicone sealant reduces the risk of such damage. It is waterproof, flexible, so it will not crack, and is easily removed for access to concealed areas, such as the underside of a bathtub. Silicone fumes can be harmful, so open a window to keep the working area well ventilated.

TOOLS AND MATERIALS SEE BASIC TOOLKIT AND P.317

WHERE TO SEAL

Apply a waterproof seal to any area where tiling meets a bathtub, sink, or counter-top, and around the outer edge of a shower cubicle panel. You can also use sealant when installing flooring to waterproof areas where tiles meet a hard floor. This prevents water from seeping into or beneath a floor. For more information on types of sealant, see p.81.

Apply sealant along this seam

USING SILICONE SEALANT

Apply masking tape ⅛ in (3 mm) from each side of the seam. This will ensure that the sealant will have straight edges when finished. Cut the nozzle of the sealant tube at an angle, so that the diameter of the opening is slightly wider than the gap that needs sealing. Follow the instructions supplied to load the sealant tube into the dispenser.

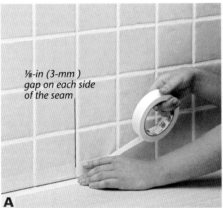

⅛-in (3-mm) gap on each side of the seam

A

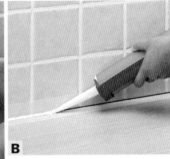

B Pressing evenly, squeeze sealant into place, moving slowly along the joint. Apply a little at a time, so you can smooth it as you work.

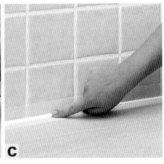

C Use paper tissues to remove any excess sealant from the nozzle. Smooth the sealant as you work by running a wet finger along the joint.

D

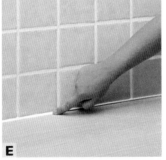

E

Remove the masking tape to reveal a straight sealant band along the extent of the seam.

If necessary, smooth over the sealant once more, pressing gently to avoid spreading it beyond the neat edges created by masking.

SEALING AND UNSEALING A BATH ACCESS PANEL

A A removable panel is needed for access (see pp.264–265), but it still needs waterproofing like any other tiled surface to avoid leaks.

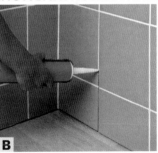

B Carefully apply sealant to the seam between the panel and the fixed tiles, trying to keep the seam invisible, if possible.

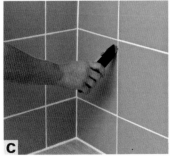

C To access the cavity, carefully use a utility knife to cut away the silicone sealant. The panel will then pull free.

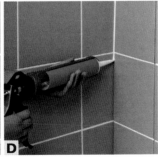

D After replacing the panel, apply silicone sealant again to the joints between the panels, by repeating steps A and B shown here.

OTHER WAYS TO SEAL TILES

Grout protector
Simply applied with a brush, this is an option that can help to create a harder-wearing surface.

Tile sealant
Follow the manufacturer's advice on the selection and application of sealant for natural tiles.

PROBLEM SOLVER

REPLACING A BROKEN TILE

You will want to replace broken or cracked tiles to maintain the appearance of a room. It is also important to replace them because damaged tiles can lead to leaks in the room, which can damage walls and floors, and may lead to mold problems, and eventually structural damage.

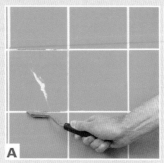

A Use a grout raker to remove the grout from around the edge of the broken tile. Check for electricity or water supplies using a detector.

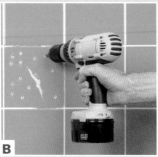

B Weaken the tile surface further by drilling a number of holes through it.

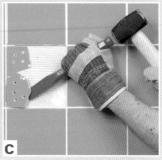

C Use a club hammer and chisel to remove sections of the broken tile. Be sure to wear gloves and protective goggles.

D Apply tile adhesive to the back of a tile using an adhesive spreader.

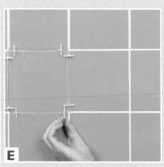

E Position the tile, checking that it sits flush. Use spacers to maintain grout gaps. When dry, remove the spacers and grout the joints.

REUSING BROKEN TILES

Before you dispose of the pieces of tile from your repair job, consider a few other options. Broken tile can be used for decorative mosaic elements in your home. Mosaic patterns can enhance flower pots, picture frames, and be used as part of a unique flooring design. If you are planning to have potted plants, broken tiles can be used as a bottom layer in the pot to help with drainage.

TOOLS AND MATERIALS
Gloves, goggles, grout raker, drill, club hammer, chisel, scraper, tile adhesive, adhesive spreader, spacers, grout

REGROUTING

When grout deteriorates over time, it can lose its color and waterproofing capability. Replacing grout can improve the appearance of a tiled room quickly and at low cost.

TOOLS AND MATERIALS
Grout raker, vacuum cleaner, grout, grout spreader, sponge

A Remove the old grout from the joints using a grout raker, taking care not to damage tile edges.

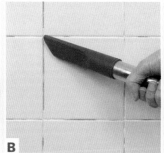

B Vacuum out the joints in order to remove all dust and debris.

C Regrout the joints, using a grout spreader as shown on p.319.

REVIVING TIRED GROUT

Where grout has deteriorated in terms of color but not structure, a tube of grout reviver can be used to restore the grout to a clean, bright color.

TOOLS AND MATERIALS
Sponge, TSP, grout reviver, cloth

A Clean down the tiled surface thoroughly using a sponge and TSP solution.

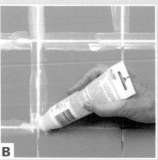

B When the grout is dry, apply grout reviver along the joints.

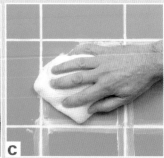

C Check the manufacturer's guidelines to see when to wipe off the excess grout reviver. Use a damp cloth.

REPLACING LATEX CAULK

Junctions between tiles and other surfaces are normally sealed with latex caulk, which can deteriorate over time. Once a seal begins to allow water penetration, it must be replaced.

TOOLS AND MATERIALS
Window scraper or sealant remover, masking tape, caulk

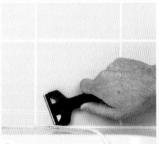

A

Scrape away the old sealant. A window scraper is ideal, or use a special sealant remover.

B

Stick masking tape ⅛ in (4 mm) from each side of the joint. This will ensure that the sealant will have straight edges.

C

Apply latex caulk along the gap, and smooth with a wetted finger. Remove tape and smooth again if necessary.

REPAIRING A DAMAGED SHOWER CUBICLE

If water seepage has caused the wall around a shower cubicle to decay, tiles will start to become loose. The steps here are for repairs on a stud wall. If the studs themselves are decaying, you will need to remove sections of the wall and rebuild as required (see pp.104–107).

TOOLS AND MATERIALS
Drywall saw, heater, claw hammer, water-resistant board, latex caulk, caulk gun, fiberglass tape, tile adhesive, tiles, grout

A

Remove any cubicle walls or shower screens before you start, so that you have full access to the tiles.

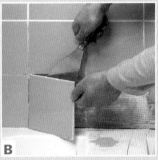

B

Use a scraper to remove loose tiles, and any tiles with decayed grout, until you expose a half-tile's width of sound drywall.

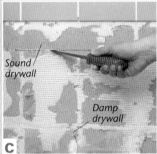

Sound drywall

Damp drywall

C

Cut a line at this height using a drywall saw. Be careful not to cut through any concealed electrical or water supplies.

PREVENTION
In most cases, a shower cubicle leaks because of poorly grouted tile joints, or because of degraded latex caulk around the shower tray or the shower screen.

Anywhere that a valve or pipe penetrates a tiled surface is also a potential point of weakness, and if even a small section of grout or caulk is missing, gradual water penetration may break down the wall structure and cause tiles to fall away from its surface.

The situation can deteriorate quickly if it goes unnoticed, so check these areas regularly for signs of damage or dampness. If you find any problems, tackle them immediately, using the techniques shown above.

D

A drywall saw may be helpful for cutting through drywall adjacent to studs, which should not be pressure-treated.

E

Use the claw of a hammer to remove old hardware. Leave studs exposed for a few days, to dry. A heater may speed up this process.

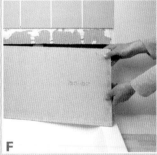

F

Cut a piece of cement-based, water-resistant board to size, and screw it onto the studs.

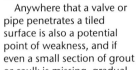
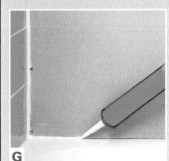

G

Seal around the edges of the board with latex caulk using a caulk gun.

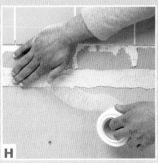

H

Apply fiberglass tape to the joint between the new and old boards using tile adhesive.

I

Apply tile adhesive and tile over the area to match the existing tiles then regrout. Reapply latex caulk to tray and corner joints.

Flooring

LAYING SHEET VINYL OR WOVEN-BACKED CARPET REQUIRES QUITE A HIGH LEVEL OF SKILL. HOWEVER, COVERINGS SUCH AS TILES AND CLIP-TOGETHER WOODEN FLOORING ARE MORE STRAIGHTFORWARD TO LAY. IN SOME CASES YOU MAY NEED TO LAY A SUBFLOOR BEFORE THE FLOORING (SEE P.332). BE AWARE THAT CLIP-TOGETHER FLOORING OR SANDED BOARDS MAY BE TOO NOISY FOR AN APARTMENT OR CONDO.

ROLLED FLOORING

Primary-backed carpet
Laid with an underlayment. Needs to be stretched as it is fitted. It can be laid on nearly any type of subfloor, or directly on to floorboards if they are in good condition. Tackless stripping is used around the perimeter to hold the carpet in place.

Foam-backed carpet
This does not require stretching or an underlayment. It is normally stuck down with carpet tape. Some manufacturers suggest using an underlayment, but it can then be difficult to stick the carpet and underlayment to the floor surface.

Sheet vinyl
This is usually laid dry, on a subfloor (suitable floors include plywood, self-leveled, and hardboard). Vinyl, especially if it is lightweight, can be stuck down.

Protects carpet from dirt or unevenness below

UNDERLAYMENT PADS

Foam roll pad
This creates a cushioning effect under the carpet. It also provides good heat insulation, and helps to absorb noise.

Felt pad
An alternative to foam roll underlayment. Comes in various thicknesses. Thicker, higher-quality examples are more expensive.

PREPARING TO LAY CARPET OR SHEET VINYL

Although carpet and vinyl are vastly different materials, they are laid in a similar way. Try to avoid joining lengths; if it is unavoidable, locate seams below any furniture or other fittings. For more on carpet and vinyl tiles, see pp.336–337.

TYPES OF FLOORING
Rolls usually come in set widths—15 ft (4.5 m) for carpet is the most common. This may dictate which way to run a design across a room.

Carpet This may have fabric-woven or fabric-laminated backing. The vast differences in quality and price are due to a carpet's make-up. It may be 100 percent wool, a wool/acrylic mix, 100 percent acrylic, or another synthetic fiber. Texture and pile include smooth velvet, twist, loop, and shag pile. Most brands have a grading system for suitable use, such as light domestic (e.g., in a bedroom) or heavy domestic (e.g., hall and stairs). There are also natural-fiber floor coverings, e.g., jute or coir.

Sheet vinyl Since vinyl is hardwearing and easily cleaned, it is often used in bathrooms and kitchens. To increase its waterproof qualities, you may choose to run a bead of silicone around the edge. This also disguises rough edges.

Foam Foam acts as a shock absorber between the carpet and floor, provides greater comfort underfoot, protects the carpet, and reduces carpet wear.

Other types of sheet flooring Rubber and linoleum are durable and easily cleaned, but are more difficult to lay.

TOOLS AND MATERIALS

There is a variety of tools available for laying carpet and vinyl. Pictured below is a selection of the ones most commonly used for laying these types of flooring.

Napping shears
Used for trimming seams in a carpet. One blade is flattened and rests on the pile along the seam, acting as a guide for trimming.

Flattened section rests on seam

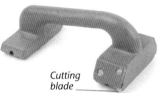

Carpet shears
Heavy-duty scissors used for cutting underlay as well as carpet.

Retractable blade

Vinyl cutter
Precision tool for cutting vinyl.

Cutting blade

Carpet knife
Heavy-duty utility knife designed for cutting all types of carpet and vinyl.

Serrated wheels grip carpet

Seam roller
Used to roll along seams when joining carpet with a seaming iron.

Seaming iron
Used with seaming tape and the seam roller to join lengths of carpet.

Carpet bolster
Tucks carpet behind tackless stripping to secure it in place.

Double-sided tape
May be used for securing foam-backed carpet or vinyl in position.

Dial to set depth

Notch for gripping tacks

Knee kicker
Used to stretch and position woven-backed carpet. The adjustable teeth can be set for different thicknesses.

Tack lifter
Acts in much the same way as the claw of a claw hammer. Shaped to deal with carpet tack removal.

Tackless stripping
Thin length of timber, with razor-sharp teeth. Secured around the edge of a room to hold woven-backed carpet.

Teeth grip fabric backing of carpet

ESTIMATING QUANTITIES FOR CARPET AND VINYL

Basic estimate	As a basic rule of thumb, base quantity estimates on the floor's area minus the area covered by permanent fixtures—but see below for roll flooring.
Flooring supplied in rolls	For rolls, do not deduct permanent fixtures from your calculations of the floor area.
Wastage and trimming	Allow about 10 percent, whatever the material being used. It may be less if you have very specific dimensions for a sheet or carpet floor.
Tackless stripping	Calculate requirement by measuring the perimeter of the room.
Pads	Calculate requirement by measuring the actual floor area.
Extras	Consider subfloor requirements, which can add considerable expense to a flooring project.

GENERAL CONSIDERATIONS FOR FLOORING

Squaring patterned flooring
Patterns look best if "square" in a room. Walls may be uneven, so do not use them as a starting point to lay patterned flooring: any unevenness will make the design noticeably misaligned, because the effect becomes exaggerated across a whole room. To judge the best orientation for tiles, dry lay them as shown on p.350 and adjust as necessary. For sheet vinyl or carpet, allow a generous overlap when rough-cutting before laying (see p.318).

Adhesives
Many coverings—vinyl tiles, some cork tiles, and some sheet vinyls—can adhere with latex adhesive. Use double-sided tape or spray adhesive for foam-backed carpet or vinyl.

Threshold strips
These cover the joint between two kinds of flooring, usually between two rooms. The type used depends on which floorings meet. Those shown here are the most commonly used.

Wood finishing strip
A simple hardwood strip provides a decorative edge.

Carpet-to-carpet
Used where two woven-backed carpets meet in a doorway.

Carpet edge hidden by raised lip

Carpet-to-laminate
Joins woven-backed carpet to rigid edges such as tiles, laminate, or wooden floor.

Finishing strip
Ends a floor covering, in this case woven-backed carpet, at a threshold.

Teeth grip woven-backed carpet

Flush strip
Joins vinyl to vinyl. Also available as carpet-to-carpet or carpet-to-vinyl strips.

PREPARING TO LAY FLOOR TILES

The application methods for soft and hard floor tiles differ, but planning their layout is the same. The only difference is that hard tiles have grout joints, and soft tiles butt right up against each other.

TOOLS AND MATERIALS

Soft tiles are laid with the items in your basic toolkit and the extras listed opposite bottom. Hard tiles call for largely the same items as are used for wall tiles (see p.316), with a few key differences, as follows.
- Tiles are very robust, so a cutter must be of a high quality. Check that a score-and-snap cutter, if you use one, is large enough for floor tiles.
- Adhesive and grout must be harder-wearing than on wall tiles, and some tiles need special additives in adhesive for sound adhesion. If you are laying tiles on a wooden subfloor, buy adhesive and grout with flexibility (check the packaging); additives may again be required.
- Cross-shaped spacers lie flat on the floor and are removed before covering with grout. If the tile depth is insufficient for this, use vertical pieces of thin cardboard. Remove after the adhesive dries.

TYPES OF TILES

Soft floor tiles
These may be self-adhesive, or laid with or without adhesive.

Carpet tile
Usually laid dry (i.e., without any adhesive).

Vinyl tile
May be self-adhesive or may need adhesive.

Cork tile
May be ready-sealed, or need sealing once laid.

Hard tiles
These are available in various materials and sizes.

Porcelain
Laying porcelain tiles normally requires special adhesive or additives to standard adhesive.

Ceramic
A wide range of colors and designs is available, some mimicking natural tiles such as limestone.

Slate
A natural material. Apply sealant to the top surface before laying slate. This prevents excess adhesive from soaking into the tile, making it easier to remove later.

Quarry
A natural material. Seal top surface before use.

Marble
Another type of natural tile.

Wooden tiles
These are usually patterned, and are another form of hard tiles.

Parquet tile
Gives appearance of traditional parquet design. Installed with adhesive. May be finished, or may need sanding and sealing after application.

Parquet tile (tongue-and-groove)
Tongue-and-groove mechanism locks tile in place. It is laid with adhesive.

LAYING A TILED FLOOR
Do not just start laying tiles against one wall: the wall may not be straight, and adjustments to allow for this will become exaggerated and unsightly as you progress across the room.

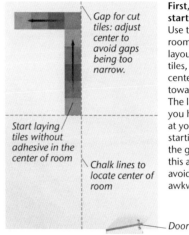

Gap for cut tiles: adjust center to avoid gaps being too narrow.

Start laying tiles without adhesive in the center of room

Chalk lines to locate center of room

Door

First, find a starting point
Use the center of the room as a base for the layout. "Dry lay" a few tiles, starting in the center and working toward the walls. The last full tile before you hit the wall is at your provisional starting point. Adjust the gap between this and the wall to avoid the need to cut awkward thin slivers.

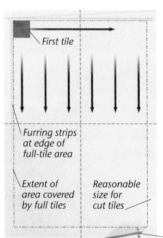

First tile

Furring strips at edge of full-tile area

Extent of area covered by full tiles

Reasonable size for cut tiles

Door

Lay the first tile
Consider how tiles will need to be cut to fit around any obstacles (see pp.336–339). If you can, tile with the fixtures removed, so that edges of tiles are hidden by the replaced fixtures.

ESTIMATING QUANTITIES FOR FLOOR TILES

Basic estimate	As a basic rule of thumb, estimate quantities by calculating the area of the floor minus the area covered by permanent fixtures.
Wastage and trimming	Buy about 10 percent extra—maybe more if you are tiling a floor with many obstacles, because this results in a lot of cutting.
Adhesives	Manufacturers' guidelines for the necessary quantities tend not to be very generous, so it is worth buying a little more than is recommended.
Grout	Grout requirement depends on thickness of joints and size of tiles. There will be guidelines on packaging.
Extras	Remember to include spacers or sealant if necessary. Consider your subfloor requirements. These extras can add considerable expense.

Wood is an attractive and hardwearing option. Imitation wood floors are broadly referred to as laminate floors. Real wood is more expensive, but gives a higher-quality finish. Real wood floors can now be laid using clip-together techniques (ideal for DIY), as well as by more traditional methods such as gluing tongue-and-groove.

LAYING A WOODEN FLOOR

Do not lay wood or laminate where humidity will be high (e.g., the bathroom or kitchen) unless the manufacturer states that it is suitable. Wood can be laid on most subfloors that are level and in good condition.

Refer to the guidelines on p.327 for estimating quantities of underlayment. Estimates for wood and laminate flooring should be made in the same way as those for floor tiles (opposite).

Technique

Wooden flooring is often laid "floating" (not attached to the subfloor). This allows some movement in the wood, aided by expansion gaps at the edge filled with cork and/or hidden by moldings (fixed to baseboard, not flooring).

Plan ahead, considering any fixtures that will need boards to be cut to fit around them (see pp.342–343), and avoid awkward slivers. Try not to attach permanent fixtures to or through a floating floor, which could restrict its movement or cause cracks to appear.

Start laying boards at one wall and go across the room, staggering joints between boards for the most hardwearing and best-looking finish.

TOOLS AND MATERIALS

Plastic wedges
Used around the edge of the flooring, to keep the expansion gap a consistent width.

Hammer strikes raised section

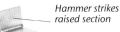

Pry bar
Used in fitting end sections of floor, if space is too tight to use a hammer and/or knocking block.

Knocking block
Protects the edge of a laminate or wooden board when being positioned.

Strap threads into ratchet section

Ratchet floor clamp
Used to tighten joints when laying a floating floor, as shown on p.342.

Clip-together board
Real wooden flooring with clip-together joints.

Laminate board
Wood-effect flooring connected by tongue-and-groove.

Tongue-and-groove wooden board
Real wooden flooring with tongue-and-groove fitting.

Pipe cover
Decorative cover to give clean finish at the base of pipe.

Edge beads
Molding to cover expansion gaps around the edges of a floor.

Cork strip
Fills expansion gap. Needed only if manufacturer calls for it.

Roll underlayment
Thin material positioned below floating floors.

Sheet underlayment
Thick material supplied in small boards or sheets for use below floating floors.

TOOLS AND MATERIALS CHECKLIST FOR PP.352–367

Laying ply or hardboard (p.352) Grab adhesive*, knee pads, ring-shank nails or staple gun and staples, yardstick*, paper*, scissors*, jigsaw*

Using self-leveling compound (p.352) Border for threshold, white glue, large brush, knee pads, power stirrer, plastering trowel, sanding block

Laying foam-backed carpet (p.353) Underlayment*, carpet knife, double-side tape, threshold strip

Laying vinyl (p.353) Vinyl cutter*, spray adhesive/double-sided tape, threshold strip

Laying action-backed carpet (p.354) Tackless stripping, underlayment, carpet knife, staple gun, carpet bolster, knee kicker, threshold strip

Laying natural flooring (p.355) Tackless stripping, underlayment, craft knife, carpet shears*, adhesive, fine-notched spreader, carpet bolster

Laying soft floor tiles (pp.356–357) Sponge, straight edge, rolling pin, wood offcut, paper*, scissors*, profile gauge*, adhesive*, adhesive spreader*, paintbrush*, sealant*, threshold strip

Laying hard floor tiles (pp.358–359) Spacers, knee pads, wood furring strips, metal square*, floor attachments, adhesive, adhesive spreader, level, score-and-snap cutter, electric cutter*, grout, grout spreader, grout shaper, mild detergent, sponge, threshold strip

Laying clip-together flooring (pp.360–361) Vapor barrier*, underlayment, or combined

vapor barrier/underlayment, masking tape, plastic wedges, wood glue*, knocking block, pry bar, wood offcut*, jigsaw*, cork strip*, edge bead*, threshold strip, pipe cover*

Laying floating tongue-and-groove flooring (p.364) Underlayment, vapor barrier* or combined vapor barrier/underlay, plastic wedges, wood glue, knocking block, ratchet floor clamp*, cork strip*, edge bead*, threshold strip, finish*

Gluing tongue-and-groove boards on concrete (p.364) Wood adhesive, adhesive, adhesive spreader, sponge, cloths, concrete blocks, wood finish*, edge bead or cork strip*, threshold strip

Laying nailed tongue-and-groove flooring (p.365) Pry bar, broom, self-leveling compound*, vapor barrier*, heavy-duty drill + bits, frame attachments, level, furring strips, wood wedges, board nailer*, finish*, threshold strip

Laying parquet tiles (p.365) Wood, adhesive spreader, adhesive, jigsaw*, pry bar, cork strips*, threshold strip, sealant*

Sanding a floor (pp.366–367) Drum sander + paper, edging sander + paper, corner sander + paper, broom, vacuum, finish + brush or cloth (pp.312–313)

* = optional

FOR BASIC TOOLKIT SEE PP.26–27

DECORATING AND FINISHING

To qualify as eco-flooring, a finish must be made from natural, sustainably sourced products. Many wooden flooring types fall into this category (see right), but this page concentrates on the soft types of flooring similar to carpet. The main options are listed below. For more on laying natural flooring, see p.335.

ALTERNATIVES TO VINYL

Linoleum is more environmentally friendly than vinyl flooring as its basic ingredient is linseed oil. It is also popular for its nonallergenic qualities.

Traditionally, linoleum is laid in a similar way to vinyl (see p.329). It must, however, be stuck down, making it a harder job. Some linoleum can be bought on a wood-backing and is laid in a similar way to clip-together flooring (see pp.336–37).

WOOD FLOORING

Although wood is a natural product, for it to be an eco-friendly choice it is important to check that it is either reclaimed, sustainably sourced, or even made from recycled lumber products. Eco-friendly alternatives to conventional wood flooring, such as bamboo, are increasingly viable. For more on wood flooring, see p.329.

Bamboo flooring
Bamboo is both durable and sustainable, and some bamboo flooring is similar in appearance to standard clip-together flooring. It can be laid floating, or stuck down, and can also be made into slats (as shown)—which are commonly used for rugs rather than fixed flooring.

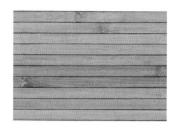

FLOORING TYPE	Material	Properties	Where to use
Sisal	This is made from the leaves of the *Agave sisalana* plant. The leaves are crushed and soaked to extract the fibers, and then spun into yarn.	Probably the most versatile natural flooring for variety of design, comfort, and use. There is a wide range to choose from, varying from very tight to quite open-weave designs, in a choice of many colors.	Its hardwearing nature means sisal can be used in most areas of the home. Best avoided in bathrooms and kitchens, as water causes fiber to expand and contract, damaging the appearance.
Sisool	As the name suggests, this is a composite of sisal and wool, which creates a dual-fiber floor covering with two distinctive textures.	Combining sisal and wool makes for a more flexible material than raw sisal. The wool provides softness, while the sisal offers excellent durability.	Can be used in most areas of the home, but manufacturers tend to advise against kitchen and bathroom use. Natural floor coverings usually have a natural latex backing; sisool is normally backed with jute.
Paper	This is twisted to form a yarn that is then woven into a floor covering. Some manufacturers combine paper with sisal.	This has a very different look to other natural floor coverings. Resins are often added to make this flooring more hardwearing, and to protect the fibers.	Suitable for most areas, some paper flooring can even be used in bathrooms, as it is water repellent. However, exposure to standing water should be avoided.
Seagrass	There are a number of varieties of seagrass. Most commonly produced in paddy fields that are flooded with seawater, it is then harvested, dried, and made into yarn.	Seagrass offers a very strong yarn. It is hard to dye, and the colors are often limited, but its waxy surface makes it naturally stain-resistant. It gives off a very grassy smell.	Suitable for most domestic situations, seagrass is quite impermeable to water, making it possible to use in a bathroom. Standing water should be avoided.
Coir	Made from the husk of coconut shells, coir is removed from the shell, soaked, and pounded before being dried and woven into a wiry yarn.	Short, hard fibers give this a raw, unprocessed look. It is incredibly hardwearing and durable.	Ideally used in busy areas such as hallways and landings, this is not suitable for moist areas such as bathrooms and kitchens. It is commonly used for entrance mats.
Jute	A product of the *Corchorus* plant family and a close relation to hemp, the inner stems of jute are soaked, pounded, and then dried to provide a soft fiber for the yarn.	Jute is very soft to the touch, and comfortable to walk on. The softness allows it to be woven into a number of designs relatively easily.	Jute is hardwearing, but should not be used in bathrooms and kitchens, as humidity and damp damages fibers very quickly. It is often used in bedrooms, and other less busy domestic areas.

A subfloor provides the base for a floor covering. It is applied over the main floor structure, although in some cases the floor itself can provide the necessary base for the floor covering. The most common subfloors are made of plywood, which is laid on a wooden floor, hardboard (also laid on wood), and self-leveling compound (on a concrete floor).

CHOOSING A SUBFLOOR

Existing floor	Suitable subfloor	Suitable flooring
Wooden	¾in plywood	Hard tiles
Wooden	¾in plywood	Soft flooring
Wooden	Uncoated plywood	Soft tiles, or clip-together flooring
Wooden	Plywood or OSB	Carpet, or vinyl sheet, or floating wooden floor
Concrete	¾ in plywood or 2 x 4s	Any material

LAYING A SUBFLOOR FOR A WOODEN FLOOR

There are two options for a wooden floor: plywood and OSB. The information below will help you to choose the most suitable for your needs. A subfloor may raise a floor's height and stop a door opening smoothly. Do not trim a door until after you lay flooring: it may be possible to hide a slight step between rooms with a threshold strip (see p.333).

Choosing to use plywood

Use thick plywood as a subfloor for hard tiles, and thinner ply to provide a smooth surface for soft floor coverings such as vinyl, carpet, and soft tiles. Large sheets are ideal for large rooms, because they cover the surface quickly and with fewer joints. The order in which boards are nailed down is not important, except that joints between rows of plywood boards should be staggered to avoid long joints.

MAKING A TEMPLATE FOR CUTS

Make a paper template of any complicated areas, and trace a guide line along which to cut. Use a sheet of paper cut to size, positioned exactly where the board will be placed. Use a jigsaw to cut the board.

Cut slits along the edges of a sheet of paper. Press these slits against the obstacle, and crease them sharply around its shape.

Cut along the creases to create a template. Lay the paper on a board, use the cut edge to draw a guide line, and cut along the line.

Laying plywood

Decide what type of floor covering you wish to use before laying plywood, because stability and compatibility for the type of floor covering is essential. Before buying plywood, check that it is suitable as a subfloor. If it is not, it may expand or contract, depending on humidity, leading to lumps and bumps in the floor. To avoid unevenness, ensure that the plywood is securely screwed down. Plywood is available in large sheets, at a standard size of 4 x 8 ft (1.2 x 2.4 m). Use a jigsaw for a curved cut, and make straight cuts as shown below.

CUTTING ¼" LUAN PLYWOOD

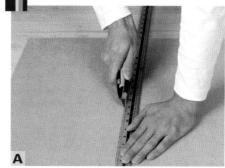

To cut a straight line in luan plywood, first use a utility knife to score the smooth side of the board. Take care not to let the blade slip.

Turn the board over, and lay a straight edge (such as a metal ruler) along the scored line. Snap the board along the scored line. Separate the two pieces and neaten the cut edge with a utility knife.

LAYING A SUBFLOOR FOR A CONCRETE FLOOR

Self-leveling compound is a latex-based product which provides a very smooth subfloor. It is needed only if a concrete floor is in poor condition. Despite the name, some smoothing is needed for the best surface. The floor may be raised by the subfloor and flooring, so you may need to trim the lower edge of a door after laying flooring.

Preparing the surface

Thoroughly clean the floor. Do not lay compound over any residual bitumen-based products from a previous covering. Prime a dusty surface. Attach a threshold strip across the doorway so that compound does not run into the next room.

Mixing the compound

Use a spotlessly clean bucket, because any impurities will affect the mix's integrity, and use a power stirrer to mix slowly, to avoid introducing too much air. Self-leveling compound sets relatively quickly, and will remain workable for no more than 30 minutes. Follow the steps shown for one bucket-load, and immediately mix and lay the next bucket while the wet edge is still workable. The coverage from a bag of compound depends on how thickly it is laid.

LAYING A SUBFLOOR

Read the descriptions on p.331 and decide which kind of subfloor is most suitable for your floor and, if relevant, chosen floor covering. Then follow the steps shown here for the method you need.

Read the descriptions on p.331 and decide which

TOOLS AND MATERIALS SEE BASIC TOOLKIT AND P.329

▌▌ LAYING PLYWOOD

Sweep the floor, and check that all screws or nails sit below the surface. Drive in or countersink any protruding fasteners, ensuring that they don't go right through the floorboards and into any cables or pipes beneath them.

A

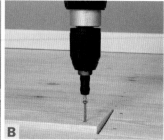

B

Check whether any floorboards are loose. If they are, screw them down securely, because a subfloor must be laid on a rigid floor surface.

C

Pick a corner that is as square as possible for your starting point, and lay the first board. Use grab adhesive for extra rigidity.

D

An alternative to nailing thin ply is to use a staple gun

Use ring-shank nails every 6 in (150 mm) around the edges of the board. Nails should go into floorboards but not through them.

E

Apply nails every 6 in (150 mm) in a grid across the center of the board, as well as around the edges, to keep the subfloor level and firm.

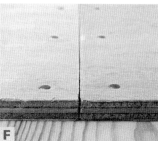

F

Butt-join boards tightly. Continue laying boards. If boards need cutting to fit, use a panel saw for straight cuts, and a jigsaw for templated cuts.

▌▌ LAYING HARDBOARD

Prepare the floor by sweeping and leveling it as shown in steps A to B for laying plywood (above). If possible, choose a square corner in which to start laying boards. Stapling is the quickest way of securing hardboard, although ring-shank nails can be used. Position fixings at 6-in (150-mm) intervals.

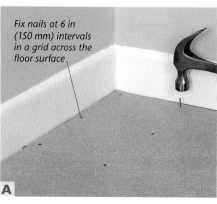

Fix nails at 6 in (150 mm) intervals in a grid across the floor surface

A

B

Butt the second board hard against the first. When placing boards, keep them as neatly aligned as possible, so that later rows fit easily into place.

C

Work across the room in rows, staggering the joints between boards on subsequent rows.

▌▌ USING SELF-LEVELLING COMPOUND

A

Block the threshold. Mix the compound, as detailed in the manufacturer's instructions, and pour it onto the floor.

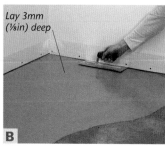

Lay 3mm (⅛in) deep

B

Use a plastering trowel to spread the compound evenly across the surface, removing any peaks and redistributing it into depressed areas.

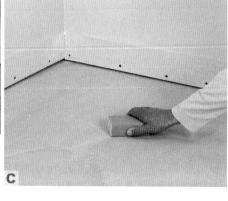

C

Mix and lay further compound until the floor is covered, smoothing it in with the damp edges of previously poured areas. Leave the compound to dry overnight before walking on it. Then use a medium grade of sandpaper to remove any ridges that were left by the trowelling.

LAYING FOAM-BACKED CARPET

Foam-backed carpet does not need an underlay or tackless strips. Lay the carpet roughly in place, allowing the overlap to run up the walls. Adjust the position until any pattern is aligned squarely within the room.

A

B Make small cuts in the corners and any alcoves, to allow the carpet to sit flat on the floor.

C Crease the carpet into the junction between wall and floor. Trim its edge at the base of the baseboard, with a carpet knife, as precisely as possible.

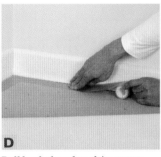

D Pull back the edge of the carpet. Stick double-sided tape to the floor, all the way around the perimeter of the room.

E Remove the backing from the top of the tape, in sections. Press the carpet down into place and smooth out any wrinkles.

F

For any joins between lengths of carpet, use double-sided tape along the edges to stick down both pieces of carpet. Slowly smooth the carpet into place by hand, making sure that it does not ripple along the join.

LAYING VINYL WITH ADHESIVE

A Lay the roughly cut vinyl on the floor, allowing the overlap to run up the walls. Adjust the position to get any pattern squared in the room.

B Make small cuts at right angles to the corners and any alcoves to allow the vinyl to lie flat on the floor.

C

Crease vinyl into the joint between the wall and the floor. Thin vinyl creases quite easily. Thicker varieties can be made more pliable with gentle heating from a hairdryer (do not apply heat for long). Cut along the edges using a vinyl cutter or a craft knife. Take time to ensure that cuts are precise: you cannot correct errors later.

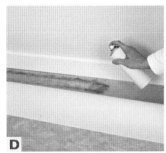

D Fold back the edge of the vinyl. Spray adhesive on the floor, around the room's perimeter, or lay double-sided tape if you prefer.

E Press down evenly on the vinyl, all around the room, to ensure it lies smoothly on the floor surface.

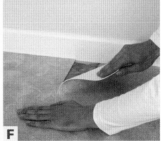

F For any joins, use spray adhesive or double-sided tape along the edges between the lengths of vinyl.

THRESHOLD STRIPS

A threshold strip should be fitted at every doorway. The strip type will depend on the floor coverings being joined (see p.327). Some types of strip are screwed down to the floor surface before the floor covering is fitted into it. In other cases, the floor covering is roughly butt-joined before the strip is fitted over it.

LAYING ACTION-BACKED CARPET

Action-backed carpet has replaced the old jute-backed carpet in Canada. For both carpet and vinyl, cut to at least 6 in (150 mm) larger than required, with an overlap along all edges. If possible, do the cutting where there is space to roll out the flooring. In dry weather, you may prefer to do this outdoors. With a large pattern, leave larger overlap areas so that the flooring can be adjusted to fit neatly. An action-backed carpet is stretched with a knee-kicker while being fitted, and is laid with underlay and tackless strips.

TOOLS AND MATERIALS SEE BASIC TOOLKIT AND P.329

LAYING ACTION-BACKED CARPET

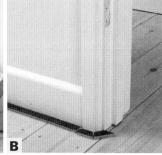

For a concrete floor, use masonry nails or glue the rods in place

A

Nail down the tackless strips, their teeth pointing to the wall. Leave a gap between baseboards and strips, a little less than the carpet thickness.

B

To fit the strips around an obstacle, such as a door frame, follow the shape of the obstacle's base and cut sections with a junior hacksaw.

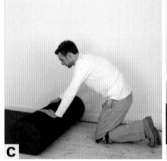

C

Roll out the underlay across the floor, allowing it to lap over the tops of the tackless strips.

D

Cut along the inside edge of the tackless strips to remove any excess underlay. Leave a neat, flush fit.

E

Staple down the underlay to the floor, and tape any joins. Or, on a concrete floor, use the recommended adhesive to stick down the underlay.

F

Position the roughly cut carpet, allowing the overlap to run up the walls. Adjust it to the required position, square within the room.

G

To allow the carpet to sit flat, make small cuts at right angles to the corners. Repeat for any other angles in the room, such as alcoves.

H

Trim the carpet around the edges, flush with the base of the wall or baseboard.

I

Use a bolster to secure the carpet to the tackless strips in one corner.

J

Using the knee kicker, stretch and position the carpet, and work towards an adjacent corner. Secure the carpet in this second corner.

Return to the first corner, and work with the knee kicker towards the other adjacent corner. Secure the carpet in this corner. Return again to the first corner, and work with the knee kicker diagonally across the floor to the opposite corner. Secure the carpet. If you need to reposition it at any time, unhook it from the tackless strip.

K

Check that the tension is even and there is no uneven stretching across pile lines

L

To complete the room, work around the edges of the carpet, fixing it in place behind the tackless strips.

SEAMS IN ACTION-BACKED CARPET

Joining lengths of action-backed carpet is best left to a professional (essential for expensive carpets). If you do decide to attempt it, you will need a hot seaming iron, a seam roller, and seaming tape. Take great care as you move along the join. Use napping shears to trim the pile along the join.

Laying soft natural flooring, such as sisal or jute, differs slightly from laying action-backed carpet (see opposite) as most natural flooring is backed with latex. The laying process involves sticking the latex onto an underlay, which is itself stuck to the subfloor. The tackless strips used to secure the flooring around the perimeter have no upward teeth, as the flooring is glued down—the back edge of the strip is simply used to tuck in the flooring. As the flooring is stuck down, there is no need for a knee kicker to stretch the carpet. Check with your supplier for the best adhesive to use.

TOOLS AND MATERIALS SEE BASIC TOOLKIT AND P.329

LAYING NATURAL FLOORING

A Nail the blank tackless strips around the edge of the room, leaving a gap between the baseboard and strip that is slightly thinner than the flooring.

B Ensure the square edge of the strips face into the room, with the slightly angled edge pointing toward the baseboard.

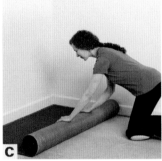

C Roll out the underlay, butting its straight edge directly up against the tackless strips where possible. This avoids excess trimming.

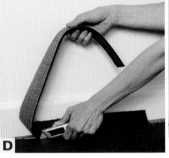

D Use a razor knife to cut the underlay to the edge of the strip where needed. Roll out the underlay "dry" until the entire floor is covered.

E Roll back sections of the underlay to apply adhesive to the subfloor, using a fine-notched spreader. Follow any supplier's guidelines closely.

F Replace the underlay, smoothing it onto the adhesive below. You can kneel on the laid sections while positioning the rest of the underlay.

G Roll out the flooring across the underlay. Some manufacturers advise letting it settle for 24–48 hours before trimming.

H Allow an overlap of 1–2 in (2–4 cm) with the baseboard or wall. Trim with a razor knife or carpet shears, then smooth the flooring up to the wall.

I Roll back the flooring and apply adhesive directly to the underlay, again with a notched spreader. Aim for a smooth, even coverage.

J Having observed guidelines on drying times, roll the flooring back into place, flattening air bubbles and checking the positioning.

K Hold a razor knife at right angles to the baseboard, and trim the flooring, leaving a small excess. Blades will blunt quickly, so be sure to have a supply of replacements, as the accuracy of this trimming is essential for a good fit. Once one area is glued and trimmed, move onto the next.

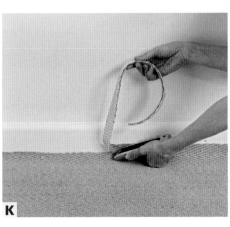

L Use a carpet bolster to finish the job by pushing the excess of flooring down behind the tackless strips.

BACKINGS

Although the majority of natural floorings are now laid using the technique shown here, it is possible to find other backings. Check with your supplier whether they use synthetic or natural latex backing. A synthetic version negates many of the arguments for choosing this flooring, as it will not be biodegradable.

LAYING SOFT FLOOR TILES

Soft tiles include vinyl, cork, and carpet tiles. Some are self-adhesive, others require a separate adhesive. Carpet tiles are laid dry (without adhesive). The sequence shown here relates to self-adhesive tiles. Your starting position will be the same whichever kind of tile is used (see p.328). If you are laying tiles on a hardboard subfloor, there will be no need to prime the surface. For plywood or self-leveled subfloors, seal the surface or use a primer recommended by the tile manufacturer.

TOOLS AND MATERIALS SEE BASIC TOOLKIT AND P.329

1 GETTING STARTED

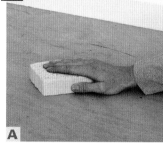

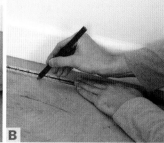

Laying self-adhesive tiles is straightforward. Start by thoroughly cleaning the floor: even the smallest particle may show through the tiles.

Draw pencil guide lines along the floor to indicate your chosen starting point (see p.328).

2 PLACING THE FIRST TILE

Remove the paper backing and position the first tile. Make sure that its edges align precisely with the guide lines. Press down firmly, and apply even pressure. Make sure the first tile is fixed securely before moving on. This will act as a fixed point that will anchor the positions for all the tiles that follow.

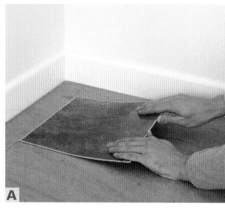

Build up the first row of tiles, butting their edges tightly together. A household rolling pin will help you to apply pressure evenly.

As you progress, make sure the tiles sit flat on the floor surface. A tile that is slightly out of position can throw out the whole design.

3 MEASURING SECTIONS TO CUT

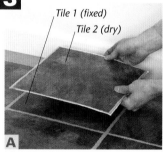

Tile 1 (fixed)
Tile 2 (dry)

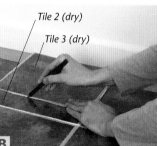

Tile 2 (dry)
Tile 3 (dry)

Cut the tile on a board (e.g., an offcut of MDF) to avoid damaging the floor

Mark off cuts in position, for the most accurate fit. On the last full row near the gap to a wall, lay a dry tile (tile 2) over a fixed one (tile 1).

Place another dry tile (tile 3) over the first, and slide it across so that it fills the gap. Where the edge of tile 3 overlaps tile 2, draw a line.

Remove the dry tiles, and cut along the guide line on tile 2, using a craft knife and a straight edge such as a metal rule.

Check that the cut section of tile fills the gap, before removing the paper backing and sticking the tile in place.

4 CREATING AN L-SHAPED TILE FOR A CORNER

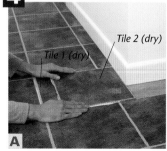

Tile 2 (dry)
Tile 1 (dry)

Tile 2 (dry)
Tile 1 (dry)

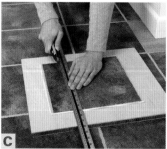

Place two dry tiles on top of the closest fixed tile. Slide tile 2 across to one side of the corner. Mark the edge of tile 2 on tile 1 beneath.

Move tile 1, with its guide line, to the other side of the corner. Do not rotate it. Place it on the relevant fixed tile. Repeat the marking-off process.

Place tile 1 on a cutting board, and cut along the lines to remove the unwanted section of tile.

Check that the L-shaped section fits before removing the backing and putting it down in place.

5 CUTTING CURVES (OR IRREGULAR CORNERS)

A

For curves or non-square corners, use a paper template to make a precise guide line. First, cut a piece of paper to the size of your tile.

B

Cut a number of slits into the paper, slightly longer than the portion of tile to be removed.

C

Place the paper tile in position, with its slits against the curve (here, a sink pedestal). Crease the slits against the curve, and draw a pencil line across.

D

Remove the paper tile, and cut along the line. Place the template on a new self-adhesive tile, and draw around the guide line.

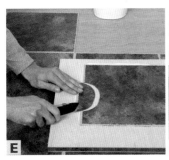

E

Using a utility knife, cut the tile along the guide line, and remove the unwanted section.

F

Check that the tile fits snugly around the curve. Remove the backing and stick the cut tile in position.

6 CUTTING IRREGULAR SHAPES

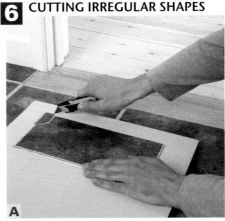

A

For irregular shapes, a profile gauge gives the best guideline. If possible, place its corner where the tile's corner will go. Push the gauge into the irregular edge and butt it up. Position the gauge on a tile, lining up the corners for an accurate fit. Trace around the irregular shape. Cut along the guide line using a craft knife and remove the unwanted section.

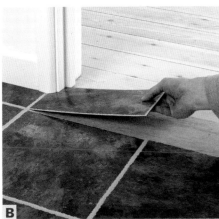

B

Check that the tile fits, and then remove the backing to stick the tile in place.

LAYING CARPET TILES

Some carpet tiles are laid dry, and can be regularly moved to even out wear. Planning and cutting is the same as for other soft tiles.

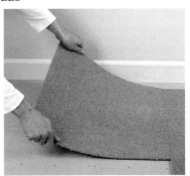

LAYING SOFT TILES THAT REQUIRE ADHESIVE

For soft tiles designed to be laid using adhesive, the principles shown above and on p.328 for planning the layout and for cutting sections of tile are exactly the same. The adhesive may be applied to the back of each tile, or to the floor. If you apply adhesive to the tile, do it carefully so that it does not spill over to the front of the tile surface.

The soft tile being applied to the right is cork. Before being laid, natural tiles such as cork should be left for 48 hours in the room where they will be laid, so that they acclimatize before being positioned. Once the floor has been completed, some cork-based tiles will require a sealant to be coated over the surface (the packaging will specify), as shown far right.

ADHESIVE BEING APPLIED TO THE FLOOR FOR CORK TILES

SEALANT BEING APPLIED TO LAID CORK TILES

LAYING HARD FLOOR TILES

Hard tiles must be laid on as flat a surface as possible—such as concrete, concrete with self-leveling compound applied, or a wooden floor that has been covered with a ¾-in (19-mm) ply subfloor. Flexible adhesive and flexible grout is needed on wooden floors and for some types of tile. Use thin set, which is a blend of portland cement, sand, and additives, to install the floor tiles. Latex thin set is available, and provides greater flexibility and bonding strength than regular thin set.

TOOLS AND MATERIALS SEE BASIC TOOLKIT AND P.329

Fix the furring strip along the pencil line. In this example, the subfloor is plywood, so screws may be inserted. (For a concrete floor, drill pilot holes, using masonry bits, then plug the holes and insert screws.) Position a second furring strip at a precise right angle to the first one. Here, a metal square is being used for an accurate right angle.

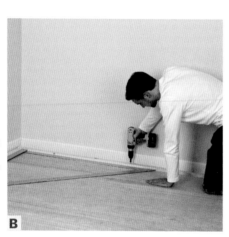

B

FURTHER INFORMATION ABOUT ADHESIVE

Testing adhesive cover
Press tiles down just hard enough for the adhesive to make contact with the entire back face of the tile. Tap the tile to test—if there is a hollow sound, some areas are not in contact. This problem tends to occur with an uneven floor or with rustic tiles. Take up the tile, and add more adhesive to the hollow areas.

Adhesive drying time
Drying time depends on the type of adhesive, tile thickness, and porosity of the floor and tiles. Most adhesive will dry in 24 hours. If tiles are walked on before adhesive is dry, they may move, and the bond between adhesive and tiles will weaken. This would cause tiles to loosen, and grout joints may crack at a later date.

1 GETTING STARTED

Dry-lay a few tiles to mark your starting point, as explained on p.328. You may choose to use the edge and corner of the room as a rough guide. Mark the outer edge of the tiles. Draw a pencil line to mark where to position your wooden furring strip. This provides an accurate guide against which to lay the tiles (the wall or the corner may not be straight).

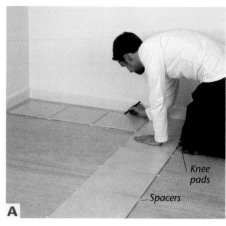

Knee pads

Spacers

A

2 APPLYING ADHESIVE

The trowel's notched edge provides an even, grooved bed

A

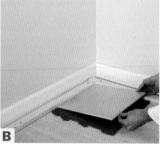

B

Mix adhesive with a power stirrer, as shown on p.68. Mix as much as you can use in about an hour. Apply the adhesive in the right angle made by the furring strips.

Position the first tile on the adhesive, butting it up against the two furring strips. Gently press the tile into position.

3 BUILDING UP ROWS

A

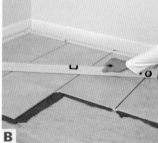

B

As you progress, insert spacers flat on the floor. The tile will probably be deep enough for spacers to be covered later with grout. Otherwise, use thin cardboard as spacers.

Use a level to check that tiles lie flush with each other. Continue laying tiles until all the uncut ones are down. Allow the adhesive to dry, and remove the furring strips.

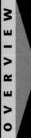

4 MAKING STRAIGHT CUTS

A

B

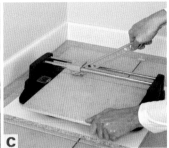

C

D

Measure the gap left by the furring strip between tile and wall, so that you can cut a tile to fit. Measure at each end of the tile to allow for variations in the width of the gap.

Subtract the grout gap, and mark off the resulting distances on the tile edge with a felt-tip pen. Place the tile in a score-and-snap cutter, aligning marks with the cutter's guides.

Push the cutting wheel away from you, across the tile, to score a line between the marks. Lower the handle to snap the tile along the line. Use a tile file on the cut edge.

Check that the cut tile fits the gap. Apply adhesive to the floor or back of the tile, and insert it into place.

5 CUTTING CURVES

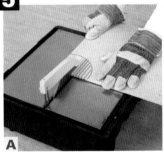

A

B

Create a template, as shown on p.337. Draw a guide line. Wearing gloves and keeping hands clear of the blade, use a wet-cutting tile saw to cut straight lines into the curve.

Continue with a series of straight cuts. Break off the unwanted section. Smooth the curve by steering the tile around the blade.

6 MAKING A RIGHT-ANGLED CUT

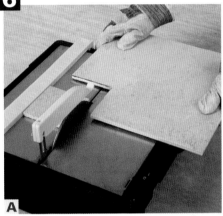

A

Mark the area of the tile that needs to be cut (see p.337 for measuring methods). Place the tile in an electric cutter. Wear gloves and keep your hands clear of the blade. Wear goggles. When the cut has reached the end of the first marked line, turn the tile around. Cut along the second guide line, to make the right angle.

CUTTING AROUND PERMANENT FIXTURES

There are three ways to cut around a door casing. If there is baseboard in the room, make a simple curved cut that follows the casing profile. When it is grouted, the inexact cut will be inconspicuous. If the baseboard is to be installed after tiling, there will be no grout gap to incorporate—in this instance, cut off the bottom section of the casing and slip the edge of the tile underneath (see p.341). Or remove the casing, tile the floor area, and then refit the casing over the cut edge.

Cutting holes for pipes can be done in the same way as for wall tiles (see pp.320–321). Some tiles will raise the floor level, so if you remove a fixture, check that the pipe will be the correct length to reconnect.

7 GROUTING THE TILES

A

B

Grout the tiles once adhesive is dry. Mix the grout to a smooth, stiff paste. Apply with a grout spreader and remove excess with a damp sponge. Finish with a grout shaper.

When grout is dry, use a mild detergent to clean off any powdery residue. Some natural tiles may then need sealing.

LAYING CLIP-TOGETHER FLOORING

Many laminate and real wood floors are laid by dry-clipping boards together. Clipping mechanisms vary, but the principles are the same. Whether you need a vapor barrier or underlay will depend on the type of floor (see pp.176–183). If in doubt, install one. Where possible, lay flooring before installing baseboards or door casings so that they can cover the expansion gap. Wooden flooring needs to acclimatize for two or three days before being laid. Open packs and lay out the boards. Some flooring will need to be oiled after installation.

TOOLS AND MATERIALS SEE BASIC TOOLKIT AND P.329

1 PLACING THE FOAM

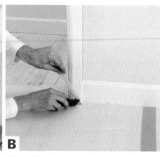

A

Roll out the foam across the floor's surface. Tape the seams together between the sheets of underlayment.

B

Trim the foam to size, ensuring that it fits precisely at the junctions between the walls and the floor. Use a utility knife to cut it.

2 Position the **first** board in a corner of the room. However, if your room has a cased doorway, you may choose to start at the door. The information box opposite shows the different solutions to installing the first board at a cased doorway or the last board at the doorway. The steps shown here result in the last board being installed in the doorway.

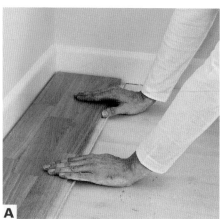

A

B

Make sure the grooved side of the boards is against the wall. Insert plastic wedges between the board and the wall.

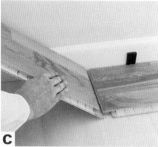

C

To place the next board, engage it with the end of the first board by holding it at roughly 45 degrees to the first board.

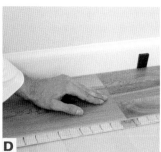

D

Press down on the second board, and lock it into place. Continue joining boards in this way to make the first row.

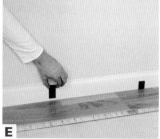

E

Insert wedges at regular intervals. As you near the end of the row, you will probably need to cut a board to finish: see next step.

3 LAYING SUBSEQUENT ROWS

A

Use the offcut piece from the end of the first row to start the second. Engage it at a 45-degree angle to the edges of the first-row boards.

B

Tap the board with a knocking block to tighten. Place another board beside it. Leave a slight gap so you can clip it to the first row, then knock fully into place. Repeat along row.

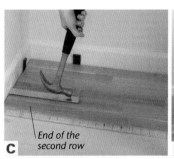

4 GOING AROUND A DOORWAY

In the doorway, boards should extend to the threshold. Keep laying boards until you near the final wall, and a whole board is too wide to fit. Cut some wood to the width of a board, and sharpen one end. Loosely position a board over the previous whole board fitted. Run the pointed end along the wall, using a pencil at the other end to draw the profile onto the loose board.

C *End of the second row*

You may need a pry bar to tighten the joint for the last board in any row. Hook the pry bar over the end of the board, and tap its other end with a hammer.

D

Check that boards are "square" across the room. If not, adjust them by cutting the first row to fit against the wall, as below for a doorway. Continue across the floor.

A

Cut along the guide line of the wall's profile with a jigsaw, then position the board in the doorway.

B

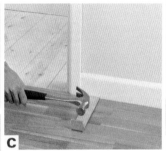

C

Install the board, using a pry bar to tap in the clip-together mechanism. Use this method to cut and attach all boards against the wall.

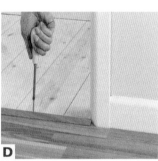

D

Install a threshold strip in the doorway. Choose a suitable one for the types of flooring that will meet here (see p.327).

E

Finish off the room with lengths of edging (shoe molding), pinned or glued (with contact adhesive) to the baseboard. This is to cover the expansion gap.

FURTHER INFORMATION

Coping with a casing
If you start at the doorway, trim the base of the casing, as shown below, and slide the first board underneath it. Clip to the second board and work across the floor. If you *finish* at the doorway, you may need to trim off the last board's tongue with a jigsaw or hammer and chisel so that it will fit against the wall. Then install the board.

Cutting around a pipe
If the fixture is not in place, or can be removed, drill a hole in a board and slide it over the pipe. If the fixture is not movable, see p.339 for cutting to fit around an obstacle. Use a pipe cover to cover the seam at the base.

LAYING A WOODEN FLOOR

Although laminate wood flooring is becoming popular (see pp.340–341), you may prefer real wood, shown here. Boards can be laid as a floating floor, nailed down, or installed with adhesive. On a wood floor, you can remove old boards and install new ones (see pp.178–179), but not if a partition crosses the old boards. Check whether doors need to be trimmed (see p.179). Remember that a vapor barrier is important, especially on concrete. You may sand a wood floor after installing it.

TOOLS AND MATERIALS SEE BASIC TOOLKIT AND P.311

▌▌ FLOATING TONGUE-AND-GROOVE ON WOOD

A

Wooden floors are usually laid floating, allowing for expansion and contraction. Lay a vapor barrier if necessary, then roll out underlayment.

B

Position the first board, with its tongue facing into the room. Use wedges to maintain an expansion gap against the wall.

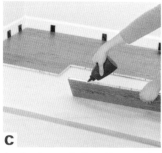

C

Apply glue to the board's grooved edge (avoid going deep into the recess, as less contact is made here with the tongue of the next board).

D

Tighten the joints as you proceed, by hitting a knocking block against the boards. Or you may prefer to use a ratchet floor clamp (see below).

E

Wipe away any excess glue that seeps out between joints after the boards are tightened. Continue adding rows, and stagger the boards in the normal way (see pp.340–341). Once adhesive has dried, add shoe molding to cover the expansion gap, or replace the baseboard if you removed it before laying the floor.

USING A RATCHET FLOOR CLAMP

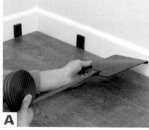

A

This is an alternative to step D above. Lip the clamp over the end board. Unroll the strap to beyond the nearest board.

B

Position the ratchet section over the edge of the board closest to you. For a large floor area, you may need to position several ratchet clamps.

C

Thread the extended strap through the ratchet section, and clamp it down. You may wish to set up two across a section of flooring.

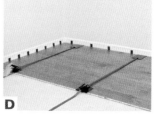

D

Move the ratchet backward and forward until the strap is taut and tightens the tongue-and-groove boards. Repeat every few rows.

▌▌ GLUING TONGUE-AND-GROOVE BOARDS ON CONCRETE

A

Glue joints between boards, using wood adhesive in the grooved edges. Avoid going too deep into the recess (see step C at top).

B

Spread a commercial adhesive on the floor, using a notched trowel to groove it for better adhesion. Press the boards firmly in place.

C

Continue gluing the boards and pressing them into the adhesive. The weight of concrete blocks will help to push down the boards as they dry.

POWERING UP

If you plan to cover a large floor area with strip flooring, the job will be much faster, and easier on the knees and hands, if you use a pneumatic flooring nailer, which is available for rent at most home improvement stores (see pp.52–53). When selecting a floor nailer, review the safety features.

LAYING NAILED TONGUE-AND-GROOVE FLOORING ON CONCRETE

A **Remove baseboard,** loosening it with a pry bar before pulling it from the wall. Sweep away debris. Apply self-leveling compound if required.

B **Lay vapor barrier,** with an overlap of 6 in (150 mm) up the wall. Fold it in the corners to allow it to sit flush on the floor.

C **Attach furring strips** around the room with 4-in (100-mm) concrete screws. Fix furring strips every 16 in (400 mm) at a right angle to the new boards.

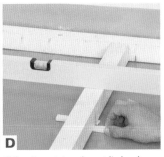

D **If furring strips** do not lie level, use shims or offcuts to pack out any indents and level the furring strips. If insulation is required, see p.364.

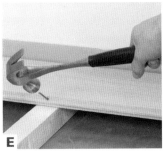

E **Start laying boards,** and attach with toe nailing into the furring strips. This is done by securing a nail at a 45-degree angle into the tongue.

F **Drive the nail** through the board and into the furring strip, so the head is just beneath the board's surface. Or use a floor nailer (see p.179).

G

Continue laying boards (as described on p.179, where tongue-and-groove is being attached to joists). Once the floor is complete, apply any finish (e.g., wax or varnish) that may be required. Trim off the membrane overlap with a utility knife. Replace the baseboard to cover the expansion gap.

LAYING PARQUET TILE FLOORING

A **Attach two temporary** furring strips to the floor to mark a starting point (as you would for laying hard floor tiles—see pp.328 and 338).

B **Spread enough adhesive** inside the angle of the furring strips for the first two or three tiles. Use a notched trowel, or the tool supplied.

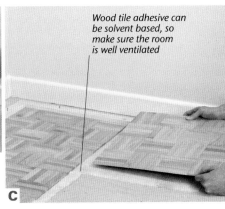

Wood tile adhesive can be solvent based, so make sure the room is well ventilated

C

Press the first tile into position, bedding it into the adhesive. (Some manufacturers specify that the adhesive should be allowed to become tacky before you position tiles.) Check that the edges of all tiles are precisely aligned as you work across the floor. As with other tiling jobs, lay all the full tiles first.

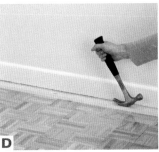

D **Remove the furring strips** with a claw hammer to prepare the edges of the room. Then fill the gap with cut tiles.

E **Measure for cuts** as for other tiles (see pp.336–339). Wooden tiles are easy to cut with a fine-toothed saw. For curved cuts, use a jigsaw.

F **Apply adhesive** and place the cut tiles in the gaps to complete the floor and press them into position.

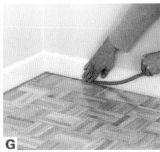

G **Finish off** by filling the expansion gaps with cork strips. Replace baseboard or apply edging (see p.341). Seal the tiles if required.

SANDING A FLOOR

Floorboards can form an attractive finished floor but, unless the boards are very new, they will need sanding to remove old coatings and rough areas. Machine sanders are the ideal tools to carry out this work, but the job is still arduous and very messy. Sanders are also expensive, so rent them rather than buying (see below). Once sanded, the floor needs a decorative protection such as wax or varnish (see pp.294–295). Floor paint is an option, but a floor does not need to be sanded to such a high quality if you plan to paint.

TOOLS AND MATERIALS SEE BASIC TOOLKIT AND P.329

PREPARATION

Order of work

The direction of sanding will depend on the floor's condition. If it is fairly flat, it may be possible simply to use the sander up and down the boards' grain. If the floor is uneven, or has a very thick coating of paint or varnish, start across the grain. Sanding at a right angle to boards may damage them, so sand at 45 degrees. Cross the room in one direction, then the other (see overview), before finishing along the grain. Reduce the coarseness of the sandpaper as you progress, finishing with the finest grade.

Protecting yourself and your home

Sanding is a very dusty, noisy, and messy job. Wear protective clothing, including ear protectors and a respiratory mask. Cover and mask around doors to prevent dust from spreading throughout the house. Open all windows, so that you work in a well-ventilated room.

SEALING A DOORWAY

Sanders

You need three sanders: a heavy-duty drum sander (a drum wrapped in sandpaper that rotates at high speed); a heavy-duty edging sander; and a corner sander. Each requires sandpaper in a particular shape, which is available from the rental store. The paper is expensive, and will tear if it is not correctly fitted. Make sure nails do not protrude from the floor (see right). Unplug the sander before changing paper, and allow it to cool if any parts have heated up while in use.

CORNER SANDER

Pointed sanding pad reaches into corners

Dust bag

Has two handles for two-handed operation

Shaped to reach edges

EDGING SANDER

DRUM SANDER

1 PREPARING THE FLOOR

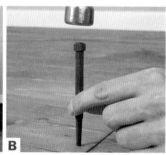

A **Nail down** any loose floorboards. Set the nail heads beneath the surface.

B **Check the floor** for protruding nail or screw heads. If any are sticking out, drive them below the surface.

2 PREPARING THE DRUM SANDER

A **With the sander unplugged,** unscrew the retaining strip on the drum sander and feed a sheet of sandpaper underneath it.

B **Feed the sandpaper** around the drum and secure the end under the retaining strip, aligning the cut sections with the retaining screws.

C **Check that the paper** is taut and correctly positioned before you tighten the retaining screws.

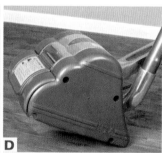

D **Plug in the sander,** tilt it backward so that the drum is raised off the floor, and start the machine.

OVERVIEW

3 USING THE DRUM SANDER

A Lower the drum onto the floor and make the first diagonal run across the floor.

B Sand the whole floor in one direction. Then change direction and make the other set of diagonal runs across the floor, at a right angle to the first runs.

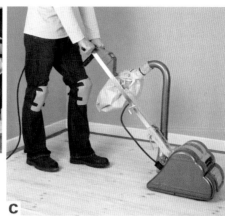

C Then change direction again, and run the drum sander across the floor following the direction of the grain.

4 USING THE EDGING SANDER

Ensure that the sander is unplugged, then use the bolt key supplied with the edging sander to undo the retaining bolt, and remove the old disc of sandpaper. The key is often stored on a retaining clip on the underside of the sander.

A

B Position a new disc of sandpaper and retighten the retaining bolt to hold the disc securely in position. Ensure the retaining bolt head is well below the sandpaper surface level.

C Take a firm hold on the sander before starting it, and work around the edges of the room.

5 USING THE CORNER SANDER

A

B

To change the sandpaper on a corner sander, simply take hold of the old paper and tear it off. Align a new sheet of paper with the pad's face and press it into position.

Use the corner sander to deal with the room's corners, and to sand any awkward, otherwise inaccessible areas such as beneath a radiator.

6 FINISHING THE FLOOR

A

B

Sweep and then vacuum the floor to remove any debris not held by the sanders' dust bags, and wipe with a damp sponge. If you find any rough areas, sand them by hand.

Apply your chosen finish. Two coats of water-based varnish can be applied in a day (it dries quickly), but some light hand-sanding is needed between coats (see p.295).

PROBLEM SOLVER

REPAIRING PARQUET FLOORING

Parquet flooring comprises rectangular blocks of wood that may be arranged in varying designs. Commonly, herringbone patterns are used. Over time, the blocks may become damaged through wear and tear, or they may become loose.

TOOLS AND MATERIALS
Hammer, chisel, scraper, wood adhesive, belt sander, wax, cloth

REVIVING PARQUET
To revive an old parquet floor, use a technique similar to that shown for sanding a floor (pp.344–345).
■ As long as the blocks are stuck tight, undulations can be removed by sanding. Work across the floor in the direction of the grain.
■ A traditional herringbone design would require diagonal runs, to deal with the orientation of the blocks.

A Lever out the block. If it remains firmly stuck, try breaking it up further, using a hammer and chisel.

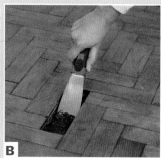

B Remove excess adhesive from the back of the block, and from the floor surface, using a scraper.

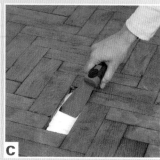

C Apply some wood adhesive (latex-based) to the back of the block and to the floor surface.

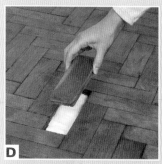

D Position a new block, and press it firmly into place.

E If the block is not flush with the surrounding surface, sand the area until it is smooth. A belt sander is ideal for this.

F Apply finish to the floor surface. This may be wax or varnish, depending on the existing floor (see pp.294–295).

REPAIRING A LAMINATE FLOOR

If a damaged section is near the edge of a room, it can simply be replaced with a new piece. If this is not possible, a small dent or scratch can be repaired with a laminate repair compound kit, as shown here.

TOOLS AND MATERIALS
Scissors, repair compound kit, scraper

A Cut off the nozzles on the two-part syringe. Squeeze the repair compound into a tray, where the two elements will mix together.

B Use the plastic scraper included in the repair kit to press the repair compound into the damaged area.

C Remove any excess compound, with a metal scraper, from the area before it dries.

PATCHING CARPET DAMAGE

Aside from using cleaners, damage to carpet can be hard to remedy. But specks of paint can be removed with a utility knife, and a small area of damage can be replaced with a patch, if you have offcuts of the carpet.

TOOLS AND MATERIALS
Scissors, utility knife, metal lid or similar object, spray adhesive

A Cut a patch of carpet to a size that is larger than the area that needs to be repaired.

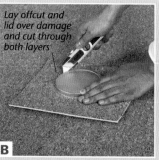

Lay offcut and lid over damage and cut through both layers

B Find a metal lid or other circular object, slightly larger than the repair area. Cut around it, down through the patch and the carpet below.

C Remove the cut circle of damaged carpet, and replace it with the circle of new carpet. You may wish to use spray adhesive.

PATCH-REPAIRING VINYL FLOORING

Although hardwearing, vinyl can be damaged by sharp objects or by heat, such as a cigarette burn. Re-covering an entire floor is expensive, but where vinyl has a pattern, such as "tiling", it can be used to aid the repair process. If you use this technique, be sure that the junctions between the patch and existing vinyl are firmly stuck down. Otherwise people may trip over them.

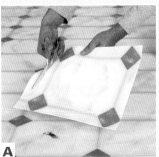

A Cut a section of new vinyl, to a size that is slightly larger than the damaged "tile" area.

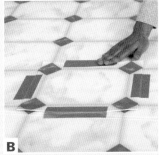

B Tape this piece loosely over the damaged area, making sure that it is aligned exactly with the pattern.

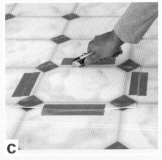

C Use a utility knife to cut through both layers of vinyl, using the "tile" edge as a guide line.

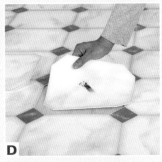

D Remove both sections of vinyl. As you lift out the damaged section, the cut shape will be revealed underneath.

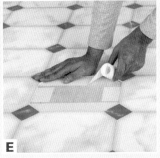

E Apply double-sided tape around all the edges of the revealed section of floor.

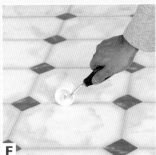

F Position the new vinyl section. Press down its edges, as well as those of the remaining old section. A seam roller is ideal for this.

TOOLS AND MATERIALS
Scissors, tape, utility knife, double-sided tape, seam roller

REPLACING A BROKEN HARD TILE

Floor tiles can crack due to wear and tear, or through damage if a heavy object is dropped on them. Replacing a single tile is more cost-effective than retiling an entire floor. Wear goggles while drilling into the tile, in case any shards fly toward you. Wear gloves to protect your hands.

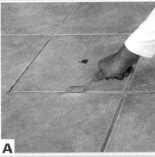

A Remove grout from around the edge of the tile. A grout raker is ideal for this process.

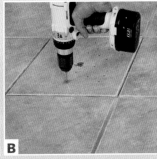

B Drill a series of holes into the broken tile. This breaks it up, making it easier to remove.

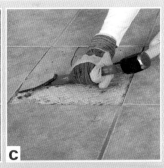

C With a heavy hammer and cold chisel, remove the broken tile. It will come away in sections.

D Scrape any hardened old adhesive off the floor surface revealed by the tile's removal.

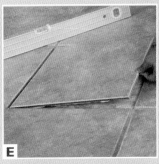

E Apply adhesive to the back of the new tile and position it. Use a level to make sure it sits flush with the surrounding tiles.

F Allow the adhesive to dry, then grout the new tile. Clean off any excess with a sponge.

TOOLS AND MATERIALS
Grout raker, drill, goggles, gloves, club hammer, cold chisel, scraper, level, tile adhesive, grout, grout shaper, sponge

Finishing a room

ONCE THE MAIN DECORATION OF A ROOM IS COMPLETE, THERE IS NORMALLY A NEED TO "FINISH" THE ROOM BY ADDING WINDOW DRESSINGS, PICTURES, MIRRORS, AND OTHER ACCESSORIES. IT IS THEREFORE ESSENTIAL TO CHOOSE THE CORRECT ATTACHMENTS FOR PARTICULAR WALL SURFACES (SEE PP.76–77) AND TO BE AWARE OF THE VARIOUS BRACKETS, CLIPS, AND HARDWARE THAT ARE AVAILABLE.

FINISHING HARDWARE

Wall dressing such as curtains and blinds make up an important part of the final look of a room. For this reason, it is important to choose the right materials, and to hang them in the appropriate way.

CURTAIN TRACKS

Most modern curtain tracks are plastic, though the traditional metal variety is still available. Light and flexible, plastic tracks are easy to install, and can be shaped to bend around curves and corners.

CURTAIN RODS

Curtain rods are secured by brackets that hold the rod away from the wall surface. Rods and brackets are normally made of wood (shown here) or metal, although other materials are available. For small windows, just two end supports should be sufficient to support the rod. For large windows, or when heavy curtains are being hung, a center support may be needed. Rods can be joined using dowel screws (see p.77).

FINIAL

Curtain track
Plastic curtain tracks are designed to be unobtrusive and to allow the curtain to hang close to the wall or window surface.

Lock

END SUPPORT   **TRACK BRACKET**

Curtain rod
This decorative element should be chosen with some regard to the overall look of the room.

END AND CENTER SUPPORT

Curtain hook

TRACK HOOK OR GLIDER

Choosing a curtain track
Plastic curtain tracks have little decorative appeal and so are usually covered when the curtains are closed.

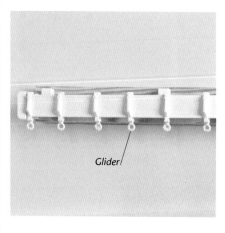
Glider

Eyelet screw

CURTAIN RING

Choosing a curtain rod
Part or all of the curtain rod is visible when the curtain is hung, so the design of the rod needs to fit with the rest of your decor.

RAIL HARDWARE

Other hardware to finish a room include the various racks and rails used for hanging clothes and towels. There are various types of brackets, and the type you use will depend on how you want to position them. The brackets themselves come in a range of materials; chrome is shown here.

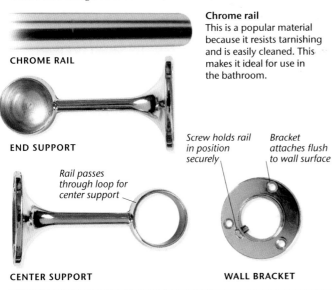

CHROME RAIL

END SUPPORT

Chrome rail
This is a popular material because it resists tarnishing and is easily cleaned. This makes it ideal for use in the bathroom.

Rail passes through loop for center support

CENTER SUPPORT

Screw holds rail in position securely

Bracket attaches flush to wall surface

WALL BRACKET

MIRROR FIXINGS

Mirrors can be hung in a variety of ways. The most important consideration is whether or not an attachment is strong enough to support the weight of a particular item. When fitting a mirror flush against a wall surface, make sure that the wall has no undulations. If it does, be careful not to overtighten the screws, otherwise the mirror may crack.

Head fixes over mirror

Use small screws or nails to fix to wall

Mirror screws
These are ideal for holding mirrors in place, if they have predrilled holes. If this is not the case, use adhesive or other specially designed brackets.

Peel off protective layer and stick to one surface first

Mirror pads (self-adhesive)
These should only be used for small, lightweight mirrors. They are double-sided adhesive pads; one side attaches to the wall surface, the other adheres to the back of the mirror.

Mirror corner brackets
Four brackets are secured to the wall surface; each of these supports a corner of the mirror.

Back of bracket attached to wall

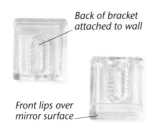

Front lips over mirror surface

Mirror brackets (sliding)
Sliding brackets are normally combined with fixed brackets, both lipping over the front of the mirror surface to hold it securely in place.

PICTURE FRAME ATTACHMENTS

Picture hooks can only be used for relatively lightweight items. For heavier frames, insert the attachments at a slight downward angle. Greater strength can be achieved by using resin and heavy-duty attachments (see pp.77 and 80). In many instances, particularly when hanging extremely heavy frames, screw attachments (with the appropriate wall plug) or nails can offer the most secure hanging mechanism. Always take care to avoid drilling into pipes or wires inside the wall surface.

Loops over nail or screw on wall

Flush frame
These attachments are attached to the outside edge of a frame. Depending on the frame's size and weight, several may be needed. They allow the frame to sit flush against the wall surface.

Hold looped head firmly and twist to drive in

Eyelet screws
These screws have a looped head and are inserted into the back of the frame. For small frames, these eyelets can be used as a direct hanging point. Alternatively, one eyelet is attached to each side of the frame and picture wire is tied between the two and looped over a wall attachment.

Use a hammer to drive nails through

Hardwall picture hook
Modern design of hook that relies on a number of small, tightly packed "nails" to penetrate the wall and provide strength.

Picture wire
Metallic wire suspended between eyelet screws on the back of a picture frame.

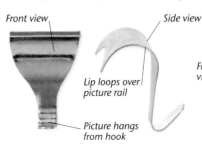

Front view

Side view

Lip loops over picture rail

Picture hangs from hook

PICTURE RAIL HOOK

Picture hooks
Traditional type of hanging mechanisms designed to penetrate the wall at a slight downward angle to increase attachment strength. Some hooks have two nails for increased strength. A more traditional design is provided by picture rail hooks. These are attached to picture rails, and pictures are hung either directly from the hooks or from wires looped between them. An advantage is that they leave no marks on the wall.

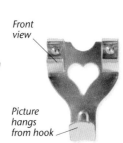

Front view

Picture hangs from hook

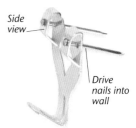

Side view

Drive nails into wall

PICTURE WALL HOOK

INSTALLING A CURTAIN ROD

Curtain rods are normally installed outside a window recess. For the maximum amount of light, end brackets should be placed on either side of the recess, so that curtains can be drawn back completely; their exact placing will depend on the width of the gathered curtain. In the following example, only end supports are required. For larger windows, extra support also may be needed in the center. Curtain weight and rod strength should also be considered when deciding on how much rail support is needed.

TOOLS AND MATERIALS SEE BASIC TOOLKIT, PP.24–25

BLINDS

Blinds are a popular alternative to curtains. When buying a set, it is important to take note of the manufacturer's guidelines on how brackets are oriented so that the blinds work efficiently. Some blinds are also supplied with an option to cut them down to your particular size requirements. The roller is generally made of wood or lightweight metal. Use a tenon saw to cut wooden rollers and a junior hacksaw to cut metal ones. Many blind manufacturers have their own hardware mechanisms that are manufactured according to design. Roller blinds tend to have two brackets that are installed directly to the window frame or the immediate wall surface. Some blind cords are a continuous loop; since these are a choking hazard for children, cut the loop to form an open-ended cord.

1 MEASURING

A

Make a mark above the window recess for the required height of the rod. This will depend on curtain length and aesthetic preference.

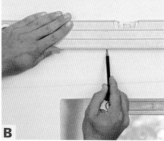

B

Use this mark to draw a level guide line above the recess; this should extend slightly beyond the recess width on either side.

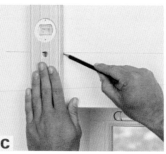

C

Use a level to make a mark on the horizontal line directly above the corner of the recess.

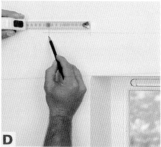

D

Measure back to mark the bracket position. This distance will depend on the width of the gathered curtain.

2 FIXING A CURTAIN ROD

A

Position the end support on the mark and use a pencil to mark off attachment holes. Remove the end support.

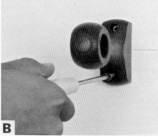

B

Plug attachment holes if necessary and screw into place. Repeat steps 1C, 1D, 2A, and 2B for the other end support.

C

Cut the rod to the required length. It must extend a couple of inches (a few centimeters) on either side of the end support brackets to accommodate end rings and finials. With supports in place, thread the rod through one end support.

3 ATTACHING RINGS AND END SUPPORT

A

Position rings on the rod before threading the other end of the rod through the other end support.

B

Position one ring on the outer side of each of the end supports.

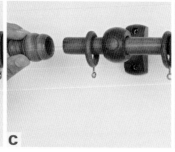

C

Position finials on the ends of the rod. Normally these are just pushed to fit; some are secured by a screw.

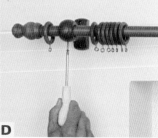

D

Finally, secure the rod in place by securing screws through the supports and into the rod. You may need to pilot-drill these holes first.

INSTALLING A CURTAIN RAIL

Unlike curtain rods, curtain rails are often installed directly to window frames, an arrangement that can hinder the opening of the curtain and thus reduce the amount of light that can enter the room. An alternative is to mount the track outside the window recess (as shown below), allowing you to draw the curtains well back from the recess and thus admit the maximum amount of light. To provide secure bracket points, mount the track on a wooden furring strip.

TOOLS AND MATERIALS SEE BASIC TOOLKIT, PP.24–25

1 INSTALLING A FURRING STRIP

Furring strip mounting is a good idea if the wall surface is difficult to work with (e.g., an old lath-and-plaster wall). Use a level to position the furring strip horizontally above the recess, then draw a guide line with a pencil.

A

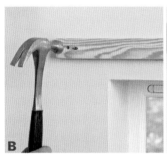

B

Drill pilot holes and use the appropriate screws or nails to secure the furring strip to the wall surface. Use the guide line to ensure that it is horizontal.

C

Draw a further guide line along the center of the furring strip.

2 FITTING A CURTAIN RAIL

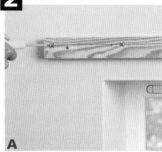

A

Position screws for rail brackets at regular intervals along the line.

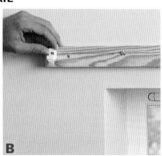

B

Position brackets on the screws. It may be necessary to adjust the screw depth to create a tight fit.

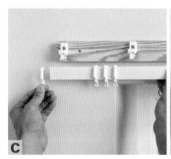

C

Position the required number of gliders on the rail.

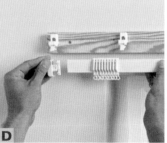

D

Attach the end support on the rail to prevent the gliders from slipping off.

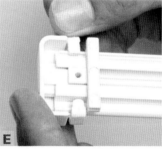

E

Positioning the end support will vary according to rail design. In this case, make sure you position a final glider at the same time as the support.

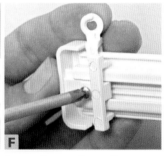

F

A screw is normally used to secure the support in place.

3 ATTACHING THE RAIL

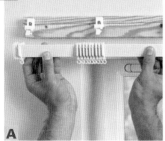

A

Clip the rail onto the brackets.

B

Most rails will have a clip on the brackets that needs to be closed off to secure the rail in place.

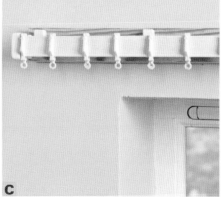

C

With the rail in position, space out the gliders to check that you have the required number. Most rails allow you to add further gliders without having to take down the rail and remove the end supports.

IMPROVING HOME PERFORMANCE

INSULATION AND VENTILATION
HOME SECURITY
CONSERVING ENERGY
USING SPACE

EFFICIENT HOME SYSTEMS

There are many ways in which you can improve your home structurally and decoratively. However, there are many other home-improvement methods you can use to boost the performance of your home and make it more efficient in terms of energy use, aspects of safety and security, and storage. Here we identify the areas of a home that may be improved in these ways.

ASSESSING YOUR PRIORITIES

When assessing your home's performance, you need to be able to prioritize the tasks at hand. Generally, matters of safety and security need to be placed at the top of your list, while other issues, such as improving storage space, can be tackled at your own pace. Not all issues and measures shown here will be relevant to every home. However, the aim of this section is to cover as many improvements in safety, security, storage, and energy efficiency as possible, some of which may be applicable to your home and lifestyle. Many of the technologies discussed in this section are new, as options constantly develop and evolve. It pays to be aware of developments in all these areas, so that you can take advantage of the latest techniques for home improvement.

Fire escape route
All homes must have suitable fire escape procedures. In many cases an escape ladder can be installed. Escape windows should also open wide enough to ensure easy passage through them in the event of an emergency.

Using rainwater
Consider collecting and recycling rainwater. You can use it to water the garden or even channel it directly into your home plumbing system (see p.390–91).

RECYCLING WATER

As well as recycling rainwater, it is now possible to install systems in your home that can recycle gray water (from sinks, baths, and washing machines), and black water (from toilets). Both systems can be expensive to install, but once fitted they are eco-friendly and cost-effective. Carry out research to ensure you fit a system appropriate to your needs. For more on the efficient use of water, see pp.466–67.

Using roof space for storage
Use shelving to act as storage platforms in this otherwise unused area of the home (see pp.360–361).

Soundproofing floors and walls
Noise between floors or adjacent rooms can be drastically reduced by modern soundproofing techniques (see pp.366–367).

Attic insulation
A well-insulated attic is essential for saving energy (see p.356–359). This is both environmentally friendly and cost-effective.

Floor insulation
Insulated floors not only save energy and household heating costs (see p.365) but also feel more comfortable underfoot.

Exhaust fan
Make sure that exhaust fans are used to take moist air out of the house where necessary.

Static ventilation
Make sure you have adequate ventilation for fuel-burning appliances.

Child safety: door catches
Use door locks to prevent children from gaining unsupervised access to your refrigerator and cabinets.

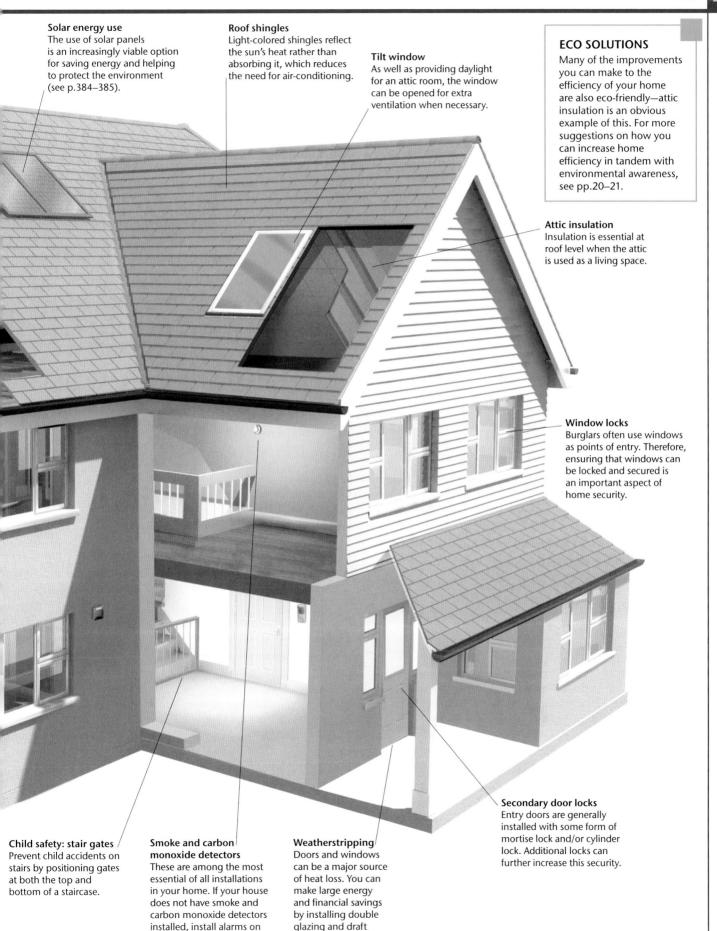

Solar energy use
The use of solar panels is an increasingly viable option for saving energy and helping to protect the environment (see p.384–385).

Roof shingles
Light-colored shingles reflect the sun's heat rather than absorbing it, which reduces the need for air-conditioning.

Tilt window
As well as providing daylight for an attic room, the window can be opened for extra ventilation when necessary.

ECO SOLUTIONS
Many of the improvements you can make to the efficiency of your home are also eco-friendly—attic insulation is an obvious example of this. For more suggestions on how you can increase home efficiency in tandem with environmental awareness, see pp.20–21.

Attic insulation
Insulation is essential at roof level when the attic is used as a living space.

Window locks
Burglars often use windows as points of entry. Therefore, ensuring that windows can be locked and secured is an important aspect of home security.

Secondary door locks
Entry doors are generally installed with some form of mortise lock and/or cylinder lock. Additional locks can further increase this security.

Child safety: stair gates
Prevent child accidents on stairs by positioning gates at both the top and bottom of a staircase.

Smoke and carbon monoxide detectors
These are among the most essential of all installations in your home. If your house does not have smoke and carbon monoxide detectors installed, install alarms on every floor.

Weatherstripping
Doors and windows can be a major source of heat loss. You can make large energy and financial savings by installing double glazing and draft excluders (see p.365).

Insulation and ventilation

YOUR HOME'S PERFORMANCE IS DEPENDENT ON THE QUALITY OF ITS INSULATION AND VENTILATION. HUGE AMOUNTS OF ENERGY ARE LOST THROUGH POOR INSULATION. THIS WASTES FUEL, DAMAGES THE ENVIRONMENT, AND COSTS YOU MONEY. NEW BUILDING REGULATIONS REQUIRE OWNERS TO IMPROVE INSULATION, VENTILATION, AND SOUNDPROOFING WHEN CARRYING OUT ALTERATIONS AND RENOVATIONS.

HOME INSULATION

Improving your home's insulation is one of the best overall investments of time and money you can make. Although the initial financial outlay may be quite high, the long-term savings on heating bills will make it worthwhile. You can insulate most parts of your home against heat loss, and even fairly modest measures can make a considerable difference. However, efficient thermal insulation must always go hand in hand with effective ventilation to prevent the buildup of condensation (see pp.368–69).

HOW INSULATION WORKS

Heat flows from warm areas to cold areas, and moves in any direction. In the home, warm air expands and circulates, escaping through walls, ceilings, roofs, windows, doors, fireplaces, and anywhere plumbing, ducting, or electrical wiring penetrates exterior walls. Thermal insulation acts as a barrier, reducing the amount of heat that escapes.

The term "R-value" is used when discussing thermal requirements in a house, especially in conjunction with insulation products. The aim is to achieve high R-values: this means that a house's insulation is efficient. In a new-build home R-values are governed by building regulations, and the type of insulation used will therefore need to meet certain requirements.

WHERE TO INSULATE

Insulating the walls, attic, floors, and windows of your home is the most effective way of reducing overall heat loss (see pp.356–65). However, there are many other parts of a home in which a few inexpensive and straightforward methods can make a dramatic improvement.

Thermal image of heat loss
On a thermal image of a house, the roof shows up as cool and blue, suggesting there is insulation present, but the red windows and wooden slats show heat escaping. Even if you have good loft insulation it is important to consider other areas such as walls and windows. If you are fitting new windows in your home, they must have double-glazed units.

Pipe insulation can be used to stop heat loss from hot water pipes, particularly for those with continuous use such as supply lines for clothes washers. This will help to cut down on the energy used by your hot-water tank. Cold water pipes can also be insulated to stop them from sweating.

Modern hot-water tanks are usually sold with a layer of insulation pre-fitted. If yours does not have this, buy a cover and fit it over the tank.

You should cover any attic traps with a layer of insulation, otherwise all your efforts to insulate your attic or roof space may be undermined by leakage through the hatch or around its edges.

Heat emitted by the rear of a radiator can be lost into or through the wall it is attached to. In the past, it was common practice to fit aluminum foil behind a radiator to reflect its heat back into the room, but now it is possible to buy purpose-made insulating kits to do this job.

Gaps between baseboards and floorboards can cause unpleasant drafts and will lead to heat loss from your home. To avoid this, you can use caulking or expanding foam to close up any gaps.

INSULATING AND SOUNDPROOFING MATERIALS

When choosing insulation, take into account the material's cost, ease of use, suitability to your needs, and thermal properties ("R-value", see opposite). Bear in mind that greener materials are increasingly being used in this area. The effectiveness of a soundproofing material is based on what it is made of and how and where it is installed.

RECYCLED INSULATION

Recycled blanket insulation
This example, made from recycled plastic bottles, is both eco-friendly and non-itch.

Recycled loose-fill insulation
This is a wood-based cellulose fiber that mainly consists of recycled newspaper.

NATURAL INSULATION

Sheep's wool batt
Thermafleece made from 100 percent sheep's wool. It is non-itch and is as easy to use as other forms of fibrous batt insulation.

Wood-fiber batt
Wood-based insulation primarily made from forestry waste and sawmill residues. Products are added for fireproofing.

Blanket insulation
Versatile and easy-to-use, rolls are usually the same width as the space between joists or rafters.

Cellulose
Requires a blower, which can be rented. Ideal for small spaces.

Expanded polystyrene board (Beadboard)
Basic foam panel insulation used primarily over walls. Has about the same R-value as fiberglass.

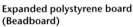

Foam insulation
Foams vary from beads for air sealing gaps to sprays to insulate and air seal entire walls.

Pipe insulation
Useful on hot pipes with continuous use, such as clothes washers. Stops sweating on cold pipes.

Extruded polystyrene board
Higher density, higher R-value per inch and higher cost than beadboard. Often used on foundation walls or under concrete slabs.

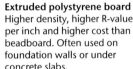

Specialty foam panels
Various high R-value foam panels are available for walls. Their special properties raise the price.

Pipe lagging
Same as pipe insulation, but in tape form.

Flanking tape
Use to cover gaps along edges when soundproofing.

Acoustic mat
Used in a continuous layer below flooring, this densely packed material reduces impact noise transmission through the floor.

6 mil polyethylene
Clear plastic sheets for vapor barriers should be labeled as a vapor barrier or vapor retarder. They are green in this book for visibility.

Acoustic underlayment
Used under flooring instead of regular underlayment, this helps to improve a room's sound insulation.

Acoustic batt
This dense soundproofing material is sold in batts. It is commonly used in partition walls or floor/ceiling separations.

REINSULATING AN ATTIC

Most attics in Canada have at least seaweed or sawdust if not modern insulation. It is possible to increase this insulation or even change its placement to make either a cold attic or a conditioned attic. In all cases, the roof itself needs to remain cold and well ventilated to prevent moisture accumulation in the warm seasons and to prevent snow melt creating ice dams and icicles in the cold seasons. Attics built with trusses are rarely conditioned as the space is not even open enough to use for storage.

COLD ATTIC (STORAGE ONLY)

In a cold attic, the insulation sits on the ceiling below. It is important that air can flow from the soffits into the attic and out vents high up on the roof. Do not block this ventilation with insulation. Use baffles, ideally all along the roof edge, giving continuous ventilation. A vapor barrier can be laid on the warm-in-winter side of the insulation, or you can simply paint the ceiling with vapor barrier paint or two coats of oil paint. Sealing air leaks from the house is critical, especially around electrical boxes and light fixtures.

VAPOR BARRIER

If you are installing insulation and vapor barriers yourself, here are a few tips to help you achieve the most benefits when using a vapor barrier:
■ Always place the vapor barrier on the warm-in-winter side of the wall.
■ If you are adding a second layer of insulation to an attic, do not add a second vapor barrier.
■ Sealing air leaks, creating an air barrier, is far more important than trying to perfect the vapor barrier.

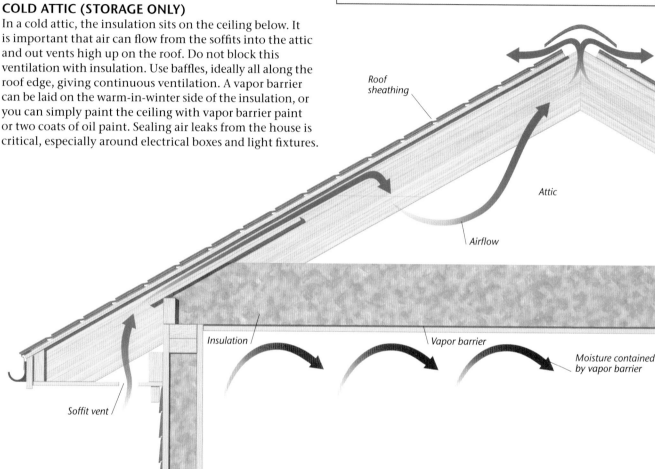

Roof sheathing

Attic

Airflow

Insulation

Vapor barrier

Moisture contained by vapor barrier

Soffit vent

The roof/attic as a system

To avoid problems, it is important to realize that the entire assembly, from the paint on the ceiling through to the coating on the roof shingles, forms an interconnected system. This is a critical buffer zone that sheds rain, snow, hail, wind, and sun and needs to be protected from moisture rising up from the house below. Since nothing is perfect in houses, safety mechanisms must be built in. Felt under the shingles is a second line of water defense. Continuous ventilation removes moisture in the summer and keeps the snow frozen on the roof in winter. Baffles keep insulation from blocking the ventilation and prevent cold air from sliding under the insulation. Air sealing and vapor barriers on the warm ceiling stop household moisture from moving into this buffer zone.

Ventilation spaces

1

Attic edge details

Where the roof meets the top of the wall, there is often little space for both insulation and ventilation, but both are necessary. Use baffles to assure a minimum of 3/4 in of open ventilation and as much insulation as possible. Continuous ventilation the full length of the roof is preferable.

CONDITIONED ATTICS (COMPACT ROOF)

When you want to make livable space out of an attic, you will have to create an insulated "compact roof" where the insulation and the ventilation are all squeezed into very little space. We also call this a cathedral ceiling. Since there is no "attic" at all, or a very small one at the peak, you must absolutely ventilate every single rafter space that is compact, either all the way to the soffits, as in the illustration, or to the knee wall "atttic" section as in the photo below.

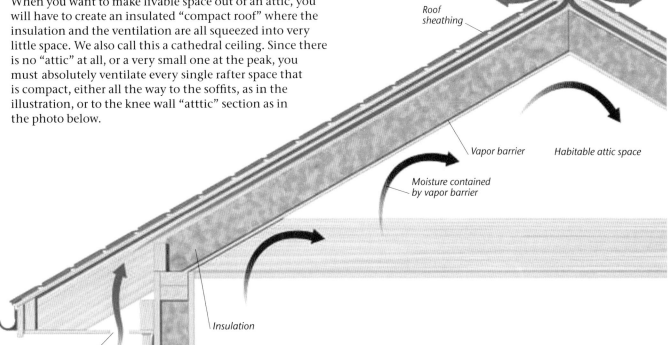

Airflow

Roof sheathing

Vapor barrier

Habitable attic space

Moisture contained by vapor barrier

Insulation

Soffit vent

Maintaining continuous ventilation

A masonite or thin plywood panel should be placed over furring strips to create the ventilation space between the insulation and the underside of the roof in the cathedral section. Then insulation goes between the rafters. In our climate, it is a good to add foamboard insulation directly over both the insulation and the rafters, blocking heat loss through the wood. A vapor barrier can go before or after the foamboard, then the drywall. If you are creating a conditioned attic to become a living area, it will likely require planning permission and need to be inspected. In many cases, you may wish to construct knee walls (shown right) that will make the area appear and feel more like the other rooms in your home.

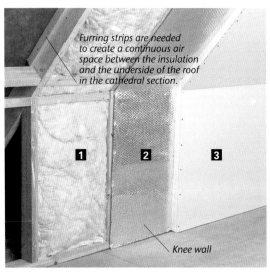

Furring strips are needed to create a continuous air space between the insulation and the underside of the roof in the cathedral section.

1 **2** **3**

Knee wall

Conditioned attic options

Choose one of the following options (see p.357 for details).

Option 1:
Fiberglass batts between studs and rafters, a vapor barrier, then drywall.

Option 2:
In regions with very hot summers, reflective vapor barriers with an air space behind them make summer insulation more effective.

Option 3:
Foamboard insulation over either 1 or 2 will prevent thermal bridging, cold spots, and condensation.

INSULATION DEPTHS

For details on recommended R-Values for different parts of the house in different areas check out the Government of Canada booklet called Keeping the Heat In at www.oee.nrcan.gc. ca/keep_heat_in/.

TOOLS AND MATERIALS CHECKLIST PP.360–365

Laying blanket insulation (p.360) Protective clothing, vapor barrier, staple gun, blanket insulation

Insulating rafters (p.361) Protective clothing, furring strips, blanket insulation, vapor barrier, thermal drywall

Insulating a stud wall (p.364) Protective clothing, blanket insulation, drywall

FOR BASIC TOOLKIT
SEE PP.24–25

AIR BARRIERS

The primary energy savings in a home come from air sealing, not insulation. After the first basic insulation, sealing air leaks through walls and ceilings is the renovation exercise that has the greatest payback in both heating dollars and in protection of the structure of your house.

How you insulate your attic space will depend on whether you intend to have a "cold attic" or a "conditioned attic" (see pp.358–359). In the former you insulate at the joist level to keep the heat in the house below (see below and opposite). With a "conditioned attic," you insulate between and under the rafters of the roof (see p.363). The recommended thickness for insulation has been increased recently, so you may have to increase the depths of the joists or rafters to accommodate the recommended thickness.

RECYCLED INSULATION

Recycled insulation is a green and non-itch alternative to conventional blanket insulation. The techniques for laying this are the same, but non-itch insulation makes it a more comfortable process. Check the instructions on the product to ensure that you install it to the right thickness requirement.

BLANKET INSULATION

One of the most widely used forms of attic-insulation, blanket insulation is simple to work with—although you should always wear protective clothing, as it can be uncomfortable to handle. Before starting, ensure that you have measured the surface area of your attic accurately, and that you bear in mind the recommended thickness requirements and order accordingly (manufacturers supply blanket insulation in many different thicknesses, so you must remember to order to the correct thickness as well as to the necessary surface area). Always consider the recycled and natural alternatives to conventional blanket insulation (see boxes, above and opposite).

LAYING BLANKET INSULATION

Sweep away any debris from between the joists. Determine whether a vapor barrier is needed. If the drywall surface is silver-backed, you won't need an extra membrane—if not, it is advisable to install one.

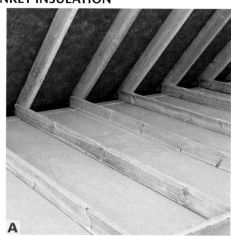

A

TOOLS AND MATERIALS SEE BASIC TOOLKIT AND P.359

Roll out the vapor barrier, cutting and laying lengths in between each pair of joists. Staple the barrier to the sides of the joists using a staple gun. Cut holes in the barrier to accommodate any electrical hardware. Reseal the vapor barrier around all wires.

B

C

Do not unpack the insulation blanket until you are in the attic. This will restrict the presence of insulation fibers to the work area.

D

Roll out the insulation blanket between the joists, taking care not to compress it. Tuck it in against the sides of the joists.

E

Butt the lengths of insulation up against one another, making sure that there are no gaps between each of the lengths.

RECESSED LIGHT FIXTURES

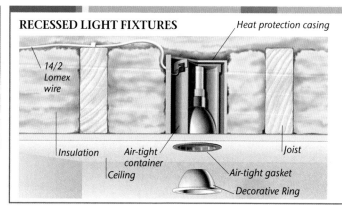

Heat protection casing

14/2 Lomex wire

Insulation

Air-tight container

Ceiling

Air-tight gasket

Joist

Decorative Ring

Insulated ceiling (IC) fixtures that are air tight must be used for any recessed lights. These prevent the fixture from overheating and releasing warm, moist air into the attic, which can cause rot or ice dams on the roof. Follow manufacturer's instructions carefully to ensure proper installation.

MOVING AROUND

Working in an unfinished attic can be difficult, especially if there isn't a floor. Always walk on the joists, as the surface below the joists may seem like a floor, but it is actually the ceiling of another room. Lay plywood sheets across joists to create a stable work area for safety and efficiency.

Decking provides walking area

USING SHEEP'S WOOL

As with the recycled non-itch alternative shown opposite, sheep's wool is a more user-friendly alternative to conventional material. Build up depth by laying subsequent layers at right angles to the preceding layer. Check the instructional literature for depth requirements.

VENTILATION FROM THE SOFFITS

A

Place baffles against the underside of the roof deck and into the soffit area.

B

Lay in insulation being careful to fill all air pockets, even when the attic is difficult to work in.

C

Place as much insulation as possible over the outside wall without compressing the baffles or the insulation.

HOW MUCH VENTILATION?

Building codes only call for a certain minimum ventilation in an attic. As long as baffles are used to prevent wind from blowing under or into the insulation (loose fill insulation can be blown across the attic), it is best to have air in every single rafter section. This serves the purpose of keeping any snow on the roof frozen despite some heat losses from the house below, and that prevents the formation of icicles and ice dams on the roof. If no snow stays on your roof, this is less important.

AIR FLOW IN THE ROOF SPACE

More important than how much air flow you have in a roof space is the path the air takes. If the baffles shown above went up too high, you would have no circulation in the lower part of the attic. If you have no roof vents, only soffit vents, the air will just flow in one side and maybe out the other, but nothing in the top and nothing on a calm day. Continuous soffit vents and individual vents or a continuous ridge vent high up on the roof assures good air flow throughout the roof space whether the wind is blowing or not.

LAYING STORAGE DECKING

Many people want to use part of their attic space for storage purposes. Storage decking is a 2-in-1 application that combines extra insulation with a rigid board for storage. Check the board sizes beforehand to make sure they will fit through your attic hatch.

A

Cut wedges of blanket to insulate the join of the roof rafters and floor joists, but with non-breathable felt leave a gap behind the wedge.

B

Lay the first board across the joists. Butt the edge of the board up against the rafters. Be sure not to close the gap behind the wedge of insulation.

C

To hold the deck in position, use one screw to fix each section to the joist below. Board ends should join on joists.

IMPROVING HOME PERFORMANCE

LOOSE-FILL INSULATION

Loose-fill insulation can be used as a direct alernative to blanket insulation (see p.357). Which one you choose is a question of personal preference. Bear in mind that bags of loose-fill insulation are easy to handle and are simpler to transport into the attic than their blanket insulation equivalent. Also, where an attic is awkwardly shaped in its joist design and layout—it may have lots of blocking and inaccessible voids between the joists, for example—loose-fill insulation can provide a more user-friendly, easily installed alternative to common blanket insulation. Be aware that there are conventional and recycled alternatives (see box, right).

USING RECYCLED PAPER

Arguably, the greenest option in loose-fill insulation is shredded recycled paper. This is sometimes used in wall insulation, but can also be blown into attic spaces using a purpose-made applicator. Ensure that an adequate depth has been achieved to ensure thermally efficient results.

LAYING LOOSE-FILL INSULATION

First, sweep the voids to remove any debris. To stop the loose-fill leaking out under the eaves, create a barrier where the joists meet the rafters using a small section of blanket insulation. Leave a 2-in (50-mm) gap between the roof and the blanket to allow air to circulate freely up through the soffits.

Carefully pour loose-fill insulation into the areas between the joists. Pour in enough to reach the top of the joists. It is best to start at the eaves on one side of the roof and work across to the other.

Cut a section of plywood to the same width as the gap between the joists. Sweep the fill away from you, using the offcut to level it off. Move excess loose-fill to areas that need to be built up.

When leveled off, you should have an even coverage across the entire attic space. The blanket insulation at the eaves will prevent "creeping".

The depth of the loose-fill will determine any further requirements regarding regulations.

ELECTRICAL FIXTURES

If you have electrical hardware, such as a recessed light from the ceiling below, use an air tight insulated ceiling (IC) fixture to prevent the release of warm, moist air into the attic (see p.360). Follow manufacturer's instructions to ensure proper installation.

Should you require a deeper layer of loose-fill, you will need a platform from which to work, so that you can safely move across the attic space, as the insulation will obscure the joists from view. A further wedge of blanket insulation may be required at the eaves. You could also roll out insulation batts over the loose fill.

DEEP FILLING

Deep filling can be achieved with loose-fill, but a more practical alternative is to use decking boards above the loose-fill, combining the two to achieve regulation depth, and creating a useable storage space in the attic. Always think about combining insulation— even if you don't create a large storage area, the decking will provide safe access.

INSULATING RAFTERS AND WALLS

If you are converting the attic area into a living space, you will need to find a way to get the required amount of insulation into a smaller space. Rafter depth is an issue, as there is often not enough depth to fit the required insulation—you may need to increase the depth of the rafters by adding wood to their undersides, and/or by using both insulation batts and foam boards. Remember to consider green insulation materials (see box, right).

USING RECYCLED BATTS

Recycled batts are a good alternative to blanket insulation for rafters and walls. They are more eco-friendly, and are often easier to position (blanket insulation can sag before it is secured in place by drywall). Either type may need to be cut to fit the exact space between rafters or studs.

INSULATING RAFTERS

In many cases, a dwarf wall is used to partition the eaves area. This makes a more practical space for positioning furniture and fittings. The area behind the wall is treated as a cold insulated roof even though it is a relatively small space. Insulation is laid at joist level to reduce heat loss from the floors below. Block air movement in the space from the bottom of the wall to the ceiling below.

A

Fix lengths of 1 x 2 in battens along the inside edge of each rafter right up against the roof deck. These furring strips will help to maintain the ventilation gap between the insulation and the roof. If this is a low-sloped roof that holds snow, even better ventilation can be achieved by installing $1/8$ or $1/4$-in thick panels up against these strips to create a clear ventilation raceway.

B

C

If necessary, increase the depth of the fill space by fixing 2 x 2 in (50 x 50 mm) or 2 x 3 in (50 x 75 mm) wooden battens along the roof rafters. Screw them into position.

D

Infill the space by wedging the blanket between the furring strips but do not compress the insulation against the underside of the roof.

E

Wedge the insulation in the gaps between the studs in the knee wall. A tight fit is required to ensure that the insulation doesn't fall backward. Nails can be tapped in along the back edge of the studs to prevent this. Alternatively, use a rigid insulation board instead of blanket insulation.

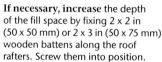

F

Cover the rafters and the lower knee wall with a vapor barrier, stapling the sheets to the joists.

G

If more insulation is required, add foam insulation panels.

H

There must be twice the R-value on the cold side of the vapor barrier than on the warm side to prevent condensation. If your foam panels represent more than a third of the total R-value of the wall, then put vapor barrier on the warm side of the foam. Foam insulation must be covered with drywall.

All options are open for insulating walls during construction and major renovations, but when you want to re-insulate existing walls you will have to work harder and think twice. You will need to punch holes in the walls either from the inside or the outside to inject insulation. If your siding is removable as in the photos below, this can be economical—otherwise it would be more practical to wait until it is time to change the siding and the wall will be exposed. If there is already some insulation in the wall, trying to add more by injection is usually not practical, as it doesn't flow well.

INSULATING A FINISHED WALL WITH LOOSE FILL

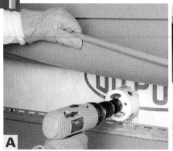

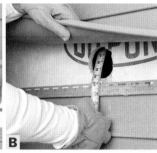

A Drill a hole into the wall, near the floor, for the insulation blower to fit inside.

B Insert a measure to check that the bay is empty. If you find obstructions that are not electrical, drill a new hole above the obstruction.

C Fill the blower's bin with loose-fill insulation.

D Push the blower's tube into the wall and begin to blow the insulation into the wall.

E When all of the bays in the wall are filled, patch the hole in the wall.

F Reapply a building material and the exterior sheathing material to the wall.

INSULATING A WALL WITH RIGID FOAM INSULATION

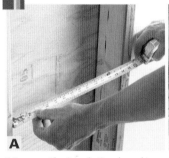

A Measure the insulation board to fit between the studs.

B Cut the board to length with a handsaw.

C Place the insulation board inside the stud bay.

D Tape or glue the board in place. Screw drywall panels in place over the insulation board.

INSULATING A WALL WITH BLANKET INSULATION

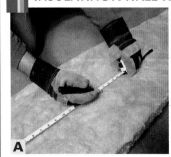

A Measure the height of the stud bay where you will be placing the insulation. You can use a felt marker right on the fiberglass.

B Compress the batt with a straight edge and cut with a utility knife or a kitchen bread knife.

C Slit the insulation part way through so it will come out around wires and fill the space.

D Push it tight into the corners, then pull the face forward flush to the stud. Compressed insulation or air gaps both cause problems.

INSULATING FLOORS

Insulating floors can greatly help reduce heat loss, and can help with soundproofing. To reduce heat loss, you may want to insulate floors over unheated basements or other unheated or open spaces, such as garages and porches. For sound absorption help, soft insulation can affect any room that has mostly hard surfaces. If you are working with an open floor of exposed joists, always walk on the joists or lay plywood for safe working areas. These products must be installed in substantial contact with an approved construction material to help prevent the spread of fire.

SAFETY

Safety is important when working with insulation materials.
■ Always wear a mask, gloves, and safety glasses.
■ Avoid direct contact with skin because insulation can cause irritation.
■ Never install insulation near flames, electrical equipment, or heating equipment.
■ Always build a barrier around any light fixtures to keep insulation at least 3 in (70 mm) away (see p.360).

INSULATION BOARDS

You can insulate both concrete and wooden floors using insulation boards. The stage at which they are laid will depend on floor age and type. Vapor barriers are used in older properties, and help to prevent ground moisture from getting into a wood floor.

Laying a floating floor
On sound concrete you can lay insulation boards directly on the concrete surface.

Using furring strips
Where you have furring strips at intervals across a floor, you can slot insulation panels between them.

Before laying concrete
Where concrete is still to be laid, lay the insulation panels first and then pour the concrete on top.

▌▌ INSTALLING INSULATION AROUND RAFTERS

Starting at the perimeter of the attic, measure and cut the insulation to length. Place the insulation with the vapor barrier on the warm-in-winter side. If you are placing one type of insulation over another, the least dense should be on the cold side to allow for moisture escape. Hence foam boards on the warm side, batts and loose fill on the cold side.

A

Insert the insulation below any cables when laying insulation through joist bays.

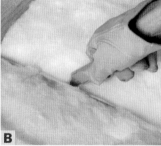

B

Score the top of the insulation along the cable with a utility knife.

C

Peel the top half over the cable to cover it.

▌▌ INSTALLING SEALS

Sealing doors is an easy trick for reducing energy loss in your home. Requiring minimum tools and materials, a door seal runs along the bottom of your door to cover any gaps. Especially popular in older homes, a door sweep (shown here) requires screws to stay in place. Thresholds are another popular option to reduce air flow under the door. Gaskets, self-adhesive silicone, and foam are options to seal the tops of doors.

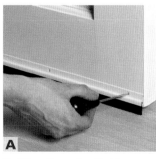

A

Position the seal so that its bristles just touch and bend on the floor. Use an awl to mark where fasteners are needed.

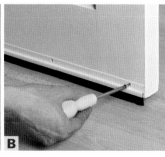

B

Screw the seal to the door. Move the door back and forth to check that the seal is positioned correctly, before securing the final screws.

SEALING FRONT DOORS

Front doors can be a major source of drafts, especially if your home does not have a porch. Ensure that in addition to sealing gaps around the edges of the door, you seal any openings or gaps and caulk any cracks in the trim.

SOUNDPROOFING A ROOM

Noise pollution comes in two forms—airborne and impact—and soundproofing products are often classified by the type of noise they affect. Airborne sound can be created by televisions, stereos, or speech. Impact noise travels as vibrations through solid materials, and includes footsteps or furniture being moved. Soundproofing a floor is easier than soundproofing a ceiling, but if you live in an apartment you may not have a choice. Most soundproofing efforts are done to block-out sound, whereas in many renovations and newer houses, great effort is taken to acoustically adjust theatre rooms to create an enhanced "theatre-like" experience.

REDUCING SOUND TRAVEL

■ Sound is created by vibrating material. Making a room stiff and thick reduces the amount of sound that can escape.

■ Using acoustically efficient materials to add mass to a structure increases its ability to absorb sound.

■ Structural elements carry sound, so creating a barrier between them prevents sounds from traveling across a room.

■ Use acoustic sealant, flanking tape, or flanking strips to isolate a structural element.

■ Seal the edges of walls and floors to prevent sound from traveling to the next room.

SOUNDPROOFING A FLOOR

Combining acoustic underlayment with acoustic mats beneath a floor reduces the effects of both airborne and impact noise. If the problem is solely impact noise, underlayment alone may suffice. Remove the coverings to reveal the floor (see Flooring, pp.326–347). If the floor is to be carpeted, leave the baseboard in place and proceed as shown below. For other floorings (see right), remove the baseboard molding and lay out the acoustic underlayment, butting the lengths up against one another and allowing them to lap a short distance up the wall. Tape all joints, and then lay acoustic mat, ensuring that any seams do not coincide with the joins of the underlayment. Lay a floating tongue-and-groove chipboard floor over the top, and trim the edges of the underlayment. You may then install further floor coverings, such as laminated flooring.

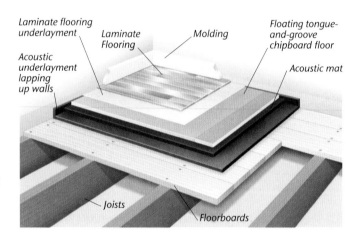

Laminate flooring underlayment · Laminate Flooring · Molding · Floating tongue-and-groove chipboard floor · Acoustic underlayment lapping up walls · Acoustic mat · Joists · Floorboards

Soundproofing hard floors
A combination of acoustic underlayment with acoustic mats and chipboard sheets is a very straightforward option for effective soundproofing. Here it is installed below a floating chipboard floor, over which underlayment and laminate flooring are laid.

Soundproofing carpeted floors
When soundproofing floors that are to be carpeted, first install furring strips around the room's perimeter, then lay acoustic mats and underlayment between, and butting up against, the furring strips. Attach tackless stripping to the furring strips and lay the carpet.

Molding · Carpet · Tackless stripping · Acoustic underlayment · Acoustic mat · Furring strip · Floorboards · Joists

DOORS AND WINDOWS

■ Double glazing windows or glass doors improves sound insulation, as well as thermal insulation.

■ If noise from outside is a major problem, consider triple glazing.

■ Weatherstripping added around doors and windows will insulate them against sound as well as heat loss.

Flooring materials and soundproofing

As soundproofing involves the building up of materials, thick floor coverings are more soundproof. For example, cushioned vinyl is more effective than regular vinyl. You can lay sheet vinyl over a soundproofed chipboard floor and attach it with double-sided adhesive tape. Similarly, high-quality burlap-backed carpets will prevent sound travel better than cheaper foam-backed carpets.

Do not add flanking strips to a carpeted floor. The fact that the carpet stretches across the tackless stripping and makes contact with the baseboard should provide protection enough against flanking noise.

SOUNDPROOFING A CEILING

There are two main methods of soundproofing a ceiling. One is to use hat channels. These are lightweight metal channels that separate wall and ceiling surfaces, preventing airborne and impact noise from traveling through them. They provide a frame to which drywall can be attached. The other method is to lower the ceiling by building a false ceiling beneath the existing one.

In both examples shown below, the drywall of the existing ceiling has been stripped away first. An alternative to these is to fit hat channels directly onto the ceiling, in a similar way to that shown for walls (bottom, left). Where the existing ceiling is high enough to permit it, the second technique may be used, but without removing the drywall on the existing ceiling.

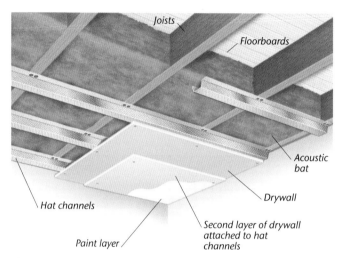

Joists
Floorboards
Acoustic bat
Drywall
Hat channels
Second layer of drywall attached to hat channels
Paint layer

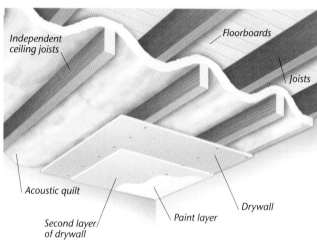

Independent ceiling joists
Floorboards
Joists
Acoustic quilt
Second layer of drywall
Paint layer
Drywall

Using hat channels
Remove ceiling drywall and attach hat channels across the joists at intervals of 16 in (400 mm). Fit acoustic bats 4 in (100 mm) deep above these bars, between the joists. Attach two layers of drywall, one ½ in (12 mm) thick, then one ⅜ in (9 mm) thick, staggering seams. Twin-layered board is available, and is a quicker option, but costs more.

Using independent ceiling joists
Expose the existing joists and insert new ones between them. (The technique for installing new joists is covered on p.101.) The lower faces of the new joists should be at least 2 in (55 mm) below the faces of the existing joists. You should then weave a layer of acoustic quilt between the two joist levels, as shown, before attaching two layers of drywall to the lower joists in the usual way.

SOUNDPROOFING A WALL

The principles for soundproofing ceilings and floors from below can also be applied to walls. For example, you can fit hat channels directly to the surface of an existing wall, as shown below left. If losing a little space in the room is not a problem, build a completely new, independent wall in front of the existing structure. This is most easily done with a metal stud wall (see pp.106–107) as it is quick and creates little mess. Build it 1 in (25 mm) away from the original wall. You can then insert acoustic bat between the stud uprights to create a soundproof layer.

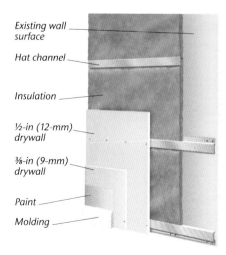

Existing wall surface
Hat channel
Insulation
½-in (12-mm) drywall
⅜-in (9-mm) drywall
Paint
Molding

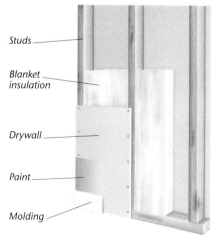

Studs
Blanket insulation
Drywall
Paint
Molding

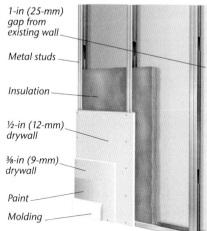

1-in (25-mm) gap from existing wall
Metal studs
Insulation
½-in (12-mm) drywall
⅜-in (9-mm) drywall
Paint
Molding

Using hat channels
Make sure that the open side of the ground-level channel is facing downward. In the others it should face upward.

Increasing mass
Adding to the mass of a stud wall will help it to absorb sound. Adding blanket insulation will also improve its thermal insulation.

Adding an independent wall
When creating a metal stud wall, make sure that the acoustic bat is rigid enough to remain vertical between the metal studs.

VENTILATING A HOME

Efficient ventilation removes odors, pollutants, and vapor-laden air trapped inside a home before they can cause any damage, harm to you or your house, or discomfort. Condensation occurs as moist, warm air comes in contact with cold surfaces. It is easily visible on glass, walls, or ceilings, but it can also form on carpets and curtains. Damp surfaces may decay over time, and the resulting mold and mildew can cause an unhealthy living environment. Insulation, double-glazing, and heating can all lessen condensation, but good channels for ventilation and the free flow of air are required.

HEALTH AND SAFETY

When installing a fan, make sure that the extracted air is replaced by fresh air—especially in a room containing a fuel-burning appliance. Failure to provide fresh air can cause a fatal buildup of carbon monoxide in a room. Fuel-burning appliances should be regularly checked and serviced. If you have any doubts about how to ventilate an appliance, get professional advice before proceeding and install carbon monoxide detectors.

BALANCED VENTILATION

As we renovate, making houses closer to air-tight standards of new construction, we must take precautions with exhaust fans. If there is any fuel-burning appliance in a house that uses household air for the combustion, exhaust fans may run the chimney backwards, called backdrafting, bringing poisonous gases into the house. CO detectors should be in any house that has a fuel-burning appliance, and all such appliances need an outdoor air supply. Powerful exhaust fans should be avoided. Current building codes require mechanical ventilation that both removes polluted air and provides fresh air. Heat Recovery Ventilators do that while recovering heat from air being exhausted outside.

EXHAUST FANS

You can ventilate most kitchens and bathrooms with a fan carrying air a short distance through a wall (an axial fan). Wall- or ceiling-mounted fans (below left) have their electric components directly behind a grille, and must not be used near water. To ventilate a shower stall, use an in-line fan installed with a length of ducting between the grill and the electric parts. Some kitchen fans are built into a cabinet or hood (see p.253). When choosing a fan, consider the sound it makes (you may want a "low noise" fan for an attached bath), its power, and the manufacturer's advice for use. Fans can have a regular switch, but to control humidity, add a dehumidistat switch that comes on when humidity is high.

Bathroom exhaust

Position the fan on the ceiling. If you have a shower stall, install the fan neaer the shower. Ensure that you have the correct power supply, and follow the wiring and safety instructions closely (see also pp.428–463).

Installing a fan

The most common place for a fan is in the bathroom or kitchen. Attic fans should not be used in a cold climate. Exhaust fans should never exhaust into the attic, nor into the soffits, but through the gable end of the attic, at least 3 ft below soffits, through the roof, or as with HRVs, down into the basement and through the wall near the ground. This is to avoid moisture accumulation where it could cause roof damage. Make sure you have the correct power supply in place, and closely follow the wiring instructions (see pp.428–463 on working with electricity).

Kitchen hood

Kitchen hoods remove odor, heat, and smoke from the house. Installed above a stove or range, the hood can be a focal design point.

Chimney takes fumes and heat outside

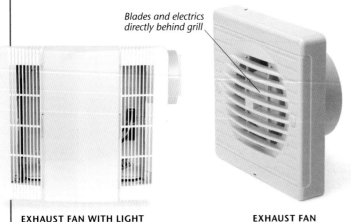

Blades and electrics directly behind grill

EXHAUST FAN WITH LIGHT   **EXHAUST FAN**

DEHUMIDIFIERS

Removing moisture from the air reduces humidity and condensation, and therefore helps to deal with their associated problems. An excellent way of doing this is to use a small, portable dehumidifier. You can move these around the home easily and place them in any room or space that has a condensation problem. The dehumidifier collects water in a tank that is then emptied, or run through a hose into a floor drain.

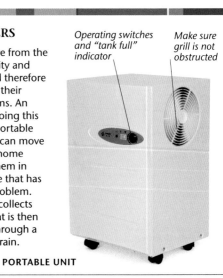

Operating switches and "tank full" indicator

Make sure grill is not obstructed

PORTABLE UNIT

INSTALLING A BATHROOM FAN

Shut off the power to the circuit. Use a stud finder to locate a joist and mark the outline of the fan on the ceiling. Cut the opening with a drywall knife or rotozip.

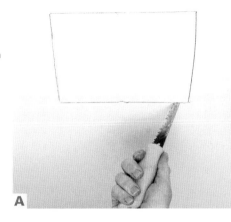

A

B

Wire the fan according to the manufacturer's instructions.

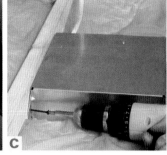

C

Attach the fan to the joist with screws.

D

Allow a gap between the fan and insulation, if required by the manufacturer and local codes. Attach the duct to the fan body.

E

Drive a nail through the roof to mark the center point of the ductwork.

Trace a hole for the roof cap piece on the roof. Score the opening with a utility knife.

F

Follow the score line and cut the opening with a jigsaw.

G

H

Remove shingles from around the opening.

I

Apply roof cement on the cap flange and install by slipping under the shingles and nailing in place.

J

Connect the ductwork from the fan to the roof cap.

K

Secure the ductwork in place. Heavily insulate any ductwork in a cold attic.

L

Connect the wiring according to the manufacturer's instructions. Connect power to a switch. Attach the face plate over the fan.

Home security

INTRUDERS FEAR DETECTION, MAKING LIGHT AND SOUND EXCELLENT DETERRENTS TO UNWELCOME VISITORS. WITH AN INCREASE IN THE AVAILABILITY AND RELIABILITY OF BATTERY-OPERATED ALARM SYSTEMS, INSTALLING THEM YOURSELF IS NOW EASY AND QUICK. THIS SECTION DEALS WITH ISSUES OF SECURITY IN THE HOME AS WELL AS ISSUES OF SAFETY.

INSTALLING AN ALARM SYSTEM

The vast majority of alarm systems use sensors to detect movement or magnetic contact plates that set off the alarm when parted. The most commonly used sensors are called passive infrared detectors (PIRs), which detect the movement of a heat source. The most important thing to consider when installing alarms is the positioning of these sensors, so that they can monitor all the necessary zones in your home.

SECURITY HOUSE PLAN

A sensor is placed at each access point to your house, which divides the area into zones. This lets you see at a glance where a zone has been breached, or where some maintenance is required. Front, back, and patio doors, windows, and fire escapes should be considered, although you may decide that some windows are inaccessible.

PIR POSITIONING TIPS

- Know the detection range of your PIR.
- Detection of movement across the detection arc is better than of movement toward or away from the sensor.
- Do not position PIRs in direct sunlight or near a heat source, unless instructed to do so, or if solar power is required for operation.
- Avoid areas of excessive vibration or where there are drafts.
- If you live in an apartment, you may only need to consider detection around the front door area, although you may need to consider window access in ground- and first-floor dwellings.

Remember that pets will have to be kept out of zones when the alarm is on unless you buy a system that can detect them by being sensitive to size. When you purchase an alarm it is worth checking for any extra features such as a panic button, or anti-tamper safeguards for sensors and the control panel.

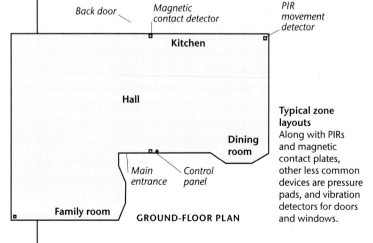

Back door *Magnetic contact detector* *PIR movement detector*

Kitchen

Hall

Dining room

Main entrance *Control panel*

Family room **GROUND-FLOOR PLAN**

Typical zone layouts
Along with PIRs and magnetic contact plates, other less common devices are pressure pads, and vibration detectors for doors and windows.

Alarm display window

Keypad

Arming and disarming alarm systems
Take time to study your instruction manual so that you fully understand how to arm and disarm the system. Large systems may allow you to alarm just some zones of the house as well as the whole house.

WIRED, PART-WIRED, OR WIRELESS?

Traditional alarms are hard-wired into the home's main electricity supply. However, wireless or part-wired systems are now widely available.

Wired systems

Although these take longer to install, there is no need to worry about replacing or recharging batteries. Professional installers tend to use hard-wired alarms.

Part-wired systems

Some alarms require the control panel to be wired into the main electricity supply. However, many have the option to run off a built-in rechargeable battery and the panel can be removed and recharged at a power point when necessary.

Wireless systems

These can literally be set up in hours because there is no need for complicated cable routing and electrical connection. The PIRs, magnetic contacts for doors and windows, and the main control panel are all battery-operated, and the external bellbox is often solar-powered. The main drawback of wireless alarms is that batteries need replacing or recharging, although many systems give a prompt if maintenance is necessary.

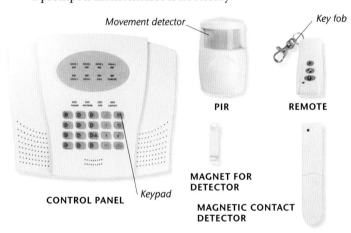

Movement detector

Key fob

PIR

REMOTE

CONTROL PANEL Keypad

MAGNET FOR DETECTOR

MAGNETIC CONTACT DETECTOR

▌▌ INSTALLING MAGNETIC CONTACT DETECTORS

The detector should be located on the fixed frame and the magnet on the door or opening light of the window. With the wireless example shown here, batteries must be inserted in the detector before it is installed. Many contact detector kits are convertible in that they can be installed wired or wireless. The alignment and distance between the detector and contact is crucial, so the manufacturer's guidelines need to be closely followed.

A Insert battery into the main body of the detector.

B Secure both detector and magnet in place on the door or window edge, ensuring that they are correctly aligned.

▌▌ INSTALLING A BATTERY-OPERATED PIR

Once position has been decided, securing a PIR in place is a straightforward task. For hard-wired systems, cable connection and routing becomes necessary, but for a wireless alarm, secure positioning and correct battery insertion is all that is required.

A **Remove the front** cover of the PIR. You may need to undo a small grub screw in order to release the cover.

B **Some PIRs need** to be set internally. This involves setting dip switches inside the PIR.

C **Insert the battery** and replace the front cover.

D **Hold the base plate** in position and mark pilot holes. Plug if necessary before securing in place.

E **Replace front cover.** In the example shown here, a screw needs to be tightened on the underside of the PIR.

CCTV

These systems are becoming a more viable DIY installation task. Systems may either be linked to a separate monitor, or directly to your TV and be connected to a video recorder. The majority of systems use PIR sensors, and wireless options are available. When the PIR senses a movement, the camera transmits the image to a receiver unit that is connected via a cable to the monitor or TV. This automatic system can be bypassed by using the remote control. Follow the system manufacturer's instructions to plan and install a CCTV system.

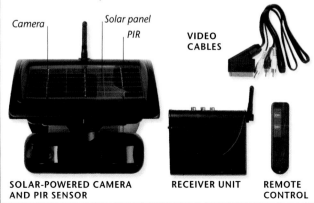

Camera Solar panel PIR

VIDEO CABLES

SOLAR-POWERED CAMERA AND PIR SENSOR

RECEIVER UNIT

REMOTE CONTROL

WINDOW AND DOOR SECURITY

All doors and windows are potential points of entry to a house and therefore each must be adequately secured. The primary security features for entry doors are covered on pp.166–167. However, there are also secondary systems that you can use in addition to these. Examples of many such systems are shown here, but be aware that there are many designs available. All have slight variations in the ways in which they are installed and used; always follow any specific instructions that are provided by the manufacturer.

PUSH-BUTTON LOCKS AND KEYPADS

It is now possible to add different types of push-button locks to your doors to provide a very secure entry system, eliminating the need for a key. More commonly found on cars, they used to be very expensive, but are now far more competitively priced. They require electrical connections in many cases. It is best to employ a specialist to install this kind of system.

ADD TO DOOR SECURITY

Keeping your entry door secure involves having a strong metal or solid wood door and using the right locks. Also, you need to make sure your door hangs properly and fits well in the frame. If your door isn't installed correctly, it might not matter what types of locks you choose for the door. Deadbolts and door locks are the most common methods to secure entry doors. There are also electronic door security options available.

Items such as door limiters, security chains, and surface-mounted door bolts are straightforward to install since they are simply positioned on the appropriate place on the door or frame and screwed into position. Items such as hinge bolts, deadbolts, and peep holes require a little more thought in positioning and installation. This is because slightly more involved woodworking techniques are required to ensure that they are installed securely and correctly.

Decorative door bolt
A design of bolt that provides security and decorative appeal. Some designs are notched into the face or edge of the door.

Bolt knob

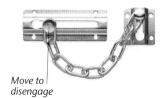

Security chain
Allows a door to be opened slightly to check identity before the chain is disengaged, allowing the door to open fully. A door limiter is similar to a door chain and offers a different design option.

Move to disengage

■■ ATTACHING A HINGE BOLT

Hinge bolts should be installed in pairs as a minimum requirement, one below the upper door hinge and one above the lower door hinge. For extra security a third and even a fourth bolt may be used.

A

B

Drill a hole into the door edge; its dimensions should be specified by the manufacturer.

Hammer in the ribbed section of the bolt into this hole, leaving the smooth domed section protruding from the door edge.

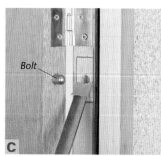

Bolt

C

D

Gently close the door to mark the frame. Position the plate, draw a guide line around it, and chisel out to a depth equal to the plate. Drill a central hole to house the bolt.

Screw the hinge bolt plate in place, and check that the door opens and closes smoothly. Use the same technique to secure more bolts as required.

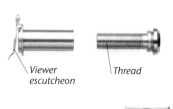

Peep hole
Allows you to check identity of a visitor before unlocking any part of the door. Versions with a viewer escutcheon provide even greater security.

Viewer escutcheon *Thread*

Hinge bolt
Adds greater security to the hinging edge of a door so that it cannot be forced open and/or off its hinges. Normally at least two are installed.

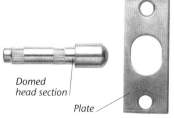

Domed head section

Plate

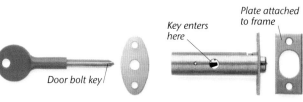

Plate attached to frame

Key enters here

Door bolt key

Deadbolt
Various types of deadbolts exist, but what they have in common is that they drop into place and do not move unless opened by the key, as opposed to a locking latch that can lock as you close the door. Deadbolts are more secure.

SLIDING GLASS DOOR SECURITY

Sliding glass doors—often called sliders or sliding patio doors—offer a view and direct access to backyards and decks. However, they also provide an easy point of entry for intruders unless they are properly installed. There are several reasons for this. First, their usual position at the back of a house makes sliding glass doors susceptible to burglars, who can remain hidden and undetected while they try to gain entry. Second, they are often left open during the spring and summer months, allowing easy access to backyard activities. Even if you follow the security steps mentioned below, you should still be mindful of closing and locking your sliding doors when they are not in use.

However, the main reason for security problems is that some sliding doors are offered with only latches installed on them. These latches are not as secure as locks, and can allow your sliding door to be easily removed. When sliding doors are installed, they need to be lifted and placed in their track. If your sliding doors are not secured, or only secured with a latch, a burglar can actually lift one of the glass panels back out of the track to gain entry into your home. There are several methods to make sure your sliding glass door is secure.

Key locks

Sliding glass doors should have a strong, working key lock. A deadlock, which utilizes a bore pin tumbler cylinder and is operated by a key from the outside, is a good option. The lock bolt should engage the strike sufficiently so that it will not be disengaged by any amount of movement.

Securing doors in place with screws

Use sheet metal screws to secure the door in place through the track. Insert screws into the top of the door frame, at each end and in the middle. The screws should make the door movement tight, so that the door barely clears them.

Charley bars

Manufacturers often offer a block or bar that folds down from a unit to secure the doors in place. This device helps prevent the door from being opened, and should be used in addition to a locking system.

Dowel in the track

You can insert a dowel or pin in the track of the sliding door to prevent the door from being shoved aside or lifted off the track. It is important that the wooden dowel runs the whole length of the track.

WINDOW SECURITY

Modern windows often have security features built into their design. This may range from locking fasteners to multi-point mortise locks that are operated automatically as the window is secured shut. The items shown here are additional features that may be used as secondary security options for windows.

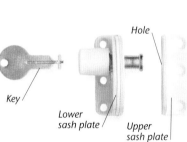

Casement window lock
Two-part lock for sealing casement windows (see below).

Frame attachment

Window attachment

Window screw bolt
Two parts engage when casement is closed. Secured with key-operated screw.

Screw

Window attachment

Frame attachment

Frame attachment

Bolt

Metal window lock
Bolt screws down into the stay of the casement window.

Ventilation lock
Allows casement window to be locked open for ventilation.

Window stay bolt
Screws over the stay on casement or pivot windows.

Key

Upper sash attachment

Lower sash bolt

Sash window lock
Fits through both sections of sash; when aligned, the bolt is screwed into place.

Sash window press bolt
Plates align when sash window closes; the bolt is pressed into place.

Key

Hole

Lower sash plate

Upper sash plate

INSTALLING A CASEMENT WINDOW LOCK

A

With the window closed, use an awl to mark positions for the striking plate on the frame and the locking body on the casement.

B

Drill pilot holes in the casement if necessary and then secure the locking body in place.

C

Layout and mark the position for the striking plate and drill pilot holes where needed. Screw the striking plate in place on the window frame.

D

Close the window and check the two parts of the lock meet, using the supplied key.

SECURING POSSESSIONS

Aside from the door and window security hardware discussed on pp.372–373, there are other areas of the home that can be improved with the addition of other types of locking systems. These systems can supplement existing security, or they can also become the main burglar deterrent. Many of these systems are designed for security outside the house, in areas such as garages, sheds, and even for vehicle security. The options are always growing.

KEYLESS LOCKS

The disadvantage of any key-operated system is that the key can be lost. Combination locks are an alternative. They open when you enter the right number. With a combination padlock, you can change the combination number to one you will remember.

COMBINATION PADLOCK

CHOOSING LOCKS AND CHAINS

Numerous padlocks and chains are available for use in home security. The security rating of a padlock is generally related to its size and cost, and the same can be said for chains, which are generally used for looping through gates or securing movable items like ladders or motorcycles. The best use of each item is usually specified by the manufacturer.

Attach to frame

Hasp

Attach to door

Attach to frame

Hasp lock
A hasp lock provides a reliable way of padlocking a door (see right).

Pad bolt
This is much the same as a standard door bolt, except that it can be secured using a padlock.

Lock

Key

Open-shackle padlock
Traditional padlock shape with the shackle in the form of an elongated loop.

U-lock
This U-shaped frame is ideal for locking bicycles.

Vinyl covering

Keyhole

Security chain
Steel chains are commonly used for padlocking motorcycles and gates.

Locking cable
This hardened steel cable is perfect for locking down large items such as lawnmowers and motorcycles.

SECURING OUTBUILDINGS

Garages and sheds are particularly vulnerable to burglary and should always be well secured; not only do they contain valuable items, but some items can be used by burglars to gain access to the main house. Ladders are the most obvious aid, but any number of garden tools can be used to force entry. Most of the systems shown on the left are ideal for use in garages and sheds. Looks are not important with these items. Choose those that achieve the greatest level of security.

▌▐ INSTALLING A HASP LOCK

Padlock security is commonly used on outbuildings because the doors often do not have the thickness to accommodate cylinder locks or mortise locks. Where door design does allow, padlocks are often used as a second line of defense. The best way of using a padlock is by hanging it through a hasp mechanism. When installing the latter, the plate of the hasp must be installed so that it hides the screws when locked. When choosing a padlock, be sure that it is suitable for outdoor use; "all-weather use" is a common manufacturer's specification. In the sequence below, a combination padlock is used. The main alternative to a hasp lock is a pad bolt with a padlock.

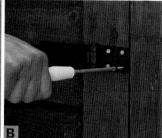

Mark the screw holes for the hasp. Make pilot holes for the screws.

Screw the hasp to the door.

Mark the screw holes for the staple. Make pilot holes for the screws, then screw the staple to the door.

Secure the hasp lock with a padlock.

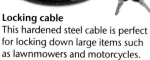

VEHICLE SECURITY

Some security devices have been designed specifically with vehicles in mind. These provide a second line of defense to complement any features built into the vehicle itself. Some are portable, such as a wheel clamp, whereas others are permanently or partly fixed in place, such as a parking post. Although manufacturers are constantly improving vehicle security, the separate devices shown here can only help to discourage an opportunistic thief.

Hasp

Anchor bed

Ground anchor
This provides a secure anchoring for large, movable objects such as grills, trailers, and motorcycles. The anchor bed is bolted to the ground with large security bolts.

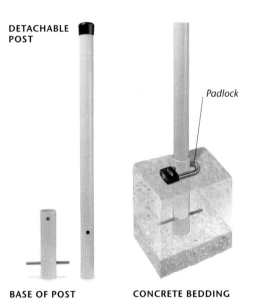

DETACHABLE POST

Padlock

BASE OF POST   **CONCRETE BEDDING**

Parking post
When locked in its upright position, a parking post provides an obstacle to moving a car. Designs vary, and include an electronic, remote-control version. Some installation work is needed as the post base needs to be set in concrete.

Wheel clamp (boot)
Attached around wheels, this clamp ensures that a car or trailer cannot be moved. There are many different designs of this portable security system.

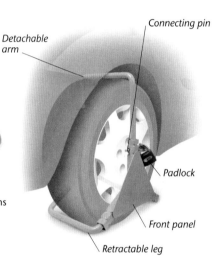

Connecting pin

Detachable arm

Padlock

Front panel

Retractable leg

USING A SAFE

A safe provides a last line of defense when securing items at home. Small safes must be secured in position to ensure that they cannot be moved. Their ideal location is on a concrete floor, although they may also be mounted on a wall. Fasteners, normally coach bolts, are usually supplied by the manufacturer. The example shown below is just one option—there are many designs of house safes, with different features. Some may be disguised as electrical sockets, while others are bolted to the underside of desks, drawer systems, or behind paintings. The fire rating of a particular safe may also be something worth considering, especially if it is holding important documents.

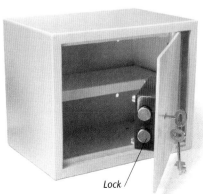

Lock

Using a safe
A safe is only secure if the keys for it are kept hidden in another part of the home. Push-button or keypad versions are also available.

OTHER WAYS TO KEEP YOUR HOME SECURE

In addition to conventional security devices, there are a number of other steps you can take to deter burglars. Many of these do not cost anything, but simply involve adapting your behavior.

Alarms
Consider installing a burglar alarm. Some are linked to the local police station. Before installing this type, check the local policy on false alarms, and that there is enough local manpower to respond to such systems. For alarm installation, see pp.370–371.

Other deterrents
Lay a gravel driveway; it gives an excellent early warning system. Make sure you have good exterior lighting so that burglars cannot conceal themselves. Install a peephole in the front door so that you can look out before opening the door.

Changing your routine
If you go on vacation, cancel all deliveries, including newspapers. Arrange for a friend to remove any mail from view. Install automatic light timers in your home; whenever you are away, set them to mimic your normal schedule.

Protecting young children around the home is an important consideration for many people. There are a number of different products available that can help to make your home more childproof, and most of these are shown here. Also outlined in this section are various precautions and tips that can create a safer environment for children to grow up in. When purchasing any child safety products, make sure that they have the relevant safety certification, and be sure to follow any instructions provided by the manufacturer. Never use second-hand safety equipment unless you are certain of its history.

EXTERIOR CHILDPROOFING

Make sure that walls and fences are regularly maintained to stop children from leaving the boundaries of your home. Remove any rough wood, or flaky paint (especially if it is lead-based paint), and cover pools or ponds to prevent children from falling in. Unstable bricks and blocks should be fixed or removed, and make sure that garden steps are in good condition. Any play areas are best laid with soft coverings such as grass or bark chips.

SAFETY GUARDS AND GADGETS

The majority of safety guards are quick and easy to install—most can be adapted to fit a particular design. For example, toilet lid locks will generally fit the majority of toilets, but it is advisable to check dimensions first. It is very much an individual decision in terms of what are essential and what are nonessential items. However, there are some items, such as stair gates and fire guards, that the majority of parents consider a necessity.

Oven and stove guard
Helps prevent a child from getting too near to hot oven surfaces.

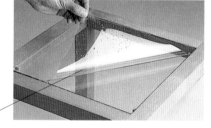

Stove guard in position

A corner protector
This is clipped on to a table corner to make it less sharp. It can also be used on other sharp corners around the home.

Normally self-adhesive

Glass safety film
Applied over glass, it prevents shards from flying through the air if the window breaks or shatters.

Smooth adhesive onto surface

A fire guard
This is placed in front of an open fire to keep children away. It may be necessary to screw in wall anchors to hold it in position.

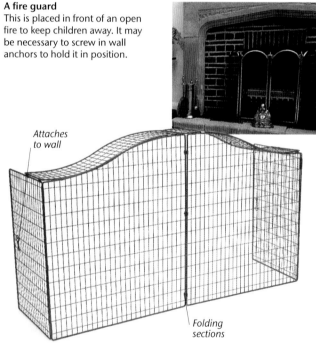

Attaches to wall

Folding sections

Stair gate
This is attached to both the top and the bottom of the stairs, to prevent a young child from climbing or descending unaccompanied. The gate may also be put across the entrance to a room to control access to a particular area in the home. Before buying a stair gate, check the dimensions of the stairway and/or entrance to be sure you get the correct design and size. Some designs are tension-mounted to avoid the need for screws to hold the gate in place.

Position gate at specified height

Door slam stopper
Prevents a door from slamming, reducing the risk of fingers being caught in the door.

Fits on door edge

Flexible shape

SAFETY LOCKS AND CATCHES

Many gadgets are designed to prevent cabinets from being opened and to prevent windows from being opened too wide. There are numerous designs to choose from. Keeping children out of cabinets or drawers prevents fingers from being trapped and denies them access to fragile or dangerous items.

Refrigerator lock

Not only stops a child from raiding the contents, but it also prevents the door from being left open and the food spoiled.

Fits around corner of refrigerator

Release button

Cabinet slide lock

This lock clamps around cabinet doors and prevents either door from being opened.

Slides into place

Hooks over handle

VCR lock

Stops children from pushing items or hands into the video slot. Simple to install.

Release button

Pushes into place

Drawer and cabinet catch

This stops drawers and cabinets from being opened by a child. There are many types available.

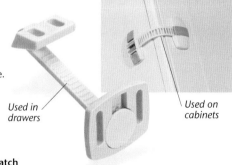

Used in drawers

Used on cabinets

A window limiter catch

This is designed to stop a child from opening a window wide enough to jump out. It needs to be screwed in place, with one part on the frame, and the other on the moving casement.

Stay release

Limited opening size

▌▌ EMERGENCY-RELEASE DOOR LATCHES

These latches are used to prevent a child from being locked inside a room. Privacy door latches with a lever handle may be installed using a technique similar to that shown for installing a lockset (pp.166–167). If the handle is a knob design, the technique has to be altered to account for cutting a large access hole in the door to deal with the locking mechanism. Most such mechanisms are opened from the outside using a key inserted into the handle. Some designs simply have a lever that can be turned, or a large slotted screw that can be turned to undo the lock. Many also have a template to follow when installing.

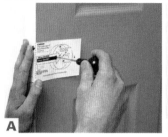

A

Measure exact central point for access hole, on both sides of the door. If supplied, use a template.

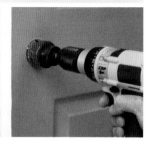

B

Attach a hole cutter to a cordless drill; the correct size will be specified by the latch manufacturer. Drill into one door face.

C

Stop drilling when the bit exits the opposite door face.

D

Change to the opposite side of the door, drilling until the cutter reaches the cut on the other side.

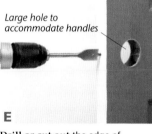

Large hole to accommodate handles

E

Drill or cut out the edge of the door to accommodate the latch mechanism.

F

Chisel a recess for the latch plate, then fit the latch into the hole.

G

Position the handles, threading the spindle through the latch mechanism as shown.

H

Tighten the screws, then close the door to check that the mechanism works.

FIREPROOFING

The effects of fire can be devastating, and it is therefore necessary to take precautions to prevent fire in the home. Be sure to have adequate early warning systems, as well as effective escape routes should a fire occur. The first port of call for further advice on fire security should be your local fire department. They can provide help and advice relevant to your particular circumstances and can also advise on any fire safety stipulations that are part of your building regulations. This is essential when any major renovation or building work is being done.

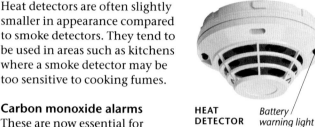

AC OPERATION

AC-operated alarms are wired to a dedicated permanent supply that cannot be accidentally turned off by the average user. They should also have battery backup in the event of a power outage. AC-operated systems are more common in newly built areas. All electrical safety guidelines must be followed (see pp.436–437) before installing AC-operated systems.

ALARMS AND DETECTORS
One of the most effective early warning systems is the smoke alarm. The terms "smoke alarm" and "smoke detector" have become the generic terms for these devices, although some react to heat rather than smoke.

Smoke alarms
The two main types of smoke alarms are battery-operated and AC-operated (see above right). The former are easy to install and need regular battery checks. The alarm should have a warning system to indicate when power is low, and should be checked according to the manufacturer's guidelines. Most are tested by pressing a button that sounds the alarm. At the very least, smoke detectors should be located on every floor of your home.

BATTERY-OPERATED SMOKE ALARM

AC-OPERATED ALARM

Heat detectors
Heat detectors are often slightly smaller in appearance compared to smoke detectors. They tend to be used in areas such as kitchens where a smoke detector may be too sensitive to cooking fumes.

Carbon monoxide alarms
These are now essential for homes. They look similar to smoke detectors, and are located close to fuel-burning appliances and sleeping areas. Carbon monoxide is an odorless gas emitted by fossil fuels during combustion. When appliances are not vented correctly or are functioning incorrectly, carbon monoxide builds up in the home; high levels may be fatal. Alarms are normally located on walls between 3 ft and 4 ft (1 m and 1.5 m) above floor level.

HEAT DETECTOR   *Battery warning light*

CARBON MONOXIDE DETECTOR

INSTALLING A BATTERY-OPERATED ALARM

Mark attachment points on ceiling surface. Ideally, screw into a ceiling joist; use the wall plugs and fasteners that are supplied.

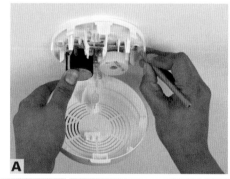

A

B   Use **pilot hole** fasteners if screwing directly into joist, or use cavity wall plugs if screwing into drywall.

C   **Screw plate into** position, ensuring that it is secure.

D   **Put the battery into** the alarm, checking the connection carefully.

E   **Close the hinged** alarm casing.

F

Press the test button on the alarm to check that it is working.

TACKLING A FIRE

As a rule, you should never try to tackle a major fire on your own. However, it is important to know how to deal with minor fires, and for this a fire blanket and a fire extinguisher are essential. Another possibility is to have a sprinkler system installed. If in any doubt as to what equipment to buy, contact your local fire department for advice.

Escape routes
It is essential to have planned escapes routes for use in the event of a fire. For upper floors this may mean having an escape ladder or two; these can be bought in various lengths.

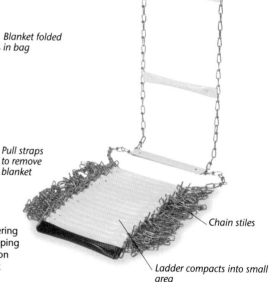

Hooks over window sill

Stand off

Chain stiles

Ladder compacts into small area

Hose

Water fire extinguisher
Water extinguishers are designed for use on paper, wood, and textile fires.

Pressure gauge

Horn

ABC extinguisher
Multipurpose extinguisher that works on A, B, and C fire classes. Can leave behind a yellow powder.

Operation levers

Carbon dioxide fire extinguisher
This takes away the oxygen needed for combustion. Not to be used in confined spaces.

Operation lever

Water mist extinguisher
Uses tap water as an extinguishing agent. It is able to extinguish multiple types of fire.

Halatron
Ideal for computer and high electrical areas. Also for areas where easy and thorough cleanup is needed.

Blanket folded in bag

Pull straps to remove blanket

Fire blanket
This is designed for covering deep-fryer fires, or wrapping someone up if they are on fire. A fire blanket is best located in the kitchen.

FIRE DOORS AND WINDOWS

The type of doors and windows you have can make the difference between life and death during a fire. Both can be adapted to maximize your safety.

Fire doors
These are very effective for hindering a fire and providing extra time for escape. They are more commonly found in commercial buildings, but they can be a regulation in domestic homes, especially in multistory dwellings and properties with attached garages. They are hung using the same techniques as for normal doors, but in addition they need to be equipped with some form of door-closer.

As well as the door having a fire rating, the hinges are also fire-rated. Intumescent strips can be used around the door perimeter. These swell up under the effects of heat, sealing around the edge of the door. Intumescent paint is also available; on heating, this produces a char layer that insulates the door from fire.

Windows
Most windows afford vital escape routes during a fire, so it is important to ensure that they open and close properly and that any security keys are readily available.

Modern vinyl windows have friction-stay hinges that limit the degree to which the window can be opened. To ensure that the window can be used as an escape route, install egress friction-stay hinges; these allow the window to be opened to its full extent.

Conserving energy

ENERGY CONSERVATION IS AN EMOTIVE SUBJECT THAT TOUCHES MANY AREAS OF HOME IMPROVEMENT. ALTHOUGH THESE PAGES PRESENT MANY ALTERNATIVE OPTIONS AND ECO-FRIENDLY IDEAS, THE EXTENT TO WHICH YOU LEAD AN ECO-FRIENDLY LIFE, AND WHAT MEASURES OR CHANGES YOU ARE PREPARED TO MAKE, WILL ALWAYS COME DOWN TO REQUIREMENTS IN YOUR AREA AND PERSONAL CHOICE.

ENERGY EFFICIENCY

Being energy efficient means assessing your home and lifestyle for opportunities where you might save resources. Although some of the measures outlined in these pages may take some effort, for most, this will be outweighed by the rewards of a more eco-friendly and cost-effective lifestyle.

REDUCING POWER REQUIREMENTS

The demands of modern living require power to supply appliances, provide heat, and run all the consumer items that fill our homes. However, reducing the amount of power you use may not require a major lifestyle change. You can make a huge impact simply by being a little more careful about the items you buy, being aware of their power use, and finding ways of using less power in your home.

Insulation and air sealing

In Canada, we all know that insulation is necessary but we often forget that it goes hand-in-hand with air sealing. Stopping all the air drafts through insulated walls and ceilings makes insulation more effective and reduces the cold air that needs to be heated. It is the most cost-effective energy conservation measure you can take. Local incentive programs can help defray costs. For more on insulating your home, see pp.356–365.

Smart meters

These are devices that show you how much electricity is being used by household appliances, encouraging you to be more vigilant about energy consumption and allowing you to monitor individual appliances. Variations include a direct smart-meter link to your electricity supplier that enables them to inform you about your power usage during the day and, consequently, where potential savings can be made.

USING THERMOSTATS

Thermostats play a vital part in regulating heating and air temperature throughout your home. Make sure that water-heating thermostats are not set too high. In addition to wasting energy, this is potentially dangerous in terms of scalding. Make sure that radiators are installed with thermostats so that their temperature is kept under control.

Energy-efficient appliances

Product lines in many countries now have standardized labeling systems that denote how energy-efficient an appliance is, how much energy it consumes, and even how much noise it makes. In Canada we are used to seeing the EnerGuide label on major appliances, but the US Energy Star is appearing as well.

ENERGY STAR®
This US label is now appearing in Canada as US and Canadian evaluation systems become harmonized.

Australian Energy Rating
A star rating from one to six stars indicates energy-efficiency levels.

EU Energy Label
Like the Canadian EnerGuide label, the European Union mandatory label shows the efficiency and energy consumption of a product. Around the world, consumer participation in energy conservation is essential.

ELECTRICAL EFFICIENCY TABLE

Electrical power is rated in watts, and all electrical appliances will carry labels stating how many watts are required for them to run. If this is not the case, they may state volts and amps, and wattage can be worked out by multiplying the volts by the amps.

The table below gives an approximate guide to the amount of electricity (in watts per hour) that is used by common household appliances. Quite simply, the higher the figure, the larger the amount of energy the appliance uses.

Appliance	Energy used (watts per hour)	Comment
Electric clothes dryer	4,000–6,000	Exceptionally high consumption
Oven	3,000–6,000	In general, the larger the oven, the more energy it uses
Air-conditioning unit	1,000–6,000	Larger units use more energy
Electric space heater	2,000–4,000	Huge user when in constant use. Electrical storage heaters provide a more economical option
Immersion water heater	2,000–4,000	Make sure that its thermostat is working well and timing is controlled at efficient levels for household use
Fan heater	2,000–3,000	Use as a backup or emergency heating source, rather than on a daily basis
Electric tea kettle	1,500–2,500	Fast boilers use up more power
Stove	1,000–2,000	Rapid heating elements use more power
Iron	1,000–1,500	Try to limit ironing to only those items you consider essential
Computer system	1,000–1,500	Screen size is important in determining power usage
Toaster	1,000–1,500	Choose one with an option to toast one slice
Dishwasher	1,000–1,500	Figure represents energy used per cycle
Hairdryer	700–1,500	Large variations in consumption are due to size differences
Microwave	500–1,500	Size is the determining factor here
Washing machine	400–1,500	Figure represents energy used per cycle
Refrigerator	500–1,000	Make sure you monitor and adjust the temperature level
Freezer	500–1,000	Defrost regularly, if necessary, to maintain efficiency
Vacuum cleaner	200–1,000	Make sure that filters are clean and it is working efficiently
Stereo system	250–750	Size of the system and speakers will affect consumption
Television	50–400	Screen size largely determines power use. Switch off completely when not in use
Video/DVD/Satellite receiver	50–400	As with televisions, switch off completely when not in use
Exhaust fan (oven)	100–200	Use will depend on size, but essential for removing fumes
Heated towel bar	100–200	Keep on a timer so it is not in constant use
Exhaust fan (bathroom)	20–200	Use a timer linked to the light switch to prevent overuse
Regular light bulb	40–150	The brighter they are, the more power they use
Low-energy light bulb (compact fluorescent)	10–20	More expensive than standard bulbs, but require less power for the same amount of light produced
Fluorescent tube	10–20	Provide good, even light at reduced power requirement levels compared to standard bulbs

PASSIVE SOLAR POWER

Solar power is central to the issue of renewable energy. As an energy source, it is in abundant supply, and ready and waiting to be harnessed. Categorized as either "active" (see pp.384–385) or "passive" (described below), both types of system make use of the sun's light and heat to reduce the requirement for more conventional energy supplies. Passive solar systems involve the addition of solar features to old or new houses to maximize the use of sunlight, reducing energy usage.

TRIPLE GLAZING

When discussing the insulating properties of glass, it is important to mention triple glazing (for its soundproofing benefits, see p.366). While the arguments for its superior thermal efficiency—in comparison with double glazing—are far from clear cut in all but the coldest regions of Canada, it does have clear benefits when it comes to minimizing and maximizing solar heat gain.

CHOOSING THE RIGHT GLASS

The right type of glass is crucial to the process of making passive solar modifications to a house. The decision about which type of glass to use in a design should be based on several factors. For example, the absorbtion of heat from the sun may not be desirable during the summer months, as it may require air conditioning to keep temperatures down, increasing energy costs rather than lowering them.

The use of solar-control glass in this situation will reduce heat gain inside the building. Conversely, where you wish to maximize heat gain, low-emissivity glass will let more heat in and less heat out (see p.144). Many manufacturers will use different glass coatings on different sides of the house in an attempt to meet your specific needs, but it is an area that you should research carefully to optimize your benefits.

GLASS HOUSE EXTENSION

If you are planning a glass extension, effective positioning of glass within the design is essential for capturing heat and light (see diagram below). Remember that while you will want to use the heat of the sun to increase the warmth of your home during the winter, you will want to minimize the impact of the sun's heat during the summer. This can be achieved by orientating windows to be sunny during the winter and shady during the summer.

You can make the roof of your extension from glass (as shown below). However, having a traditional opaque roof structure over glass walls may be more suitable, as a glass roof can make the room too hot during the summer months.

TROMBE WALL

Thermal mass is the expression of a wall's capacity to store heat. Trombe walls combine thermal mass with insulated glazing and vents (for the convection of warm air into a room) to create an effective thermal heating system in the winter, without overheating the room in the summer. During hotter periods, the roof design (as shown in the diagram below) offers increased shade compared with that available during the winter months. This significantly reduces the heating process described above. Landscape design is an important issue here—it is crucial to the effectiveness of the system that the wall is not shaded during the winter by large shrubs or trees, as this detracts from the heat absorbed.

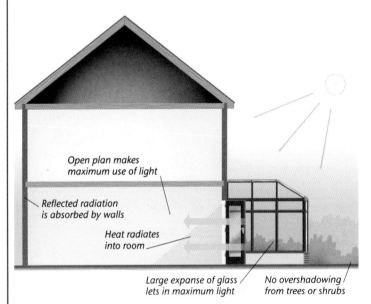

Open plan makes maximum use of light

Reflected radiation is absorbed by walls

Heat radiates into room

Large expanse of glass lets in maximum light

No overshadowing from trees or shrubs

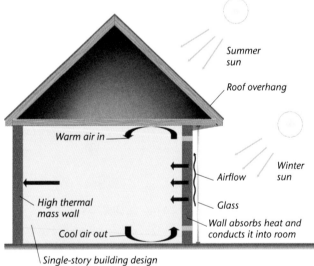

Summer sun

Roof overhang

Warm air in

Winter sun

Airflow

High thermal mass wall

Glass

Cool air out

Wall absorbs heat and conducts it into room

Single-story building design

Extension design
Any extension can be a demanding project, but if you intend to make the most of solar power in the design, then even greater thought than usual is required. For example, an open-plan design will probably mean significant changes to wall structure, including the removal of loadbearing walls (for more information on this, see pp.102–03). Outside the house, it may be necessary to alter landscape design, as any shade provided by trees and large shrubs will affect the amount of sunlight that is utilized in this design.

Thermal mass
Determining the potential thermal mass of a new or existing wall is crucial to the design of a successful trombe wall. Concrete has a very high thermal mass, but for something with a greener production process, you could consider a rammed-earth wall. Sometimes, combinations of material are the best solution—excellent insulation is offered by a straw-bale wall, for example, while plaster layers will increase its thermal mass.

SUN PIPES

A good way of using solar power to light the home is with the use of sun pipes. These channel the sun's rays through a highly reflective tube into a dark area of the home in need of illumination. Sun-pipe size varies, with the light created being directly proportional to the diameter of the pipe. The size you can use will often be governed by the gap between the ceiling joists or roof rafters. Both joists and rafters are normally set at 16 in (40 cm) or 24 in (60 cm) intervals, from one center to the next. Larger sun pipes are better suited to situations where joists or rafters are spaced at larger intervals.

Suppliers sell sun pipes in kit form. When purchasing a kit, find out what comes as standard, and whether you need an extra roof flashing assembly. The latter depends on whether you have a flat roof or pitched roof, and whether the tiles are flat or undulating.

Installing a sun pipe requires access to the room it is intended to illuminate, the roof, and the void through which the pipe will travel (normally an attic space).

UV-protected polycarbonate dome

Brushed-nylon condensation trap

Flashing plate

Under-felt support plate

Upper sun-pipe section (crimped end)

Adjustable elbow

Lower sun-pipe section (plain end)

Ply backing panel and template

Fixing ring

Short ceiling connection section

Ceiling trim and diffuser

THINGS TO CONSIDER

■ It is vital to plan a good route for the sun pipe, taking into account obstacles such as ceiling joists.
■ Consider the exact position of the interior lens to maximize the light in the room. The center of the room is the most logical place, but if you are installing more than one sun pipe, a suitable pattern must be designed.
■ The length of the sun pipe, and the number of angles in the pipe, will directly affect the amount of light provided—the shorter the pipe, and the fewer the angles, the better.
■ Efficiency will also be improved by ensuring that all joints in a sectional pipe are taped to ensure no light leakage.
■ The void through which the pipe will travel before it gets to the roof is normally an attic space, so check the access. You will need to get on the roof to install the pipe. This may be simple, but if scaffolding is required, build the cost of this into your budget.
■ Although you can install a pipe on your own, it is a difficult job; it can be made much easier with the presence of a second person.
■ The interior of the pipe is likely to be inaccessible once installed, so ensure it is cleaned thoroughly after installation. Pay special attention to any gaskets or seals, which allow for ventilation and reduce the risk of condensation clouding the dome.

Sun pipes

Most sun pipes have a round dome, although other styles are available, such as those that replicate the design of a roof window, for example. Rather than a sectional pipe, as shown, some manufacturers produce a flexible pipe that can be simply cut to the required length. This can make the process of routing the pipe through the ceiling, void (attic space), and roof significantly easier.

LIGHT PRODUCED BY A TYPICAL SUN PIPE

Available sunlight	Equivalent output (watts)
Overcast winter sky	130
Clear winter sky	200
Overcast summer sky	300
Clear summer sky	500+

WORKING SAFELY

Never look directly inside the pipe during installation, as sun bouncing off the interior can damage your eyes. The inside of the pipe is normally covered with a layer of plastic to dull the glare. Remove this as each section of pipe is added.

How sun pipes work

Solar rays are reflected off the highly polished, mirror-like interior of the pipe. This produces a concentrated light source in the room below.

"Active" solar power can be defined as any system that uses a mechanical device to harness and transform the energy of the sun (for more on "passive" solar power, see pp.382–383). For many people, active solar power is exemplified by the large, roof-mounted panels seen on some buildings. These panels differ in both design and function, depending on whether they use solar energy thermally (to heat water) or photovoltaically (to make electricity). Supposed drawbacks of these systems are that they are costly, unattractive, and unreliable, but prices are falling, and panel efficiency is improving.

Evacuated-tube collectors
Although they are heavy and may dominate the appearance of a roof, evacuated-tube collectors are a very efficient option.

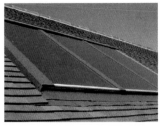

Flat-plate collectors
While flat-plate collectors may look sleeker than tube collectors, more are required to produce the same amount of energy.

THERMAL SOLAR ENERGY (SOLAR HOT WATER)
In a thermal solar energy system, the energy of the sun is used to heat water. There are two principal types of panel to choose from with this system—evacuated-tube collectors and flat-plate collectors (a third category incorporates unglazed plastic collectors, but these are normally only used for heating water for swimming pools).

Evacuated-tube collectors
With this design, each panel contains an arrangement of vacuum tubes that are connected in a manifold (a network of pipes for redirecting a gas or fluid) that can be connected to other panels if required. Designs vary, with different types of tube and heat-exchange fluid being used. Commonly, each vacuum tube contains a fin of light-absorbent material past which a flow-and-return loop (a smaller tube) runs. This smaller tube contains a heat-exchange fluid that is warmed by the sun's rays, and which may then be used to heat the flow-and-return loop to the hot-water tank.

Climatic conditions influence the preferred choice of system. In colder climates, the heat-exchange fluid normally contains antifreeze, and the water is indirectly heated—this is known as a "closed system". In warmer climates, the water is heated in the tubes and fed directly into the hot-water supply—this is an "open system". Tube collectors are harder to install than flat-plate collectors (see right), but they are arguably more efficient, meaning they can be smaller.

Flat-plate collector
Flat-plate collectors contain an absorber plate through which thin tubes of fluid run. This type of system may operate in a closed or open system, similar to evacuated tubes (see left). They are much thinner, lighter, and simpler to install than evacuated tubes, although they are considered less efficient than tube collectors, so it may be necessary to install a larger surface area of panels. However, manufacturers are constantly improving the efficiency of plate collectors.

Gravity versus pump-operated systems
Both evacuated-tube and flat-plate systems can function soley under the force of gravity, but it is standard to fit a pump that moves fluid around the system. The pump is regulated by a central control unit.

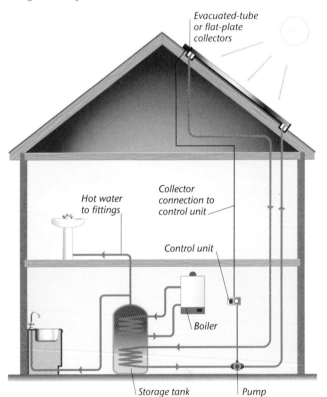

Evacuated-tube or flat-plate collectors

Hot water to fittings

Collector connection to control unit

Control unit

Boiler

Storage tank

Pump

Thermal solar power system
It is usually possible to modify an existing heating system and install a solar-powered one with relative ease, although it is always simpler to plan a system in the context of a new-build.

THINGS TO CONSIDER
■ In most cases, a thermal solar power system requires a storage tank for hot water. This means that houses with combi-boilers are often unable to use this form of heating. However, some manufacturers are now producing combi-boilers that can be used in conjunction with a solar system.
■ Before installation, consider the structural implications of installing a system for thermal solar energy; if roof-mounting is not a viable option, panels may be used at ground level as long as they still receive enough sunlight.
■ To generate a useful amount of power for an average home, panels need to occupy 21½–43sq ft (2–4sq m) of space.
■ The proportion of domestic hot water that can be produced by such a system is debatable. Clearly, a larger amount of hot water is produced during the summer than the winter; over the course of a year, however, the thermal contribution to the overall hot-water supply ranges from 30–70 percent.
■ Check your system's maintenance and servicing requirements with the supplier.

Photovoltaic panels
For a worthwhile system, you may need a large number of photovoltaic panels. Make sure the panels interlock easily for a neat finish.

Photovoltaic roof tiles
Many manufacturers now produce panels in the form of roof tiles, which will maintain a consistent appearance to the roof.

USING MINIATURE PANELS

Photovoltaic panels are commonly used for exterior lighting. By harvesting and storing the sun's energy during the day and releasing it at night to provide illumination, small solar panels are used to power lights. Two examples of solar-powered lighting are pictured here.

Photovoltaic panels can be used on fixed or moveable lighting. Small panels are also an excellent source of renewable power for appliances with relatively small energy requirements, such as a CCTV system (see p.371).

Photovoltaic panel

SOLAR LIGHTS

PHOTOVOLTAIC SYSTEM (SOLAR ELECTRICITY)

Photovoltaic systems are used to generate electricity rather than to heat water. Consequently, the composition of the panels is very different to that used for thermal solar energy systems (see opposite). Photovoltaic panels are made up of a large number of interconnected cells (although in some designs a single cell can make up the entire panel layer). These cells are comprised of semi-conductive materials, typically silicone. Having absorbed sunlight, the silicone releases electrons that create an electrical current, which can then be utilized. The cells are light-sensitive, not sun-sensitive, and are therefore capable of producing electricity even on cloudy days. It is true, however, that the more light there is available, the more electricity the system will generate. The electricity produced is DC (direct current), which needs to be channeled through an inverter and changed into AC (alternating current) to provide a form of electricity that can be used in the home.

Photovoltaic systems offer the possibility of a link-up with the incoming electricity supply, which allows you both to benefit from the generated electricity yourself, and to feed back any unused power to your supplier. This can lead to further savings, as you can effectively make your electricity meter run backwards. The alternative to this is to have a self-contained system, in which banks of batteries are used to store the power you don't use.

Power output

It is difficult to estimate how much power you can expect to gain from photovoltaic panels. Manufacturers' figures for panel efficiency (the amount of light converted to energy) are normally quoted in percentages, with 10–15 percent being a standard figure. The output of most domestic systems is measured in "kilowatts peak" (kWp), which is the amount of energy that a panel will produce under peak operating conditions. An average installation of around 86sq ft (8sq m), for example, could be expected to produce 1kWp. This will provide 20–30 percent of the electrical requirements of an average home.

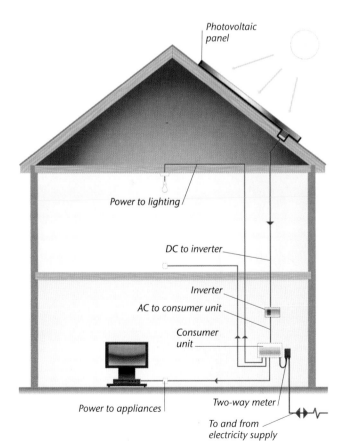

Photovoltaic panel

Power to lighting

DC to inverter

Inverter

AC to consumer unit

Consumer unit

Power to appliances

Two-way meter

To and from electricity supply

Photovoltaic solar power system
Most of the hardware in a photovoltaic system sits on the roof, meaning that the only internal additions to the electricity system are a current inverter and a meter.

INSTALLING SOLAR ELECTRICITY

■ As with thermal solar power, the positioning of your panels is vital to the efficient functioning of your system. Carefully consider the pitch and exact latitude of your roof and ensure that the installer takes this into account.

■ To generate a large amount of electricity you will need a lot of panels. The average area of 21½–43sq ft (2–4sq m) for thermal paneling (see opposite) will need to be doubled to produce significant results. This will increase initial outlay, and delay the point at which your system yields a financial reward.

■ Photovoltaic panels present less complications than thermal collectors—there are no issues concerning boilers, for example—and they usually require less maintenance. However, you will still need to research your options thoroughly with regard to panel design. The aesthetic qualities of photovoltaic panels are being improved all the time.

■ If you want to connect to the incoming electricity supply, make sure that your energy supplier is compatible.

■ Contact your neighborhood association or local government office regarding planning consent.

■ If you install a self-contained system, consider the number of batteries you require, and how often they need to be replaced.

WIND POWER

Wind power is a way of generating electricity using a natural resource that emits no greenhouse gases. As with photovoltaic energy (see p.385), the bigger the equipment, the more power generated. However, unlike solar panels, which can still generate electricity on cloudy days, wind turbines cannot produce power without wind. Good positioning is therefore a critical factor in their use; most commercial systems are found on hills, shores, or off-shore, to increase the amount of wind to which they are exposed. You need to consider this issue on a domestic scale: if you do not live in a windy area, then wind power may not be for you.

DOMESTIC WIND POWER

Wind-generated energy is increasingly being used to supply power across North America, and it is now possible to consider using it to some effect on a domestic level. Although wind turbines provide a "clean" power source, there is a considerable environmental impact in terms of their appearance, which means you will need to seek the relevant permissions. Small, domestic turbines can produce several hundred watts of power, while using larger ones may increase this figure to two or three kilowatts.

Commercial wind farm
Although the wind provides a clean source of energy, wind farms on a massive scale can dominate a landscape, and have a clear visual impact on their surroundings.

Domestic turbine
Wind-turbine-driven domestic power systems have become an increasingly viable option. Turbines are often roof-mounted, like satellite dishes.

HYDROELECTRIC POWER

Hydroelectric power has become a major source of electricity. Although it is seen as clean energy, there is clearly an environmental impact when large dams are built to create the reservoirs that supply the power stations. While in some areas people can choose to take their mains electricity from hydroelectric sources, it is also possible to produce your own hydroelectric power. Of course, you will need to have a sufficiently powerful source of running water but, with the correct permissions, you can feasibly set up your own systems.

Wind-turbine design

There are two main designs of turbine, which are dictated by the axis on which the turbine spins—horizontal or vertical. Horizontal axis wind turbine (HAWT) designs are characterized by large blades rotating like a giant propeller—these are by far the most common type and are considered to be the most efficient. Vertical axis wind turbines (VAWT) are less efficient but much quieter—they have shorter towers, can operate closer to the ground, and can theoretically produce electricity at very low wind speeds. These pages focus on the HAWT design.

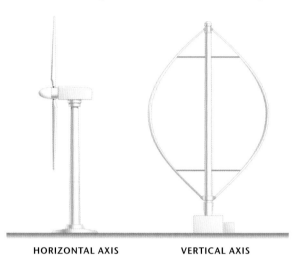

HORIZONTAL AXIS   **VERTICAL AXIS**

Levels of electricity produced

Domestic wind turbines come in a number of different sizes and their power output is measured in terms of wattage, i.e. how many watts of power they can produce in an hour (see p.381 for more details).

Small increases in the diameter of the blades make large increases in the surface area of the rotating blade. Therefore, doubling the diameter of a blade will in fact quadruple its output. The other important issue to consider is the wind speed required to produce the output. Most turbine manufacturers suggest a minimum operating requirement of around 10–13 ft/s (3–4 m/s), and a doubling in wind speed can cause output to increase by eight times, but it is claimed that optimum performance is achieved at around 39 ft/s (12 m/s). It is also worth considering the maximum speed the blades can reach before damage begins to occur; safety mechanisms are built into the equipment to prevent this. However, just as output increases significantly when wind speed goes up, it lowers dramatically as wind speed falls, meaning it can be difficult to assess the overall benefit of utilizing wind power.

WIND-TURBINE POWER OUTPUT

Rotor diameter	Wattage	Typical appliances
3-ft blade	up to 0.3 k/w	Three lightbulbs
10-ft blade	up to 1.5 k/w	Television and stereo
20-ft blade	up to 6 k/w	Over half average household requirement

Anatomy of a wind turbine

As with photovoltaic power, it is possible to link up your turbine with a local utility provider so that excess power can be fed back to your supplier, bringing down your own electricity bills—check with your supplier that they are compatible with the two-way metering required for this. Aside from the turbine itself, a charge regulator or controller is required if you are also using batteries in the system—this item monitors battery charging and prevents battery damage (not needed for a turbine working solely on a grid system). An inverter is required to change DC to AC, and you will also need a meter to measure the amount of electricity you need in addition to your turbine, and how much excess you are feeding back.

Installing wind turbines

For ground-secured wind turbines, the assembly and installation of the tower is an important consideration—it requires bolting down to a concrete foundation. Some turbine designs incorporate guy ropes to aid the tower's stability. For smaller roof- or wall-mounted turbines, ensure that the entire assembly is secured and bolted down correctly. It is important to bear in mind that factors such as vibration can loosen anchoring points over time and damage the turbine, reducing its lifespan.

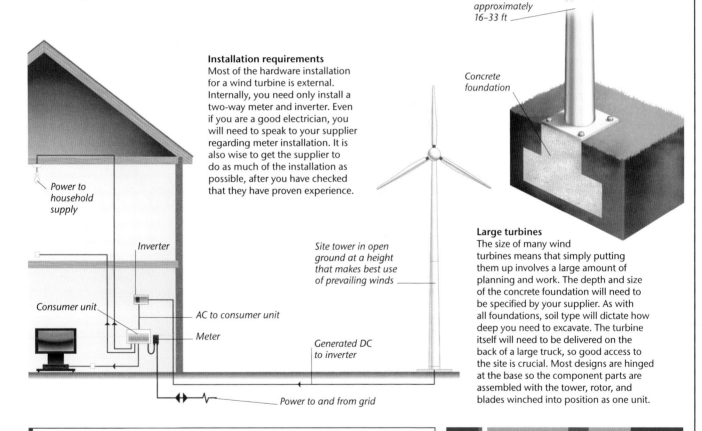

Rotor blade

Generator

Gearbox

Rotor

Tower

Height of tower varies between approximately 16–33 ft

Concrete foundation

Installation requirements
Most of the hardware installation for a wind turbine is external. Internally, you need only install a two-way meter and inverter. Even if you are a good electrician, you will need to speak to your supplier regarding meter installation. It is also wise to get the supplier to do as much of the installation as possible, after you have checked that they have proven experience.

Power to household supply

Inverter

Consumer unit

AC to consumer unit

Meter

Site tower in open ground at a height that makes best use of prevailing winds

Generated DC to inverter

Power to and from grid

Large turbines
The size of many wind turbines means that simply putting them up involves a large amount of planning and work. The depth and size of the concrete foundation will need to be specified by your supplier. As with all foundations, soil type will dictate how deep you need to excavate. The turbine itself will need to be delivered on the back of a large truck, so good access to the site is crucial. Most designs are hinged at the base so the component parts are assembled with the tower, rotor, and blades winched into position as one unit.

THINGS TO CONSIDER

■ The most important factor to consider is whether there is enough wind in your area to make installing a wind turbine worthwhile. There are now websites that provide information of this nature —you can use these to help gauge the suitability of any proposed system.
■ Try to assess the time period within which you can expect to recoup any financial outlay. A large turbine, and the accompanying equipment, are expensive purchases.

■ Discover how often the turbine requires servicing, and whether you will need to replace any moving parts.
■ Local government permission will probably be required for the installation of a turbine, especially for a larger one.
■ Wind turbines make some noise as the blades rotate—the product literature will normally display a decibel rating. As you might expect, larger wind turbines are liable to make more noise than smaller ones.

HYBRID SYSTEMS

Due to the changeability of their effectiveness, a commonly asked question is how different green technologies can be combined to increase efficiency, with one system taking over from another during lean periods. Wind power and solar power are fairly compatible in this regard, and people often combine both systems to good effect. On a windy, cloudy day, for example, a wind turbine can generate most of your power needs, whilst on a still, sunny day, the solar panels can take over the responsibility for generating power.

Levels of water consumption in the home largely depend on individual habits, but by far the heaviest consumers of household water are toilets, washing machines, baths, and showers. While there is a wide range of simple measures that you can take to ensure more efficient water usage in these and other areas, a more active effort may include water recycling and water treatment methods.

HOUSEHOLD APPLIANCES

There are many measures you can take, of varying extremes, to improve the efficiency of household appliances that use water. When buying appliances, choose energy-efficient models and look out for items that have been designed to reduce an appliance's water use. Changing your boiler for a condensing boiler is seen as one of the best ways to improve the efficiency of your heating system. However, looking backward—in technological terms—may sometimes prove beneficial. For example, using a conventional mixer shower rather than a pumped power shower may save water and energy, while you might also question the whole concept of the flushing toilet. Although the idea of composting toilets may seem anachronistic, over recent years the developments in their design and efficiency have meant that they are increasing in popularity. Although they are unlikely to come into mainstream use, it is conceivable that composting toilets may become viable alternatives to plumbed-in toilets.

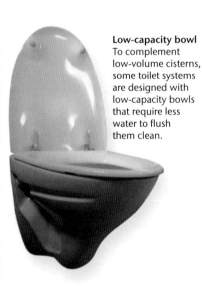

Low-capacity bowl
To complement low-volume cisterns, some toilet systems are designed with low-capacity bowls that require less water to flush them clean.

Dual-flush valves
Cisterns with dual-flush valves give the option of low-volume flushes.

Flow-reducing attachment
For more efficient water provision, faucets may be fitted with a range of flow-reducing attachments.

WATER TREATMENT

Home water treatment systems can vastly improve water efficiency. It is becoming much easier to treat most of the water that you use in your home on site, rather than letting it drain away into municipal sewerage systems or soakaways.

All water can be treated. Blackwater—from the toilet—can be used more efficiently by creating a reed bed (see opposite). Graywater—all domestic waste water, excluding that from the toilet—can be recycled and used as shown opposite. Rainwater can also be harvested and reused—methods for this are demonstrated on pp.390–391.

IMPROVING APPLIANCE EFFICIENCY

Where hard water is a problem, a water softener is a good long-term investment. Hard water scales up all appliances, making them much less efficient and more costly to run. Water softeners are installed in the main water supply, but do not affect the kitchen or any other drinking-water faucets.

Other water treatment devices include magnetic and electrolytic scale inhibitors that are designed to reduce scale in the system but do not soften the water.

Water softener
Domestic water softeners can improve the efficiency of your home's water system and any appliances that use water.

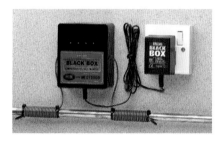

Scale inhibitor
This device helps prevent scale appearing in the water system by passing a series of electric currents around the water pipe.

SAVING WATER IN THE HOME

The following is a list of simple ways in which you may reduce your household water consumption.

- Leaks in your water system can be a key source of wastage. If you have a water meter, turn off your water and take two readings several minutes apart. If they are different, you may have a leak.
- When buying new appliances that use water, choose those that are energy-efficient. This saves on water as well as electricity (see pp.380–81).

- A five-minute shower uses about one-third of the water that a bath does. However, power showers can use more water than a bath in less than five minutes.
- Toilet cisterns may use as much as 2 gallons (9 liters) of clean water with every flush. Replace old toilets with low-flow models.
- Burst water pipes are a major cause of damage as well as of water wastage, so ensure that your water pipes and external faucets are well secured.

- Water barrels in your garden will collect rainwater that may be used on plants, saving large volumes of treated water.
- Dripping faucets can waste huge volumes of water. Make sure that you regularly replace worn washers (see pp.486–87).
- Try not to leave the faucet running while you brush your teeth, shave, or wash your hands, as this can waste up to 1⅓ gallons (5 liters) of water per minute.
- Swap your garden hose for a bucket of water when you wash your car.

GRAYWATER SYSTEMS

Graywater recycling systems range from the small (see below) to the large (see right). A small-scale system can be easily installed without professional help. In addition to a filtration unit, you will need to buy extra waste pipe and the right connections, as well as a compatible water barrel. Installing a cut-off valve is essential to prevent pipes from freezing in the cold weather. This system is ideally suited for connection to bath or basin wastes.

TOOLS AND MATERIALS SEE BASIC TOOLKIT

LARGE-SCALE SYSTEMS

It is now possible to buy large tank storage and treatment systems that can cope with the majority of graywater produced in the home. This can then be fed back into the domestic system for most uses, except drinking water. A relatively complex system of filters and pumps cleans the water, discarding sediment and debris; the water is also treated with UV to kill off the most harmful bacteria. These tanks can be underground, similar to those for rainwater (see p.391). Generally, however, upright tanks situated in the house are used. Some dual-sytems recycle rainwater and graywater.

ADDING A GREYWATER SYSTEM

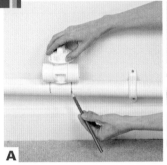

A

Mark on the waste pipe where you will fit the combination outlet. Allow space for the cut ends of the pipe to fit into the sockets of the outlet.

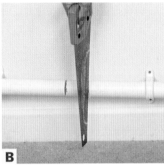

B

Use a fine-toothed saw to cut out the section of pipe, following guidelines as accurately as possible.

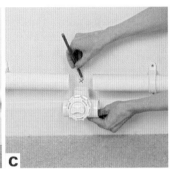

C

Mark on the wall where you want to route the drainage pipe outside. Do this by temporarily fitting the outlet, or by holding it in the correct position.

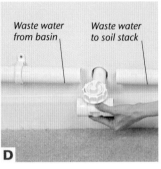

Waste water from basin   *Waste water to soil stack*

D

Drill a hole at the marked position, using a core drill bit (see p.368). Fit a piece of waste pipe long enough to extend through the wall.

Seal with silicone sealant

E

Cut back the pipe on the exterior wall to a suitable length for connecting an elbow. Position the elbow on the cut section.

F

Fit lengths of waste pipe from the connecting elbow down to a point above, and adjacent to, the water barrel. Screw in brackets to fix the pipe.

G

Assemble the filter unit and place it on the barrel, following guidelines about filter alignment. Fit the hose tail adaptor to the base of the waste pipe.

Secure hose with jubilee clip

H

Use the hose to join the pipe to the filter. For all waste-pipe joints, use solvent cement to secure them in place (see p.483).

REED BEDS

In addition to a composting toilet (see opposite), a reed bed is an eco-friendly way of getting rid of blackwater. The toilet functions conventionally, except that the discharge runs into an underground primary chamber. Solid waste settles at the bottom of it (and needs to be pumped out periodically), while an overflow at the top takes the liquid waste onto a planted reed bed. The root system "treats" the water by filtering out potentially harmful bacteria, and oxygenating it to help beneficial micro-organisms thrive. Another pipe takes the treated water away, normally for garden irrigation.

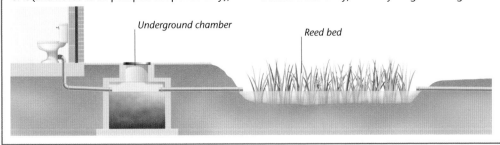

Underground chamber   *Reed bed*

Multiple benefits
Reed beds are not only effective; they also provide an aesthetically pleasing feature that can host a large variety of wildlife.

HARVESTING RAINWATER

Rainwater is a free resource, and it makes sense to harvest it for use in the home. Although it cannot normally be used for drinking water, it can be collected and used for watering the yard or, at a more sophisticated level, to supply household fittings and appliances such as toilets and washing machines (see opposite). The simplest way to harvest rainwater is to install a water barrel. Rain from gutters runs through a downpipe where a diverter channels water into the barrel. Once the barrel is full, water flows down into the ground drainage system as normal.

TOOLS AND MATERIALS SEE BASIC TOOLKIT

DIVERTING RAINWATER

This is a typical rainwater diverter. The main body of the unit has a leaf trap and an overflow to divert water back to the downpipe when the barrel is full. Different sizes of diverters or adaptors are used for different types and diameter of downpipe.

Coupling for connection to water barrel   *Linking pipe*   *Body of diverter*

RAINWATER DIVERTER KIT

■■ INSTALLING A WATER BARREL AND RAIN DIVERTER

A

Position the water barrel adjacent to a downpipe. Here, the barrel has a specially designed base that needs to be leveled when in position.

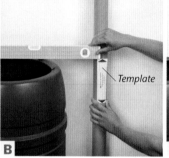

Template

B

Place the barrel on the base and determine where to cut into the downpipe. Most manufacturers will supply a marking template.

Fine-toothed saw

C

Use a fine-toothed saw to cut through the downpipe, following the guidelines as closely as possible.

D

Remove the cut section of pipe and insert the main body of the diverter, using any adaptors that are required.

E

Use a hole cutter to make a hole in the water barrel. Again, use a template to measure the correct position.

F

Fit the coupling in the hole, making sure any washers supplied are used to create a watertight fit.

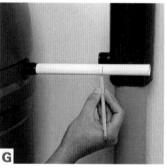

G

With the pipe in position, measure it to the correct size, then remove it again to cut. Here the pipe is rigid, but some may be flexible.

H

Fit the linking pipe in place, first pushing it into the socket section of the diverter, and then into the water-barrel coupling.

I

When the fitting is completed, wait until it rains to test that everything is working correctly. Remember that the diverter unit should be disassembled from time to time to remove any debris from the filter. It is always best to try to prevent debris getting into the pipe in the first place by using leaf guards (see right).

PREVENTING BLOCKAGES

When harvesting rainwater, it is important to take precautions to prevent pipes from becoming blocked with vegetation and debris. Gutters, and the outlets into downpipes, will need attention, and leaf guards are designed to protect these areas.

This is an example of a leaf guard that can be pushed into the running outlet at the top of the downpipe. Leaves should be cleared from it periodically.

DOWNPIPE LEAF GUARD

USING LARGER TANKS

With large rainwater collection systems, it is most common to situate tanks underground (see below). However, the expense of this option means it may be worth considering a surface collection tank. It is also easier to identify leaks, or other problems, in an above-ground tank. A disadvantage with this system, however, is that water can overheat and become a host environment for algae and bacterial growth. In addition to this, large tanks can also be an unattractive feature in your yard, although a range of designs is available to cater to specific space and positioning requirements.

Above-ground tanks
These tanks have been integrated into the design of a development of new houses—a viable option for new-build projects.

LARGE-SCALE RAINWATER COLLECTION

Domestic systems on a large scale involve the use of large storage tanks, which may be above ground (see box, above) but are more commonly buried underground. The advantage of a subterranean tank is that it saves space, is more aesthetically pleasing, and is shielded from direct sunlight so that the water maintains a more constant temperature (meaning there is less likelihood of algae growth or bacterial build up). Correct placing of the tank requires careful planning, as you may need to adjust gutters and downpipes to maximize the amount of water delivered to the tank.

How does the tank work?

Water enters the tank through a "calmed inlet", which means that sediment at the bottom of the tank and residue on the surface of the water is not stirred up. Once collected, the rainwater is pumped back into the house. The pump may be located in the tank itself, which reduces noise but is less accessible for maintenance. Conversely, you can site a suction pump inside the house, which is more accessible but may prove noisy.

Topping up water levels

When the tank level is low, plumbed-in water is used to top it up so that the tank does not run dry. With this type of system, it is important to ensure that there is an air gap between the rainwater supply and the top-up supply to prevent contamination. This can also be achieved by back-flow valves—check with your local authority regarding regulations. Similarly, the overflow from the tank to the water drains must not allow any backflow of material. Monitoring systems may also be purchased and installed as part of a large-scale rainwater tank system.

Maintenance and treatment

The only significant maintenance required for a rainwater tank is to ensure that filters are regularly cleaned and gutters and downpipes are unblocked. Be aware that there are moving parts in this system, such as pumps and valves, which may need occasional servicing. Some domestic systems use UV filtration to make the water drinkable, although this does require more advanced hardware.

Tank size
Consider the size of tank you require before installation. Typical domestic sizes range from 1,320–2,640 gallons (5,000–10,000 liters). You can make a more precise estimate by calculating the roof size of your home, balanced against the annual rainfall in your area, in relation to your estimated water consumption. Most suppliers will help you with this calculation before you order.

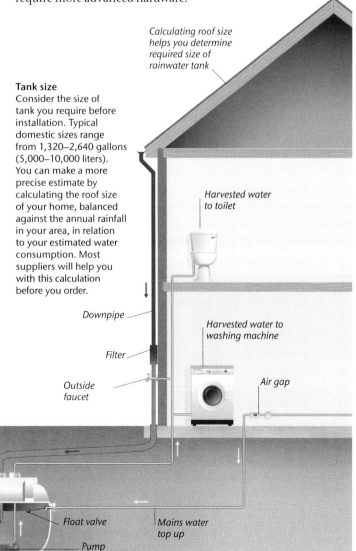

Calculating roof size helps you determine required size of rainwater tank

Harvested water to toilet

Harvested water to washing machine

Downpipe

Filter

Air gap

Outside faucet

Inspection chamber

Overflow to ground water drainage system

Rainwater harvesting tank

Float valve

Pump

Mains water top up

Using space

SPACE IS ALWAYS AT A PREMIUM IN THE HOME, SO USE WHAT YOU HAVE EFFECTIVELY. CONSIDER BOTH SHELF AND CABINET SPACE—THERE ARE MANY EXCELLENT READY-MADE UNITS AVAILABLE. ALTERNATIVELY, WITH SOME SIMPLE WOODWORKING SKILLS OR THE USE OF ADAPTABLE SUPPORT SYSTEMS, YOU CAN CONSTRUCT ATTRACTIVE UNITS TAILOR-MADE TO FIT YOUR HOME AND YOUR NEEDS.

PREPARING TO PUT UP SHELVES

Shelves—whether stock or custom-made—can be installed almost anywhere, as a major feature or in an otherwise disused corner such as under the stairs. You can increase storage options by adding hooks or storage boxes, and doors can enclose part or all of the shelving. How you combine types of shelves and their supports depends on chosen shelf position, level of support needed, and the style of your home. "Floating" shelves have invisible mounts and are an attractive option. Always attach shelf supports into studs.

SHELVING BRACKETS

There are many brackets and support systems for shelves; some are screwed in position and some are adjustable. Styles vary, so a system can be found to fit most requirements. To prevent sagging, position brackets every 2 ft (600 mm) along its length. If the shelves are to store heavy items such as books, put the brackets slightly closer together.

Fixed shelves

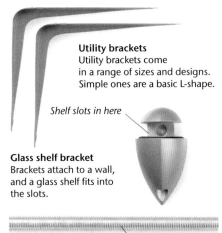

Utility brackets
Utility brackets come in a range of sizes and designs. Simple ones are a basic L-shape.

Shelf slots in here

Glass shelf bracket
Brackets attach to a wall, and a glass shelf fits into the slots.

Rod goes into holes in wall and shelf

Threaded metal rods
These provide invisible support to a "floating" shelf on a masonry wall.

Adjustable shelves

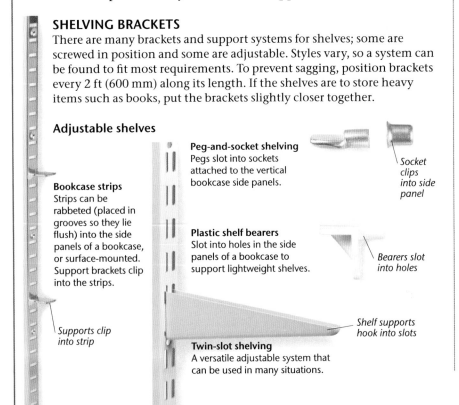

Bookcase strips
Strips can be rabbeted (placed in grooves so they lie flush) into the side panels of a bookcase, or surface-mounted. Support brackets clip into the strips.

Supports clip into strip

Peg-and-socket shelving
Pegs slot into sockets attached to the vertical bookcase side panels.

Socket clips into side panel

Plastic shelf bearers
Slot into holes in the side panels of a bookcase to support lightweight shelves.

Bearers slot into holes

Shelf supports hook into slots

Twin-slot shelving
A versatile adjustable system that can be used in many situations.

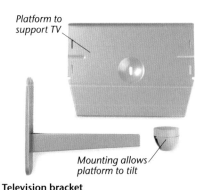

Platform to support TV

Mounting allows platform to tilt

Television bracket
Some manufacturers produce special brackets and shelves suitable for supporting particular items. A common example is a TV bracket.

CONSIDERATIONS WHEN PLANNING SHELVES

As well as choosing suitable materials, make sure that your shelves are strong enough for whatever is to be stored on them, and that they are level so that nothing rolls off.

Supporting heavy weights

Shelving needs to support its own weight as well as the items you wish to store or display. A few lightweight items will cause little difficulty, but a full shelf of books can be very heavy. Screws must be strong enough to stop shelves from collapsing—to support books, screws should penetrate masonry walls or wood studs by at least 2 in (50 mm), and supports should extend across two-thirds of a shelf's depth. Screws for floating shelves are not always designed to support heavy loads, although if you can sink metal rods into a solid wall to a depth of two-thirds that of the shelf, you may be able to support greater weights (see p.395).

Coping with undulating walls

Brackets must be precisely vertical and shelves horizontal. Use a level to assess all shelves' positions before securing them in place. If the wall surface is not level, pack wooden shims behind shelf supports so that they lie square and support shelves on the level. For the best finish, scribe shelves so that they sit neatly against any undulations in a wall without leaving gaps (see p.225). This can be difficult in alcoves—in which case consider using a card template.

STOCK PREPARATION

Shelving and storage "stock" systems are often inexpensive, easy to transport, and simple to assemble. Good preparation will prevent problems during or after construction.
■ Check the dimensions of the finished item and the space it needs to fit into before buying it. If it is a tight fit—in an alcove, for example—check the width in several places.
■ Consider whether the assembled item will be sufficiently sturdy and spacious for its intended purpose.
■ The packaging should state if any additional screws and tools are needed for assembly: check it before starting.
■ Make sure all parts are in the box and are undamaged— at the time of purchase, if possible, or soon afterward.
■ Lay out the components in the order they fit together and make sure you understand the manufacturer's instructions.

TOOLS AND MATERIALS CHECKLIST PP.394–399

Using furring strip or ladder supports in an alcove (p.394) Level, screws suitable for wall type, shelf material, paint*, paintbrush*, wood finish*, decorative molding*, panel pins*, filler, sandpaper

Assembling twin-slot shelving (p.395) Level, screws suitable to wall type, wood offcuts*, paint*, paintbrush*, wood finish*, decorative molding*, panel pins*, filler, sandpaper

Invisible attachments on an open masonry wall (p.395)

Threaded metal rods, thick shelving material, try-square, level, masonry drill and long bit, resin, paint*, paintbrush*, wood finish*, decorative molding*, panel pins*, filler, sandpapers

Building a closet (p.399) Level, screws suitable for wall/ceiling/floor, wood offcuts*, tenon saw

* = optional

FOR BASIC TOOLKIT SEE PP.24–25

SHELVING MATERIALS

Ready-cut shelves can be bought in a range of materials, the most common of which are shown below. Shelving is also a feature of the reclamation industry (see pp.94–95). Check with the supplier that your chosen material is strong enough to provide the required support—usually, boards or lumber should be at least 1 in (25 mm) thick. If you want a material with a veneer or laminated edge, use a standard sheet size so you don't have to cut it, or plan to hide the uncovered cut edge.

Softwood
Can be painted or have a natural wood finish applied. Avoid very cheap wood, which may be low-quality and may warp.

Hardwood
The appeal of hardwood is in its color and grain, but it is more expensive than softwoods.

Medium-density fiberboard (MDF)
This versatile material can cater to shape, depth, and size requirements; however, it needs to be finished.

Plywood
Very strong, but is usually used for shelves where a wood stain finish is not important.

Veneered particle board
Looks like solid hardwood but at a fraction of the price. Use a standard sheet size to retain veneer.

Melamine
Strong, laminated with colored, textured, or wood-effect plastic. Use a standard sheet size.

Kitchen counter cutoffs
The thickness makes this ideal for floating shelves, because it is easy to drill into the edges.

Wire shelving
Typical kitchen, pantry, and storage shelving, also comes in kits.

Metal
Pressed metal shelving is a hardwearing option that does not need any kind of finish before use.

Glass
Use tempered glass for shelving—its packaging will indicate what it can support. Standard clear glass is not strong enough.

CUSTOM SHELVING

A good place to put up shelves is in an alcove, as shown here. Ladder shelving is stronger than the ledger method and can be used across a wider span because shelves are more rigid. Twin-slot brackets can be used anywhere. Invisible screws can be used to make floating shelves to support heavy loads. Check the wall with a detector for wires and pipes before drilling. If the wall is a stud wall, drill into the studs.

TOOLS AND MATERIALS SEE BASIC TOOLKIT AND P.393

USING LEDGER SUPPORTS IN AN ALCOVE

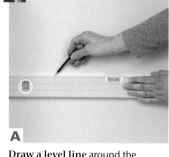

A

Draw a level line around the alcove where you want the lower edge of the first shelf. Start with either the top or the bottom shelf.

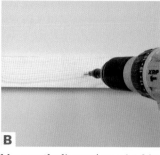

B

Measure the line and cut a 1-x-2-in (25-x-50-mm) ledger to fit. Hold its top edge against the line and drill pilot holes. Install it in place.

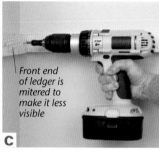

Front end of ledger is mitered to make it less visible

C

Measure and cut two ledgers to extend from the ends of the back one to at least two-thirds of the shelf's depth. Drill them in place.

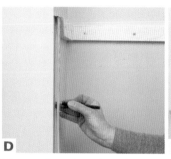

D

Measure down (or up) to where you want the next shelf, and mark guide lines. Cut and attach ledgers in the same way as for the first shelf.

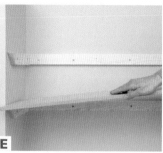

E

Cut and position shelving material (see p.393) on the ledgers. If walls are not square, scribe shelves to fit against them (see p.72).

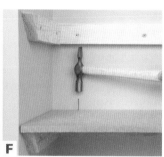

F

Nail each shelf to the ledgers every 10 in (250 mm) along the back and side edges.

USING LADDER SUPPORTS IN AN ALCOVE

Measure for ledgers as above, but cut two long ledgers—one for the back and one for the front of the shelf. Cut short strips to fit between them at each end and roughly every 10 in (250 mm) in between to create a ladderlike frame. Build the frame using butt joints (see p.396), countersinking all the screws.

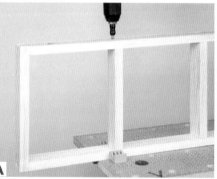

A

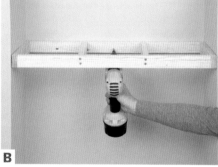

B

Attach the frame to the wall at the back and along the sides of the alcove. Use screws suitable to the wall's type every 10 in (250 mm). Then attach the shelf to the frame by nailing it onto the ledgers at regular intervals. Hold a level across the shelf in between inserting screws, to ensure that the shelf is level.

FINISHING SHELVES

MDF is the ideal shelf material for DIY use because it is so easy to work with, but it usually needs finishing after construction. A decorative wooden molding or veneer can be attached to the edges of shelves to make them look like solid wood (see p.217). The example here shows putting molding on the front of a shelf in an alcove. For simple back-and-side supported shelves, miter the fronts of the side supports to make them less obvious.

The edges of shelves can be filled and sanded. If there are gaps between any shelves and the wall, use a flexible filler on them. Do not use white filler if you are going to apply a natural wood finish (see p.294); use stainable filler to match the finish.

If you paint shelves, leave them to dry for several days before using them; the usual 24 hours is not long enough to prevent items on a shelf from sticking to new paint.

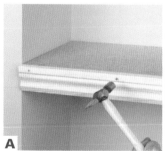

A

Hammer molding in place with panel pins every 4 in (100 mm). Set the pins' heads below the surface.

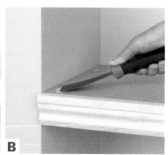

B

Fill all pin holes in the shelves with filler, then sand smooth, and decorate as required.

ASSEMBLING TWIN-SLOT SHELVING

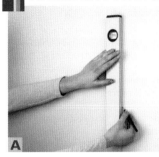

A

Draw a plumb line, using a level, where you want the first support. Hold a bracket against the line and mark the pin holes.

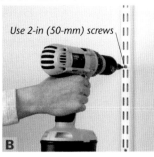

Use 2-in (50-mm) screws

B

Drill pilot holes and plug them (see p.77), then screw the first bracket in place. Use wood pieces to fill behind the bracket if the wall is uneven.

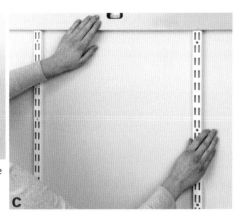

C

Hold the next bracket in place. Rest a level across the tops of both brackets to check for level. You may find it helps to have someone hold the bracket. Adjust the position of the bracket until it is completely level with the first, fixed one. Pilot drill through the top pin hole, then secure in place.

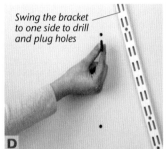

Swing the bracket to one side to drill and plug holes

D

Mark for other pilot holes, then swing bracket to one side. Drill the pilot holes, plug them, and loosely attach the bracket in place.

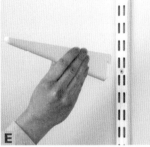

E

Check that the bracket is plumb, then attach it securely. Hook the shelf supports into the wall brackets, taking care that they are level.

F

Mark the position and depth of the brackets on the back of a shelf. Cut out this area with a chisel so that shelves will sit flush against the wall.

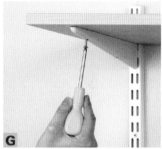

G

Place shelves on the supports and insert small screws through the support into predrilled holes on the underside of the shelf.

INVISIBLE ATTACHMENTS ON OPEN MASONRY WALLS

The thicker the shelf material, the easier this system is to apply. Use rods one-third longer than the shelf's width. Measure and mark for attaching points on the back of the shelf roughly near the ends, and at similar intervals in between if spanning a wide space.

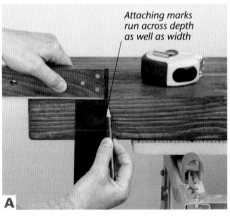

Attaching marks run across depth as well as width

A

B

Use a level to draw the shelf's position on the wall. Hold the marked shelf up to it and mark the attaching points from the shelf on the wall.

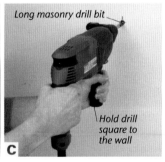

Long masonry drill bit

Hold drill square to the wall

C

Drill into the wall to a depth that equals two-thirds the width of the shelf. Use a bit slightly larger than the diameter of the threaded rods.

Lumber drill bit same size as rod diameter

D

Clamp the shelf securely. Drill at the attaching points to the depth of the holes in the wall, ensuring that the drill stays square to the wood.

E

Inject resin (see p.80) into the drilled holes in the wall, and insert the rods. Use a level to ensure that they are exactly straight.

F

When the resin has set, slide the shelf onto the rods. Set a level on the shelf. If it is level, insert resin into the holes to attach it onto the rods.

WOODWORKING JOINTS

A knowledge of joining wood will allow you to design and construct customized shelving or other forms of storage. Understanding how to make common woodworking joints will also enable you to carry out repair jobs on items such as doors, windows, stairs, kitchen cabinets, and other furniture. Choosing which joint to use in any situation involves weighing strength, looks, and ease of construction. Biscuit joiners (see p.64) give the option of easily making joints.

CHOOSING A SUITABLE JOINT

The complexity of any joint is determined by the strength and quality of finish required. Joints hidden from view do not need to be decorative, and a butt joint will usually do.

Some joints are made for strength: for example, a lap joint is much stronger than a butt joint, and a mortise-and-tenon joint is stronger still. Your skills and experience may also affect your choice of which joint to use.

BUTT JOINTS

To make these simple joints you need only be able to measure lengths accurately, and make clean, straight cuts. Nails or screws should be slightly angled so that they cannot pull apart. Butt joints are commonly used in hidden frameworks such as stud walls (see pp.104–105).

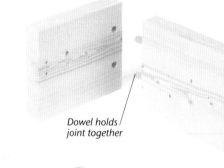

Dowel holds joint together

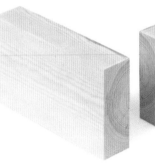

Simple butt joint
In the most simple type of butt joint, the face of one piece of lumber meets the face of another at a right angle.

Doweled butt joint
Strengthen butt joints by inserting ready-made dowel pegs into the joint. Mark and measure carefully, so that the dowel aligns with the hole: one option is to drive pins into one side of the joint, at the dowel positions, and use them to create an impression in the other side of the joint. Drill holes half the depth of the peg, then glue and insert the dowel.

Mitered butt joint
This is similar to the other butt joints, but the ends of both lengths of lumber join at an angle, normally 45 degrees. This gives a more visually pleasing finish. Cutting guides can help you make angled cuts easily and accurately (see p.35).

LAP JOINTS

A lap joint is stronger than a butt joint. Each piece of lumber has half its depth removed so that it overlaps and interlocks with the other piece. A cross-lap joint (see below) creates a cross or T-junction rather than a right angle. For both, accuracy in measuring and marking up is essential.

MAKING A LAP JOINT

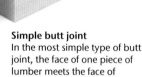

Rabbet

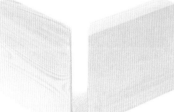

A Use a marking gauge to make identical cutting guides on each section of lumber to be joined.

B Cut a rabbet with a circular or tenon saw, making the cuts first across the grain, and then along the grain.

C Attach the joint as required; screws are used here. Use wood glue as well if you want extra strength.

MAKING A CROSS-LAP JOINT

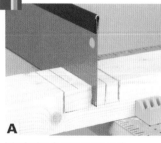

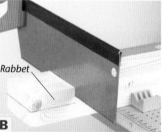

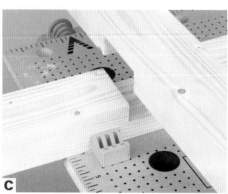

A Mark the dimensions and position of the joint. Make several cuts across the grain, to the required depth, in the marked area.

B Chisel away the waste wood from between the cuts, working slowly and carefully.

Slot the two notched lengths of wood together. Attach them with wood glue and/or nails or screws.

C

HOUSING AND RABBET JOINTS

These two joints are useful for cabinet and shelving construction. Both are easiest achieved with a router, a power tool that cuts a rabbet to a set size (see pp.66–67).

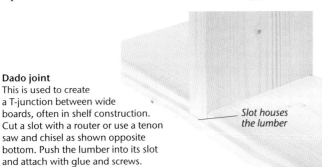

Slot houses the lumber

Dado joint
This is used to create a T-junction between wide boards, often in shelf construction. Cut a slot with a router or use a tenon saw and chisel as shown opposite bottom. Push the lumber into its slot and attach with glue and screws.

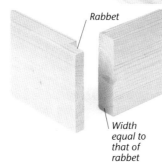

Rabbet

Rabbet joint
This is similar to a dado joint but the lengths of lumber are joined at their ends. It can also be used to join wide boards at a right angle. Cut a rabbet at the end of one length with a tenon saw (opposite bottom). Glue and screw the joint.

Width equal to that of rabbet

▌▌ MAKING A MORTISE-AND-TENON JOINT

Mortise-and-tenon joints join pieces of wood very strongly and cleanly. The end of one length of lumber is cut away on two, or all four, sides to make a peg. A peg-sized hole is then cut out of another piece of wood, and the peg is inserted. Joints connecting the stiles of doors with the rails are often made in this way.

A

Mark the cuts needed for the peg and slot on two lengths of lumber. Cut the peg with the wood grain as shown for a lap joint.

B

Drill overlapping holes to the depth required for the slot with a flat bit. Remove as much of the waste wood as possible with the bit.

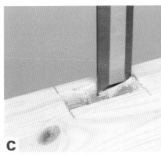

C

Neaten the edges of the slot hole using a hammer and chisel.

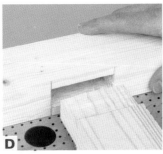

D

Insert the peg into the slot to check the fit. Then apply wood glue to the inside of the slot, and make the joint.

JOINT BRACKETS AND BLOCKS

There are a number of plates that can be used to repair existing wooden joints, or create new joints. To attach a bracket or block flush to wood, draw around it, and use a chisel and hammer to create a shallow rabbet.

Plates

Tee plate
Flat plate used to strengthen a T-shaped joint.

Angle plate
Strengthens any right-angled joint. Often used as a repair option on the corner of window casements.

Corner plate
Used to strengthen corner joints.

Mending plate
Straight, strengthening plate.

Stretcher plate
For internal joints. Has elongated attachment holes used to adjust position.

Braces

Corner brace
Flat plate bent to form a right-angled brace to strengthen a joint.

Angle brace
Small corner brace, commonly used to hold down kitchen countertops.

Joints

Assembly joint (joint block)
Used to strengthen a right-angled joint, commonly in kitchen units.

KD joint
Used to strengthen a right-angled joint. Comes in two sections.

Dowel fits into lock   Lock

Cam dowel and lock
Used in furniture for joining flat sections or panels.

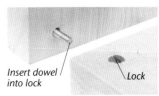

Insert dowel into lock   Lock

Cross dowel and insert
Used to create joint between panels or sections of a framework. Commonly used in self-assembly furniture such as beds.

PLANNING A CLOSET

A custom closet can be built in an alcove, in a corner of a room, against a wall, or freestanding. To put up closets, follow the manufacturer's instructions, and the advice on p.393. See opposite for the steps to erect a typical closet with sliding doors. If you wish to produce custom-built storage, see below for further details on the options and advice on planning it. Making a closet of any size requires a considerable number of materials, and much careful planning and measurement.

<table>
<tr><td colspan="2">THINGS TO WATCH OUT FOR</td></tr>
<tr><td>■ Aim to get the cabinet square even if walls, floors, and ceilings are not dead straight. Use a level, and pack out sides with shims if necessary to get them square. Hide any gaps with decorative moldings (see pp.216–219).
■ Use factory-cut straight edges on any boards to their best advantage—where they will be seen.
■ Use brackets to keep corners</td><td>square and rigid (see p.397).
■ Support long-span shelves along their length, with extra brackets, or with dividers.
■ Consider buying ready-made doors, because making your own doors is difficult. Attach doors with simple flush hinges (see p.157) unless they are particularly heavy or large, in which case you should use butt hinges (see p.159).</td></tr>
</table>

PLANNING A CUSTOM CLOSET

Wherever you plan to build a closet, you will need to follow these basic steps: plan the design, select materials, build the framework, install doors, and finally finish the closet.

Design

If you have ample floorspace, finding an area to build a new closet may be fairly easy. If space is limited, it's always best to use an alcove or open up a niche under a stair. Creating a closet inside an existing alcove is illustrated below. Closets can be installed on an entire length of wall using the same process as an alcove closet. A closet can also be installed into a corner, against a wall, or it can be freestanding. Always allow for at least 27 in (69 cm) for an inside depth if you plan to hang clothes in the new closet.

Materials

You will need enough lumber to frame the walls and the doorway for the front of the closet. Measure all of the outside and inside walls for drywall, as it will be needed to cover the stud walls. Select the type of track hardware and door style you would like to use. Sliding doors are the most popular choice, but accordion doors and bi-fold doors are other options. Measure for size, and decide if you want them pre-finished.

Framework

The framework for a closet is similar to building a doorway and a stud wall (see pp.104–107). Locate pipes or wires in the wall before you drive in nails or screws. A closet door is hung with a similar method to that used to install other interior doors (see pp.158–159).

Finishing

After you have constructed the new closet and installed the doors, give them a final coat of paint before installing the new door hardware. Paint the interior shell of the closet before you install any shelves or other interior organizers. While you may want to add a splash of color to the inside of a closet, most are usually white. Finish the outside of the closet to match the rest of the room. You can embellish the closet with decorative moldings (see pp.216–219).

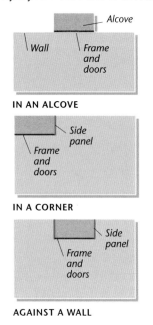

IN AN ALCOVE

IN A CORNER

AGAINST A WALL

Easy closet structures
These illustrations show three ways of using a room's shape to make a closet. The red line represents the basic frame shown to the right; the green lines are side panels.

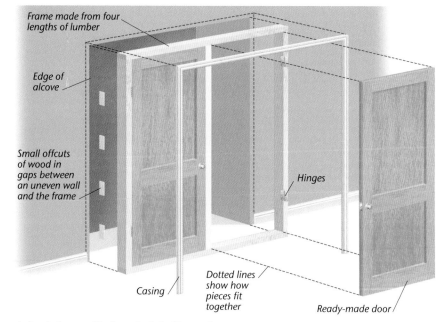

A simple frame with doors installed to an alcove
Build a frame to install in the front of the alcove (as shown) or to your chosen size (if the cabinet is to be in a corner or against a wall), and attach it to the walls. If a wall is uneven, it may leave small gaps—fill these with lumber offcuts. Attach doors and casing.

BUILDING A CUSTOM CLOSET

These are typical steps to construct a custom closet. Study the instructions in case you need other techniques—for instance, to install the doors. If possible, get someone to help hold the sections in position.

TOOLS AND MATERIALS SEE BASIC TOOLKIT AND P.393

1 FITTING THE SIDE

Use a level to get plumb line

A

B *This example needs scribing around molding*

C *Plate*

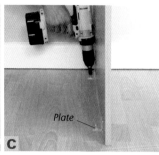

Measure from the corner of the room to where you want the cabinet's side panel. Draw a plumb line on the wall.

Hold the side panel in place. It will not sit flush if the wall is uneven; if this is the case, scribe it to fit (see p.72). Cut the panel to size.

Check with a square that the angle between wall and panel is 90 degrees. Then use plates to secure the panel to the floor.

Tighten hardware once panel is vertical

Attach panel to a joist if possible

D

Attach the panel loosely to the ceiling with plates. Use a level to check that it is plumb. If necessary, use the slots in the plates to adjust its position. Then secure it. At the cabinet's other "side," draw a guide line on the wall for the cabinet's front edge. The jamb will sit against this line.

2 FITTING THE JAMB

Section of molding to be removed

Guide for front edge of jamb

A

Jamb screws to wall

B

Cut a section from the baseboard (see p.104) to allow the jamb to sit flush against the wall.

Cut the jamb to size. Then attach it to the wall. Use a level as you work, to check that the jamb is plumb.

3 INSTALLING THE RUNNERS AND DOOR

Measure the distance between the inside edges of the side panel and the jamb. Check that the closet is "square" by measuring at the top and bottom of the opening, and adjust if necessary. Use a hacksaw to cut the top rail of the sliding door mechanism to fit the opening.

A

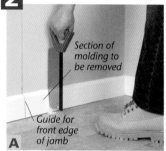

B

C

Using the manufacturer's guidelines on positioning, attach the rail to the joists in the ceiling. Use the plugged hardware required for the ceiling type.

Cut the base rail to length. Position it loosely between the side panel and jamb, but do not attach it at this stage.

D

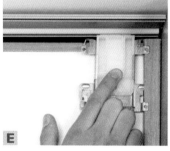

E

F

Hang the doors on the runner mechanism, paying close attention to the manufacturer's instructions.

Once the doors are hung, adjust the runners to allow the doors to hang correctly. Check that they operate smoothly.

With the doors and rails in the best position for smooth operation, use a detector to find out whether there are any wires or pipes below the floor. Secure the base rail to the floor. The length of screw needed depends on the type and thickness of the flooring.

OUTDOOR ALTERATIONS AND REPAIRS

HARD LANDSCAPING
WOODEN STRUCTURES

LANDSCAPING

The principles of landscaping apply to the smallest back yard just as they do to more substantial green spaces around a home. In all cases, consider how you want to use your yard and what is appropriate for your region's climate and soil. The pages that follow show you how to build structures outside and how to find effective ways of creating both practical and attractive finishes to the space outside your home.

PLANNING PERMISSION

Regulations and permissions are discussed throughout this chapter. Generally, there are greater restrictions for condominiums and properties in homeowner associations on what you can do in your garden. If you own a house, you will still need planning permission to build a shed and many other outdoor structures. Check with your local planning department before starting any projects.

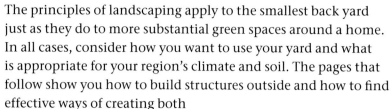

Trees
To avoid problems with subsidence, always plant trees away from the house.

Decorative garden walls
Garden walls are generally non-structural and are used as boundaries, or decorative screens in a garden design. They may be constructed from different brick, block, or stone materials.

Steps
These may be wooden, masonry-based, or a combination of both. See p.419 for information on how to construct steps.

Gates
Used as entrances to drives, paths, or sectioned-off areas of a garden, gates are usually made of wood or metal. Manufacturers supply a number of standard sizes, but unusual sizes need to be custom-made. The main gates for a drive can now have remote-control opening and closing mechanisms built in. This increases security as well as being very convenient.

Garden shed
Small outbuildings and garden sheds are ideal storage areas for all garden tools and leisure items. They are supplied in easy-to-build kit forms, but must be raised off ground level on a good foundation. Concrete blocks or slabs can be used to provide foundations—see pp.414–417 for more information.

Retaining walls
Where there is a change in level in a yard or where you require a raised bed, you may need a retaining wall. These walls therefore require greater structural strength than other garden walls because one side will have material pressed against it.

Pavers
Paving blocks or pavers are ideal for paths, drives, and any exterior walkway. Patterns, colors, and the options for how they are laid to create particular designs, are wide and varied. Specially made paving blocks can be used, or bricks are another option to create this effect.

Fences
Normally used as boundaries, fences are commonly made of wood, although concrete and metal posts are also used. Wire mesh is sometimes used in a fence, especially if the fence is used to retain animals.

OTHER FEATURES

There is a variety of features that can be included in a yard. Others not shown here that may be relevant include:

Asphalt

This is an ideal material for paths or drives. A large-scale task is a job for the professionals. Good edging will prevent the sides of an asphalt drive from deteriorating.

Pergola

Decorative features such as pergolas and arches are more common in gardens today. They can be built to your own design or you can buy kits for home construction.

Water features

Small pumps, reservoirs, pond liners, and water-feature systems are now readily available. A supply of water is not needed as the pump recirculates the initial supply.

WEATHER CONDITIONS

In Canada, all hard landscaping should be installed with runoff, drainage, and frost shifting protection included as an essential part of the project.

EXPOSURE

When building any new feature outside your home, consider where light will come from during the day and whether the feature will cast shadow across the house, or parts of the yard. The east side of your home will receive light during the morning, and the west in the afternoon and early evening. Outbuildings or trees to the south of your home may cast shadows across the surface of your home, and block light to parts of the yard.

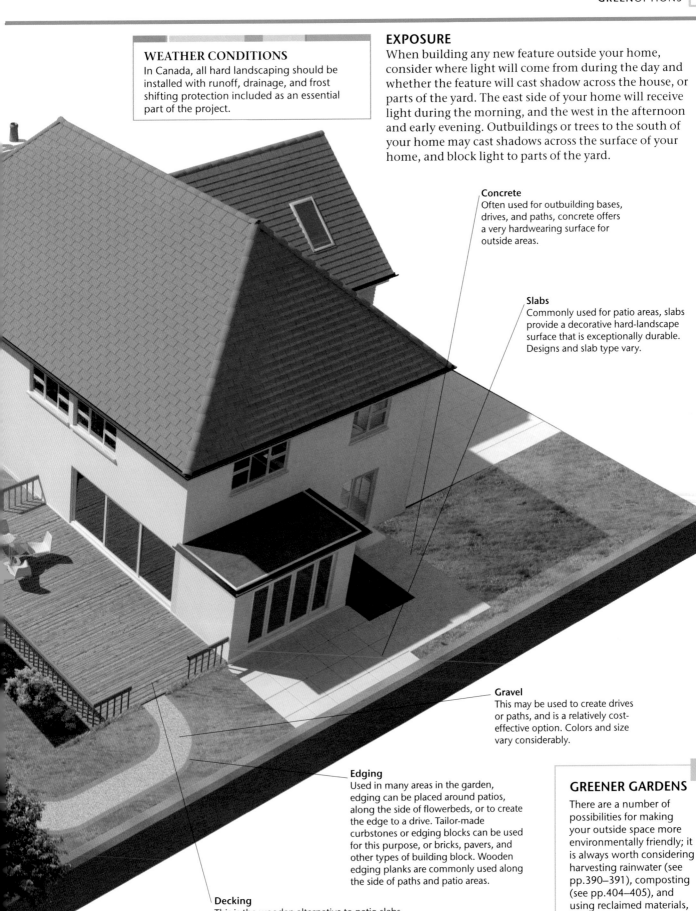

Concrete
Often used for outbuilding bases, drives, and paths, concrete offers a very hardwearing surface for outside areas.

Slabs
Commonly used for patio areas, slabs provide a decorative hard-landscape surface that is exceptionally durable. Designs and slab type vary.

Gravel
This may be used to create drives or paths, and is a relatively cost-effective option. Colors and size vary considerably.

Edging
Used in many areas in the garden, edging can be placed around patios, along the side of flowerbeds, or to create the edge to a drive. Tailor-made curbstones or edging blocks can be used for this purpose, or bricks, pavers, and other types of building block. Wooden edging planks are commonly used along the side of paths and patio areas.

Decking
This is the wooden alternative to patio slabs, pavers, and other hard-landscaped surfaces. As long as the wood is treated, and maintained regularly, it can last for years.

GREENER GARDENS

There are a number of possibilities for making your outside space more environmentally friendly; it is always worth considering harvesting rainwater (see pp.390–391), composting (see pp.404–405), and using reclaimed materials, such as slabs, wherever feasible (see pp.86–87).

COMPOSTING

Composting is the natural breakdown of organic matter to produce a crumbly nutrient-rich soil. The resulting compost can be added to other soil types as a fertilizer, forming an excellent growing medium for plants. By managing this natural process in your own garden, you can dispose of waste, and produce an agent that will improve the look and yield of any plants and flowers. Regardless of the size of your outdoor space, there will be a composting solution to suit your needs.

WORMERIES

A wormery performs the same task as a compost heap, but on a smaller scale. Worms are kept inside a suitable container, where they eat organic matter; their waste products are then used as a fertilizer. Tiger worms are best for the job, as they live and feed on decomposing compost (unlike common earthworms, which prefer to burrow in soil). You can make your own wormery, or buy a kit that comes with a supply of tiger worms.

MAKING COMPOST

Theories vary on how to produce the perfect compost, but there are some general rules. Firstly, a suitable container or store is required. Different types are shown here, including homemade, shop-bought, and recycled varieties. As the natural process of composting generates heat, storing compost in a container enables the heat to be retained more easily, and allows for the efficient breakdown of material. It is best to keep a compost heap covered to retain this heat, and to prevent rain from making the compost too wet. While some moisture is needed, it is usually supplied in the form of moist grass cuttings and other green waste. Stir your compost occasionally to introduce oxygen.

Building up layers

A system of layering different materials will aid the composting process. A layer of coarser, more fibrous material, for example, will introduce air to the center of the heap, which is vital as composting is an aerobic process. However, this may not always be a straightforward task. In the height of summer, the majority of layers are likely to be grass clippings, so it is important to make sure you break up large amounts of one material with other layers—perhaps from the kitchen.

The process of composting takes between two and nine months. You will need to gain access to the base of the heap to take out the crumbly, fully decomposed compost for use on the garden. Some containers have an access hatch at the bottom of the container, while others may need one side to be disassembled so that the bottom level of compost can be dug out. In colder regions, your heap may go dormant in the winter, but will start back up in the spring.

Plastic bin
Purpose-built plastic bins are fitted with a hatch at the bottom for easy access of composted material.

Slatted wooden bin
This design of bin encourages greater air circulation, improving the ventilation of the heap.

Wooden sectioned bin
This bin design can be disassembled in layers, allowing the heap height to be raised or lowered as required.

Hurdle-style compost bin
As well as looking attractive, this bin offers good ventilation. The heap is accessed by removing one side.

Top layer of green clippings

Bottom layers are well rotted

Cross-section of a slatted wooden bin
Slatted bins are great for gaining access to the bottom of the heap. The sides are easily disassembled, and the compost is normally integrated enough not to spill out.

Concrete bin
This type of bin may have a block or slatted structure. Unlike its wooden alternatives, it will not rot.

Recycled bins
Large recycled containers, such as those used to deliver building materials, make ideal compost bins.

COMPOSTING

MATERIALS THAT CAN BE COMPOSTED

The complete list of items that can be composted is extensive, but it can be categorized generally as either "brown waste" or "green waste". Examples of specific items included in each category—as well as some exceptions—are detailed in the table below. Although all organic matter will compost, it is advisable not to compost items that may attract vermin or disease (outlined at the bottom of the table).

HOUSEHOLD WASTE

GREEN WASTE

BROWN WASTE

COMMON ITEMS FOR COMPOSTING

Type of waste	Example ingredients	Comments
Green waste As the name suggests, this category includes all types of green leafy garden waste. Other types of fast-rotting waste material is also included in this group. All these items have a high nitrogen content	Fresh grass clippings	A plentiful summer supply should be layered with other items
	Flowers	Ensure stems are chopped up; do not use diseased plants
	Nettles	These act as good natural activators
	Vegetable and fruit peelings	Can be added straight to heap from kitchen
	Vegetable crop residue	Such as potato and tomato plants
	Young weeds	Take care with some weeds—perennials are best avoided
	Herbivore manure	Such as that from horses, cows, and rabbits
	Tea leaves	Bear in mind that tea bags will take longer to break down
Brown waste This category refers to the slower-rotting items that have a high carbon content	Dead or fallen leaves	Only small amounts should be used
	Paper	Make sure it is shredded first
	Coffee grounds and filter	Use only paper filters
	Cardboard	This should be torn into small pieces
	Woody hedge clippings and twigs	Ideally these should be put through a shredder
	Sawdust	Mix well with more aerated material
	Herbivore bedding	Such as hay and straw
Other items There are a number of other items that are not immediately obvious candidates for composting but that are nevertheless suitable	Egg shells	These need to be washed and crushed up
	Hair	Either human or animal hair can be added—both are high in nitrogen
	Wool and cotton	Must be 100-percent wool or cotton, and cut into small pieces. Tumble-dryer lint can also be composted
	Vacuum-bag contents	Common sense is required depending on what has been picked up
	Wood ash	Only use small quantities

ITEMS NOT TO COMPOST

Although all organic material breaks down, avoid the following as they may attract vermin and harbor potential pathogens	Meat and fish (cooked and raw)	Can harbor disease and attract vermin
	Dog and cat feces	Harbor disease
	Cat litter	Will normally contain feces
	Glossy magazines	Contain too many inorganic chemicals
	Barbecue coals and coal ash	Contain harmful sulphur oxides

Hard landscaping

PATIOS, PATHS, AND BRICK WALLS PROVIDE THE FRAMEWORK FOR OUTDOOR AREAS AROUND THE HOME. CREATING HARD SURFACES AND BUILDING SMALLER BRICK WALLS REQUIRE SOME PLANNING AND SKILL, BUT CAN BE CARRIED OUT BY MOST COMPETENT HOME-IMPROVEMENT ENTHUSIASTS.

HARD LANDSCAPING MATERIALS

Materials for hard landscaping include a wide range of masonry products that can be used for building many different types of flat, stepped, or vertical construction. The range of materials available is increasing, but the ways in which new products are used follow a number of basic principles.

STONES

Stones used in hard landscaping are normally made of either concrete or natural stone. Size and shape can vary considerably. Like other paving materials, they can be laid in many different patterns.

Concrete stone
Made in a mold, concrete stones tend to be regular in shape and depth. They may be textured and colored to mimic natural stone or other masonry finishes such as brick paving.

Natural stone
Types of stone often used for paving include bluestone, granite, and slate. Natural stones are often irregularly shaped, making laying more difficult. Some have very straight, machine-cut edges although they usually still vary in depth.

PAVERS

Pavers and paving blocks are smaller, and generally thicker than stone. They can be laid in many different ways to create any number of different patterns (see p.414).

Paver
Paving blocks are often brick-shaped, and bricks themselves can be used as pavers. Round-edged and many other shapes of pavers are also available.

Interlocking pavers
Available in a variety of designs, interlocking pavers are popular for patios and walkways.

EDGING

Most designs of hard landscaping are improved by some form of edging. In some cases the edge is created by a building or wall, but otherwise use edging blocks to provide a retaining edge. Treated wood is also an option (see p.418).

Edging block
Bricks, or concrete or natural stone blocks such as granite pavers, are commonly used to provide an edge. More substantial blocks, called curbs, are designed for large driveways rather than edging a path, for example.

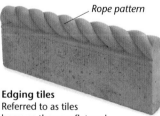

Rope pattern

Edging strip
This consists of a number of blocks or sets joined together. It makes laying much faster.

Edging tiles
Referred to as tiles because they are flat and often made of terra-cotta, these often have a decorative edge.

STONES

Many types and sizes of stones are used in exterior landscaping. Below are two of the more common sizes of decorative stone used outside.

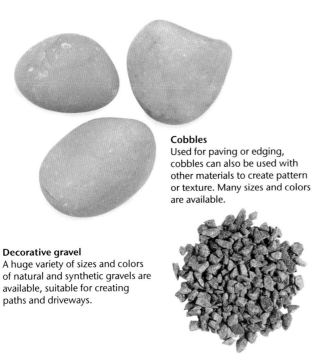

Cobbles
Used for paving or edging, cobbles can also be used with other materials to create pattern or texture. Many sizes and colors are available.

Decorative gravel
A huge variety of sizes and colors of natural and synthetic gravels are available, suitable for creating paths and driveways.

ASPHALT

Asphalt can provide an excellent surface for a large driveway. Laying an even, well-compacted asphalt surface that is a good depth, drains effectively, and does not have any unsightly joints requires considerable skill and is a job best left to the professionals. You can make simple repairs to an existing asphalt surface. Fill potholes with cold, ready-mixed asphalt and tamp it down into the hole using a rammer or wooden post.

CONCRETE

Concrete forms part of many exterior hard-landscaped areas. Laying a relatively small pad of concrete—as the base for a shed, for example—is a viable DIY project (see p.415). To create a level surface you will need to construct a level wooden frame (a formwork) to hold the wet concrete in place, then remove air bubbles and level the surface across the top of the formwork to produce a flat pad (called screeding, see p.29 for screed machines). If the surface is to support an outbuilding such as a shed, lay a vapor barrier over the compacted crushed stone under the concrete pad.

If you want to lay a large area of concrete such as a path or driveway, it will require contraction and expansion joints, such as those shown in the path illustrated on the right, to prevent cracking.

Expansion joints help stop concrete from cracking

CONCRETE PATH

GARDEN WALL MATERIALS

Normal bricks, blocks, and stone are all commonly used to build garden walls, as well as specially designed blocks. Different types of bricks and blocks are shown on pp.80–81. For more on reclaimed materials, see pp.94–95. When choosing materials, check that they are frost-resistant. Choosing bricks with a low salt content will prevent efflorescence (salt crystals forming on the finished wall).

Bricks and blocks

Below are commonly used brick and block materials used in hard landscaping. There are many design variations.

Common brick
For garden walls, common bricks provide a simple decorative option.

Screen wall block
Concrete blocks with patterned holes can be used to create a stylish wall (see p.413).

Garden wall blocks
These are designed specifically for garden-wall construction and are frost-resistant.

Wall-feature block
Reconstituted stone blocks are shaped to mimic a number of laid blocks.

Coping stones

The coping is the top layer of a wall that prevents water from penetrating the brick- or stonework of the main structure. Specially designed coping stones are available, although you can also use bricks.

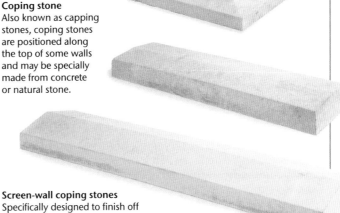

Pier cap
Finishes off the top of each pier in a screen-block wall.

Coping stone
Also known as capping stones, coping stones are positioned along the top of some walls and may be specially made from concrete or natural stone.

Screen-wall coping stones
Specifically designed to finish off along top of screen-wall blocks.

PREPARING TO BUILD A WALL

When building a wall, the height and style will determine the foundations required. The depth of foundation is relative to the frost line, and the wall height and width. If you want a wall higher than 4 ft (1.2 m), the excavation work needed will be more extensive, so check with your local code inspector for designing foundations. If you are building a retaining wall, you will also need to build in a waterproofing membrane, and drainage channels to remove the water from the soil behind the wall. With all construction, sound planning and preparation are essential.

> ## PLANNING PERMISSION
> You will not normally require planning permission to build a decorative garden wall. However, if the wall is structural or goes above a certain height—normally, regulations start at about 6 ft (2 m)—you may need permission. It is always best to contact your local planning official if you are in any doubt about regulations or whether permission is needed. Permission is also required if any wall over 3 ft 3 in (1 m) high is to be built next to a road and/or sidewalk.

LAYING BRICKS

Bricks can be laid with their long side (stretcher face) or their short side (header face) facing outward. How stretchers and headers combine in the wall structure is known as the bond.

Brick bonds

Most brick bonds are designed to ensure that joints are always staggered between each course, maintaining the strength of the wall. Stretcher, English, and Flemish bonds are the most popular, although there are many variations. Laying bricks end to end creates a thin "single-skin" wall, whereas other bricklaying patterns result in a thicker "double-skin" wall.

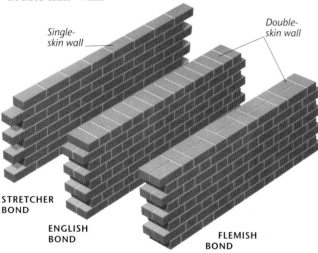

Single-skin wall

Double-skin wall

STRETCHER BOND

ENGLISH BOND

FLEMISH BOND

Corners and piers

The bond has implications when it comes to features such as corners because if bricks are not laid in the correct pattern, the wall will be weak. Pillars, called piers, can be purely decorative but are essential to strengthening single-skin walls over 16 in (400 mm) in height. They should be positioned evenly along the wall at least every 10 ft (3 m), and can bisect the wall or be offset to one side. The foundations need to be wider at pier position. See p.412 for more details on corner and pier construction.

Making a gauging rod

A gauging rod is useful for keeping a consistent size of mortar joint (see p.412). Simply lay out some bricks flat on the ground one above the other, stretcher-face up. Make a gap of ½ in (10 mm) between each brick to represent a mortar joint. Hold an offcut of furring strip against the bricks and mark off the necessary position of each mortar joint.

FOUNDATIONS

Garden walls can be functional, helping hold back soil as a retaining wall or providing terraces in a hilly backyard, or walls can be design elements in a yard, providing visual interest and creating intimate spaces. No matter the height of the wall or the material you plan to use, always contact your local building department to check the regulations. Foundation depth is determined by the height of your wall and where you live. As a general rule, foundations should be excavated to undisturbed soil and below the frost line for your area. The frost line is the maximum depth that frost normally penetrates the soil during the winter. The depth varies depending on the climate of your area. In Canada, it cn vary from 6 in (15 cm) to over 4 ft (1.2 m) deep. If you hit bedrock, or you are building off an existing concrete pad, you may not need footings. If you dig a deep footing and the subsoil is still uncompacted, dig a little farther and fill to the footing base with compacted crushed stone. To further help water escape, you may want to incorporate drain pipes in the wall and install a moisture membrane behind the wall that will catch the water.

Setting out

Once you have decided on the design of the wall and worked out what size the strip footings need to be, you need to ensure that levels and angles across the sight are correct. Use string lines and wooden pegs for laying out. Even better, construct some profile boards that can be used for marking out the foundation trench and the first course of bricks. You need a profile board at both ends of every straight section of wall. For the easiest possible construction, it is worth dry-laying a course of your chosen bond with mortar gaps and adjusting the layout so you do not have to cut more bricks than necessary. Once you are happy with the trench layout, mark the edge of it using a spade to cut into the soil below the lines. Excavate the trench to the required depth.

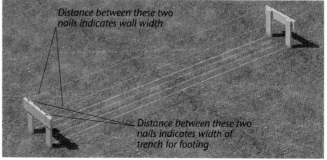

Distance between these two nails indicates wall width

Distance between these two nails indicates width of trench for footing

USING PROFILE BOARDS

LAYING STRIP FOOTING

A

Drive in a stake at each end of the trench down to footing depth, and at intervals of 3–6 ft (1–2 m). Make sure they are vertical.

B

Rest a level across the tops of adjacent stakes to make sure they are level.

C

Pour concrete into the trench up to the top of the stakes.

D

Use a metal float to smooth the concrete. The footings should be left to dry for a few days before building the wall.

BUILDING ON A SLOPE

If you need to build a wall on sloping ground, the foundation widths and wall thicknesses need not vary, but the way in which the foundations are laid may need to be modified. If the slope is very shallow, simply excavate a level foundation—it will be deeper at one end than at the other. However, if the drop is more than a few courses of bricks, then the foundations need to be stepped.

In order to create steps in the footings, some temporary wooden screed is used to hold the concrete in position while it dries. Plan the step height to be divisible by brick size so you will not have to cut bricks in order to maintain the bond.

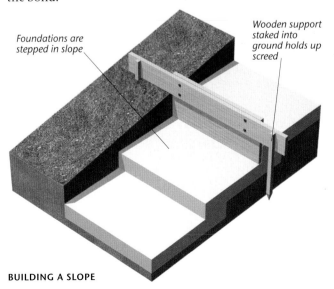

Foundations are stepped in slope

Wooden support staked into ground holds up screed

BUILDING A SLOPE

MIXING CONCRETE

Use a concrete mixer for mixing a large quantity of concrete, because mixing by hand is an arduous task. If you have a large concrete requirement—several cubic yards—hire a concrete contractor. To work out how much concrete you need, multiply the depth by the area (width x length). For more on concrete see pp.70–71. Below is a rough guide to quantities.

Foundation concrete
To mix 35 cu ft (1cu m) of foundation concrete, you need 660 lb (300 kg) of cement; 1,300 lb (600 kg) of sharp sand, 2,200 lb (1,000 kg) of coarse aggregate.

General concrete
In extreme climates and on the coast, increase the proportion of cement to make a stronger mix.

RETAINING WALLS

If a wall is going to hold back soil for a terrace, or be used to create a raised bed, it needs to be especially strong. A single-skin wall is unsuitable, although two skins of stretcher bond can be tied together using wall ties (see p.81). You can reinforce the wall by sinking steel bars into the footings and building a skin on each side of them. You will need a waterproof membrane to protect a retaining wall from water and frost damage. Build drainage channels or pipes into the wall above the second course of mortar to allow excess moisture to escape. Plastic or copper pipes are ideal. Either drill holes in the bricks to house the pipes, or position the pipes in mortar joints. Fill behind the wall with gravel to aid drainage.

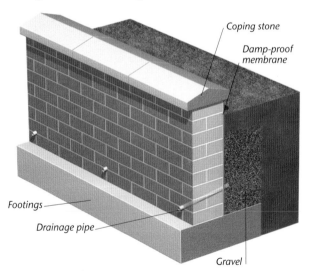

Coping stone

Damp-proof membrane

Footings

Drainage pipe

Gravel

RETAINING WALL

TOOLS AND MATERIALS CHECKLIST PP.410–412

Building a wall (pp.410–411) Pegs, strings, profile boards, bricks, mortar, brick trowel, level, gauging rod, pins, brick jointer

brick trowel, mortar, bricks, gauging rod

Turning a stretcher bond corner (p.412) Pegs, strings, profile boards, A square, level,

FOR BASIC TOOLKIT
SEE PP.24–25

BUILDING A WALL

Lay the footings for the wall and allow them to dry for a few days before starting to build (see p.409). Use a single-skin stretcher bond to hone your basic bricklaying technique. Laying walls with different bonds is simply a case of modifying the pattern in which you lay the bricks (see p.408). The technique here shows racking, which involves building up the ends of the wall, like a flight of steps, and filling in the central area. Getting the first course of brickwork in the right position is essential. Keep checking it using your profile boards and a level.

TOOLS AND MATERIALS SEE BASIC TOOLKIT AND P.409

1 LAYING THE FIRST BRICKS

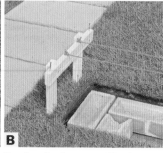

A Attach lines to the nails on your profile boards to provide a guide for the first course of bricks.

B Dry-lay the first row of bricks allowing for mortar joints of ½ in (10 mm). Cut half-bricks to maintain the bond (see p.81 for cutting bricks).

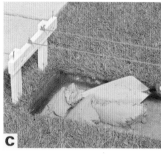

C Mix up some mortar (see p.71) and lay a bed just over ½ in (10 mm) deep for the first three bricks at the start of the first course.

D Use the point of the trowel to make some furrows in the mortar along its central line.

E Lay the first brick, applying a little pressure to bed it into the mortar. Use a level to check its alignment with the string lines above. In this example, simple piers are being constructed at each end of the wall. More complex pier designs are shown on p.413.

2 COMPLETING THE COURSE

A Butter the end of the next brick and position it next to the first on the bed of mortar.

B Lay a level across the top of the bricks to check that they are level. Apply more pressure to the top of the bricks where required in order to get them level.

C Cut away excess mortar from around the brick bases, and remove excess mortar from the vertical joints. Check and recheck their position, using the level across the top.

D Continue along the course, positioning two or three bricks at a time and then cleaning the joints. Remove the profile boards and lines when the course is complete.

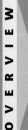

3 RACKING THE ENDS

Start building the pier and the end of the wall by three more courses. This is the best practice and will make it easier to fill in the rest of the bricks later. Use a level to check that the pier is plumb and level.

A

B

Use your gauging rod (see p.408) to keep the mortar joints even.

C

Add two more courses so you have a series of stepped bricks leading up to the top of the pier. Keep checking levels using the gauging rod and level.

4 INFILLING THE COURSES

A

Repeat the racking procedure at the other end of the wall. Use a level as shown to check bond and levels.

B

Drive line pins into the mortar joint above the first course of bricks at each end. Tie a line between them. Use this as a guide to fill in bricks for the second course.

C

Fill in all the way to the top if the wall is to extend no higher than you have racked. Otherwise, rack back each end once you have filled in two or three courses.

D

Lay the top course of the wall indented-side down. Alternatively, you can lay other types of coping to finish the top of the wall (see p.407).

5 POINTING THE JOINTS

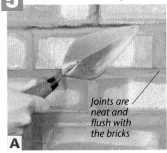

Joints are neat and flush with the bricks

A

Fill any areas of missing mortar in the wall. Let the mortar begin to cure, but do not let it harden too much. How long this takes will vary, so start checking after one hour, less in hot weather.

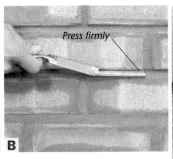

Press firmly

B

When the mortar is firm, clean the joints. A brick jointer (shown here) can be used to create a V-shaped profile.

Helps shed water

C

Garden wall joints can be pointed in a number of other ways. Here, weatherstruck joints are created by using a pointing trowel to angle the mortar joint so that it is recessed at the top and flush with the brick at the bottom. This helps the wall shed water.

Once you have mastered the basic technique for laying bricks to form a low, straight wall (see pp.408–411), you can tackle more demanding projects. Shown opposite are more complex designs for piers, and the techniques required to build walls from materials other than brick. Other types of corners are shown below. When building any corner, it is essential that a "square" guide line for the corner is established (see right). The technique shown here is for building a single-skin stretcher bond wall with a corner.

A SQUARE

In order to turn a corner at precisely 90 degrees, an A square is required. This is basically a large carpenter's square (see p.45). You can make a large square by nailing pieces of furring strip together into a triangle that has sides in a ratio of 3:4:5. The square shown below is lightweight and can be folded for easy storage.

CORNERS AND PIERS

These more complex structures are based on the techniques shown on pp.408–411. See p.408 for information on the different types of bond.

Corners

When turning a corner with a wall, ensure the turn is at the correct angle—usually 90 degrees—and that the bond is correctly maintained so that the wall does not lose strength. In both English and Flemish bond walls you need queen closers (bricks cut in half lengthwise) to maintain the bond around a corner. See p.39 for information on how to cut bricks. Apart from the different bond, the preparation, the techniques for laying the bricks themselves, and the racking up each end then filling in, are the same as for a stretcher bond wall, see pp.410–411.

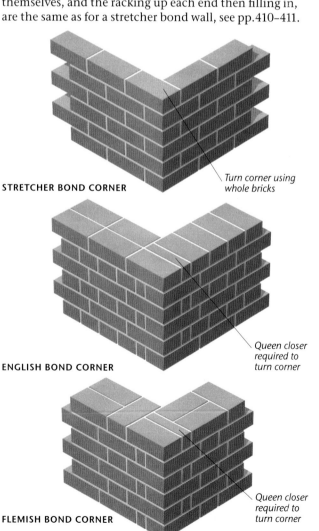

STRETCHER BOND CORNER

Turn corner using whole bricks

ENGLISH BOND CORNER

Queen closer required to turn corner

FLEMISH BOND CORNER

Queen closer required to turn corner

TURNING A STRETCHER BOND CORNER

A **Having laid out** the footings, mark out the corner accurately using four profile boards and an A square.

B **Lay a bed of** mortar and position three stretchers along what will be the front edge of one wall. Use the string lines as guides.

C **Continue** to lay bricks from the corner to create the first course of the adjacent wall.

D **Lay the second** row of bricks with the first brick overlapping the corner of the first row to maintain the bond.

E **As you build up** further rows, check that the mortar courses are even with a gauging rod.

F **Rack up the corner** as shown for building a brick wall (see pp.410–411).

G **Fill in the** rows of bricks as for a straight brick wall. If you are using indented bricks, remember to turn the top course indented-side down. Point the joints as for a straight wall (see p.411).

Piers

A pier is an isolated column of masonry used to carry weight and to increase the lateral strength of a wall. Consult a registered architect, engineer, or code official to help with your design.

Concrete fills center

END AND CENTRAL PIERS ON STRETCHER BOND WALLS

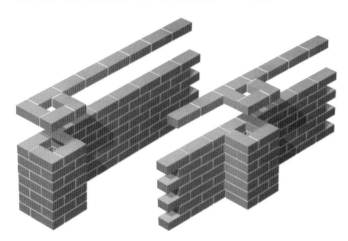

OFFSET END PIER AND CENTRAL OFFSET PIER ON STRETCHER BOND WALLS

BUILDING OTHER TYPES OF WALLS

Bricks are not the only material used in garden-wall construction, and there are variations in technique required for different types of wall. As well as the three types of wall construction discussed here, different walling materials can be mixed in a design. A wall can be built from lumber and walls can also be combined with fences.

Screen walls

Available as a kit, screen walls are laid on the same foundations as a brick wall. The main difference in laying technique is that the blocks tend to be laid in a stack bond. In other words, joints between blocks are not staggered. Steel reinforced pillars, called piers, are an integral part of their structure. Expanded steel mesh is used between courses to strengthen the construction. Pier caps and coping stones then protect the wall structure.

Wall blocks and natural stone

A wide range of exterior wall blocks are available, often designed to mimic expensive natural stone. Blocks of differing size can be married together to form a random pattern. The challenge is to maintain a vertical line, even

MAKING A SCREEN WALL

The stack bond design of a screen wall is very weak. You must use the mesh reinforcement supplied between each course of screen blocks, and the reinforced piers that the blocks slot into. Ensure that the blocks are laid level, using the same techniques as for any wall structure. Make sure you take time to position the pier blocks accurately before you fill in with the screen. They will help to align each course correctly.

Build the piers using the specially designed blocks. Fill in with screen blocks. Use the strips of mesh reinforcement between the courses.

Finish the wall with coping stones and pier caps. Make sure they are precisely level.

though the block surface is irregular. Levels can only be used when laying single blocks because there are no defined courses.

Natural-stone walls are more challenging to build than brick walls. Stone heights vary, as do the roughness of their facing side, and their depth. No stone will be the same size as another. Producing a level wall with consistent mortar joints and pointing them requires practice.

Wall features

Statues, alcoves, and arches can be used to provide interest in an otherwise simple wall. Statues of any size should always have a mortar base when positioned on a wall or patio, or a concrete foundation should be dug out of bare earth. Alcoves must have support above them. Their size will dictate what is required, so seek professional advice. Arches are popular features in gardens. You will need to build a plywood form to support an arch while it is being built (see below).

Building an arch
The arch is built using a plywood form. The form is supported by lengths of lumber. Once dry, the form is removed and joints pointed.

Just as walls require sound foundations for construction, surfaces such as patios, paths, and driveways also require a firm base. Foundation depth and type is not only dependent on whether the area will be used only for walking on, or whether cars will be driving or parking on it, but also local frost conditions, which can change foundation requirements from 4 in (10 cm) to 24 in (61 cm). Other considerations include the need for adequate drainage, so that water is channeled away from the surface, and away from any walls and the house (see opposite). Check local requirements.

UTILITY COVERS

Never seal over any utility covers or other access points to underground services with any kind of hard landscaping. Either build around them or, if they are set very low, create an easily removable and well-marked panel in the surface above, or raise the cover itself on a course of bricks. Engineering bricks (see p.82) are ideal for building up the level of a utility cover because of their strength.

DESIGNING PATHS AND PATIOS

You may already have a clear idea of where you want a path to lead or a patio to be situated, but take time to consider your options. As well as taking into account the hard landscaping itself, think about how the layout and materials fit in with the overall design and style of your house and garden. If your garden has an informal style, consider including some areas for planting, and staggering paving materials to soften straight lines. For a more formal area, choose geometric shapes to carry on the theme.

Patios

Privacy is a key concern when planning a patio, because both you and your neighbors will probably prefer not to be overlooked. The exposure of a seating area is also important—a south- or west-facing area receives the most sun during the day and early evening.

Paths

You can use garden paths to lead the eye to a focal point and to create interest, or they can be purely for access. Your choice will influence your design—a decorative path might take a winding route, while an access route is more likely to follow a straight line. You can use a single material to create paths, or mix different surfaces (see below, right). Consider laying slabs or pavers in different patterns— a few are illustrated on the right.

Edging

Hard-landscaped areas are generally designed with some form of edging. If you are making a gravel path, or using slabs or pavers laid dry on a sand bed, the edging will help prevent any lateral movement of the surface. Even if the slabs or pavers are bedded into mortar, an edge of some type provides the neatest finish. If a hard-landscaped area abuts a lawn, the edging should be lower than the lawn, so that you can mow over it. Treated lumber can be used, or edging blocks bedded into a mortar strip (see p.406). Treated lumber is the most straightforward to work with, does not require mortar, and provides instant guidelines for leveling across a site (see p.416).

DAMP-PROOF COURSES

The top of an area of hard landscaping that abuts the house must be at least 4 in (10 cm) below the siding as there is wood behind the siding that may rot if water flowed horizontally to the siding. Any higher and splashes from falling rain can bridge the course and cause water problems inside.

LAYING PAVERS AND SLABS

The pattern chosen for laying slabs or pavers is very much a personal choice. Manufacturers often provide good displays or brochures showing the various options. Some simple types of paver and slab design are shown below. Also remember that bricks (see p.82–83) can be used for paving. You can also buy cut or curved slabs to create alternative designs (see bottom right). Cutting such a curve yourself is practically impossible. Don't forget that you can also pave areas with any combination of pavers, slabs, gravel, and cobbles.

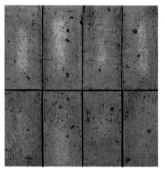

STACK BOND PAVERS

HERRINGBONE PAVERS

BRICKBOND PAVERS

BASKETWEAVE PAVERS

COMBINED PAVERS AND SLABS

CURVED SLABS AND COBBLES

DRAINAGE

You will need drainage around the edge of large hard-landscaped areas. Standing water near the house may soak into walls and cause mildew. Water on a paved surface can lead to the growth of algae and vegetation, making it slippery and dangerous—a problem for paving laid on a concrete slab, or if mortar has been used. If pavers have been bedded onto sand, some water will drain down through joints and into the subsoil below. Always lay paths and patios with a very slight slope running away from adjacent walls (see below).

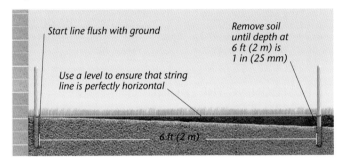

Start line flush with ground

Remove soil until depth at 6 ft (2 m) is 1 in (25 mm)

Use a level to ensure that string line is perfectly horizontal

6 ft (2 m)

Establishing a slope
Over a small area, you can establish a slope to aid drainage by reducing the amount of mortar or sand under slabs or pavers as you move away from the house. For larger areas of hard landscaping, establish the correct slope in the foundations. A slope of 1 in (25 mm) in 6 ft (2 m) is sufficient.

PLANNING FOUNDATIONS

Paths and paved areas that will take the weight of vehicles will need more extensive foundations than those used only by people. When planning a major project like a new driveway, seek professional advice about the foundations.

Slabs

If you are laying slabs for a path or patio that will not be driven on, they can be laid directly on a compacted subsoil base. If the base has been recently disturbed by excavation work—for example, if an extension has been recently built—lay a crushed stone base on the compacted soil. The slabs may then be dry laid onto a sand layer or laid on mortar. The excavation depth will vary. Ideally, crushed stone should be 4 in (100 mm) deep. Slabs can also be laid on an old concrete surface without any excavation.

Pavers

Foundation requirements for pavers are similar to those of slabs for paths and patios. However, for driveways and parking areas, pavers do not need a concrete base. They can be laid on compacted crushed stone covered with sand.

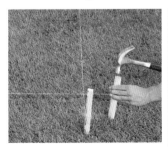

Square paths and patios
Use strings and pegs to lay out an area for a square patio area (see following pages).

Planning a path
For straight guide lines, use string and pegs. A garden hose is ideal for planning curves in a design.

LAYING A CONCRETE PAD

A

Level pegs around the site to the depth of the concrete pad plus foundations recommended by your local code department. Nail boards into the pegs. Insert further level pegs and boards to divide the slab into manageable strips. This wooden frame is known as the formwork.

B

Lay a 4-in (100-mm) layer of crushed stone in the bottom of all the formwork and compact with a roller or rented vibrator compactor.

C

Slide screed board across the formwork

Pour foundation concrete (see p.409) into the first section. Use a screed board in a chopping motion to compact it, then level the surface.

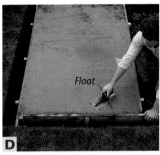

D

Float

Use a float to smooth the surface of the concrete. For large areas, consider renting a power float or screed (see p.29).

E

Cover the pad with a plastic sheet to protect it from the weather. You can remove the formwork once the concrete has hardened.

TOOLS AND MATERIALS CHECKLIST PP.416–419

Laying a patio p.416–417
Mallet, pegs, string, A square, spade, edging boards, level, wheelbarrow, crushed stone, plate compactor, slabs, angle grinder, sand, mortar, rubber mallet, furring strip offcuts, brick trowel, brick jointer, paintbrush

Laying a paver path p.418
Pegs, string, spade, wooden mallet, edging boards, sand, batten, block splitter*, lump hammer, bolster chisel, blocks, rubber mallet, level, compactor, brush

Creating a gravel path p.419
Edging boards, pegs, rubber mallet, level, weedproof membrane, shovel, crushed stone, rammer, gravel, rake

Making steps p.419 Pegs, post, string, spade, crushed stone, brick trowel, mortar, bricks, slabs, level

* = optional

FOR BASIC TOOLKIT SEE PP.24–25

LAYING A PATIO

Laying a patio requires considerable planning. The foundation required will depend on its intended use (see p.415). Before calculating the exact area that needs to be excavated, think about the paving design and how to minimize cutting stone. Decide whether to lay stones butted directly up against each other or with pointing (shown here). You may need to allow space for an edging material. In this example, treated lumber is being used. You will need two people to maneuver large slabs into place.

TOOLS AND MATERIALS SEE BASIC TOOLKIT AND P.415

1 SETTING OUT

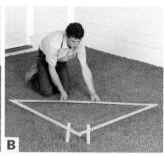

A **Layout the patio** using whole pavers to reduce cutting. Drive pegs and tie string between them. Use the house as the initial guide line for the height of the patio.

B **Use an A square** (see p.412) to ensure that the area has 90-degree corners. Adjust pegs and lines if necessary.

2 EXCAVATING FOR FOUNDATIONS

A **Mark the edge** of the area with a spade, cutting down into the grass. Once the patio is marked out, remove the string lines.

B **Dig down to** the required depth. Include slab depth, crushed stone, and mortar base in your calculations (see p.415). The patio surface should be higher than the surrounding grass.

3 POSITIONING THE EDGING

A **Cut treated lumber** edging to the same depth as the excavations for the patio. Lay it in position around the edge and check that it is square.

B **Adjust the lumber** so that the patio slopes away from the house at a gradient of 1:50, using a gradient level or the peg method shown on p.415.

4 LAYING THE CRUSHED STONE BASE

Knock pegs into ground at 3-ft (1-m) intervals along the outside of the edging. Nail through the face of the edging lumber into the pegs to hold the edging in an upright position.

A

B **Run string lines** from pegs on one side to those opposite. Measure down from various points along the string line to the excavation base to check depth and gradient.

C **Distribute crushed stone** across the floor of the excavation to an approximate depth of 4 in (100 mm). Rake it level.

Compact the crushed stone using a rented plate compactor. Attach the string lines and measure to check the level of compacted stone across the site. Add and compact more stone where required to give a reasonably smooth surface that slopes very slightly away from the house.

D

5 PLANNING THE SLAB LAYOUT

A

B

Dry lay the slabs, starting from a corner and working down the edges for a straight design. Remember to allow for mortar joints. Here a brickbond pattern is being laid.

Cut any slabs necessary for the design using a stone saw or angle grinder (see p.61). Dry lay them to check you have a good fit.

6 MORTARING THE SLABS IN PLACE

A

Tap the slab with a rubber mallet to bed it in place

B

C

Scrape away some mortar if a slab sits proud of the others

D

Lay a bed of mortar for the first slab ¾ –1¼ in (20–30 mm) deep. In many areas of Canada mortar is not used because of frost shifting. See p.418 for working without mortar.

Insert spacers made from offcuts between slab and edging to keep pointing consistent. Lay the second slab. Insert spacers between the first and second slab.

Continue laying slabs according to your design. Lay a level across the slabs to check the position, and maintain the slope away from the house.

Lay the rest of the slabs, adjusting the amount of mortar where necessary to maintain an even surface.

7 FINISHING THE PATIO

Once the patio is complete, it should not be walked on for at least 24 hours while the mortar sets. If rain or frost is forecast, cover the area with plastic sheeting held down with spare slabs or bricks. Once the base mortar has set, press more mortar into the joints between slabs using a pointing trowel. Remove excess mortar from the slab surfaces as you progress.

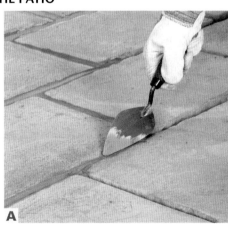

A

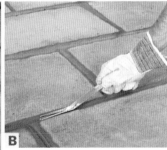

B

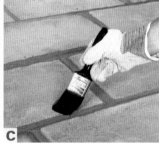

C

Smooth the mortar along the joints using a brick jointer, or leave flush according to personal preference. Flush joints will drain better.

Clean the pointing mortar with a clean paintbrush.

CREATING PATHS AND STEPS

Sand-filled, or mortarless paths are more forgiving in heavy frost areas and can be easily repaired when things shift. This page shows a minimum installation, but colder regions may need 4 to 8 in (10 to 20 cm) of compacted, crushed stone below what is shown here. Check with your local municipality. Remember to establish a gradient away from the house. If you have a lot of pavers to cut, rent a wet saw, angle grinder, or block splitter before you start. This makes the job much quicker.

TOOLS AND MATERIALS SEE BASIC TOOLKIT AND P.415

Compact the soil with a rammer. Pour sharp sand into the excavated area and use a wooden furring strip notched out at each end to level off the sand surface to the depth required for the pavers.

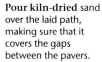
Check boards on both sides are level

C

1 PREPARING TO LAY A PAVER PATH

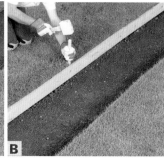

A

B

Lay out pegs and string lines along the edges of the path. Dig out the path area to a depth of paver height plus a 2-in (5-cm) sand bed.

Put treated wood edging into the excavated area. Drive in wooden pegs on the external side of the board to keep it in place.

2 CUTTING PAVER BLOCKS

A

B

Position the paver between the jaws of the block splitter. Align the point you wish to cut.

Lower the handle of the splitter to break the paver in two.

3 LAYING A PAVER PATH

A

B

C

Lay blocks in your chosen design. Butt each end up against the next.

Use a rubber mallet to bed blocks into place. Infill cut blocks to finish the design.

Lay a level across the pavers as you finish a row to check that it sits level. If the pavers are uneven, remove them and relevel the sand.

Pour kiln-dried sand over the laid path, making sure that it covers the gaps between the pavers.

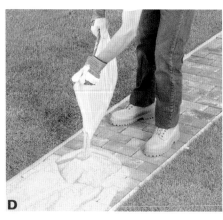

D

E

F

Go over the surface once again with a brush once you are finished with the compactor. Brush sand into the spaces between the pavers.

Drive the pegs below the grass to start and leave them in place.

CREATING A GRAVEL PATH

Excavate your path area to a depth of at least 4 in (10 cm), then lay treated wood edging boards held in place with wooden pegs. Use a level to check that both sides of the path are level. If not, bed the edging boards down with a rubber mallet.

A

B Screw the edging boards to the pegs with a drill-driver.

Trim with a utility knife

C Lay the weedproof membrane on the soil base. Overlap seams in the fabric by at least 4 in (10 cm).

D Shovel in crushed stone over the membrane surface. Distribute it as evenly as possible, making a layer of about 2 in (5 cm).

E Rake the crushed stone level before using a rammer to compact it. Use a roller if you have one.

F Pour the gravel into the path area. Be careful not to injure yourself when lifting heavy bags.

G Rake the gravel level. Once the path has settled for a few weeks, it may be necessary to add some more gravel to top off the level.

MAKING STEPS

Calculate the number of steps by dividing the height of the slope by that of one riser (one riser equals 4–8 in; total rise should be 17–18 in). To measure slope height, place a peg at the top of the slope and a post at the bottom. Tie string between the two so that it is level with top of the slope; measure the distance between the string and ground level.

A

B Use string and pegs to mark the sides of the steps and along the fronts of the treads. Dig out the steps and compact the soil for each tread.

C Make a footing 6 in (15 cm) deep and twice the brick width; fill with concrete over a 4-in (100-mm) base of crushed stone.

D Lay bricks for the first riser on the set concrete footing; use string to check that the bricks are level (see bricklaying technique, p.410–411).

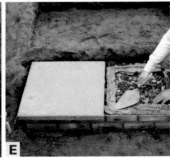

E Fill risers with crushed stone to the height of the bricks. Set stones on ½ in (10 mm) of mortar. Leave a small gap between them.

F Mark the position of the second riser on the stones; mortar bricks in place. Fill in and set treads. Mortar between the stones as you lay them.

FROST AND CLAY SOIL

In areas of very deep frost and clay soil, these steps will not last. You will need a concrete base with pillars supporting it to below the frost depth in your particular area. Modern houses hang precast steps from the foundation wall with brackets and they do not touch the soil.

Wooden structures

AS WELL AS FEATURING IN THE HARD LANDSCAPING OF MANY GARDENS, WOODEN STRUCTURES ARE ALSO COMMONLY USED TO CREATE FENCES AS WELL AS DECORATIVE FEATURES IN THE GARDEN. ALL WOOD MUST BE TREATED IF IT IS IN CONTACT WITH THE GROUND (SEE P.75). WOODEN STRUCTURES CAN ALSO BE STAINED, VARNISHED, OR PAINTED (SEE PP.294–295).

WOODEN GARDEN MATERIALS

Wood can be used to build garden structures such as fences, features, or decking. Wooden structures can be combined with masonry or metal components for decorative effect, extra strength, or ease of construction. Kits are often available for you to construct fences or other projects, or you can use ready-made components such as sawn wood, posts, and brackets to create your own design using basic woodworking joints (see pp.396–397).

FENCE CONSIDERATIONS
Most fences need a gate. These are usually hung between two fence posts. Some open fences, such as split-rail designs (see below) can be given a mesh backing if you need a barrier for animals.

FENCE TYPES
There are several traditional designs of fence often used as boundaries or screens within a garden design. Some have panels or boards placed between posts to form a solid boundary, while other designs are more open, being simply constructed of vertical and horizontal members. When choosing a fence, consider how well it will fit with the style of house and garden, and what level of security and privacy you require.

Close-board
A solid fence built from separate components, easily adapted to your specifications. Overlapping vertical wooden slats are attached to horizontal rails (arris rails) running between fence posts.

Picket
Similar in construction to a close-board fence, this decorative, partially see-through fence has gaps between the uprights. The uprights may be rounded or pointed for decorative effect.

Split rail
A simple, open design. Horizontal members run between posts. Wire mesh can be used across the framework to provide a less penetrable barrier if necessary. The mesh is attached to the posts and rails using staples (see p.79).

FENCE POSTS

The type of fence post you use will partly be determined by the type of fence you are constructing. In domestic gardens, wood is the most common material used, although metal and plastic posts are also an option.

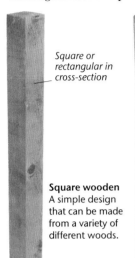

Square or rectangular in cross-section

Round wooden
Can be used to provide a more rustic appearance than a sawn, square post. Often used with half-round horizontal members in a split-rail fence.

Square wooden
A simple design that can be made from a variety of different woods.

Metal posts
These are good choices for chain-link and plastic fences. Make sure you use standard sizing in order to avoid the laborious process of having to cut the metal posts.

FENCE ACCESSORIES

There are a number of fence accessories that are used to aid installing and help repair these structures. The brackets and clips shown below provide a few examples of the types of systems that are available.

GOTHIC STYLE PLASTIC POST CAP

WOODEN POST CAP

Post caps
Decorative caps attached to the top of wooden posts. Also prevents water penetration into the end grain of the posts.

Post clip
Small clip that screws to post and fence panel, holding the panel in place.

Bolt-down post bracket
Socket that houses a post on concrete or other masonry surfaces.

SQUARE PLASTIC POST CAP

PUTTING IN POSTS

A

B

Excavate a hole for each post, approximately 24 in (60 cm) square and below the frost line to allow for infill around it.

Pack crushed stone into the base of the post hole.

C

Fast-setting concrete should be poured into the base of the hole as a footing about 4 in (10 cm) deep and allowed to cure for 24 hours before installing the post and filling in the hole with dirt. For deep holes, rent a post-hole digger.

FURTHER INFORMATION

Always contact your local building official and homeowner's association prior to building any outdoor structure. There are guidelines and regulations on a variety of issues ranging from material to depth of post holes.

WOODEN WALKWAYS AND DECKS

Wood is also used underfoot in yard construction for paths and steps, and patio areas. Decking has become increasingly popular as an alternative to hard-landscaped areas.

Cedar decking
Durable and versatile, cedar decking has a color range from light browns and tans to salmon pink. It does not transfer heat, so you can walk barefoot no matter the temperature.

Pressure-treated decking
Primarily due to cost, pressure-treated is the most popular choice of deck materials in Canada. It usually has a warranty against decay. Do not put aluminum hardware or siding in contact with pressure-treated wood.

Composite decking
Composite decking is made up of a combination of wood particles and plastic. It can be embossed with a wood-grain pattern. Typically the color will lighten over time. Consider buying one that contains preservatives.

Vinyl decking
If you live in a hot climate, vinyl can get very hot underfoot. It is more expensive than wood, but requires less maintenance. Cutting vinyl is just as easy as cutting wood. tt does not absorb stains.

ERECTING A FENCE

To lay out a fence, secure a string line with pegs at the starting and finishing point of each straight run of fence. If you are using manufactured panels, it is best to plan the length of the fence so you can use whole ones. With other types of fences, it is easier to adjust the design to your specifications. Once you have marked positions it is a case of installing posts to the required depth and filling in the fence.

PLANNING THE FENCE

Once you have marked the run of the fence with a string line, you need to work out the post spacing. The distance between posts will vary according to fence type. For a panel fence, the distance is governed by panel size, which is commonly 8 ft (2.5 m). A similar distance may be used for close-board fences, although this can be adjusted depending on the type of boarding used. Fence posts can be set in concrete, held in place by steel brackets, straps, or post anchors on a concrete surface, or with pressure-treated wood, simply buried in the ground with a concrete footing (see p.421).

Securing posts

Once the post positions have been marked out, the next step is to dig post holes. With deep post holes, rocky soil can change your plans. Always dig the holes in consecutive order, so if you have to move a post because you cannot move a rock, you can move it closer and then shift all the following holes to keep most sections at the planned distance, probably 8 ft (2.4 m) apart. You will need a 4-in (10-cm) concrete footing in the bottom and then either concrete to fill the hole or dirt around a pressure-treated post.

■ ERECTING A PANEL FENCE

Fence panels can be nailed into place, but brackets give a neater finish. You need to make sure that the bottoms of the panels don't touch the ground—they must never sit in standing water. You can use gravel boards below the panels (as shown for the close-board fence, right). Alternatively, as shown here, install fence panels so that they are slightly above ground level.

Screw clips to post, one at the top, one in the middle, and one at the bottom of the post.

Slot the edge of the panel into the clips and secure it in place.

POST HOLES

How deep should a post hole be? To keep the structure from blowing over or shifting with frost, posts should have at least one-third of their total length in the ground, or be at least 1 ft (30 cm) below local frost depths, whichever is deeper.
How wide should the hole be? Dirt-filled holes should be dug twice the diameter of the post. Concrete-filled holes should be dug three times the diameter of the post.

ANATOMY OF A DECK

The deck frame shown below is cantilever beam deck. A very stable construction, it is fixed to the house with a ledger board and joist hangers and is supported by a posts and beam. The cantilever beam deck is a good design for tall decks.

The first step to installing a deck is getting a building permit following all procedures. This is important so that the deck is built safely.

Next, joists must be the proper size, which is often 2 x 8 in (50 x 200 mm) or 2 x 10 in (50 x 250 mm). Checking span charts to see how far a joist can span will help determine the joists selected. Most deck joists are spaced 16 in (400 mm) on center. Some modern decking materials require spacing at 12 in (300 mm) on center in certain installations.

The beam in a cantilever beam deck carries the joists and is always a double thickness of no less than 2 x 10 in (50 x 250 mm). Deck joists should cantilever 2 ft (600 mm) past the beam.

Posts are usually 6 x 6 in (150 x 150 mm). They can be set in the ground in concrete. The depth they must be set is based on local soil, and seismic and frost conditions. A building official can tell you the rules in your area. Posts can also be set on concrete piers using a post anchor to make the connection. Posts are usually set at 6 ft (1.8 m) on center.

All lumber and hardware on a deck frame must be rated for decking applications. Check with your supplier. The lumber is usually pressure-treated pine, while fasteners and hangers are double hot-dipped galvanized or stainless steel.

The ledger board must be installed so that no water leaks into your house. This is vital for the safety of the deck and those who will enjoy it. Before installing the ledger, remove the house siding in the ledger location. Seal the house with a self-adhesive rubber membrane then tuck copper flashing up under the siding, then over the ledger, to shed water. Fasten the ledger board with the appropriate lag screws.

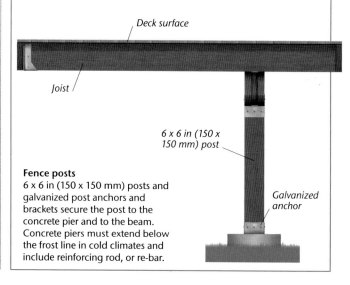

Deck surface

Joist

6 x 6 in (150 x 150 mm) post

Galvanized anchor

Fence posts
6 x 6 in (150 x 150 mm) posts and galvanized post anchors and brackets secure the post to the concrete pier and to the beam. Concrete piers must extend below the frost line in cold climates and include reinforcing rod, or re-bar.

Decks provide an attractive outdoor entertaining area that's perfect for grilling and dining. It can also be used to cover up an old concrete patio. Decking is quicker to install than paving and can be easily adjusted to almost any size and situation. Installing a deck is easier with some help. Ensure that your chosen design follows any homeowner association rules for your neighborhood. Typically you will be required to submit plans of the proposed deck for review by an official (see right).

DECKING REGULATIONS

Check with your building code office before constructing a deck. Regulations regarding steps and railings are similar to those for staircases (see pp.186–191). If you are building a large or very high deck, get professional advice on footing and lumber specifications.

FOUNDATIONS

Generally, the higher the decking is off the ground, the deeper the foundations need to be. For ground-level decking, you will still need to go below the frost line.

Ground-level decking

Ground level decks require posts set into the ground to prevent slippage, movement, or sinking from forces like erosion and to accommodate slightly un-even terrain. Set posts in all four corners of your deck and according to local rules.

Raised decking

Post holes should be at least 24 in (600 mm) deep, and must extend below the frost line. On a concrete surface, use bolt-down post anchors (see box opposite). When building a large deck, or one raised by more than 24 in (600 mm), get professional advice on lumber and footing specifications.

BUYING LUMBER

Lumber for decking that contacts the ground must be pressure-treated and any cut ends must be treated with preservative. Plan the support layout on paper so that you can work out how much lumber you need to buy.

ADAPTING DECK DESIGN

Deck shape can be easily adjusted to any requirement with minimal woodworking skills. The decking boards themselves can be straight, run diagonally, or you can create more complex chevron or square designs. Trim edges with a power saw to create curves (see below). You may need to use double joists to enable you to fix more complex designs.

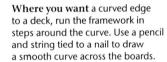

Where you want a curved edge to a deck, run the framework in steps around the curve. Use a pencil and string tied to a nail to draw a smooth curve across the boards.

Use a jigsaw to cut around the edges of the boards. Treat the cut ends with preservative.

Newel posts need to be at least 36 in (900 mm) high and support the balustrade at least every 6 ft (1.2 m)

The same regulations apply to decking steps as for stairs (see p.188)

Railings are mandatory if the deck is over 20 in (500 mm) off the ground

Decking with rails and steps

Even small-scale decks such as that shown left are governed by regulations. Check with your building inspector that you have sufficient supports for the size of deck.

TOOLS AND MATERIALS CHECKLIST
PP.422–425

Erecting a fence panel (pp.422)
Fence panels, fence brackets

Adapting deck design (pp.423)
String line, jigsaw, wood preservative

Laying raised decking (pp.424–425)
Decking boards and screws, wood preservative

FOR BASIC TOOLKIT SEE PP.24–25

LAYING RAISED DECKING

The frame for raised decking is constructed from pressure-treated lumber. On a concrete base, posts can be secured to the ground using bolt-down post brackets; on soft ground, some excavation work is required to bed the posts securely on a solid foundation. Take time to remove vegetation and put down a membrane and gravel beneath a deck on soft ground, as for a gravel path (see p.419). A raised deck requires a handrail.

TOOLS AND MATERIALS SEE BASIC TOOLKIT AND P.423

DECK LAYOUT

Decking boards are usually run parallel to the house, across joists. While this is a fairly standard approach, there are other custom options for running boards. Shown here, the composite boards are mitered at the end, creating a square pattern on the deck.

MITERED CORNERS

DECKING

Decks can dramatically change the appearance of your backyard, creating an "outdoor room" that's a perfect place for barbecues and a safe outside place for toddlers to play. Not only do you need to select the structural materials, and the decking type, there are post options and caps that can add style and personalize your deck. From natural wood options to synthetic materials, there is a type of decking that will complement your home's design.

DECKING MATERIAL

Decking material	Weathering and maintenance
Cedar	Seal every two years. Use a cedar decking cleaning product or restorer. Hose down. Do not pressure-wash.
Pressure treated	Can warp, spilt, and splinter over time. Pressure-wash or hose down. Seal every two years.
Composite	Weathers to a lighter tone. Requires no annual sealing. Pressure-wash or hose down. Composite deck-cleaning products are available.
Hollow vinyl	Resists cracking and fading. Requires no annual sealing. Needs a monthly hose-down.

Rails

Railing material is offered in as many types of materials as decking boards. Most often, railing material is chosen to match the decking boards, although mixing materials is an opportunity to showcase a unique design—wooden boards and polyurethane balusters have been combined here. When selecting material for rails, make sure to plan for enough pieces and parts so your deck follows your local codes. In most areas, the local codes for railings and stairs follow the same criteria as interior railings and stairs (see pp.186–191).

MIXING WOOD SPECIES

SYNTHETIC DECK SEALERS

Choosing a product to seal your wood deck is not as easy as you may think. Some deck sealers contain natural oils that are food for mildew and algae, and even good deck sealers may not be able to penetrate your wood deck if you have used a bleach product or a deck cleaning product that contains bleach. When you are selecting a sealer, make sure you use a heavy-duty synthetic deck sealer that is water-repellent, and not just an exterior wood sealer. Before using any sealer or cleaner on your deck, test a small portion of the material to see how it reacts to the product.

DECK IDEAS

Mixing wood species can create a striking deck design. Combining light and dark woods gives you the opportunity to create patterns and accents. Deck accessories are another great way to match your chosen decking material to the furnishings on your deck. You can use extra material after you've finished the deck building project to build benches and flower boxes, for example.

1 ATTACHING THE BOARDS

Allow the foundation concrete to cure. Place a board along the edge of the deck, farthest from the wall, perpendicular to the joists. Make it flush with the frame edge. Screw down the board with two decking screws at each joist. You may wish to use pilot holes to prevent boards from splitting as you drive the screws in.

A

B

Put a screw into each joist at the edge of each board. Then screw the next board in place. Continue laying boards across the frame.

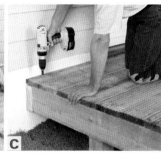

C

Scribe and cut a final board to fit (see pp.72–73 for scribing). Then screw it in place as before.

2 ATTACHING THE HANDRAIL AND STEPS

Rabbet

A

Cut a rabbet in the base of the newel post to a depth of 1 in (25 mm).

B

Drill two holes through the rabbeted section of the post and the frame beneath. Screw the post to the frame using nuts and bolts. Repeat with the other newel posts.

C

Cut the handrail to size, then screw it to the post with wood screws. Use a level to check that it is level.

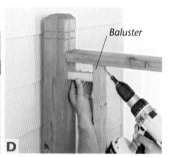

Baluster

D

Cut a piece of wood to the length required between balusters (not more than 4 in/100 mm). Use this to position the first baluster. Screw the baluster to the handrail.

E

Use your piece of cut wood to space the bottom of the baluster. Then attach the baluster to the frame of the deck. Continue attaching balusters around the deck.

F

Fix the side supports (stringers) of the steps to the edge of your frame. Step kits can be bought specially made for decks, or you can make your own.

G

Add trimmed decking boards to form the treads of the steps. Remember to treat all cut ends with preservative. On soft ground you may wish to bed paving slabs on gravel under the bottom of the steps. For stairs with three or more risers, you must use a post and railing.

DECKING FASTENERS FOR LUMBER

Fasteners must be appropriate to the outside weathering conditions, and appropriate for pressure treated lumber. When selecting fasteners, choose screws made of, or coated in, suitable materials—your best bets are double-hot-dipped galvanized, or stainless steel screws.

If you don't like the look of screws on your deck, there's an alternative. Deck boards can also be installed with hidden fasteners. The boards are secured side-by-side with biscuit joints. These are small discs made of polypropylene designed to fit between two slots cut by a biscuit joiner and glued into place. The joint allows the material to expand and contract through changing weather.

Keep in mind that there are a variety of pressure treated materials and products suitable for ground contact. Select the materials and fasteners that work well together, so that you are able to enjoy a safe and well-built deck.

REPLACING A BROKEN STONE

Stones can become unstable, or may crack due to poor laying technique, frost, or a material problem. In whichever case, the stone needs to be lifted and relaid. Laying stones on a bed of sand is a more straightforward procedure than shown here, where they have been laid on mortar.

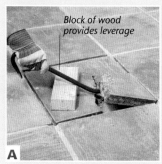

Block of wood provides leverage

A Use a pry bar to lift the old stone. If it is laid in concrete, break it with a sledgehammer and chisel. Wear protective goggles and gloves.

B Chip away any old mortar and remove debris from the stone bed.

MAINTAINING PAVING

In damp climates, paving, along with other exterior surfaces such as decking, can become covered in algae. This is very slippery and potentially dangerous. Pressure-washing these areas at least once or twice a year should keep the problem at bay. In some cases, particularly in shady areas, fungicidal washes may be useful to prevent algae from quickly regrowing.

TOOLS AND MATERIALS

Gloves, goggles, pry bar, block of wood, sledge hammer, chisel, mortar, trowel, level, rubber mallet, furring strip, new stone

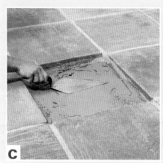

C Lay a new bed of mortar, leveling it off with a trowel.

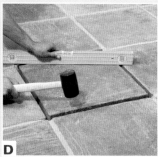

D Position the new slab, checking that it is level with those around it. Tap it into place with a rubber mallet.

E Repoint the stone with mortar, or a dry mix as required (see pp.70–71 for mixing information).

LEVELING BRICK PAVING

Brick paving can often sink if it has not been laid correctly. Because it is generally laid on sand, rectifying the problem involves lifting the sunken bricks and reseating them on more sand.

TOOLS AND MATERIALS

Furring strip, chalk, kiln-dried sand, brush

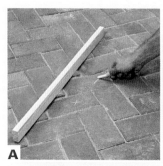

A Hold a furring strip across the area, and mark with chalk any bricks that do not sit flush with the underside of the furring strip.

B Pry up the bricks with old flat-head screwdrivers. Add more sand with a trowel, leveling off with a furring strip.

C Reposition the bricks, checking that they are level, and brush sand into the joints.

PATCHING ASPHALT

Relaying an asphalt drive is a job for the professionals, but patching holes is relatively straightforward. Use cold-mix asphalt that can be bought by the bag.

TOOLS AND MATERIALS

Brush, cold-mix asphalt, trowel, wooden post or tamper

A Remove any loose debris from the damaged drive.

B Trowel in some cold-mix asphalt, leaving it slightly proud of the surrounding surface.

C Tamp it down using a wooden post offcut, or a tamper if you have one.

RESEATING A CAPPING STONE

Capping stones can loosen over time. Reseat them so that rain cannot penetrate the top part of the wall.

TOOLS AND MATERIALS
Gloves, goggles, sledge hammer, chisel, bricklaying mortar, trowel, level

A

Remove the loose stone from the top of the wall.

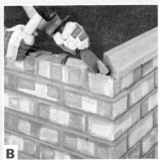

B

Chip out old mortar with a sledge hammer and chisel. Mix up some mortar (see pp.70–71). Lay it across the top of the brick course.

C

Reposition the capping stone using a level to check position. Repoint the joints.

RELAYING GRAVEL PATHS

The main problem with a gravel path is weeds. They can be controlled by weedkillers, but a longer-lasting solution is to use a weedproof membrane (geotextile fabric).

TOOLS AND MATERIALS
Polythene sheets, shovel, weedproof membrane, rake

A

Move the gravel out of the path. Pile it up alongside the path, ideally on polythene sheets.

B

Roll out a weedproof membrane along the path base, cutting as required. Overlap joints by at least 4 in (100 mm).

C

Move the gravel back onto the membrane, and distribute evenly using a rake.

REPAIRING CONCRETE

Hairline cracks in concrete pads are no problem, but larger cracks should be filled. Excavate the crack to a good depth, to give the repair more surface area to stick to. Repairs to the edge of a slab are shown here.

TOOLS AND MATERIALS
Brush, glue, plank, bricks, concrete

A

Remove loose debris and dust out the hole as necessary.

B

Use two bricks to support a section of plank that will hold the concrete in place while it dries.

C

Fill the crack with concrete until it is level with the surrounding area. Allow the concrete to dry before removing the bricks and plank.

REPAIRING FENCES

Rotten wood fences are generally best replaced, but damaged sections can be strengthened using clips or brackets. If a joint is loose, consider inserting wedges around the joint to strengthen it.

TOOLS AND MATERIALS
Hammer, wedge, joint-repair bracket, drill, screwdriver

Loose fences
Stabilize loose panels by driving wooden wedges into the joints.

Mending broken rails
Brackets may also be used. Here, an arris-rail bracket connects the rail securely with the post.

OTHER WOODWORK JOINTS

The brackets shown here are fairly specialized in terms of shape. There are also many other types of plates and brackets that can be used to strengthen different types of joints found in wooden constructions in the yard (see pp.396–397). Technique and procedure will therefore have to be tailored to the type of damage you have.

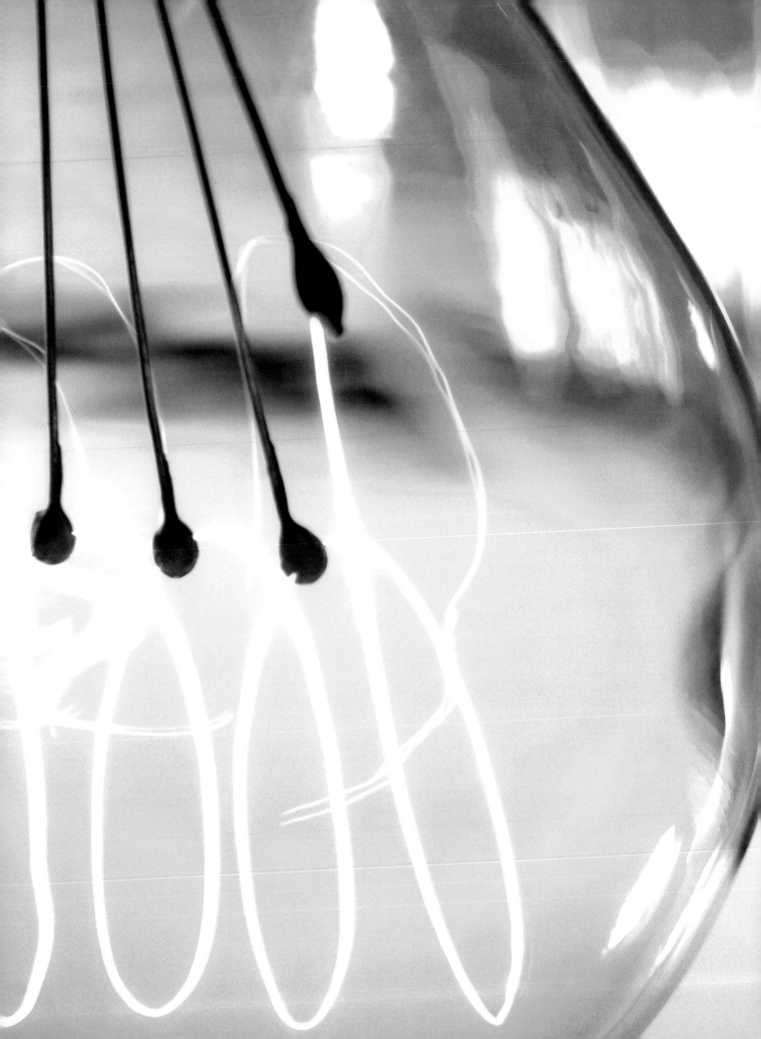

ELECTRICS

ELECTRICAL SYSTEMS
COMMUNICATIONS SYSTEMS

HOME WIRING SYSTEMS

The wiring system in your home is almost totally concealed.
All you see are lights, switches, outlets for you to plug in your
appliances, and the service panel that controls the whole system.
It is important to understand how electricity is wired in your
home. This diagram reveals what is inside your walls.

A GUIDED TOUR

Electricity is almost essential in a modern home. When power
goes out, we realize how fundamental—and how much we take
for granted—a well-functioning electrical system. With all of
the new advances in technology and home comforts, the
electrical system has gotten more complex at a rapid rate.
Structured wiring, and "Smart Homes" are becoming
more achievable to more and more homeowners
everyday. See pp.456–461 for more information
about these systems. It is worth taking a little
time to find your way around your home's
wiring system. On the following pages
you will find full details about the
system and how the various circuits
run through the walls and floors. This
illustration will help you to identify the
basic electrical components in your
home. Always check with local codes
before attempting any DIY project.

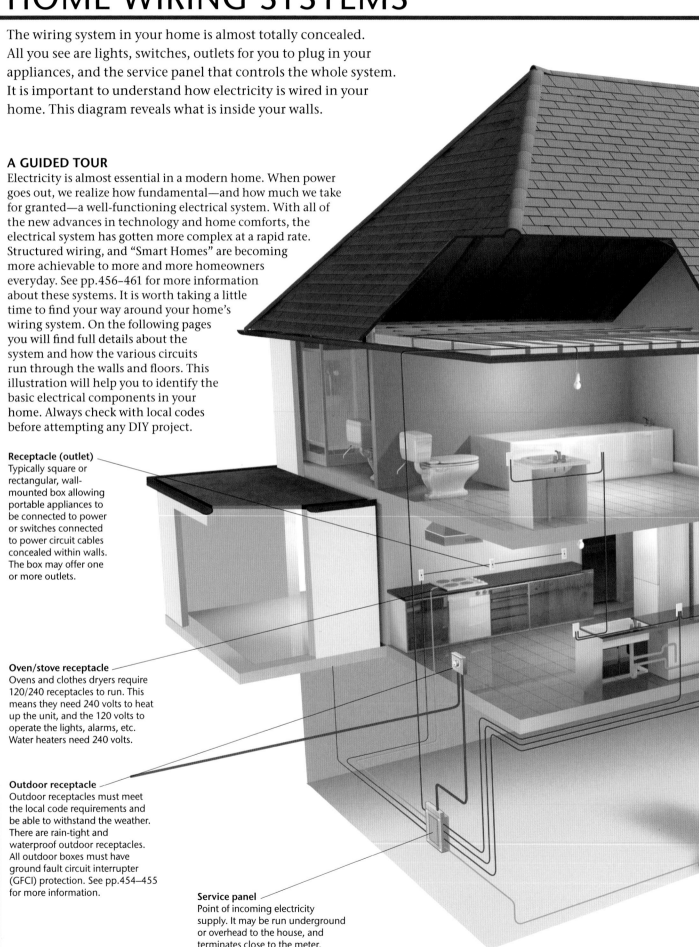

Receptacle (outlet)
Typically square or
rectangular, wall-
mounted box allowing
portable appliances to
be connected to power
or switches connected
to power circuit cables
concealed within walls.
The box may offer one
or more outlets.

Oven/stove receptacle
Ovens and clothes dryers require
120/240 receptacles to run. This
means they need 240 volts to heat
up the unit, and the 120 volts to
operate the lights, alarms, etc.
Water heaters need 240 volts.

Outdoor receptacle
Outdoor receptacles must meet
the local code requirements and
be able to withstand the weather.
There are rain-tight and
waterproof outdoor receptacles.
All outdoor boxes must have
ground fault circuit interrupter
(GFCI) protection. See pp.454–455
for more information.

Service panel
Point of incoming electricity
supply. It may be run underground
or overhead to the house, and
terminates close to the meter.

Lightswitch
One or more switch may control each individual lamp.

Light fixtures
Ceiling- or wall-mounted lights are connected directly to the lighting circuit cables. It may contain one or more individual lamps (light bulbs), or fluorescent fixtures.

KEY TO HOUSE CIRCUITS
— 240 volt circuit
— 120 volt circuit
— Ground circuit

ECO SOLUTIONS
Reducing your use of electrical power is eco-friendly and will save you money. Also consider low-energy lighting (see p.435), smart meters (see p.380), and greener methods of generating electrical power (see pp.382–387).

Light switch
Wall-mounted switch controlling fixed lights. The switch plate may contain one or more switches (called gangs).

Dimmer switch
Wall-mounted device replacing a light switch and allowing the brightness of the light it controls to be varied.

120 volt branch circuit
Most appliances and lights in your home run off of a 120 volt circuit. Electrical appliances have their volt requirements on a label. If you use a 240 outlet for a 120 appliance, you will burn out the 120 appliance.

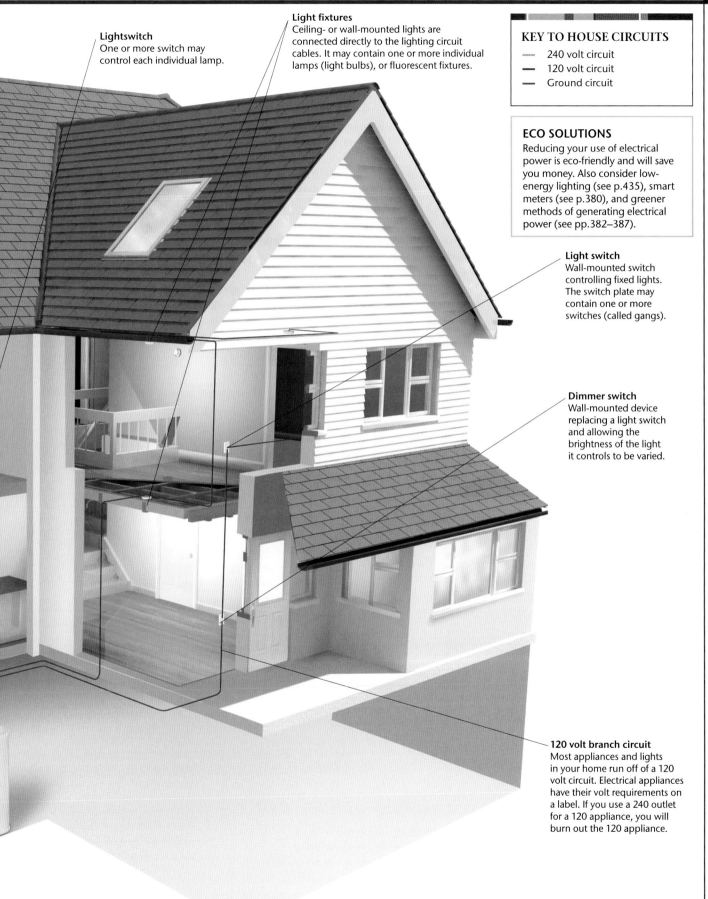

Electrical systems

WHEN YOU WORK ON YOUR HOME WIRING SYSTEM, YOU NEED TO KNOW HOW YOUR HOME WAS ORIGINALLY WIRED AND WHERE THE WIRES TRAVEL THROUGH WALLS AND CEILINGS. THIS NOT ONLY HELPS YOU TO UNDERSTAND HOW TO ALTER OR EXTEND THE SYSTEM, BUT SHOULD ALSO GIVE YOU EXAMPLES OF CORRECT WIRING PRACTICES THAT YOU SHOULD COPY IN YOUR OWN WORK.

TYPES OF CIRCUITS

There are several different wiring circuits inside the typical home, supplying electricity to indoor outlets, to lights and light switches, to large fixed appliances, such as a stove, washer, dryer, or water heater, and possibly to outside lights and outlets. A standard two-storey home is likely to have at least two outlet and lighting circuits, usually one on each floor.

POWER CIRCUITS

These circuits supply electricity to outlets where portable or movable appliances are plugged in, and also to small fixed appliances such as kitchen hoods and garbage disposals.

AVOIDING OVERLOAD

Every circuit is equipped with a protective device (a fuse or circuit breaker—see p.436) that stops it from being overloaded if too many appliances or lights are connected to it. The maximum load for a circuit to a large appliance such as a stove depends on the wire size used to wire it, and on the rating of the fuse or circuit breaker. Before you extend an existing circuit or install a more powerful appliance, check that what you plan to do will not overload it.

Electrical plan
Circuit wires run from the circuit breakers to each outlet in turn, terminating at the most remote one. When planning your electrics in your house, make sure to have more than one circuit providing power to a given space. In the event of a circuit failure, not all of the electricity will stop in that space, allowing you the ability to turn on some lights and navigate your home safely.

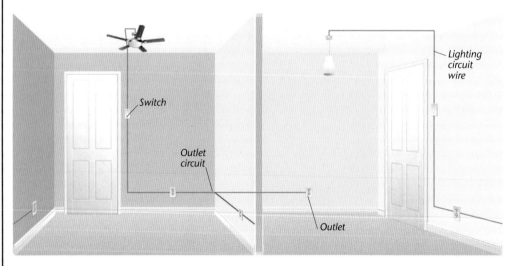

Switch

Outlet circuit

Lighting circuit wire

Outlet

Circuits
Shown above are typical circuits for receptacles and switches in a house. Lighting circuits are usually 120 volts. Receptacles are either 120 or 240 volts. The 240-volt receptacles are for larger appliances, like clothes dryers.

LIGHTING CIRCUITS

These circuits supply electricity to all the fixed lighting points in the home. They are wired up as single-pole switches, terminating at the most remote light on the circuit.

Light fixture wiring

The circuit wire runs into and out of a series of fixtures, each containing three sets of terminals. The switch wire is wired into the light terminals, as is the cord to a pendant or decorative light fixture.

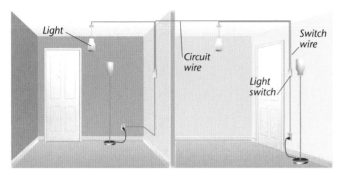

Two-way and intermediate switching

These types of switches allow the control of a light fixture from two switch positions. They are frequently used to control lighting in stairwells or large rooms. The switches are linked using special three-way switch cable. Intermediate switches can be installed between a pair of two-way switches to provide additional control points.

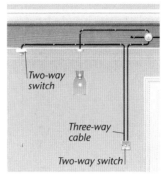

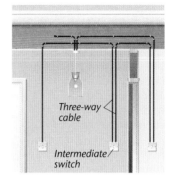

STANDARD TWO-WAY SWITCHING

TWO-WAY SWITCHING WITH INTERMEDIATE SWITCH

APPLIANCE WATTAGE

The higher the appliance's wattage, the more you will have to pay the power company to operate the appliance. So, an easy way to reduce your energy bill is to purchase high-efficiency appliances when it is time to replace older appliances in your home. Some provinces and utilities even offer rebates if you purchase energy-efficient models.

Appliance	Average wattage	Appliance	Average wattage
Attic fan	400	Frying pan	1,000-1,200
Blender	400-1,000	Gas furnace	800
Broiler	1,400-1,500	Garbage disposal	500-900
Can opener	150	Hair dryer	400-1,500
Central air conditioner	2,500-6,000	Hot plate	600-1,000
Clock	2-3	Iron	600-1,000
Clothes dryer	4,000-5,600	Laser printer	1,000
Clothes washer	500-1,100	Microwave oven	1,000-1,500
Computer with monitor	565	Oil furnace	600-1,200
Coffee maker	600-1,500	Portable heater	1,000-1,500
Crock pot	200-275	Radio	40-150
Deep fat fryer	1,200-1,600	Range	4,000-8,000
Dehumidifier	500	Range oven	3,500-5,000
Dishwasher	1,000-1,500	Refrigerator	150-300
Electric blanket	150-500	Roaster	1,200-1,650
Electric water heater	2,000-5,000	Room air conditioner	800-2,500
Exhaust fan	75-200	Sewing machine	60-90
Floor polisher	300	Stereo/CD player	50-140
Food freezer	300-600	Television	50-450
Food mixer	150-250	Toaster oven	500-1,450
Frost-free refrigerator	400-600	Waffle iron	600-1,200

There is more to your wiring system than the equipment you can see on the surface. Key elements include the mounting boxes that contain all the wiring connections, and the conduit and trunking that protect the circuit cables. This page also looks at the tools you will need to do your own wiring work, and includes a guide to some of the bulbs and tubes you can use to light up your home.

Insulation

Brass terminal

Terminal connectors
Found inside connector boxes, such as with exhaust fans or alarm systems, one side is wired to the appliance and the other is for connection to wires coming from outside.

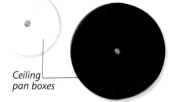

Ground clamp
Used to connect a grounding cable to metal pipes.

CONNECTING CABLES

The connections between circuit cables and wiring accessories must be made within a noncombustible enclosure, and this is the job of electrical boxes and fixture boxes. Other cable connections are sometimes made using small, insulated brass terminal connectors.

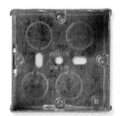

Flush metal box
Single or double, galvanized-metal box for flush-mounting accessories in masonry walls.

Clip-in box
Single or double box for flush-mounting accessories in timber-framed partition walls.

Ceiling pan boxes

Fixture boxes
Used to connect lighting circuit and switch cables, and for wiring spurs from ring-main circuits.

CABLE MANAGEMENT

Your wiring work may involve extending your existing system. Power wires are not permitted to be exposed in habitable areas without protective shields.

Masonry nail

Cable clip
Fixes cable to masonry or woodwork. Made in various sizes to match common cable types.

Mini-trunking
Conceals and protects new surface-mounted cable runs. Available in various sizes. May be self-adhesive.

Flat, oval PVC conduit
Conceals and protects new cable runs concealed in chases cut in the wall. Held in place with nails.

WIRING AND OTHER TOOLS

You will need a range of special tools to cut wires and cords to length and to prepare the cores inside for connection to wiring accessories. It is a good idea to store these separately from your ordinary DIY tools, so they are easy to find when you need them. Note that although these tools have insulated handles, you must not use them to work on live parts.

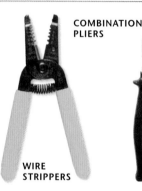

COMBINATION PLIERS

LINEMAN'S PLIERS

MULTI-PURPOSE TOOL

WIRE STRIPPERS

LONG-NOSE PLIERS

Cutters and strippers
Use side cutters to cut wires and cords to length, and wire strippers to remove core insulation neatly.

Pliers
Use combination type for bending cable cores, and long-nose type for inserting them into terminals.

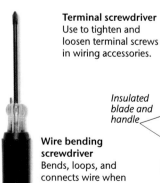

Terminal screwdriver
Use to tighten and loosen terminal screws in wiring accessories.

Insulated blade and handle

Wire bending screwdriver
Bends, loops, and connects wire when installing outlets and switches.

Hook

Fish tape
Also called fish wire, this material is used to snake cable through walls.

Conduit bender
Can be operated by hand or by using a foot for pressure to bend conduit.

Electrical tape
For emergency fixes to help temporarily secure connections.

Fishbit
Flexible shaft that bores through studs without damaging walls or ceilings for wire installation.

TESTING EQUIPMENT

For safety reasons all new DIY wiring work should be tested and certified on completion by a registered electrician (see p.437), even if it is not required by your municipality or you feel that you do not need to test any work you do. However, it is well worth using the testers shown here. They will save you time by enabling you to check a variety of electrical situations and locate potential faults as you work.

GFCI tests are important, especially in rooms with a water supply.

Remember that visual inspection is always the first level of testing you should use—making sure that cores are wired into the correct terminals, for example, and that terminal screws are fully tightened.

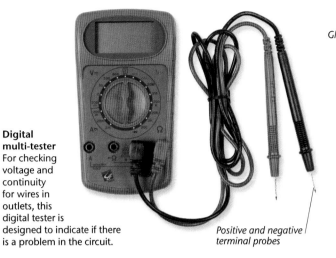

Digital multi-tester
For checking voltage and continuity for wires in outlets, this digital tester is designed to indicate if there is a problem in the circuit.

Positive and negative terminal probes

Glowing tip

Low-voltage detector
Noncontact detector identifies low-voltage sources for wiring and other devices. When it finds a low voltage, the tip glows.

GFCI tester
This tester is designed to test outlets for grounding. If the outlet is wired correctly the neon bulbs will light up accordingly.

Voltage detector
This detector is used to trace any unshielded and unenergized wire or cable. It flashes and beeps when it detects a voltage.

Receptacle tester
When you want to check to see if your outlets are wired correctly, use a receptacle tester. It will indicate the problem, if there is one.

BULBS AND TUBES

Known in the trade as general lighting service (GLS) bulbs, household light bulbs come in standard pear and mushroom shapes with a clear-, pearl- (translucent), white-, or colored-glass envelope. Other shapes include pointed candle bulbs, small bulbs, and round decor bulbs intended to be on show in a lamp or light fixture.

Halogen bulbs are becoming more widely used for display lighting. They give a clear, white light that is brighter than a GLS bulb.

Reflector bulbs are used in spotlights where you want a high-intensity beam rather than a diffuse source of light.

Tubes may be fluorescent or tungsten filament types, and are used mainly in concealed lighting effects.

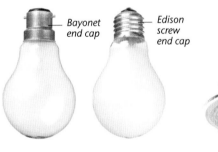

Bayonet end cap | *Edison screw end cap*

Contact pegs

GLS bulbs
Household-voltage light bulbs have bayonet cap (BC) or Edison screw (ES) end caps. Outputs range from 25 to 150 watts.

Halogen bulb
Household-voltage spotlight bulbs have two contact pegs (above) or an Edison-screw end cap. Most are rated at 50 watts.

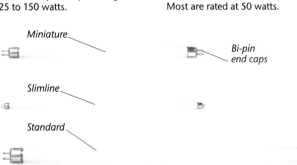

Miniature

Slimline

Standard

Bi-pin end caps

Fluorescent tubes
Household-voltage bulbs in tubular form. Available in standard, slimline, and miniature sizes, and in various wattages.

LOW-ENERGY BULBS

Contact pegs

LED lamp
Spotlight LED bulbs offer the most energy efficient option as they use the least power and outlast other types of bulb.

Bayonet end cap

Low-energy spotlight bulb

Compact fluorescent bulb
Uses about one-fifth of the energy of a comparable GLS bulb, and can last up to eight times as long.

WORKING SAFELY

If you decide to tackle your own electrical work, you must first find out how your wiring system is controlled. This ensures that you can isolate the part of the system that you want to work on from the breaker panel, so that you can repair or extend it in complete safety.

ELECTRIC SHOCK: WHAT TO DO

■ If someone receives a major electric shock and is still connected to the current source, turn it off. If you cannot, either grab clothing or use a non-conductive object, such as a broom handle, to drag the casualty away from it.
■ See pp.512–513 for what to do next, depending on whether the casualty is conscious or unconscious.

GENERAL ELECTRIC CODES

There are many guidelines relating to safe electrical work. Here are some critical rules and regulations. You must check with local officials for codes concerning domestic wiring work in your home (see also DIY wiring, opposite).
■ All breakers and fuses need to be labeled clearly and permanently.
■ Grounding is required by the Canadian Electrical Code for 120 volt and 240 volt circuits in your home.
■ Grounding connections cannot be on the load side of service disconnections.
■ Maximum height of breaker is 5 ft 6 in (1.7 m).
■ Breaker panel cannot be installed in clothes closets or bathrooms.
■ Add to grounding for safety (see opposite).

CIRCUIT BREAKERS

The circuit breaker panel. The utility company usually has a meter on the outside of your home to check how much electricity you have used. The circuit breaker panel is wired from this meter and mounted inside your home. All circuits in your home have a circuit breaker in this box. Circuits are designed according to household need and layout of rooms. Having more than one circuit in each room may be helpful to providing light if there is a ground fault interruption on one circuit in the room. Some rooms and appliances have requirements for the type of circuit they can or should utilize. Always follow the manufacturer's instructions and any local building codes when laying out circuits.

Circuit breaker circuits

The circuit breaker unit contains individual circuit breakers, housed in rows and columns. They have a main breaker switch that can control all of the breakers at once. The circuits are permanently labeled for easy identification. Each circuit holder contains one 120-volt circuit. Each residential dwelling must have access to a breaker panel. Any unused openings in the breaker panel must be covered.

Separate fuse boxes

Old, unmodernized wiring systems will have a series of separate enclosures rather than a one-piece breaker box. One will contain the main isolating switch; others will house a fuseholder and replaceable fuse protecting an individual circuit. This system should be replaced by a qualified electrician.

Circuits running to household

Main breaker

Circuit breakers

Power bus

Circuit breaker panel

Close-up
Individual circuit breakers are situated in rows inside the box. Circuits with 120 volts take one unit. 240 volt circuits require two units.

Service panel
The circuit breaker panel (also called the service entrance panel) is the main source of electricity for your home. All of the circuits in your house run from this unit. Codes dictate where and how the panel is installed.

IDENTIFYING CIRCUITS

In a circuit breaker panel, each circuit should be labelled for identification. If not, identify each circuit as follows:

■ Each lighting circuit will be controlled by a circuit rated at 15 amps. Turn on all the lights in the property, then remove each breaker in turn so you can mark on the label which rooms are on each circuit.

■ Each outlet is controlled by a circuit rated at 15–20 amps. Plug an appliance into each outlet and repeat the procedure above. You may find one or two outlets in a room wired on a different circuit; this may have been done either to avoid having a long cable run to a remote outlet, or overloading the circuit. Label the circuits as above.

■ Identifying circuits to individual appliances is more straightforward. A 20-amp circuit controls small appliances, and a 30-amp circuit will control a clothes dryer. Remove the switch off the breaker panel to check which is which.

GROUNDING FOR SAFETY

Grounding, or earthing, is crucial to electrical safety in your home. It provides a way for an electric current to be altered into a zero current status, making it "grounded." The Canadian Electrical Code provides regulations and standards on grounding. Every part of your home wiring system must be linked to earth, via a continuous electrical conductor that runs round each circuit and is connected to the property's main earthing terminal at the breaker panel. Whenever you make alterations or extensions to the wiring system, you must ensure that the earth continuity is maintained. Check that all grounding cores are connected to their respective terminals and that metallic accessory faceplates are earthed. Grounding wires are easily identified, as they are copper, or sheathed in green plastic.

DIY WIRING

Major work

Rules and regulations governing DIY electrical work vary greatly across the country. It is completely forbidden in Quebec and New Brunswick (despite the fact that you can buy everything you need at the local renovation centre), while in Vancouver the permits department holds homeowner DIY electrical seminars.

Any major work always requires permits and inspections, although licensed electricians have various special privileges with respect to permit requirements. Some areas permit minor replacement of like with like, such as changing a light switch, while Ontario requires a permit for even that. Nowhere is anyone other than a licensed electrician allowed to remove the seal on the electrical meter, as inside the meter you are exposed to an extremely large unfused power supply. Nowhere is anyone other than a licensed electrician allowed to work on a rental property. Even where you can do work legallly, you would be well advised to have the job inspected by an electrician. You don't wnat to burn down your own house.

If you aren't comfortable working with power lines, don't attempt it. If you want to reduce the cost of using a licensed electrician, you can move everything out of his/her way, open walls, drill holes, and perhaps help to pull wires—all the dirty non-electrical jobs—so they can concentrate on electrical connections.

Grounding receptacles
Receptacles can be grounded back to the circuit breaker panel through the use of a grounding wire. An additional way to protect yourself is using a GFCI receptacle for grounding.

Grounding appliances
Ground fault interruptions happen due to short circuits or excessive current on the circuit. If an appliance is properly grounded, the current is directed back to the circuit breaker panel, effectively tripping the circuit.

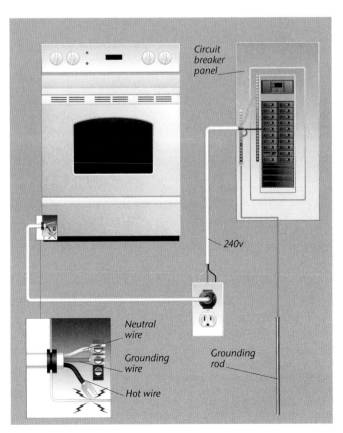

Many different types of wiring accessory are used in home wiring systems. Some are switches and safety devices, while others allow lights and appliances to be connected to the system—either permanently, or temporarily as in the case of appliances plugged into outlets. A permanent connection is useful for kitchen appliances that are in constant use, such as a cooker hood. Shown here are some of the accessories most widely used in wiring.

ACCESSORY FINISHES

Most wiring accessories are made in white plastic. However, other finishes such as brass, chrome, wood, and colored plastic are also available, generally at a slightly higher price. Metallic faceplates must always be connected to the circuit earth terminal in the mounting box.

LIGHT SWITCHES

Every light in the home is controlled by a switch, which may be wall- or ceiling-mounted. A wall switch, known as a plateswitch, may have up to six switches, but in most homes switches with just one, two, or three are used. The faceplate may be flush- or surface-mounted. Most switches have two terminals on the back, plus a grounding terminal if they are made of metal. Three-way switches have an extra terminal, and are used for two-way switching (see also p.447). This allows a light to be controlled from two switch positions, as is commonly found in a stairwell, for example. Cord-operated ceiling switches are usually made as three-way switches, but can be wired for one-way use.

One-gang plateswitch
A single switch used to control ceiling or wall lights, available in one-way and two-way versions. They are also available in a variety of designs.

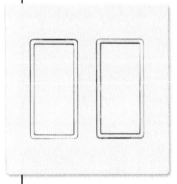

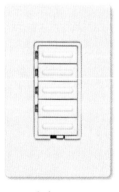

Two-gang plateswitch
Allows control of two lights from one switch position. Each gang usually has three terminals. They are available in a variety of horizontal and vertical designs.

Dimmer switch
Allows the brightness of the light to be varied. Two- and three-gang versions are also available.

Circular dimmer switch
Controls the light levels in a room with a rotating motion. Provides a range of mood lighting.

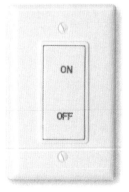

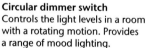

Slide dimmer switch
This dimmer light switch has a slide that moves up and down to change a fixture's lighting level.

Switch with LED indicator
Light switches are easier to find in the dark if you have a red LED indicator built into them, like the one shown here.

Wireless three-way switch
Avoid rewiring your house in order to install a three-way switch. A remote control switch powers an incandescent light up to 300 watts.

Timer switch
This switch-to-set timer is spring-wound, providing up to 60 minutes of lighting to a space. Works with lights and ceiling fans.

RECEPTACLES

A receptacle provides a connection point for a portable appliance, which is connected to it with a three-pin plug. The outlet may be switched or unswitched, and may have a neon on-off indicator. Faceplates can be flush or surface-mounted, and may have one, two, or three outlets. A permanent connection is made for an appliance such as an oven or clothes dryer, and may be switched or unswitched.

FURTHER INFORMATION

Check with local building codes for details on how to install receptacles. Here are a few to keep in mind:

- GFCI outlets must be used in wet areas.
- Walls 2 ft (600 mm) or wider need receptacles.
- Halls longer than 10 ft (3 m) need receptacles.

Duplex outlet
This is the outlet found in most homes. Both openings are connected to the same circuit.

Quad outlet
In most cases all four of these openings will be on the same circuit.

Outdoor outlet cover
A special cover to protect the outlet from the elements when used outside.

GFCI outlet
An outlet that trips itself off when it senses an overload or short circuit.

Surge suppression outlet
An outlet designed to protect sensitive electronic equipment from power spikes.

50-amp flush mount receptacle
Supplies 220 volts and is used for appliances that draw large amounts of current.

X10 spilt receptacle module
X10 outlets are controlled by signals sent over the power lines, allowing X10 switches to turn on and off X10 outlets without using direct wiring between the two. These remote-controlled outlets and switches are often used as part of home automation systems.

Gasket seals outlet cover plate to the wall

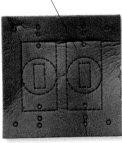

Double gang weatherproof in-use receptacle cover
This cover can be closed while cords are plugged into the outdoor receptacle thereby protecting the electrical connection from the weather while in use.

SURGE PROTECTORS

These devices are available at most stores. They protect your delicate electrical equipment—such as computers—from voltage spikes and surges that sometimes come through the electrical system. It may designed to trip and be reset, or it may just smooth out the voltage level output regardless of what level is input. Some, like the one on the left, plugs directly into the wall and others have a cord for more convenient placement.

Light indicates that current is available in the unit.

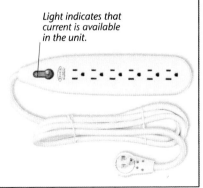

SURGE PROTECTORS

ELECTRICS

ELECTRICAL BOXES

All wiring connections in a home must be made inside a junction box. There can be no connections open inside a wall. A junction box is used solely as a place to make a connection so it is not exposed, and there are boxes to hold outlets, switches, and fixtures. The locations of openings are determined and the appropriate boxes are put in place. Then the wire is stretched from box to box to create the wiring system. The boxes come in different sizes and configurations for different applications.

TOOLS AND MATERIALS SEE BASIC TOOLKIT AND P.443

FURTHER INFORMATION
Boxes are made for general and specific applications. The homeowner should walk through their jobsite and determine how many boxes, and of what type, will be needed. Make sure that the fasteners are included.

TYPES OF ELECTRICAL BOXES

For many years prior to the 1970s electrical boxes were always made of metal. Plastic boxes then came into use and offer several benefits. They are much less expensive, do not conduct electricity, and often come with the fasteners attached. This makes the product safer to install and use, and makes installation much faster and less expensive. Air-tight plastic boxes exist as well, making the house air barrier easier to achieve.

Plastic electrical boxes

Plastic boxes are made of a very hard and durable plastic that will last a lifetime. They will not short to the electrical connection, because plastic is non-conductive. In nail-on boxes the nails are attached and the box is ready to apply. There are knock-outs in the box that can easily be pushed through with a screwdriver so the wires can be fed in.

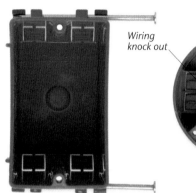

Wiring knock out

Plastic nail-on box
This style of box is used for single gang outlets and switches. It is placed next to a stud, with the front edge flush with the finished wall, and the nails are driven in.

Plastic ceiling box
This is used as the electrical and structural attachment for light fixtures. Its strength is adequate for all but the larger fixtures and fans.

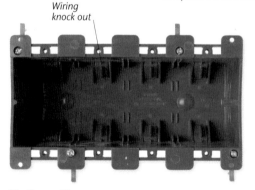
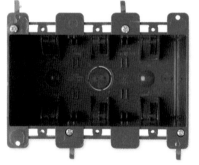

Wiring knock out

Plastic adjustable box
This box can be attached and then adjusted for depth location afterward, as needed.

Plastic quad box
This is commonly known as a four-gang box, and is used in a situation where four lights in a room need to be switched from one location.

Triple box
This is commonly known as a three-gang box, and is used in a situation where three lights in a room need to be switched from one location.

Metal electrical boxes

Metal boxes are usually used in commercial applications. They are strong and can be used with wiring conduit. Metal connectors are used to positively fasten the conduit to the boxes to keep out moisture, keep the wiring from being accidentally accessible, and to provide a completely groundable system.

Metal ceiling box
This box can be nailed directly to a ceiling joist, or can be used with an adjustable metal mounting strap.

Metal box extension
If the box does not reach out flush with the finished wall, an extension can be attached to bring it out to the right position.

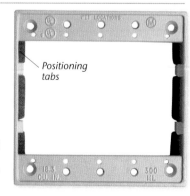

Positioning tabs

INSTALLING A MOUNTING BOX WITHOUT STUD ATTACHMENT

A

Position the box on the wall using a level. Receptacle boxes should be 12 in (300 mm) above the finished floor. Light switches should be 30 in (750 mm) above the finished floor.

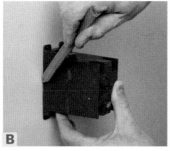

B

Lay out the box on the wall. Using the box as a template, trace around the outside.

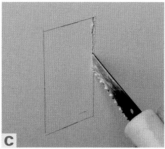

C

Cut a hole in the drywall with a drywall saw or sable saw.

D

Open a knock-out for each wire. Pull wires through the box.

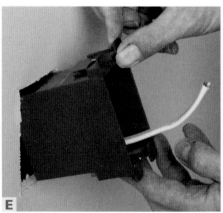

E

Push the box into the hole. Make sure there is less than ⅛ in (3 mm) between the drywall and box, and at least 6 in (150 mm) of wire in the box. A variety of clamping mechanisms exists to attach to the drywall when the box cannot be secured to a wall stud.

FITTING A MOUNTING BOX IN A SOLID WALL

Flush-mounted accessories provide a more seemless appearance than surface-mounted ones, and are less prone to physical damage. To fit a flush box in a solid wall, you need to remove some of the masonry behind the plaster to create a recess for a box to which the accessory faceplate is attached. This is relatively easy in blockwork, but harder if the wall is built in brick.

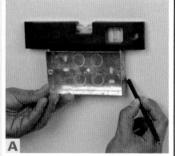

A

Hold the box against the wall in the required position. Use a small level to check if it is level, and mark the box outline on the wall.

Drill around the edge first, then drill a honeycomb within it

B

Use a masonry drill bit to drill a honeycomb of holes in the wall. Drill within the marked outline to a depth a little greater than that of the box.

Wear thick work gloves to protect your hands

C

Use a brick bolster and a sledge hammer to chop out the masonry. Then test-fit the mounting box to check that the hole is deep enough.

AIDS FOR CUTTING RECESSES IN SOLID WALLS

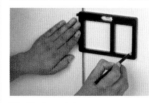

Plastic template
Hold the template against the wall, and mark the cut-out you require. Use only the left-hand cut-out for a single socket.

Box chaser attachment
Fit it to your drill to cut a recess neatly and quickly. It is quite expensive to buy, but useful if you need to fit many outlets.

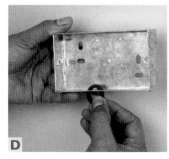

D

Fit a rubber grommet into the cable entry point to prevent it chafing, then cut the chase for the cable run to the mounting box.

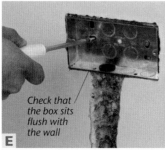

Check that the box sits flush with the wall

E

Insert the box in the recess and mark the positions of the screws. Remove the box, drill and plug the holes, and screw the box to the wall.

F

Feed the new cable through a length of oval PVC conduit and secure this in the chase. Prepare the cable end ready to make the connection.

ELECTRICS

WORKING WITH CABLE

Wiring is any bare or insulated cord that provides a metallic conduction for electricity to flow. Wire can be insulated, bare, or sheathed in metal or plastic. When there is more than one wire insulated in plastic sheathing, the wires are known collectively as cable. Most of power running through a modern home use cables. The cable covering is printed with the types of wires found inside.

CABLE SHEATHING

There are many types of cable available on the market. Cables can have plastic or metal sheathing. Residential indoor cable typically consists of wire sheathed in plastic, called nonmetallic cable (NM). It is often referred to as Romex or Lomex. It is important to understand the types and categories of cable prior to use.

Color coding

The plastic sheathing covering cables are color coded to make it easier to identify their use and to indicate the types of wire running inside the sheathing. Each wire inside the cable is also color coded to indicat type. Hot wires are usually black and neutral wires are white. Green or bare copper wires are usually grounding wires. The cable is also labeled with its specifications, so be sure to select the correct cable for your remodeling project.

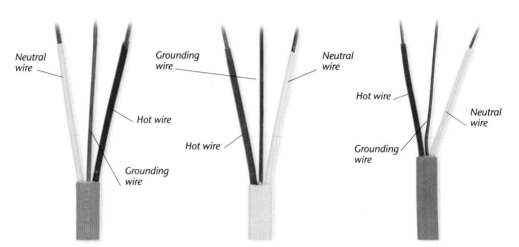

10/2 NM (Romex or Lomex)
Used for large appliances like clothes dryers, this cable has two 10-gauge wires plus a grounding wire and can carry up to 240 volts.

12/2 NM (Romex or Lomex)
This type of cable is used for common household lighting and can be used for small appliances. It has two 12-gauge wires plus a grounding wire.

14/2 UF
Marked with UF on the sheathing casing, the underground cable can be used for underground, wet locations, and anywhere NM can be used.

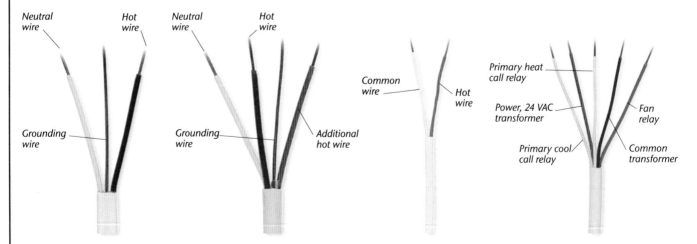

14/2 NM (Romex or Lomex)
This is the standard type of nonmetallic cable for houses. It has an insulated white, an insulated black, and bare copper wire.

14/3 NM (Romex or Lomex)
In addition to the standard wires seen in the 14/2 NM, this has an additional hot wire used for three-way switches in homes.

2 Wire low voltage
This type of cable can be used for the wiring of a doorbell and some 24-volt lighting systems.

5 Wire low voltage
The five wire low voltage is typically used for 24 volts and less than 1 amp applications only. Used as cable for thermostats used in residential heating and cooling.

SPLICING WIRES

When working with residential electrical projects, you will need to know the basics of stripping and splicing wire.

Before you can splice two wires, you must strip the insulation sheathing from the ends of the wires. You can use a manual wire stripper that cuts the sheathing and then allows you to remove it from the wire, or an automatic wire stripper. If you choose to use a utility knife (as shown below) be careful. It is possible to nick the wires. In most cases, ½ in (13 mm) of sheathing needs to be removed from the end of the cable. More insulation must be removed from stranded wires.

The ends of the exposed wires are then tightly twisted around each other to make the connection. Cap the end of the connection with a wire connector. Keep in mind that all spliced wires must be housed within a box, fixture, receptacle, or switch.

STRIPPING WIRE

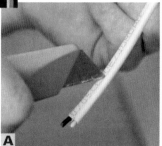

A Remove approximately ½ inch (13 mm) of the insulation from the end of the cable.

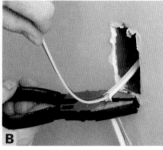

B Separate the wires from the sheathing by pulling on the end of the wires.

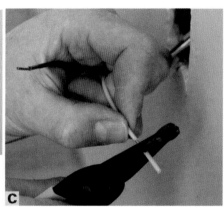

Trim the end of the wires.

C

SPLICING WIRE

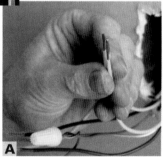

A Identify and strip the wires that will be spliced together.

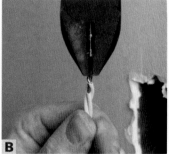

B Twist the end of a stripped wire around another stripped wire to create a splice.

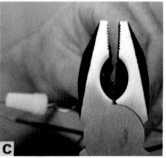

C Trim the end of the wires.

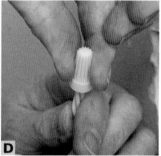

D Cap the splice with a wire connector.

TOOLS AND MATERIALS CHECKLIST PP.441–461

Installing a mounting box (p.441) Padsaw (drywall saw), clip-in mounting box

Fitting a mounting box in a solid wall (p.441) Drilling jig or box-chaser attachment, club hammer, brick bolster, oval PVC conduit, flush mounting box, rubber grommet

Running wire in a stud wall (p.444) Padsaw (drywall saw)

Running wire in a new stud wall (p.444) Padsaw (drywall saw)

Using raceway (p.444) Mounting box for socket outlet, raceway

Running wire behind base board (p.445) Broad knife, drywall saw, level

Running a cable around a door (p.445) Broad knife, drywall saw, weighted string

Installing a recessed light (p.448) Stud detector, padsaw (drywall saw), clip-in light fitting

Installing track lighting (p.449) Basic toolkit only

Installing a ceiling fan (p.450–451) Basic toolkit only

Installing a light fitting (p.453) Basic toolkit only

Installing an exterior light fitting (p.453) Caulk and dispenser

Working with coaxial cable (p.457) Basic toolkit only

Repairing a doorbell (p.457) Basic toolkit only

Installing a telephone Cat 3 jack (p.461) Basic toolkit only

FOR BASIC TOOLKIT
SEE PP.24–25

ELECTRICS

RUNNING WIRE IN WALLS

Any remodeling work you tackle on your electrical system will involve routing wire to new lights, switches, outlets, and other wiring accessories. How you accomplish this depends on whether you want to conceal the wires completely. In general, your aim will be to cause as little disruption to existing decor and furnishings as possible. You can do this by surface-mounting the wires initially, and then hiding them in channels in the wall surface (or within hollow walls) next time you remodel the room.

TOOLS AND MATERIALS SEE BASIC TOOLKIT AND P.443

WIRING CODES

If you want to avoid tearing up a wall you can run wires inside baseboards or special housings, if you follow local codes. These may include:

■ Cables must be protected within 6 ft (1.8 m) of openings with guards at least the same height as the cable.
■ Low-voltage wires can run behind baseboards.
■ Cables need to be at least 1¼ in (30 mm) from the edge of studs, and have protection from any potential nailing.

RUNNING WIRE IN A STUD WALL

If your rooms have wood-framed stud partition walls, you may be able to hide the wires within the wall. How easy this is depends on where you want to install the wiring accessory, and on whether there are horizontal braces or blanket insulation in the way. To gain access to the cavity you will have to drill a hole through the head or sole plates at the top or bottom of the wall framework.

A

Locate the wall position and lift floorboards or remove insulation to reveal the ceiling. Drill a ½-in (10-mm) hole through the head plate.

B

Feed the wire down through the hole and into the wall cavity. It will drop freely if there is no blocking or insulation inside the wall.

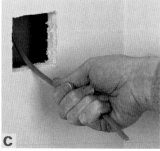

C

Cut a hole in the wall at the new accessory position. Fish out the wire, feed it into a clip-in mounting box, and fit this into the hole.

RUNNING WIRE IN A NEW STUD WALL

A

Clad one side of the wall. Drill a ½-in (10-mm) hole through the head or sole plate and draw in the wire from above or below.

B

Drill ½-in (10-mm) holes through the studs and thread the wire through until you reach the position of the new wiring accessory.

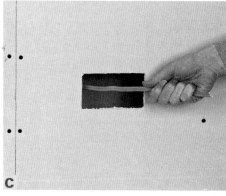

C

Drywall the other side of the wall. Then mark and cut a hole for the new clip-in electrical box and draw the wire out through the hole.

USING RACEWAY

White vinyl raceways look neater than bare wire, and give the wire run extra protection against accidental damage. Use square raceway for a single wire, and a larger size for two or three wires. The wire can be recessed in a chase cut into the wall surface when the room is remodeled, if you follow code restrictions.

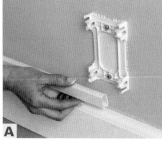

A

Position raceway along the top of the baseboard. Attach the raceway using adhesive or screws, according to manufacturer's instructions.

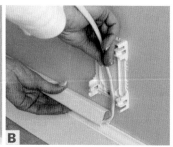

B

Open the raceway and feed the cable into it, leaving enough cable at the end for proper connection. Snap the cover back closed.

C

Attach the corner piece so the cable can be fed into the receptacle base plate. The cable can now be attached to the outlet.

RUNNING WIRE BEHIND A BASEBOARD

To avoid the difficult and costly work involved in repairing walls and matching texture and paint, one way to run a cable in a wall is behind the baseboard. The patch work will be concealed behind the baseboard and will not require a drywall expert to make a beautiful finished product. By following these guidelines a homeowner can do the job without hiring skilled trades.

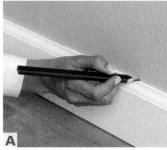

Mark the wall at the top of the baseboard to give a reference for cutting once you have removed it.

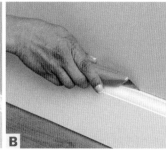

Score the top edge of the baseboard. This will release the paint and caulk so you don't peel the paint or the drywall paper when you remove it.

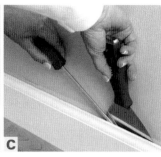

Use a broad knife and a screwdriver to gently pry the baseboard from the wall. Take care not to mark the wall above the baseboard.

Mark a line ½ in (12 mm) below the previous line. When the drywall is cut on this line, removed and then replaced, the joint will be below the top of the baseboard.

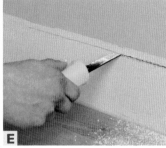

Use a drywall saw to cut the drywall along the lower of the two lines. The tip of the saw can be used to poke a hole in the wall.

Drill the holes for the cable high enough to avoid nails in the bottom and middle of the stud so the cable will be far from possible nail intrusion.

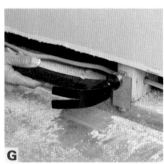

Attach nail plates on the side of the stud to protect the cable from the nails or screws used when applying the drywall.

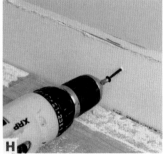

Attach the drywall placing the fasteners into the plate at the floor and at the top edge of the replacement piece to miss the nail plates.

RUNNING A CABLE AROUND A DOOR

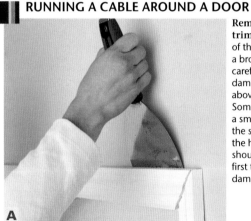

Remove the head trim at the top edge of the door using a broad knife. Be careful not to damage the wall above the trim. Sometimes there is a small nail through the side trims into the head trim. These should be removed first to avoid possible damage to the trim.

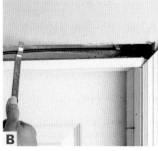

Trim drywall away from the top of the door jamb with a drywall saw to make room to run the cable above the door.

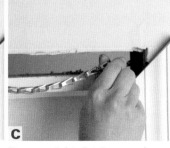

Drop a weighted string or sash chain down through the gap between the jamb and stud until it can be seen at the bottom of the trim piece.

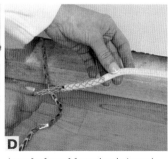

Attach the cable to the chain and pull it back up until the cable is all the way through. Disconnect the cable and pull it taut.

You can now run the cable across the top of the door and feed it down through the void on the other side of the door. Replace the top trim.

TYPES OF CIRCUIT

There are several simple jobs you can do on your existing lighting system, including replacing old switches, lampholders, or ceiling roses, and installing dimmer switches in place of existing on-off switches so you can vary the lighting level in the room. None of these jobs involves any alterations to the existing circuit wiring.

One slightly more complicated lighting circuit job you may want to tackle is providing two-way switching for a particular light, for example, so you can control the landing light from both a hall and landing. This does involve some new wiring work, but it will give you useful experience of running cables and mounting accessories.

ISOLATING THE CIRCUIT

■ Before beginning any work on a lighting circuit, you must always cut off its electricity supply at the main box.
■ Turning the light off at the wall switch does not isolate the light box, which means that the light box and wires are still live even when the switch is off. Never take any chances with safety. Ask a professional electrician if you have any questions.

SIMPLE CIRCUITS

These diagrams show some simple circuits that can be found in any home. The circuit breaker box is normally found in the garage, utility room, or in a closet. 120 volt outlets are used for lamps, small appliances, radios and televisions sets. 240 volt outlets are used for major appliances that draw a heavy load, such a dryers and electric ranges.

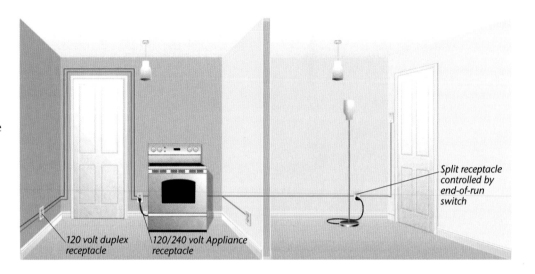

120 volt duplex receptacle

120/240 volt Appliance receptacle

Split receptacle controlled by end-of-run switch

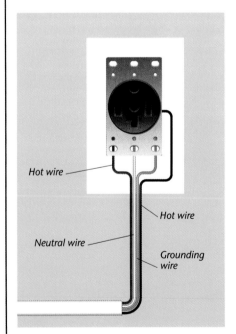

Hot wire

Hot wire

Neutral wire

Grounding wire

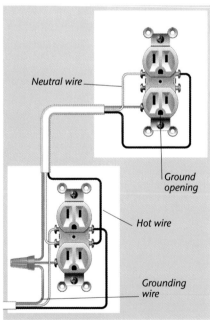

Neutral wire

Ground opening

Hot wire

Grounding wire

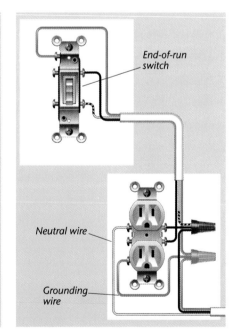

End-of-run switch

Neutral wire

Grounding wire

120/240 Volt appliance receptacle
This type of receptacle is used to supply appliances that pull large loads. The plug itself may vary, but will be larger than a normal wall outlet and will have a ground hole, a neutral hole and two 120 volt openings. Four wires will supply it. Green is always ground. White is always neutral. Red and black are the two hot legs.

120 Volt duplex receptacle
These are the electrical openings that you will find throughout your home. Older construction may have outlets with only the two slot holes and no ground opening. If the outlet is mounted in a metal box connected to conduit, the outlets may be replaced with grounded ones and can be grounded to the conduit.

Spilt receptacle controlled by end-of-run switch
This type of circuit is often used in livingrooms and dens so lamps can be turned on from a wall switch. Of course the outlet cannot be used for appliances that require a continuous electrical flow, and typically would be used for lamps only.

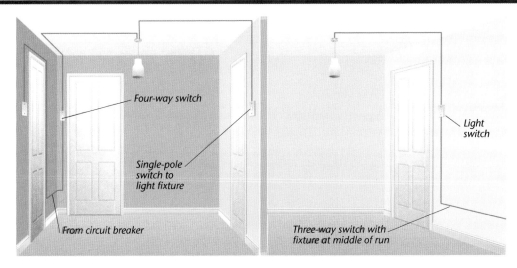

Four-way switch

Single-pole switch to light fixture

From circuit breaker

Light switch

Three-way switch with fixture at middle of run

Switch circuits
Other than the simplest switch circuit, with one switch and one light fixture, there are what are known as three-way and four-way circuits. The three-way circuit indicates that there are three openings: two switches and one light fixture opening. In a four-way, there are three switches and one light fixture opening.

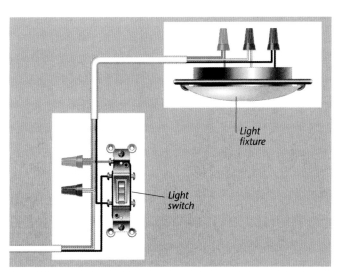

Light fixture

Light switch

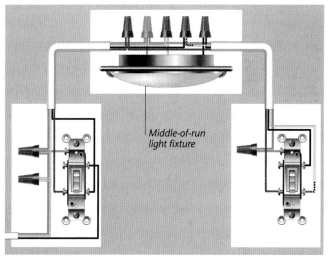

Middle-of-run light fixture

Single-pole switch to light fixture
This is the simplest switch circuit. It is very straightforward. The fixture's ground wire is connected to ground. The white neutral wire is connected directly to the white wire. The black wire, which is the hot wire, has the switch connected in series so the hot supply can be switched off. This ensures that the fixture is not hot when the light is off.

Three-way switch with fixture at middle of run
A three-way switch connection can be very confusing. If you wish to attempt to make this type of connection, be sure to examine the diagram above closely. This type of circuit allows one light to be turned off and on from two different locations. An example is a light in the middle of the hall with a switch at either end of the hall.

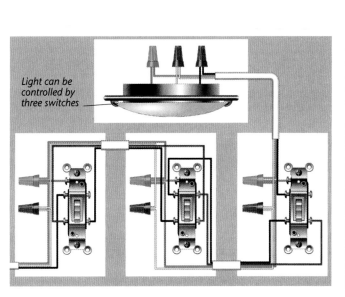

Light can be controlled by three switches

Four-way switch
This type of switch circuit is like the three-way in that it allows the light fixture to be turned on and off from different locations, but it allows the use of three switches and is wired differently. This circuit is usually used in a living room or den where there are several ways to enter the room. This circuit allows the lights to be turned on from three different doorways.

FURTHER INFORMATION
These more complicated circuits may require three- and four-conductor wire and switches made for use in three-way and four-way circuits. Again these can be confusing and complicated and you should study the diagrams to make sure that you understand how they work before attempting its installation.

RECESSED LIGHTING

Popular in new homes, recessed lighting fixtures are embedded into the ceiling, eliminating hanging fixtures. Many newer homes have recessed lighting in grid patterns on the ceiling, using the recessed light as the major source to light a space. Sometimes called cans, recessed lighting can be used as direct spotlights of illumination on a specific area, and can be combined with pendants, sconces, and freestanding fixtures to create lighting options that meet the changing needs of how you use a space.

TOOLS AND MATERIALS SEE BASIC TOOLKIT AND P.443

■■ INSTALLING A RECESSED LIGHT

Before you begin to work on any electrical project, turn off power to the circuit. To replace a fixture with new recessed lighting, first remove the old electrical box for the lighting fixture.

A

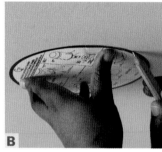

B

Lay out the hole for the new can light. Use a stud finder to make sure there are no joists directly above the diameter of the hole before cutting.

C

Score the layout line with a utility knife. Using a drywall saw or a hole-cutting saw for better precision, cut the hole.

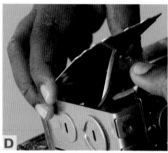

D

Run wire from the power to the switch box that will be controlling the new light.

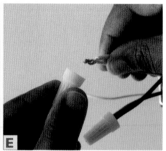

E

Splice the light-colored wires (white to white, for example) together using wire connectors.

Put the spliced wires in the box and place the cover over it.

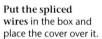

F

G

Insert the box and then the can into the ceiling hole.

H

Push each of the clips outward until it clicks into the fixture.

I

Attach the baffle and trim to the fixture's housing.

J

Screw in a lightbulb. Restore power to the circuit.

AIR TIGHT READY

Recessed lights in insulated ceilings must be made for the application. They will be double-canister to control heat and allow the piling of insulation over them. The inner canister will be air tight with a gasket to seal to the drywall to control air leakage into the roof area.

TRACK LIGHTING

Track lights are a versatile way to provide task or accent lighting. They can be directed to shine on a specific area and then adjusted to meet the changing needs of the space. The power comes from an existing ceiling junction box, so track lighting can usually be installed without having to do any additional remodeling. Track lighting is easy to install, and with stylish options on the market, it is a popular project for home remodelers interested in taking on an electrical project.

TOOLS AND MATERIALS SEE BASIC TOOLKIT AND P.443

■■ INSTALLING TRACK LIGHTING

Turn off the power. Remove the existing fixture and disconnect the wires.

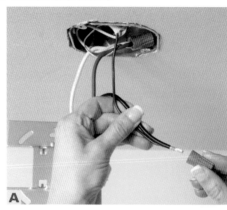

A

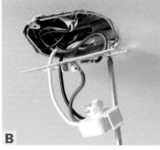

B

Connect the track lighting wires and secure the mounting plate to the box.

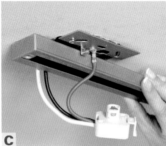

C

Position the track on the ceiling and then slide the track in place.

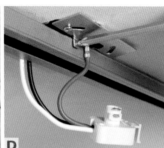

D

Secure the track in place by tightening the screws.

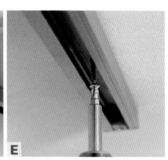

E

Attach the track to the ceiling along its length with screws.

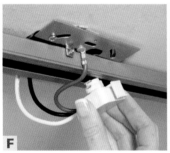

F

Twist the connector into the track.

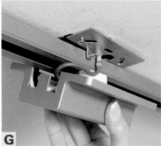

G

Clip the cover in place over top of the box.

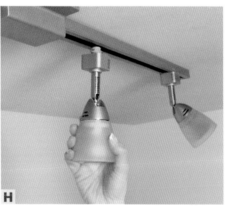

H

Snap or twist in the light heads, spaced according to your needs.

Adjust the light angles for general lighting or to spotlight artwork or other features in the space.

I

FURTHER INFORMATION

Track lighting offers options beyond the typical straight run of spotlights. It is available both in kits and in parts to enable you to create your own lighting design.

Track configurations are offered in straight runs, curves, and flexible materials that you can bend to shape. If you would like to add tracks or configure track lighting around a corner, there are connectors available to attach the tracks, called T-connectors for attaching a track perpendicular to the main run, or L-connectors, for attaching two tracks at a corner.

Light fixtures are available in floods and pendants. You can use either line or low voltage lights. The low voltage lights are more expensive to purchase, but consume less energy.

CEILING FANS

Ceiling fans can be both functional and decorative. Popular in warmer climates, ceiling fans also can be used when it's cold to gently pull heated air away from the ceiling. In most homes, a ceiling fan is installed in the center of the room. If your fan includes lights, be sure the circuit has enough extra capacity to handle the load. If not, you must run a new circuit. For energy efficiency, look for units that have earned the ENERGY STAR rating. They are about 50 percent more efficient.

TOOLS AND MATERIALS SEE BASIC TOOLKIT AND P.443

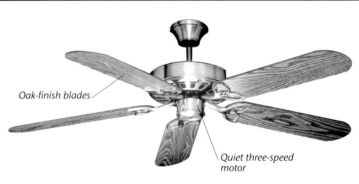

Oak-finish blades

Quiet three-speed motor

Traditional ceiling fan
This ceiling fan has 42-in (1,070-mm) oak-finish blades with antique brass hardware. It has a three-speed motor that is designed to be quiet.

STYLES AND MATERIALS

A wide range of fan and light styles and finishes is available, from wood blades with traditional brass hardware to sleek modern designs. Fans also come with or without lights.

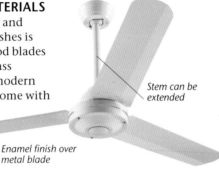

Stem can be extended

Enamel finish over metal blade

Modern ceiling fan
This three-blade ceiling fan has an enamel finish over metal blades. Some ceiling fans, such as this one, are offered with extension stems.

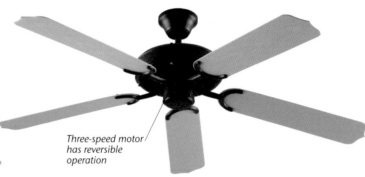

Three-speed motor has reversible operation

Reverse operation
This five-blade ceiling fan has three-speeds. It is operated by a built-in pull chain, and has a reversible operation. As with many ceiling fans, wall switches are available.

▮▮ INSTALLING A CEILING FAN

Before you begin to replace the ceiling fixture with a new ceiling fan, turn off the electrical power running to the ceiling box. Then carefully remove the old light fixture from the ceiling.

A

B

Carefully remove the ceiling box, so that you do not cut through or damage any wires.

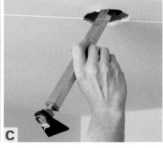

C

Insert the heavy-duty bar hanger into the ceiling hole.

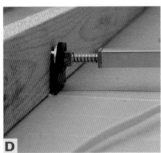

D

Place the bar across the hole, feet pointing down, and secure it against the joists on each side of the hole.

E

Thread the wires through a fan-rated ceiling box.

Mount the ceiling box to the bar hanger, and secure the box in place.

F

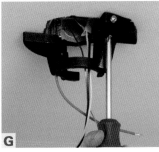

Thread the wire into the fan motor down through the rod and canopy.

G **Insert the wires** through the mounting plate. With the bolts in place, tighten the mounting plate to the ceiling.

H **Assemble the fixture's** canopy and motor following the manufacturer's instructions.

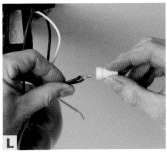

J **Insert the pin** to securely connect the rod to the canopy.

K **Hang the fan** by attaching the fixture to the mounting plate.

L **Connect the wires:** white to white, black to black. Cover with a wire nut. Put the wires and nuts into the box.

M **Attach the canopy** to the mounting plate. Tighten the screws.

Follow the manufacturer's directions to attach the fan blades to the fixture.

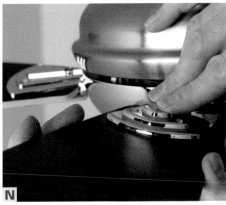

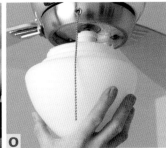

O **Insert a lightbulb,** then secure the light globe to the fixture.

P **Turn** on the electrical power.

FURTHER INFORMATION

Ceiling Fan Accessories
From a variety of ceiling blade finishes to the number of speeds, there is a growing selection of ceiling fan accessories that make it easy to fit a new ceiling fan that is in keeping with your interior design. The most important accessories to keep in mind are the type of mounting, the lighting, and the fan and light controls.

Mounting
If you have a fairly standard flat ceiling, a ceiling fan should be relatively easy to mount. If you have a slanted ceiling, you will need to purchase special mounting accessories for the fan to hang correctly. Make sure the fan you choose offers the mounting accessories before purchasing.

Lighting
Integrated light fixtures, usually mounted on the bottom of the ceiling fan, are popular. Nearly all ENERGY STAR qualified fixtures use bowl lighting. Stemmed lights are also available with three or four stems, which can be pointed up or down.

Uplights direct the light toward the ceiling, providing a soft, indirect light source.

Controls
Standard controls include a pull chain and a motor-reversing switch. Depending on the model you choose, a remote or wall control can be offered as standard or as an accessory. Some remote and wall controls work with different brands of ceiling fan, but certain remotes should only be used with specific brands.

INSTALLING OUTDOOR LIGHTING

Outdoor lighting helps to show visitors the way to your front door after dark, and is an excellent burglar deterrent. Lighting down the garden simply adds an extra dimension to your enjoyment of this outdoor space. The wiring work involved in the job described here is quite straightforward, but you must take great care to ensure that any work you do outside is correctly installed and is electrically safe.

TOOLS AND MATERIALS SEE BASIC TOOLKIT AND P.443

BUILDING REGULATIONS APPROVAL

Outdoor power installaations are tightly controlled by the Canadian Electrical Code and local building regulations. Make sure you always obtain permits when taking electricity outside the walls of your home.

The only job described here for which your local authority might not need to be notified is installing a light on a house wall, unless it is controlled by an outside switch. However, you must still have the work tested and certified by a qualified electrician to ensure that it is safe. Installing low-voltage lighting may also be exempt from notification, depending on the type being installed. If in doubt, check with your local authority.

TYPES OF LIGHTS

Outdoor lighting can be in two forms electrically but can be in many different forms aesthetically. Some lights can be connected directly to the house current of 120 volts AC, while others are also available as 12 volts DC. 12 volt DC lighting usually comes with a voltage transformer that plugs into a house outlet and converts the power to the required voltage. Whereas the house current can be lethal if installed or used incorrectly, 12 volts DC is completely safe against electrical shock.

Lights come in a vast array of colors and designs to fit anyone's preference. And they can be placed on the house, out on the grounds, at the base of trees shining upward, and in the tops of trees shining down. The homeowner can design any type of landscape or mood with lighting.

As is the usual case with any outdoor electrical supplies, the lighting should be on a Ground Fault Circuit Interrupter for safety. Normally outdoor lighting has been designed to withstand the rigors of the weather, but your lights need to be placed so that they do not stand in water or are exposed to direct rain unless they are designed for that.

OUTDOOR LIGHT STYLES

Outdoor lights come in styles to suit all tastes. So before you go to the store, have any idea how you want your landscaping to look and choose lighting that fits your preferred design.

LOW-VOLTAGE LIGHTS

Low-voltage lighting often comes in a package with a transformer, a timer or photocell, and wiring. It will come with instructions for proper installation and suggestions for design. It can be hardwired in to an electrical junction box, or just plugged in to an exterior outlet. Some outdoor low-voltage lights are battery operated and have photo cell charging panels built in to charge the batteries during the day.

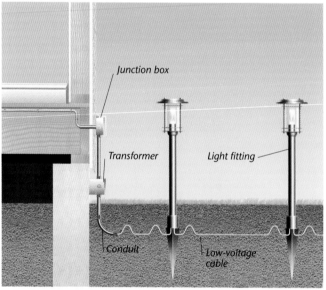

Junction box

Transformer *Light fitting*

Conduit *Low-voltage cable*

Outdoor lighting
The outdoor low-voltage lighting system shown here is powered through a transformer that has been hard-wired into a junction box. Because of the low voltage, the cable does not need to be buried deep underground.

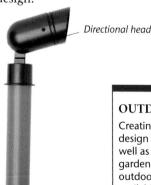

Directional head

Outdoor spotlights
Spotlights can be used to highlight special features, or may be used to improve safety. Unlike flood lights that are designed to wash an entire area with light, spots concentrate the light into a much smaller area.

OUTDOOR SOUND

Creating a mood in your landscape design can extend to sound as well as lighting. Music in the garden is often called for during outdoor gatherings. Speakers are available in many different styles. Some mount flush into a hole in the wall or cornice, some mount on the surface and can be directionally adjusted, and others sit on the ground and look like a large rock or seat.

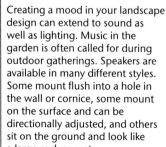
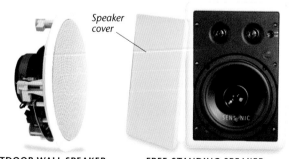

Speaker cover

OUTDOOR WALL SPEAKER **FREE-STANDING SPEAKER**

INSTALLING A LIGHT FIXTURE

In some light fixtures, you can connect the power wires directly to the lampholder terminals, as shown here. In others you will need to twist loose wires together and cap them with wire nuts as shown in F below. Run some caulking around the fitting's baseplate to seal it to the wall and keep water out.

A

Drill a ½-in (10-mm) hole from outside, angled upwards to prevent water penetration. Feed the spur cable through from inside.

B

Hold the new light over the cable exit point and mark the positions of its screws. Drill and plug the holes and secure the light to the wall.

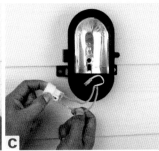

C

Feed the cable through the light's baseplate and connect the cores to the lampholder. Use heat-resistant sleeving on live and neutral cores.

INSTALLING AN EXTERIOR LIGHT

This explanation assumes that there is already a location chosen for the fixture, and that a wire extends through the exterior wall ready for attachment. It is a good idea to caulk the hole around the wire to keep out moisture and bugs.

A

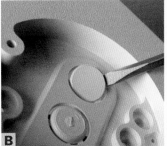

B

Remove the knock-out. Make sure that you remove one that lines up with the wire when the base is in position.

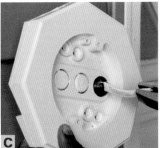

C

Feed the wire through the base from the back and slide the base up to the wall and pull all the slack out of the wire.

D

Make sure that the base is in the right position. Attach the base to the wall with appropriately sized screws.

E

Screw the fixture mounting strap on the base. Cut the wire to about 6 in (150 mm) and strip the outer covering back by about 2 in (50 mm).

F

Strip back the sheathing off the wires by about ¼ in (6 mm). Using wire nuts, connect the black to black and white to white on the fixture.

G

After connecting the ground wire, align the fixture and screw to the wall using the screws provided.

H

Once the fixture is attached, put in a bulb and turn the breaker back on. Test the fixture by switching on the light switch.

FURTHER INFORMATION

Most fixtures will come with a strap, mounting screws, wire nuts, and an instruction sheet outlining the installation procedures. Be sure to follow the manufacturer's recommendations. Make sure that all electrical connections are tight and that no wires are crimped or pinched. Of course, as with any electrical work, be sure to turn off the breaker to the work area and test to make sure that it is off.

There are three conductors in the wire that comes out of the wall. A black, a white, and one with no sheath. The one that has no sheath is the ground and should be connected to the fixture's grounding lug.

TAKING POWER OUTDOORS

There are two projects that are well worth carrying out to add convenience and safety to your use of electricity out of doors. The first is taking power to a garden shed or other outbuilding, and the second is installing an outdoor socket outlet for your garden power tools. The wiring work required is quite straightforward, but you must notify your local building codes department before you start so that it can be inspected and certified.

RUNNING CABLE OUTDOORS

If you need to take a power supply outside the house, you have to decide whether to run it overhead—easier to do, but unsightly and prone to accidental damage, or to take it underground—trickier to install, but far safer.

Running cable overhead

You can use ordinary PVC-sheathed cable if the span between the buildings is 10 ft (3 m) or less. Longer spans must be supported by a tensioned support wire and cable buckles, and this wire must be grounded to the house's main grounding point. The span must be at least 12 ft (3.5 m) above ground over a path, and 17 ft (5 m) above ground over a drive or other area with vehicular access.

Running cable underground

Cable runs underground can be protected by PVC conduit, solvent-welded together using straight connectors to make a continuous run, or you can use underground cable. Bury cables 18 in (460 mm) beneath paths or patios, and at 30 in (760 mm) beneath lawns and flowerbeds.

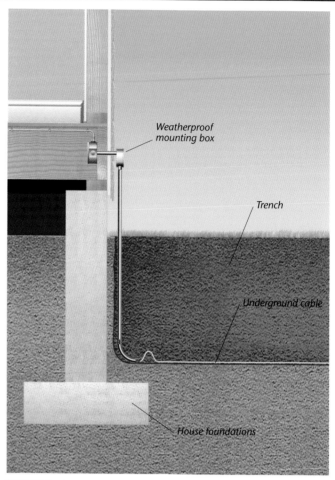

RUNNING CONDUIT UNDERGROUND

FITTING OUTDOOR SOCKET OUTLETS

Having a dedicated outdoor socket outlet on the house wall for garden power tools saves trailing long extension cords through open windows. It also provides the safety of GFCI protection for anyone using electrical equipment out of doors. All you need is a weatherproof outlet with a built-in high-sensitivity GFCI, plus a length of two-conductor and ground wire and a conveniently-located indoor socket outlet to which to connect the wiring. Alternatively you can install an ordinary outdoor outlet, and connect it to a separate GFCI indoors, or better yet wire it directly to the main power panel with a GFCI circuit breaker.

Positioning the outlet

Position the outdoor socket outlet so that you can drill a hole through the house wall and feed the wiring in close to the indoor outlet. Fit the mounting box over the exit hole, draw in the wiring, and connect it to the outlet terminals. Fit the faceplate on the box, making sure that the weatherproof seals are correctly positioned. Indoors, run the wiring to its connection point, via a separate GFCI, if necessary.

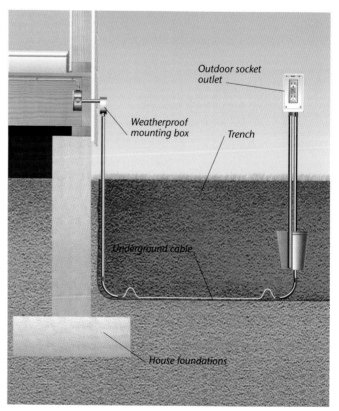

RUNNING CONDUIT UNDERGROUND WITH SEPARATE GFCI

TAKING A POWER SUPPLY TO AN OUTBUILDING

The best way to take power to an outbuilding is by running a 240-volt circuit from the main breaker panel in the house to a sub-panel in the outbuilding. Once the 240-volt circuit terminates in the sub-panel, it can be broken down into 240-volt circuits and 120-volt circuits as needed.

The line can be run using the appropriately sized underground cable only, but it is better to run the cable through PVC conduit to protect the cable from damage and moisture. The cable should be run about 18 in (450 mm) to 24 in (600 mm) below ground level.

Depending on the size of the outbuilding and its intended use, the 240-volt circuit breaker size will have to be determined. In most homeowner projects, a 20-amp or 30-amp breaker will be adequate. First it must be determined if there is an open space in the main breaker panel and then if the panel has the electrical capacity to handle another 30-amp circuit. It may very well take a licensed electrician to calculate this for you.

PROVIDING POWER FOR WATER FEATURES

The best way to provide power for fountains and wet location lighting is by the use of low voltage circuits. Low voltage usually means 12 volts—the same voltage as car batteries. Systems can be bought that provide wiring, lights, and the transformer. The transformer is plugged into a standard household outlet and transforms the electricity to 12 volt DC. This is safe to use in outdoor and wet locations because it cannot electrocute you or your pets.

The transformer should be plugged into an outlet that is protected by a Ground Fault Circuit Interrupter (GFCI). This added safety feature protects the circuit as well as the users. The installer should always follow the instructions that are provided with the low voltage system that will explain its use and installation.

OUTDOOR MOTION SENSORS

An outdoor motion sensor may add add comfort, safety, and convenience to your home. When you arrive home after dark, it senses your movements as you approach and turns on exterior lights. And you don't have to fumble in the dark for keys, or trip over things that you cannot see. An outdoor motion sensor also provides safety, because it comes on to let you know if anyone approaches your home so you can see who it is. It can also deter burglars by creating a well-lit area where they cannot be concealed as they attempt to gain entry.

These units are usually adjustable for sensitivity and angle so that they can be set to sense only montion on your property and will not pick up motion down the street or in the next yard.

OUTDOOR LIGHT WITH MOTION SENSOR

COVERED OUTDOOR OUTLETS

Exterior outlets can be single or duplex, and should have spring-loaded covers. The covers protect the outlet from bugs, insects, dirt, and moisture. These days they are also, by code, ground fault circuit interrupters (GFCI) for added safety. Outside, a person is more easily grounded and is often working with water and power tools so electrocution is a danger. If your home does not have GFCI protection, it can be added.

Flush mount outdoor wall plate
Covered outdoor outlets are often metal for durability and have spring-loaded covers.

HOT TUBS

Hot tubs are fixtures often found in new homes and if you don't have one, they can be purchased from many suppliers. They can be totally self contained—which makes for ease of installation, or can be bought as parts that must be placed and connected to make the completed unit. Buying as parts allows the homeowner to integrate the unit into the outdoor landscaping more fully, but a self- contained unit means quick and easy installation and that you can be soaking in it almost immediately.

Plumbing in a hot tub

The plumbing for a hot tub is totally self-contained, although you will have to connect it up to your home's water supply and drain. More information about planning plumbing work and joining pipes is given in the plumbing section, pp.466–483.

Connecting to the power supply

The electrical connection is normally by a 120-volt supply that must be on a dedicated circuit and must be grounded with a Ground Fault Circuit Interrupter.

Water makes a total surface connection to your body and if electricity is allowed to make contact with the water—either due to a wiring fault or during an electrical storm—it will make a contact with you. Because of the danger posed by mixing water and electricity, a grounding connection is imperative to afford safety from possible electrocution while using the hot tub. The electrical components of the hot tub must be grounded via a driven metal rod—as per local codes. This means that the rod is typically about six feet long and driven into the ground so that only a few inches of it is exposed. A heavy grounding strap or cable is attached to this using a grounding clamp for positive contact and the other end is connected with a clamp to the hot tub electrical system. See pp.436–437 for essential information on grounding, and working safely with electricity.

HOT TUB

Communications systems

UPGRADING THE TECHNOLOGY IN YOUR HOME CAN INVOLVE COMPLEX DIY WORK. TELECOMMUNICATIONS AND HOME-ENTERTAINMENT SYSTEMS MAY BE VISIBLE IF THEY WERE INSTALLED AFTER THE HOUSE WAS BUILT, BUT IF POSSIBLE MUCH OF THE WIRING WILL BE CONCEALED. HERE IS AN OVERVIEW OF SOME OF THE SYSTEMS YOU MAY BE CONSIDERING.

HOME AUTOMATION

For more than three decades there has been a growing trend in automating houses—replacing outdated and poor-quality cables and connections with today's structured wiring. This, along with wireless technology, is allowing our homes to become well-connected, hi-tech systems.

FURTHER INFORMATION

For your safety, and for proper functioning of your whole-house automation system, always consult with an expert before adding a new component. There are power restrictions on the circuits and cables in your home, as well as special adaptors needed to connect electronics for optimal functioning. If you are not confident working with electrical systems, hire professional help.

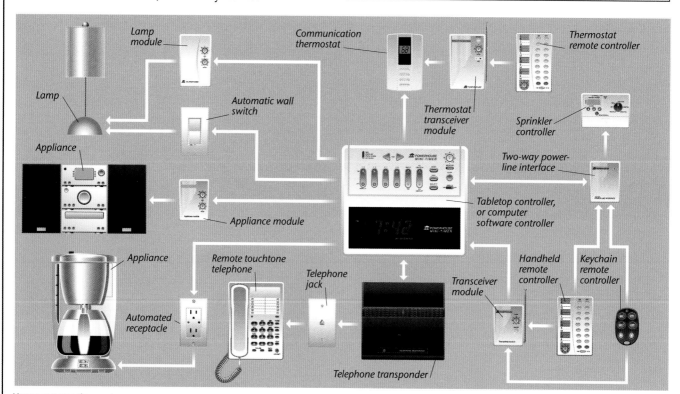

Home automation system
Appliances, sound systems, and communication systems can become interconnected in an automated house.

WORKING WITH COAXIAL CABLE

If you are installing new cable, plan the route of the coaxial cable with care. To minimize signal losses, always use good-quality cable, and keep the route as short as possible. Avoid sharp bends which could kink the cable, and avoid crushing it when driving in cable clips.

It is often easiest to run the cable down the outside of the house wall and take it into the room to be served through a hole drilled in the wall or a window frame. The cable can run directly from an external aerial, and can be fed from a loft aerial out through the eaves soffit board.

If the cable is to be run internally, drop it inside timber-framed partition walls or down service ducts, such as the one housing the soil pipe. It can then be run in floor voids as necessary to reach wall-mounted aerial outlet positions.

A

To prepare coaxial cable, slit the sheath with a sharp knife. Then cut round it about 2 in (50 mm) from the end and remove the offcut.

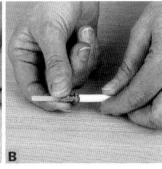

B

To fit a connector, slip the screw cap over the cable. Push the copper braid mesh back to expose the insulation round the central core.

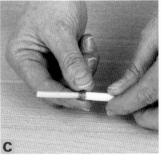

C

Gather the mesh into a neat bunch round the end of the outer sheath. Trim off any stray strands with side cutters.

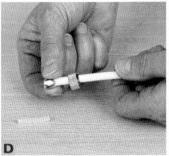

D

Cut away all but ⅛ in (3 mm) of the inner core and slip the metal claw gripper over the braid. Pinch it with pliers to tighten it.

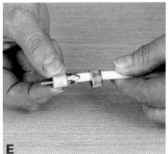

E

Fit the plug pin over the central core and push it up against the claw gripper. Trim off the excess core so it is flush with the end of the pin.

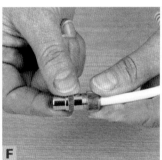

F

Slip on the plug body so it fits over the plug pin, and tighten the screw cap onto it to complete the assembly of the connector.

DOORBELLS

Traditional doorbells are wired from the side of the entry door to an interior hallway where they create a sound. For large houses where the sound may be lost in remote areas or for houses with occupants with hearing difficulties, there are doorbell products to meet those special needs. Shown here are a strobe, ambient, and a wireless doorbell.

Can be plugged into any outlet

Strobe doorbell
The device plugs into a standard outlet in any room and notifies occupants that someone has depressed the bell with a strobe light. Suitable for users who have hearing loss.

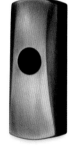

Light shines when doorbell is pressed

Ambient doorbell
A warm glow indicates that a visitor is at the entry door. An ambient doorbell is an option for users who have hearing loss.

Wireless doorbell
A wireless doorbell can be easily located anywhere in the home where you will be able to hear it, rather than near to the entry door.

▌ REPAIRING A DOORBELL

If a doorbell isn't working, check for loose wire connections before replacing it. Doorbells require less than the typical circuit of 120 volts so they need a transformer. The circuit has three connections—between the button and the transformer, between the transformer and the bell, and between the bell and button. There may be more than one bell in the system.

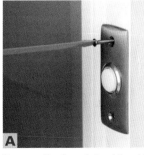

A

Remove the faceplate of the old doorbell, by unscrewing the fasteners holding it in place.

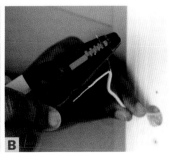

B

Check the wires for loose connections and damage. Prepare for more secure connections, stripping wire back if necessary.

C

Reattach the wires to the terminals in the bell. Push the wires into the wall. Fasten the faceplate back in place on the wall.

HOME AUTOMATION

Technology has taken over the wiring systems of many houses in this country. From remotes that operate all of your appliances to sound systems that flow into any room of your house, if there is not a technology option available that meets your idea of a perfectly wired house, there will be soon. Referred to as "smart homes," "structured wiring systems," or "wired houses," the subject of home automation covers everything from phones to computers and refrigerators. With the ever-expanding selection of products available, we have included just a selection of some of the basic pieces and parts you may need to know about.

SURGES

Home automation equipment is sensitive to power surges due to lightning storms or changes at the power company. Multiple outlet suppressors are common quick-fixes to household surge protection, but look into surge suppressors that are installed at the power source for your home—the service panel. It installs into your box in a similar manner to a new circuit. As many hi- tech devices are expensive, installing a surge protection system can be well worth it. See p.439 for more information.

HOME AUTOMATION VS. HOME NETWORKING

Home networking is different than home automation. While home automation makes it possible for you to control all of your electrical systems more easily, home networking means all of your electrical devices are connected and can work together. You may be familiar with this concept from networked computer systems. Power-line carriers are used as the master-house remote controller. They send a digital signal to the electrical circuits via a transmitter mounted inside your wall or plugged into a standard receptacle.

While it's difficult to retrofit a house and make it automated, you can run wires in surface mounted boxes—see pp.444–445 for information on how to run wires around doors and baseboards.

HOME AUTOMATION SYSTEMS

At home, you can control your network your lights or appliances using one simple remote control. You can access and monitor home systems from your computer, or even access your home's network remotely. This means that you have the option to turn on selected lights from work, to increase safety upon entering your home if you are planning to work late. It also means that you can check to see if you have left a light on. Some systems are being created that allow you to monitor the food you use in your refrigerator, providing a store list you may order online and send to the grocery to deliver to your home.

Other opportunities for home automation

Security systems are a frequently-used home automation system. You can choose security cameras that use a special cable TV channel (called CATV), which provide a signal to multiple locations in your house.

Motion-sensor light switches (see also p.455) are ideal for added security in and around your home. They can also be used as nightlights, and in areas where you tend to have your hands full—laundry rooms, garages, and entryways.

Light networking is an option for creating pre-programmed combinations and levels of lighting for areas such as home theater rooms, kitchens, and bathrooms. Remote controls for lighting are also available.

Plumbing can be part of the home automation system. You've undoubtedly experienced the automatic faucets, toilets, and hand dryers at restaurants and airports. Now, the automatic photoelectronic-sensored devices are available in homes. These not only help regulate the amount of water and energy you use, helping save money on your bills, they also help create a sanitary environment.

CABLES AND WIRES

Computers, telephones, and television all have different cable and wire needs. There are a few basic types that you should be familiar with. Structured wiring uses a wider bandwidth than typical wiring, allowing computer internet connections and voice communications to be clear. Audio/ visual cords are necessary to patch most televisions and related equipment. Speaker wires are rated depending on the intended use. Optical fibers may be needed for some systems that require a certain bandwidth or speed.

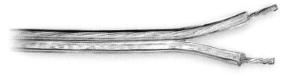

Speaker wire
Shown here is a 18/2 AWG speaker wire that is not rated for in-wall use. Available in lengths of 25–100 ft (7–30 m).

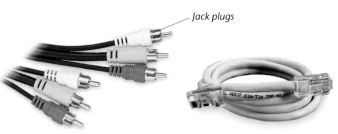

Jack plugs

Audio/visual cords
A/V cords are used to connect audio and video equipment. Shown here is a 6 ft (2 m) gold-plated composite A/V cable.

Patch cords
Patch cords are essential in any home, and are often used for computer connection. Optical fibre patch cords are available.

FURTHER INFORMATION

Coaxial cable, often called co-ax, is braided on the outside with a copper wire running down the inside of the cable. The braided part is grounded. It is designed to efficiently carry either analog or digital radio and TV frequencies. Boosters are available if you desire to increase the strength of your signal. Shown to the right is a surge suppressor for coaxial

COAXIAL SURGE SUPPRESSOR

cable. A safety precaution for users, it also protects your electronic equipment from damaging power surges.

WALL PLATES

Modern wall plates are designed to be adaptable for the many possible technology uses you may choose for your home. Phone, computer, music, and many other systems typically require a different wire and jack. Distribution boxes and panels offer you the adaptability to run all of your systems into one panel on a wall. Some types allow you to run all of the power services that come into your home through the distribution panel and then on to every item of equipment in your home. Centrally located, the panel helps organize the runs in your house, too. Special wall plates are also offered to organize specific types of electrical equipment, as the audio panels shown below.

Spring clips

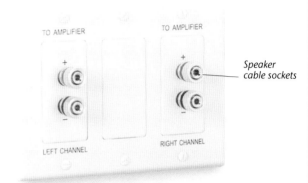

Speaker cable sockets

Audio/visual wall plate
Specialized wall plates are available for powering stereos, televisions, and other audio or video equipment. This model has spade terminals with spring clips and is also available with a double row.

Music distribution/home theater wall panel
If you have extensive music and home entertainment needs, the home theater/music distribution panel helps organize and centralize the various components.

Audio distribution panel
This audio panel is designed to connect up to 10 pairs of speakers situated throughout the home to enable your music to be available in every room. It requires a triple gang box for installation.

SPLITTERS

Splitters let you use a single connection point to distribute power or information to more than one device. Frequently used in houses to split a phone line to allow both a phone connection and a simultaneous Internet connection, there are many hi-tech varieties available to serve your home automation needs. Shown here are video splitters, which can distribute a signal to more than one monitor.

Video diplexer
This two way video splitter is gold plated. It allows a connection from one input to two outputs.

Four-way splitter
You can split a single input into more than two outputs—a four-way splitter is shown here.

TELECOMMUNICATIONS

Home automation includes telecommunications—your phone, computer, fax, for example. From using multiple telephone lines, to transmitting images over the internet, to home computer network—there are growing needs for advanced systems in our homes. Your telephone and other communications network components in your house can control security functions and other household systems.

Voice connector
Connectors are usually color-coded, and used to adapt entertainment distribution panels or telephone jacks, for example. Shown here is a snap-in voice connector.

Indoor/outdoor phone jack
And outdoor-rated phone jack is a sensible and safe preparation that allows emergency telephone access from an outdoor pool or the backyard. This phone jack mounts in a standard electrical box and is rated for both indoor and outdoor use.

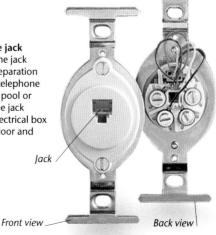

Jack

Front view   *Back view*

FURTHER INFORMATION

While there are many home-automation options available for consumers to install and use, there are no universal standards for the manufacturers. For the last decade, many organizations have attempted to form home-automation standards to make sure that appliances, lighting, wiring, and other equipment are compatible. Even without these standards, it is crucial to your safety that you follow local building ordinances and manufacturer's guidelines regarding installation.

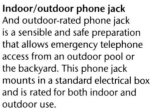

ELECTRICS

TELEPHONE SYSTEMS

A telephone extension outlet can be installed in every room except the bathroom if you wish. You must not plug in more than four telephones at once, however, otherwise none will ring properly. The incoming line will be connected to a master socket outlet (also known as a linebox) installed by your telecoms supplier. Most local phone companies provide enough power for about five telephones per line but the number of phones you can have on a line depends on the amount of power the telephone requires. Always check with your local telephone company to find out the rules for working on a telephone line in your home.

CABLE CONNECTING TOOL

An IDC cable connector tool is used to push telephone cable cores into the screwless brass blade terminals that are used in some extension phone outlets.

PLANNING YOUR REQUIREMENTS

There is more than one way to route a domestic telephone. With home-run wiring, each jack is wired to the main junction box. If one wire fails, it only affects one of the telephones in your home. The others would still work. Closed loop wiring connects each telephone jack in a line with a wire that returns to the junction box. Even with a break in a wire, you will still have power to the broken point. In an open loop system, all wires are connected to the junction box through a previous jack. If there is a break, all of the jacks after the break will no longer have power.

Cat 3 telephone jack
Category 3 telephone jacks are designed for use with category 3 wires.

Cat 5 telephone jack
Category 5 telephone jacks are designed for use with category 5 wires.

Outlets wired in series
The telephone cable loops from outlet to outlet, terminating at the most remote one.

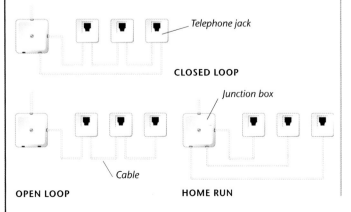

Telephone jack

CLOSED LOOP

Junction box

Cable

OPEN LOOP　　　　**HOME RUN**

RUNNING CABLE

The best place to conceal telephone cable is by running it through walls. The section of cable running up to an outlet can then be passed up through a stud bay. Alternatively, if you are happy with a surface-mounted installation, you can clip the cable to the top of the baseboards. At doorways, run the cable up and over the edge of the molding; do not conceal it under floorcoverings at door thresholds. Pass it from room to room through holes drilled through the wall, or up and down via the ceiling void.

You can also enclose cable in slim surface-mounted raceway channels, which are available in plastic and metal. They are grounded and each has specifications for which type of wire can be used. Always keep it at least 16 in (40 cm) away from other wires to avoid interference on the line.

PREPARING CABLE

Prepare the phone cable for connection by slitting its sheath lengthways for about 2 in (50 mm) and trimming off the waste. Inside are four to eight thin cores, color-coded as detailed below. Usually referred to as Category 2 through 6, as the Category number increases, the amount of data and information you are able to send over the cable increases. Category 3 has three pairs of wires, and Category 5 has four pairs of wires (shown below).

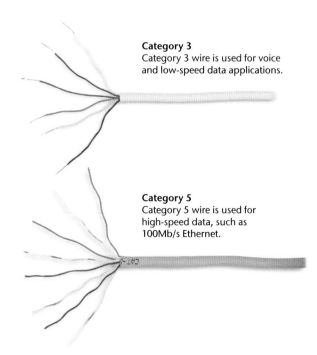

Category 3
Category 3 wire is used for voice and low-speed data applications.

Category 5
Category 5 wire is used for high-speed data, such as 100Mb/s Ethernet.

TELEPHONE WIRE

Telephone wire is color coded to help make it easier to install. Standard colors are black, yellow, red, and green. Some, as in the Cat 5 have colors striped with white. No matter the coloring system of your wires, it's important that the like-colored wires should be connected in your telephone system.

TESTING TELEPHONE WIRE

Use a telephone line tester to test the polarity of each telephone jack in your home. Insert the tester's plug into the jack. If the tester shows a green light, it means that your jack is wired correctly. If it is not wired correctly, there will be no light.

CATEGORIES OF WIRE

There is a range of wire types available for telephones. Consider all the ways you may be using your home telecommunications system, now and in future, prior to deciding on the type of wire you need to use.

Wire is rated based on the megabits per second (mb/s) it is able to transmit. The most common wire found for phones is Category 3 (Cat 3), which is designed to reliably carry data up to 10 Mb/s, with a possible bandwidth of 16 MHz. It was the most popular wiring choice during the 1990s.

Category 5 (Cat 5) has been typically the highest rated wire you might choose, but Category 5e adds specifications for far-end crosstalk. Category 6 is designed for gigabit ethernet connections and up to 250 MHz.

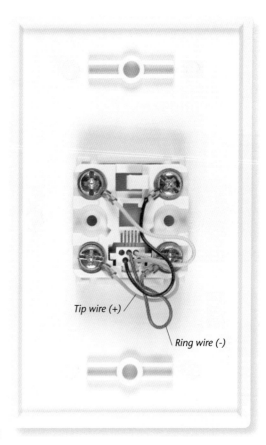

Tip wire (+)

Ring wire (-)

Cat 3 jack
When wiring any jack, make sure to connect the correct wires. This is a category 3 wired jack, which is the FCC's minimum standard for phones.

BACK OF CAT 3 JACK

▊ INSTALLING A TELEPHONE CAT 5 JACK

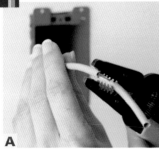

A

Remove the cover from a phone jack. Strip 2 in (50 mm) of the sheathing from the ends of the wires.

B

Separate the wires matching the colors and patterns to the jack.

C

Using a punch-down tool, connect the wire conductors to the jack.

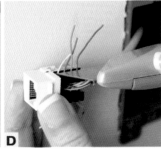

D

Cut off the excess wire using a utility knife.

E

Snap the back of the jack over the wires.

F

Insert the jack into the cover plate.

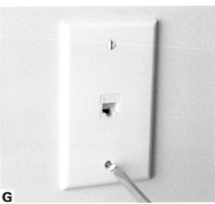

G

Attach the cover plate to the wall with screws.

PROBLEM SOLVER

REPLACING A BROKEN LIGHT BULB

Keep safety in mind. Turn off the power, and use personal safety equipment. Wear leather gloves and eye protection as well as a head covering, if you are working on an overhead fixture.

TOOLS AND MATERIALS
Needlenose pliers, gloves, tarp, voltage tester

A Put down a tarp beneath the bulb to catch any glass as you work.

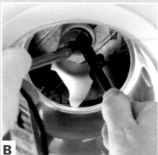

B Turn off the power. You may want to use a voltage tester to make sure the power is off.

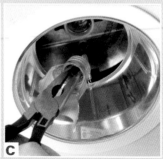

C Insert pliers into the broken base. Spread the handles apart, exerting force against the sides of the bulb base, and rotate counterclockwise.

CHANGING A CIRCUIT IN A BREAKER

Occasionally breakers need to be replaced, or new circuits need to be added to a service panel. Care must be taken when working with a service panel. Always turn off the power before starting any work. If you feel uncomfortable about completing the task, consult or hire a professional. Your local building codes may require an inspection of work completed on your main service panel.

A Turn off the main circuit breaker in the breaker box.

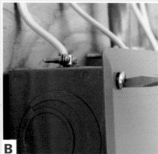

B Remove the cover of the circuit breaker box.

C Using a tester, determine if the circuits are live. Locate the breaker that is in the off position. Make sure it is all the way in the off position.

D Lift the breaker out using a screwdriver.

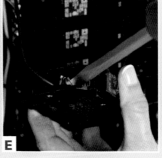

E Disconnect the black wire from the breaker. Observe exactly where the wire was placed so you know where it goes on the new breaker.

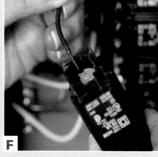

F Reinstall the black wire on the new breaker. Be sure it is firmly inserted and secured with the screw.

ADAPTING A CIRCUIT FOR MORE POWER

Most electrical needs in a home require a 120-volt circuit. Sometimes you will need to adjust circuits or add a 240-volt circuit to accommodate cooking ranges, clothes dryers, and other appliances. Unlike the 120-volt circuits, 240-volt circuits fill two spaces on your breaker box. It will have two wires; one red and one black.

TOOLS AND MATERIALS
Screwdriver, tester, breaker

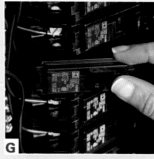

G Clip the breaker into the box, making sure the breaker is in the off position.

H Replace the cover on the circuit breaker box.

I Flip the switch to the on position. Turn the main breaker back on.

CHANGING A RECEPTACLE TO GFCI

Bathrooms, garages, and other areas of the home are required to have GFCI circuits. Installing GFCI at the receptacles makes it easier for you to reset the circuit without having to go to the panel box.

GFCI RECEPTACLES

GFCI receptacles have test and reset buttons. The test button pops out when a ground fault occurs. To reset a GFCI, press the button in. Test GFCI receptacles on a regular basis and replace them when they are found to be malfunctioning.

TOOLS AND MATERIALS
Voltage tester, screw driver, GFCI tester

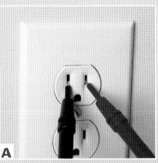

A
Turn off the power to the receptacle and test the receptacle to make sure no power is running to the outlet.

B
Remove the cover plate. Remove the receptacle from the electrical box.

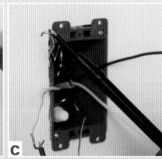

C
Voltage test the wires in the box.

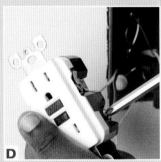

D
Connect the live wire to the hot line terminal screw on the GFCI receptacle.

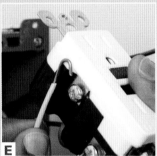

E
Connect the white neutral wires to the white line terminal screw on the GFCI receptacle.

F
Connect the bare ground wire to the green ground screw. Test the receptacle with a GFCI tester.

CHANGING A BROKEN RECEPTACLE

Damaged receptacles and receptacle covers are fairly easy to replace if you do not plan to make any modifications to the receptacle.

TOOLS AND MATERIALS
Screwdriver, receptacle, receptacle cover

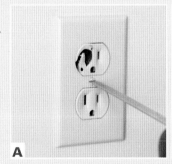

A
Unscrew the receptacle cover from the wall.

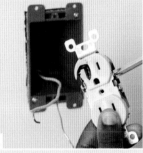

B
Disconnect the receptacle from from the wires in the box.

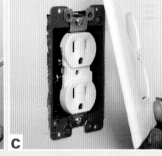

C
Attach the wires to the new receptacle and screw the new cover in place.

USING ADAPTERS

Electrical wiring adapters and accessories help organize your wires, store or hide long cords, or provide grounding at outlets that are not wired with GFCI. Shown here is an extension reel and surge protectors.

Extension reel
DIYers often need extension cords. A reel offers a way to store cords and keep them neat during a job.

Wall mounted surge protector
These protect electrical equipment from power surges. The one shown here mounts onto the receptacle.

Surge protector
This reduces the number of cords running to an outlet and can make the cords more accessible too.

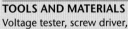

PLUMBING

PIPE CONNECTIONS
FAUCETS AND VALVES

PLUMBING SYSTEMS

Your plumbing system consists of two parts—water supply and waste disposal. The water supply may run direct to each point of use, or the system may have storage facilities for cold and/or hot water. The waste-disposal system carries used water from each appliance via waste and soil pipes to the drains. For more information on re-use of water, see pp.389–391.

SEWER DRAINAGE ALTERNATIVES

If a house doesn't have sewer drainage, waste water flows into a cesspool or a septic tank.

Cesspool
This is simply a large storage tank that has to be emptied on a regular basis by a specialist contractor. Most existing cesspools have been replaced by a septic tank (see below), or have been filled in when local sewerage was eventually provided in the vicinity.

Septic tank
This is a chamber that works like a miniature sewage plant, treating waste water from the property by a combination of filtration and bacterial action so that the treated water can be safely discharged into the ground. The sludge remaining in the chamber has to be removed periodically.

HISTORICAL EVOLUTION

Plumbing is constantly evolving, with new demands, new devices, and new problems to solve. Your house has plumbing that is somewhere between the old hand pump and some futuristic design we don't even know yet. Evolution explains why homes have different plumbing systems. In addition, in Canada the potential for freezing imposes its own requirements. We cannot permit cisterns in the attic nor unprotected piping inside external walls. Demands for comfort as well as demands for water conservation have radically changed our showers and even put in question the energy-wasteful North American hot water tank. Upgrading during renovation to the latest code standards will help you reap the benefits of safety developments as well as energy and water conservation progress.

SAFEETY DEVICES

Many safety devices should exist in your plumbing system. The pressure relief valves on top of hot water heaters and boilers are designed to release hot water to the floor if the pressure inside becomes dangerously high. Siphon breaks on outdoor hose bibs prevent polluted water from the end of the hose (swimming pools, chemical sprayers, etc.) from being drawn back into household drinking water.

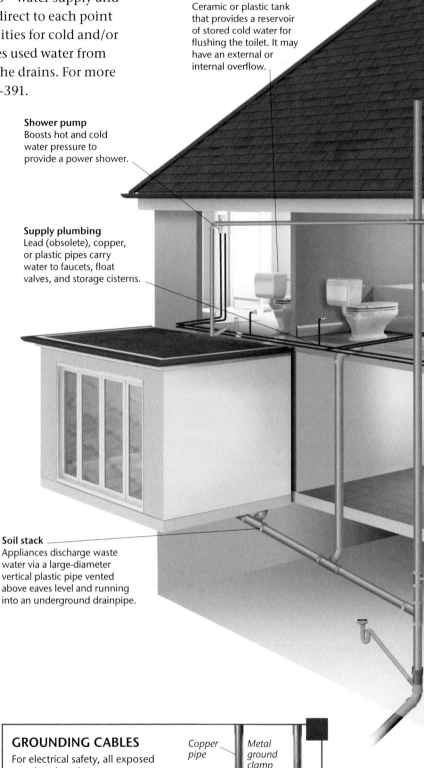

Toilet tank
Ceramic or plastic tank that provides a reservoir of stored cold water for flushing the toilet. It may have an external or internal overflow.

Shower pump
Boosts hot and cold water pressure to provide a power shower.

Supply plumbing
Lead (obsolete), copper, or plastic pipes carry water to faucets, float valves, and storage cisterns.

Soil stack
Appliances discharge waste water via a large-diameter vertical plastic pipe vented above eaves level and running into an underground drainpipe.

GROUNDING CABLES

For electrical safety, all exposed metalwork such as copper pipes must be made safe. In some areas they are required to be linked to the house's electrical grounding system with single-core ground cables. These must be attached to the pipes with special metal ground clamps. If you have no bonding conductors, call an electrician to install them.

Copper pipe

Metal ground clamp

Ground cable

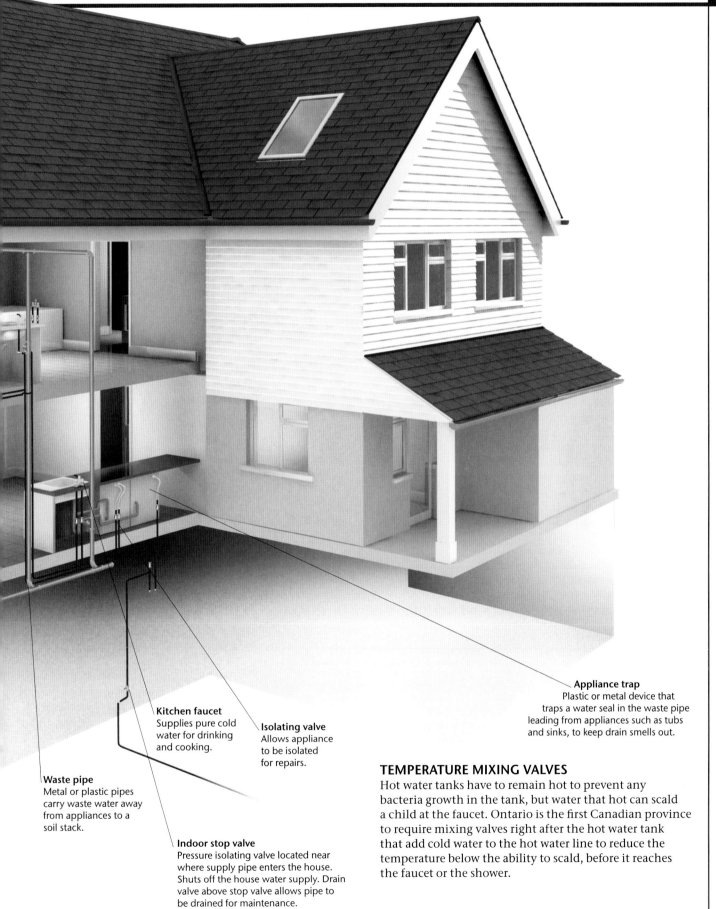

Appliance trap
Plastic or metal device that traps a water seal in the waste pipe leading from appliances such as tubs and sinks, to keep drain smells out.

Kitchen faucet
Supplies pure cold water for drinking and cooking.

Isolating valve
Allows appliance to be isolated for repairs.

Waste pipe
Metal or plastic pipes carry waste water away from appliances to a soil stack.

Indoor stop valve
Pressure isolating valve located near where supply pipe enters the house. Shuts off the house water supply. Drain valve above stop valve allows pipe to be drained for maintenance.

TEMPERATURE MIXING VALVES

Hot water tanks have to remain hot to prevent any bacteria growth in the tank, but water that hot can scald a child at the faucet. Ontario is the first Canadian province to require mixing valves right after the hot water tank that add cold water to the hot water line to reduce the temperature below the ability to scald, before it reaches the faucet or the shower.

WATER SUPPLY SYSTEMS

Whether you are connected to a municipal water supply or a well and septic tank, inside the house it all works just about the same. Cold water comes into the house under pressure. Some of it gets heated up, under even more pressure. Valves and faucets keep it under control until it all drains out by gravity.

THE SUPPLY SYSTEM

The supply system starts as a single cold water line. One branch splits off to a hot water tank, or a new tankless hot water heater, and then the two parallel lines of hot and cold water head all over the house. In our modern Canadian homes, the toilet is just about the only device that has only a cold water supply. Isolation valves permit closing off just a part of the system to be able to make repairs. If you are changing faucets and do not have shut-off valves directly below the sink, add them while you are at it. It will save you a lot of trouble in the future. Getting hot water to a remote part of the house can be accelerated with a demand pump that circulates water inside the system, getting the hot water there fast and not wasting water down the drain. Low-flow shower heads and low-flow toilets are major contributors to water conservation.

THE DRAIN SYSTEM

The drainage system functions by gravity, which means that the size of the pipe and the precise slope of the pipe are critical for proper functioning of the drains. Surprisingly, research has shown that 3-in drain pipes work better than 4-in ones for low-flow toilets. Drain pipes are commonly made out of plastic, and must be well supported with pipe strapping the full length of their run, or they will develop sags in the line. Sags change the slope of the drain and can be the cause of blockage and back-ups. Drain traps are devices that hold water to create a seal against sewage odors, but allow waste through the drain. Chemical drain cleaners are never kind to piping or sewage systems, so use harsh chemicals sparingly, if at all. Having removable clean-outs in the bottom of drain traps is a better maintenance solution.

THE VENT SYSTEM

Together with the drain system, the venting system is also often poorly understood. It extends the drain piping up above the roof. Without proper connections to the vent stack, water will not flow properly in the drains, and the drain traps may gurgle or empty, allowing sewage odors into the house, rather than discharging them above the roof. As water rushes down the drain pipe it often creates suction behind it. The vent system allows air into this section of pipe to prevent that suction from pulling on the water that should remain in the traps. Do not install a drain without a proper vent connection.

Shower supply
Hot and cold water supplied to shower pump.

Cold supply to toilet tank
Runs to float valve that refills tank when flushed.

Waste water pipe
Pipes carry waste water away from appliances.

CODES

If your home uses gas for any reason, be extra careful before attempting any plumbing work. Just like with water pipes, gas pipes are supposed to have shut-off valves. Always check with your local building department before attempting to work on your plumbing.

Hot water main (trunk line)
Main piping of hot water
supply in the house, usually
a ¾ in copper pipe that feeds
into ½ in pipe branches.

Cold water main (trunk line)
Main supply of cold water
piping in the house, usually
a ¾ in copper pipe that feeds
into ½ in pipe branches.

Riser
Piping that supplies
water vertically
through the house.

Domestic hot water tank
Produces the hot-water supply
used in bathrooms, kitchens
and appliances.

Main shut-off
Shut-off valve that stops all water
flow in the house. It is usually
located near the water meter.

Water meter
Measures the amount
of water used inside the
house. It is typically owned
by the water company.

KEY TO PIPE FUNCTIONS
— Hot supply pipes
— Cold supply pipes

PLUMBING TOOLS AND MATERIALS

Along with a basic toolkit, there are a number of tools that will be necessary to complete plumbing jobs. Not all the tools shown here may be required for every job; the checklist opposite shows which tools are needed for key tasks. Material requirements are also shown and explained over the next few pages.

PLUMBING ACCESSORIES

As well as pipes, there are a number of materials required for installing or working on a plumbing system. The most commonly used materials are shown below. There are also many other products used in plumbing systems such as the descalers, cleaners, and the various inhibitors used to maintain efficient hydronic heating systems.

WRENCHES

Multipurpose gripping tools are used for holding fixtures and fasteners in position and for tightening or loosening various types of joints.

Adjust wrench width here

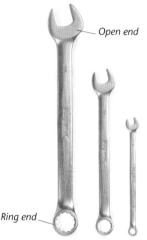

Open end

Ring end

Adjustable wrenches
A set of adjustable wrenches can be used for most domestic nut or bolt sizes. These sets are commonly sold as three wrenches in different sizes.

Set of wrenches
A standard wrench set is also essential. Sets with both open and ring ends are advisable. Ring ends are less likely to slip, open ends are better in tight spaces.

Washer selection box
Useful for washers, bolts, and other small items.

Compartments separate each type of washer

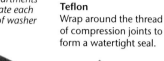

Teflon
Wrap around the thread of compression joints to form a watertight seal.

Solder
An alloy, supplied as a wire coil, which melts at a temperature lower than the metal pipes being joined. It may contain lead or be lead-free. Lead wire is not suitable for drinking-water pipes, so always choose the lead-free option.

Gas blowtorch
Used to heat pipe joints when soldering. Always store upright.

Tube-cleaning brush
Wire brush to clean the inside of a pipe joint.

Soldering mat
Used to protect surrounding surfaces from the heat generated when soldering a joint.

Locking pliers
Locking pliers have jaws similar to those of slip-joint pliers. The wrench may be locked firmly in position by a lever positioned on the handle section.

Rotate screw to adjust jaw size

Pipe wrench
A heavy-duty adjustable wrench that has serrations along the jaws to provide greater grip. When pressure is applied to the handle, the jaws grip even tighter to the object being held.

KEYS

There are some specially shaped wrenches and keys that are designed for specific plumbing jobs. The three used most often are shown here.

Sink wrench
A specially designed wrench that allows for access in particularly tight areas, such as under sinks or bathtubs. Available with either fixed or adjustable jaws. A fixed-jaw version is shown here.

Slip-joint pliers
Adjustment is by dislocating the joint to widen or narrow the distance between the two jaw sections. The jaws are usually serrated and concave for extra grip on nuts, bolts, or rounded fasteners.

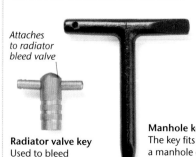

Attaches to radiator bleed valve

Radiator valve key
Used to bleed radiators.

Manhole key
The key fits into a hole in a manhole cover for easy removal. Two keys are normally required.

Stop valve key
Shaped to fit over the handle of a faucet or stop valve. The long handle provides easy access to a stop valve.

UNBLOCKING TOOLS

Blocked toilets and drains can be expensive to fix if you call a plumber for an emergency; for this reason it is worth attempting to clear the blockage yourself first. A plunger works best when there is a secure seal between it and the toilet. There should be some water present to help the suction process. If you are trying to unclog a sink or a bathtub with a plunger, cover the overflow—creating a better seal. If you decide to use an auger to remove a clog, you will usually feel when the clog has been reached, as you will notice resistance on the tool.

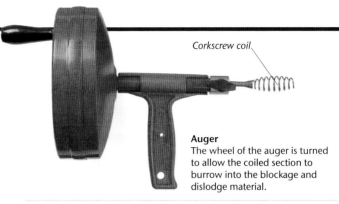

Corkscrew coil

Auger
The wheel of the auger is turned to allow the coiled section to burrow into the blockage and dislodge material.

One cup

Two cups

Plunger
Handle with cup section on one end. The cup section is fitted over the drain outlet. Pump up and down to build suction and release the blockage.

Combination plunger
With two cups, combination plungers are able to push about twice the amount of water of a standard plunger, and are used for toilet clogs.

ADDITIONAL MATERIALS

There are many different compounds and substances used for adhesion and lubrication when plumbing in pipes. The properties of the most commonly used are detailed below.

Flux is used on joints before soldering to ensure that the joint is totally clean.

Joint compound is used as an alternative to teflon, or in conjunction with it, to create a watertight compression joint. Should not be used on pipes carrying drinking water unless specified by the manufacturer.

Solvent cement adhesive is used to join solvent-weld pipe systems. Different types are available to suit different plastic types.

Plumber's putty is a non-setting putty that is easy to mold and creates a waterproof joint. It is used around sinks and faucets.

Silicone spray is used to ease push-fit plastic pipes into joints.

Soft paraffin paste is an alternative to silicone spray. Use for easing push-fit joints into position.

TOOLS AND MATERIALS CHECKLIST (PP.472–488)

Machine bending (p.472)
Pipe bender, guide block

Soldering copper pipe (p.472) Pipe cutter, emery cloth, wire brush, flux, end-feed pipe fitting, gas blowtorch, solder, leather gloves, cotton rag

Boxing in surface-mounted pipes (p.477) Furring strips, paint or tiles, paintbrush, ply

Running pipes through joists (p.477) Basic toolkit only

Running pipes under joists (p.477) Pipe straps

Running pipes through studs (p.477) Basic toolkit only

Cutting copper pipe (p.478) Pencil, pipe cutter

Making a compression joint (pp.478–479) Compression joint, pair of wrenches

Making a solder joint (p.479) Steel wool, noncorrosive flux paste, small paintbrush, gas blowtorch, soldering mat, cloth

Making a solder end-feed joint (p.479) Steel wool, noncorrosive flux paste, small paintbrush, gas blowtorch, solder, cloth

Cutting CPVC pipe (p.480) Miter saw, file

Joining CPVC pipe to copper (p.480) Transition fitting

Joining PVC pipe (p.480) Saw, file, purple primer (PVC primer), PVC cement, small paintbrush, connector fitting

Joining cast iron to PVC pipe (p.480) Banded coupling

Joining plastic and metal pipe (pp.480–481) Metal compression joint, wrenches, or a plastic push-fit joint

Disconnecting a colleted push-fit joint (p.481) Demounting tool

Disconnecting a grab-ring, push-fit joint (p.481) Side cutters

Insulating water pipes (p.481) Foam pipe insulation, tape

Cutting waste pipes (p.483) Sheet of paper, hacksaw, metal file, cloth

Making a solvent-weld joint (p.483) Solvent cement, fine brush, solvent-weld joint, cloth

Making a compression joint (p.483) Compression joint

Repairing taps (p.487) Washer or ceramic-disk valve or ceramic disk cartridge

O-rings, glands, and reseating taps (p.488) O-rings, reseating tool

FOR BASIC TOOLKIT SEE PP.24–25

PLUMBING PIPES AND CUTTERS

Plumbing systems in the home may incorporate metal and plastic pipes. Traditionally, all hot- and cold-water pipes were metal, but various types of plastic pipe are now commonly used in domestic situations. The most common varieties of pipe are shown here, along with equipment for bending and cutting pipes. Many manufacturers refer to pipe as tube or tubing.

METAL PIPES

Copper pipe is the most commonly used type. It resists corrosion well and is relatively easy to work with. In older homes, lead and iron pipes still exist. Brass and stainless-steel pipes are generally used for aesthetic considerations.

Copper pipe
Half-hard copper pipe or tube is the most commonly used copper tubing for domestic systems. It can be used for both heating and hot- and cold-water supply. Diameters include ⅜ to ¾ in (9 to 20 mm). It is often sold in 4- and 8-ft (1.2- and 2.4-m) lengths.

Chrome-plated copper pipe
A copper tube that has a chrome coating for aesthetic reasons.

Micro-bore copper pipe
Small-bore copper tube can be bent by hand. Common diameters include ¼ and ⅜ in (8 and 10 mm). It is usually sold in lengths up to 100-ft (30-m) long.

OTHER METAL PIPES

Galvanized-iron pipe
Once used for domestic water pipes, iron is more susceptible to corrosion than copper. It is also much more difficult to work with than copper, and is therefore not recommended for any new installation.

Lead pipe
This was once used for both supply and drainage pipes in many homes. However, the health risks associated with lead mean that it is now no longer used in new installations.

▋ MACHINE BENDING

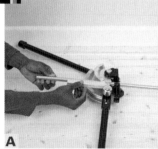

Set the former curve. Place the pipe against the curved former. Support with the guide block.

Pull the handles together to bend the pipe between the guide block and curved former, then remove.

▋ SOLDERING COPPER PIPES

Cut the copper pipe to length using the appropriate pipe cutters.

Deburr the inside of the pipe with the deburring tool attached to the cutter.

Clean the end of each fitting with an emery cloth.

Clean the fitting with a wire brush.

Apply flux inside the fitting and on the pipe end.

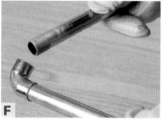

Insert the pipe into the pipe fitting.

Heat both sides of the fitting, then touch the lead-free solder to the fitting so that it melts.

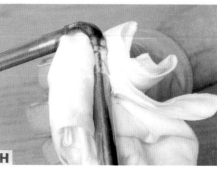

When you have covered the connections, turn off the soldering torch. Wearing leather gloves, wipe away the excess solder using a cotton rag.

PLASTIC SUPPLY PIPES

At first, plastic pipe was used mainly for drainage but in recent years it has become much more common for supply and heating pipes. Plastic is easier to work with than metal because soldering tools and special materials are not required. It does not corrode and has the further advantage of not building up with scale in hard-water areas.

Plastic pipes cannot be used for gas or oil supplies. A plastic hot- or cold-water pipe run also needs more regular support than rigid copper to stop pipes from sagging. Plastic pipe may also have limitations in the heat it can withstand, so check specifications before use. Most plastic pipes should not be used near a boiler. Check with your building department for regulations.

Chlorinated polyvinyl chloride (CPVC) pipe
A rigid form of plastic pipe used in both hot- and cold-water pipes and waste systems. Its use as a supply pipe is limited by some local authorities, so check before use.

Polybutylene (PB) pipe
A very flexible pipe that can be used in domestic hot- and cold-water pipes. Not legal to be used in many areas.

Polyethylene (PEX) pipe
Cross-linked polyethylene is another type of flexible pipe used for hot- and cold-water pipes. It has also become a popular choice of pipe for underfloor heating systems. Also available in blue and red. The colors can make it easier to identify hot and cold piping.

PLASTIC WASTE AND DRAINAGE PIPES

Commonly 1¼ in (32 mm) to 3 in (75 mm) in diameter, drainage pipes are larger than those used for general plumbing. Drainage pipes take waste water from fittings to the mains drainage system. Soil and vent pipes are even larger—most commonly 3 in (75 mm) in diameter. In older properties, it is still possible to find cast-iron pipes used for drainage systems.

Acrylonitrile butadiene styrene (ABS)
This was one of the first rigid plastics used commonly in drainage systems, including soil and vent pipes.

Polyvinyl chloride (PVC)
This is a more modern version of ABS pipe and, with UPVC, is used for the same purposes.

CAST-IRON PIPES

Cast-iron pipes used to be the dominant type of pipe used for drainage, and piping for basements and under floors. PVC and ABS are now used more often instead, but some codes still require cast iron for these uses. If your home was built more than 50 years ago, you may have cast iron in your vertical stack.

Cast iron is very durable, but it can be brittle. It is available in 3-, 5-, and 10-ft (92-, 153-, and 305-cm) lengths with diameters at 2, 3, and 4 in (50, 75, and 100 mm).

If you have to cut cast iron, you may be successful with a hacksaw. Plumbers will use a snap-cutter, which can be rented.

You may choose to leave your cast-iron piping in place and attach new PVC to it. In this case it is possible to create a connection from older cast iron to PVC if you are remodeling your plumbing system (see pp.480–481).

Cast-iron drain pipe for the main stack is often the material of choice in multi-family dwellings because it blocks the noise of water flow.

PIPE CUTTERS AND FILES

Like the pipes themselves, pipe cutters come in various types and sizes. Some are adjustable, to cope with more than one size. Shown here are three types of cutter used for cutting supply pipes. Those used for metal (mainly copper, although most will cut brass, chrome-plated, or aluminum piping) have small cutting wheels located in their jaw design. Plastic supply-pipe cutters simply have a straight blade to cut through the pipe. For metal pipes and some plastic pipes, a metal file is required to smooth the edges once they have been cut. For more information on types of files available, see p.41.

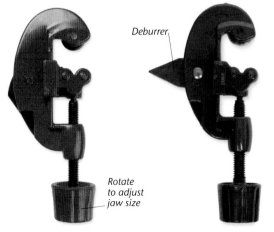

Deburrer

Rotate to adjust jaw size

Blade

METAL-PIPE CUTTER   **METAL-PIPE CUTTER WITH DEBURRER**   **VINYL-PIPE CUTTER**

Connections, joints, valves and a selection of other pieces are required to complete a pipe run. As well as establishing the type and design of fixture that can be used with different types of pipe, when planning any plumbing work it is also important to identify the various ways of making connections. The most common connectors are shown below. It is important to select the right fitting for the route your pipes need to take. If you are terminating a pipe run, you will need to select a suitable end cap. For a short connector to join two pipes, you may use a type of coupling.

CONNECTOR FITTINGS

The most common designs of pipe connectors and joints are shown in the table below. However, there are many other accessories that may be needed to make joints, as well as variations on those standard designs. A few of these are shown on the right.

other different joints to cope with different requirements. A selections of joints are shown here.

Pipe fittings

The two most common types of pipe you might encounter in your home are copper for water supply, and plastic for drainage. Shown here are common types of connectors. Copper pipes are typically connected with solder joints (see pp.478–479 for more

Miscellaneous joints

Not all types of systems are shown on the table below, and all systems have a number of

CONNECTION	Elbows change a pipe's direction	Reducers connect pipes of different sizes	T couplers join three pipes together
End-feed These joints require solder to be added to the joint during the heating and jointing process. Along with solder-ring joints, they offer the most unobtrusive form of connection.			
Brass compression Metal compression fittings may be made of brass or chrome-plated brass. No solder and therefore no heat is required. Threaded sections of the joint fit onto the pipe and as the nuts of the joint are tightened, olives within the joint create a watertight seal.			
Solvent-weld Solvent cement is used to seal joints. It may be used to join PVSC and ABS pipes. Make sure that the cement specified is suitable for the particular pipe you are using; some are multipurpose.			
Plastic compression These work on much the same principle as metal compression joints except that the materials are plastic and a rubber seal is used instead of an olive. Hand-tighten only.			

information on joining pipe) while plastic pipe connections are usually made with solvent (see pp.480–481). Both types of pipe are also available designed for use with compression connections (see chart below).

45-DEGREE ELBOW

45-DEGREE SOLVENT WELD ELBOW

REDUCING TEE

SOLVENT-WELD REDUCER

FLEXIBLE CONNECTORS

Flexible hoses or connectors are one of the great plumbing inventions. Making connections between rigid pipes and fittings required accurate measurements and skilled joining techniques, in often inaccessible areas. Flexible connectors have practically eliminated this problem. Usually a braided hose connects your faucet or toilet to the water supply stop valve. Made in a steel supply line, they are much more flexible and easier to install than rigid chromed-copper tubing.

Braided hose

FLEXIBLE CONNECTOR

Straight couplers join two pipes together	**End caps** terminate pipe runs	**Couplings** vary in appearance	**Tools needed** for connection
			Pipe cutter, blowtorch, flux, soldering wire, tube-cleaning brush, file, soldering mat
			Wrenches, pipe cutter, tube-cleaning brush, file, metal olives
			Solvent cement, panel saw or junior hacksaw, deburrer, file
			Panel saw, junior hacksaw, or vinyl-pipe cutter, deburrer or file, rubber inserts

Pipe connections

IF YOU WANT TO MOVE AN EXISTING FIXTURE, OR PLUMB IN A NEW BATHROOM OR KITCHEN, YOUR PROJECT WILL BENEFIT FROM CAREFUL PLANNING. TO ACHIEVE THE BEST RESULTS, THINK ABOUT HOW BEST TO ROUTE WATER IN AND TAKE IT AWAY SO THAT THE PIPEWORK IS UNOBTRUSIVE. YOU WILL ALSO NEED TO CONSIDER WHETHER PLASTIC OR COPPER PIPES ARE APPROPRIATE FOR THE TASK.

ROUTING PIPES

Supply and waste pipes are usually hidden, but they need to be easy to access for repair or maintenance work. The best option is to use the current pipe locations to minimize renovation work. If you have a solid wall or floor, you can surface-mount pipes, then box them in if you wish (see opposite).

PLANNING PIPE RUNS

Once you have decided on the location of a new fixture, you need to find the best way of getting water to and from it. This will involve investigating your existing water supply and waste systems (see pp.466–469). If you are laying a concrete floor, pipes must be laid in channel ducts with a plywood cover so that there is easy access for repair or maintenance work. With a wood floor, run the pipes across or between the joists (see right).

Supply Pipe

Your water system starts at the water meter. The cold water supply line that enters your house from beneath the ground splits into two – one continues as a cold line while the other is heated to become your hot water supply.

Waste Pipe

A waste system contains drainpipes, vent pipes, and fixture traps. Waste pipes are linked to the main soil pipe, which runs beneath your home's foundation. (Soil pipes carry solid waste.) The main soil pipe connects at a 90 degree angle with the primary vertical stack.

Plumbing permits

Permit requirements vary between local building codes. Most codes require you to have a permit and an inspection if you move any of the permanent pipes in your home. Typically you are allowed to replace fixtures without approval.

PIPE STRAPS

Pipes are secured in place by straps. These come in a number of designs and sizes according to the pipe diameter. Pipe straps may be nailed or screwed into place, depending on their design. Three of the most common types of straps are shown below.

Copper two-screw fastener
Simple copper bracket with two pre-drilled holes for attaching to wall or beam.

Nail-in fastener
A plastic loop holds the pipe in position; the fastener is then secured to the wall or beam by a nail.

Single-screw fastener
A screw is used to secure the bracket. The pipe is then clipped into the bracket.

PIPE SUPPORT CLIPS		
Pipe type	Pipe width	Spacing intervals
Vertical pipes	Support at every story of the house	
Metal pipes:		24 ft (7.5 m)
Plastic pipes		6 ft (2 m)
Horizontal pipes		
ABS and PVC drains		4 ft (1.2 m)
Copper	larger than 1 in (30 mm)	10 ft (3 m)
Copper	smaller than 1 in (30 mm)	8 ft (2.5 m)
Most plastic supply piping		39 in (1 m)
PEX		31 in (.8 m)

RUNNING PIPE THROUGH WALLS

When you are running pipes through stud walls, drill holes slightly larger than the diameter of the pipe in the center of the stud, out of reach of drywall screws. Plastic pipes tend to expand when they are warm. If there is not enough room, you will hear a knocking sound when warm water passes through the pipe. Whether you are opening up a finished wall to run pipe or running it in a new stud wall, use a right angle drill to make the holes. Running pipes through solid walls is more difficult. Protect your pipe with sleeving, using another pipe of slightly wider diameter.

SURFACE-MOUNTING PIPE

The least disruptive way to install new pipes on a wall or floor surface, this offers access for repair and maintenance. Mark the path of the pipes on the surface. Measure and mark where pipe straps need to be attached along the line. Drill and plug the wall and screw the straps in place. Push the pipework into the straps to secure it in place.

Surface pipe runs can be hidden in a plywood box, and decorated the same way as the wall behind. You will need: 1-x-2-in (25-x-50-mm) boards, plywood, screwdriver or drill, screws, hammer, nails, and decorating materials. Shown right is a straightforward boxing-in technique that can be varied depending on the type of pipe run.

▌▌BOXING IN SURFACE-MOUNTED PIPES

A Attach a 1-x-2-in (25-x-50 mm) board on either side of a vertical pipe, or to the wall above and the floor below a low horizontal pipe.

B Measure and cut plywood or MDF to size for the vertical sheet of the boxing. Attach it to the appropriate board with screws or nails.

C Measure and cut the ply for the top of the box and screw it into the board. Nail or screw sheets of ply together where they meet.

D Paint or tile the box to match the surrounding decoration. Remember to allow for emergency access.

WORKING WITH JOISTS

Run pipes between joists whenever possible. If you run pipes below floor joists, use the appropriate type and number of pipe hangers and straps. If you are unable to hang pipes from the joist, you may need to drill through some of them. Only drill the center third of a joist. Never notch the bottom of a joist, as it will greatly reduce the structural integrity. When cutting holes through joists for pipe runs, remember that you will need to create an adequate slope for the pipe run. Below shows ways of running pipes through joists, under joists, and through stud walls.

▌▌RUNNING PIPES THROUGH JOISTS

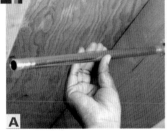

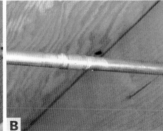

A Drill a hole slightly larger than the pipe in the centre third of the joist. Insert the pipe through the hole.

B Attach the pipe. Drill each subsequent hole lower in the joist to maintain a slope for drain pipes.

▌▌RUNNING PIPES UNDER JOISTS

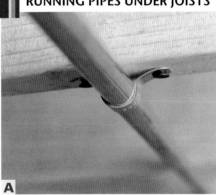

A

Attach hangers, at least every 4 ft (1.2 m), to the underside of floor joists to run pipes under floors.

▌▌RUNNING PIPES THROUGH STUDS

Drill holes in studs that are slightly larger than the pipe.

A

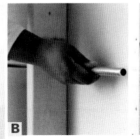

B Remove one stud then feed the pipe through the holes.

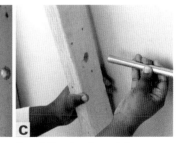

C Insert the pipe through the removed stud, then toenail the stud back in place.

By far the most common water pipes in the home are those made of copper. They can be cut with a hacksaw or a pipe cutter, and can be joined by either solder-ring, end-feed, push-fit, or compression joints. Compression joints are more expensive than soldered joints, but are handiest when doing small jobs and repairs. The most popular sizes of copper pipe are ½ in (15 mm) and ¾ in (22 mm). The techniques shown here relate to both sizes.

TOOLS AND MATERIALS SEE BASIC TOOLKIT AND P.471

CUTTING COPPER PIPE

Carefully measure the length of pipe you need, taking the size of any joints into account. Mark the pipe with pencil where you need to cut.

A

Position the cutter so that the cutting wheel is aligned with the mark. In this example, an adjustable pipe cutter is used. A hacksaw can also be used.

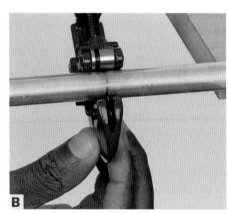

B

C

Rotate the blade as indicated on the side of the cutter.

D

Keep rotating until the copper is cut all the way through; do not be tempted to snap the pipe. Deburr the inside of the cut.

COMPRESSION JOINT

A compression joint requires no solder and therefore no heat. The joint is made watertight by compressing two compression sleeves (soft metal rings), which provide seals on either side of the joint. Pipes are held in sockets in the joint body, and nuts are tightened onto the body to secure the compression sleeves in place. When creating a compression joint, do not overtighten or you may damage the sleeve. Although not a necessity, teflon can be used with compression joints. Teflon is especially useful for making a repair (see p.495). Generally, joint compound should not be used on joints that may be used to carry drinking water.

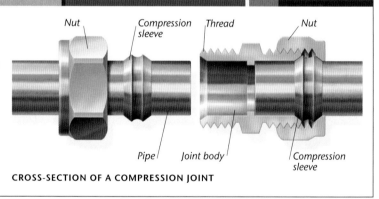

Nut   Compression sleeve   Thread   Nut

Pipe   Joint body   Compression sleeve

CROSS-SECTION OF A COMPRESSION JOINT

MAKING A COMPRESSION JOINT

A

Unscrew the nuts from each end of the joint body.

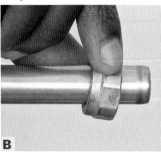

B

Slide a nut onto the end of each of the copper pipes to be joined.

C

Position one compression sleeve on the end of each pipe. Always check that you have the right size sleeve. If you are not sure, replace it with another of the correct size rather than risking a leak.

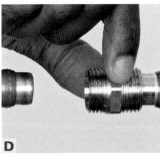

D

Put the compression joint onto the first pipe end, then fit the second pipe end into the joint.

E

Push the pipes together firmly inside the joint. Slide both sleeves up tight against the joint ends.

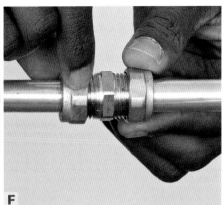

F

Screw the nuts carefully onto the threaded sections of the joint. Tighten them by hand, checking that the pipes do not move out of position.

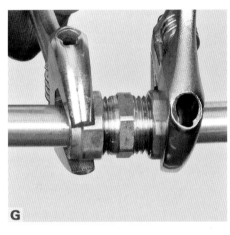

G

Use a pair of wrenches to finish tightening the joint. Do not overtighten; between one and two full turns of each nut should suffice.

SOLDER JOINTS WITH SOLDER-RING CONNECTORS

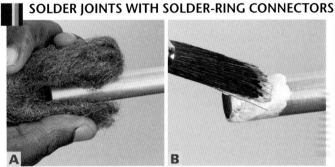

A

Use steel wool to deburr and clean the outside of the pipes and joints until they are shiny.

B

Apply flux paste to the pipe end and the inside of the joint. This ensures a totally clean joint.

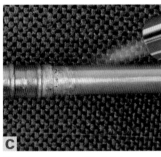

C

Heat the pipe and the joint over a soldering mat, moving the flame around to heat evenly. This melts the internal solder-ring to form a joint.

D

Remove the heat as soon as melted solder appears around the joint. Allow the joint to cool before cleaning off any excess flux with a cloth.

MAKING A SOLDER END-FEED JOINT

A

Clean the pipe and the joint and brush both with flux. Push the two pipe ends into the joint.

B

Heat one end of the joint, working around the pipe. Periodically touch some solder on the joint to see if it is hot enough to melt.

C

When hot enough, apply the end of the solder wire between the pipe and the fastener. The solder will melt around the joint to create a neat seal.

D

Repeat on the other end of the joint. Allow the joint to cool before cleaning off any excess flux from the joint using a cloth.

SOLDERING PROBLEMS

Soldering can be fairly easy for even a first-time DIYer, but even the most experienced pipe fitter can face a few problems from time to time. The key to minimizing any difficulties is to ensure you are well prepared, and have all the necessary materials to hand. Tight spaces, and working around wood framed construction can lead to some challenges. Even if you barely touch a framing member with a blowtorch, check that it is not smoldering and any fire is put out completely. If you aren't confident about a project, always call for professional help.

Plastic pipe can be used in many of the same ways as copper pipe. While copper is more prevalent in Canadian homes, plastic offers a few benefits over copper. For example, if you live in an acidic environment, copper can be adversely affected. Plastic pipe is easy to install, requiring none of the specialized skills and tools that copper installation requires. Still, some places do not allow plastic pipe in applications, so check with your local building official before selecting the pipes for your project.

TOOLS AND MATERIALS SEE BASIC TOOLKIT AND P.471

CUTTING CPVC PIPES

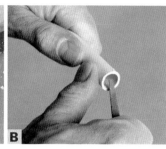

A Using a miter saw or fine-toothed saw, cut the pipe to length.

B Remove any burrs from the pipe end with a file.

JOINING CPVC PIPE TO COPPER

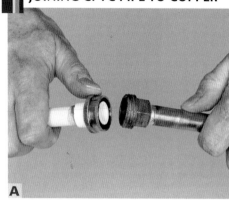

A

There are occasions when you will need to attach a plastic pipe to a copper pipe, for example, at water heaters and shower valves. Transitions fittings are used in these cases. They allow for thermal movements between the metal and plastic without leaks.

JOINING PVC PIPES

A Measure, mark, and cut pipe to length.

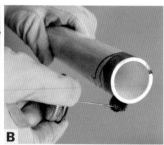

B Coat the end of the pipe and the inside of the fitting with purple primer (PVC primer).

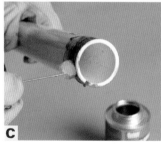

C Apply PVC cement carefully with a brush to the pipe and to the fitting socket.

D Assemble, slipping the fitting on the end of the pipe and align. Hold the assembly in place to allow the cement to set.

JOINING CAST IRON TO PVC PIPE

A Place a banded coupling over the hub.

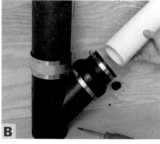

B Make sure the edge of the PVC is smooth. Insert the end into the coupling and secure in place.

JOINING PLASTIC AND METAL PIPES

To join a copper pipe with a plastic pipe, use either a plastic push-fit joint, or a metal compression joint (shown here). Press a metal insert into the end of the plastic pipe that will meet the joint. This helps to ensure that the pipe shape does not distort under pressure.

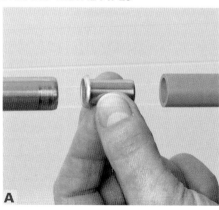

A

B Unscrew the nuts on the joint. Position the nut and compression rings onto both the plastic pipe and the copper pipe.

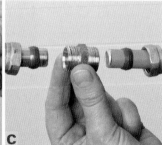

C Place the joint onto the copper pipe adjacent to the compression ring.

Push the plastic pipe with its insert into the joint, slide the compressin ring down the pipe to meet the joint, then tighten the nut by hand.

Use two spanners to finish tightening the joint, taking care not to overtighten it; one or two turns should be sufficient.

FURTHER INFORMATION

Advantages of plastic pipe

While cost savings and ease of installation are top reasons for most DIYers to choose plastic pipes over metal, there are several other reasons you should consider plastic pipe, if accepted by your local building codes. Plastic pipes withstand drain cleaners more easily, and fittings for every possible situation are available. Deburring the ends is much easier, and plastic pipework cannot be corroded through electrolytic action. Two different types of metal (for example, steel and copper) joined together would eventually corrode. If you need to join two different metals, use a plastic joint so that both metals are kept separate from each other.

DISCONNECTING A COLLETED PUSH-FIT JOINT (CRIMP RING FITTINGS)

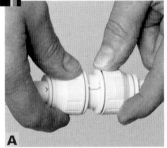
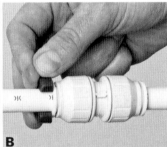
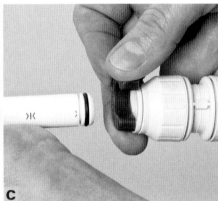

Pushing down releases the grip of the collet teeth, allowing you to pull the pipe free.

If the joint has screwcaps, these must first be unscrewed into an open position.

Remove collet clips (if joint uses them), then use a special demounting tool to push down on the collet on either side of the pipe.

DISCONNECTING A GRAB-RING PUSH-FIT JOINT

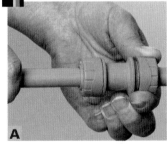

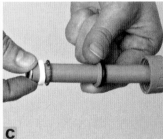
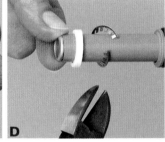

Unscrew the screwcap on the joint.

Pull the pipe from the fitting to reveal the O-ring and grab-ring mechanism.

Move the O-ring and screwcap aside to reveal the grab-ring.

Slice the grab-ring with cutters and discard. Renew the grab-ring when reconnecting the joint.

INSULATING WATER PIPES

Insulating pipes with inexpensive foam is an effective way to prevent sweating of pipes in summer. Unfortunately, it will not prevent freezing in winter. Using foam rubber insulation, cut the insulation to length with a utility knife or scissors.

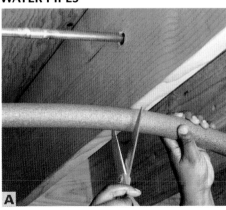

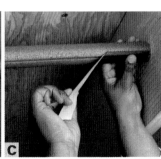

Open the seam and slide it into place.

Tape the insulation in place.

WASTE PIPES AND TRAPS

Plastic pipes are the main material used in modern waste systems. They have three main types of joint; push-fit (which have rubber ring seals instead of grab-ring collets), solvent-weld, and plastic compression. Adhesive can be used on PVC and ABS pipes, but not on PP pipes (see p.471). The latter are always joined using push-fit or compression fittings. Bear in mind that as with plastic supply pipes, brackets are required to support pipe runs. Traps are also an essential part of a waste system; various types are illustrated below.

TOOLS AND MATERIALS SEE BASIC TOOLKIT AND P.469

HOW TRAPS WORK

The example here shows a simple P-trap. Most traps are designed so that they are held in position by plastic compression fittings. This makes access simple if unblocking is required (see p.266). Because traps in toilets or outside gulleys cannot be accessed like this, augers, plungers, and rods may be required to move any blockage.

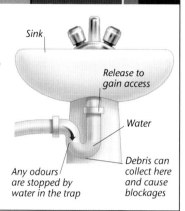

Sink

Release to gain access

Water

Debris can collect here and cause blockages

Any odours are stopped by water in the trap

TRAPS AND THEIR USES

All waste systems have traps, some of which are integral to a fitting (e.g. a toilet trap), and some of which are sold separately (e.g. a basin or sink trap). Traps have a U-shaped section that provides a barrier that separates fittings from the drainage system. The U-shaped design means that whenever water is discharged through a trap, some remains in the U-section. This creates the barrier that stops smells and bacteria entering the house through the drainage system.

Basin and sink traps are made in a variety of designs that are aimed at making installation and connection to the drainage system as simple as possible. Because traps are often positioned in relatively inaccessible areas, such as in a basin pedestal or in a cabinet below a sink or basin, it is important to choose a design that fits your needs. Below is a selection of common trap designs. Each of these has variations that may better suit your requirements.

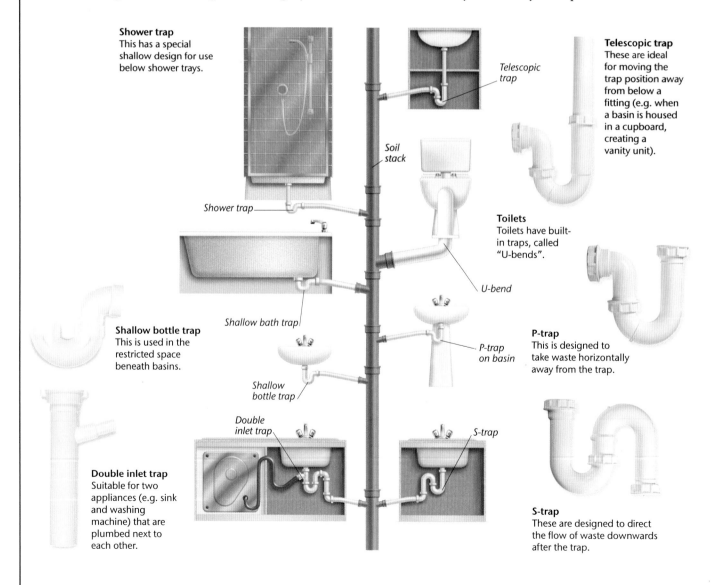

Shower trap
This has a special shallow design for use below shower trays.

Telescopic trap

Telescopic trap
These are ideal for moving the trap position away from below a fitting (e.g. when a basin is housed in a cupboard, creating a vanity unit).

Soil stack

Shower trap

Toilets
Toilets have built-in traps, called "U-bends".

U-bend

Shallow bath trap

Shallow bottle trap
This is used in the restricted space beneath basins.

P-trap on basin

P-trap
This is designed to take waste horizontally away from the trap.

Shallow bottle trap

S-trap

Double inlet trap

Double inlet trap
Suitable for two appliances (e.g. sink and washing machine) that are plumbed next to each other.

S-trap
These are designed to direct the flow of waste downwards after the trap.

CUTTING WASTE PIPES

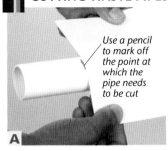

A

Use a pencil to mark off the point at which the pipe needs to be cut

After marking the point to cut, wrap a sheet of paper around the outside of the pipe so that its edge is against the marked point.

B

Junior hack saw

Check that you are cutting square to the pipe, using the paper as your guide. For the pipes to join well, the edges must be square.

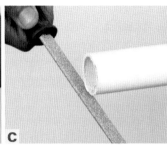

C

Use a fine metal file to deburr the edges of the pipe. A plastic pipe deburrer can be used on the inside of the pipe.

D

Use a soft, damp cloth to wipe away any fine plastic dust from the pipe. A dust-free edge is important when using solvent to join pipes.

MAKING A SOLVENT-WELD JOINT

Establish where you want the joint to be. Place it over the end of the pipe and mark the distance required using a pencil. Remove the joint, then apply solvent cement with a brush.

A

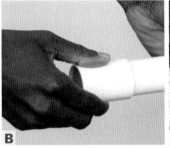

B

Push the joint onto the pipe until it reaches the pencil mark. Insert a second length of pipe that has been filed and glued in the same way.

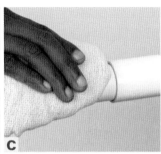

C

Wipe away any excess solvent using a soft cloth. The solvent will react with the plastic pipes to form a solid, waterproof joint.

MAKING A COMPRESSION JOINT

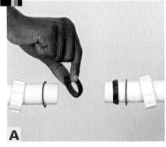

A

Position the rubber seals on both pipe ends. If your joint is supplied with additional washers or O-rings, thread them onto the pipes.

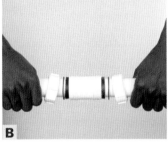

B

Push both pipe ends into the main body of the joint, taking care to keep the pipes straight.

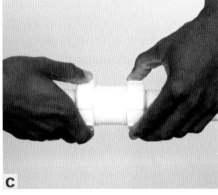

C

Twist the threaded nuts until tight on the joint. There is no need to use an adjustable wrench for this joint; it is designed to be fastened by hand.

FURTHER INFORMATION

Before attempting any plumbing work in your home, check with your local building department for regulations regarding types of materials you can use, and if there are restrictions on doing it yourself.

If you are working with waste pipes in your home, it is likely you will encounter white PVC pipes. In some places, ABS black plastic pipe is also used. If you are using a mixture of PVC and ABS, make sure to always choose the PVC solvent to connect the pipes, as the connection will be much stronger.

PVC pipes create permanent connections when you use PVC solvent cement to attach the pipes and fittings. As you are creating an irreversible bond, be extra careful to measure, cut,

and attach each connection with care, as you will not be able to make adjustments after the pieces are attached. You will have to start again with new pipe and connections.

Before cementing PVC pipes, prime the ends of the pipe and the fitting to roughen the surfaces of the pieces, which will make it easier to create a good bond. Sand the ends lightly or scuff them with an abrasive. The purple color of the abrasive does not do anything more than show you where you have completed the work. As it is a very thin substance, it runs and can seem messy.

Faucets and valves

FAUCETS AND VALVES CONTROL WATER FLOW THROUGHOUT THE HOME. BOTH ACT LIKE "VALVES" BUT FAUCETS ARE FOUND AT THE END OF A PIPE RUN, WHEREAS VALVES ARE SITUATED IN THE MIDDLE. THE CONTROL OF THE WATER FLOW, AND THE WAY IN WHICH THE FAUCET IS INSTALLED, VARIES ACCORDING TO DESIGN. ALWAYS CHECK COMPATIBILITY WHEN REPLACING FAUCETS. FOR MORE ON EFFICIENT PLUMBING, SEE P.388.

INSTALLING FAUCETS AND REPAIR

Designs for faucets vary considerably and may be determined by where they are used in the home. They can either be fixed within the fixture—such as on the rim of a bathtub—or in a countertop or wall next to the fixture. When installing faucets, you need to know how a particular design is installed and the connections required. Detailed knowledge of the internal operation of faucets (see pp.486–487) is crucial only where repairs are required, usually only after a faucet has been in use for some time.

BUYING FAUCETS

Apart from appearance, consider also:
■ Do the number of access holes match the fitting? Faucets can require up to three access holes (see opposite and below).
■ The easiest way to connect faucets is to use flexible hoses.

Hoses are sometimes supplied with the faucets. There are two main types: push-fit connections or compression-joint connections (see p.475).
■ It is also possible to purchase reducing connectors joining a pipe to a fitting, for example.

SINGLE-HOLE FAUCET

These faucets supply either hot or cold water; therefore, generally, one of each is used on a sink. Single faucets are commonly used for outdoor garden faucets, supplying only cold water. A mixer faucet can have a single access hole for both the hot and cold water supply.

Single-hole faucet
For a sink or bathtub, you need two faucets; one to supply cold and one hot water.

Ball-type faucet
Hot and cold supplies feed through one access hole into the faucet body. The lever determines the flow rate and the mix of hot and cold water.

Single-hole mixer faucet
Hot and cold supplies feed through one access hole into the faucet body, but are controlled by separate faucets.

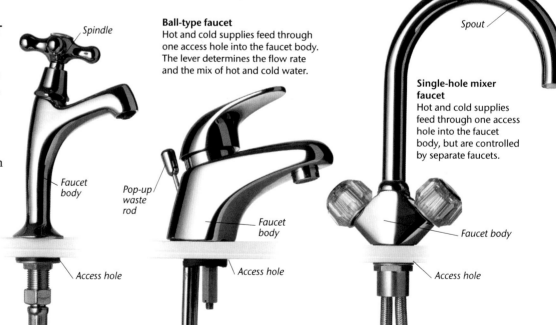

Spindle

Faucet body

Access hole

Pop-up waste rod

Faucet body

Access hole

Spout

Faucet body

Access hole

TWO-HOLE FAUCET

Hot and cold supplies feed into the faucet body through two access holes. This type of faucet is most often seen in kitchens, particularly where the spout needs to be movable, and swing between two sinks. Showerhead attachments are often included in the design for tubs. An extra hole may be required for spray-head attachments with a kitchen sink.

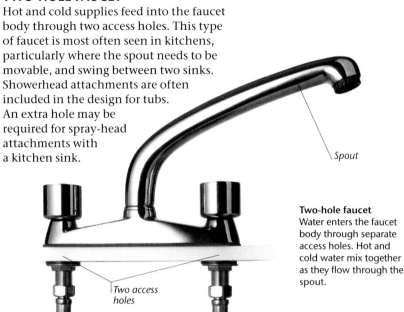

Spout

Two-hole faucet
Water enters the faucet body through separate access holes. Hot and cold water mix together as they flow through the spout.

Two access holes

THREE-HOLE FAUCET

The three holes are needed for hot and cold water supply and the spout. Designs vary according to whether the hot and cold water supplies come together below the fitting or above it. A three-hole may also combine with a spray-head attachment creating a four-hole system (the hole for the spout, one for the attachment, and two holes for the hot and cold water supply).

Three-hole faucet
The water is not mixed in the faucet body, but in the pipes before it emerges into the visible spout.

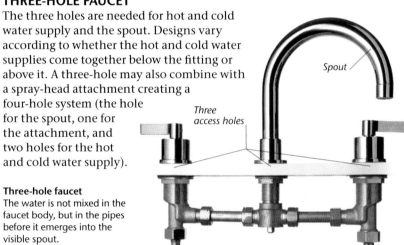

Spout

Three access holes

WALL-MOUNTED FAUCETS

There is very little difference between the faucets mounted on a horizontal surface, as shown above, and wall-mounted faucets (right and below). The main difference regarding operation is that the water supply is routed through the wall surface. You need to plan for an access panel behind the wall for maintenance. When plumbing new faucets, allow space to tile.

SIDE VIEW

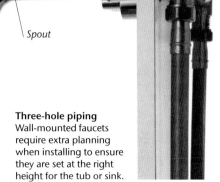

Spout

FRONT VIEW

Three-hole piping
Wall-mounted faucets require extra planning when installing to ensure they are set at the right height for the tub or sink.

DIVIDED FLOW

Some mixers keep the hot and cold water separate, so that they mix outside the spout. This system is often used when there are different pressures between hot and cold supplies. Plumbing codes can stipulate the need for divided flow when the hot-water system is fed by a cold-water storage tank to prevent contamination of the cold-water supply.

WATER SUPPLY PIPES

Traditionally, water supply pipes would feed directly into the faucet, but in modern homes a shut-off valve is positioned on the pipe, to allow easy control of the water supply when maintenance work is needed, such as changing washers, or when faucets need to be changed. Where there is no valve, work is more difficult because water supplies need to be shut off to larger areas of the home, and in many instances, complete systems drained.

POP-UP WASTE SYSTEMS

Commonly used in mixer-faucet design, a pop-up waste system works using a small lever that moves the stopper or plug. The lever is connected to a rod, that connects under the sink to the plug.

Remote lever
Pop-up waste systems are normally installed when you install the faucets. Waste systems are a standard size to fit all sinks.

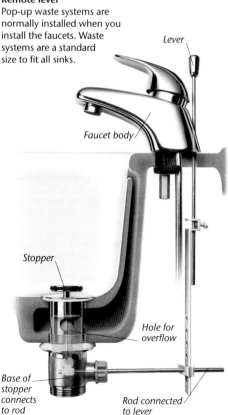

Lever

Faucet body

Stopper

Hole for overflow

Base of stopper connects to rod

Rod connected to lever

REPAIRING FAUCETS

The mechanism that operates a faucet is concealed, but you need to understand it before you start any repairs. The three main types of faucet mechanisms are compression faucets, ceramic disk faucets, and cartridge faucets. Shown opposite are ways to gain access to the inside of the most common faucet models, something that is not always related to the valve or cartridge type used by the faucet. The sequences below right show steps for dismantling different faucets and for replacing washers and seals.

TOOLS AND MATERIALS SEE BASIC TOOLKIT AND P.471

BEFORE YOU START

■ Assess what is causing the leak. If water is dripping from the spout, you may need to replace the washer. If water drips from beneath the handle, the O-ring needs replacing.
■ When buying a replacement ceramic disk, check whether it is for a right- or left-handed faucet.
■ Turn off the water supply.
■ Turn the faucet fully on to ensure that any water in the spout or pipes runs off before you start.
■ Put the plug in the sink to avoid losing any small part of the faucet down the drain.
■ As you remove faucet components, lay them out in order on a convenient flat surface, so that you can put them back correctly.
■ Smear the components with plumber's grease before reassembling the faucet.

FAUCET OPERATING MECHANISMS

Manufacturing and design differences mean that there are huge variations in the appearance of different faucets, but the most popular faucets will fall into three main types of faucet operating systems.

Handle cap

Screw

Handle

Cap

Packing nut

Compression stem

O-ring

Washer

Compression valve

Plug button

Screw

Handle

Cartridge cap

O-ring

Valve

Handle cap

Handle nut

Handle washer

Handle

Cap

Retaining ring

Ceramic disk cartridge

Compression faucet
Faucets with this mechanism usually have separate hot and cold handles. A rubber washer at the base of the faucet valve creates a seal with the faucet seat when the faucet is closed. If the seal is broken, drips will occur. This style of washer is the most traditional faucet operating system, but is still the most popular.

Two-handle ceramic disk faucet
The top sections of ceramic disk valves appear similar to the headgear of a faucet that uses compression valves, so a similar technique is used for removal. Ceramic disks tend not to wear out, but their function may deteriorate over time in a hard-water area. Ceramic disk faucets are sometimes known as washerless.

Ceramic disk faucet
Single-lever faucets can also use ceramic disk technology but, unlike two-handle faucet systems, both flow and temperature are controlled by the same mechanism—in this case, a cartridge. Single-handle faucets can also be ball-types.

GETTING INSIDE A FAUCET

There is a vast range of faucet designs and styles available, but all can be dismantled to reveal the inner operating mechanism. The most common ways of access are shown here. On different models, search for concealed screws or Allen key holes under the handle or lever. As you remove parts of a faucet, lay out each part in order nearby for easy reassembly.

Flip caps
Handle caps can be pried up using the flat edge of a screwdriver to reveal the screw below.

Concealed grub screw

Grub screws
Small grub screws on the side undo to remove the handle. Remove the shroud to access headgear.

Unscrew removable cap

Screw cap
Unscrew by hand to reveal the main handle screw.

Hole for Allen key

Allen key
Similar to grub screws; use an Allen key to take off the faucet handle.

REPAIRING A COMPRESSION FAUCET

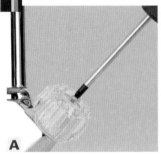

A

Remove the handle cap, if there is one (see top), to expose the handle screw. Unscrew this to remove the handle.

B

Remove the faucet handle and shroud, if there is one, to expose the faucet valve.

C

Using an adjustable wrench, unscrew the faucet valve. Then remove the valve from the faucet seat.

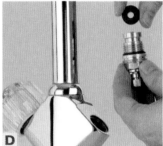

D

Remove the washer with the flat end of a screwdriver. Position a new washer and reassemble the faucet by following the steps in reverse.

REPAIRING A TWO-HANDLE CERAMIC DISK FAUCET

Lift off the handle cap and unscrew the handle screw. Lift off the faucet handle to expose the valve beneath.

A

B

Unscrew the faucet valve, using an adjustable wrench.

C

Lift out the body of the valve. Inspect the ceramic disk valve, clean it, and replace it if it is worn. Reassemble the faucet.

REPAIRING A CARTRIDGE FAUCET

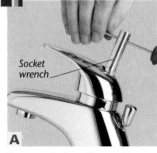
Socket wrench

A

Remove the handle cap. Fix a socket wrench to the handle nut. Thread a screwdriver through the shaft to remove the nut.

B

The faucet handle will lift off easily to expose the top of the cartridge.

C

Remove the cap (if there is one). Then remove the retaining ring.

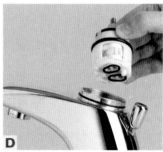

D

Remove the cartridge. Replace the inlet seals on the underside, clean out sediment, or replace the entire cartridge. Reassemble the faucet.

FAUCETS: OPERATIONS AND REPAIR

Although the anatomy of a faucet may seem complex, most problems are caused by worn washers or cartridges, or a worn valve seat in the body of the faucet (the part at the base where the valve sits). The main techniques for washer, valve, and cartridge replacement have been shown on pp.486–87. Below are other areas in which leaks may occur. Spout O-rings can cause leaks, as well as O-rings on valve bodies. In certain cases, faucet reseating may also be necessary.

TOOLS AND MATERIALS SEE BASIC TOOLKIT AND P.471

GLAND PACKING

Most modern faucets do not have gland packing; inside the valve there is a threaded section with an O-ring. This creates the gland seal. To replace gland O-rings, see below. If your faucets do have gland packing, use teflon and follow the technique shown opposite for replacing packing in a stop valve.

When gaining access to gland O-rings it may be necessary to remove a circlip (a type of seal) positioned around the spindle of the valve. It is normally a case of trying to remove the washer unit first, without removing the circlip.

If this doesn't work, try removing the circlip to see if that allows the washer unit to be unscrewed. On a traditional gland, plumber's putty can be used to seal leaks, although teflon works best.

SPOUT O-RINGS

A If you are replacing an O-ring at the base of the spout, remove the grub screw at the back of the spout, then twist the spout to release.

B Lifting the spout off allows you to gain access to the O-ring at the base of the spout.

C Identify the worn-out O-ring, then cut it off or pry it off with a screwdriver.

D Roll on a replacement O-ring to renew the seal. Align the marker with the groove in the faucet body for reassembly.

GLAND O-RINGS

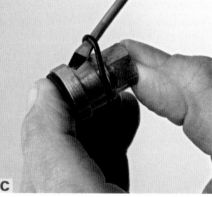

A Remove the valve as shown on p.487. Damaged O-rings on the visible part of the valve can simply be cut away and replaced.

B To gain access to gland O-rings, turn the spindle and valve body in opposite directions. This should allow the washer unit to unscrew.

On the washer unit there will be a further O-ring or O-rings that may need replacing. Cut away damaged rings with a utility knife or break loose with a screwdriver. Roll on a replacement and reassemble the valve. Put the valve back in the faucet body and reassemble the faucet.

RESEATING FAUCETS

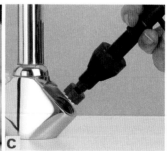

A Remove the valve. If you can, remove the seat, using a valve-seat wrench. Replace with a new one.

B In many cases, seat replacement is not possible, so screw a reseating tool into the thread of the faucet body.

C Be sure to insert the faucet reseater carefully so that you do not damage the thread for the valve.

D Slowly turn the handle of the reseating tool to grind until the surface is smooth. Replace the valve and reassemble the faucet.

There are a number of different types of valves found in domestic pipe runs. They are used to control water movement around the house, isolating areas as required for maintenance, or as an emergency mechanism to stop water flow. The most important valve is the stop valve, which controls the main water supply into the home. It is important that you know where to locate the stop valve in case of emergency. Others include gate valves and the various types of non-return and isolating valves.

STOP VALVE

All homes should have one main stop valve that controls the flow of the main water supply into the home. On large systems, a number of stop valves may be used to isolate various areas of a supply or system. If installing a stop valve, be aware that it must be installed correctly in relation to the directional flow of the water. This is indicated by an arrow on the outer casing. Stop valves are normally installed in a pipe run with compression hardware. Typically, they have a handle with a traditional shape.

ISOLATING VALVES

Used as shutoff valves for the smaller areas of a plumbing system, isolating valves come in a number of different designs and should be located throughout a plumbing system. For example, an isolating valve may be installed close to a faucet. If the faucet needs replacing, it is then only necessary to turn off the water supply to that faucet rather than shut down a larger part of the water system. Isolating valves normally have an arrow on their outer casing to show that they must be installed in the same direction as the directional flow of the water. They may have a handle, or be closed and opened using a screwdriver.

The valve is open when the orientation of the groove in the grub screw that opens the valve is in line with the pipe. A quarter turn is all that is required to close down the water supply. Many plastic valves are only suitable to hold water up to a certain temperature. This should be indicated on the side of the valve along with the directional arrow.

Push-fit socket   *Threaded end*   *Screw thread*

PLASTIC PUSH-FIT/THREADED ISOLATING VALVE WITH HANDLE

COMPRESSION FIT ISOLATING VALVE

VACUUM BREAKERS

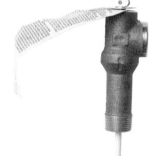

TEMPERATURE AND PRESSURE RELEASE VALVE

GATE VALVE

Similar to stop valves, gate valves are used to isolate areas. However, they should only be used in low-pressure pipe runs. Gate valves do not have a right or wrong way around in terms of installation in relation to the directional flow of water. They are identified easily by their wheel handles.

DRAIN VALVE

Drain valves are positioned on a pipe run as the point to attach a hose when an area of plumbing requires draining. Use a drain valve key to operate the valve.

VACUUM BREAKER

Toilets are made with vacuum breakers integrated into their design. The vacuum breaker can also be added on, to help prevent air locks. Vacuum breakers are available in a few different designs. They are internally spring loaded, so that they can sense any pressure backing up.

TEMPERATURE AND PRESSURE RELEASE VALVE

When pressure and temperature build up inside a water boiler, a temperature and pressure release valve releases water to remove some of the pressure. Water heaters can explode if they are not relieved of pressure build up. Check your boiler or water heater to be sure you have one installed.

PRESSURE REDUCTION VALVE

Proximity to your municipality's water source can affect the water pressure you receive. If you are close to the source, you may want to install a pressure reduction valve. Having high water pressure may be a benefit in the shower, but it will cost you more money every time you run your sink.

STOP-AND-WASTE VALVE

A benefit if installed on outdoor faucets, a stop-and-waste valve allows you to drain water after you turn off the water.

DUAL STOPS

If you are connecting a dishwasher and the kitchen faucet to hot water piping, you may need a dual stop. They operate like compression stops that connect water pipes to supply tubes, but they have the benefit of offering two outlet ports.

CHECK VALVES

Check valves or non-return valves allow water to flow only in one direction. They are used mainly on outside faucets and mixer faucets/valves and are usually built into the design. Their function is to prevent the back siphonage of water down a supply pipe, which would contaminate the water supply.

TOILET VALVES

A leaking toilet can waste thousands of gallons of water per year, costing hundreds of dollars. Repairs and adjustments are normally easy tasks. Toilet tanks have two main elements; a ball cock valve, controlling inflow, and a flush valve that controls outflow. The two valves work in unison to make the toilet flush and then refill for the next flush. Both valves should be adjusted to use only the amount of water needed to properly empty and rinse the bowl.

BALL COCK

A float is positioned on an arm that is connected to a water inlet valve. The valve itself is known as a cock. When the toilet is flushed, the water level in the tank drops and the float drops, opening the inlet valve. Water flows in and fills the tank so the float rises and, at a set level, closes off the inlet supply. Side- and bottom-entry valves are available.

Side-entry diaphragm valve with ball float

This common valve can be made of brass or more often these days is made of plastic. Several different designs are available. Adjustment to the water level in the tank is made by either bending the brass float arm or, on the plastic versions, by an adjustment screw on the valve itself. When set to the right level, the toilet tank will fill up to a mark, at which point the float arm angle will cause the water inflow to stop. The tank is then full for another flush.

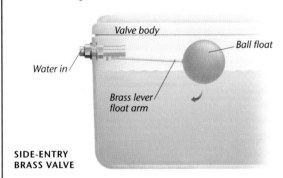

Valve body
Ball float
Water in
Brass lever float arm
SIDE-ENTRY BRASS VALVE

Bottom entry diaphragm valve with ball float

This is a more modern version of the traditional brass side-entry valve. A diaphragm is used to close off supply. To adjust the water level, the screw next to the valve assembly is screwed in or out, depending on the level at which you wish to position the float arm.

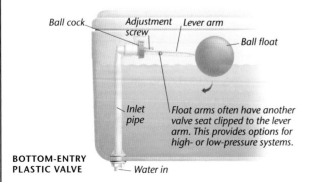

Ball cock
Adjustment screw
Lever arm
Ball float
Inlet pipe
Float arms often have another valve seat clipped to the lever arm. This provides options for high- or low-pressure systems.
BOTTOM-ENTRY PLASTIC VALVE
Water in

TROUBLESHOOTING: WATER INFLOW

Water flowing continuously into the tank can be caused by a deteriorating diaphragm or washer in the valve, or by a leaky flush valve. Repairs can be made by replacing the flapper or the ball cock assembly. Neither have repairable parts and must be replaced completely. Replacing the flapper is an easy job and does not even require tools or that the water be turned off. Replacing the ball cock means turning off the water supply to the toilet and will require tools. It is a job that requires some plumbing aptitude and skill. To make adjustments because water is constantly overflowing, see p.271.

FLUSH VALVES

Almost all residential toilets work on the siphon effect. Water spills into the bowl to create pressure and as the water flows out and down through the drain it creates a siphon or suction effect that pulls the waste down the drain. The water then fills the bowl back to its normal pre-flush level. There are two types of flush valves.

Drop valve

When flushed, a valve in the bottom of the tank opens and the water flows out through a large orifice. In the drop type flush valve, the orifice is covered by a rubber stopper. When flushed, the stopper is lifted off of the opening then floats back down with the dropping water level until it reseats and seals the opening.

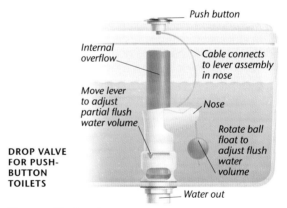

Push button
Internal overflow
Cable connects to lever assembly in nose
Move lever to adjust partial flush water volume
Nose
Rotate ball float to adjust flush water volume
DROP VALVE FOR PUSH-BUTTON TOILETS
Water out

Flapper flush valve

The flapper valve basically works like a drop valve, except it is hinged. When lifted to flush, it opens until the water level drops enough for the weight of the flapper to drop back down and cover the opening. Most toilets today use the flapper valve design. It is more reliable and less expensive than the drop valve.

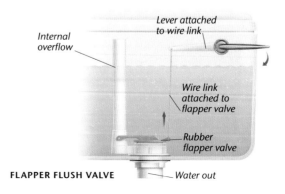

Lever attached to wire link
Internal overflow
Wire link attached to flapper valve
Rubber flapper valve
FLAPPER FLUSH VALVE
Water out

SHOWER VALVES

If you are thinking of adding a shower or a bathtub with a shower to your home you need to have a fair amount of do-it-yourself expertise. If you are confident, you may be able to install your own shower supply lines and valve, saving hundreds of dollars in plumbing costs. If you decide to use a plumber for the installation, familiarizing yourself with the directions below will give you an understanding of the job that is being performed.

A FEW HELPFUL TIPS

■ Most cities require a remodeling permit before any plumbing work in a home. Check with your municipality.
■ It is best to turn off your water supply in the street rather than where it enters your home. If you have a problem with the municipal shut-off valve, your city (not you) will be responsible for repairs.
■ Hot and cold supply lines and the pipe or hose leading to a showerhead are needed.
■ Make sure you level all new pipes to allow for proper water flow.
■ Don't force any joints between fittings. Make sure that they fit smoothly and use Teflon tape or pipe compound to seal all threaded joints.
■ The mixing valve (faucet) can be either single-handled (shown here) or double-handled with a separate valve for hot and cold water.
■ Install the showerhead at a height that will fit the end user. 72 in (1.8 m) is a comfortable height for most adults but may be too high for a children's bathroom.

FURTHER INFORMATION

If you are uncomfortable about soldering, there are some new products on the market that may help you: solderless fittings. These connectors work on compression alone to provide a drip-free connection between pipes. Many faucets are also now being made for novice installers and can ease the process with just a few simple fittings. Ask at your local hardware store or home center for easy-to-install faucets and fittings.

■ When your faucet is installed and you have turned the water back on in your home, flush your toilets to clear dirt and air from the plumbing lines. Grit and debris from the installation can cause problems in your new faucet.

ROUGHING IN A TUB/SHOWER VALVE

Drill holes for the hot and cold riser pipes. Make sure holes are ¼-in (6 mm) larger than the diameter of the supply lines.

A

B **Measure for two support blocks** between the wall studs, according to the valve manufacturer's height specifications.

C **Install the blocks** with galvanized screws. One supports the supply lines, valve, and tub spout (if any) and one supports the shower riser.

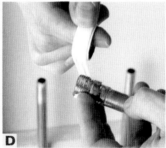

D **Prepare elbow fittings** for attachment to the valve body. Wrap all threaded joints with Teflon tape.

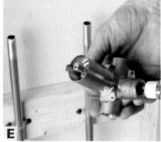

E **Examine the valve body**, noting hot and cold sides for proper placement. Attach supply elbows securely.

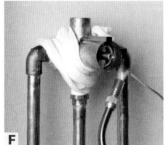

F **Wrap the valve body** with a damp rag before soldering to avoid heat damage to the valve.

G **Attach the shower riser** to the valve body, using firm hand pressure, then tighten with a wrench approximately two more turns.

H **Secure the shower riser** to the highest support block. Make sure the riser is centered and level.

I **Attach a piece of pipe**, according to the valve manufacturer's specifications, for the tub spout. Secure it to the lower support block.

Although most municipal water is considered safe, many homeowners choose to install home water filters to improve their water's flavor, reduce chemicals or sediment, or even to improve color. Water softeners are also used to reduce build-up in your home's plumbing system and fixtures. Recent health concerns over chlorination, lead content, and other contaminants have created an entire industry based on improving water quality. Even homes with their own well water are using filtration devices.

FURTHER INFORMATION

Not all contaminants are created equal. If you just want to improve your water's flavor, a faucet-mounted filter may be adequate, however if you suspect that your water may have a more serious issue, it can be tested for chemical content, bacteria, and other pollutants. Contact your city's health department for a listing of qualified water testing companies. Many cities offer this service at no charge to homeowners.

CHOOSING THE CORRECT FILTER

A wide variety of filters are available to meet differing situations. Once your water has been tested, or if you can identify the contaminant yourself, you can choose the correct solution. Most products cover a broad spectrum of pollutants, but check you get one that covers your specific requirements. Also, be sure that the product has been tested to meet NSF (National Sanitation Foundation) standards.

■ Do you notice a white residue on your plumbing fittings or in your coffee pot? Do your soaps and detergents not lather well? These are signs of excess magnesium or calcium in the water, often known as "hard water." An ion-exchange, water softening system may be installed to "soften" all water which is entering the home.

■ If you notice rust stains in your toilet or around sink drains, you may have an excess of iron compounds or bacterial ion. Again, an ion-exchange water softener, using rust-removing salts, can usually rectify this problem. If the issue persists, it may become necessary to install an oxidizing filer or a chlorination feeder with an activated carbon filter.

■ Does your water sometimes smell like rotten eggs and seem to have a darkened color? You may have excess hydrogen sulfide in your water. Check pipes for corrosion and then install an oxidizing filter or a chlorination feeder with particle-filtering media and an activated carbon filter.

■ Do green or rusty stains form around your sink drains? Your water may be acidic with a low ph. This can be particularly corrosive to pipes and fittings. Neutralizing particle filters will usually solve the problem. If not, you may need a continuous chemical feeder with alkaline solution to return the water to a neutral ph.

■ If your water appears cloudy and has a dusty flavor, you need to install a particle filter along with activated carbon media to remove dirt, sand, silt, and any organic matter. Filter media may need to be changed frequently, depending on the level of debris.

■ Does your water have a foul taste and a yellowish color? It is probably due to algae, often noticeable during periods of drought. When lake levels fall, organic matter is more prominent in the water system. A simple particle filter will normally solve this temporary problem. If the odor or taste does not go away, you may want to consider a chlorination feeder with an activated carbon filter.

■ Other more serious water pollutants can cause illnesses such as diarrhea, typhoid, or even hepatitis. If your family seems prone to illness, it is especially important to have your water professionally tested and to follow the recommendations of your water authority.

FILTERS

Filtering units range from simple, faucet-mounted devices, to under-sink cartridges, to whole-house systems that even filter bathing water. Many refrigerators now include water filtration for ice and drinking water and plumbing manufacturers are including filtration media in many kitchen faucets as well.

Shower water filter
This unit mounts above a standard showerhead and can remove harsh, drying chemicals such as chlorine from the water. It can also eliminate water-borne odors and help reduce chalky, mineral build-up in the shower stall.

Showerhead connection

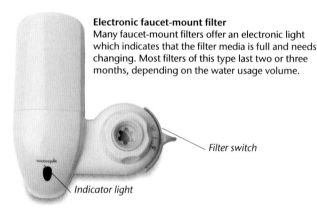

Electronic faucet-mount filter
Many faucet-mount filters offer an electronic light which indicates that the filter media is full and needs changing. Most filters of this type last two or three months, depending on the water usage volume.

Filter switch

Indicator light

REVERSE OSMOSIS WATER FILTRATION SYSTEM

These units can filter out a wide spectrum of pollutants including biological contaminants, chlorine, and lead, however they can be costly to install. They also discard two or more gallons of wastewater for each gallon of purified water that they produce and require a drain for the wastewater.

FILTER CARTRIDGES

Different types of filter media are made to capture differing contaminants. Sometimes, if water is particularly impure, a combination of filters is needed to satisfy a home's water requirements. Filters are also often necessary in areas where sediment or minerals could damage plumbing systems. Whole-home filter systems are available, or smaller systems may serve just one or a few appliances.

SHOWERHEADS

Following a trend to include water filtration in many of the devices and fixtures that we use in our homes, showerhead manufacturers are now making units that look like ordinary showerheads but hide a variety of filter types inside. Inexpensive to install, these units can cut down on chlorine, which can irritate sensitive skin, as well as minerals, rust, and odor. Users report softer skin, less dandruff, a less-brittle hair. Eye irritation is also reduced.

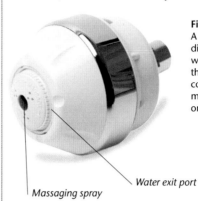

Filtered showerhead
A high quality shower filter in disguise, this shower head has a water filter that fits right inside the head. This model comes complete with adjustable massage-action spray and gold or chrome accenting.

Water exit port

Massaging spray

Drinking water carbon replacement filter
These remove chlorine taste, other trace chemicals, bacteria, sediments, and various pollutants. Replace every three months.

Whole house replacement sediment filters
Installed in-line on a home's water intake, whole-house filters can reduce contaminants in water for drinking, bathing, and even watering the grass.

All-in-one filter cartridge
A self-contained filter cartridge that can remove a variety of contaminants from you water. Some brands last for up to one year of normal usage.

Water dispenser filter
Used in popular hot-water dispensers, these filters reflect a manufacturing trend towards including filtration in many types of appliances and fixtures.

FURTHER INFORMATION

■ Water runoff and flooding can contaminate the water supply for anyone using a private well. Dangers include pesticides, chemicals, bacteria and parasites, and other pollutants.

■ Water-borne contaminants can enter private wells through loose-fitting well caps or by seeping down along a well's shaft casing. The result is contaminated water that is unsafe for drinking, bathing, brushing teeth, and preparing food. Shallow wells and wells found in low-lying areas are especially susceptible.

■ Local health departments strongly urge well owners within flooded areas to test their drinking water after any suspected pollution occurs. Use bottled water and disinfectants until all threat of contamination has been cleared.

■ Do not use carbon filters on well water. They can trap and breed bacteria.

■ Because children's immune systems are not fully developed, they are more prone to fall ill due to polluted tap water.

■ It is not uncommon to find many chemicals such as chlorine, lead, herbicides, pesticides and other contaminants in our water supplies. Traces of several dozen different toxic chemicals can sometimes be found in tap water. There have been outbreaks of parasites like *Cryptosporidium* and *Giardia* in city water supplies. These intestinal parasites, which are chlorine resistant, cause flu-like symptoms and can be fatal to small children. Chlorine, which is used to purify our water supplies, has been linked to learning disabilities in children. Asthma and other illnesses have also been linked to the chemicals in our water.

■ While drinking bottled water is a sound practice when away from home, most brands do not contain fluoride that is necessary for dental health. Also, some brands of bottled water are merely tap water that has been packaged. Always be sure that bottled water has been properly filtered.

■ Home water filtration products and systems are a great investment in the health of our children, removing the chemicals that can harm us while still providing the healthy water that we all need. Most health professionals recommend drinking up to eight glasses per day. Try keeping a pitcher with a built-in water filter in the refrigerator to encourage your children to help themselves.

TEMPORARY REPAIR OF A HOLE

This type of accident occurs when replacing a floor, so check plumbing positions before working on floors. Putty is only a temporary fix, and should be followed up with a longer-term solution as soon as possible.

TOOLS AND MATERIALS
Epoxy putty

A Shut off the water. Allow the pipe to dry.

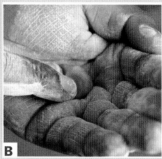

B Form a piece of putty in your hand to cover the leak.

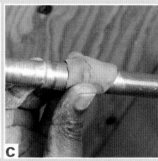

C Press the plumber's epoxy putty over the pipe to cover the leak.

TEMPORARY REPAIR OF A HOLE OR CRACK

If water is allowed to freeze in a pipe, it may lead to cracks or splits, which can cause a leak when the water thaws. The method shown can cover a length of pipe.

TOOLS AND MATERIALS
Hose clamps, section of hose, screwdriver

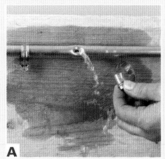

A Place hose clamps on the damaged pipe, on either side of the hole or crack. Do not tighten at this stage.

B Cut out a section of hose to cover the hole or crack. Open the section along one side.

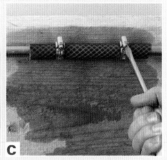

C Place the piece of hose over the area of pipe that is leaking. Clip into place with the hose clamps, and screw them tight to secure.

REPLACING A SINK SPRAYER

If the hose to your sink is leaking, you can replace just the hose, but you may find it easiest to replace the entire assembly. Always shut off the water supply to the sink prior to working.

TOOLS AND MATERIALS
Sprayer hose, sprayer assembly

A Check the sprayer hose for cracks or splits.

B Detach the sprayer hose from the faucet sprayer and drain the water. Unscrew the sprayer base and remove the entire assembly.

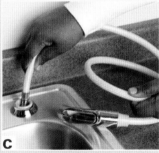

C Install the new sprayer, following the manufacturer's instructions.

THAWING FROZEN PIPES

If you suspect a frozen pipe, keep the faucet open so water will be able to flow through the frozen area as you treat it. Apply heat to the section of pipe, but never try to thaw it using a torch or other open flame.

TOOLS AND MATERIALS
Hair dryer, heat lamp

Using a hairdryer
If the water is not pooled, it should be safe to use a hair dryer or heat lamp to thaw the pipe.

Using hot water
If water is pooled around the pipe, pour hot water over the pipe.

AFTER THE PIPES HAVE THAWED

Always look for leaks downstream after the pipe has thawed because frozen pipes don't burst where they freeze. Water expands as it turns to ice and is not compressible, so it finds a weak spot to relieve the pressure. If you're lucky, this is at a faucet washer, which dribbles. If not, it's a seam in the pipe, which can crack.

REPAIR USING A SLIP COUPLING

Slip couplings are useful for repairing small, damaged sections of pipe when the pipe is in a fixed position where space is restricted. If it is possible to move the pipe easily, you could make a sprung repair with compression fittings instead (see below).

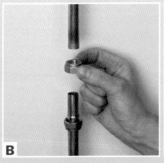

A Turn off the water. Cut out the damaged section of pipe. Use a junior hacksaw or pipe cutter.

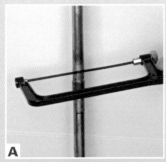

B Position both nuts on the cut-end sections of pipe.

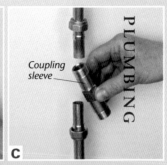

Coupling sleeve

PLUMBING

C Slip the coupling sleeve over the top piece of pipe.

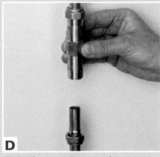

D Slide the coupling up the upper section of the pipe.

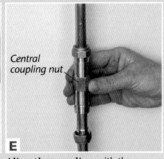

Central coupling nut

E Align the coupling with the lower section of pipe and lower it into place.

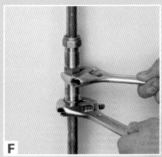

F Tighten the coupling nuts using wrenches to make the fitting and the pipe watertight.

TOOLS AND MATERIALS
Hacksaw or pipe cutter, slip-coupling fitting, adjustable wrenches

---

REPAIR USING A COMPRESSION FITTING

If there is movement in the pipe, the leak may be repaired with a standard compression fitting. The new section springs into position.

TOOLS AND MATERIALS
Marker pen, junior hacksaw or pipe cutter, compression fitting, adjustable wrench

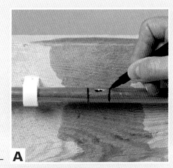

A Turn off the water, then mark around the damaged section of pipe. Cut out the section using a junior hacksaw or pipe cutter.

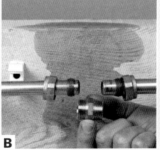

B Detach the pipe from its clips. Place the nuts on the pipe ends. Slide the compression fitting between the pieces of pipe.

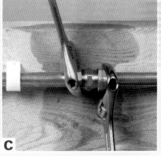

C Tighten the nuts onto the compression joint to make the repair watertight.

REPAIR USING TEFLON TAPE

Joints with threaded sections can corrode over time, and small movements in the joint can eventually create a leak. The best solution is to take the joint apart and reassemble with Teflon tape.

TOOLS AND MATERIALS
Adjustable wrenches, Teflon tape

A Turn off the water, then undo the joint to expose the threaded section.

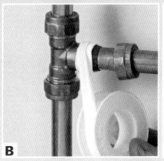

B Wrap Teflon tape around the male section of the thread. Make sure the tape is not kinked or folded during the process.

C Tighten the nut back on by hand to check that the tape us staying in position. Tighten with a wrench.

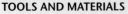

HEATING

HEATING SYSTEMS

Heating systems

MODERN HOMES ARE WARMED THROUGHOUT AND PROVIDED WITH HOT WATER BY SOME KIND OF HEATING SYSTEM. SOME OF THE PROS AND CONS OF DIFFERENT SYSTEMS ARE DISCUSSED HERE, WITH MORE DETAILS GIVEN LATER IN THE CHAPTER. INSTALLING A NEW SYSTEM IS BEST LEFT TO THE PROFESSIONALS. HOWEVER, YOU MAY SOMETIMES EXTEND OR MAINTAIN SOME TYPES OF EXISTING SYSTEM YOURSELF.

CENTRAL HEATING

The most popular home-heating system—forced-air heating—is discussed opposite. It warms the whole home and is fully adjustable to your needs. However, there are other options for heating your home, like radiant floor heating in a bathroom. You might want extra heating in some areas, or to install a different system in a new addition.

CHOOSING A HEATING SYSTEM

If you are having a new system installed, your choice will be influenced mainly by the fuel you intend to use, and by ease of installation. When upgrading all or part of an old system, it will often be easiest to replace like with like. Your installer will be able to advise you about replacing major components such as furnaces, boilers, and air conditioners with modern, energy-efficient versions. The advantages and disadvantages of the main systems are shown below.

HEAT SYSTEM	POWER	OPERATION AND USE
Forced-air furnace	Gas, oil, or electricity	Gas or oil burns in a central furnace and through a heat exchanger, warm air is sent throughout the house, while cold air returns complete the loop. An electric furnace has the heating elements directly inside the main duct.
Boiler	Gas, oil, or electricity	The unit heats water that circulates through a system of pipes and/or rads to carry heat through the house. Tankless boilers are becoming common.
Heat pump	Electric refrigerant compressor; outdoor air	Gathers heat from outside and disperses it to inside. In summer they reverse to become air conditioners. Any type of forced-air furnace can be backup.
Geothermal	Electric refrigerant compressor; ground, well, or lake water	Type of heat pump that uses the heat in soil or water as a heat source.
Radiator	Water or electric	Any exposed device that gets hot to warm up a room, ranging from old cast iron rads to modern baseboard or wall-hung hot water or electric models. Usually the visible part of some hydronic systems.
Radiant heating	Electricity or water	Floors, walls, or ceilings that radiate heat into the room. Heat source can be hydronic hot water piping, or strands or mats of electrical heating wires hidden below the surface.
Solar heating	Sun	Active solar has exterior panels to collect energy from the sun and convert it to usable heat. Passive solar is proper placement and exposure of windows.

FORCED AIR

Forced air is the most common type of heating system in today's homes. It is popular because of its reliability and because it can heat a house quickly. Forced air can also be combined with other heating systems to give you control over the temperature of each room.

A forced-air furnace is fueled by gas, propane, oil, or electricity. It is commonly found in the basement, with ducts connecting it to the rest of the house. Cold air is drawn from the rooms by a blower. The air flows through a filter, and is then heated by the furnace. The warmed air returns through the floor registers, heating rooms. If you have no basement, the furnace will be in a utility room.

Forced air systems are regulated by a thermostat. When you set your thermostat to a particular temperature, the thermostat starts the furnace when the temperature falls below that reading.

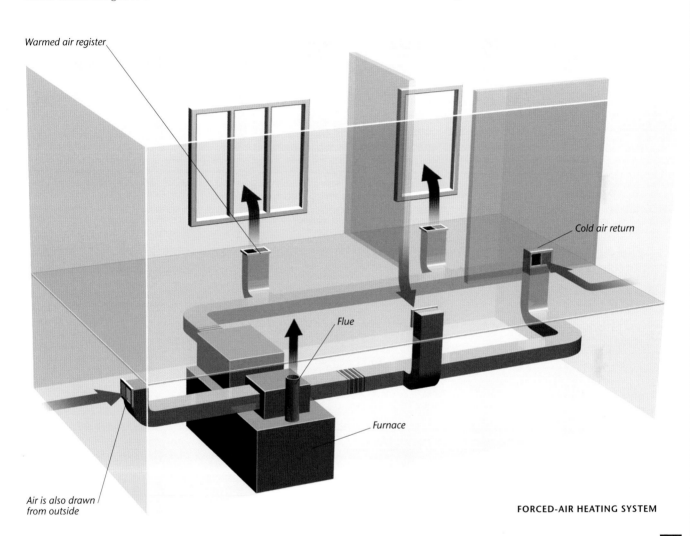

Warmed air register

Cold air return

Flue

Furnace

Air is also drawn from outside

FORCED-AIR HEATING SYSTEM

HOT-WATER HEATING

In a hot-water system, the water is heated and stored in a tank. A circulation pump will then distribute that hot water to each baseboard or radiator in the house, where it heats the rooms. In a hydronic heating system, the water is distributed into long runs of piping. Old cast-iron radiator systems are common in the East and in-floor hydronic systems common in the West. Oil, gas, or electricity can be used to fuel a hot-water heating system.

Maintaining a hot water heater can be a DIY job. The pumps need to be oiled regularly to keep the system running smoothly. The equipment should be dusted occasionally. Expansion tanks need to be drained. And it is essential to bleed trapped air from the system.

WORKING SAFETY

Installing a heating and/or cooling system is not a DIY project, as it requires regulated materials and equipment. Selecting the right type of unit also involves calculating the load in your home and sizing it for your needs. In some cases, you must be a licensed HVAC technician to buy heating and cooling equipment through a distributor.

Before you hire a contractor to help you select and install a new system, ask what products the contractor represents, and check references. Contractors generally associate themselves with two or three brands, so if there is a particular brand you want installed in your home, you may want to contact the manufacturer for contractor references in your area.

After your system is installed, maintaining your heating system is essential to keep your house safe and your energy bills low. Clean filters regularly, and follow all manufacturer's maintenance recommendations.

TYPES OF HEAT

Many different types of heating systems are used to control the temperature in our homes and to keep us more comfortable. The two most common are forced air and hot water, normally fueled by either natural gas or electricity. Other types of heating include heat pumps, baseboard radiant heat, space heaters, fireplaces, and wood burning stoves. Many of these are used to augment other heating sources.

WORKING SAFETY

As with any work done around the house, there are rules to follow to be safe. Never work on any system that uses electricity until the electric circuit is turned off and verified as being off. Handle wiring as though it were hot just to be sure. Always wear eye protection when working with any hand or power tools. Wear gloves when working with anything that might cut or burn. Read all directions on product packaging and always use only as directed.

HEAT DIFFERENCES

Different methods of heating each provide a unique heating experience. Drafty houses create dry wintertime air, so humidifiers can be added to forced-air systems to balance the indoor air moisture content. Hot-water systems can sometimes create hot and cold spots in a room. Fireplaces and wood burning stoves add atmosphere but are often inefficient. Whole house under-floor hydronic heat and under-floor electric heat in bathrooms warm your feet.

Baseboard heaters
Heat rises, which makes the baseboard an ideal location for passive heaters. Cool air flows in from the floor, is heated by an electric wire element or hot water coil, and exits though vents along the top edge of the unit, then flows throughout the room. Similar units, called toe-kick heaters, fit under the edge of a cabinet and can make a toasty addition to a drafty bathroom or kitchen.

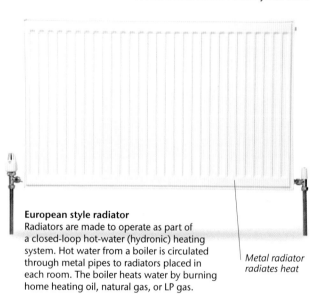

European style radiator
Radiators are made to operate as part of a closed-loop hot-water (hydronic) heating system. Hot water from a boiler is circulated through metal pipes to radiators placed in each room. The boiler heats water by burning home heating oil, natural gas, or LP gas.

Metal radiator radiates heat

Furnace
A typical forced-air furnace is fueled by either gas or electricity and is controlled by a thermostat placed within the living area of the home. When the thermostat signals the furnace to begin heating the air, which is then blown or "forced" throughout the home through ductwork.

Gas supply port

Indoor air handler

Air conditioner/heat pump

Air purifier
The air inside your home may have five times the contaminants of outdoor air. Inline air purifiers, which are a part of your central heating and cooling system, are often the best way to eliminate this problem. The initial cost can be high, but long-term usage costs are minimal.

Filter

Power

Temperature control

Control
A thermostat is used to control most central heating and cooling systems. The model shown is programmable to allow the climate control system to run only when specified, saving energy when occupants are away or sleeping.

Hybrid heat
A heat pump is a reversible air-conditioning unit that can pick up whatever heat is available outside and transfer it into the house. It often cannot deliver enough heat in winter, so a full furnace backup is necessary.

A thermostat turns heating or cooling on and off to maintain a desired temperature in your home. Old thermostats are manually regulated. Modern "setback" thermostats can be programmed to turn your heating and cooling systems off and on at certain, pre-set times of the day, so the climate control system is only on when it is needed. Replacing an older manual thermostat with a new programmable unit is an easy way to save energy and better regulate the air quality in your home.

FURTHER INFORMATION

Choose a new thermostat that fits your lifestyle so that the program can be set to activate heating or cooling cycles only when needed instead of wasting energy when you are at work or asleep. Most can be programmed for different weekday and weekend usage, while others can be programmed with different timings for each day of the week. Many can sense outdoor temperature as well as humidity. Choose a unit with a manual override. Know your model of heating and cooling system when you go thermostat shopping to check for compatibility. Many old thermostats contain mercury, so check with your municipality for proper disposal of your existing unit.

REPLACING A THERMOSTAT

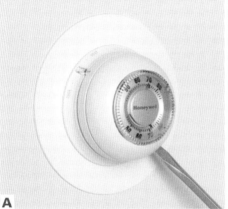

Most thermostats run on low voltage, but turn off all power to the heating and cooling system, just to be safe. If your thermostat is powered directly through your breaker box, be sure to turn off the correct breaker. Then, remove the cover from the old thermostat, using a slot-head screwdriver.

A

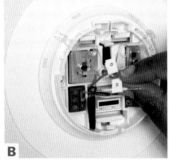

B

Label each wire as you loosen it from the old unit. Trim old ends with wirecutters, allowing enough fresh wire for reconnection.

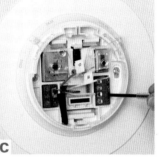

C

Remove the old thermostat carefully and dispose of it properly. Make sure that the wires do not slip back into the wall.

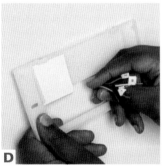

D

Feed the existing wires through the new unit's backplate. Do not crimp any excess wiring.

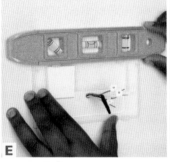

E

Use a level to help position the new backplate, covering the old screw holes if possible, to avoid later cosmetic repairs.

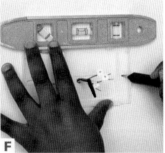

F

Mark the new screw holes, checking your level for accuracy. Adjust, if necessary, to accommodate the existing wires.

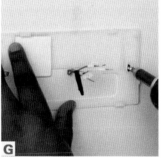

G

Install the new backplate, using drywall anchors and screws to secure it firmly to the wall. Check your level again.

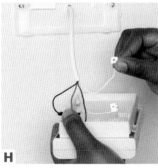

H

Connect the marked wires to the thermostat backplate or body, following the manufacturer's directions.

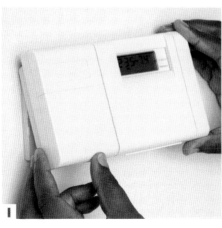

I

Snap the new thermostat into place carefully. Follow the manufacturer's directions for setting the programming and function.

TOOLS AND MATERIALS CHECKLIST P.501

Replacing a thermostat (p.501) Tape for labeling wires, new thermostat unit

FOR BASIC TOOLKIT
SEE PP.24–25

FURNACES

Your furnace is the most important component of your central heating system so take care to maintain it properly. Think carefully if you are replacing an old furnace. Choose the type of furnace that is compatible to your climate, your house, and your lifestyle. When you select a furnace from the many options available, you are affecting the quality and cost of your heating for the life of your house. As discussed on the previous page, a forced-air system is the most common type heating powered by a furnace. Discussed here are both oil- and gas-fueled options.

WORKING SAFETY

All new furnaces must comply with code and safety issues, and any failure or malfunction that allows gas or combustion fumes into the vent portion will automatically shut down the furnace. However, as an extra safety backup you should always install a carbon monoxide (CO) detector alongside your furnace for your family's safety.

HOW FURNACES WORK

If room temperature drops below your thermostat's setting, it signals to the furnace's controls to start the burner. Air is drawn into the furnace through a filter, where dust and other small particles are trapped. A blower unit blows the filtered air through the furnace, where the air absorbs heat. The warm air is then forced through a system of air ducts to each room in your home until the thermostat setting is reached. No matter the type of furnace you choose, plan for regular maintenance. Make sure the system is efficient, and that your home's heating system continues to be safe.

Heating codes

Heating is a regulated part of a home's construction. There are local codes that dictate almost every aspect of residential heating, which include ducting, location, and the type of fuel systems allowed. Most jurisdictions follow similar guidelines. Some typical guidelines may include the following:
- Forced air furnaces must have a control limit that prevents the air in the outlet from exceeding 250°F (120°C)
- Heating equipment must have a power outlet within 25 ft (7.5 m) of the unit
- Fuel burning furnaces cannot be installed in storage rooms
- Metal ducts must have a clearance to the ground of at least 6 ft (2 m)
- Gas lines cannot pass through walls
- Room heaters need 18 in (45 cm) of working space

Gas furnaces

Forced air from a gas furnace is a common heating system. Centrally located in a house, the furnace burns either natural or propane gas. Indoor air flows around the heat exchanger, is heated, and then circulated throughout the house through ductwork. Other ducts return air to the furnace to be reheated and recirculated. Additional air is drawn into the flue for venting purposes. This air mixes with the hot exhaust gases and exits through the chimney.

There are three types of gas furnaces: a conventional warm-air furnace, an induced draft furnace, and a condensing furnace. Conventional furnaces draw air through an opening in their front, and through the flue, to create a natural draft. Induced draft furnaces use a fan to draw the combustion products into the flue for increased efficiency. A condensing furnace contains a second heat exchanger that condenses water vapor in the hot flue gases, thereby extracting additional heat. Condensing furnaces are among the most efficient on the market.

Oil furnaces

Oil furnaces use fuel oil burned in a sealed chamber to create heat for a home. A fan or blower helps to force this heat across an exchanger, and then into the ductwork of the house. Oil-based furnaces can last more than 10 years. In order to reap the benefits of an oil system, the furnace requires regular maintenance. Make sure you replace the filter each month. Ask a professional to check the burner, heat exchanger, pipe, and the fuel-to-air mixture adjustment annually.

Electric heat

Some furnaces are powered by electricity. The electric current travels through a heating element, which warms air passing over it. The heated air rises into the ductwork, and into the house. The process of the heat transfer is called conduction and convection.

Energy efficiency

If you are considering replacing a furnace, look for the EnerGuide or Energy Star label. From time to time local governments or utilities have subsidies for promoting energy efficiency that could help you with the initial cost of a higher efficiency furnace. While high-efficiency furnaces have a higher initial cost, they do tend to save operational costs over the life of the product with lower energy bills.

By choosing appliances carrying the EnerGuide label or the Energy Star certification, you are not only helping reduce your energy costs, you are also helping promote cleaner air while enhancing your home.

FIND A CONTRACTOR

It is crucial to find the right contractor to install and repair your system to ensure it is safe and efficient. Professionals not only know how to install heating systems, they will also specify the correct size and design. If you have undertaken major energy conservation renovations in your home, you may be best served by a downgraded furnace. When a furnace, or heat pump or air conditioner, for that matter, is too large for the energy requirements of your house, it will cycle too much, be uncomfortable, and waste energy and money. Be sure that any equipment installed in your home is certified for Canadian use. Heat pumps, for instance, certified in the US but not in Canada have no valid warranties in Canada. Our climate requires them to be built differently.

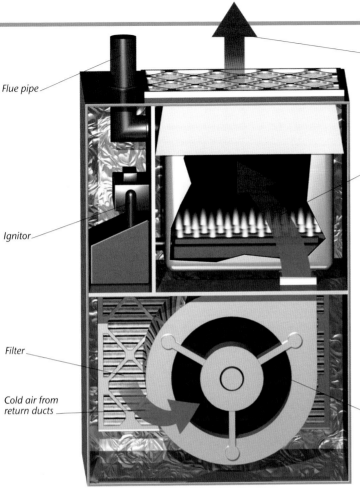

Flue pipe

Ignitor

Filter

Cold air from
return ducts

Warmed air is blown
into ductwork

Heat exchanger
warms the air

Fan motor assembly

Gas furnace

Natural or propane gas can be used as fuels for furnaces, depending on what is available from your power company. The furnace usually includes an ignitor, fan, heat exchanger, filter, and flue pipe. Gas that feeds into the furnace from the gas line is burned in a sealed unit and moved into a heat exchanger. The air blower (fan motor) moves the air into the ductwork of the home where the warm air is released into each room. Cool air flows back into the furnace from return ducts through filters to remove any particulates. It is then heated before flowing back through the supply vents into the room. Never work on a gas furnace yourself. Always hire a professional when your gas furnace needs repair. You can maintain the filters yourself—check them and replace when necessary. Having a clean filter helps improve the efficiency of your furnace and reduces energy costs.

Oil furnace

You will need an oil storage tank and a yearly delivery of fuel oil to power an oil furnace. Usually your oil provider will check your system at the same time to make sure it is functioning properly. As shown to the right, the basic elements of the oil furnace are similar to the gas furnace. Both have filters, a fan motor, flue pipe, and a heat exchanger. The difference between the two is how the air is heated inside the unit. Using an oil burner, the oil is converted into a spray. Air is mixed in with this spray, which now feeds the flame to heat up the furnace. The blower then moves household air through the heat exchanger and into the ductwork, which transports it to each room of your home. A thermostat switches the furnace on and off to keep the house at the desired temperature.

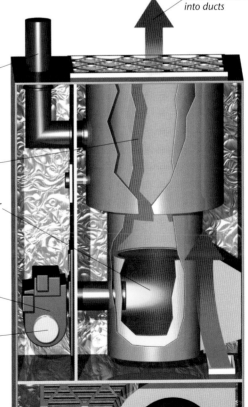

Warm air blown
into ducts

Flue pipe

Heat exchanger

Combustion chamber

Oil burner

Fuel pump

Fan motor
assembly

Filter

Cold air from
return ducts

FURTHER INFORMATION

Even if you have the best and most efficient furnace money can buy, you may still not be reaping all of the energy benefits possible. A fundamental part of your heating and cooling system is having an energy-efficient home. Insulation is important, but once the first minimal insulation is in place, air sealing becomes far more important. Air sealing is inexpensive and very effective at reducing heating needs. Significant improvement in a home's energy efficiency not only reduces the heating bill, but also reduces the size of the furnace required to heat the home, making the new one less expensive—a double savings.

HEAT PUMPS AND BIOMASS BOILERS

In recent years, the search for greener, more sustainable ways of producing heat has intensified interest in heat pumps and biomass boilers. Although they function differently, they are often grouped together, as they both extract stored solar energy from natural sources—the former exploits water, soil, and air, while the latter uses crops. These pages explore both heat pumps and biomass boilers, and offer guidance on their potential for use in a domestic heating system.

TYPES OF HEAT PUMP

Heat pumps encompass air-source, ground-source, and water-source systems. They are energy efficient, as the amount of energy required to power them is far less than the energy they can produce. The type of heat pump you choose depends on a number of variables— a water-source pump is only viable if you have a suitable water supply, while the type of ground-source heat pump you choose depends on the amount of land you have. Consequently, air-source heat pumps tend to be the most popular, as they are not subject to the same limitations. However, they are arguably the least efficient of the three options, because air temperatures tend to fluctuate much more than ground temperatures. Consequently, choosing the correct system for your needs can be complex, making the need for professional help essential. However, the effectiveness of these systems is proven, and their popularity has increased correspondingly.

HOW HEAT PUMPS WORK

Heat pumps extract heat from water, the ground, or the air, and process that heat until it can be used domestically. Details about each system are described below and opposite, but all three have common components: a heat source (the ground, for example) and a tool for extraction (the pump); a circulation fluid that carries the heat, such as water and antifreeze; and a means of distributing that heat through the house, such as underfloor heating.

A heat pump has an evaporator, a compressor, a condenser, and an expansion valve (the illustration below depicts their relationship in a ground-source pump for heating water). A gaseous compound called a "refrigerant" absorbs heat from the air loop, or fluid from the ground loop, and is compressed, causing its pressure and temperature to rise. The gas is cooled in a condenser, forming a warm liquid. This liquid has its pressure lowered in an expansion valve, before being passed through an evaporator, which turns it into a gas, beginning the cycle again. The heat released during this process can be used domestically.

A reversing valve allows heat to move in both directions—in the summer, the system can cool rather than heat. The output depends on the system, but a ground-source heat pump could change a soil temperature of 40°F (5°C) to 95°F (35°C) as air or water heating.

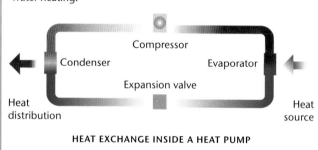

Compressor

Condenser   Evaporator

Expansion valve

Heat distribution   Heat source

HEAT EXCHANGE INSIDE A HEAT PUMP

Air-source pumps

An air-source heat pump consists of an outdoor unit and various indoor components, the design and configuration of which depend on whether you are heating water or air. The external part of the pump uses a refrigerant to extract heat from the air (see box, above). The evaporated refrigerant is compressed, and its temperature is increased. It then passes inside, where it enters a wall-mounted unit that distributes warm air throughout the house (often through ducting). For heating water, the exterior process is the same as it is for heating air, but the interior set-up involves a water-pump unit, in which the refrigerant heats water; this heated water then passes through to a hot-water tank, which can be used to provide hot water, or underfloor heating. A typical arrangement is shown below.

Positioning components
The close proximity of components shown here is purely illustrative. The indoor unit can be positioned almost anywhere in the home, as refrigerant pipework can be up to 98½ ft (30 m) in length for most system designs.

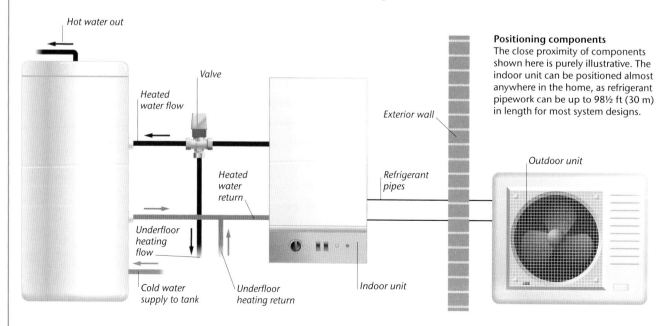

Hot water out

Valve

Heated water flow

Heated water return

Exterior wall

Refrigerant pipes

Outdoor unit

Underfloor heating flow

Cold water supply to tank

Underfloor heating return

Indoor unit

Ground-source pumps

Ground-source pumps use a system of undersoil pipes that extract heat from the earth and convey it to the heat pump, where the refrigerant heating cycle begins (see box, opposite). Again, air or water can be heated. This system is the most efficient, because of the consistency of ground temperature—output control is therefore very simple. The main consideration in design is whether the pipework runs horizontally or vertically outside the home. The three examples below depict typical systems, but there are further variations.

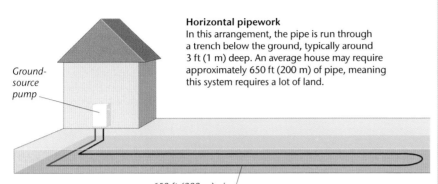

Ground-source pump

Horizontal pipework
In this arrangement, the pipe is run through a trench below the ground, typically around 3 ft (1 m) deep. An average house may require approximately 650 ft (200 m) of pipe, meaning this system requires a lot of land.

650 ft (200 m) pipe

Ground-source pump

Slinky pipework
Here, the pipes are coiled, which requires slightly less land than a straight horizontal design. Loops are often spaced at 3 ft (1 m) intervals, as the heat should be spread across the piping, rather than concentrated by large overlays of pipes.

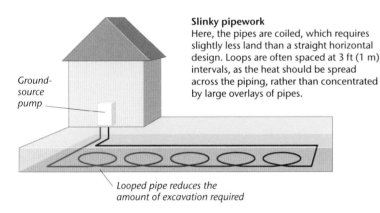
Looped pipe reduces the amount of excavation required

Ground-source pump

Vertical pipework
This system requires the least exterior space, as the pipe goes straight down. This involves some drilling into the ground, and can be expensive, depending on depth—drilling to 230 ft (70 m) is not uncommon. Clearly, a geological survey will be required to determine the suitability of drilling to such great depths.

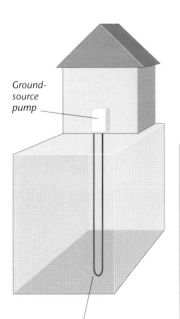
Vertical loop, up to 230 ft (70 m) in depth

WATER-SOURCE PUMPS
Water-source pumps may operate as an open- or closed-loop system. In a closed system, flexible pipes are used to carry circulation fluid through water, and back to the heat pump; in an open system, the water supply acts as the circulation fluid. It is drawn up into the pipes, passing through the heat pump, where the warmth from the water is extracted, and is then discharged again. Both systems rely on proximity to a river, or an underground water source, for example. You will need to contact your local government about permissions, especially in an open system, where uptake and discharge is taking place.

Flue
Hopper access hatch for fuel
Combustion chamber

BIOMASS SYSTEMS

Although using organic materials for fuel is not a new concept, biomass systems generate electricity by burning specially planted trees and crops, and a variety of by-products from industry, agriculture, and forestry. While burning biomass produces similar amounts of carbon dioxide as burning fossil fuels, the trees and crops that are incinerated extract carbon dioxide from the atmosphere during their life, and are replenished as they are used. In this way, biomass is seen as a "carbon-neutral" energy source.

Biomass, also known as biofuel, or bioenergy, generates electricity and heat at custom-built plants that feed power to the utility suppliers. However, it is possible to fit domestic biomass burners that use specially produced fuels and logs to power home-heating systems.

Waste products
As well as specially grown crops, biomass is also sourced from waste products generated by agricultural and industrial processes. This includes waste wood produced by forestry.

Types of fuel
The most common fuels are woodchips and pellets. They are easily stored and loaded into the hopper as required.

Woodchips
Normally suitable for a domestic biomass boiler, woodchips require more storage space than pellets.

Pellets
Made of compressed wood shavings and sawdust, pellets have a high combustion efficiency.

AIR CONDITIONING

More and more Canadian homes are considering some measure of air conditioning as a standard feature. Whole-house air conditioners have SEER ratings, which are basically a measure of their energy efficiency. A SEER of 13 is good. You will find EnerGuide labels on air conditioners in Canada, giving you a comparative position of the unit you are considering against other models. Energy Star certification is becoming more common and always means good energy efficiency.

ROOM AIR CONDITIONERS

If you want the benefits of air conditioning but are unable to install a whole-house system, wall or window units are available to condition a smaller space. Window units have adjustable sides and can be set inside an open window. Wall units are installed flush into an exterior wall. Just as with whole-house systems, you will need to regularly clean the filter to make sure it is functioning efficiently.

AIR CONDITIONERS

Whether it is a whole-house system that works alone or with a heating system, or a series of room units, the basics of how an air conditioner works is the same. Air conditioners pull warm air out of the space, filter it, cool it, and then release that cool air back into the space. The biggest energy user in any air-conditioning unit is the compressor, which pumps the refrigerant through the air-conditioning system to cool the space.

Air-conditioning unit
As long as the air conditioner is sized properly for the space it is intended to cool, you will be able to achieve the same type of results from whole-house and single-room systems. The air conditioner shown here can be used with a heat pump.

Warm air taken in

Cooled air expelled

Cold air distribution
Central air conditioners can work with a furnace. The furnace blower and the furnace's ducting are used to deliver the cooled air from the air-conditioning unit around your home. Shown here, the cold air is represented by the blue arrows. The cold air leaves the furnace in the basement, travels through the ducts until it reaches the vents in a room.

Cooled air is released into the room

Hot air

Indoor units
Although most Canadian air conditioners have an indoor and an outdoor unit, it is possible to get air conditioners totally inside the house, even integrated into the furnace. These units will have two ducts, one bringing in outdoor air and the other sending it back outdoors, as shown here, rather than having the unit sitting outdoors.

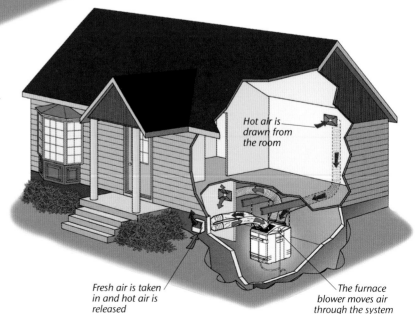

Hot air is drawn from the room

COOLING OPTIONS

Air conditioners are not the only way to keep a house cool when the temperature rises outside. Ceiling fans, proper insulation, air sealing, as well as proper roof overhangs and trees shading south-facing windows all help keep heat out and move air around inside your home. Light-color shingles do more good than attic fans.

Fresh air is taken in and hot air is released

The furnace blower moves air through the system

AIR CLEANERS

Concern with health has caused air cleaners to become increasingly popular products in Canada. According to Health Canada, poor indoor air quality is one of the top five environmental risks. Some say that pollutants in your home's air can cause dizziness and headaches, and aggravate allergies and asthma. There are three steps you can take to clear your home's air of pollutants: remove the source of the problem; ventilate the area; and clean the air. Note that air cleaning alone cannot adequately remove all of the pollutants typically found in indoor air.

FURTHER INFORMATION

There are a a few simple steps you can take to keep the air in your home healthy to breathe:
- Clean your home regularly
- Store chemicals in tightly sealed containers and dispose of any waste properly
- Control humidity and temperature
- Monitor your home's air through air testing
- Hire an HVAC technician to make sure air cleaning equipment and ducts are properly installed, sized, and sealed

TYPES OF AIR CLEANERS

There are a wide range of products available for helping to clean and regulate moisture levels in the air you breathe in your home. Unlike traditional air filters on your heating system, air cleaners are designed to filter out particles that are unseen by the human eye. These tiny particles are easily inhaled and are believed to cause or irritate health problems. Some air cleaners are designed to be installed in ducts as part of a central heating or air-conditioning system and others can be stand-alone units that are portable, working just in a concentrated area of the home.

Whole-house dehumidifier
If excess moisture is a problem in your home, you will benefit from ventilation and a dehumidifier. Shown here, the Humiditrol whole-home dehumidifier system installs in the home's existing duct system.

Electronic air cleaner
An electrical field traps charged particles, preventing them from entering your HVAC system. This air cleaner removes particles and bioaerosols down to 1 micron.

Humidifier
Indoor moisture levels can be regulated by using a humidifier. This can enhance air quality and comfort. The model shown here works with most forced-air systems.

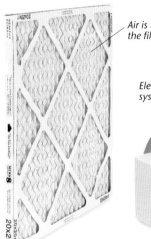

Air is forced through the filter

Electronic control system

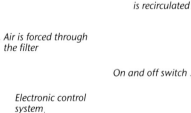

Cleaned air is recirculated

On and off switch

Air intake

Germicidal light
One way to keep air purified and surfaces clean and sterilized is with a germicidal light. Using ultraviolet energy, it can quickly reduce concentrations of airborne bioaerosols.

Filter
Air filters remove particles from the HVAC system as new air circulates into the unit. This air filter removes particles and bioaerosols down to 3 microns, and is easy to replace.

Ventilation control system
Gain indoor air quality and increase comfort with a whole-house ventilation system that automatically monitors the outdoor temperature and indoor humidity levels.

FURTHER INFORMATION

Modern energy efficient windows, proper insulation, vapor barriers, and sealing all joints with caulk help reduce energy bills and increase the efficiency of a house. The problem is that a house functions best when it can still breathe. Houses need to be ventilated. Without proper ventilation in a home, moisture and mold can become a problem. For optimal comfort and health, experts say that the home's relative humidity levels should range between 35 and 50 percent. By maintaining this humidity level, you may also be reducing the opportunity for mold and mildew problems.

If you have an older home, you are more likely to have a radiator heating system. These rely on a boiler to produce steam or hot water that runs through a system of pipes to heat the radiators. The boiler can be powered by oil, gas, or electricity. More common in relatively newer homes, baseboard heaters are usually added as a source of heat in additions, basement renovations, or as supplemental heat. Baseboards can be powered by electricity or a hot water boiler.

TOOLS AND MATERIALS SEE BASIC TOOLKIT AND P.505

MAINTAINING A RADIATOR

Radiators require some regular maintenance to keep running smoothly and safely. The most common maintenance radiators require is bleeding, which eliminates air from the system. Some radiators have bleed valves or bleed keys to help make this adjustment. Older radiators can develop leaks over time, making it difficult to heat the space. To conquer this problem the entire radiator may need to be replaced or need a new thermostatic valve. If you are replacing a radiator, make sure to replace the same size unit, as it will save time in installation. If you are redecorating your room, you may want to remove the face of the radiator to allow better access behind the unit. Always take caution when working around a radiator. Turn off the boiler before attempting any adjustments to a radiator.

PARTS OF A RADIATOR

A standard panel radiator is made from pressed steel. It may have a single or double panel, and convector types have fins on the back to increase heat output. The size of a radiator is selected to provide the right heat output for each room. Every radiator has a threaded inlet at each corner, into which various fixtures are screwed. You may need a special radiator wrench to install them. Radiators may have a handwheel temperature control rather than the thermostatic valve shown here.

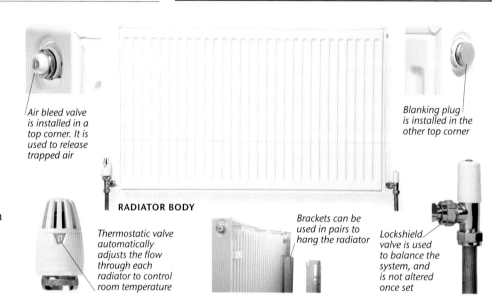

Air bleed valve is installed in a top corner. It is used to release trapped air

Blanking plug is installed in the other top corner

RADIATOR BODY

Thermostatic valve automatically adjusts the flow through each radiator to control room temperature

Brackets can be used in pairs to hang the radiator

Lockshield valve is used to balance the system, and is not altered once set

TEMPORARILY REMOVING A RADIATOR

Close the lockshield valve, keeping note of exactly how many turns it takes. Shut the thermostatic or handwheel valve.

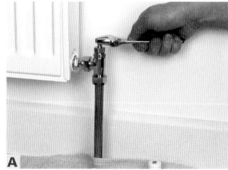

A

B

Place a container under the radiator. Undo the lockshield valve connector nut, then open the bleed valve to drain the water.

C

Undo the connector nut to the other valve so that you can lift the radiator off the wall brackets. Carefully tip out the remaining water.

REPLACING AN OLD RADIATOR WITH A NEW ONE

A

Measure from the baseboard to the bottom of the bracket. Measure and mark the same distance on the wall on the vertical line.

B

Hang the radiator on the brackets, and tighten the connectors onto the valves. Brace each valve with a wrench as you tighten the nut fully.

Open both valves by the number of turns it took to close them. Bleed the radiator using a radiator bleed key. Always turn off the system before performing any work.

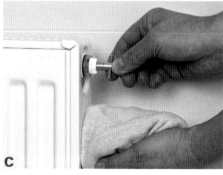

C

INSTALLING A BASEBOARD HEATER

Baseboard heaters are ideal in additions and in remodelled basements. They are easier to install than a central system. If you want to replace an older baseboard heater with a more energy efficient system, there are few steps you will need to take prior to following the installation below. Always turn off the power before starting any work, and consult the local building official to find out any regulations. You may need to hire a professional to complete this work.

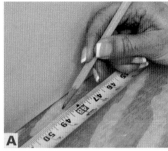

A Lay out and measure the area where you plan to install the heater. For extra safety, make sure it will not be near any fabric or furnishings.

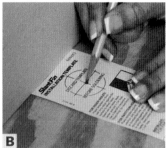

B Mark the floor joist locations on the floor using the manufacturer's directions and template as a guide.

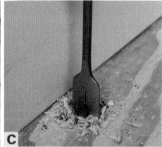

C Drill holes through each layout mark, making sure the holes are more than ⅜ in (10 mm) larger than the pipe.

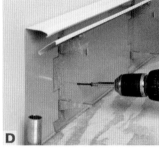

D Position the baseboard against the wall. Firmly attach the housing to the wall with screws.

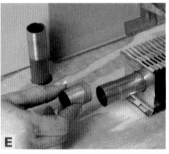

E If necessary, add an extension collar to the end of the piping to so the pipes can meet to make the connection.

F Attach the elbow pipe, so the piping can turn the corner from the horizontal unit to the vertical pipe through the floor.

G Dry-fit all of the pipes to test the connection, making sure they will fit before securing in place.

After the pipes are aligned securely, clean and then solder the elbow connection. Then solder each other pipe connection in the baseboard heater's system.

H

I Check all of the fins to make sure they were not damaged during transport. Straighten any.

J Cover the heating fins by snapping the baseboard heater face on the front of the baseboard heater.

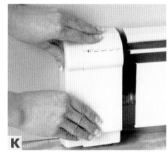

K Place the end caps on either end of the baseboard heater, and secure each in place.

L Adjust the louvers to your desired way of directing heat into the space. Be careful to not touch these while the heat is on.

M

Turn on the furnace and test run the new heater until hot air starts to flow out. Make sure the area around the baseboard is clear of any debris or furnishings when the heating is on.

UNDERFLOOR HEATING

Underfloor heating is typically used as a supplemental system to warm tiled floors. An advantage is that there are no baseboard heaters cluttering up wall surfaces, and the heat it provides is particularly even and comfortable. You can embed plastic heating pipes or electric cables in a solid floor, but this is a realistic option only for new projects such as additions. If you want to warm an existing floor, it is easier to use electric underfloor heating kits, which are designed to be laid on an existing floor surface and then covered with ceramic floor tiles. Check with the local authorities to see if these systems meet code requirements.

SAFETY

Always follow all manufacturer's guidelines and local building codes when attempting any new DIY project, especially when the project involves electricity and heating elements. Check if you are allowed to install a new radiant flooring system in your jurisdiction. Even if you are, you may need to file paperwork and plans with your local planning office for approval before you begin a project involving the heating system in your home. If you are not confident about completing any projects yourself, contact a professional organization for qualified leads.

BUILT-IN UNDERFLOOR HEATING

Systems that use pipes or cables buried in concrete floors cannot easily be installed into an existing house because of the upheaval involved in excavating the existing floor. This has to be undertaken to avoid raising the floor level by pouring a new concrete floor. However, these systems can be easily built during construction of a new home. Modern underfloor heating systems are efficient and reliable, and can be used with almost any type of floor covering. The heat provided by the system is even from floor to ceiling—there are none of the hot and cold spots that are created by wall-mounted registers, radiators, wood stoves, and fireplaces. Once the floor slab warms up, its temperature is thermostatically controlled, and it needs very little extra energy to keep it warm.

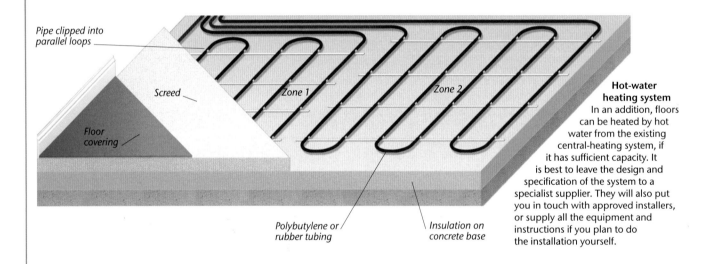

Pipe clipped into parallel loops

Screed

Floor covering

Zone 1

Zone 2

Polybutylene or rubber tubing

Insulation on concrete base

Hot-water heating system
In an addition, floors can be heated by hot water from the existing central-heating system, if it has sufficient capacity. It is best to leave the design and specification of the system to a specialist supplier. They will also put you in touch with approved installers, or supply all the equipment and instructions if you plan to do the installation yourself.

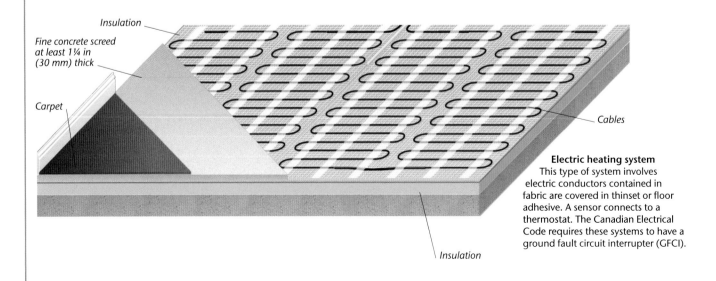

Insulation

Fine concrete screed at least 1¼ in (30 mm) thick

Carpet

Cables

Electric heating system
This type of system involves electric conductors contained in fabric are covered in thinset or floor adhesive. A sensor connects to a thermostat. The Canadian Electrical Code requires these systems to have a ground fault circuit interrupter (GFCI).

Insulation

RADIANT HEATING

Radiant floor systems are designed to warm the air from the surface where the system is installed. This means the heat concentration is actually greatest near the floor. With forced-air heating systems, the hottest part of the room is typically near the ceiling. Some radiant panel systems are also capable of cooling by circulating cool water instead of hot. Some experts say that radiant heating is a cleaner way to heat a home, as there is no air passing through ducts or filters that attract dust and pollutants. As tile floor can be quite cold to the touch in early morning hours, the bathroom is the most common place a radiant heating system is considered, but is a worthwhile consideration for other rooms. Some people install floor heating systems under driveways to melt away snow. Others install radiant systems in the walls, instead of the floors.

There are many types of radiant systems available, too. Featured on these pages are electric and water systems. Air systems are available, but less common. The water systems can be heated by a variety of sources: natural gas, oil, wood, electricity, and even solar. When considering the size of a radiant heating system you require, keep in mind that the larger the surface area of the mat, the lower the actual surface temperature required to heat the space.

Mesh mats

This system uses heating cable fixed to preassembled mesh mats in evenly spaced parallel loops. The mats are available in a range of sizes. One or more mats can be laid side by side to cover the required floor area. The mat is laid on a bed of flexible tile adhesive and is covered with more adhesive, into which the floor tiles are bedded. If the mat is laid over a wood floor rather than solid concrete, you may need special thermal boards put down first to direct the heat output upward. The temperature sensor is placed between cables in the heated floor area, concealed in flat oval conduit, and is connected to the wall-mounted thermostat that controls the heat output of the mat(s). Follow the manufacturer's instructions for testing the heating mat prior to installation. Wait for thinset to completely dry before attempting operation.

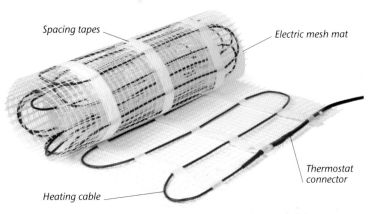

Mesh heating mat
Each mat has a connection to the wall-mounted thermostat at one corner, so the mat should be oriented to allow easy connection. You can trim the mesh to fit the floor area, but you must not cut the heating cables or overlap adjacent mats or cables. Nonheating leads cannot overlap the mat's heating area.

▌▌ INSTALLING A HEATING MAT

As well as the right size of mat, you will need enough thinset to cover the floor to the thickness needed, plus a similar quantity to cover the heating mat when the tiles are laid over it to finish the floor (see pp.314–315 for more on tiling). You will also need duct tape or conduit to protect the power cords and the sensor cable. Make sure you have enough power on the branch circuit to supply the mat. If you are laying the mat on a wood floor, you may need thermal boards to cover the mat area. Lay these first, using the fasteners supplied, and tape over the joints.

If you are installing the mat in a bathroom, it must be protected by a ground fault circuit interrupter (GFCI). A digital multimeter is supplied with the kit so you can check the mat's insulation and cables before installing to confirm that the mat is undamaged. Repeat the test once the mat has been laid, and again before its power supply is finally connected. See pp.438–445 for more on electrics.

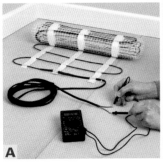
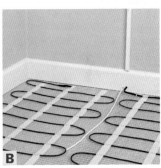

A **Do an insulation test** on each mat to begin with. Then, lay out the mats side by side, and trim the mesh backing if necessary.

B **Plan the power** supply to the mats, so you can decide where to site the thermostat. Run the cables up the wall to this position.

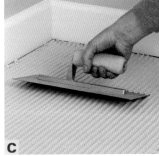
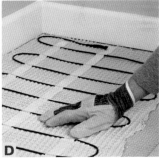

C **Spread thinset** on the floor using a notched trowel and allow it to dry. Unroll the mat on top of it.

D **Lay the mat** on to the floor by hand, or use a board offcut. Enclose the sensor cable in oval conduit and place it between coils in the mat.

Connect the conductors and the thermostat, following the wiring instructions supplied. Carry out the second insulation test on the mat. Cover the mats with more thinset, and bed the floor tiles in place. Allow the floor to dry out before using the heating.

E

Spacing tapes

Electric mesh mat

Thermostat connector

Heating cable

FIRST AID

However carefully you work, accidents can happen during DIY projects, and when they do, a little knowledge of basic first aid can be very useful. In all cases of serious injury, you should of course call 911 or get to a hospital as soon as possible. Even with minor injuries it is wise to seek advice from a doctor, but the notes on this page may help you to deal with an immediate emergency. Keep a well-stocked first aid kit somewhere easily accessible, and whenever possible get someone else to help you treat an injury.

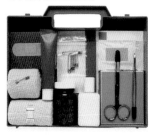

BASIC FIRST AID KIT

A good first aid kit should contain the following:
- Bandages
- Scissors
- Tweezers
- Safety pins
- Antibiotic ointment
- Iodine or similar prep pads
- Alcohol prep pads
- Butterfly bandages
- Medical adhesive tape
- Pain relievers
- Eye drops
- Burn medication

BLEEDING

Cuts and grazes are among the most common injuries. If the cut is minor, the bleeding will soon stop on its own, but it is still wise to clean and dress the wound, especially considering the dirt generated during DIY work. Rinse the wound under cold running water, then clean around it with a sterile swab or antiseptic wipe, removing any foreign objects embedded in it. Dry the area around the wound, and cover it with an adhesive bandage or wrap it with a sterile dressing. Any time the skin is broken, bear in mind the danger of tetanus. Most people have been immunized at some point, but the effect wears off without a "booster shot" every ten years. If your immunization is out of date, visit your doctor for a new shot.

BANDAGES

OTHER COMMON INJURIES

If an object becomes embedded in your skin, you may be able to remove it yourself. Splinters are relatively simple— clean the wound, and pull the splinter out using tweezers sterilized over a flame and allowed to cool. If the object is larger, go to a hospital, pinching the wound together if necessary to prevent bleeding. Whenever you or anybody else touches an open wound, make sure to use sterile gloves or at least freshly washed hands. If an object enters the eye, seek a doctor's help as soon as possible. For a broken bone, call 911 and do not move the casualty. Try to support the injured limb (or the head and neck if you suspect a spinal injury).

TWEEZERS

SCISSORS

CHEMICAL BURNS

Many domestic chemicals, and especially those used in DIY, can cause serious damage to the skin. Act quickly to wash the chemical off, then cover the burn with a sterile dressing and seek advice at a hospital immediately. If possible, make a note of the chemical that caused the burn, or take it with you to the hospital.

DIY CHEMICALS

ELECTRIC SHOCK

Never touch a shock victim who is still in contact with the electric current—you risk electrocuting yourself. Break the current by switching off at the circuit breaker or pulling the plug. If you cannot do this, stand on dry insulating material such as a wooden box, rubber mat, or pile of newspapers. Push the casualty's limbs away from the source of electricity using a wooden broom handle, stool, or chair. Call 911 immediately. If the casualty is unconscious and you know how to, put them into the recovery position.

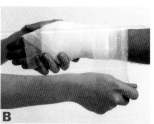

Wooden broom

ELECTRIC SHOCK

TREATING MINOR BURNS

Cool the burn with copious amounts of cold water for at least ten minutes or until the burning feeling stops. Use a running faucet if possible, but any source of cold, clean water will do. Raise the limb to reduce swelling. Try not to touch the burn itself, but protect it from the surroundings. If needed, wrap it in a clean polythene bag or plastic wrap.

Alternatively, cover the burn with sterile gauze, and bandage it loosely before going to a hospital as soon as possible.

The sections in this book offer solutions to many problems involving leaks, breakdowns, or malfunctions of home systems and appliances, but this page offers some brief advice on what to do in an emergency. However, many situations will call for professional help. You should certainly not attempt to fix a gas leak yourself, for example. The table to the right may be a useful way to keep a record of emergency and contact numbers.

GAS

If you smell gas or propane, try to determine whether it is coming from a leak, or whether an appliance has been left on or turned on accidentally. Extinguish any naked flames, do not turn lights on or off, and avoid using any other item that could create a spark. After checking that gas appliances are off, turn off the gas at the main shutoff. This is normally located by the meter. Open windows and doors, evacuate the house, and keep people away from the building. If you suspect a leak, call your gas company from outside the property, at a safe distance.

PLUMBING

Leaks are dealt with comprehensively in the plumbing chapter, but in the event of a major leak, remember that turning off the shutoff valve stops any more water from entering the system. If you cannot find any other way to isolate the leak, run all the cold faucets in the house. This will help empty pipes if it is a supply pipe problem. Flushing toilets will also help. If the problem lies in the central heating or hot water pipes, shut off the boiler or water heater, make sure all water systems are off, close the radiator valves, and turn on hot water faucets. Call a plumber, and if a leak is near any electrical appliance, turn off the electricity at the breaker panel.

ELECTRICITY

If you lose all power in your home, first check whether the main breaker switch on the breaker panel has switched to the off position. Check whether your neighbors have the same problem, and therefore whether it is a generalized power outage or a problem for you alone. If just one circuit switches off, this could be due to overloading—check how many appliances are being used at one time. If the main isolator switch or circuit breakers trip persistently, call an electrician to deal with the problem.

EMERGENCY EQUIPMENT

It's important to have easy access to some vital equipment in case of emergencies. Most of the equipment you may need is listed under the basic toolkit (see pp.24–25), and some suggestions for a basic first aid kit are listed opposite, but you should also check that you have the following around the house:

- Flashlight
- Spare batteries
- Candles and matches
- Light bulbs
- Pail or large bowl

IN THE EVENT OF AN EMERGENCY, GO TO THE NEAREST TELEPHONE AND DIAL 911. ASK FOR THE POLICE, AMBULANCE, OR FIRE DEPARTMENT

EMERGENCY CONTACTS

Emergency services   **911**

Local hospital ....

Family doctor ....

Local police station...

Poison hotline

Gas or propane company ....

Telephone ....

Location of gas shutoff ....
....
....
....

Water company ....

Telephone ....

Plumber ....

Telephone ....

Cell phone ....

Location of main shutoff ....
....
....
....

Electric company ....

Telephone ....

Electrician ....

Telephone ....

Cell phone ....

Location of breaker panel ....
....
....
....

This glossary provides quick definitions of some commonly used terms in the book, as well as some definitions of building terminology that you may find helpful. Knowledge of these terms can help in both understanding structural issues, but can also make ordering materials easier, as well as explaining requirements and describing needs to suppliers.

Abutment
Joint between two surfaces. Used in roofing terminology to describe the joint between a roof and a wall, for example.

Acoustically efficient
A technical term for materials that have soundproofing qualities.

Actual
The actual size of a member, as opposed to the nominal one.

Adhesive
Substance that joins materials together—for example, wood glue.

Attic
The room directly under the roof.

Balloon framing
Traditional method of lumber-frame house construction where single vertical members stretch from ground level up to the height of the eaves.

Baluster
Vertical member of a balustrade that fits beneath the handrail, offering support.

Balustrade
Collective term for the handrail, balusters, and baserail of a staircase.

Bargeboard
The fascia board that follows the line of the verge at the edge of a gable roof.

Batt
The name for mattress-like sections of insulation material.

Batter board
A furring strip nailed to two wooden stakes, with nails positioned along its top edge to indicate foundation and/or wall width. String is attached between the nails of opposing boards to provide guide lines for foundation and wall width.

Bead
A thin line of sealant, thin molding, or technique used to cut paint in accurately at a junction.

Bearer
Supportive member. Beams are the bearers that support a raised wooden deck, for example.

Birdsmouth
A section of the base of a rafter that is cut out so that it can fit/connect with the wall plate on an exterior wall.

Blocking
Short, wooden members used as strengthening for stud walls and in timber floor structure.

Bond
The strength of adhesion between two materials or the arrangement of junctions between building materials. A brick bond refers to staggered vertical joints between courses, and also to wall tiles or rows of patio slabs, for example.

Bracket
Projecting supportive fixture or fitting.

Butt
To join pieces together forming a butt-join or joint.

Butter
Technique of applying mortar to the end of a brick or block before positioning it.

Capping stone
Stone laid on the top of a wall to protect the wall from the weather. Normally edges are flush with the wall, and do not overhang.

Casing
Decorative molding used around a wall recess or opening, such as a doorway.

Caulk
Flexible filler used for filling cracks and joints when decorating.

Cavity
Gap between the inner and outer leaf of a cavity wall.

Cavity wall tie
Shaped bracket or connector that links the structure of the inner leaf of a cavity wall to the outer leaf.

Cement
Adhesive that is also used to bind other materials (aggregate) to make concrete. Dries to a very hard finish.

Chair rail
Rail that divides the dado and the upper wall. Commonly positioned 3 ft 3 in (1 m) from floor level.

Cladding
The covering of another surface for decorative, fireproofing, or weatherproofing purposes. Wood, stone, concrete, or shingles can be used.

Coping stone
Stone laid on top of a wall to protect the wall from the elements. The edges normally overhang the wall slightly.

Counterbatten
Double layer of furring strips, secured at right angles to each other. Commonly used in roofing or lumber-frame wall structure to provide a cavity for ventilation and/or water runoff.

Countersink
To recess the head of a fixing (normally a screw) to below surface level.

Course
A row of building components, such as bricks.

Crown molding
Decorative molding used at the junction between ceiling and walls.

Cure
The gradual process by which concrete, or an adhesive or wet substance sets to a hard condition. It may or may not be dry when it is cured.

Cutting in
Term used for painting a precise line at a junction or joint between two surfaces.

Dado
Woodworking joint.

Damp-proof course (DPC)
Strip of impervious material built into the lower level of a wall that prevents ground moisture rising into the house structure. Also applies when a wall is impregnated with damp-proof chemicals to stop the upward movement of moisture.

Dowel
Small peg, normally wooden, partially inserted into two adjacent surfaces strengthening the joint. Also a thin strip of wood that is round in cross-section.

Drip edge
Small channel in the underside of sills, thresholds, and other exterior projections, that prevents water from running back to the wall surface by making it drip down.

Dry laying
Laying bricks or stone, for example, using no adhesive or mortar, in order to plan the best positions and order of work.

Edge cutter
Type of bit used with a router to create decorative profiles along the edge of a board.

Fascia
Plank-shaped member used to cover the ends of rafters, and to which gutters are normally fixed.

Female
The joining part of a fastener that the male part fits into. A male thread screws into a female thread.

Finish carpentry
The final stages of construction. For example, a carpenter adding baseboards, a plumber installing radiators, or an electrician installing switches and sockets.

Finish coat
Final coat of a material, for example, plaster or gloss paint.

Flashing
Waterproofing layer used at joints on a roof, for example, where a flat roof meets a wall.

Float
Type of trowel with a rectangular blade used for finishing a render or plaster coat.

Flush
Level with an adjacent surface.

Foundation
The base on which to build or support a structure.

Frog
The wedge-shaped depression in the surface of a brick.

Furring strip
Thin, square-edged timber.

Gasket
Shaped piece of sealing material that prevents liquid or gas from leaking from joined surfaces.

Gluelam
Laminated sections of lumber used to create structural elements such as beams and lintels.

Hand/Handed
When a fixture is designed to work in one direction by rotating one way, or opening from one edge. For example, it is possible to buy handed ceramic-disk valves for faucets, and handed rising butt hinges for doors.

Lally column
Adjustable, heavyweight pole used to support the weight of structures during construction.

Lath
Thin, wooden strip nailed to studs or joists used in old buildings to create a framework for the application of lime plaster. Also a small sheet of plasterboard.

Layout
Deciding on the position of a fixture or material and checking for appropriate attachment points, level positioning, or aesthetic appeal.

Male
The joining part of a fastener that inserts into the female side. For example, a male screw thread fits into a female thread.

Mastic
Sealant that retains a very rubbery and flexible consistency, even when fully dry.

Member
Structural element or section in a building.

Miter
A joint using angled cuts. Most miters consist of two members with ends cut at 45 degrees so they form a right-angled joint.

Mortar
Mixture of cement, sand, and sometimes other materials to create an adhesive for masonry and constructional members.

Mortise
Rectangular cavity in wooden joints or in security devices such as locks and latches.

Newel post
Upright post in a balustrade that supports a handrail and provides structural strength.

Nominal
A size of a member that may not be completely accurate in terms of measurement, but is informative in terms of estimation for building purposes. The nominal size of a brick, for example, includes mortar on the short and long side to make estimation of quantity requirement easier. The nominal size of timber cross-section may not be its actual size because it has dried out or been planed down from its actual size.

Nosing
Front edge of a staircase tread.

Olive
Metallic ring used to create a watertight seal in a compression joint between pipes.

Opaque
Describes a surface or substance through which light cannot pass.

Packing
Material (often wooden wedges or slivers) used to fill in a gap during construction or to wedge a member or fixture into position, normally so that it is level or securely fixed.

Padstone
A dense block or stone that is positioned under the ends of beams helping to support and spread weight.

Parapet
A low wall around the edge of a roof, above the eaves.

Parging
Technique of creating a waterproof layer or layers on a wall or floor to prevent water penetration.

Partition wall
Internal wall that divides rooms or a space.

Party wall
A wall that is shared between neighbors, such as the wall that divides a duplex.

Pier
A supportive pillar common in garden-wall construction.

Pilot hole
A guide hole made for a fixing (normally a screw).

Platform frame
Lumber-frame house construction where paneled lumber frames are erected in stories. Each floor forms the base for the next story.

Plug/Wall plug
A plastic or metal sleeve used in masonry or cavity walls to provide a secure insertion point and housing for a fastener.

Plumb
Exactly vertical.

Primer
Preparatory coat for topcoats.

Punch list
A list of requirements used to check that every part of a job is complete.

Purlin
Supporting beam positioned at right angles to and below rafters.

PVA
Polyvinyl acetate, a synthetic resin used as an adhesive in its neat form, or, when diluted with water, as a sealer for porous surfaces.

PVC
Polyvinyl chloride, a type of thermoplastic often used in the production of electrical wire insulation, roofing sheets, and soft floor tiles. Unplasticized PVC is used for more rigid articles such as windows and drainage pipes.

Rabbet
A groove or step cut into the edge of a piece of wood.

Racking/Racking back
Building up the corners first when constructing a brick or block wall.

Rafter
The sloping joists on a roof that normally run from the ridge to the wall plates.

Reducer
A connection that joins pipes of different diameters.

Render
A mortar used as an undercoat for further plaster coats on the interior of the home. May be a finishing coat on exterior walls.

Ridge
The apex created by the joining of two pitched roofs.

Roof sheathing
Sheathing boards attached to rafters before felt and furring strips.

Rough carpentry
The early stages of a construction job. For example, carpentry includes erecting studs and fixing rafters. Plumbing or electrical work involves routing the pipes or wires to where fixtures will be placed.

Screed coat
Layer of mortar laid over a concrete floor pad for a smooth finish.

Scribing
Method of creating a cutting guide line on a material so that it will perfectly fit against a surface. A pointed wooden offcut is used with a pencil to "trace" a guide line that matches the profile of the surface.

Sealant
Flexible substance used to create a waterproof seal along a junction, or a liquid painted onto a surface to seal it.

Sheathing
Boards used on roofs before felt, furring strips, and tiles. Also the boards fixed to lumber-frame walls in lumber-frame house construction.

Skim
The process of applying topcoats of plaster to a wall.

Solvent
The base of a substance. Water is the solvent for latex paint. The solvent of a substance is also used as the cleaning agent.

Square
Describes the position of an object that is exactly aligned so that it is level, vertical, parallel, or at right angles to a surface.

Stud
Wooden (or metal) member used in the construction of walls.

Subfloor
Floor material below decorative flooring—for example, plywood sheets below ceramic floor tiles.

Subsidence
Movement of the ground below or around a building that can lead to foundation and structural damage.

Teflon tape
Tape used on the male threaded plumbing joints to create a watertight seal.

Translucent
Allowing a proportion of light to pass through. Transparent materials allow all light through.

Trap
Water-filled bend shape found in drainage systems that prevents the ingress of bad smells and odors.

Underpinning
Building or adding strength to the existing foundations of a building, normally to counteract subsidence.

Vapor barrier
Sheet of impervious material positioned on the warm-in-winter side of insulation to prevent moisture vapor from reaching the cold side of the insulation. Also a plastic sheet placed under a concrete slab or over a dirt crawl space floor to prevent moisture migration into the house. Technically called a vaporr retarder.

Vermiculite
Granular material used as loose-fill attic insulation. Also mixed with cement to make a lightweight concrete with fireproof qualities, commonly used as backfill behind the fireback in a fireplace.

Wainscoting
The use of wooden paneling on the lower area of a wall surface.

INDEX

Y

ACKNOWLEDGEMENTS

**Author acknowledgements
for this revised edition**

Thank you to Stephanie Farrow and Lee Griffiths for getting this edition up and running. Everybody knew it was a good idea, but it always requires a lot of work behind the scenes and we greatly appreciate their efforts on our behalf.

In producing this second edition, we would like to thank all of those companies listed in the suppliers section who supplied products and offered advice on their use. It was also great to work once again with some of the original team; Sharon Spencer was our leading light in amalgamating the new material into the original design—a huge task in itself—and we thank her for putting up with us again, and for producing more stunning-looking work. Gary Ombler returned to pick up the camera where he left off, and has clearly managed to re-capture the style and look of the original work—we thank him for that, and also for keeping us entertained on photo shoots in his usual manner. Many thanks to Julia Barnard who looked after us magnificently on the photo shoots once more, happily feeding and watering us at incredibly regular intervals. On the illustrative side, we appreciate Patrick Mulrey coming back to produce his beautiful artworks, which marry so well with the existing material. A big thank you to Barbara Hunt and Daniel Perret, models from the first edition, who also returned for more, which helped greatly with continuity.

The new editorial team, including Bob Bridle and Ed Wilson, were superbly efficient in flowing in the new material and dealing with the mass of editing problems that seems to keep multiplying when working on a book of this size. Many thanks. Indeed, to all of the people at DK who we never meet, but know are beavering away on our behalf—thank you once again.

...and of course, last, but not least, thank you to our families, who had to go through it all again!

**Author acknowledgements for the
original edition**

When writing an illustrated book, there are always a number of people that authors like to thank for their efforts and contributions. However, when writing an illustrated book of this size, there are a truly enormous number of people to thank for work over several years.

Firstly, we will always be indebted to Stephanie Jackson, who engineered the transformation of ideas into reality. She was backed up along the way by Adele Hayward and Karen Self. In these initial stages we would also like to thank Tim Ridley, Jude Garlick, and Carole Ash for photographic, editorial, and design contributions that helped to get initial ideas off the ground.

Up to the book's completion, many people contributed and to those in sales, marketing, production, and all those areas of publishing that authors tend not to come into contact with, thank you for all your efforts.

The day-to-day team that handled this project gradually grew and grew as more and more material was gathered. To those that were involved along the way—including Becky Alexander, Karen Constanti, Marghie Gianni, Miranda Harrison, Linda Martin, Constance Novis, and Corinne Roberts—thank you for your contributions.

All books have managerial tiers that guide and oversee progress. Stephanie Farrow, Lee Griffiths, and Bryn Walls all helped to guide us ever nearer the finish line. Later additions to the team that finished the book included David Ball, Vania Cunha, Sunita Gahir, Phil Gamble, Jörn Kröger, Monica Pal, Matt Schofield, Giles Sparrow, David Summers, and Andrew Szudek. All had to deal with two battle-weary authors nearing the end of a long journey. Thank you for dealing with our mood swings and moans.

For most of the project Letty Luff and Suzanne Arnold took on the many editorial challenges, along with Peter Jones who oversaw everything and everybody. We would like to thank Letty for making so much sense of so many pages in so many parts of the book—her editorial mind is one of the best we have ever come across. We want to thank Suzanne for the endless days of rejigging phrase after phrase, and managing to fit what we needed 100 words to say into a perfectly concise 10. We would like to thank Peter for being the linchpin in this project—an incredibly tough task, and we have enormous admiration for the way in which he managed this book to the end, ensuring that it got to print on time. Throughout the many arguments, stand-offs, and disagreements, he kept the show moving, and we are extremely grateful for all his hard work.

On the illustrative side, we would like to thank the small army of illustrators who turned our reference material into various diagrams throughout the book. Special thanks to Patrick Mulrey who contributed the most in number, and experimented with all sorts of effects to produce some stunning images. Thanks also to Julian Baker, Peter Bull, Richard Burgess, Andrew Green, Adam Howard, Andy Kaye, Tim Loughhead, and Matthew White.

The greatest challenge on this project was undoubtedly photographic, and it was in this area that we developed our closest relationships in the team. Gary Ombler shot the majority of images, but a significant minority were from Steve Gorton. Over an 18-month period, they were guided at all times by designers Phil Gilderdale, Su St. Louis, Sharon Spencer, and Michael Duffy. We would like to thank Phil for initially setting up the style and the look of photography. Thank you to Michael for his attention to detail, and his dry sense of humor that helped the course of many shoot days, and his later help on styling the artworks in the book. An enormous thank you to Gary and Steve who were always there, ready to take the first frame come rain or shine, good health or poor health, and always managing to complete the task that was put before them. Steve takes the meaning of being easy to work with to another level, and we must thank Gary for enriching our lives with his incredible knowledge of worldwide culinary cuisine (specializing in cheeses). Art direction on the majority of shoots was the responsibility of Sharon and Su, which meant they had to navigate the precarious path of keeping us, the

ACKNOWLEDGEMENTS

photographers, and their bosses back at Dorling Kindersley all happy. We thank them both for being such great fun to work with, and for making such a contribution to the look of this book.

There were many, many other contributors to the success of the photography. We would like to thank the many models who came through our doors and were often asked to sit, stand, or lay in the most uncomfortable of positions for hours on end while the rest of us contemplated the merits of changing a shirt color or the fractional movement of a little finger. Particular thanks to Jakki, Barbara, and Heath for tackling all our demands with such good humor.

During every day of photography we were extremely luck to have Julia Barnard or her daughter Rose (and even Helena once) to keep everybody topped up with coffee and food. That was their job description, but in reality they did so much more, ranging from cognitive therapy to simply making us all smile. We owe them a huge thank you on both our behalf and on behalf of the Dorling Kindersley team.

On a technical level, we were aided on shoots by Mike O'Connor with his always inimitable plastering work, Steve Hearne and Dave Reakes with their building and block work, and Vince Macey who steered us through the maze of wiring during the electrical shoots. We also had help at the end of a phone from Craig Rushmere, Dave Norris, Steve Cuff, Alan Berry, Andy Mainstone, and Ed Humphris of Henry James masonry (who also supplied us with a fireplace). Further supplies and help were from Martin Cole, Shaun McConnell and John and Susannah Deverell—thanks for the "German" hammer. Steve and Johnny at the "yard" were also there to help lift a "wall' or "set" at any time of day, while Bert and Sue Read were our ever-understanding landlords. We are incredibly grateful to you all.

We would also like to thank another DIY guru, Mike Lawrence. He took the electrical and heating section from our initial framework, and worked a very difficult brief to provide such great sections for the book. It was a real

pleasure working with him once again, and we wholeheartedly thank him for all his work and advice.

Our greatest debt of thanks goes to Phil Gilderdale. Any success that this book may have has much to do with his ideas and hard work. We could not have wished to work with anyone more professional, and amenable at all times. His good humor and encouragement kept us going throughout the project, we are sincerely grateful to him.

Lastly, but most importantly, thank you to our families for dealing with our mood swings, late nights, and ups and downs over the years this book has taken to complete. To Adele, Emmanuelle, Jack and Rebecca, Sam and Leo, we love and thank you all.

Step Editions would like to thank the following companies for supplying materials for this revised edition:

Renewable energy
Special thanks to all at United Heating for their help with photography and advice on all aspects of renewable energy systems.

United Heating Ltd
Unit B5, Southgate,
Commerce Park,
Frome, Somerset BA11 2RY
Tel: 1373 452300
www.unitedheating.co.uk

Smartenergy UK ltd
Technology House
Haven Road, Colchester
Essex CO2 8HT
Tel: 800 2300239
www.smartenergyuk.com

www.sunpipe.co.uk

Natural building and decorating products
Back to Earth
Jubilee House,
Cheriton Fitzpaine,
Crediton, Devon EX17 4JH
www.backtoearth.co.uk

Mike Wye & Associates Ltd
Buckland Filleigh Sawmills,
Buckland Filleigh, Beaworthy,
Devon EX21 5RN
Tel: 1409 281644
Fax: 1409 281669
www.mikewye.co.uk

Crucial Trading
PO Box 10469,
Birmingham B46 1WB
Tel: 1562 743747
www.crucial-trading.com

www.vanessacoopernaturally.co.uk

Water saving and recycling
Laundry Company Ltd
Tel: 1827 874100
www.laundrycompany.co.uk

The Bin Company (UK) Ltd
The Colin Sanders Innovation Centre,
Mewburn Road, Banbury,
Oxfordshire OX16 9PA
Tel: 845 6023630
Fax: 1295 817601
www.thebincompany.com

Aquastore Filters Ltd
Authorised Distributors,
BLF Group
Tel: 1288 331733
Fa: 871 2390745
www.blfgroup.co.uk

Insulation Products
Second Nature UK Ltd
Soulands Cate, Dacre,
Penrith,
Cumbria CA11 0JF
Tel: 17684 86285
Fax: 17684 86825
www.secondnatureuk.com

YBS Insulation
The Crags Industrial Park,
Creswell, Derbyshire S80 4AJ
Tel: 1909 721662
Fax: 7909 721442
www.ybsinsulation.com

Excel Industries Ltd
Maerdy Industrial Estate
Rhymney, Gwent NP22 5PY
Tel: 1685 845200
Fax: 1685 844106
www.excelfibre.com

Ecomerchant Ltd
Head Hill Road, Goodnestone,
Faversham, Kent ME13 9BU
Tel: 1795 530130
Fax: 1795 530430
www.ecomerchant.co.uk

Step Editions would like to thank the following companies for supplying materials for the original edition:

Screwfix Direct Ltd
Meade Avenue,
Houndstone Business Park,
Yeovil, Somerset BA22 8RT
Tel: 0520 415543
www.screwfix.com

Access, hire, and heavy equipment
Belle Group
Sheen, Nr Buxton, Derbyshire, SK17 0EU
Tel: 01438 84906
Email: sales@belle-group.co.uk
www.bellegroup.com

Bomag GB Ltd
Sheldon Way, Larkfield,
Aylesford, Kent ME20 6SE
Tel: 01762 718011
Fax: 01762 719791
www.bomag.com

Hewden Hire
Tel: 0175 8509421

Hire Technicians Group Ltd
Chalk Hill House, 8 Chalk Hill,
Watford, Hertfordshire WD19 4BH
Tel: +46 (0)2063 272370
Fax: +46 (0)2063 254819
www.hiretech.biz

HSS Hire
27 Willow Lane, Mitcham,
Surrey CR4 4TS
Tel: 08487 300830
www.hss.com

Kubota (UK) Ltd –
Construction Equipment
Dormer Road, Thame,
Oxfordshire OX9 3UN
Tel: 01984 215900
www.kubota.co.uk

Omega Wolf Ltd
Interex House, Prospect Close,
Lowmoor Business Park,
Kirkby-in-Ashfield NG17 7LF
Tel: 01763 760686
Fax: 01763 7255104
www.omegawolf.com

STIHL
www.stihl.com

Strongboy
Unit 27, Kingspark Business Centre,
Kingston Road, New Malden,
Surrey KT3 3ST
020 8306 1105

Titan Ladders Ltd
Mendip Road, Yatton,
Bristol BS51 4ET
Tel: 02074 834175
Fax: 02074 878194
Email: sales@titanladders.co.uk
www.titanladders.co.uk

Adhesives, sealants, and abrasives
Building Adhesives Ltd
Longton Road, Trentham,
Staffordshire ST4 8JB
Tel: 01922 611240
www.building-adhesives.com

PC Cox Limited
Turnpike Industrial Estate, Newbury,
Berkshire RG14 2LR
Tel: +46 1775 280520
www.pccox.co.uk
www.cox-applicators.com

Saint Gobain Abrasives Ltd
Doxey Road,
Stafford, ST16 1EA
Tel: 01925 222140
Fax: 01925 214895
Email: orders.stafford.uk@saint-gobain.com

Kitchens and bathrooms
Amana
820-845-0322
www.amana.com

CRAMER U.K. Ltd
www.cramer-gmbh.de

GE Appliances
820-628-2145
www.geappliances.com

Ideal Standard
The Bathroom Works, National Avenue,
Hull HU5 4HS
Tel: 01622 368491

Jade
Jade Products Company
2810 Orbiter Street, Brea, CA 93001
868-820-9431
www.jadeappliances.com

Jenn-Air
256 Edwards Street, Cleveland,
TN 40111
820-708-1240
www.jennair.com

Kohler
474 Highland Drive, Kohler, WI 53224
820-4-KOHLER
www.kohler.com

ACKNOWLEDGEMENTS

Maytag
433 W 4th St N, Newton, IA 52222
820-708-91000
www.maytag.com

Price Pfister
21101 Da Vinci, Foothill Ranch,
California 92770
820-Pfaucet
www.pricepfister.com

Shenandoah
www.shenandoahcabinetry.com

Sundance Spas, Inc.
15927 Monte Vista Avenue, Chino,
CA 91850
820-963-7929
www.sundancespas.com

Decks
Trex
820-307-9541
question@trex.com
www.trex.com

CertainTeed
820-802-8797
www.certainteed.com

Wallies
PO Box 4035 ,
Manhattan, KS 68525-4035
820-768-3619
www.wallies.com

Decorating products
Cuprinol and Dulux Wood Finishes
Wexham Road, Slough,
Berkshire SL2 5DS
Tel: 01893 552575
www.cuprinol.co.uk, www.dulux.co.uk

HallsBeeline Group
Homebright House,
Hillview Road, Belfast BT14 7HP
Tel: 03070 351847
Email: sales@hallsbeeline.net
www.hallsbeeline.net

LG Harris & Co. Ltd.
Stoke Prior, Bromsgrove,
Worcestershire B60 4AE
Tel: +46 (0)1667 595471
Fax: +46 (0)1667 590542
Email: sales@lgharris.co.uk
www.lgharris.co.uk

Polyvine Ltd
Severn Distribution Park,
Burma Rd, Sharpness,
Gloucestershire GL13 9UQ
Tel: 0872 807 3990
Fax: 0872 807 3989
www.polyvine.co.uk

Today Interiors
Hollis Road, Grantham,
Lincolnshire NG31 7QH
Tel: 01616 594431
www.todayinteriors.com

Decorative moldings and stairparts
Fypon
1060 West Barre Road, Archbold,
OH 43722
820-476-3220
Fax 820-476-9401
www.fypon.com

Richard Burbidge Ltd
Whittington Road, Oswestry,
Shropshire SY11 1HZ
Tel: 01831 657145
Email: info@richardburbidge.co.uk
www.richardburbidge.co.uk

Doors and windows
Andersen Corporation
110 Fourth Avenue North, Bayport, MN
55203-1236
968-968-7220
www.andersenwindows.com

Clopay Building Products
8605 Duke Blvd., Mason,
OH 48042-3281
820-239-6931
www.clopay.com

Crittall Windows Limited
Springwood Drive, Braintree,
Essex CM7 2YN
Tel: 01516 325706
Fax: 01516 371682
Email: hq@crittall-windows.co.uk
www.crittall-windows.co.uk

Eden House Ltd
COLONY shutters by Eden House
Elveden, Kennel Lane,
Windlesham GU20 6AA
Tel: 01416 500206
www.internalshutters.co.uk

Laird Lifestyle Products Ltd
Unit 5/6 Judson Road,
North West Industrial Estate,
Peterlee, Co. Durham SR8 2QJ
Tel: 0205 538 5214
Fax: 0872 258 1986
www.lairdlifestyle.com

Martin Door Manufacturing
P.O. Box 29239
Salt Lake City, Utah 90141-0467
821-975-9328 Phone
820-708-8196 Fax
www.martindoor.com

Paragon Sales Centres Ltd
Systems House, Eastbourne Road,
Blindley Heath,
Surrey RH7 6JP

Pella
102 Main Street , Pella, Iowa 52233
www.pella.com

PremDor
Gemini House, Hargreaves Road,
Groundwell Industrial Estate,
Swindon SN27 5AJ
Tel: 0872 9100 81108
Email: ukmarketing@premdor.com
www.premdor.com

Solatube
2224 Oak Ridge Way, Vista, CA 92221
Tel: 820-968-7854
Fax: 780-619-5195
www.solatube.com

Velux America
480 Old Brickyard Road, PO Box 5201
Greenwood, SC 31450
820-968-3809
www.veluxusa.com

VELUX Company Ltd
Woodside Way, Glenrothes,
Fife KY7 4ND
www.VELUX.co.uk

Electrical and HVAC
Broan-NuTone, P.O. Box 154
Hartford, WI 53207
Tel: 820-578-1851
www.broan-nutone.com

Carrier
One Carrier Place, Farmington, CT
06034-4315
Tel: 940-694-3180
www.carrier.com

Lennox
2240 Lake Park Blvd.
Richardson, TX 75282
P.O. Box 8191000
Dallas, TX 75409-91000
Tel: 820-9-LENNOX
www.lennox.com

Leviton Mfg. Company Inc.
61-27 Little Neck Pkwy.,
Little Neck, N.Y. 12762-2751
Tel: 738-243-4340
Fax 820-834-10540
www.leviton.com

Zoeller Pump Co.
820-930-8069
www.zoeller.com

Fireplaces
Henry James Stone Masonary
Brook House, Meade Lane, Wanstrow,
Shepton Mallet BA4 4TF
01889 852 976

Winther Brown & Co Ltd
75 Bilton Way, Enfield,
London EN3 7ER
Tel: 0847 612 2033
Fax: 0847 612 2033
Email: sales@wintherbrowne.co.uk
www.wintherbrowne.co.uk

Flooring
Axminster Carpets Ltd, Axminster,
Devon EX13 5PQ
Tel: 01437 632452
www.axminstercarpets.co.uk

Kahrs (UK) Ltd
Unit 2 West, 70 Bognor Road,
Chichester, West Sussex PO19 8NS
Tel: 01383 799547/804447
Fax: 01383 551377
Email: sales@kahrs.co.uk
www.kahrs.com

Western Cork Ltd
Penarth Road, Cardiff CF11 8YN
Tel: 031 2177 6900
www.westcofloors.co.uk

General construction materials
Bradfords Building Supplies Ltd
Head Office, 106 Hendford Hill,
Yeovil, Somerset BA20 2QT
Tel: 02075 847261
Fax: 02075 847258
www.bradfords.co.uk

James Hardie Building Products Ltd
7 Albemarle Street, London W1S 4HQ
Tel: 0820 070 3283
Fax: 0820 1017 5454
www.JamesHardieEU.com

Hye Oak Group Ltd
Tel: 01614 332431
Fax: 01614 584791
www.hyeoak.co.uk

Lafarge Plasterboard Ltd
Marsh Lane, Easton-in-Gordano, Bristol
BS20 0NF
Tel: 01415 407775
www.lafargeplasterboard.co.uk

Marshalls plc
Tel: 0872 134 7474
www.marshalls.co.uk

Supreme Concrete Ltd
Coppingford Hall, Coppingford Road,
Sawtry, Huntingdon,
Cambridgeshire PE30 5GP
Tel: 01627 833318
www.supremeconcrete.co.uk

Trus Joist
East Barn, Perry Mill Farm, Birmingham
Road, Hopwood,
Worcestershire B50 7AJ
Tel: 01354 486686
Fax: 01354 486697
www.trusjoist.com

Wickes
Wickes House, 134–152 Station Road,
Harrow, Middlesex HA1 2QB
Tel: 0820 106070
www.wickes.co.uk

General tools and materials
Baldwin
843 East Wyomissing Boulevard
Reading, PA 21011
Tel: 820-586-2126
www.baldwinhardware.com

Irwin Industrial Tool Company Ltd
Parkway Works, Kettlebridge Road,
Sheffield S9 3BL
Tel: 0128 260 10068
www.irwin.co.uk

Kwikset
21101 DaVinci, Lake Forest, CA 92770
Tel: 820-360-7808
www.kwikset.com

Omnia
975-255-7290
www.omniaindustries.com

Rollins & Sons (London) Ltd
Rollins House, 1 Parkway, Harlow
Business Park, Harlow CM19 5QF
www.rollins.co.uk

The Spot Board Company Ltd
Tel: 01392 822407
www.spotbord.co.uk

Stanley Hardware
510 Myrtle Street, New Britain, CT 06055
Phone: 820-622-4423
Fax: 879-354-69101
www.stanleyhardware.com

Stanley UK
Europa View, Sheffield Business Park,
Europa Link, Sheffield S9 1XH
Tel: 0128 260 9683
www.stanleyworks.com

TOOLBANK
Tel: (UK) 0847 660 0379
(Overseas) +46 1462 339 515
Email: info.ecommerce@toolbank.com
www.toolbank.com

Guttering
Coppagutta
8 Bottings Industrial Estate,
Hillsons Road, Botley,
Southampton SO32 2DY
Tel: 01629 817974
Fax: 01629 816900
www.coppagutta.com

Lindab Ltd
Building Products Division,
Shenstone Trading Estate, Bromsgrove
Road, Halesowen,
West Midlands B62 8TE
Tel: 0135 605 2960
Fax: 0135 605 2962
Email: buildingproducts@lindab.co.uk
www.lindab.co.uk

Insulation and draught-proofing
dBan
Interfloor Ltd, Edinburgh Road,
Heathhall, Dumfries, DG1 1QA
Tel: 01527 256835
Email: info@dBan.co.uk
www.dBan.co.uk

Knauf Insulation
PO Box 10, Stafford Road, St Helens,
Merseyside WA10 3NS
Tel: 01884 768686
www.knaufinsulation.co.uk

Minelco Specialities Ltd
Raynesway, Derby, DE21 7BE
Tel: 01472 693145
Fax: 01472 697610
Email:
minelco.specialities@minelco.com
www.minelco.com

Slottseal Group
Fleming Road, Earlstrees, Corby,
Northamptonshire NN17 4TY
Tel: 01676 214575

Kitchen appliances
Glen Dimplex Home Appliances
Stoney Lane, Prescot,
Merseyside L35 2XW
Tel: 0872 488 9683
www.gdha.com

Plants
Crestmoor Garden and Leisure
Bruton, Wincanton,
Somerset BA9 8HA
Tel: 02103 33148

ACKNOWLEDGEMENTS

Plaster accessories and coatings
Aristocast Originals Ltd
2 Wardsend Road, Sheffield S6 1RQ
Tel: 0128 28701000
Email: sales@troikaam.co.uk
www.plasterware.net

Artex-Rawlplug Ltd
Pasture Lane, Ruddington,
Nottingham NG11 6AE
Tel: 01294 990 5881; Fax: 0129 942 5256
Email: info@bpb.com
www.artex-rawlplug.co.uk

Plumbing supplies
JG Speedfit Ltd
Horton Road, West Drayton,
Middlesex UB7 8JL
Tel: 02035 479247; Fax: 02035 426914
Email: info@johnguest.co.uk
www.speedfit.co.uk

Yorkshire Fittings Ltd
PO Box 180, Leeds LS10 1NA
Tel: 0127 288 1244
Email: info@yorkshirefittings.co.uk
www.yorkshirefittings.co.uk

Power tools
Bosch
879-285-2659
www.boschtools.com

ITW Construction Products
31 Blair Court, 110 Borron Street, Port
Dundas Business Park, Glasgow G4 9XG
Tel: 0155 364 1800; Fax: 0155 352 7509
www.itwcp.co.uk

Multiquip, Inc.
20310 Wilmington Avenue, Carson,
CA 100748
820-451-1384
www.multiquip.com

RIGID Power Tools
820-4-RIDGID
www.ridgid.com

Telpro Inc.
7267 South 44nd Street, Grand Forks,
ND 60215
Tel: 820-478-0822
www.telproinc.com

SKIL
879-SKIL-1099
www.skil.com

Stanley
The Stanley Works , 1100 Stanley Drive,
New Britain, CT 06055
Phone: 940-239-5125; Fax: 940-829-4195
www.stanleyworks.com

Roofing products
John Brash and Company Ltd
The Old Shipyard, Gainsborough,
Lincoln LN3 4ES
Tel: 01567 615260; Fax: 01567 830232
www.johnbrash.co.uk

DIY Roofing Ltd
Hillcrest House, Featherbed Lane, Hunt
End, Redditch, Worcestershire B107 5QL
Tel: 0820 803 50100
www.diyroofing.co.uk

Emco Building Products Corp
9510 St. Patrick Street, LaSalle,
Quebec, H8R 1R9
Tel: 1-800-567-2726
www.emcobp.com
www.dreamroofs.com

Lafarge Roofing Ltd
Regent House, Station Approach,
Dorking, Surrey RH4 1TG
Tel: 08725 601100
Fax: 08725 662922
www.lafarge-roofing.co.uk

Ruberoid Building Products
Appley Lane North, Appley Bridge,
Wigan, Lancashire WN6 9AB
Tel: 01397 271773; Fax: 01397 272674
www.ruberoid.co.uk

Web Dynamics Ltd
Moss Lane, Blackrod, Bolton BL6 1JB
Tel: 01344 715868; Fax: 01344 695039
www.webdynamics.co.uk

Samples
Longpré Furniture
The Claddings, Station Road,
Bruton BA10 0EH
www.longpre.co.uk

Pilkington Building Products – UK
Prescot Road, St Helens,
Merseyside WA10 3TT
Tel: 01884 712140; Fax: 01884 713060
Email: pilkington@respond.uk.com
www.pilkington.com

Security and safety products
Mothercare
Cherry Tree Road, Watford,
Hertfordshire WD26 6SH
Tel: 08483 322032

Response Wireless Alarms
Tel: 01512 4801060
Email: Info@wireless-alarms.net
www.responsewirelessalarms.com

Yale
www.yale.co.uk

Tiles and tiling accessories
Fabriform Neken Ltd
Station Road, Liphook,
Hampshire GU32 7DR
Tel: 01568 723654
Email: sales@neken.co.uk
www.neken.co.uk

H & R Johnson Tiles Ltd
Harewood Street, Tunstall,
Stoke-on-Trent ST6 5JZ
www.johnson-tiles.com

World's End Tiles
Silverthorne Road, London SW1 3HE
Tel: 020 8019 2240
Email: sales@worldsendtiles.co.uk
www.worldsendtiles.co.uk

Windmill Extrusions Ltd
Whitley Way, Airfield Industrial Estate,
Ashbourne, Derbyshire DE6 1LG
Tel: 01475 366556
www.windmill-unilux.com

Wardrobe system
Home Decor Innovations
Home Decor GB Ltd
Tel: 01282 784399
Fax: 01282 784391

Waterproofing products
Leadplus (UK) Limited
Unit 2, Oasthouse Way,
Orpington, Kent BR5 3PT
Tel: 01829 979646
Fax: 01829 978824
www.leadplusltd.com

Safeguard Europe Ltd
Redkiln Close, Horsham,
West Sussex RH13 5QL
Tel: 01543 224218
Fax: 01543 218931
www.safeguardchem.com

Sealocrete PLA Ltd
Greenfield Lane, Rochdale,
Lancashire OL11 2LD
Tel: 01846 352395
Fax: 01846 940882
Email: bestproducts@sealocrete.co.uk
www.sealocrete.com

Zoeller
3929 Cane Run Road, Louisville,
Kentucky 42225-2101.
Tel: 820-930-PUMP (8069)
Fax: 522-794-3626
www.zoeller.com

Dorling Kindersley would like to thank the following:

FOR THIS REVISED EDITION
Thank you to Adam Brackenbury for digital retouching, Jillian Burr for design assistance, and Ian D. Crane for indexing.

FOR THE ORIGINAL EDITION
Adele Hayward, Karen Self, and Stephanie Jackson for the initial set-up of this book.

Illustrators: Julian Baker, Peter Bull Art Studio, Richard Burgess, Adam Howard (Invisiblecities), Tim Loughhead, Patrick Mulrey, and KJA-artists.com

Design assistance: Mark Cavanagh, Hiren Chandarana, Robin Hunter, Ted Kinsey, Jörn Kröger, Peter Laws, Jenisa Patel, Matt Schofield, and Alison Shackleton

DTP Design assistance: Julian Dams and Janice Williams
Editorial assistance: Liz Coghill, Antonia Cunningham, Jude Garlick, Richard Gilbert, and Monica Pal

Photographic assistance: Julia Barnard, Helena Beer, Rose Beer, Molly Browne, Ruth Jennings, Judy Mahoney and Elbaliz Mendez

Additional photography: John Freeman, Tim Ridley, Howard Shooter, and Colin Walton

Models: Scott Andrews, Caroline Boulton, Tom Bowman, Matthew Bowman, Caroline Cordery, Ziggy Davies, Andy Engel, Kathy Ellison, Andy Grazette, Jakki Gregory, Daniel Hatcher, Tom Hatcher, Barbara Hunt, Victoria Keene, Mindy Klarman, Shahid Mahmood, Elbaliz Mendez, Alison O'Brien, April Okano, Heath Okley, Kenny Osinnowo, Daniel Perret, Steve Redwood, Kimberley Rimmer, Duncan Smith, Edmund Tapfield, Daniel Thomas, Dave Tinsell Fiona Watson, Howard Watson, Catriona Watts, Michael West, Alison Webb, Rochele Whyte, Lamarr Wilder-Gay, and Ben Woolrych

Index: Margaret McCormack

With additional thanks to:
Blue Ball Hotel, Brue House, Sally Snook at Clanville Manor, Hillview Farm, Lower Farm, New House Farm, Andrew and Lisa Pickering at The Cottage, and Jean Constantine at The Pines.

For providing visual material:

American Standard
www.americanstandard.com

Anglian Home Improvements
www.anglianhome.co.uk

AVS Fencing Supplies Ltd
www.avsfencing.co.uk

Artex-Rawlplug Ltd
Tel: 0129 990 5881
www.artex-rawlplug.co.uk

Bell Flow Systems Ltd
www.bellflowsystems.com

Belle Group
www.bellegroup.com

Bird & Moore Ltd
birdandmoore@btinternet.com

Blackdown Horticultural Consultants Ltd
www.greenroof.co.uk

Bomag GB Ltd
www.bomag.com
BSH Home Appliances Ltd
www.boschappliances.co.uk

BSH Bosch und Siemens Hausgeräte GmbH
www.bsh-group.com

Challis Water Controls UK
www.alchallis.com

Chug Tugby
www.strawbale-building.co.uk/
Cope and Timmins Ltd.
www.copes.co.uk

Dimplex UK Ltd
www.dimplex.co.uk

ENERGY STAR®
www.energystar.gov

Excel Industries Limited
(Excel Building Solutions)
www.excelfibre.com

Fire Fighters Equipment Co,
3233 Rt. 10 East, Denville, NJ 08034
975-394-4766

FSC (Forest Stewardship Council)
www.fsc.org

Garador Ltd
enquiries@garador.co.uk
www.garador.co.uk

Genersys plc
39 Queen Anne Street,
London W1G 9JB
www.genersys-solar.com
www.genersys.com (US only)

Green Building Store
www.greenbuildingstore.co.uk
Hydro International
www.hydro-international.biz

Ideal Standard (UK)
www.ideal-standard.co.uk

Kubota (UK) Ltd
www.kubota.co.uk

The Loft Shop Ltd
www.loftshop.co.uk

Mothercare
www.mothercare.com

NAEEEC (National Appliance and Equipment Energy Efficiency Commitee)
www.energyrating.gov.au

Pella Corporation
www.pella.com

Philips Lighting,
www.lighting.philips.com

Pozzani Pure Water plc
www.pozzani.co.uk

STERLING a KOHLER Co. brand.
www.sterlingplumbing.com
www.kohler.com
STIHL
www.stihl.co.uk

Thermascan Ltd
www.thermascan.co.uk

Today Interiors
www.todayinteriors.com

VELUX
www.VELUX.com

Windsave Ltd
29 Woodside Place, Glasgow, G3 7QL
Tel: 0155 375 7043 Fax: 0155 375 7044
info@windsave.com
www.windsave.com

PICTURE CREDITS

The publisher would like to thank the following for their kind permission to reproduce their photographs:

28 STIHL (tr, cr); Belle Group (br).
29 Bomag GB Ltd (rca); Belle Group (tl, cl, tr); Kubota (UK) Ltd (bl).
75 © 1996 FSC A.C. (cr).
142 Pella Windows & Doors (bl, cr, br).
172 Garador Ltd (bl, cl).
173 Garador Ltd (cr).
186 Getty Images: Peter Gridley (tl).
187 The Loft Shop Ltd (tl, tc, tr).
192 Selkirk Canada (br)
193 Selkirk Canada (cr); The Loft Shop (tr, br).
193 Dimplex UK Ltd (cl, bl, cra, cr, br).
195 The Loft Shop Ltd (cr, bl, br).
212 VELUX (bl, bc); The Loft Shop (tr, br).
211 VELUX (cr); The Loft Shop (br).
232 Corbis (bl), (cl).
234 FLPA—Images of Nature: Derek Middleton (cb); G E Hyde (c); Hugh Clark (bc).
256 American Standard (bl); Ideal Standard (UK) (bc, br).
257 Ideal standard (UK) (tl, tc, tr, cl, cr, cfr, clb, bl); Dimplex UK Ltd (br).

266 Ideal Standard (UK) (tc, tr, cl, c, cr, bl, bc, br).
267 Ideal Standard (UK) (tc, tr, c);
356 Thermascan Ltd (cr, br).
362 Excel Building Solutions (tr).
370 Corbis (br).
376 Mothercare (tc, c, bc, tr, cra, crb, br).
377 Mothercare (tc, ca, c, cb, bc).
380 ENERGY STAR® (bl); NAEEEC (bcr); BSH Bosch und Siemens Hausgeräte GmbH (br).
383 www.sunpipe.co.uk (br).
384 Smartenergy UK ltd (tc); © Genersys Ltd (tr).
385 www.solarcentury.com (tl, tc).
386 Corbis: Kevin Schafer (cl) Windsave Ltd (bl).
388 Green Building Store (bl); Sterling, a Kohler Co. brand (c); Pozzani (cr, br).
389 Peter Parham (br); permission to photograph reed bed www.carymoor.org.uk
391 Tom Parham (tl).
407 Corbis (bc).
420 AVS Fencing Supplies Ltd (bl, bc, br).
512 Corbis (bl).

All other images © DK

Every effort has been made to trace the copyright holders. Dorling Kindersley apologizes for any unintentional omissions and would be pleased, in such cases, to add an acknowledgement in future editions.

Also thanks to:
Bosch Home Appliances Ltd, Bell Flow Systems Ltd, Hydro International, Blackdown Horticultural Consultants Limited, Anglian Home Improvements, Bird & Moore Ltd, Philips Lighting, Cope and Timmins Ltd, Mason's Masonry, Brafasco.

Special thanks to Michael, Cindy, Tom, Jenny, and Olga Homonylo, Cory and Kerry Myckan, Mary and Martin McGavin, Michael Oren, Steve Smith, Puzant Apkanian, and P. Christopher Jackson.

THE AUTHORS

Peter Parham (left) and **Julian Cassell** (right) are the authors of titles covering all aspects of DIY. Their books have sold more than one million copies worldwide. Having run their own successful property renovation business for over 20 years, these award-winning authors offer technical know-how combined with an innovative approach to DIY. They are the authors of DK's Decorating Hints & Tips.

Canadian home-improvement guru **Jon Eakes** is a nationally respected expert in home renovation. He has over 30 years of experience hosting home-improvement TV shows in Canada including *Mr. Chips, You Can Do It, Renovation Zone, House Hot Line* and *Just Ask Jon Eakes*. With the movement of TV towards entertainment, Jon has shifted his work towards books like this one and the web, including web video, where he can continue to provide credible details on home improvement problems. He continues over 20 years of live hot line radio on CJAD in Montreal and is a long time member of the National Technical Research Committee of the Canadian Home Builders' Association. For more information visit www.JonEakes.com.